Seventh Joint Conference on Lexical and Computational Semantics (*SEM 2018)

New Orleans, Louisiana, USA
5 – 6 June 2018

ISBN: 978-1-5108-6352-1

NAACL HLT 2018

**Lexical and Computational Semantics
(*SEM 2018)**

Proceedings of the 7th Conference

June 5-6, 2018
New Orleans

Association for Computational Linguistics (ACL)
209 N. Eighth Street
Stroudsburg, PA 18360
USA
Tel: +1-570-476-8006
Fax: +1-570-476-0860
acl@aclweb.org

Introduction

Preface by the General Chair

*SEM, the Joint Conference on Lexical and Computational Semantics is the major venue for research on all aspects of semantics since 2012. This 2018 edition is therefore the seventh in a series that we envisage to be a lot longer in the future.

As in previous years, *SEM 2018 has attracted a substantial number of submissions, and offers a high quality programme covering a wide spectrum of semantic areas. The overall goal of the *SEM series, which is bringing together different communities that treat the computational modeling of semantics from different angles, is beautifully met in this year's edition, which includes distributional and formal/linguistic semantics approaches, spanning from lexical to discourse issues, with an eye to applications.

We hope that the diversity and richness of the programme will provide not only an interesting event for a broad audience of NLP researchers, but also serve to stimulate new ideas and synergies that can significantly impact the field.

As always, *SEM would not have been possible without the active involvement of our community. Aside from our dedicated programme committee, to whom we give an extended acknowledgement further in this introduction, we are very thankful to Johannes Bjerva (Publicity Chair) and Emmanuele Chersoni (Publication Chair) for their efficiency and hard work in making the conference a visible and shared event, from website to proceedings. We are grateful to ACL SIGLEX and SIGSEM for endorsing and staying behind this event, and to Google, who thanks to its sponsorship to *SEM 2018, made it possible to assign a few student grants, as a partial reimbursement of the *SEM participation costs.

As General Chair, I am particularly grateful to the Programme Chairs, Jonathan Berant and Alessandro Lenci, to whom we all owe the excellence and variety of the programme, and to whom I personally owe a very rewarding experience in sharing responsibility for this important event. I hope you will enjoy *SEM 2018 in all its diversity, and you will find it as stimulating and enriching as it strives to be.

Malvina Nissim
General Chair of *SEM 2018

Preface by the Program Chairs

We are pleased to present this volume containing the papers accepted at the Seventh Joint Conference on Lexical and Computational Semantics (*SEM 2018, co-located with NAACL in New Orleans, USA, on June 5-6, 2018). Like for the last edition, *SEM received a high number of submissions, which allowed us to compile a diverse and high-quality program. The number of submissions was 82. Out of these, 35 papers were accepted (22 long, 14 short). Thus, the acceptance rate was 35.6% overall, 42.3% for the long papers and 28.6% for the short submissions. Some of the papers were withdrawn after acceptance, due to multiple submissions to other conferences (the 2018 schedule was particularly complicated, with significant intersection of *SEM with ACL, COLING, and other venues). The final number of papers in the program is 32 (19 long, 13 short).

Submissions were reviewed in 5 different areas: Distributional Semantics, Discourse and Dialogue, Lexical Semantics, Theoretical and Formal Semantics, and Applied Semantics.

The papers were evaluated by a program committee of 10 area chairs from Europe and North America, assisted by a panel of 115 reviewers. Each submission was reviewed by three reviewers, who were furthermore encouraged to discuss any divergence in evaluation. The papers in each area were subsequently ranked by the area chairs. The final selection was made by the program co-chairs after an independent check of all reviews and discussion with the area chairs. Reviewers' recommendations were also used to shortlist a set of papers nominated for the Best Paper Award.

The final *SEM 2018 program consists of 18 oral presentations and 14 posters, as well as two keynote talks by Ellie Pavlick (Brown University & Google Research, joint keynote with SemEval 2018) and Christopher Potts (Stanford University).

We are deeply thankful to all area chairs and reviewers for their help in the selection of the program, for their readiness in engaging in thoughtful discussions about individual papers, and for providing valuable feedback to the authors. We are also grateful to Johannes Bjerva for his precious help in publicizing the conference, and to Emmanuele Chersoni for his dedication and thoroughness in turning the program into the proceedings you now have under your eyes. Last but not least, we are indebted to our General Chair, Malvina Nissim, for her continuous guidance and support throughout the process of organizing this installment of *SEM.

We hope you enjoy the conference!
Jonathan Berant and Alessandro Lenci

General Chair:

Malvina Nissim, University of Groningen

Program Chairs:

Jonathan Berant, Tel-Aviv University
Alessandro Lenci, University of Pisa

Publication Chair:

Emmanuele Chersoni, Aix-Marseille University

Publicity Chair:

Johannes Bjerva, University of Copenaghen

Area Chairs:

Distributional Semantics
Omer Levy, University of Washington
Sebastian Padó, University of Stuttgart

Discourse and Dialogue
Ani Nenkova, University of Pennsylvania
Marta Recasens, Google Research

Lexical Semantics
Núria Bel, Pompeu Fabra University
Enrico Santus, Massachusetts Institute of Technology

Theoretical and Formal Semantics
Sam Bowman, New York University
Kilian Evang, University of Düsseldorf

Applied Semantics
Svetlana Kiritchenko, National Research Council Canada
Lonneke van der Plas, University of Malta

Invited Talk: Why Should we Care about Linguistics?

Ellie Pavlick
(Joint Invited Speaker with SemEval 2018)

Brown University & Google Research

In just the past few months, a flurry of adversarial studies have pushed back on the apparent progress of neural networks, with multiple analyses suggesting that deep models of text fail to capture even basic properties of language, such as negation, word order, and compositionality. Alongside this wave of negative results, our field has stated ambitions to move beyond task-specific models and toward "general purpose" word, sentence, and even document embeddings. This is a tall order for the field of NLP, and, I argue, marks a significant shift in the way we approach our research. I will discuss what we can learn from the field of linguistics about the challenges of codifying all of language in a "general purpose" way. Then, more importantly, I will discuss what we cannot learn from linguistics. I will argue that the state-of-the-art of NLP research is operating close to the limits of what we know about natural language semantics, both within our field and outside it. I will conclude with thoughts on why this opens opportunities for NLP to advance both technology and basic science as it relates to language, and the implications for the way we should conduct empirical research.

Invited Talk: Linguists for Deep Learning; or How I Learned to Stop Worrying and Love Neural Networks

Christopher Potts
Stanford University, USA

The rise of deep learning (DL) might seem initially to mark a low point for linguists hoping to learn from, and contribute to, the field of statistical NLP. In building DL systems, the decisive factors tend to be data, computational resources, and optimization techniques, with domain expertise in a supporting role. Nonetheless, at least for semantics and pragmatics, I argue that DL models are potentially the *best* computational implementations of linguists' ideas and theories that we've ever seen. At the lexical level, symbolic representations are inevitably incomplete, whereas learned distributed representations have the potential to capture the dense interconnections that exist between words, and DL methods allow us to infuse these representations with information from contexts of use and from structured lexical resources. For semantic composition, previous approaches tended to represent phrases and sentences in partial, idiosyncratic ways; DL models support *comprehensive* representations and might yield insights into flexible modes of semantic composition that would be unexpected from the point of view of traditional logical theories. And when it comes to pragmatics, DL is arguably what the field has been looking for all along: a flexible set of tools for representing language and context together, and for capturing the nuanced, fallible ways in which langage users reason about each other's intentions. Thus, while linguists might find it dispiriting that the day-to-day work of DL involves mainly fund-raising to support hyperparameter tuning on expensive machines, I argue that it is worth the tedium for the insights into language that this can (unexpectedly) deliver.

Table of Contents

Resolving Event Coreference with Supervised Representation Learning and Clustering-Oriented Regularization
Kian Kenyon-Dean, Jackie Chi Kit Cheung and Doina Precup 1

Learning distributed event representations with a multi-task approach
Xudong Hong, Asad Sayeed and Vera Demberg 11

Assessing Meaning Components in German Complex Verbs: A Collection of Source-Target Domains and Directionality
Sabine Schulte im Walde, Maximilian Köper and Sylvia Springorum 22

Learning Neural Word Salience Scores
Krasen Samardzhiev, Andrew Gargett and Danushka Bollegala 33

Examining Gender and Race Bias in Two Hundred Sentiment Analysis Systems
Svetlana Kiritchenko and Saif Mohammad 43

Graph Algebraic Combinatory Categorial Grammar
Sebastian Beschke and Wolfgang Menzel 54

Mixing Context Granularities for Improved Entity Linking on Question Answering Data across Entity Categories
Daniil Sorokin and Iryna Gurevych 65

Quantitative Semantic Variation in the Contexts of Concrete and Abstract Words
Daniela Naumann, Diego Frassinelli and Sabine Schulte im Walde 76

EmoWordNet: Automatic Expansion of Emotion Lexicon Using English WordNet
Gilbert Badaro, Hussein Jundi, Hazem Hajj and Wassim El-Hajj 86

The Limitations of Cross-language Word Embeddings Evaluation
Amir Bakarov, Roman Suvorov and Ilya Sochenkov 94

How Gender and Skin Tone Modifiers Affect Emoji Semantics in Twitter
Francesco Barbieri and Jose Camacho-Collados 101

Element-wise Bilinear Interaction for Sentence Matching
Jihun Choi, Taeuk Kim and Sang-goo Lee 107

Named Graphs for Semantic Representation
Richard Crouch and Aikaterini-Lida Kalouli 113

Learning Patient Representations from Text
Dmitriy Dligach and Timothy Miller 119

Polarity Computations in Flexible Categorial Grammar
Hai Hu and Larry Moss 124

Coarse Lexical Frame Acquisition at the Syntax–Semantics Interface Using a Latent-Variable PCFG Model
Laura Kallmeyer, Behrang QasemiZadeh and Jackie Chi Kit Cheung 130

Halo: Learning Semantics-Aware Representations for Cross-Lingual Information Extraction
Hongyuan Mei, Sheng Zhang, Kevin Duh and Benjamin Van Durme........................142

Exploiting Partially Annotated Data in Temporal Relation Extraction
Qiang Ning, Zhongzhi Yu, Chuchu Fan and Dan Roth.....................................148

Predicting Word Embeddings Variability
Benedicte Pierrejean and Ludovic Tanguy..154

Integrating Multiplicative Features into Supervised Distributional Methods for Lexical Entailment
Tu Vu and Vered Shwartz..160

Deep Affix Features Improve Neural Named Entity Recognizers
Vikas Yadav, Rebecca Sharp and Steven Bethard..167

Fine-grained Entity Typing through Increased Discourse Context and Adaptive Classification Thresholds
Sheng Zhang, Kevin Duh and Benjamin Van Durme..173

Hypothesis Only Baselines in Natural Language Inference
Adam Poliak, Jason Naradowsky, Aparajita Haldar, Rachel Rudinger and Benjamin Van Durme180

Quality Signals in Generated Stories
Manasvi Sagarkar, John Wieting, Lifu Tu and Kevin Gimpel...............................192

Term Definitions Help Hypernymy Detection
Wenpeng Yin and Dan Roth...203

Agree or Disagree: Predicting Judgments on Nuanced Assertions
Michael Wojatzki, Torsten Zesch, Saif Mohammad and Svetlana Kiritchenko................214

A Multimodal Translation-Based Approach for Knowledge Graph Representation Learning
Hatem Mousselly Sergieh, Teresa Botschen, Iryna Gurevych and Stefan Roth...............225

Putting Semantics into Semantic Roles
James Allen and Choh Man Teng..235

Measuring Frame Instance Relatedness
Valerio Basile, Roque Lopez Condori and Elena Cabrio..................................245

Solving Feature Sparseness in Text Classification using Core-Periphery Decomposition
Xia Cui, Sadamori Kojaku, Naoki Masuda and Danushka Bollegala.........................255

Robust Handling of Polysemy via Sparse Representations
Abhijit Mahabal, Dan Roth and Sid Mittal...265

Multiplicative Tree-Structured Long Short-Term Memory Networks for Semantic Representations
Nam Khanh Tran and Weiwei Cheng..276

Conference Program

June 5th, 2018

9:00–10:30   **Session 1**

9:15–9:30   *Opening Remarks*

9:30–10:30   *Invited Talk by Ellie Pavlick (Brown University): Why Should we Care about Linguistics?*

10:30–11:00   *Coffee Break*

11:00–12:30   **Session 2**

11:00–11:30   *Resolving Event Coreference with Supervised Representation Learning and Clustering-Oriented Regularization*
Kian Kenyon-Dean, Jackie Chi Kit Cheung and Doina Precup

11:30–12:00   *Learning distributed event representations with a multi-task approach*
Xudong Hong, Asad Sayeed and Vera Demberg

12:00–12:15   *Assessing Meaning Components in German Complex Verbs: A Collection of Source-Target Domains and Directionality*
Sabine Schulte im Walde, Maximilian Köper and Sylvia Springorum

12:15–12:30   *Learning Neural Word Salience Scores*
Krasen Samardzhiev, Andrew Gargett and Danushka Bollegala

12:30–14:00   *Lunch Break*

June 5th, 2018 (continued)

14:00–15:30   **Session 3**

14:00–14:30   *Examining Gender and Race Bias in Two Hundred Sentiment Analysis Systems*
Svetlana Kiritchenko and Saif Mohammad

14:30–15:00   *Graph Algebraic Combinatory Categorial Grammar*
Sebastian Beschke and Wolfgang Menzel

15:00–15:15   *Mixing Context Granularities for Improved Entity Linking on Question Answering Data across Entity Categories*
Daniil Sorokin and Iryna Gurevych

15:15–15:30   *Quantitative Semantic Variation in the Contexts of Concrete and Abstract Words*
Daniela Naumann, Diego Frassinelli and Sabine Schulte im Walde

15:30–16:00   *Coffee Break*

16:00–18:00   **Session 4**

16:00–16:50   ***Poster Booster***

16:50–18:00   ***Poster Session***

EmoWordNet: Automatic Expansion of Emotion Lexicon Using English WordNet
Gilbert Badaro, Hussein Jundi, Hazem Hajj and Wassim El-Hajj

The Limitations of Cross-language Word Embeddings Evaluation
Amir Bakarov, Roman Suvorov and Ilya Sochenkov

How Gender and Skin Tone Modifiers Affect Emoji Semantics in Twitter
Francesco Barbieri and Jose Camacho-Collados

Element-wise Bilinear Interaction for Sentence Matching
Jihun Choi, Taeuk Kim and Sang-goo Lee

Named Graphs for Semantic Representation
Richard Crouch and Aikaterini-Lida Kalouli

Learning Patient Representations from Text
Dmitriy Dligach and Timothy Miller

Polarity Computations in Flexible Categorial Grammar
Hai Hu and Larry Moss

Coarse Lexical Frame Acquisition at the Syntax–Semantics Interface Using a Latent-Variable PCFG Model
Laura Kallmeyer, Behrang QasemiZadeh and Jackie Chi Kit Cheung

Halo: Learning Semantics-Aware Representations for Cross-Lingual Information Extraction
Hongyuan Mei, Sheng Zhang, Kevin Duh and Benjamin Van Durme

Exploiting Partially Annotated Data in Temporal Relation Extraction
Qiang Ning, Zhongzhi Yu, Chuchu Fan and Dan Roth

Predicting Word Embeddings Variability
Benedicte Pierrejean and Ludovic Tanguy

Integrating Multiplicative Features into Supervised Distributional Methods for Lexical Entailment
Tu Vu and Vered Shwartz

Deep Affix Features Improve Neural Named Entity Recognizers
Vikas Yadav, Rebecca Sharp and Steven Bethard

Fine-grained Entity Typing through Increased Discourse Context and Adaptive Classification Thresholds
Sheng Zhang, Kevin Duh and Benjamin Van Durme

June 6th, 2018

<table>
<tr><td>9:00–10:30</td><td>Session 5</td></tr>
</table>

9:00–10:30 **Session 5**

9:00–10:00 *Invited Talk by Christopher Potts (Stanford University): Linguists for Deep Learning; or How I Learned to Stop Worrying and Love Neural Networks*

10:00–10:30 *Hypothesis Only Baselines in Natural Language Inference*
Adam Poliak, Jason Naradowsky, Aparajita Haldar, Rachel Rudinger and Benjamin Van Durme

10:30–11:00 *Coffee Break*

11:00–12:15 **Session 6**

11:00–11:30 *Quality Signals in Generated Stories*
Manasvi Sagarkar, John Wieting, Lifu Tu and Kevin Gimpel

11:30–12:00 *Term Definitions Help Hypernymy Detection*
Wenpeng Yin and Dan Roth

12:00–12:15 *Agree or Disagree: Predicting Judgments on Nuanced Assertions*
Michael Wojatzki, Torsten Zesch, Saif Mohammad and Svetlana Kiritchenko

12:15–14:00 *Lunch Break*

June 6th, 2018 (continued)

14:00–15:30   Session 7

14:00–14:30   *A Multimodal Translation-Based Approach for Knowledge Graph Representation Learning*
Hatem Mousselly Sergieh, Teresa Botschen, Iryna Gurevych and Stefan Roth

14:30–15:30   *Putting Semantics into Semantic Roles*
James Allen and Choh Man Teng

15:00–15:30   *Measuring Frame Instance Relatedness*
Valerio Basile, Roque Lopez Condori and Elena Cabrio

15:30–16:00   *Coffee Break*

16:00–16:30   *Solving Feature Sparseness in Text Classification using Core-Periphery Decomposition*
Xia Cui, Sadamori Kojaku, Naoki Masuda and Danushka Bollegala

16:30–17:00   *Robust Handling of Polysemy via Sparse Representations*
Abhijit Mahabal, Dan Roth and Sid Mittal

17:00–17:30   *Multiplicative Tree-Structured Long Short-Term Memory Networks for Semantic Representations*
Nam Khanh Tran and Weiwei Cheng

Resolving Event Coreference with Supervised Representation Learning and Clustering-Oriented Regularization

Kian Kenyon-Dean
School of Computer Science
McGill University
`kian.kenyon-dean`
`@mail.mcgill.ca`

Jackie Chi Kit Cheung
School of Computer Science
McGill University
`jcheung@cs.mcgill.ca`

Doina Precup
School of Computer Science
McGill University
`dprecup@cs.mcgill.ca`

Abstract

We present an approach to event coreference resolution by developing a general framework for clustering that uses supervised representation learning. We propose a neural network architecture with novel Clustering-Oriented Regularization (CORE) terms in the objective function. These terms encourage the model to create embeddings of event mentions that are amenable to clustering. We then use agglomerative clustering on these embeddings to build event coreference chains. For both within- and cross-document coreference on the ECB+ corpus, our model obtains better results than models that require significantly more pre-annotated information. This work provides insight and motivating results for a new general approach to solving coreference and clustering problems with representation learning.

1 Introduction

Event coreference resolution is the task of determining which *event mentions* expressed in language refer to the same real-world event instances. The ability to resolve event coreference has improved the quality of downstream tasks such as automatic text summarization (Vanderwende et al., 2004), questioning-answering (Berant et al., 2014), headline generation (Sun et al., 2015), and text-mining in the medical domain (Ferracane et al., 2016).

Event mentions are comprised of an action component (or, head) and surrounding arguments. Consider the following passages, drawn from two different documents; the heads of the event mentions are in boldface and the subscripts indicate mention IDs:

(1) The president's **speech**$_{m1}$ **shocked**$_{m2}$ the audience. He **announced**$_{m3}$ several new controversial policies.

(2) The policies **proposed**$_{m4}$ by the president will not **surprise**$_{m5}$ those who **followed**$_{m6}$ his **campaign**$_{m7}$.

In this example, $m1$, $m3$, and $m4$ form a chain of coreferent event mentions (underlined), because they refer to the same real-world event in which the president gave a speech. The other four are singletons, meaning that they all refer to separate events and do not corefer with any other mention.

This work investigates how to learn useful representations of event mentions. Event mentions are complex objects, and both the event mention heads and the surrounding arguments are important for the event coreference resolution task. In our example above, the head words of mentions $m2$, *shocked*, and $m5$, *surprise*, are lexically similar, but the event mentions do not corefer. This task therefore necessitates a model that can capture the distributional relationships between event mentions and their surrounding contexts.

We hypothesize that prior knowledge about the task itself can be usefully encoded into the representation learning objective. For our task, this prior means that the embeddings of corefential event mentions should have similar embeddings to each other (a "natural clustering", using the terminology of Bengio et al. (2013)). With this prior, our model creates embeddings of event mentions that are directly conducive for the clustering task of building event coreference chains. This is contrary to the indirect methods of previous work that rely on pairwise decision making followed by a separate model that aggregates the sometimes inconsistent decisions into clusters (Section 2).

We demonstrate these points by proposing a method that learns to embed event mentions into a space that is tuned specifically for clustering. The representation learner is trained to predict which event cluster the event mention belongs to,

1

*Proceedings of the 7th Joint Conference on Lexical and Computational Semantics (*SEM)*, pages 1–10
New Orleans, June 5-6, 2018. ©2018 Association for Computational Linguistics

using an hourglass-shaped neural network. We propose a mechanism to modulate this training by introducing *Clustering-Oriented Regularization* (CORE) terms into the objective function of the learner; these terms impel the model to produce similar embeddings for coreferential event mentions, and dissimilar embeddings otherwise.

Our model obtains strong results on within- and cross-document event coreference resolution, matching or outperforming the system of Cybulska and Vossen (2015) on the ECB+ corpus on all six evaluation measures. We achieve these gains despite the fact that our model requires significantly less pre-annotated or pre-detected information in terms of the internal event structure. Our model's improvements upon the baselines show that our supervised representation learning framework creates new embeddings that capture the abstract distributional relations between samples and their clusters, suggesting that our framework can be generalized to other clustering tasks[1].

2   Related Work

The recent work on event coreference can be categorized according to the assumed level of event representation. In the predicate-argument alignment paradigm (Roth and Frank, 2012; Wolfe et al., 2013), links are simply drawn between predicates in different documents. This work only considers cross-document event coreference (Wolfe et al., 2013, 2015), and no within-document coreference. At the other extreme, the ACE and ERE datasets annotate rich internal event structure, with specific taxonomies that describe the annotated events and their types (Linguistic Data Consortium, 2005, 2016). In these datasets, only within-document coreference is annotated.

The creators of the ECB (Bejan and Harabagiu, 2008) and ECB+ (Cybulska and Vossen, 2014), annotate events according to a level of abstraction between that of the predicate-argument approach and the ACE approach, being most similar to the TimeML paradigm (Pustejovsky et al., 2003). In these datasets, both within-document and cross-document coreference relations are annotated. We use the ECB+ corpus in our experiments because it solves the lack of lexical diversity found within the ECB by adding 502 new annotated documents, providing a total of 982 documents.

Previous work on model design for event coreference has focused on clustering over a linguistically rich set of features. Most models require a pairwise-prediction based supervised learning step which predicts whether or not a pair of event mentions is coreferential (Bagga and Baldwin, 1999; Chen et al., 2009; Cybulska and Vossen, 2015). Other work focuses on the clustering step itself, aggregating local pairwise decisions into clusters, for example by graph partitioning (Chen and Ji, 2009). There has also been work using nonparametric Bayesian clustering techniques (Bejan and Harabagiu, 2014; Yang et al., 2015), as well as other probabilistic models (Lu and Ng, 2017). Some recent work uses intuitions combining representation learning with clustering, but does not augment the loss function for the purpose of building clusterable representations (Krause et al., 2016; Choubey and Huang, 2017).

3   Event Coreference Resolution Model

We formulate the task of event coreference resolution as creating clusters of event mentions which refer to the same event. For the purposes of this work, we define an event mention to be a set of tokens that correspond to the *action* of some event. Consider the sentence below (borrowed from Cybulska and Vossen (2014)):

(3) On Monday Lindsay Lohan **checked into** rehab in Malibu, California after a car **crash**.

Our model would take, as input, feature vectors (see Section 4) extracted from the two event mentions (in bold) independently. In this paper, we use the gold-standard event mentions provided by the dataset, and leave mention detection to other work.

3.1   Model Overview

Our approach to resolving event coreference consists of the following steps:

1. Train a supervised neural network model which learns event mention embeddings by predicting the event cluster in the training set to which the mention belongs (Figure 1).

2. At test time, use the previously trained model's embedding layer to derive representations of unseen event mentions. Then, perform agglomerative clustering with these embeddings to create event coreference chains (Figure 2).

---

[1] All code used in this paper can be found here:
`https://github.com/kiankd/events`

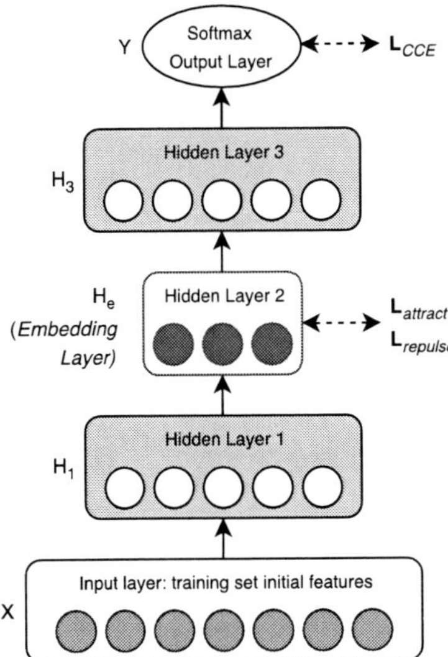

Figure 1: Our supervised representation learning model during the training step. Dashed arrows indicate contributions to the loss function.

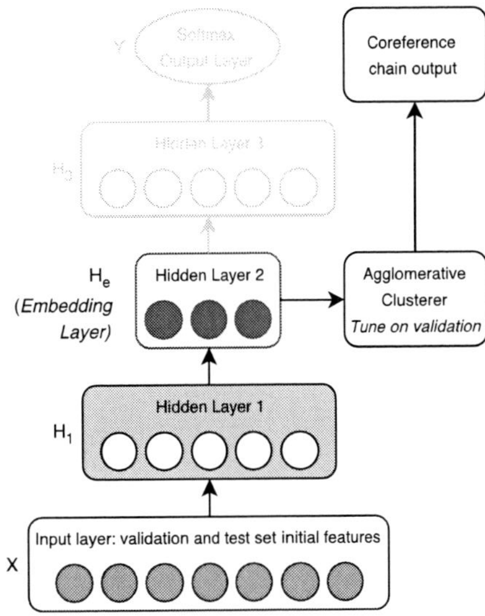

Figure 2: Our trained model at inference time, used for validation tuning and final testing. Note that H_3 and Y are not used in this step.

3.2 Supervised Representation Learning

We propose a representation learning framework based on training a multi-layer artificial neural network, with one layer H_e chosen to be the embedding layer. In the training set, there are a certain number of event mentions, each of which belongs to some gold standard cluster, making C total non-singleton clusters in the training set. The network is trained as if it were encountering a $C+1$-class classification problem, where the class of an event mention corresponds to a single output node, and all singleton mentions belong to class $C+1$[2].

When using this model to cluster a new set of mentions, the final layer's output will not be directly informative since the output node structure corresponds to the clusters within the training set. However, we hypothesize that the trained model will have learned to capture the abstract distributional relationships between event mentions and clusters in the intermediate layer H_e. We thus use the activations in H_e as the embedding of an event mention for the clustering step (see Figure 2). A similar hourglass-like neural architecture design has been successful in automatic speech recogni-

tion (Grézl et al., 2007; Gehring et al., 2013), but has not to our knowledge been used to pre-train embeddings for clustering.

3.3 Categorical-Cross-Entropy (CCE)

Using CCE as the loss function trains the model to correctly predict a training set mention's corresponding cluster. With model prediction y_{ic} as the probability that sample i belongs to class c, and indicator variable $t_{ic} = 1$ if sample i belongs to class c (else $t_{ic} = 0$), we have the mean categorical-cross entropy loss over a randomly sampled training input batch X:

$$\mathbf{L}_{CCE} = -\frac{1}{|\mathbf{X}|} \sum_{i=1}^{|\mathbf{X}|} \sum_{c=1}^{C+1} t_{ic} \log(y_{ic}) \quad (1)$$

3.4 Clustering-Oriented Regularization (CORE)

With CCE, the model may overfit towards accurate prediction performance for those particular clusters found in the training set without learning an embedding that captures the nature of events in general. This therefore motivates introducing regularization terms based on the intuition that embeddings of mentions belonging to the same cluster should be similar, and that embeddings of mentions belonging to different clusters should be dissimilar. Accordingly, we define dissimilarity between two vector embeddings $(\vec{e_1}, \vec{e_2})$ according

---

[2]If each singleton mention (i.e., a mention that does not corefer with anything else) had its own class then the model would be confronted with a classification problem with thousands of classes, many of which would only have one sample; this is much too ill-posed, so we merge all singletons together during the training step.

to the cosine-distance function $\mathbf{d}$:

$$\mathbf{d}(\vec{e_1}, \vec{e_2}) = \frac{1}{2}\left(1 - \frac{\vec{e_1} \cdot \vec{e_2}}{||\vec{e_1}||\,||\vec{e_2}||}\right) \quad (2)$$

Given input batch X, we create two sets $\mathcal{S}$ and $\mathcal{D}$, where $\mathcal{S}$ is the set of all pairs (a, b) of mentions in X that belong to the same cluster, and $\mathcal{D}$ is the set of all pairs (c, d) in X that belong to different clusters. Note that all vector embeddings $\vec{e_i} = H_e(i)$; i.e., they are obtained by feeding the event mention i's features through to embedding layer H_e. We now define the following *Attractive* and *Repulsive* CORE terms.

3.4.1 Attractive Regularization

The first desirable property for the embeddings is that mentions that belong to the same cluster should have low cosine distance between each others' embeddings, since the agglomerative clustering algorithm uses cosine distance to make coreference decisions.

Formally, for all pairs of mentions a and b that belong to the same cluster, we would like to minimize the distance between their embeddings $\vec{e_a}$ and $\vec{e_b}$. We call this "attractive" regularization because we want to attract embeddings closer to each other by minimizing their distance $\mathbf{d}(\vec{e_a}, \vec{e_b})$ so that they will be as similar as possible.

$$\mathbf{L}_{attract} = \frac{1}{|\mathcal{S}|} \sum_{(a,b) \in \mathcal{S}} \mathbf{d}(\vec{e_a}, \vec{e_b}) \quad (3)$$

3.4.2 Repulsive Regularization

The second desirable property is that the embeddings corresponding to mentions that belong to different clusters should have high cosine distance between each other. Thus, for all pairs of mentions c and d that belong to different clusters, the goal is to maximize their distance $\mathbf{d}(\vec{e_c}, \vec{e_d})$. This is "repulsive" because we train the model to push away the embeddings from each other to be as distant as possible.

$$\mathbf{L}_{repulse} = 1 - \frac{1}{|\mathcal{D}|} \sum_{(c,d) \in \mathcal{D}} \mathbf{d}(\vec{e_c}, \vec{e_d}) \quad (4)$$

3.5 Loss Function

Equation 5 below shows the final loss function[3]. The attractive and repulsive terms are weighted by

hyperparameter constants λ_1 and λ_2 respectively:

$$\mathbf{L} = \mathbf{L}_{CCE} + \lambda_1 \mathbf{L}_{attract} + \lambda_2 \mathbf{L}_{repulse} \quad (5)$$

By adding these regularization terms to the loss function, we hypothesize that the new embeddings of test set mentions (obtained by feeding-forward their features into the trained model) will exemplify the desired properties represented by the loss function, thus assisting the agglomerative clustering task in producing correct coreference-chains.

3.6 Agglomerative Clustering

Agglomerative clustering is a non-parametric "bottom-up" approach to hierarchical clustering, in which each sample starts as its own cluster, and at each step, the two most similar clusters are merged, where similarity between two clusters is measured according to some similarity metric. After each merge, clustering similarities are recomputed according to a preset criterion (e.g., single- or complete-linkage). In our models, clustering proceeds until a pre-determined similarity threshold, τ, is reached. We tuned τ on the validation set, doing grid search for $\tau \in [0, 1]$ to maximize B^3 accuracy[4]. Preliminary experimentation led us to use cosine-similarity (see cosine distance in Equation 2) to measure vector similarity, and single-linkage for clustering decisions.

We experimented with two initialization schemes for agglomerative clustering. In the first scheme, each event mention is initialized as its own cluster, as is standard. In the second, we initialized clusters using the lemma-δ baseline defined by Upadhyay et al. (2016). This baseline merges all event mentions with the same head lemma that are in documents with document-level similarity that is higher than a threshold δ. Upadhyay et al. showed that it is a strong indicator of event coreference, so we experimented with initializing our clustering algorithm in this way. We call this model variant CORE+CCE+LEMMA, and describe the parameter tuning procedures in more detail in Section 5.

4 Feature Extraction

We extract features that do not require the pre-processing step of event-template construction to represent the context (unlike Cybulska and Vossen

---

[3]Note that, while we present Equations 3 and 4 as summations over pairs from the input batch, the computation is actually reasonable when written in terms of matrix multiplications. The most expensive operation multiplying the embedded batch of input samples times its transpose.

[4]We optimize with B^3 F1-score because the other measures are either too expensive to compute (CEAF-M, CEAF-E, BLANC), or are less discriminative (MUC).

1.action	*checked into, crash*
2.time	*On Monday*
3.location	*rehab in Malibu, California*
4.participant	*Lindsay Lohan* (human)
	car (non-human)

Table 1: An event template of the sentence in Example 3, borrowed from Cybulska and Vossen (2014; 2015). Our model only requires as input the *action*, not the *time*, *location*, nor *participant* arguments.

(2015), see Table 1); instead, we represent the surrounding context by using the tokens in the general vicinity of the event's action. We thus only require the event's action – which is what we define as an *event mention* – to be previously detected, not all of its arguments. We motivate this by arguing that it would be preferable to build high quality coreference chains without event template features since since extracting event templates can be a difficult process, with the possibility of errors cascading into the event coreference step.

4.1 Contextual

Inspired by the approach of Clark and Manning (2016) in the entity coreference task, we extract, for the token sets below, (i) the token's *word2vec* word embedding (Mikolov et al., 2013) (or average if there are multiple); and, (ii) the one-hot count vector of the token's lemma[5] (or sum if there are multiple), for each event mention, em:

- the first token of em;
- the last token of em;
- all tokens in the em;
- each of the two tokens preceding em;
- each of the two tokens following em;
- all of the five tokens preceding em;
- all of the five tokens following em;
- all of the tokens in em's sentence.

4.2 Document

It is necessary to include features that characterize the mention's document, hoping that the model learns a latent understanding of relations between documents. We extract features from the event mention's document by building lemma-based TF-IDF vector representations of the document. We use log normalization of the raw term frequency

---

[5]This is a 500-dimensional vector where the first 499 entries correspond to the 499 most frequently occurring lemmas in the training set, and the 500th entry indicates if the lemma is not in that set of most frequently occurring lemmas.

of token lemma t in document d, $f_{t,d}$, where $TF_t = 1 + \log(f_{t,d})$. For the IDF term we use smoothed inverse document frequency, with N as the number of documents and n_t as the number of documents that contain the lemma, we have $IDF_t = \log(1 + \frac{N}{n_t})$. By performing a component-wise multiplication of the *IDF* vector with each row in term-frequency matrix *TF*, we create TF-IDF vectors of each document in the training and test sets (with length corresponding to the number of unique lemmas in the training set). We compress these vectors to 100 dimensions with principal component analysis fitted onto the train set document vectors, which is used to transform the validation and test set document vectors.

4.3 Comparative

We include comparative features to relate a mention to the other mentions in its document and to the mentions in the set of documents the model would be requested to extract event coreference chains from. This is motivated by the fact that coreference decisions must be informed by the relationship mentions have with each other. Firstly, we encode the position of the mention in its document with specific binary features indicating if it is first or last; for example, if there were five mentions and it were the third, this feature would correspond to the vector $[0, \frac{3}{5}, 0]$.

Next, we define two sets of mentions we would like to compare with: the first contains all mentions in the same document as the current mention em, and the second contains all mentions in the data we are asked to cluster. For each of these sets, we compute: the average word overlap and average lemma overlap (measured by harmonic similarity) between em and each of the other mentions in the set. We thus add two feature vector entries for each of the sets: the average word overlap between em and the other mentions in the set, and the average lemma overlap between em and the other mentions in the set.

5 Experimental Design

We run our experiments on the ECB+ corpus, the largest corpus that contains both within- and cross-document event coreference annotations. We followed the train/test split of Cybulska and Vossen (2015), using topics 1-35 as the train set and 36-45 as the test set. During training, we split off a validation set[6] for hyperparameter tuning.

Following Cybulska and Vossen, we used the portion of the corpus that has been manually reviewed and checked for correctness. Some previous work (Yang et al., 2015; Upadhyay et al., 2016; Choubey and Huang, 2017) do not appear to have followed this guideline from the corpus creators, as they report different corpus statistics compared to those reported by Cybulska and Vossen. As a result, those papers may report results on a data set with known annotation errors.

5.1 Evaluation Measures

Since there is no consensus in the coreference resolution literature on the best evaluation measure, we present results obtained according to six different measures, as is common in previous work. We use the scorer presented by Pradhan et al. (2014). In this task, the term "coreference chain" is synonymous with "cluster".

MUC (Vilain et al., 1995). Link-level measure which counts the minimum number of link changes required to obtain the correct clustering from the predictions; it does not account for correctly predicted singletons.

B^3 (Bagga and Baldwin, 1998). Mention-level measure which computes precision and recall for each individual mention, overcoming the singleton problem of MUC, but can problematically count the same coreference chain multiple times.

CEAF-M (Luo, 2005). Mention-level measure which reflects the percentage of mentions that are in the correct coreference chains. Note that precision and recall are the same in this measure since we use pre-annotated mentions.

CEAF-E (Luo, 2005). Entity-level measure computed by aligning predicted with the gold chains, not allowing one chain to have more than one alignment, overcoming the problem of B^3.

BLANC (Luo et al., 2014). Computes two F-scores in terms of the pairwise quality of coreference decisions and non-coreference decisions, and averages these scores together for the final results.

CoNLL. The mean of MUC, B^3, and CEAF-E.

5.2 Models

We compare our representation-learning model variants to three baselines: a deterministic lemma-

based baseline, a lemma-δ baseline, and an unsupervised baseline which clusters the originally extracted features. We also compare with the results of Cybulska and Vossen (2015).

5.2.1 Baselines

LEMMA. This algorithm clusters event mentions which share the same head word lemma into the same coreference chains across all documents.

LEMMA-δ. Proposed by Upadhyay et al. (2016), this method provides a difficult baseline to beat. A δ-similarity threshold is introduced, and we merge two mentions with the same head-lemma if and only if the cosine-similarity between the TF-IDF vectors of their corresponding documents is greater than δ. This δ parameter is tuned to maximize B^3 performance on the validation set, which we found occurs when $\delta = 0.67$.

UNSUPERVISED. This is the result obtained by agglomerative clustering over the original unweighted features. Again, we optimize the τ similarity threshold over the validation set.

5.2.2 Sentence Templates (CV2015)

Cybulska and Vossen (2015) propose a model that uses sentence-level event templates (see Table 1), requiring more annotated information than our models. See (Vossen and Cybulska, 2017) for further elaboration of this model. To our knowledge, this is the best previous model on ECB+ using the same data and evaluation criteria as our work.

5.2.3 Representation Learning.

We test four different model variants:

- CCE: uses only categorical-cross-entropy in the loss function (Equation 1);

- CORE: uses only clustering-oriented regularization; i.e., the attract and repulse terms (Equations 3 and 4);

- CORE+CCE: includes categorical-cross-entropy and the attract and repulse terms (Equation 5);

- CORE+CCE+LEMMA: initializes the agglomerative clustering with clusters computed by lemma-δ (with a differently tuned value of δ than the baseline) and continues the clustering process using the similarities between the embeddings created by CORE+CCE.

---

[6]Topics 2, 5, 12, 18, 21, 23, 34, 35 (randomly chosen).

Model	λ_1	λ_2	B^3	τ
Baselines				
UNSUPERVISED	-	-	0.590	0.657
LEMMA	-	-	0.597	-
LEMMA-δ	-	-	0.612	-
Model Variants				
CORE+CCE+L	2.0	0.0	**0.678**	0.843
CORE+CCE	2.0	2.0	0.663	0.776
	2.0	1.0	0.666	0.773
	2.0	0.1	0.665	0.843
	2.0	0.0	**0.669**	0.843
	0.0	2.0	0.662	0.710
CORE	2.0	2.0	0.631	0.701
	1.0	1.0	0.625	0.689
CCE	-	-	0.644	0.853

Table 2: Model comparison based on validation set B^3 accuracy with optimized τ cluster-similarity threshold. For CORE+CCE+LEMMA (indicated as CORE+CCE+L) we tuned to $\delta = 0.89$; for LEMMA-δ we tuned to $\delta = 0.67$.

5.3 Hyper-parameter Tuning

For the representation learning models, we performed a non-exhaustive hyper-parameter search optimized for validation set performance. We keep the following parameters constant across the model variants:

- 1000 neurons in H_1 and H_3; 250 neurons in H_e, the embedding layer (see Figure 1);

- Softmax output layer with $C + 1$ units;

- ReLU activation functions for all neurons;

- *Adam* gradient descent (Kingma and Ba, 2014);

- 25% dropout between each layer;

- Learning rate of 0.00085 (times 10^{-1} for CORE);

- Randomly sampled batches of 272 mentions, where a batch is forced to contain pairs of coreferential and non-coreferential mentions.

Models are trained for 100 epochs. At each epoch, we optimize τ (our agglomerative clustering similarity threshold) using a two-pass approach: we first test 20 different settings of τ, then τ is further optimized around the best value from the first pass. For CORE+CCE+LEMMA, we tune the δ parameter of the lemma-δ clustering approach to the validation set by testing 100 different values of δ; these different δ values initialize the clusters, and we then continue clustering by testing validation results obtained when using the similarities between the embeddings created by CORE+CCE for different values of τ.

Some of the results of hyperparameter tuning on the validation set are shown in Table 2. Interestingly, we observe that CORE+CCE performs slightly better with $\lambda_2 = 0$; i.e., without repulsive regularization. This suggests that enforcing representation similarity is more important than enforcing division, although we cannot conclusively state that repulsive regularization would not be useful for other tasks. Nonetheless, for test set results we use the optimal hyperparameter configurations found during this validation-tuning step; e.g., for CORE+CCE we set $\lambda_1 = 2$ and $\lambda_2 = 0$.

6 Results

Table 3 presents the performance of the models for combined within- and cross-document event coreference. Results for these models are obtained with the hyper-parameter settings that achieved optimal accuracy during validation-tuning.

Firstly, we observe that CORE+CCE offers marked improvements upon the UNSUPERVISED baseline, CORE model, and CCE model. From these results we conclude: (i) supervised representation learning provides more informative embeddings than the original feature vectors; and, (ii) that combining Clustering-Oriented Regularization with categorical-cross-entropy is better than just using one or the other, indicating that our introduction of these novel terms into the loss function is a useful contribution.

We also note that CORE+CCE+LEMMA (which obtains the best validation set results) beats the strong LEMMA-δ baseline. Our model offers marked improvements or roughly equivalent scores in each evaluation measure except BLANC, where the baseline offers a 3 point F-score improvement. This is due to the very high precision of the baseline, whereas CORE+CCE+LEMMA seems to trade precision for recall.

We finally observe that CORE+CCE+LEMMA improves upon the results of Cybulska and Vossen (2015). We obtain improvements of 14 points in MUC, 3 points in entity-based CEAF, 5 points in CoNLL, and 1 point in BLANC, with equivalent results in B^3 and mention-based CEAF. These re-

Model	MUC			B^3			CM	CE			BLANC			CoNLL
	R	P	F	R	P	F	F	R	P	F	R	P	F	F
Baselines														
Lemma	66	58	62	66	58	62	51	87	39	54	64	61	63	61
Lemma-δ	55	68	61	61	80	**69**	**59**	73	60	66	62	80	**67**	66
Unsupervised	39	63	48	55	81	66	51	72	49	58	57	58	58	57
Previous Work														
CV2015	43	77	55	58	86	**69**	58	-	-	66	60	69	63	64
Model Variants														
CCE	66	63	65	69	60	64	50	59	63	61	69	56	59	63
CORE	58	58	58	66	58	62	44	53	53	53	66	54	56	57
CORE+CCE	62	70	66	67	69	68	56	73	64	68	68	59	62	67
CORE+CCE+Lemma	67	71	**69**	71	67	**69**	58	71	67	**69**	72	60	64	**69**

Table 3: Combined within- and cross-document test set results on ECB+. Measures CM and CE stand for mention-based CEAF and entity-based CEAF, respectively.

Model	MUC			B^3			CM	CE			BLANC			CoNLL
	R	P	F	R	P	F	F	R	P	F	R	P	F	F
Baselines														
Lemma-δ	41	77	53	86	97	**92**	85	92	82	87	65	86	71	77
Unsupervised	32	36	34	85	86	85	74	80	78	79	65	55	57	66
Model Variants														
CCE	44	49	46	87	89	88	79	82	80	81	67	67	67	72
CORE	55	32	40	89	70	78	65	64	79	71	75	54	56	63
CORE+CCE	43	68	53	87	95	91	84	90	82	86	67	76	70	76
CORE+CCE+Lemma	57	69	**63**	90	94	**92**	**86**	90	86	**88**	73	78	**75**	**81**

Table 4: Within-document test set results on ECB+. Note that Lemma is equivalent to Lemma-δ in the within-document setting. Cybulska and Vossen (2015) did not report the performance of their model in this setting.

sults suggest that high quality coreference chains can be built without necessitating event templates.

In Table 4, we see the performance of our models on within-document coreference resolution in isolation. These results are obtained by cutting all links drawn across documents for the gold standard chains and the predicted chains. We observe that, across all models, scores on the mention- and entity-based measures are substantially higher than the link-based measures (e.g., MUC and BLANC). The usefulness of CORE+CCE+Lemma (which initializes the clustering with the lemma-δ predictions and then continues to cluster with CORE+CCE) is exemplified by the improvements or matches in every measure when compared to both Lemma-δ and CORE+CCE. The most vivid improvement here is observed with the 10 point improvement in MUC over both models as well as the 4 and 5 point improvements in BLANC respectively, where the higher recall entails that CORE+CCE+Lemma confidently predicts coreference links that would otherwise have been false negatives.

7 Conclusions and Future Work

We have presented a novel approach to event coreference resolution by combining supervised representation learning with non-parametric clustering. We train an hourglass-shaped neural network to learn how to represent event mentions in a useful way for an agglomerative clustering algorithm. By adding the novel Clustering-Oriented Regularization (CORE) terms into the loss function, the model learns to construct embeddings that are easily clusterable; i.e., the prior that embeddings of samples belonging to the same cluster should be similar, and those of samples belonging to different clusters should be dissimilar.

Our results suggest that clustering embeddings created with representation learning is much better than clustering of the original feature vectors, when using the same agglomerative clustering algorithm. We show that including CORE in the loss function improves performance more than when only using categorical-cross-entropy to train the representation learner model. Our top-performing model obtains results that improve upon previous work despite the fact that our model requires less annotated information in order to perform the task.

Future work involves applying our model to automatically annotated event mentions and other event coreference datasets, and extending this framework toward a full end-to-end system that does not rely on manual feature engineering at the input level. Additionally, our model may be useful for other clustering tasks, such as entity coreference and document clustering. Lastly, we seek to determine how CORE and its imposition of a clusterable latent space structure may or may not assist in improving the quality of latent representations in general.

Acknowledgements

This work was funded with grants from the Natural Sciences and Engineering Research Council of Canada (NSERC) and the Fonds de recherche du Québec - Nature et Technologies (FRQNT). We thank the anonymous reviewers for their helpful comments and suggestions.

References

Amit Bagga and Breck Baldwin. 1998. Algorithms for scoring coreference chains. In *The first international conference on language resources and evaluation workshop on linguistics coreference*, volume 1, pages 563–566.

Amit Bagga and Breck Baldwin. 1999. Cross-document event coreference: Annotations, experiments, and observations. In *Proceedings of the Workshop on Coreference and its Applications*, pages 1–8. ACL.

Cosmin Adrian Bejan and Sanda Harabagiu. 2014. Unsupervised Event Coreference Resolution. *Computational Linguistics*, 40(2):311–347.

Cosmin Adrian Bejan and Sanda M Harabagiu. 2008. A Linguistic Resource for Discovering Event Structures and Resolving Event Coreference. In *LREC*.

Yoshua Bengio, Aaron Courville, and Pascal Vincent. 2013. Representation learning: A review and new perspectives. *IEEE transactions on pattern analysis and machine intelligence*, 35(8):1798–1828.

Jonathan Berant, Vivek Srikumar, Pei-Chun Chen, Abby Vander Linden, Brittany Harding, Brad Huang, Peter Clark, and Christopher D Manning. 2014. Modeling Biological Processes for Reading Comprehension. In *Proceedings of the 2014 Conference on EMNLP*, pages 1499–1510.

Zheng Chen and Heng Ji. 2009. Graph-based event coreference resolution. In *Proceedings of the 2009 Workshop on Graph-based Methods for NLP*, pages 54–57. ACL.

Zheng Chen, Heng Ji, and Robert Haralick. 2009. A Pairwise Event Coreference Model, Feature Impact and Evaluation for Event Coreference Resolution. In *Proceedings of the workshop on events in emerging text types*, pages 17–22. ACL.

Prafulla Kumar Choubey and Ruihong Huang. 2017. Event coreference resolution by iteratively unfolding inter-dependencies among events. *arXiv preprint arXiv:1707.07344*.

Kevin Clark and Christopher D Manning. 2016. Improving Coreference Resolution by Learning Entity-Level Distributed Representations. *arXiv preprint arXiv:1606.01323*.

Agata Cybulska and Piek Vossen. 2014. Using a sledgehammer to crack a nut? Lexical diversity and event coreference resolution. In *LREC*, pages 4545–4552.

Agata Cybulska and Piek Vossen. 2015. Translating Granularity of Event Slots into Features for Event Coreference Resolution. In *Proceedings of the 3rd Workshop on EVENTS at the NAACL-HLT*, pages 1–10.

Elisa Ferracane, Iain Marshall, Byron C Wallace, and Katrin Erk. 2016. Leveraging coreference to identify arms in medical abstracts: An experimental study. *EMNLP*, pages 86–95.

Jonas Gehring, Yajie Miao, Florian Metze, and Alex Waibel. 2013. Extracting deep bottleneck features using stacked auto-encoders. In *Acoustics, Speech and Signal Processing (ICASSP), 2013 IEEE International Conference on*, pages 3377–3381. IEEE.

Frantisek Grézl, Martin Karafiát, Stanislav Kontár, and Jan Cernocky. 2007. Probabilistic and bottle-neck features for LVCSR of meetings. In *Acoustics, Speech and Signal Processing, 2007. ICASSP 2007. IEEE International Conference on*, volume 4, pages IV–757. IEEE.

Diederik Kingma and Jimmy Ba. 2014. Adam: A method for stochastic optimization. *arXiv preprint arXiv:1412.6980*.

Sebastian Krause, Feiyu Xu, Hans Uszkoreit, and Dirk Weissenborn. 2016. Event linking with sentential features from convolutional neural networks. In *Proceedings of the 20th SIGNLL Conference on Computational Natural Language Learning*, pages 239–249.

Linguistic Data Consortium. 2005. ACE (Automatic Content Extraction) English Annotation Guidelines for Events. Version 5.4.3 2005.07.01.

Linguistic Data Consortium. 2016. Rich ERE Annotation Guidelines Overview. V4.2.

Jing Lu and Vincent Ng. 2017. Learning antecedent structures for event coreference resolution. In *Machine Learning and Applications (ICMLA), 2017*

16th IEEE International Conference on, pages 113–118. IEEE.

Xiaoqiang Luo. 2005. On coreference resolution performance metrics. In *Proceedings of the conference on Human Language Technology and EMNLP*, pages 25–32. ACL.

Xiaoqiang Luo, Sameer Pradhan, Marta Recasens, and Eduard H Hovy. 2014. An Extension of BLANC to System Mentions. In *ACL (2)*, pages 24–29.

Tomas Mikolov, Ilya Sutskever, Kai Chen, Greg S Corrado, and Jeff Dean. 2013. Distributed representations of words and phrases and their compositionality. In *Advances in neural information processing systems*, pages 3111–3119.

Sameer Pradhan, Xiaoqiang Luo, Marta Recasens, Eduard H Hovy, Vincent Ng, and Michael Strube. 2014. Scoring coreference partitions of predicted mentions: A reference implementation. In *ACL (2)*, pages 30–35.

James Pustejovsky, José M Castano, Robert Ingria, Roser Sauri, Robert J Gaizauskas, Andrea Setzer, Graham Katz, and Dragomir R Radev. 2003. TimeML: Robust specification of event and temporal expressions in text. *New directions in question answering*, 3:28–34.

Michael Roth and Anette Frank. 2012. Aligning predicate argument structures in monolingual comparable texts: A new corpus for a new task. In *Proceedings of the First Joint Conference on Lexical and Computational Semantics-Volume 1: Proceedings of the main conference and the shared task, and Volume 2: Proceedings of the Sixth International Workshop on Semantic Evaluation*, pages 218–227. ACL.

Rui Sun, Yue Zhang, Meishan Zhang, and Donghong Ji. 2015. Event-driven headline generation. In *Proceedings of ACL*, pages 462–472.

Shyam Upadhyay, Nitish Gupta, Christos Christodoulopoulos, and Dan Roth. 2016. Revisiting the Evaluation for Cross Document Event Coreference. In *COLING*.

Lucy Vanderwende, Michele Banko, and Arul Menezes. 2004. Event-centric summary generation. *Working notes of DUC*, pages 127–132.

Marc Vilain, John Burger, John Aberdeen, Dennis Connolly, and Lynette Hirschman. 1995. A model-theoretic coreference scoring scheme. In *Proceedings of the 6th conference on Message understanding*, pages 45–52. ACL.

Piek Vossen and Agata Cybulska. 2017. Identity and granularity of events in text. *arXiv preprint arXiv:1704.04259*.

Travis Wolfe, Mark Dredze, and Benjamin Van Durme. 2015. Predicate argument alignment using a global coherence model. In *Proceedings of the 2015 Conference of NAACL: Human Language Technologies*, pages 11–20.

Travis Wolfe, Benjamin Van Durme, Mark Dredze, Nicholas Andrews, Charley Beller, Chris Callison-Burch, Jay DeYoung, Justin Snyder, Jonathan Weese, Tan Xu, et al. 2013. PARMA: A Predicate Argument Aligner. In *ACL (2)*, pages 63–68.

Bishan Yang, Claire Cardie, and Peter Frazier. 2015. A Hierarchical Distance-dependent Bayesian Model for Event Coreference Resolution. *Transactions of the Association for Computational Linguistics*, 3:517–528.

Learning Distributed Event Representations with a Multi-Task Approach

Xudong Hong†, Asad Sayeed*, Vera Demberg†
†Dept. of Language Science and Technology, Saarland University
{xhong,vera}@coli.uni-saarland.de
*Dept. of Philosophy, Linguistics, and Theory of Science, University of Gothenburg
asad.sayeed@gu.se

Abstract

Human world knowledge contains information about prototypical events and their participants and locations. In this paper, we train the first models using multi-task learning that can both predict missing event participants and also perform semantic role classification based on semantic plausibility. Our best-performing model is an improvement over the previous state-of-the-art on thematic fit modelling tasks. The event embeddings learned by the model can additionally be used effectively in an event similarity task, also outperforming the state-of-the-art.

1 Introduction

Event representations consist, at minimum, of a predicate, the entities that participate in the event, and the thematic roles of those participants (Fillmore, 1968). *The cook cut the cake with the knife* expresses an event of cutting in which a cook is the "agent", the cake is the "patient", and the knife is the "instrument" of the action. Experiments have shown that event knowledge, in terms of the prototypical participants of events and their structured compositions, plays a crucial role in human sentence processing, especially from the perspective of *thematic fit*: the extent to which humans perceive given event participants as "fitting" given predicate-role combinations (Ferretti et al., 2001; McRae et al., 2005; Bicknell et al., 2010). Therefore, computational models of language processing should also consist of event representations that reflect thematic fit. To evaluate this aspect empirically, a popular approach in previous work has been to compare model output to human judgements (Sayeed et al., 2016).

The best-performing recent work has been the model of Tilk et al. (2016), who effectively simulate thematic fit via *selectional preferences*: generating a probability distribution over the full vocabulary of potential role-fillers. Given event context as input, including a predicate and a given set of semantic roles and their role-fillers as well as one target role, its training objective is to predict the correct role-filler for the target role. The objective of predicting upcoming role-fillers is cognitively plausible: there is ample evidence that humans anticipate upcoming input during sentence processing and learn from prediction error (Kuperberg and Jaeger, 2016; Friston, 2010) (even if other details of the implementation like back-propagation may not have much to do with how errors are propagated in humans).

An analysis of role filler predictions by Tilk et al.'s model shows that the model does not make sufficient use of the thematic role input. For instance, the representation of *apple eats boy* is similar to the representation of *boy eats apple*, even though the events are very dissimilar from one another. Interestingly, humans have been found to make similar errors. For instance, humans have been shown to frequently misinterpret a sentence with inverse role assignment, when the plausibility of the sentence with swapped role assignment is very high, as in *The mother gave the candle the daughter*, which is often erroneously interpreted as the daughter receiving the candle, instead of the literal syntax which says that the candle receives the daughter (Gibson et al., 2013).

Tilk et al.'s model design makes it more susceptible to this type of error than humans. The model lacks the ability to process in both directions, i.e., to both comprehend *and* produce thematic role marking (approximated here as thematic role assignment). We therefore propose to add a secondary role prediction task to the model, training it to both produce and comprehend language.

In this paper, we train the first model using multi-task learning (Caruana, 1998) which can ef-

11

*Proceedings of the 7th Joint Conference on Lexical and Computational Semantics (*SEM)*, pages 11–21
New Orleans, June 5-6, 2018. ©2018 Association for Computational Linguistics

fectively predict semantic roles for event participants as well as perform role-filler prediction[1]. Furthermore, we obtain significant improvements and better-performing event embeddings by an adjustment to the architecture (parametric weighted average of role-filler embeddings) which helps to capture role-specific information for participants during the composition process. The new event embeddings exhibit state-of-the-art performance on a correlation task with human thematic fit judgements and an event similarity task.

Our model is the first joint model for selectional preferences (**SPs**) prediction and semantic role classification (**SRC**) to the best of our knowledge. Previous works used distributional similarity-based (Zapirain et al., 2013) or LDA-based (Wu and Palmer, 2015) SPs for semantic role labelling to leverage lexical sparsity. However, when it comes to a situation with domain shift, single task SP models that rely heavily on syntax have high generalisation error. We show that the multi-task architecture is better suited to generalise in that situation and can be potentially applied to improve current semantic role labelling systems which rely on small annotated corpora.

Our approach is a conceptual improvement on previous models because we address multiple event-representation tasks in a single model: thematic fit evaluation, role-filler prediction/generation, semantic role classification, event participant composition, and structured event similarity evaluation.

2 Role-Filler Prediction Model

Tilk et al. (2016) proposed a neural network, the non-incremental role-filler (**NNRF**) model, for role-filler prediction which takes a combination of words and roles as input to predict the filler of a target role. For example, the model would take "waiter/ARG0" and "serve/PRD" and target role "ARG1" as input and return high probabilities to words like "breakfast", "dish", and "drinks".

The original NNRF model can be seen in Figure 1 (excluding the part of the architecture shown in the red box). The input layer is a role-specific embedding tensor $\mathbf{T} \in \mathbb{R}^{|V| \times |R| \times d}$ that is indexed by two one-hot encoded vectors $\mathbf{w}_i$ and $\mathbf{r}_i$ for input word w_i and input role r_i, where V is the set of

words and R is the set of semantic roles in our vocabulary. Tilk et al. applied *Tensor Factorisation*, which reduces the number of parameters to $(|V| + |R| + d) \times k$. The embedding tensor is factorised into three matrices[2]: $\mathbf{A}_e \in \mathbb{R}^{|V| \times k}$, $\mathbf{B}_e \in \mathbb{R}^{|R| \times k}$ and $\mathbf{C}_e \in \mathbb{R}^{k \times d}$. The overall embedding for a pair consisting of a word and its role, referred to as an *event participant embedding*, is represented as:

$$\mathbf{p}_l = (\mathbf{w}_i \mathbf{A}_e \circ \mathbf{r}_i \mathbf{B}_e) \mathbf{C}_e \tag{1}$$

where "$\circ$" is the Hadamard product.

When several word-role pairs $l = (w_i, r_i) \in C$, where C is the event context, are given as input, the model sums up their event participant embedding vectors to yield an *event representation* e. Then it passes through one non-linearity layer with a parametric rectified linear unit (He et al., 2015): $\mathbf{h} = PReLU(\mathbf{e} + \mathbf{b}_e)$ where $\mathbf{b}_e$ is a bias vector.

The output layer consists of a softmax regression classifier computed as:

$$\mathbf{o}_w = Softmax_w(\mathbf{h}\mathbf{W}_w + \mathbf{b}_w) \tag{2}$$

where $\mathbf{b}_w$ is a bias vector. For each target role r_t, the model learns a target role-specific classifier with weight matrix of $\mathbf{W}_w^{(r_t)} \in \mathbb{R}^{d \times |V|}$, using r_t and event context C to predict the target word w_t. The weight matrices are stacked into an order-3 tensor and then factorised as:

$$\mathbf{W}_w^{(r_t)} = \mathbf{C}_w \, diag(\mathbf{r}_t \mathbf{B}_w) \, \mathbf{A}_w \tag{3}$$

where $diag(\mathbf{v})$ is a diagonal matrix with vector $\mathbf{v}$ on its main diagonal.

However, we found that the NNRF model in some cases relies heavily on lexical features but is not sensitive enough to semantic role assignments and hence represents phrases like "boy eats apple" in a similar way as "apple eats boy". We believe that a reason for this lies in the fact that the correct filler can often be predicted even when the role assignment is ignored, i.e., with the current objective, the model can often neglect the thematic role information. One could easily imagine that even humans might show similar behaviour if they only had to guess meanings from words they hear and are not required to produce correctly marked language themselves. We thus propose to add a second task to the network in order to approximate the dual comprehension and production tasks in human language learning.

[2]Further explanations are in the supplemental material.

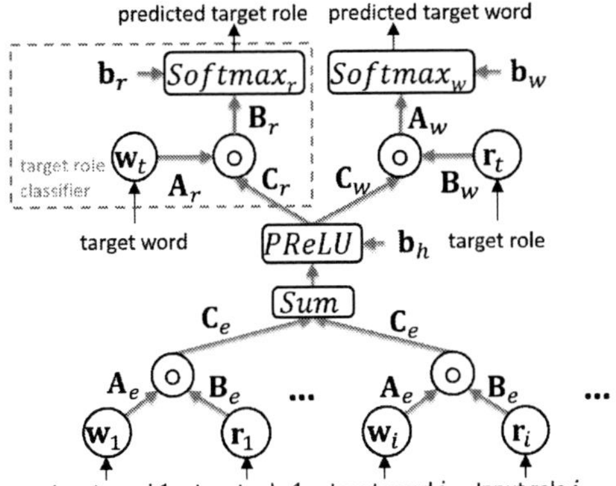

Figure 1: Architecture of multi-task role-filler model.

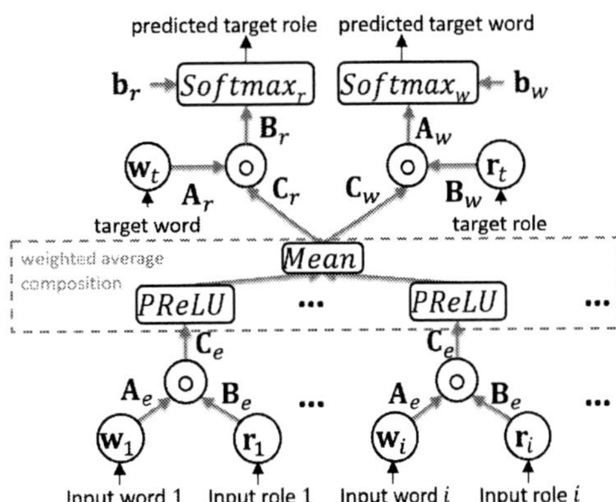

Figure 2: Architecture of role-filler averaging model.

3 Multi-Task Model

Our core idea is to add a second task, semantic role classification, such that the role-filler prediction model needs to predict the correct semantic role label for a target role-filler and a given set of input word-role pairs, i.e., the event context. Multi-task learning can integrate different objectives into one model and has previously been shown to help improve model generalisation (e.g., Caruana, 1998). The auxiliary task can be considered a regularisation of the objective function of the main task.

A neural model can be extended to multi-task architecture straightforwardly via sharing the low-level distributed representations. We design a multi-task model (**NNRF-MT**) which shares the event participant embedding for the event context and tackles role-filler prediction and semantic role classification simultaneously.

Figure 1 shows the NNRF-MT model with an additional role prediction classifier in the last layer, indicated by the red box. The new target role classifier mirrors the design of the original target word classifier. The output vector of the new target role classifier is computed as:

$$\mathbf{o}_r = Softmax_r(\mathbf{h}\mathbf{W}_r + \mathbf{b}_r) \quad (4)$$

where $\mathbf{W}_r \in \mathbb{R}^{d \times |R|}$ is the weight matrix of the target role classifier, and $\mathbf{b}_r$ is its bias vector. Like Equation (3), the weight matrix $\mathbf{W}_r^{(w_t)}$ for the target word w_t is factorised as:

$$\mathbf{W}_r^{(w_t)} = \mathbf{C}_r \, diag(\mathbf{w}_t \mathbf{A}_r) \, \mathbf{B}_r \quad (5)$$

where $\mathbf{A}_r \in \mathbb{R}^{|V| \times k^{(r)}}$.

3.1 Parametric Role-Filler Composition

In the NNRF-MT model, the embedding vectors of each word-role pair are simply summed up to represent the event. But in many cases, event participants contribute to the event differently. This has the disadvantage that some important participants are not correctly composed. Even worse, there is no normalization between cases where different numbers of role-filler pairs are available as context.

We thus propose a parametric architecture where PReLU is applied to each word-role pair embedding, and the resulting vectors are then combined by using the **mean** composition function. Parameters inside PReLU can now act as weights for each role-filler embedding. Computing the mean can be considered as the normalisation of role-filler representations within the event boundary, which can prevent the possible over-/underflow of the weights of the hidden vector.

With this method, the event embedding is computed as:

$$\mathbf{e} = \frac{1}{|C|} \sum_{l \in C} PReLU_l(\mathbf{p}_l) \quad (6)$$

and then directly fed into the classifier as the hidden vector $\mathbf{h}$. Figure 2 shows the resulting model named Role-Filler Averaging model (**RoFA-MT**), which is identical to the NNRF-MT model, except for the composition of event participant embeddings (marked by the red box).

3.2 Residual Learning

An additional way to reduce the challenge of exploding or vanishing gradients in factorised tensor is to apply *residual learning* (He et al., 2016).

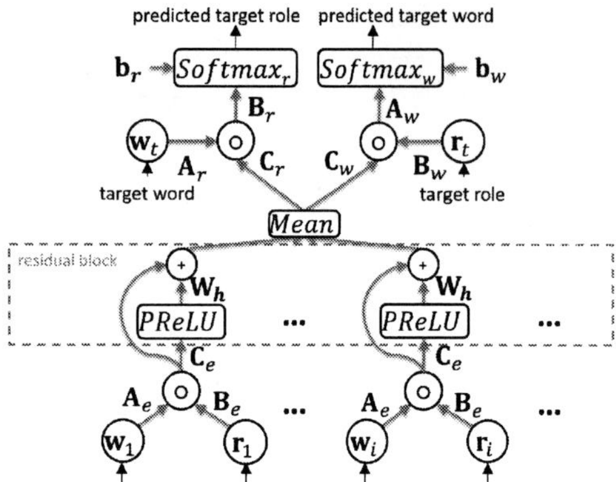

Figure 3: Architecture of residual role-filler averaging model.

The key idea in residual learning is that an identity mapping over other layers may be combined with a model that encodes information through several layers in order to simultaneously capture lower-level and higher-level information. We therefore experiment with residual learning in our RoFA-MT model (henceforth called **ResRoFA-MT**): the event participant vector now consists of a "raw" vector and a weighted vector that has been fed through a linear hidden layer, see Figure 3.

The original weight of the role-filler embedding is passed into the non-linear layer as:
$\mathbf{h}_l = PReLU_l(\mathbf{r}_l\mathbf{C}_e)$ where $\mathbf{r}_l = \mathbf{w}_i\mathbf{A}_e \circ \mathbf{r}_j\mathbf{B}_e$ is the residual (i.e., the composition of word embedding and semantic role embedding). Then the combination of the output hidden vector $\mathbf{h}_l$ and the residual vector goes into the event embedding as:

$$\mathbf{e} = \frac{1}{|C|} \sum_{l \in C} (\mathbf{h}_l\mathbf{W}_h + \mathbf{r}_l) \qquad (7)$$

where $\mathbf{W}_h$ is the weight matrix. After that, the event embedding goes directly into the classifier.

3.3 Multi-Task Training

The multi-task model is trained to optimise two objective functions in parallel. For each clause in the training data, we extract the predicate and all participants. We then choose each word-role pair as the target and the remainder as context C for one training sample. We use the multi-task model to predict the target role given the target filler as an input and to predict the target filler given the target role. We use a weighted combination of the probabilities of the target role and target word to

obtain the overall loss function as:

$$\mathcal{L} = \mathcal{L}^{(w)}(C, r_t) + \alpha\mathcal{L}^{(r)}(C, w_t)$$

where α is the hyper-parameter of the weight of the semantic role classification task and can be tuned for different training purposes. In this paper, we choose 1.0 as the weight of semantic role prediction α to balance between two tasks.

4 Experiments

To learn an event representation from language resources with access to generalised event knowledge, we use the Rollenwechsel-English (**RW-eng**) corpus[3], a large-scale corpus based on BNC and ukWaC with about 2B tokens, which contains automatically generated PropBank-style semantic role labels for the head words of each argument (Sayeed et al., 2018).

We choose the first 99.2% as training data, the next 0.4% as validation data and the last 0.4% as test data, which follows Tilk's setting to make a fair comparison. From the training data, we extract a word list of the 50K most frequent head words (nouns, verbs, adjectives and adverbs) and add one OOV symbol[4]. For training the model, we distinguish between seven role labels: PRD for predicates, ARG0, ARG1, ARGM-MNR, ARGM-LOC, ARGM-TMP; all other roles are mapped onto a category OTHER.

NNRF is the current state-of-the-art model for event representation; we reimplement this model and use it as the baseline for our evaluation tasks. For a fair comparison, we train the NNRF model and our three multi-task models on the newest version of RW-eng corpus. Each model is trained for 27 iterations (or less if the model converged earlier)[5].

Because we use random parameter initialisation, to observe its effect to our evaluations, we train 10 instances of each model and report average performance (we do not use these 10 models as an ensemble method such as labelling by majority voting).

---

[3]http://rollen.mmci.uni-saarland.de/RW-eng

[4]A detailed description of data preprocessing is in the supplemental.

[5]The details of hyper-parameter setting are in the supplemental.

Model	Accuracy	p-value
NNRF-MT	89.1	-
RoFA-MT	94.8	< 0.0001
ResRoFA-MT	94.7	< 0.0001

Table 1: Semantic role classification results for the three multi-task architectures.

5 Evaluation: Semantic Role Classification

We begin by testing the new component of the model in terms of how well the model can predict semantic role labels.

5.1 Role Prediction Given Event Context

We evaluate our models on semantic role prediction accuracy given the predicate and other arguments with their roles on the test dataset of the RW-eng corpus. Table 1 shows that the RoFA-MT and ResRoFA-MT models outperform the NNRF-MT model by a statistically significant margin (tested with McNemar's test), showing that the parametric weighted average composition method leads to significant improvements.

5.2 Classification for Verb-Head Pairs

Semantic role classification systems make heavy use of syntactic features but can be further improved by integrating models of selectional preferences (Zapirain et al., 2009). Here we compare the semantics-based role assignments produced by our model to predictions made by various selectional preference (SP) models in the first evaluation of Zapirain et al. (2013). E.g., the model is to predict ARG1 for the pair (eat_{verb}, $apple$) without any other feature.

Zapirain et al. (2013) combined a verb-role SP model built on training data and an additional distributional similarity model trained on a large scale corpus for estimating the fit between verbs and their arguments for different roles. These thematic fit estimates are used to select the best role label for each predicate-argument pair.

We consider only following best variants as baselines:

Zapirain13^{Pado07}: This variant uses a distributional similarity model constructed on a general corpus (BNC) with Padó and Lapata (2007)'s syntax-based method.

Zapirain13$^{Lin98}_{in-domain}$: This variant contains Lin (1998)'s distributional similarity model which uses syntax-based clustering. The model is pre-computed on a mixed corpus (including WSJ) which is in the same domain as the WSJ test set.

We apply our trained role labelling model directly to the test set, without touching the WSJ training/validation set. Following the baselines, for semantic roles which are not represented in our model, we do not make any prediction (this is reflected in lower recall for those cases).

The model is evaluated on the data set from the CoNLL-2005 shared task (Carreras and Màrquez, 2005), which contains the WSJ corpus as part of its training/validation/test sets and the Brown corpus as an out-of-domain test set (marked in Table 2 as **Brown**). We estimate 99% confidence intervals using the bootstrapping method, with 100 replications. We also construct a trivial baseline model, the ZeroR classifier, which predicts the majority class ARG1 given any input.

Table 2 shows that the baseline model using Lin's similarities (Zapirain13$^{Lin98}_{in-domain}$) works best on the WSJ test dataset, statistically significantly outperforming each of the other methods ($p < 0.01$). However, this can be explained by the fact that this model is using semantic similarities obtained from the same domain as the WSJ test set. Among the models without using in-domain semantic similarity, ResRoFA-MT is significantly better than all others ($p < 0.01$).

On the Brown data, which is out-of-domain for all models, the ResRoFA-MT model achieves the best result and outperforms previous baselines significantly ($p < 0.01$). Without any training on the WSJ corpus, our best model has a much smaller gap between test and ood dataset (only about 3 F_1 points), which indicates that our multi-task models generalise better than previous baselines.

5.3 End-to-End Semantic Role Labelling

Future work will need to investigate in more detail whether the multi-task models proposed here can be used to improve the performance of existing semantic role labellers. While our model cannot be directly applied to a standard semantic role labelling task (because it assigns roles only to head words), we were able to combine the model with an existing semantic role labeller and obtained promising results. Adding embeddings based on the predicate and target word $\mathbf{h}C_r diag(\mathbf{w}_t \mathbf{A}_r)$ from the NNRF-MT model (see Equation (4), (5)) as a feature to the MATE semantic role labeller

Model	In domain: WSJ test			Out-of-domain: Brown			$F_1^{test} - F_1^{ood}$
	P	R	F_1	P	R	F_1	
ZeroR baseline	36.11	36.11	36.11	32.46	32.46	32.46	3.65
Zapirain13^{Pado07}	53.13	50.44	51.75	43.24	35.27	38.85	12.90
Zapirain13$^{Lin98}_{in-domain}$	59.93	**59.38**	**59.65****	50.79	48.39	49.56	10.09
NNRF-MT	55.80	49.16	52.27	53.43	45.42	49.10	3.17
RoFA-MT	67.93	51.19	58.39	65.71	47.36	55.05	3.34
ResRoFA-MT	**68.03**	51.27	58.47	**66.39**	**47.85**	**55.62****	2.85

Table 2: Results of semantic role classification given verb-head pairs. P is precision, R is recall and F_1 is F-measure. F_1 values with a mark are significantly higher than all other values in the same column, where (**) $p < 0.01$.

(Björkelund et al., 2010; Roth and Woodsend, 2014) leads to a small but statistically significant improvement of 0.11 points in F_1 score on the out-of-domain dataset used in the CoNLL-2009 semantic role labelling task (Hajič et al., 2009).

6 Evaluation: Thematic Fit Modelling

Next, we evaluate our multi-task models against human thematic fit ratings in order to assess whether the inclusion of the multi-task architecture leads to improvements on this task, following Padó et al. (2009); Baroni and Lenci (2010); Greenberg et al. (2015b); Sayeed et al. (2016).

6.1 Datasets

The human judgement data consists of verbs, a verbal argument with its role, and an average fit judgement score on a scale from 1 (least common) to 7 (most common), e.g., $ask, police$/AGENT, 6.5. We used:

Pado07: the dataset proposed by Pado (2007) consists of 414 predicate-participant pairs with judgements. The roles are agent and patient.

McRae05: the dataset from McRae et al. (2005) contains 1444 judgements of verbs with an agent or patient.

Ferretti01: the dataset proposed by Ferretti et al. (2001) contains 274 ratings for predicate-location pairs (**F-Loc**) and 248 rating for predicate-instrument pairs (**F-Inst**).

GDS: the dataset from Greenberg et al. (2015a) contains 720 ratings for predicates and patients.

6.2 Baseline Models

We compare our models against previous distributional semantic models used for thematic fit tasks; many of these are from the Distributional Memory (DM) framework (Baroni and Lenci, 2010) whose tensor space is a high-dimensional count space

of verb-noun-relation tuples from a large-scale mixed corpus smoothed by local mutual information. The key idea in applying DM models to the thematic fit rating task is to construct a "prototype filler", and compare candidate fillers against the prototype using cosine similarity. The baseline models we compare against include NNRF and:

TypeDM: This is best-performing DM model from Baroni and Lenci (2010). Relations of verb-noun pairs are obtained using hand-crafted rules. The results of this model are from reimplementations in Greenberg et al. (2015a,b).

SDDM-mo: This DM comes from Sayeed and Demberg (2014) and is constructed with automatically-extracted semantic information.

GSD15: This is the overall best-performing model from Greenberg et al. (2015b) using hierarchical clustering of typical role-fillers to construct prototype on TypeDM.

SCLB17: This is the best-performing model on F-Inst from Santus et al. (2017). The number of fillers used in prototype construction is 30 and the number of top features is 2000. We report the highest results among the different types of dependency contexts in their framework.

6.3 Methods and Results

We correlated the human judgements with the output probability of the role-filler given the predicate and the role. To avoid conflation between frequency in the training dataset and plausibility of the role-filler, we adopt the practice proposed in Tilk et al. (2016) to set the bias of the output layer to zero during the evaluation. We consider the NNRF model as our baseline and perform a two-tailed t-test to calculate statistical significance between the baseline model and each of the three models proposed in this paper.

Model	Pado07	McRae05	F-Loc	F-Inst	GDS	avg
TypeDM	53	33	23	36	46	40.8
SDDM-mo	**56**	27	13	28	-	-
GSD15	50	36	29	42	48	40.5
SCLB17	49	28	37	50	-	-
NNRF	43.3	35.9	**46.5**	**52.1**	57.6	44.2
NNRF-MT	43.2	36.1	46.3	50.0*	57.2	44.0
RoFA-MT	52.2**	41.9**	45.9	49.4*	60.7**	48.6**
ResRoFA-MT	53.0**	**42.5****	46.3	47.7**	**60.8**	**48.9****

Table 3: Results on human thematic fit judgement correlation task (Spearman's $\rho \times 100$) compared to previous work. The last column reports the weighted average results by numbers of entries of all five datasets. Values with a mark are significantly different from the baseline model (NNRF), where (*) $p < 0.05$, (**) $p < 0.01$.

Table 3 shows results for all models and datasets. The ResRoFA-MT model performs best overall, improving more than 4 points over the baseline. The multi-task model (NNRF-MT) has performance similar to baseline (NNRF). Our new architecture using a parametric weighted average over event participant embeddings (RoFA-MT) outperforms simple summation (NNRF-MT), especially on the Pado07, McRae05 and GDS datasets. The residual method leads to further minor improvements on the Pado07, F-Loc and GDS datasets. However, on predicate-instrument pairs of the F-Inst dataset, NNRF outperforms other models significantly. We think that multi-task models are biased towards roles with a larger frequency like `ARG0` or `ARG1`, which is proved in the ablation study (see Section 8).

7 Evaluation: Compositionality

The thematic fit judgements from the tasks discussed in section 6 only contain ratings of the fit between the predicate and one role-filler. However, other event participants contained in a clause can affect human expectations of the upcoming role-fillers. For instance, mechanics are likely to check tires, while journalists are likely to check spellings. The **B10** dataset (Bicknell et al., 2010) contains human judgements for 64 pairs of agent-verb-patient triples, where one triple in each pair is plausible (e.g., "journalist check spelling"), and one is implausible (e.g., "journalist check type"). A model is evaluated based on whether it successfully assigns a higher likelihood/rating to the plausible than to the implausible object (also referred to as the *Accuracy 1* metric in Tilk et al. (2016)). The baseline models are NNRF as well as:

Random: The naive baseline model consists of choosing the tags uniformly at random.

Lenci11: Lenci (2011) proposed a composition model for TypeDM.

Table 4 shows that our new composition method based on parametric weighted average outperforms previous models; the RoFA-MT model achieves the highest accuracy overall and outperforms the baseline (NNRF) significantly.

7.1 Event Similarity

Lastly, we evaluate the quality of the event embeddings learned via the multi-task network models. While word embeddings from tools like word2vec (Mikolov et al., 2013) are standard methods for obtaining word similarities, identifying a suitable method for more general event similarity estimation is still a relevant problem. The model proposed here constitutes an interesting method for obtaining event embeddings, as it is trained on two semantics-focused prediction tasks.

For evaluation, we use the sentence similarity task proposed by Grefenstette and Sadrzadeh (2015) (second experiment in their paper). For evaluation, we use the re-annotated dataset, named **GS13**, constructed in 2013 by Kartsaklis and Sadrzadeh (2014). Each row in the dataset contains a participant ID, two sentences, a human evaluation score of their similarity from 1 to 7, and a `HIGH`/`LOW` tag indicating the similarity group of two sentences. An example entry is:

p1, (table, draw, eye), (table, attract, eye), 7, `HIGH`

where p1 is the participant ID. We compare our models' performance to NNRF, as well as:

Kronecker: The best-performing model in Grefenstette and Sadrzadeh (2015) using Kronecker product as its composition method.

W2V: The sentence representations in W2V are

	Random	Lenci11	NNRF	NNRF-MT	RoFA-MT	ResRoFA-MT
Accuracy 1	0.50	0.67	0.73	0.71	**0.76***	0.75

Table 4: Results on agent-patient compositionality evaluation comparing to previous models. Values with a mark are significantly different from the baseline model (NNRF), where (*) $p < 0.05$.

	W2V	Kronecker	NNRF	NNRF-MT	RoFA-MT	ResRoFA-MT	Human
$\rho \times 100$	13	26	34.2	35.7	34.0	**36.7****	60

Table 5: Results on event similarity evaluation comparing to previous models. Values with a mark are significantly different from the baseline model (NNRF), where (*) $p < 0.05$, (**) $p < 0.01$.

constructed by element-wise addition of pre-trained word2vec (Mikolov et al., 2013) word embeddings.

Human: Mean inter-annotator correlation using Spearman's ρ. This can be considered to be the upper bound of the task.

To estimate sentence similarity, we feed all three words and their roles (`ARG0/PRD/ARG1`) into each model. We then extract the event representation vectors for both sentences and compute their cosine similarity. Table 5 shows correlation coefficients in Spearman's $\rho \times 100$ between sentence-pair similarities and human judgement scores. ResRoFA-MT obtains best results, indicating that the secondary task helped also to improve the network-internal event representations. These results indicate that ResRoFA-MT-based event embeddings may be suitable for applications and tasks where similarity estimates for larger phrases are needed (cf. Wanzare et al., 2017).

8 Ablation Study: Single-task Variants

From the evaluations above, we notice that the performance of the multi-task model with simple addition composition method (NNRF-MT) is not significantly different from the single task model (NNRF). In order to test whether the additional training task improves model performance, we develop single-task variants for RoFA-MT and ResRoFA-MT models, named RoFA-ST and ResRoFA-ST correspondingly, by taking out the semantic role classifiers. We then perform one-trial experiments and evaluate the models on thematic fit modelling and compositionality tasks by comparing the one-trial results of single-task variants versus the confidence intervals obtained from the 10 runs of the multi-task models.

The results in Table 6 show that multi-task models significantly outperform single-task models on Pado07, McRae05, F-Loc, GDS and over-

all. However, single-task variants are superior to multi-task models on F-Inst dataset, which is consistent with our findings in Section 6.2. On the compositionality tasks, the multi-task architecture improves only the performance of the residual weighted average model (ResRoFA-MT) but harms the event similarity performance of the weighted average model (RoFA-MT).

9 Related Work

Modi et al. (2017) proposed a compositional neural model for referent prediction in which event embeddings were constructed via the sum of predicate and argument embeddings. Weber et al. (2017) proposed a tensor-based composition model to construct event embeddings with agents and patients. They represented predicates as tensors and arguments as vectors. Cheng and Erk (2018) proposed a neural-based model to predict implicit arguments with event knowledge in which the event embeddings are composed with a two-layer feed-forward neural network.

10 Conclusions

This paper introduced two innovations to the modelling of events and their participants at the clause level: (1) we proposed a multi-task model of role-filler prediction and semantic role classification; (2) we proposed a parametric weighted average method which improves the composition of event participants in the input.

The introduction of semantic role classification as a secondary task addressed a weakness of Tilk et al. (2016)'s model. The semantic role classification task requires a much stronger internal representation of the semantic roles on top of lexical information. Thanks to the internal hidden layer shared between the two tasks, the event representation profited from the additional learning objective, increasing the models' performance on esti-

Model	Pado07	McRae05	F-Loc	F-Inst	GDS	avg	B10	GS13
RoFA-ST	44.1***	36.6***	44.4*	**56.7***	57.3***	44.5***	75.0	36.3**
RoFA-MT	52.2	41.9	45.9	49.4	60.7	48.6	**76.1**	34.0
ResRoFA-ST	42.3***	35.8***	44.5**	50.4*	56.9***	43.6***	67.2***	32.5***
ResRoFA-MT	**53.0**	**42.5**	**46.3**	47.7	**60.8**	**48.9**	74.5	**36.7**

Table 6: Ablation study of single task variants. Underlined values indicate the best values with the same composition method, and bold values indicate the best values on that data set. Values with a mark are significantly different from the multi-task baseline models (RoFA-MT / ResRoFA-MT), where (*) $p < 0.05$, (**) $p < 0.01$, (***) $p < 0.001$.

mating event similarity.

We also performed a study regarding the usefulness of our purely semantics-based representations for semantic role labelling. While many semantic role labellers rely predominantly on syntax, our approach addresses the likelihood that a semantic role should be assigned purely based on its plausibility to fill that role content-wise. We showed that the semantics-based role label predictions generated by our multi-task model outperform the ones based on earlier syntax-based selectional preference methods and observe promising results for integrating the model with a semantic role labeller on out-of-domain data.

Our parametric composition method (RoFA-MT) composes event embeddings in the hidden layer, which captures role-specific information during the composition process and reduces the risk of overflow and underflow of the hidden layer weights. We additionally included the residual learning method alongside RoFA-MT (ResRoFA-MT), further mitigating the vanishing/exploding gradient problem and allowing the transmission of information from lower levels directly into the event embedding. This approach provided the overall best result of all models on the thematic fit human judgement task as well as the event similarity task and competitive results on the tasks individually.

10.1 Future Work

In future work, the model may be improved by including visual information from photos and videos. Common-sense reasoning is becoming a new focus (Mostafazadeh et al., 2016; Baroni et al., 2017). One characteristic of common-sense knowledge is that it is often not explicitly mentioned in language precisely *because* it constitutes common-sense knowledge and is hence uninformative as it can easily be inferred (Mukuze et al., 2018). Syntactically optional event participants (such as the kitchen as location for the predicate "cook") are thus often omitted in text; this sets a limit to what can be learned from text only.

The prospect of applying our models independently to SRL tasks suggests an area of potential future work. Our models currently use only the predicates and head words of arguments. Instead of depending on corpora with extracted head words, we can integrate an attention mechanism (Vaswani et al., 2017) to capture the position of syntactic heads. We are working on extending our models to use all words, which will enable testing as an SRL tool.

Finally, the predictive nature of this type of model can potentially enable its deployment in incremental semantic parsing (Konstas et al., 2014; Konstas and Keller, 2015) by combining the multi-task design with the incremental architecture in (Tilk et al., 2016). We are continuing to develop this and other ways of employing models of event representation that simultaneously predict event participants and assess the fit of given participants.

Acknowledgements

This research was funded in part by the German Research Foundation (DFG) as part of SFB 1102 "Information Density and Linguistic Encoding", EXC 284 Cluster of Excellence "Multimodal Computing and Interaction", and a Swedish Research Council (VR) grant for the Centre for Linguistic Theory and Studies in Probability (CLASP). We thank Dr. Michael Roth for conducting the semantic role labelling evaluation using features from our model to see whether it is beneficial. We sincerely thank the anonymous reviewers for their insightful comments that helped us to improve this paper.

References

Marco Baroni, Armand Joulin, Allan Jabri, Germàn Kruszewski, Angeliki Lazaridou, Klemen Simonic, and Tomas Mikolov. 2017. CommAI: Evaluating the first steps towards a useful general AI. *arXiv preprint arXiv:1701.08954* .

Marco Baroni and Alessandro Lenci. 2010. Distributional memory: A general framework for corpus-based semantics. *Computational Linguistics* 36(4):673–721.

Klinton Bicknell, Jeffrey L Elman, Mary Hare, Ken McRae, and Marta Kutas. 2010. Effects of event knowledge in processing verbal arguments. *Journal of memory and language* 63(4):489–505.

Anders Björkelund, Bernd Bohnet, Love Hafdell, and Pierre Nugues. 2010. A high-performance syntactic and semantic dependency parser. In *Proceedings of the 23rd International Conference on Computational Linguistics: Demonstrations*. Association for Computational Linguistics, pages 33–36.

Xavier Carreras and Lluís Màrquez. 2005. Introduction to the CoNLL-2005 shared task: Semantic role labeling. In *Proceedings of the Ninth Conference on Computational Natural Language Learning (CoNLL-2005)*. Association for Computational Linguistics, Ann Arbor, Michigan, pages 152–164.

Rich Caruana. 1998. Multitask learning. In *Learning to learn*, Springer, pages 95–133.

Pengxiang Cheng and Katrin Erk. 2018. Implicit argument prediction with event knowledge. *arXiv preprint arXiv:1802.07226* .

Todd R Ferretti, Ken McRae, and Andrea Hatherell. 2001. Integrating verbs, situation schemas, and thematic role concepts. *Journal of Memory and Language* 44(4):516–547.

C. J. Fillmore. 1968. The case for case. *Universals in Linguistic Theory* pages 1–25(Part Two).

Karl Friston. 2010. The free-energy principle: a unified brain theory? *Nature Reviews Neuroscience* 11(2):127.

Edward Gibson, Leon Bergen, and Steven T Piantadosi. 2013. Rational integration of noisy evidence and prior semantic expectations in sentence interpretation. *Proceedings of the National Academy of Sciences* 110(20):8051–8056.

Clayton Greenberg, Vera Demberg, and Asad Sayeed. 2015a. Verb polysemy and frequency effects in thematic fit modeling. In *Proceedings of the 6th Workshop on Cognitive Modeling and Computational Linguistics*. Association for Computational Linguistics, Denver, Colorado, pages 48–57.

Clayton Greenberg, Asad Sayeed, and Vera Demberg. 2015b. Improving unsupervised vector-space thematic fit evaluation via role-filler prototype clustering. In *Proceedings of the 2015 Conference of the North American Chapter of the Association for Computational Linguistics: Human Language Technologies*. Association for Computational Linguistics, Denver, Colorado, pages 21–31.

Edward Grefenstette and Mehrnoosh Sadrzadeh. 2015. Concrete models and empirical evaluations for the categorical compositional distributional model of meaning. *Computational Linguistics* 41(1):71–118.

Jan Hajič, Massimiliano Ciaramita, Richard Johansson, Daisuke Kawahara, Maria Antònia Martí, Lluís Màrquez, Adam Meyers, Joakim Nivre, Sebastian Padó, Jan Štěpánek, Pavel Straňák, Mihai Surdeanu, Nianwen Xue, and Yi Zhang. 2009. The CoNLL-2009 shared task: Syntactic and semantic dependencies in multiple languages. In *Proceedings of the Thirteenth Conference on Computational Natural Language Learning (CoNLL 2009): Shared Task*. Association for Computational Linguistics, Boulder, Colorado, pages 1–18.

Kaiming He, Xiangyu Zhang, Shaoqing Ren, and Jian Sun. 2015. Delving deep into rectifiers: Surpassing human-level performance on imagenet classification. In *Proceedings of the IEEE international conference on computer vision*. pages 1026–1034.

Kaiming He, Xiangyu Zhang, Shaoqing Ren, and Jian Sun. 2016. Deep residual learning for image recognition. In *Proceedings of the IEEE conference on computer vision and pattern recognition*. pages 770–778.

Dimitri Kartsaklis and Mehrnoosh Sadrzadeh. 2014. A study of entanglement in a categorical framework of natural language. *arXiv preprint arXiv:1405.2874* .

Ioannis Konstas and Frank Keller. 2015. Semantic role labeling improves incremental parsing. In *Proceedings of the 53rd Annual Meeting of the Association for Computational Linguistics and the 7th International Joint Conference on Natural Language Processing (Volume 1: Long Papers)*. Association for Computational Linguistics, Beijing, China, pages 1191–1201.

Ioannis Konstas, Frank Keller, Vera Demberg, and Mirella Lapata. 2014. Incremental semantic role labeling with Tree Adjoining Grammar. In *Proceedings of the 2014 Conference on Empirical Methods in Natural Language Processing (EMNLP)*. Association for Computational Linguistics, Doha, Qatar, pages 301–312.

Gina R Kuperberg and T Florian Jaeger. 2016. What do we mean by prediction in language comprehension? *Language, cognition and neuroscience* 31(1):32–59.

Alessandro Lenci. 2011. Composing and updating verb argument expectations: A distributional semantic model. In *Proceedings of the 2nd Workshop on

Cognitive Modeling and Computational Linguistics. Association for Computational Linguistics, Stroudsburg, PA, USA, CMCL 2011, pages 58–66.

Dekang Lin. 1998. Automatic retrieval and clustering of similar words. In *Proceedings of the 17th international conference on Computational linguistics-Volume 2*. Association for Computational Linguistics, pages 768–774.

Ken McRae, Mary Hare, Jeffrey L Elman, and Todd Ferretti. 2005. A basis for generating expectancies for verbs from nouns. *Memory & Cognition* 33(7):1174–1184.

Tomas Mikolov, Ilya Sutskever, Kai Chen, Greg S Corrado, and Jeff Dean. 2013. Distributed representations of words and phrases and their compositionality. In *Advances in neural information processing systems*. pages 3111–3119.

Ashutosh Modi, Ivan Titov, Vera Demberg, Asad Sayeed, and Manfred Pinkal. 2017. Modelling semantic expectation: Using script knowledge for referent prediction. *Transactions of the Association of Computational Linguistics* 5(1):31–44.

Nasrin Mostafazadeh, Nathanael Chambers, Xiaodong He, Devi Parikh, Dhruv Batra, Lucy Vanderwende, Pushmeet Kohli, and James Allen. 2016. A corpus and evaluation framework for deeper understanding of commonsense stories. *arXiv preprint arXiv:1604.01696* .

Nelson Mukuze, Anna Rohrbach, Vera Demberg, and Bernt Schiele. 2018. A vision-grounded dataset for predicting typical locations for verbs. In *The 11th edition of the Language Resources and Evaluation Conference (LREC)*.

Sebastian Padó and Mirella Lapata. 2007. Dependency-based construction of semantic space models. *Computational Linguistics* 33(2):161–199.

Ulrike Pado. 2007. *The Integration of Syntax and Semantic Plausibility in a Wide-Coverage Model of Human Sentence Processing*. Ph.D. thesis, Saarland University.

Ulrike Padó, Matthew W Crocker, and Frank Keller. 2009. A probabilistic model of semantic plausibility in sentence processing. *Cognitive Science* 33(5):794–838.

Michael Roth and Kristian Woodsend. 2014. Composition of word representations improves semantic role labelling. In *Proceedings of the 2014 Conference on Empirical Methods in Natural Language Processing (EMNLP)*. pages 407–413.

Enrico Santus, Emmanuele Chersoni, Alessandro Lenci, and Philippe Blache. 2017. Measuring thematic fit with distributional feature overlap. In *Proceedings of the 2017 Conference on Empirical Methods in Natural Language Processing*. Association for Computational Linguistics, Copenhagen, Denmark, pages 659–669.

Asad Sayeed and Vera Demberg. 2014. Combining unsupervised syntactic and semantic models of thematic fit. In *Proceedings of the first Italian Conference on Computational Linguistics (CLiC-it 2014)*.

Asad Sayeed, Clayton Greenberg, and Vera Demberg. 2016. Thematic fit evaluation: an aspect of selectional preferences. In *Proceedings of the 1st Workshop on Evaluating Vector-Space Representations for NLP*. Association for Computational Linguistics, Berlin, Germany, pages 99–105.

Asad Sayeed, Pavel Shkadzko, and Vera Demberg. 2018. Rollenwechsel-English: a large-scale semantic role corpus. In *Proceedings of the 11th edition of the Language Resources and Evaluation Conference*.

Ottokar Tilk, Vera Demberg, Asad Sayeed, Dietrich Klakow, and Stefan Thater. 2016. Event participant modelling with neural networks. In *Proceedings of the 2016 Conference on Empirical Methods in Natural Language Processing*. Association for Computational Linguistics, Austin, Texas, pages 171–182.

Ashish Vaswani, Noam Shazeer, Niki Parmar, Jakob Uszkoreit, Llion Jones, Aidan N Gomez, Łukasz Kaiser, and Illia Polosukhin. 2017. Attention is all you need. In *Advances in Neural Information Processing Systems*. pages 6000–6010.

Lilian DA Wanzare, Alessandra Zarcone, Stefan Thater, and Manfred Pinkal. 2017. Inducing script structure from crowdsourced event descriptions via semi-supervised clustering. *LSDSem 2017* page 1.

Noah Weber, Niranjan Balasubramanian, and Nathanael Chambers. 2017. Event representations with tensor-based compositions. *arXiv preprint arXiv:1711.07611* .

Shumin Wu and Martha Palmer. 2015. Can selectional preferences help automatic semantic role labeling? In *Proceedings of the Fourth Joint Conference on Lexical and Computational Semantics*. pages 222–227.

Beñat Zapirain, Eneko Agirre, and Lluís Màrquez. 2009. Generalizing over lexical features: Selectional preferences for semantic role classification. In *Proceedings of the ACL-IJCNLP 2009 conference short papers*. Association for Computational Linguistics, pages 73–76.

Benat Zapirain, Eneko Agirre, Lluis Marquez, and Mihai Surdeanu. 2013. Selectional preferences for semantic role classification. *Computational Linguistics* 39(3):631–663.

Assessing Meaning Components in German Complex Verbs:
A Collection of Source–Target Domains and Directionality

Sabine Schulte im Walde and **Maximilian Köper** and **Sylvia Springorum**
Institut für Maschinelle Sprachverarbeitung
Universität Stuttgart, Germany
{schulte,maximilian.koeper,sylvia.springorum}@ims.uni-stuttgart.de

Abstract

This paper presents a collection to assess meaning components in German complex verbs, which frequently undergo meaning shifts. We use a novel strategy to obtain source and target domain characterisations via sentence generation rather than sentence annotation. A selection of arrows adds spatial directional information to the generated contexts. We provide a broad qualitative description of the dataset, and a series of standard classification experiments verifies the quantitative reliability of the presented resource. The setup for collecting the meaning components is applicable also to other languages, regarding complex verbs as well as other language-specific targets that involve meaning shifts.

1 Introduction

German particle verbs (PVs) are complex verb structures such as *anstrahlen* 'to beam/smile at' that combine a prefix particle (*an*) with a base verb (*strahlen* 'to beam'). PVs represent a type of multi-word expressions, which are generally known as a *"pain in the neck for NLP"* (Sag et al., 2002). Even more, German PVs pose a specific challenge for NLP tasks and applications, because the particles are highly ***ambiguous***; e.g., the particle *an* has a partitive meaning in *anbeißen* 'to take a bite', a cumulative meaning in *anhäufen* 'to pile up', and a topological meaning in *anbinden* 'to tie to' (Springorum, 2011). In addition, they often trigger ***meaning shifts*** of the base verbs (BVs), cf. Springorum et al. (2013); e.g., the PV *abschminken* with the BV *schminken* 'to put on make-up' has a literal meaning ('to remove make-up') and a shifted, non-literal meaning ('to forget about something').[1]

With PVs representing a large and challenging class in the lexicon, their meaning components and their mechanisms of compositionality have received a considerable amount of interdisciplinary research interest. For example, a series of formal-semantic analyses manually classified German PVs (with particles *ab, an, auf, nach*) into soft semantic classes (Lechler and Roßdeutscher, 2009; Haselbach, 2011; Kliche, 2011; Springorum, 2011). Corpus studies and annotations demonstrated the potential of German PVs to appear in non-literal language usage, and to trigger meaning shifts (Springorum et al., 2013; Köper and Schulte im Walde, 2016b). Regarding computational models, the majority of existing approaches to PV meaning addressed the automatic prediction of German PV compositionality (Salehi et al., 2014; Bott and Schulte im Walde, 2015; Köper and Schulte im Walde, 2017b), in a similar vein as computational approaches for English PVs (Baldwin et al., 2003; Bannard, 2005; McCarthy et al., 2003; Kim and Baldwin, 2007; Salehi and Cook, 2013; Salehi et al., 2014). Only few approaches to German and English PVs have included the meaning contributions of the particles into the prediction of PV meaning (Bannard, 2005; Cook and Stevenson, 2006; Köper et al., 2016).

Overall, we are faced with a variety of interdisciplinary approaches to identifying and modelling the meaning components and the composite meanings of German PVs. Current and future research activities are however hindered by a lack of resources that go beyond PV–BV compositionality and can serve as gold standards for assessing

(i) the meaning contributions of the notoriously ambiguous particles, and

(ii) meaning shifts of PVs in comparison to their BVs.

---

[1] We deliberately make use of the general term "meaning shift" in comparison to specific instances such as metaphor and metonymy because non-literal language usage of PVs is not restricted to a specific type of meaning shift.

*Proceedings of the 7th Joint Conference on Lexical and Computational Semantics (*SEM)*, pages 22–32
New Orleans, June 5-6, 2018. ©2018 Association for Computational Linguistics

In this paper, we present a new collection for German PVs that aims to improve on this situation. The dataset includes 138 German BVs and their 323 existing PVs with particle prefixes *ab, an, auf, aus*. For all target verbs, we collected

1. sentences from 15 human participants across a specified set of domains, to address their ambiguity in context; and

2. spatial directional information (UP, DOWN, RIGHT, LEFT), also in context.

Meaning shifts are typically represented as a mapping from a rather concrete source-domain meaning to a rather abstract target-domain meaning (Lakoff and Johnson, 1980). For example, the abstract conceptual domain TIME may be illustrated in terms of the structurally similar, more concrete domain MONEY, enabling non-literal language such as *to save time* and *to spend time*. For German PVs, meaning shifts frequently take place when combining a BV from a concrete source domain with a particle (as in the *abschminken* example above, where the BV *schminken* is taken from the domain HUMAN BODY), resulting in a PV meaning (possibly among other meanings) related to an abstract target domain such as DESIRE.

Targeting the representation of meaning shifts with our collection, we specified source domains for the BVs (such as MENSCHLICHER KÖRPER 'HUMAN BODY') and target domains for the PVs (such as ZEIT 'TIME'). In this way, our dataset offers source–target domain combinations for assessing BV–PV meaning shifts across PVs and particle types. Our domains were taken from conceptual specifications in (Kövecses, 2002), which cluster semantically and encyclopedically related concepts to ensure a generally applicable set of domains involved in meaning shifts. The spatial directional information is captured through simple directional arrows and enables a view on spatial meaning components of particle types and PVs, which supposedly represent core meaning dimensions of PVs (Frassinelli et al., 2017).

While the collection focuses on German PVs, the representation of the meaning components (source and target domains, as well as directions) is language-independent. Therefore, the setup for collecting the meaning components that we present below should also be applicable to other languages, regarding complex verbs as well as regarding other language-specific targets that undergo meaning shifts.

2   Related Work

PV Meaning Components and Classifications
So far, the most extensive manual resources regarding German PV meaning components rely on formal semantic research within the framework of Discourse Representation Theory (DRT), cf. Kamp and Reyle (1993). Here, detailed word-syntactic analyses and soft classifications were created for German PVs with the particles *auf* (Lechler and Roßdeutscher, 2009), *nach* (Haselbach, 2011), *ab* (Kliche, 2011), and *an* (Springorum, 2011).

PV Compositionality   Most manual and computational research on PV meaning addressed the meaning of a PV through its degree of compositionality, for German as well as for English complex verbs. McCarthy et al. (2003) exploited various measures on distributional descriptions and nearest neighbours to predict the degree of compositionality of English PVs with regard to their BVs. Baldwin et al. (2003) defined Latent Semantic Analysis (LSA) models (Deerwester et al., 1990) for English PVs and their constituents, to determine the degree of compositionality through distributional similarity, and evaluated the predictions against various WordNet-based gold standards. Bannard (2005) defined the compositionality of an English PV as an entailment relationship between the PV and its constituents, and compared four distributional models against human entailment judgements. Cook and Stevenson (2006) addressed not only the compositionality but also the meanings of English particles and PVs. Focusing on the particle *up*, they performed a type-based classification using window-driven and syntactic distributional information about the PVs, particles and BVs. Kim and Baldwin (2007) combined standard distributional similarity measures with WordNet-based hypernymy information to predict English PV compositionality. Kühner and Schulte im Walde (2010), Bott and Schulte im Walde (2017) and Köper and Schulte im Walde (2017a) used unsupervised (soft) clustering and multi-sense embeddings to determine the degree of compositionality of German PVs. Salehi and Cook (2013) and Salehi et al. (2014) relied on translations into multiple languages in order to predict the degree of compositionality for English PVs. Bott and Schulte im Walde (2014) and Bott and Schulte im Walde (2015) explored and compared word-based and syntax-based distributional models in the prediction of German PVs. Köper and Schulte im Walde (2017b) integrated visual information into a similar textual distributional model.

Altogether, most PV gold standards that are used for evaluation within the above approaches to compositionality rate the similarity between PV and BV, ignoring the contribution of the particle meaning. Exceptions to this is the gold standard by Bannard (2005), rating the entailment between the PV and its particle as well as between the PV and its BV. In addition, all PV gold standards are type-based, i.e., rating the compositionality for a PV type, rather than for PV senses in context.

Spatial Meaning Components The Grounding Theory indicates that the mental representation of a concept is built not only through linguistic exposure but also incorporating multi-modal information extracted from real-world situations, including auditory, visual, etc. stimuli (Barsalou, 1999; Glenberg and Kaschak, 2002; Shapiro, 2007). Spatial meaning plays an important role in grounding information. For example, Richardson et al. (2003) showed an interaction between spatial properties of verbs and their positions in language comprehension. Dudschig et al. (2012) and Kaup et al. (2012) demonstrated effects of typical locations of a word's referent in language processing. Specifically for German PVs, Frassinelli et al. (2017) found spatial meaning (mis)matches for PVs with particles *an* and *auf*, when combining them with primarily vertical vs. horizontal BVs. The spatial information in our dataset provides an opportunity to further explore spatial meaning components in German BVs and PVs.

Meaning Shift Datasets Lakoff and Johnson (1980) and Gentner (1983) were the first to specify systematic conceptual mappings between two domains, within their theories of conventional metaphors and analogy by structure-mapping, respectively. In contrast, practical advice and projects on the actual annotation of source/domain categorisations or meaning shifts are sparse. The *Master Metaphor List (MML)* represents an extensive manual collection of metaphorical mappings between source and target domains (Lakoff et al., 1991) but from a practical point of view has been critised for its incoherent levels of specificity and its lack of coverage by Lönneker-Rodman (2008),

who relied on the MML next to EuroWordNet when annotating a total of 1,650 French and German metaphor instances. Similarly, Shutova and Teufel (2010) used the source and target domains from the MML but relied only on a subset of the domains, which they then extended for their annotation purposes.

As to our knowledge, there is no previous dataset on meaning shifts of complex verbs, other than a smaller-scale collection developed in parallel by ourselves, which however focuses on analogies in meaning shifts rather than source–target domains (Köper and Schulte im Walde, 2018). Some datasets include non-literal meanings of verbs (Birke and Sarkar, 2006; Turney et al., 2011; Shutova et al., 2013; Köper and Schulte im Walde, 2016b), and the MML-based meaning shift annotations by Lönneker-Rodman (2008) and Shutova and Teufel (2010) also include verbs but are less target-specific than our work. In addition, while both Lönneker-Rodman (2008) and Shutova and Teufel (2010) asked their annotators to label words in their corpus data, we follow a different strategy and ask our participants to generate sentences according to domain-specific target senses.

3 Target Verbs, Domains, Directionalities

In this section, we describe our selections and representations of BV and PV targets (Section 3.1), the source and target domains (Section 3.2), and the directional arrows (Section 3.3).

3.1 German Base and Particle Verbs

Based on the source domain descriptions by Kövecses (2002), cf. Section 3.2 below, we identified BVs which (i) supposedly belong to the respective source domain, and (ii) we expected to undergo meaning shifts when combined with one of our target particle types, as based on our linguistic expertise from previous work (see related work above).

All of the BVs were systematically combined with the four prefix particles *ab, an, auf, aus*, resulting in a total of 552 PVs. Since we did not want to include neologisms into our PV targets, we then checked the PV existence in the online version of the German dictionary *DUDEN*[2]. The final list of target PVs that were found in the dictionary comprised 323 verbs.

---

[2]www.duden.de/suchen/dudenonline/

Source Domains		Target Domains	
Menschlicher Körper	Human Body	Emotion und Gefühl	Emotion and Feeling
Gesundheit und Krankheit	Health and Illness	Wunsch und Sehnsucht	Desire
Tiere	Animals	Moral	Morality
Pflanzen	Plants	Gedanke	Thought
Gebäude und Konstruktion	Buildings and Construction	Gesellschaft und Nation	Society and Nation
Maschinen und Werkzeuge	Machines and Tools	Wirtschaft und Ökonomie	Economy
Spiele und Sport	Games and Sports	Menschliche Beziehungen	Human Relationships
Geld und Handel	Money and Economic Transaction	Kommunikation	Communication
Kochen und Essen	Cooking and Food	Zeit	Time
Hitze und Kälte	Heat and Cold	Leben und Tod	Life and Death
Licht und Dunkelheit	Light and Darkness	Religion	Religion
Kräfte	Forces	Ereignis und Handlung	Event and Action
Bewegung und Richtung	Movement and Direction		
Geräusch und Klang	Sound		

Table 1: Source and target domains.

3.2 Domains of Meaning Shifts

The *Master Metaphor List (MML)* provides the most extensive list of source–domain shift definitions but has been criticised for being incomplete regarding corpus annotations (Lönneker-Rodman, 2008; Shutova and Teufel, 2010), cf. Section 2. In addition, we found the MML and an extended subset as provided by Shutova and Teufel (2010) impractical to apply because the lists use too many categories that are based on too diverse motivations, such as event structures (e.g., change, causality, existence, creation) vs. event types (e.g., mental objects, beliefs, social forces).

Instead, our source and target domains were taken from specifications in (Kövecses, 2002), which we assumed to ensure a more stratified and generally applicable set of domains involved in meaning shifts. Table 1 lists all 13 source and 12 target domains by Kövecses (2002), including both the original English terms from Kövecses (2002) and the German translations that we used in our collection. Regarding the source domains, we added one domain to Kövecses' original list, i.e., SOUND, which we expected to play a role in BV–PV meaning shifts (Springorum et al., 2013).

3.3 Spatial Directionality Arrows

According to Viberg (1983), spatial experience provides a cognitive structure for the concepts underlying language. Given that we focus on PVs with prepositional particles (*ab, an, auf, aus*), we assume that the particles are spatially grounded, similar to preposition meanings which indicate spatial fundamentals (Herskovits, 1986; Dirven, 1993) and structure space regarding location, orientation, and direction (Zwarts, 2017).

We decided to focus on directionality as a central function in space, and to use arrows as visual expressions of directional meaning, given that (i) visual expressions are supposedly analogous expressions in language and categorise meaning, cf. Tversky (2011); (ii) arrows are asymmetric lines that "fly in the direction of the arrowhead" and provide structural organisation (Heiser and Tversky, 2006; Tversky, 2011); and (iii) directed arrows provide a simple but unambiguous depictive expression for direction in space. Our selection of arrows uses the four basic directions

$$\text{UP} \uparrow \qquad\qquad \text{LEFT} \leftarrow$$
$$\text{DOWN} \downarrow \qquad\qquad \text{RIGHT} \rightarrow$$

4 Dataset[3]

In this section, we describe our collection of meaning components from three different perspectives: the instructions for annotators (Section 4.1), a broad qualitative description of the dataset (Section 4.2), and classification experiments to verify the quantitative value of the resource (Section 4.3).

4.1 Annotation Instructions

We randomly distributed BVs and PVs over lists with 35 verbs each. The annotators were asked

(i) to choose one or more pre-defined semantic domain classes for each verb,

(ii) to provide an example sentence to illustrate the class assignment, and

(iii) to select an arrow that intuitively corresponds to the generated example sentence.

---

[3]The dataset is publicly available from `www.ims.uni-stuttgart.de/data/pv-bv-domains/`.

heulen

Menschliche Körper	☒	*Das Kind heult schon den ganzen Tag.*	↑ ☒ ← →
Gesundheit/ Krankheit	☐		↑ ↓ ← →
Tiere	☐		↑ ↓ ← →
Pflanzen	☐		↑ ↓ ← →
Gebäude/ Konstruktion	☐		↑ ↓ ← →
Maschinen/ Werkzeuge	☒	*Die Maschine heult durch die Halle.*	↑ ↓ ← ☒
Spiele/ Sport	☐		↑ ↓ ← →
Geld/Handel	☐		↑ ↓ ← →
Kochen/Essen	☐		↑ ↓ ← →
Hitze/Kälte	☐		↑ ↓ ← →
Licht/ Dunkelheit	☐		↑ ↓ ← →
Kräfte	☐		↑ ↓ ← →
Bewegung/ Richtung	☐		↑ ↓ ← →
Klang/ Geräusch	☒	*Die Sirene heult sehr laut.*	☒ ↓ ← →

Figure 1: Example annotation for the verb *heulen* 'to howl' with (i) a selection of three source domain classes, (ii) the corresponding three sentences, and (iii) the corresponding three arrows.

The classes (i.e., the source domains in the BV lists, and the target domains in the PV lists) were described by key words (e.g., the German equivalents of *appearance, growth, cultivation, care, use* for the source domain PFLANZEN 'PLANTS'). Then, the annotators were provided one example annotation (cf. Figure 1 for the verb *heulen* 'to howl') before they started the annotation process.

4.2 Qualitative Description

The annotations enable multiple views into meaning components of the underlying BVs and PVs on a token basis. In the following, we provide selected analyses and interactions regarding domains and directions (Section 4.2.1) and non-literal language and meaning shifts (Section 4.2.2).

4.2.1 Analyses of Domains and Directions

Table 2 shows the total number of sentences that were generated by the participants, and the pro-

portions per domain. Similarly, Table 3 shows the proportions per arrow type across the generated sentences.

In total, we collected 2,933 sentences across the 138 BVs and the 14 source domains, and 4,487 sentences across the 323 PVs and the 12 target domains. We find a rather skewed distribution for the number of sentences per verb type, varying between 2–47 for BVs and 1–30 for PVs; still, the collection comprises ≥10 sentences per verb for 134 out of 138 BVs (97%), and for 277 out of 323 PVs (86%), as illustrated in the number of sentences per verb type in Figures 2 and 3.

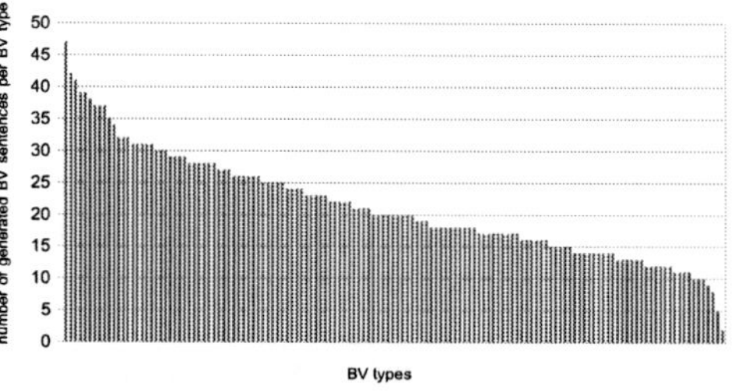

Figure 2: Number of generated sentences per BV.

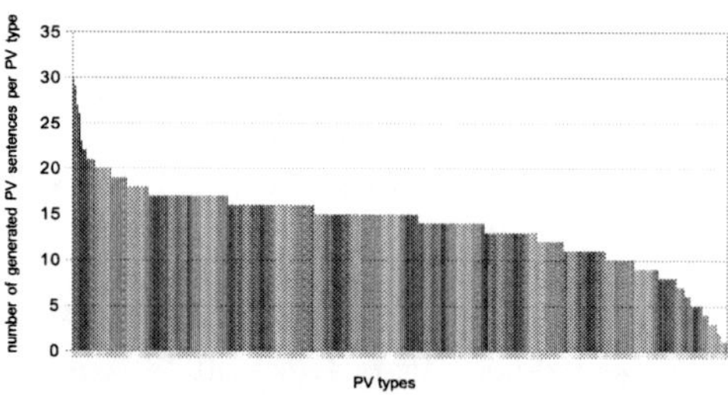

Figure 3: Number of generated sentences per PV.

The distribution of source domain sentences across domains ranges from a proportion of 3.41% for the domain FORCES up to 14.69% for the domain HUMAN BODY. The distribution of target domain sentences is more skewed, ranging from 0.47% for the domain RELIGION up to 33.88% for the domain EVENT/ACTION. Regarding directional information, we find a considerably low proportion of ≈10% for the left arrow (←), while the other three directions (up, down, right) received between 22% and 30%. Table 3 also shows that participants often chose more than one arrow for a specific generated sentence. We list those nine arrows and arrow combinations that were selected >50 times in total, i.e., across BV and PV sentences.

Source Domains	No. of Sentences		Target Domains	No. of Sentences	
Human Body	431	14.69%	Event/Action	1,520	33.88%
Animals	322	10.98%	Economy	460	10.25%
Health/Illness	251	8.56%	Emotion/Feeling	452	10.07%
Machines/Tools	242	8.25%	Human Relationships	383	8.54%
Games/Sports	211	7.19%	Life/Death	365	8.13%
Cooking/Food	210	7.16%	Time	292	6.51%
Plants	207	7.06%	Thought	284	6.33%
Economic Transaction	190	6.48%	Communication	280	6.24%
Buildings/Construction	167	5.69%	Society/Nation	181	4.03%
Sound	165	5.63%	Desire	150	3.34%
Heat/Cold	156	5.32%	Morality	99	2.21%
Movement/Direction	154	5.25%	Religion	21	0.47%
Light/Darkness	127	4.33%			
Forces	100	3.41%			
Total:	2,933	100.00%	*Total:*	4,487	100.00%

Table 2: Source and target domains: number and proportions of generated sentences per domain.

Source Domain Directions	No. of Sentences		Target Domain Directions	No. of Sentences	
↓	879	29.97%	→	1,300	28.97%
↑	782	26.66%	↓	1,218	27.15%
→	648	22.09%	↑	1,113	24.80%
←	270	9.21%	←	462	10.30%
↔	128	4.36%	↔	178	3.97%
↔ ↕	58	1.98%	↓ →	52	1.16%
↕	50	1.70%	↑ →	44	0.98%
↑ →	16	0.55%	↕ ↔	28	0.62%
↓ →	12	0.41%	↕	27	0.60%
other combinations	69	0.24%	*other combinations*	54	1.20%
no choice	21	0.72%	*no choice*	21	0.47%
Total:	2,933	100.00%	*Total:*	4,487	100.00%

Table 3: Directional information: number and proportions of selected arrows and arrow combinations.

BV/PV	Domain	Direction	Sentence
BV	LIGHT/DARKNESS	↑	*Der Diamant **funkelt** im Licht.* 'The diamond sparkles in the light.'
BV	PLANTS	↓	*Die Blätter **fallen** von den Bäumen.* 'The leaves fall from the trees.'
BV	FORCES	←	*Er **bog** das Kupferrohr.* 'He bent the copper pipe.'
BV	ANIMALS	↔	*Die Bullen **fechten** miteinander.* 'The bulls fence with each other.'
BV	HEAT/COLD	↔ ↕	*Das Feuer **brennt** heiß.* 'The fire is burning hot.'
PV	MORALITY	↓	*Du solltest von deinem hohen Ross **absteigen**.* 'You should step down off your pedestal.'
PV	EMOTION/FEELING	↑	*Der Druck **wächst** kurz vor der Präsentation **an**.* 'The pressure increases shortly before the presentation.'
PV	HUMAN-RELATIONSHIPS	→	*Sie lässt ihn eiskalt **abblitzen**.* 'She turns him down cold-bloodedly.'
PV	LIFE/DEATH	↕	*Musst du mein ganzes Leben **aufwühlen**?* 'Do you have to chum up my whole life?'
PV	COMMUNICATION	↔	*Er **kauft** ihr die Lüge problemlos **ab**.* 'He believes her lie without any doubts.'

Table 4: Example BV and PV sentences with selected domains and directions.

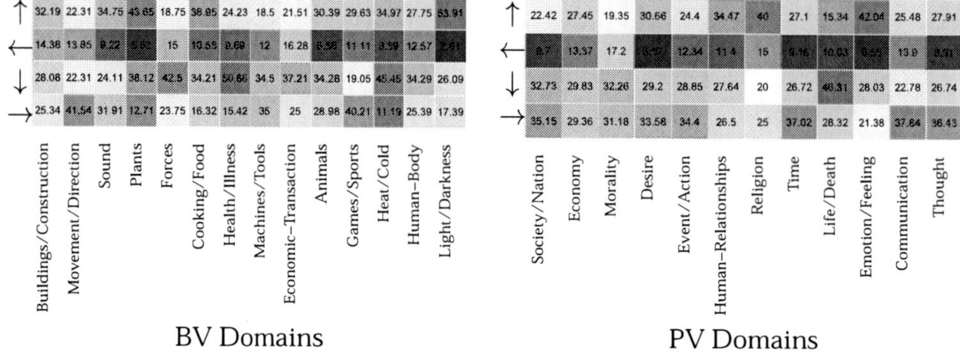

(a) BV source domains and directionality.

(b) PV target domains and directionality.

Figure 4: Interaction of domains and directionality.

Figure 4 illustrates how source and target domains interact with the arrows as indicators of directionality. As in the overall picture in Table 3, the proportions for the direction LEFT are considerably lower than for the other directions, with few domains receiving up to 15–17%: FORCES and MONEY/ECONOMIC TRANSACTION in the source sentences, and MORALITY and RELIGION in the target sentences. The direction RIGHT is a very strong indicator of the source domains MOVEMENT/DIRECTION, GAMES/SPORTS, MACHINES/TOOLS and the target domains COMMUNICATION, TIME, THOUGHT, SOCIETY/NATION; the direction UP is a very strong indicator of the source domains LIGHT/DARKNESS, PLANTS and COOKING/FOOD and the target domains EMOTION/FEELING and RELIGION; the direction DOWN is a very strong indicator of the source domains HEALTH/ILLNESS, HEAT/COLD, FORCES, PLANTS and the target domain LIFE/DEATH; all of these strong indicators received proportions >35%. Table 4 presents example sentences for some BV and PV domain/arrow combinations.

Figure 5 breaks down the information on arrow directions across the four particle types. While the particles are notoriously ambiguous, we can see that across the PV target domain sentences three of the particle types (*ab, auf, aus*) show a predominant directional meaning, i.e., DOWN, UP, RIGHT, respectively. The particle *an* is more flexible in its directional meaning, which confirms prior assumptions (Frassinelli et al., 2017).

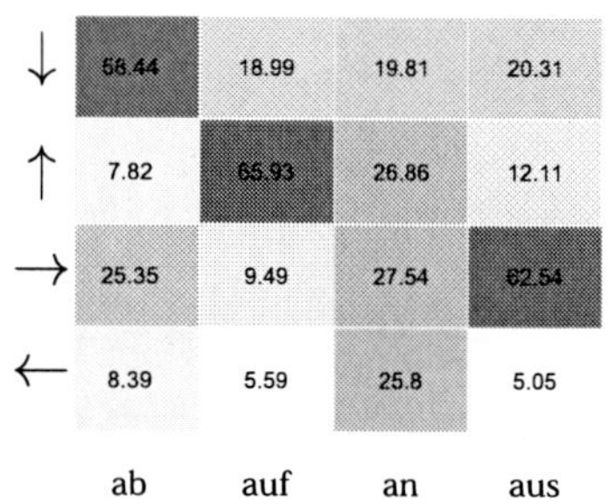

Figure 5: Directionality of particle types.

4.2.2 Analyses of Meaning Shifts

We now take the first steps into analysing non-literal language and meaning shifts within our collection. We started out by assuming that "meaning shifts for German PVs frequently take place when combining a BV from a concrete source domain with a particle, resulting in a PV meaning (possibly among other meanings) related to an abstract target domain". Consequently, the generated PV sentences are expected to (i) represent shifted, non-literal language meanings and to (ii) exhibit abstract meanings, both considerably more often than the generated BV sentences.

(Non-)Literal BV/PV Language Usage We asked three German native speakers to annotate the 2,933/4,487 BV/PV sentences with ratings on a 6-point scale [0,5], ranging from clearly literal (0) to clearly non-literal (5) language. Dividing the scale into two disjunctive ranges [0, 2] and [3, 5] broke down the ratings into binary decisions.

Table 5 shows the numbers and proportions of BV/PV sentences that were annotated as literal vs. non-literal language usage, distinguishing between full agreement (i.e., all annotators agreed on the binary category) and majority agreement (i.e., at least two out of three annotators agreed on the binary category). We can see that the proportions of non-literal sentences are indeed considerably larger for PVs than for BVs (14.8% vs. 3.2% for full agreement, and 29.5% vs. 14.8% for majority agreement), thus indicating a stronger non-literal language potential for German PVs in comparison to their BVs. Contrary to our assumptions, the participants in the generation experiment also produced a large number of literal sentences for PVs. In our opinion this indicates (a) the ambiguity of German PVs, which led participants to refer to literal as well as non-literal senses; and (b) that the presumably strongly abstract target domain definitions did not necessarily enforce non-literal senses.

		literal		non-literal	
BVs	full	2,443	83.3%	94	3.2%
	maj	2,674	91.2%	259	8.8%
PVs	full	2,174	48.5%	666	14.8%
	maj	3,150	70.2%	1,337	29.5%

Table 5: (Non-)literal language usage in generated BV/PV sentences.

Abstractness in BV/PV Sentences As meaning shifts typically take place as a mapping from a source to a target domain, where the target domain is supposedly more abstract than the source domain, we expect our sentences in the target domains to be more abstract than those in the source domains. Figure 6 shows that this is the case:

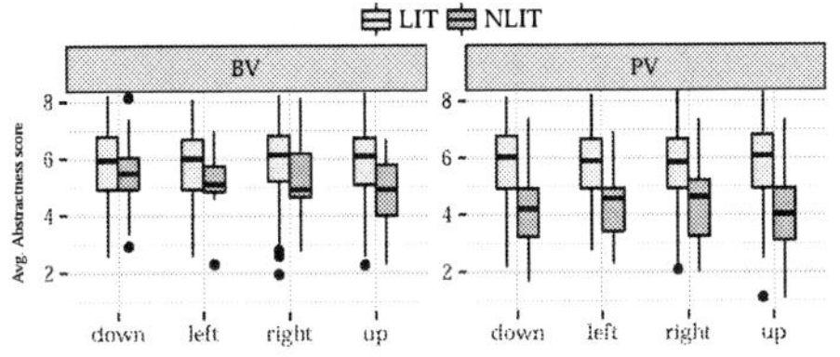

Figure 6: Average concreteness of nouns in BV/PV sentences, categorised by directionality.

Relying on abstractness/concreteness ratings of a semi-automatically created database (Köper and Schulte im Walde, 2016a), we looked up and averaged over the ratings of all nouns in a sentence.

The ratings range from 0 (very abstract) to 10 (very concrete). We can see that across directions the literal sentences are more concrete than the non-literal sentences. In addition, we can see that the differences in abstractness are much stronger for the PV target-domain sentences than for the BV source-domain sentences.

Particle Meaning Shifts Figure 7 once more illustrates preferences in arrow directions across the four particle types, but is –in contrast to Figure 5– restricted to the non-literal PV sentences (full agreement). For particles *ab* and *auf* we hardly find differences when specifying on non-literal language usage; for both *an* and *aus* we find an increase of DOWN meanings in non-literal language usage, which goes along with a decrease of LEFT meanings for *an* and a decrease of RIGHT meanings for *aus*. So within our collection we find some evidence for meaning shifts within PV types for the two particle types *an* and *aus* but not for *ab* and *auf*, which seem to stay with their predominant vertical meanings also in non-literal language.

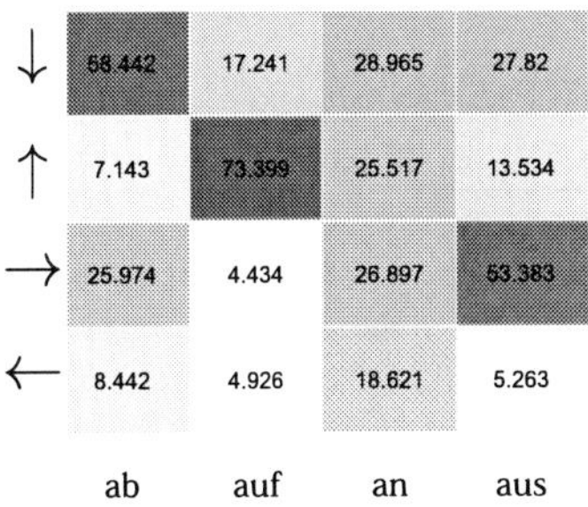

Figure 7: Directionality of particle types restricted to non-literal sentences.

Source–Target Domain Meaning Shifts Figure 8 presents meaning shifts as strengths of relationships between source and target domains, when looking at only literal BV sentences and non-literal PV sentences. The cells in the heat map present the results of multiplying the target domain degrees of membership across all PVs with the source domain degrees of membership of their respective BVs. We applied positive pointwise mutual information (PPMI) weighting to avoid a bias towards popular classes. Examples of particularly strong combinations are PLANTS → TIME (e.g., *blühen → aufblühen*); and SOUND → COMMUNICATION (e.g., *bellen → anbellen*).

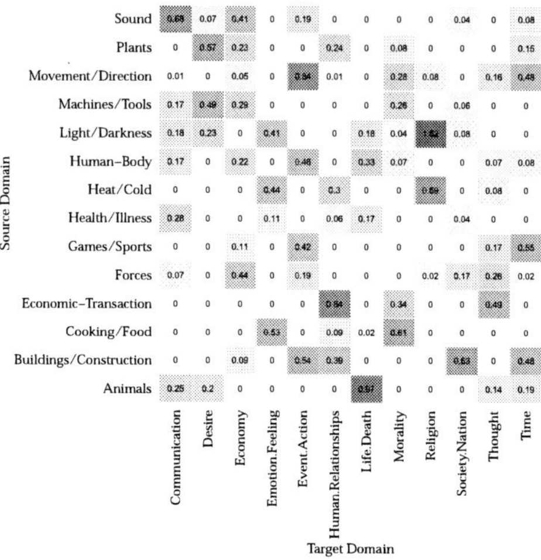

Figure 8: Source–target domain shifts.

4.3 Verification

While the previous section illustrated the value of the collection from a qualitative perspective, we also verified the information through computational approaches. We applied standard classifiers to predict source domains, target domains as well as directionality, given the underlying sentences. Our baseline is provided by *Majority*, which refers to the performance obtained by guessing always the largest class. For the target domains this majority provides a considerably high baseline with an accuracy of 33.95%, due to the very large class EVENT/ACTION. We therefore added a branch of experiments excluding this class (Target$_2$).

As the most general set of features we used Uni_{word}, a simple bag-of-words method where we counted how many times a certain unigram has been seen for a class. We implemented this method using Multinomial Naive Bayes. Similarly, we conducted experiments using Uni_{lemma} instead of Uni_{word}, which we expected to increase the chance of observing the unigram features.

Affective is a meaning-shift-related feature type. It relies on a range of psycholinguistic norms such as valency, arousal and concreteness/abstractness, which are supposedly salient features for meaning shifts and directions (Turney et al., 2011; Dudschig et al., 2015; Köper and Schulte im Walde, 2016b). We represented each sentence by providing an average affective score over all nouns, as taken from the semi-automatically created database by Köper and Schulte im Walde (2016a).

Finally we combined the above features (*Combination*). We relied on the affective norms, the lemma unigram features as well as the directionality information for domain prediction, or the domain information for directionality prediction.

Tables 6 and 7 present the accuracy results of classifying the generated sentences into domains and directionalities, respectively. According to the χ^2 test and $p < 0.001$, all our feature sets except for the affective norms in Table 7 outperform the baseline significantly, both individually and in combination. We thus conclude that also from a quantitative perspective the collection represents a valuable resource for complex verb meaning.

Feature Set	Method	Source	Target	Target$_2$
Majority	Baseline	14.82	33.45	15.46
Affective	SVM	30.95	40.61	31.50
Uni_{word}	Naive Bayes	54.15	43.40	42.60
Uni_{lemma}	Naive Bayes	57.09	44.74	43.84
Combination	SVM	**60.74**	**49.87**	**45.46**

Table 6: Predicting domains.

Feature Set	Method	Source	Target
Majority	Baseline	34.09	31.74
Affective	SVM	40.93	35.63
Uni_{word}	Naive Bayes	48.56	55.27
Uni_{lemma}	Naive Bayes	**52.28**	**56.94**
Combination	SVM	49.18	55.93

Table 7: Predicting directionality.

5 Conclusion

We presented a new collection to assess meaning components in German complex verbs, by relying on a novel strategy to obtain source and target domain characterisations as well as spatial directional information via sentence generation rather than sentence annotation. A broad qualitative description of the dataset and a series of standard classification experiments assessed the reliability of the novel collection.

Acknowledgments

The research was supported by the DFG Collaborative Research Centre SFB 732. In addition, we particularly thank our student researchers Ingrid Kasimir, Daniela Naumann and Florian Lux for their help in collecting and cleaning the dataset.

References

Timothy Baldwin, Colin Bannard, Takaaki Tanaka, and Dominic Widdows. 2003. An Empirical Model of Multiword Expression Decomposability. In *Proceedings of the ACL Workshop on Multiword Expressions: Analysis, Acquisition and Treatment.* Sapporo, Japan, pages 89–96.

Collin Bannard. 2005. Learning about the Meaning of Verb–Particle Constructions from Corpora. *Computer Speech and Language* 19:467–478.

Lawrence W. Barsalou. 1999. Perceptual Symbol Systems. *Behavioral and Brain Sciences* 22:577–660.

Julia Birke and Anoop Sarkar. 2006. A Clustering Approach for the Nearly Unsupervised Recognition of Nonliteral Language. In *Proceedings of the 11th Conference of the European Chapter of the ACL.* Trento, Italy, pages 329–336.

Stefan Bott and Sabine Schulte im Walde. 2014. Optimizing a Distributional Semantic Model for the Prediction of German Particle Verb Compositionality. In *Proceedings of the 9th International Conference on Language Resources and Evaluation.* Reykjavik, Iceland, pages 509–516.

Stefan Bott and Sabine Schulte im Walde. 2015. Exploiting Fine-grained Syntactic Transfer Features to Predict the Compositionality of German Particle Verbs. In *Proceedings of the 11th Conference on Computational Semantics.* London, UK, pages 34–39.

Stefan Bott and Sabine Schulte im Walde. 2017. Factoring Ambiguity out of the Prediction of Compositionality for German Multi-Word Expressions. In *Proceedings of the 13th Workshop on Multiword Expressions.* Valencia, Spain, pages 66–72.

Paul Cook and Suzanne Stevenson. 2006. Classifying Particle Semantics in English Verb-Particle Constructions. In *Proceedings of the ACL/COLING Workshop on Multiword Expressions: Identifying and Exploiting Underlying Properties.* Sydney, Australia, pages 45–53.

Scott Deerwester, Susan T. Dumais, George W. Furnas, Thomas K. Landauer, and Richard Harshman. 1990. Indexing by Latent Semantic Analysis. *Journal of the American Society of Information Science* 41(6):391–407.

René Dirven. 1993. Dividing up Physical and Mental Space into Conceptual Categories by Means of English Prepositions. In Zelinksy C. Wibbelt, editor, *The Semantics of Prepositions – From Mental Processing to Natural Language Processing*, Mouton de Gruyter, volume 3 of *Natural Language Processing*, pages 73–98.

Carolin Dudschig, Irmgard de la Vega, and Barbara Kaup. 2015. What's up? Emotion-specific Activation of Vertical Space during Language Processing. *Acta Psychologica* 156:143–155.

Carolin Dudschig, Martin Lachmair, Irmgard de la Vega, Monica De Filippis, and Barbara Kaup. 2012. From Top to Bottom: Spatial Shifts of Attention caused by Linguistic Stimuli. *Cognitive Processes* 13:S151–S154.

Diego Frassinelli, Alla Abrosimova, Sylvia Springorum, and Sabine Schulte im Walde. 2017. Meaning (Mis-)Match in the Directionality of German Particle Verbs. Poster at the 30th Annual CUNY Conference on Human Sentence Processing.

Dedre Gentner. 1983. Structure-Mapping: A Theoretical Framework for Analogy. *Cognitive Science* 7:155–170.

Arthur M. Glenberg and Michael P. Kaschak. 2002. Grounding Language in Action. *Psychonomic Bulletin and Review* 9(3):558–565.

Boris Haselbach. 2011. Deconstructing the Meaning of the German Temporal Verb Particle *"nach"* at the Syntax-Semantics Interface. In *Proceedings of Generative Grammar in Geneva.* Geneva, Switzerland, pages 71–92.

Julie Heiser and Barbara Tversky. 2006. Arrows in Comprehending and Producing Mechanical Diagrams. *Cognitive Science* 30:581–592.

Anette Herskovits. 1986. *Language and Spatial Cognition: An Interdisciplinary Study of the Prepositions in English.* Studies in Natural Language Processing. Cambridge University Press, London.

Hans Kamp and Uwe Reyle. 1993. *From Discourse to Logic.* Kluwer Academic Publishers.

Barbara Kaup, Monica De Filippis, Martin Lachmair, Irmgard de la Vega, and Carolin Dudschig. 2012. When Up-Words meet Down-Sentences: Evidence for Word- or Sentence-based Compatibility Effects? *Cognitive Process* 13:S203–S207.

Su Nam Kim and Timothy Baldwin. 2007. Detecting Compositionality of English Verb-Particle Constructions using Semantic Similarity. In *Proceedings of the 7th Meeting of the Pacific Association for Computational Linguistics.* Melbourne, Australia, pages 40–48.

Fritz Kliche. 2011. Semantic Variants of German Particle Verbs with *"ab"*. *Leuvense Bijdragen* 97:3–27.

Maximilian Köper and Sabine Schulte im Walde. 2016a. Automatically Generated Affective Norms of Abstractness, Arousal, Imageability and Valence for 350 000 German Lemmas. In *Proceedings of the 10th International Conference on Language Resources and Evaluation.* Portoroz, Slovenia, pages 2595–2598.

Maximilian Köper and Sabine Schulte im Walde. 2016b. Distinguishing Literal and Non-Literal Usage of German Particle Verbs. In *Proceedings of the Conference of the North American Chapter of the Association for Computational Linguistics: Human Language Technologies*. San Diego, California, USA, pages 353–362.

Maximilian Köper and Sabine Schulte im Walde. 2017a. Applying Multi-Sense Embeddings for German Verbs to Determine Semantic Relatedness and to Detect Non-Literal Language. In *Proceedings of the 15th Conference of the European Chapter of the Association for Computational Linguistics*. Valencia, Spain, pages 535–542.

Maximilian Köper and Sabine Schulte im Walde. 2017b. Complex Verbs are Different: Exploring the Visual Modality in Multi-Modal Models to Predict Compositionality. In *Proceedings of the 13th Workshop on Multiword Expressions*. Valencia, Spain, pages 200–206.

Maximilian Köper and Sabine Schulte im Walde. 2018. Analogies in Complex Verb Meaning Shifts: The Effect of Affect in Semantic Similarity Models. In *Proceedings of the 16th Annual Conference of the North American Chapter of the Association for Computational Linguistics: Human Language Technologies*. New Orleans, LA, USA. To appear.

Maximilian Köper, Sabine Schulte im Walde, Max Kisselew, and Sebastian Padó. 2016. Improving Zero-Shot-Learning for German Particle Verbs by using Training-Space Restrictions and Local Scaling. In *Proceedings of the 5th Joint Conference on Lexical and Computational Semantics*. Berlin, Germany, pages 91–96.

Zolzan Kövecses. 2002. *Metaphor: A Practical Introduction*. Oxford University Press, New York.

Natalie Kühner and Sabine Schulte im Walde. 2010. Determining the Degree of Compositionality of German Particle Verbs by Clustering Approaches. In *Proceedings of the 10th Conference on Natural Language Processing*. Saarbrücken, Germany, pages 47–56.

George Lakoff, Jane Espenson, and Alan Schwartz. 1991. Master Metaphor List. Technical Report.

George Lakoff and Mark Johnson. 1980. *Metaphors we live by*. University of Chicago Press.

Andrea Lechler and Antje Roßdeutscher. 2009. German Particle Verbs with *"auf"*. Reconstructing their Composition in a DRT-based Framework. *Linguistische Berichte* 220:439–478.

Birte Lönneker-Rodman. 2008. The Hamburg Metaphor Database Project: Issues in Resource Creation. *Language Resources and Evaluation* 42:293–318.

Diana McCarthy, Bill Keller, and John Carroll. 2003. Detecting a Continuum of Compositionality in Phrasal Verbs. In *Proceedings of the ACL Workshop on Multiword Expressions: Analysis, Acquisition and Treatment*. Sapporo, Japan, pages 73–80.

Daniel C. Richardson, Michael J. Spivey, Lawrence W. Barsalou, and Ken McRae. 2003. Spatial Representations activated during Real-Time Comprehension of Verbs. *Cognitive Science* 27:767–780.

Ivan A. Sag, Timothy Baldwin, Francis Bond, Ann Copestake, and Dan Flickinger. 2002. Multiword Expressions: A Pain in the Neck for NLP. In *Proceedings of the Conference on Intelligent Text Processing and Computational Linguistics*. Mexico City, Mexico.

Bahar Salehi and Paul Cook. 2013. Predicting the Compositionality of Multiword Expressions Using Translations in Multiple Languages. In *Proceedings of the 2nd Joint Conference on Lexical and Computational Semantics*. Atlanta, GA, USA, pages 266–275.

Bahar Salehi, Paul Cook, and Timothy Baldwin. 2014. Using Distributional Similarity of Multi-way Translations to Predict Multiword Expression Compositionality. In *Proceedings of the 14th Conference of the European Chapter of the Association for Computational Linguistics*. Gothenburg, Sweden, pages 472–481.

Larry Shapiro. 2007. The Embodied Cognition Research Programme. *Philosophy Compass* 2(2):338–346.

Ekaterina Shutova and Simone Teufel. 2010. Metaphor Corpus Annotated for Source – Target Domain Mappings. In *Proceedings of the 7th International Conference on Language Resources and Evaluation*. Valletta, Malta, pages 3255–3261.

Ekaterina Shutova, Simone Teufel, and Anna Korhonen. 2013. Statistical Metaphor Processing. *Computational Linguistics* 39(2):301–353.

Sylvia Springorum. 2011. DRT-based Analysis of the German Verb Particle *"an"*. *Leuvense Bijdragen* 97:80–105.

Sylvia Springorum, Jason Utt, and Sabine Schulte im Walde. 2013. Regular Meaning Shifts in German Particle Verbs: A Case Study. In *Proceedings of the 10th International Conference on Computational Semantics*. Potsdam, Germany, pages 228–239.

Peter Turney, Yair Neuman, Dan Assaf, and Yohai Cohen. 2011. Literal and Metaphorical Sense Identification through Concrete and Abstract Context. In *Proceedings of the Conference on Empirical Methods in Natural Language Processing*. Edinburgh, UK, pages 680–690.

Barbara Tversky. 2011. Visualizing Thought. *Topics in Cognitive Science* 3:499–535.

Ake Viberg. 1983. The Verbs of Perception: A Typological Study. *Linguistics* 21(1):123–162.

Joost Zwarts. 2017. Spatial semantics: Modeling the meaning of prepositions. *Language and Linguistics Compass* 11(5):1–20.

Learning Neural Word Salience Scores

Krasen Samardzhiev   **Andrew Gargett**   **Danushka Bollegala**
Department of Computer Science, University of Liverpool
Science and Technology Facilities Council.
`krasensam@gmail.com, danushka@liverpool.ac.uk`
`andrew.gargett@stfc.ac.uk`

Abstract

Measuring the salience of a word is an essential step in numerous NLP tasks. Heuristic approaches such as tfidf have been used so far to estimate the salience of words. We propose *Neural Word Salience* (NWS) scores, unlike heuristics, are learnt from a corpus. Specifically, we learn word salience scores such that, using pre-trained word embeddings as the input, can accurately predict the words that appear in a sentence, given the words that appear in the sentences preceding or succeeding that sentence. Experimental results on sentence similarity prediction show that the learnt word salience scores perform comparably or better than some of the state-of-the-art approaches for representing sentences on benchmark datasets for sentence similarity, while using only a fraction of the training and prediction times required by prior methods. Moreover, our NWS scores positively correlate with psycholinguistic measures such as concreteness, and imageability implying a close connection to the salience as perceived by humans.

1 Introduction

Humans can easily recognise the words that contribute to the meaning of a sentence (i.e. content words) from words that serve only a grammatical functionality (i.e. functional words). For example, functional words such as *the, an, a* etc. have limited contributions towards the overall meaning of a document and are often filtered out as *stop words* in information retrieval systems (Salton and Buckley, 1983). We define the *salience* $q(w)$ of a word w in a given text T as the semantic contribution made by w towards the overall meaning of T. If we can accurately compute the salience of words, then we can develop better representations of texts that can be used in downstream NLP tasks such as similarity measurement (Arora et al., 2017) or text

(e.g. sentiment, entailment) classification (Socher et al., 2011).

As described later in section 2, existing methods for detecting word salience can be classified into two groups: (a) lexicon-based filtering methods such as stop word lists, or (b) word frequency-based heuristics such as the popular term-frequency inverse document frequency (tfidf) (Jones, 1972) measure and its variants. Unfortunately, two main drawbacks can be identified in common to both stop words lists and frequency-based salience scores.

First, such methods do not take into account the semantics associated with individual words when determining their salience. For example, consider the following two adjacent sentences extracted from a newspaper article related to the visit of the Japanese Prime Minister, *Shinzo Abe*, to the White House in Washington, to meet the US President *Donald Trump*.

(a) *Abe visited Washington in February and met Trump in the White House.*

(b) *Because the trade relations between US and Japan have been fragile after the recent comments by the US President, the Prime Minister's visit to the US can be seen as an attempt to reinforce the trade relations.*

In Sentence (a), the Japanese person name *Abe* or American person name *Trump* would occur less in a corpus than the US state name *Washington*. Nevertheless, for the main theme of this sentence, *Japanese Prime minister met US President*, the two person names are equally important as the location they met. Therefore, we must look into the semantics of the individual words when computing their saliences.

Second, words do not occur independently of one another in a text, and methods that compute

33

*Proceedings of the 7th Joint Conference on Lexical and Computational Semantics (*SEM)*, pages 33–42
New Orleans, June 5-6, 2018. ©2018 Association for Computational Linguistics

word salience using frequency or pre-compiled stop words lists alone do not consider the contextual information. For example, the two sentences (a) and (b) in our previous example are extracted from the same newspaper article and are adjacent. The words in the two sentences are highly related. For example, *Abe* in sentence (a) refers to the *Prime Minister* in sentence (b), and *Trump* in sentence (a) is refers to the *US President* in sentence (b). A human reader who reads sentence (a) before sentence (b) would expect to see some relationship between the topic discussed in (a) and that in the next sentence (b). Unfortunately, methods that compute word salience scores considering each word independently from all other words in near by contexts, ignore such proximity relationships.

To overcome the above-mentioned disfluencies in existing word salience scores, we propose an unsupervised method that first randomly initialises word salience scores, and subsequently updates them such that we can accurately predict the words in local contexts. Specifically, we train a two-layer neural network where in the first layer we take pre-trained word embeddings of the words in a sentence S_i as the input and compute a representation for S_i (here onwards referred to as a *sentence embedding*) as the *weighted average* of the input word embeddings. The weights correspond to the word salience scores of the words in S_i. Likewise, we apply the same approach to compute the sentence embedding for the sentence S_{i-1} preceding S_i and S_{i+1} succeeding S_i in a sentence-ordered corpus. Because S_{i-1}, S_i and S_{i+1} are adjacent sentences, we would expect the sentence pairs (S_i, S_{i-1}) and (S_i, S_{i+1}) to be topically related.[1]

We would expect a high degree of cosine similarity between s_i and s_{i-1}, and s_i and s_{i+1}, where boldface symbols indicate vectors. Likewise, for a randomly selected sentence $S_j \notin \{S_{i-1}, S_i, S_{i+1}\}$, the expect similarity between S_j and S_i would be low. We model this as a supervised similarity prediction task and use backpropagation to update the word salience scores, keeping word embeddings fixed. We refer to the word

---

[1] S_{i-1} and S_{i+1} could also be topically related and produce a positive training examples in some cases. However, they are non-adjacent and possibly less related compared to adjacent sentence pairs. Because we have an abundant supply of sentences, and we want to reduce label noise in positive examples, we do not consider (S_{i-1}, S_{i+1}) as a positive example.

salience scores learnt by the proposed method as the *Neural Word Salience* (NWS) scores. We will use the contextual information of a word to learn its salience. However, once learnt, we consider salience as a property of a word that holds independently of its context. This enables us to use the same salience score for a word after training, without having to modify it considering the context in which it occurs.

Several remarks can be made about the proposed method for learning NWS scores. First, we do *not* require labelled data for learning NWS scores. Although we require semantically similar (positive) and semantically dissimilar (negative) pairs of sentences for learning the NWS scores, both positive and negative examples are automatically extracted from the given corpus. Second, we use pre-trained word embeddings as the input, and do *not* learn the word embeddings as part of the learning process. This design choice differentiates our work from previously proposed sentence embedding learning methods that jointly learn word embeddings as well as sentence embeddings (Hill et al., 2016; Kiros et al., 2015; Kenter et al., 2016). Moreover, it decouples the word salience score learning problem from word or sentence embedding learning problem, thereby simplifying the optimisation task and speeding up the learning process.

We use the NWS scores to compute sentence embeddings and measure the similarity between two sentences using 18 benchmark datasets for semantic textual similarity in past SemEval tasks (Agirre et al., 2012). Experimental results show that the sentence similarity scores computed using the NWS scores and pre-trained word embeddings show a high degree of correlation with human similarity ratings in those benchmark datasets. Moreover, we compare the NWS scores against the human ratings for psycholinguistic properties of words such as arousal, valence, dominance, imageability, and concreteness. Our analysis shows that NWS scores demonstrate a moderate level of correlation with concreteness and imageability ratings, despite not being specifically trained to predict such psycholinguistic properties of words.

2   Related Work

Word salience scores have long been studied in the information retrieval community (Salton and

Buckley, 1983). Given a user query described in terms of one or more keywords, an information retrieval system must find the most relevant documents to the user query from a potentially large collection of documents. Word salience scores based on term frequency, document frequency, and document length have been proposed such as tfidf and BM25 (Robertson, 1997).

Our proposed method learns word salience scores by creating sentence embeddings. Next, we briefly review such sentence embedding methods and explain the differences between the sentence embedding learning problem and word salience learning problem.

Sentences have a syntactic structure and the ordering of words affects the meaning expressed in the sentence. Consequently, compositional approaches for computing sentence-level semantic representations from word-level semantic representations have used numerous linear algebraic operators such as vector addition, element-wise multiplication, multiplying by a matrix or a tensor (Blacoe and Lapata, 2012; Mitchell and Lapata, 2008).

Alternatively to applying nonparametric operators on word embeddings to create sentence embeddings, recurrent neural networks can learn the optimal weight matrix that can produce an accurate sentence embedding when repeatedly applied to the constituent word embeddings. For example, skip-thought vectors (Kiros et al., 2015) use bi-directional LSTMs to predict the words in the order they appear in the previous and next sentences given the current sentence. Although skip-thought vectors have shown superior performances in supervised tasks, its performance on unsupervised tasks has been sub-optimal (Arora et al., 2017). Moreover, training bi-directional LSTMs from large datasets is time consuming and we also need to perform LSTM inference in order to create the embedding for unseen sentences at test time, which is time consuming compared to weighted addition of the input word embeddings. FastSent (Hill et al., 2016) was proposed as an alternative lightweight approach for sentence embedding where a softmax objective is optimised to predict the occurrences of words in the next and the previous sentences, ignoring the ordering of the words in the sentence.

Surprisingly, averaging word embeddings to create sentence embeddings has shown compara-

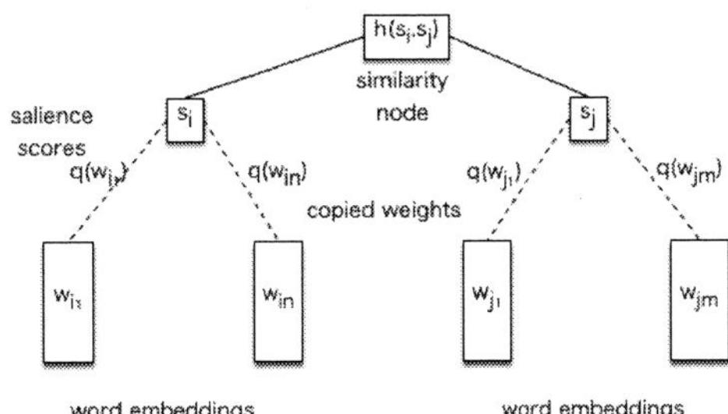

Figure 1: Overview of the proposed neural word salience learning method. Given two sentences (S_i, S_j), we learn the salience scores of words $q(w)$ such that we can predict the similarity between the two sentences using their embeddings s_i, s_j. Difference between predicted similarity and actual label is considered as the error and its gradient is backpropagated through the network to update $q(w)$.

ble performances to sentence embeddings that are learnt using more sophisticated word-order sensitive methods. For example, (Arora et al., 2017) proposed a method to find the optimal weights for combining word embeddings when creating sentence embeddings using unigram probabilities, by maximising the likelihood of the occurrences of words in a corpus. Siamese CBOW (Kenter et al., 2016) learns word embeddings such that we can accurately compute sentence embeddings by averaging the word embeddings. Although averaging is an order insensitive operator, (Adi et al., 2016) empirically showed that it can accurately predict the content and word order in sentences. This can be understood intuitively by recalling that words that appear between two words are often different in contexts where those two words are swapped. For example, in the two sentences "*Ostrich* is a large *bird* that lives in Africa" and "Large *birds* such as *Ostriches* live in Africa", the words that appear in between *ostrich* and *bird* are different, giving rise to different sentence embeddings even when sentence embeddings are computed by averaging the individual word embeddings. Instead of considering all words equally for sentence embedding purposes, attention-based models (Hahn and Keller, 2016; Yin et al., 2016; Wang et al., 2016) learn the amount of weight (attention) we must assign to each word in a given context.

Our proposed method for learning NWS scores is based on the prior observation that averaging is an effective heuristic for creating sentence embeddings from word embeddings. However, unlike sentence embedding learning methods that do not learn word salience scores (He and Lin, 2016; Yin

35

et al., 2016) , our goal in this paper is to learn word salience scores and not sentence embeddings. We compute sentence embeddings only for the purpose of evaluating the word salience scores we learn. Moreover, our work differs from Siamese CBOW (Kenter et al., 2016) in that we do not learn word embeddings but take pre-trained word embeddings as the input for learning word salience scores. NWS scores we learn in this paper are also different from the salience scores learnt by (Arora et al., 2017) because they do not constrain their word salience scores such that they can be used to predict the words that occur in adjacent sentences.

3 Neural Word Salience Scores

Let us consider a vocabulary $\mathcal{V}$ of words $w \in \mathcal{V}$. For the simplicity of exposition, we limit the vocabulary to unigrams but note that the proposed method can be used to learn salience scores for arbitrary length n-grams. We assume that we are given d-dimensional pre-trained word embeddings $\boldsymbol{w} \in \mathbb{R}^d$ for the words in $\mathcal{V}$. Let us denote the NWS score of w by $q(w) \in R$. We learn $q(w)$ such that the similarity between two adjacent sentences $\mathcal{S}_i$ and $\mathcal{S}_{i-1}$, or $\mathcal{S}_i$ and $\mathcal{S}_{i+1}$ in a sentence-ordered corpus $\mathcal{C}$ is larger than that between two non-adjacent sentences $\mathcal{S}_i$ and $\mathcal{S}_j$, where $j \notin \{i - 1, i, i + 1\}$. Let us further represent the two sentence $\mathcal{S}_i = \{w_{i1}, \ldots, w_{in}\}$ and $\mathcal{S}_j = \{w_{j1}, \ldots, w_{jm}\}$ by the sets of words in those sentences. Here, we assume the corpus to contain sequences of ordered sentence such as in a newspaper article, a book chapter or a blog post.

The neural network we use for learning $q(w)$ is shown in Figure 1. The first layer computes the embedding of a sentence $\mathcal{S}$, $\boldsymbol{s} \in \mathbb{R}^d$ using Equation 1, which is the weighted-average of the individual word embeddings.

$$\boldsymbol{s} = \sum_{w \in \mathcal{S}} q(w)\boldsymbol{w} \qquad (1)$$

We use (1) to compute embeddings for two sentences $\mathcal{S}_i$ and $\mathcal{S}_j$ denoted respectively by $\boldsymbol{s}_i$ and $\boldsymbol{s}_j$. Here, the same set of salience scores $q(w)$ are used for computing both $\boldsymbol{s}_i$ and $\boldsymbol{s}_j$, which resembles a Siamese neural network architecture.

The root node computes the similarity $h(\boldsymbol{s}_i, \boldsymbol{s}_j)$ between two sentence embeddings. Different similarity (alternatively dissimilarity or divergence) functions such as cosine similarity, ℓ_1 distance, ℓ_2 distance, Jenson-Shannon divergence etc. can be

used as h. As a concrete example, here we use softmax of the inner-products as follows:

$$h(\boldsymbol{s}_i, \boldsymbol{s}_j) = \frac{\exp\left(\boldsymbol{s}_i^\top \boldsymbol{s}_j\right)}{\sum_{\mathcal{S}_k \in \mathcal{C}} \exp\left(\boldsymbol{s}_i^\top \boldsymbol{s}_k\right)} \qquad (2)$$

Ideally, the normalisation term in the denominator in the softmax must be taken over all the sentences $\mathcal{S}_k$ in the corpus (Andreas and Klein, 2015). However, this is computationally expensive in most cases except for extremely small corpora. Therefore, following noise-contrastive estimation (Gutmann and Hyvärinen, 2012), we approximate the normalisation term using a randomly sampled set of K sentences, where K is typically less than 10. Because the similarity between two randomly sampled sentences is likely to be smaller than, for example, two adjacent sentences, we can see this sampling process as randomly sampling *negative* training instances from the corpus.

For two sentences $\mathcal{S}_i$ and $\mathcal{S}_j$ we consider them to be similar (positive training instance) if $j \in \{i - 1, i + 1\}$, and denote this by the target label $t = 1$. On the other hand, if the two sentences are non-adjacent (i.e. $j \notin \{i - 1, i + 1\}$), then we consider the pair $(\mathcal{S}_i, \mathcal{S}_j)$ to form a negative training instance, and denote this by $t = 0$.[2] This assumption enables us to use a sentence-ordered corpus for selecting both positive and negative training instances required for learning NWS scores.

Specifically, the model is trained using the two adjacent sentences to $\mathcal{S}_i$ - $\{i - 1, i + 1\}$ as positive examples, and K=2 negative examples not in $\{i - 1, i + 1\}$. These are sampled from the whole text corpus using a uniformly. Similar to (Kenter et al., 2016), we found that increasing the number of negative examples increases the training time, but does not have a significant impact on model accuracy.

Using t and $h(\boldsymbol{s}_i, \boldsymbol{s}_j)$ above, we compute the cross-entropy error $E(t, (\mathcal{S}_i, \mathcal{S}_j))$ for an instance $(t, (\mathcal{S}_i, \mathcal{S}_j))$ as follows:

$$E(t, (\mathcal{S}_i, \mathcal{S}_j)) = t \log\left(h(\boldsymbol{s}_i, \boldsymbol{s}_j)\right) + (1-t) \log\left(1 - h(\boldsymbol{s}_i, \boldsymbol{s}_j)\right) \qquad (3)$$

Next, we backpropagate the error gradients via the network to compute the updates as follows:

$$\frac{\partial E}{\partial q(w)} = \frac{(t - h(\boldsymbol{s}_i, \boldsymbol{s}_j))}{h(\boldsymbol{s}_i, \boldsymbol{s}_j)(1 - h(\boldsymbol{s}_i, \boldsymbol{s}_j))} \frac{\partial h(\boldsymbol{s}_i, \boldsymbol{s}_j)}{\partial q(w)} \qquad (4)$$

---

[2] It is possible in theory that two non-adjacent sentences could be similar, but the likelihood of this event is small and can be safely ignored in practice.

Here, we drop the arguments of the error and simply write it as E to simplify the notation. To compute $\frac{\partial h(\boldsymbol{s}_i, \boldsymbol{s}_j)}{\partial q(w)}$ let us define

$$g(\boldsymbol{s}_i, \boldsymbol{s}_j) = \log\left(h(\boldsymbol{s}_i, \boldsymbol{s}_j)\right) \qquad (5)$$

From which we have,

$$\frac{\partial h(\boldsymbol{s}_i, \boldsymbol{s}_j)}{\partial q(w)} = h(\boldsymbol{s}_i, \boldsymbol{s}_j)\frac{\partial g(\boldsymbol{s}_i, \boldsymbol{s}_j)}{\partial q(w)}. \qquad (6)$$

We can then compute $\frac{\partial g}{\partial q(w)}$ as follows:

$$\mathcal{I}[w \in \mathcal{S}_i]\boldsymbol{w}^\top \boldsymbol{s}_j + \mathcal{I}[w \in \mathcal{S}_j]\boldsymbol{w}^\top \boldsymbol{s}_i \qquad (7)$$

$$-\log(\sum_k \exp\left(\boldsymbol{s}_i{}^\top \boldsymbol{s}_j\right) \mathcal{I}[w \in \mathcal{S}_i]\boldsymbol{w}^\top \boldsymbol{s}_k + \qquad (8)$$

$$\mathcal{I}[w \in \mathcal{S}_k]\boldsymbol{w}^\top \boldsymbol{s}_i)) \qquad (9)$$

Here, the indicator function $\mathcal{I}$ is given by (10).

$$\mathcal{I}[\theta] = \begin{cases} 1 & \theta \text{ is True} \\ 0 & \text{otherwise} \end{cases} \qquad (10)$$

Substituting (10), (7), in (4) we compute $\frac{\partial E}{\partial q(w)}$ and use stochastic gradient descent with initial learning rate set to 0.01 and subsequently scheduled by AdaGrad (Duchi et al., 2011). The NWS scores can be either randomly initialised or set to some other values such as ISF scores. We found experimentally that the best performing models are the ones with the weights initialised with ISF. Source code of our implementation is available[3].

4 Experiments

We use the Toronto books corpus[4] as our training dataset. This corpus contains 81 million sentences from 11,038 books, and has been used as a training dataset in several prior work on sentence embedding learning. Note that only 7,807 books in this corpus are unique. Specifically, for 2,098 books there exist one duplicate, for 733 there are two and for 95 books there are more than two duplicates. However, following the training protocol used in prior work (Kiros et al., 2015), we do not remove those duplicates from the corpus, and use the entire collection of books for training. We convert all sentences to lowercase and tokenise using the Python NLTK[5] punctuation tokeniser. No further pre-processing is conduced beyond tokenisation. The proposed method is implemented using TensorFlow[6] and executed on a NVIDIA Tesla K40c 2880 GPU.

[3]https://bitbucket.org/u3ks/year3
[4]http://yknzhu.wixsite.com/mbweb
[5]http://www.nltk.org/
[6]https://www.tensorflow.org/

4.1 Measuring Semantic Textual Similarity

It is difficult to evaluate the accuracy of word salience scores by direct manual inspection. Moreover, no such dataset exists where human annotators have manually rated words for their salience. Therefore, we resort to extrinsic evaluation, where, we first use (1) to create the sentence embedding for a given sentence using pre-trained word embeddings and the NWS scores computed using the proposed method. Next, we measure the semantic textual similarity (STS) between two sentences by the cosine similarity between the corresponding sentence embeddings. Finally, we compute the correlation between human similarity ratings for sentence pairs in benchmark datasets for STS and the similarity scores computed following the above-mentioned procedure. If there exists a high degree of correlation between the sentence similarity scores computed using the NWS scores and human ratings, then it can be considered as empirical support for the accuracy of the NWS scores. Note that we have not trained the word salience model on the SemEval datasets, but are only using them to test the effectiveness of the computed NWS scores. As shown in Table 1, we use 18 benchmark datasets from SemEval STS tasks from years 2012 (Agirre et al., 2012), 2013 (Agirre et al., 2013), 2014 (Agirre et al., 2014), and 2015 (Agirre et al., 2015). Note that the tasks with the same name in different years actually represent different tasks.

We use Pearson correlation coefficient as the evaluation measure. For a list of n ordered pairs of ratings $\{(x_i, y_i)\}_{i=1}^n$, the Pearson correlation coefficient between the two ratings, $r(\boldsymbol{x}, \boldsymbol{y})$, is computed as follows:

$$r(\boldsymbol{x}, \boldsymbol{y}) = \frac{\sum_{i=1}^n (x_i - \bar{x})(y_i - \bar{y})}{\sqrt{\sum_{i=1}^n (x_i - \bar{x})^2}\sqrt{\sum_{i=1}^n (y_i - \bar{y})^2}} \qquad (11)$$

Here, $\bar{x} = \frac{1}{n}\sum_{i=1}^n x_i$ and $\bar{y} = \frac{1}{n}\sum_{i=1}^n y_i$. Pearson correlation coefficient is invariant against linear transformations of the similarity scores, which is suitable for comparing similarity scores assigned to the same set of items by two different methods (human ratings vs. system ratings).

We use the Fisher transformation (Fisher, 1915) to test for the statistical significance of Pearson correlation coefficients. Fisher transformation, $F(r)$, of the Pearson correlation coefficient r is given by (12).

$$F(r) = \frac{1}{2}\log\left(\frac{1+r}{1-r}\right) \qquad (12)$$

Then, 95% confidence intervals are given by (13).

$$\tanh\left(F(r) \pm \frac{1.96}{\sqrt{n-3}}\right) \qquad (13)$$

We consider two baseline methods in our evaluations as described next.

Averaged Word Embeddings (AVG) As a baseline that does not use any salience scores for words when computing sentence embeddings, we use *Averaged Word Embeddings* (AVG) where we simply add all the word embeddings of the words in a sentence and divide from the total number of words to create a sentence embedding. This baseline demonstrates the level of performance we would obtain if we did not perform any word salience-based weighting in (1).

Inverse Sentence Frequency (ISF) As described earlier in section 2, term frequency is not a useful measure for discriminating salient vs. non-salient words in short-texts because it is rare for a particular word to occur multiple times in a short text such as a sentence. However, (inverse of) the number of different sentences in which a particular word occurs is a useful method for identifying salient features because non-content stop words are likely to occur in any sentence, irrespective of the semantic contribution to the topic of the sentence. Following the success of Inverse Document Frequency (IDF) in filtering out high frequent words in text classification tasks (Joachims, 1998), we define *Inverse Sentence Frequency* (ISF) of a word as the reciprocal of the number of sentences in which that word appears in a corpus. Specifically, ISF is computed as follows:

$$\mathrm{ISF}(w) = \log\left(1 + \frac{\text{no. of sentences in the corpus}}{\text{no. of sentences containing } w}\right) \qquad (14)$$

In Table 1, we compare NWS against AVG, ISF baselines. **SMOOTH** is the unigram probability-based smoothing method proposed by (Arora et al., 2017).[7] We compute sentence embeddings for NWS, AVG and ISF using pre-trained 300 dimensional GloVe embeddings trained from the Toronto books corpus using contextual windows

of 10 tokens.[8] For reference purposes we show the level of performance we would obtain if we had used sentence embedding methods such as, skip-thought (Kiros et al., 2015), and Siamese-CBOW (Kenter et al., 2016). Note that however, sentence embedding methods do not necessarily compute word salience scores. For skip-thought, Siamese CBOW and SMOOTH methods we report the published results in the original papers. Because (Kiros et al., 2015) did not report results for skip-thought on all 18 benchmark datasets used here, we report the re-evaluation of skip-thought on all 18 benchmark datasets by (Wieting et al., 2016).

Statistically significant improvements over the ISF baseline are indicated by an asterisk $*$, whereas the best results on each benchmark dataset are shown in bold. From Table 1, we see that between the two baselines AVG and ISF, ISF consistently outperforms AVG in all benchmark datasets. In 9 out of the 18 benchmarks, the proposed NWS scores report the best performance. We suspect that the word salience model has the best performance in the OWNs datasets because they are closest to the training data. However, it outperforms the other models in other datasets such as images, and student-answers which talks about the generalisability of the model. Moreover, in 9 datasets NWS statistically significantly outperforms the ISF baseline. Siamese-CBOW reports the best results in 5 datasets, whereas SMOOTH reports the best results in 2 datasets. Overall, NWS stands out as the best performing method among the methods compared in Table 1.

Our proposed method for learning NWS scores does not assume any specific properties of a particular word embedding learning algorithm. Therefore, in principle, we can learn NWS scores using *any* pre-trained set of word embeddings. To evaluate the accuracy of the word salience scores computed using different word embeddings, we conduct the following experiment. We use SGNS, CBOW and GloVe word embedding learning algorithms to learn 300 dimensional word embeddings from the Toronto books corpus.[9] The vocabulary size, cut-off frequency for selecting words, context window size are are kept fixed across differ-

---

[7]Corresponds to the GloVe-W method in the original publication.

[8]We use the GloVe implementation by the original authors available at `https://nlp.stanford.edu/projects/glove/`

[9]We use the implementation of word2vec from `https://github.com/dav/word2vec`

Table 1: Performance on STS benchmarks.

Dataset	SMOOTH	skip-thought	Siamese-CBOW	AVG	ISF	NWS
<u>2012</u>						
MSRpar	43.6	5.6	**43.8**	28.4	39.1	28.5
OnWN	54.3	60.5	64.4	47.1	60.5	**65.5***
SMTeuroparl	**51.1***	42.0	45.0	37.1	44.5	50.1
SMTnews	42.2	39.1	39.0	32.2	34.9	**44.7***
<u>2013</u>						
FNWN	23.0	**31.2**	23.2	26.9	29.4	25.2
OnWN	68.0*	24.2	49.9	25.0	63.2	**78.1***
headlines	63.8	38.6	**65.3***	40.2	59.4	57.0
<u>2014</u>						
OnWN	68.0	46.8	60.7	41.1	68.5	**80.8***
deft-forum	29.1	37.4	**40.8**	27.1	37.1	29.9
deft-news	**68.5**	46.2	59.1	48.8	63.6	65.4
headlines	59.3	40.3	**63.6***	41.9	58.8	56.2
images	74.1*	42.6	65.0	35.3	66.3	**75.9***
tweet-news	57.3	51.4	**73.2***	41.7	57.1	64.5*
<u>2015</u>						
answers-forums	41.4	27.8	21.8	25.7	37.6	**49.6***
answers-students	61.5	26.6	36.7	56.5	67.1	**68.0**
belief	47.7	45.8	47.7	29.3	43.2	**54.3***
headlines	64.0	12.5	21.5	49.3	**65.4**	65.3
images	75.4*	21	25.6	49.8	66.1	**76.6***
Overall Average	55.1	35.5	47.0	38.0	53.4	**57.6**

ent word embedding learning methods for the consistency of the evaluation. We then trained NWS with each set of word embeddings. Performance on STS benchmarks is shown in Table 2, where the best performance is bolded.

From Table 2, we see that GloVe is the best among the three word embedding learning methods compared in Table 2 for producing pre-trained word embeddings for the purpose of learning NWS scores. In particular, NWS scores reports best results with GloVe embeddings in 10 out of the 18 benchmark datasets, whereas with CBOW embeddings it obtains the best results in the remaining 8 benchmark datasets.

Figures 2a and 2b show the Pearson correlation coefficients on STS benchmarks obtained by NWS scores computed respectively for GloVe and SGNS embeddings. We plot training curves for the average correlation over each year's benchmarks as well as the overall average over the 18 benchmarks. We see that for both embeddings the training saturates after about five or six epochs. This ability to learn quickly with a small number of epochs is attractive because it reduces the training time.

4.2 Correlation with Psycholinguistic Scores

Prior work in psycholinguistics show that there is a close connection between the emotions felt by humans and the words they read in a text. *Valence* (the pleasantness of the stimulus), *arousal* (the intensity of emotion provoked by the stimulus), and *dominance* (the degree of control exerted by the stimulus) contribute to how the meanings of words affect human psychology, and often referred to as the *affective* meanings of words. (Mandera et al., 2015) show that by using SGNS embeddings as features in a k-Nearest Neighbour classifier, it is possible to accurately extrapolate the affective meanings of words. Moreover, perceived psycholinguistic properties of words such as *concreteness* (how "palpable" the object the word refers to) and *imageability* (the intensity with which a word arouses images) have been successfully predicted using word embeddings (Turney et al., 2011; Paetzold and Specia, 2016). For example, (Turney et al., 2011) used the cosine similarity between word embeddings obtained via La-

39

Table 2: Effect of word embeddings.

Dataset	NWS with pre-trained		
	SGNS	CBOW	GloVe
2012			
MSRpar	14.27	24.15	**28.47**
OnWN	59.76	61.25	**65.50**
SMTeuroparl	41.04	45.51	**50.12**
SMTnews	43.42	**46.94**	44.73
2013			
FNWN	21.47	**29.31**	25.21
OnWN	67.37	70.04	**78.06**
headlines	57.05	**57.46**	57.02
2014			
OnWN	73.06	73.71	**80.83**
deft-forum	28.62	**32.49**	29.90
deft-news	59.63	61.95	**65.35**
headlines	56.05	55.64	**56.20**
images	76.94	**78.08**	75.88
tweet-news	61.49	**66.41**	64.46
2015			
answers-forums	36.35	46.78	**49.65**
answers-students	59.53	59.92	**68.01**
belief	51.97	**55.65**	54.27
headlines	61.24	63.04	**65.32**
images	77.67	**78.39**	76.55
Overall Average	52.60	55.92	**57.52**

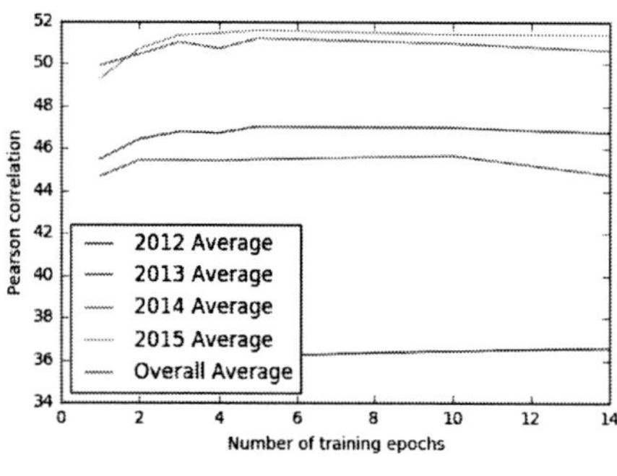

(a) GloVe

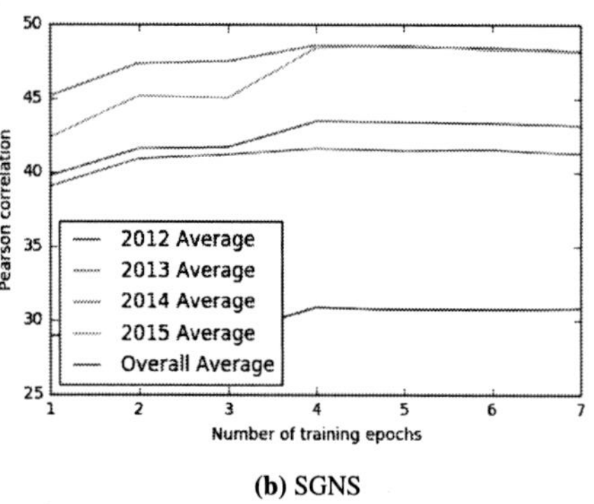

(b) SGNS

Figure 2: Pearson correlations on STS benchmarks against the number of training epochs

tent Semantic Analysis (LSA) (Deerwester et al., 1990) to predict the concreteness and imageability

Table 3: Pearson correlation coefficients against Psycholinguistic ratings of words in the ANEW and MRC databases.

Embed.	Arousal	Conc.	Dom.	Img.	Valance
GloVe	0.03	0.26	0.09	0.25	0.03
CBOW	0.04	-0.35	-0.04	-0.37	0.04
SGNS	-0.01	0.27	0.06	0.27	-0.01

ratings of words.

On the other hand, prior work studying the relationship between human reading patterns using eye-tracking devices show that there exist a high positive correlation between word salience and reading times (Dziemianko et al., 2013; Hahn and Keller, 2016). For example, humans pay more attention to words that carry meaning as indicated by the longer fixation times. Therefore, an interesting open question is that *what psycholinguistic properties of words, if any, are related to the NWS scores we learn in a purely unsupervised manner from a large corpus?* To answer this question empirically, we conduct the following experiment. We used the Affected Norms for English Words (ANEW) dataset created by Warriner et al. (2013), which contains valence, arousal, and dominance ratings collected via crowd sourcing for 13,915 words. Moreover, we obtained concreteness and imageability ratings for 3364 words from the MRC psycholinguistic database. We then measure the Pearson correlation coefficient between NWS scores and each of the psycholinguistic ratings as shown in Table 3.

We see a certain degree of correlation between NWS scores computed for all three word embeddings and the concreteness scores. Both GloVe and SGNS show moderate positive correlations for concreteness, whereas CBOW shows a moderate negative correlation for the same. A similar trend can be observed for imageability ratings in Table 3, where GloVe and SGNS correlates positively with imageability, while CBOW correlates negatively. Moreover, no correlation could be observed for arousal, valance and dominance ratings. This result shows that NWS scores are not correlated with affective meanings of words (arousal, dominance, and valance), but show a moderate level of correlation with perceived meaning scores (concreteness and imageability).

4.3 Sample Salience Scores

Tables 4 and 5 show respectively low and high salient words for ISF, NWS (ISF initialised) and NWS (randomly initialised) methods. words) se-

ISF	NWS (ISF init.)	NWS (rand init.)
the	your	alexis
to	our	tobias
i	we	copyright
and	my	rupert
a	you	spotted
of	us	vehicle
was	me	sword
he	i	isaac
his	voice	fletcher
you	has	cook

Table 5: Sample words with the high salience

ISF	NWS (ISF init.)	NWS (rand init.)
pathways	guess	hurdling
conspiratorial	boulder	happen
henna	autopsy	weird
alejandro	hippy	alejo
bedpost	alejandro	bolivians
swiveling	philosophy	his
confederate	arrow	answer
mid-morning	germany	her
alejo	spotted	yesterday
phd	bookstore	replied

lected from a sample of 1000 words. The probability of each word appearing in the sample was based on its frequency in the text corpus. The fact that the top ranked words with NWS differ from that of ISF suggests that the proposed method learns salience scores based on attributes other than frequency and provides a finer differentiation between words. The effectiveness of the NWS scores when initialised with ISF might be due to incorporating frequency information in addition to salience.

5 Conclusion

We proposed a method for learning Neural Word Salience scores from a sentence-ordered corpus, without requiring any manual data annotations. To evaluate the learnt salience scores, we computed sentence embeddings as the linearly weighted sum over pre-trained word embeddings. Our experimental results show that the proposed NWS scores outperform baseline methods, previously proposed word salience scores and sentence embedding methods on a range of benchmark datasets selected from past SemEval STS tasks. Moreover, the NWS scores shows interesting correlations with perceived meaning of words indicated by concreteness and imageability psycholinguistic ratings.

References

Yossi Adi, Einat Kermany, Yonatan Belinkov, Ofer Lavi, and Yoav Goldberg. 2016. Fine-grained analysis of sentence embeddings using auxiliary prediction tasks. *arXiv* .

Eneko Agirre, Carmen Banea, Claire Cardie, Daniel Cer, Mona Diab, Aitor Gonzalez-Agirre, Weiwei Guo, Iñigo Lopez-Gazpio, Montese Martxalar, Rada Mihalcea, German Rigau, Larraitz Uria, and Janyce M. Wiebe. 2015. Semeval-2015 task 2: Semantic textual similarity, english, spanish and pilot on interpretability. In *Proc. of SemEval*. pages 252 – 263.

Eneko Agirre, Carmen Banea, Claire Cardie, Daniel Cer, Mona Diab, Aitor Gonzalez-Agirre, Weiwei Guo, Rada Mihalcea, German Rigau, and Janyce Weibe. 2014. Semeval-2014 task 10: Multilingual semantic textual similarity. In *Proc. of the 8th International Workshop on Semantic Evaluation (SemEval)*. pages 81–91.

Eneko Agirre, Daniel Cer, Mona Diab, and Aitor Gonzalez-Agirre. 2012. Semeval-2012 task 6: A pilot on semantic textual similarity. In *Proc. of the first Joint Conference on Lexical and Computational Semantics (*SEM)*. pages 385 – 393.

Eneko Agirre, Daniel Cer, Mona Diab, Aitor Gonzalez-Agirre, and Weiwei Guo. 2013. shared task: Semantic textual similarity. In *Proc. of the Second Joint Conference on Lexical and Computational Semantics (*SEM):*. pages 32–43.

Jacob Andreas and Dan Klein. 2015. When and why are log-linear models self-normalizing? In *Proc. of the North American Chapter of the Association for Computational Linguistics: Human Language Technologies*. pages 244–249.

Sanjeev Arora, Yingyu Liang, and Tengyu Ma. 2017. A simple but tough-to-beat baseline for sentence embeddings. In *Proc. of International Conference on Learning Representations (ICLR)*.

William Blacoe and Mirella Lapata. 2012. A comparison of vector-based representations for semantic composition. In *Proc. of the Joint Conference on Empirical Methods in Natural Language Processing and Computational Natural Language Learning*. pages 546–556.

Scott Deerwester, Susan T. Dumais, George W. Furnas, Thomas K. Landauer, and Richard Harshman. 1990. Indexing by latent semantic analysis. *JOURNAL OF THE AMERICAN SOCIETY FOR INFORMATION SCIENCE* 41(6):391–407.

John Duchi, Elad Hazan, and Yoram Singer. 2011. Adaptive subgradient methods for online learning and stochastic optimization. *Journal of Machine Learning Research* 12:2121 – 2159.

Michal Dziemianko, Alasdair Clarke, and Frank Keller. 2013. Object-based saliency as a predictor of attention in visual tasks. In *Proc. of the 35thth Annual Conference of the Cognitive Science Society.* pages 2237–2242.

R. A. Fisher. 1915. Frequency distribution of the values of the correlation coefficient in samples of an indefinitely large population. *Biometrika* 10(4):507–521.

Michael U. Gutmann and Aapo Hyvärinen. 2012. Noise-contrastive estimation of unnormalized statistical models, with applications to natural image statistics. *Journal of Machine Learning Research* 13:307 – 361.

Michael Hahn and Frank Keller. 2016. Modeling human reading with neural attention. In *Proc. of Empirical Methods in Natural Language Processing (EMNLP).* pages 85–95.

Hua He and Jimmy Lin. 2016. Pairwise word interaction modeling with deep neural networks for semantic similarity measurement. In *Proc. of the North American Chapter of the Association for Computational Linguistics: Human Language Technologies.* pages 937–948.

Felix Hill, Kyunghyun Cho, and Anna Korhonen. 2016. Learning disributed representations of sentences from unlabelled data. In *Proc. of the North American Chapter of the Association for Computational Linguistics: Human Language Technologies.* pages 1367–1377.

Thorsten Joachims. 1998. Text categorization with support vector machines: Learning with many relevant features. In *Proc. of the European Conference on Machine Learning (ECML).* pages 137–142.

Karen Spärck Jones. 1972. A statistical interpretation of term specificity and its application in retrieval. *Journal of Documentation* 28:11–21.

Tom Kenter, Alexey Borisov, and Maarten de Rijke. 2016. Siamese cbow: Optimizing word embeddings for sentence representations. In *Proc, of the Annual Meeting of the Association for Computational Linguistics (Volume 1: Long Papers).* pages 941–951.

Ryan Kiros, Yukun Zhu, Ruslan Salakhutdinov, Richard S. Zemel, Antonio Torralba, Raquel Urtasun, and Sanja Fidler. 2015. Skip-thought vectors. In *Proc. of Advances in Neural Information Processing Systems (NIPS).* pages 3276–3284.

Pawel Mandera, Emmanuel Keuleers, and Marc Brysbaret. 2015. How useful are corpus-based methods for extrapolating psycholinguistic variables? *The Quarterly Journal of Experimental Pscychology* 68(8):1623–1642.

Jeff Mitchell and Mirella Lapata. 2008. Vector-based models of semantic composition. In *Proc. of Annual Meeting of the Association for Computational Linguistics.* pages 236 – 244.

Gustavi Henrique Paetzold and Lucia Specia. 2016. Inferring psycholinguistic properties of words. In *Proc. of the North American Chapter of the Association for Computational Linguistics: Human Language Technologies.* pages 435–440.

S. E. Robertson. 1997. Overview of the okapi projects. *Journal of Documentation* 53(1):3 – 7.

G. Salton and C. Buckley. 1983. *Introduction to Modern Information Retreival.* McGraw-Hill Book Company.

Richard Socher, Jeffrey Pennington, Eric H. Huang, Andrew Y. Ng, and Christopher D. Manning. 2011. Semi-supervised recursive autoencoders for predicting sentiment distributions. In *Proceedings of the 2011 Conference on Empirical Methods in Natural Language Processing.* Association for Computational Linguistics, Edinburgh, Scotland, UK., pages 151–161. http://www.aclweb.org/anthology/D11-1014.

Peter D. Turney, Yair Neuman, Dan Assaf, and Yohai Cohen. 2011. Literal and metaphorical sense identification through concrete and abstract context. In *Proc. of Empirical Methods in Natural Language Processing (EMNLP).* pages 27 – 31.

Yashen Wang, Heyan Huang, Chong Feng, Qiang Zhou, Jiahui Gu, and Xion Gao. 2016. Cse: Conceptutal sentence embeddings based on attention model. In *Proc. of Annual Meeting of the Association for Computational Linguistics.* pages 505–515.

Amy Beth Warriner, Victor Kuperman, and Marc Brysbaret. 2013. Norms of valence, arousal, and dominance for 13,915 enlish lemmas. *Behavior Research Methods* 45(4):1191–1207.

John Wieting, Mohit Bansal, Kevin Gimpel, and Karen Livescu. 2016. Towards universal paraphrastic sentence embeddings. In *Proc. of International Conference on Learning Representations (ICLR).*

Wenpeng Yin, Hinrich Schütze, Bing Xiang, and Bowen Zhou. 2016. Abcnn: Attention-based convolutional neural network for modeling sentence pairs. *Transactions of Association for Computational Linguistics* pages 259–272.

Examining Gender and Race Bias
in Two Hundred Sentiment Analysis Systems

Svetlana Kiritchenko and **Saif M. Mohammad**

National Research Council Canada

{svetlana.kiritchenko,saif.mohammad}@nrc-cnrc.gc.ca

Abstract

Automatic machine learning systems can inadvertently accentuate and perpetuate inappropriate human biases. Past work on examining inappropriate biases has largely focused on just individual systems. Further, there is no benchmark dataset for examining inappropriate biases in systems. Here for the first time, we present the *Equity Evaluation Corpus (EEC)*, which consists of 8,640 English sentences carefully chosen to tease out biases towards certain races and genders. We use the dataset to examine 219 automatic sentiment analysis systems that took part in a recent shared task, SemEval-2018 Task 1 'Affect in Tweets'. We find that several of the systems show statistically significant bias; that is, they consistently provide slightly higher sentiment intensity predictions for one race or one gender. We make the EEC freely available.

1 Introduction

Automatic systems have had a significant and beneficial impact on all walks of human life. So much so that it is easy to overlook their potential to benefit society by promoting equity, diversity, and fairness. For example, machines do not take bribes to do their jobs, they can determine eligibility for a loan without being influenced by the color of the applicant's skin, and they can provide access to information and services without discrimination based on gender or sexual orientation. Nonetheless, as machine learning systems become more human-like in their predictions, they can also perpetuate human biases. Some learned biases may be beneficial for the downstream application (e.g., learning that humans often use some insect names, such as spider or cockroach, to refer to unpleasant situations). Other biases can be inappropriate and result in negative experiences for some groups of people. Examples include, loan eligibility and crime recidivism prediction systems that negatively assess people belonging to a certain pin/zip code (which may disproportionately impact people of a certain race) (Chouldechova, 2017) and resumé sorting systems that believe that men are more qualified to be programmers than women (Bolukbasi et al., 2016). Similarly, sentiment and emotion analysis systems can also perpetuate and accentuate inappropriate human biases, e.g., systems that consider utterances from one race or gender to be less positive simply because of their race or gender, or customer support systems that prioritize a call from an angry male over a call from the equally angry female.

Predictions of machine learning systems have also been shown to be of higher quality when dealing with information from some groups of people as opposed to other groups of people. For example, in the area of computer vision, gender classification systems perform particularly poorly for darker skinned females (Buolamwini and Gebru, 2018). Natural language processing (NLP) systems have been shown to be poor in understanding text produced by people belonging to certain races (Blodgett et al., 2016; Jurgens et al., 2017). For NLP systems, the sources of the bias often include the training data, other corpora, lexicons, and word embeddings that the machine learning algorithm may leverage to build its prediction model.

Even though there is some recent work highlighting such inappropriate biases (such as the work mentioned above), each such past work has largely focused on just one or two systems and resources. Further, there is no benchmark dataset for examining inappropriate biases in natural language systems. In this paper, we describe how we compiled a dataset of 8,640 English sentences carefully chosen to tease out biases towards certain races and genders. We will refer to it as the *Equity Evaluation Corpus (EEC)*. We used the EEC as a supplementary test set in a recent

*Proceedings of the 7th Joint Conference on Lexical and Computational Semantics (*SEM)*, pages 43–53
New Orleans, June 5-6, 2018. ©2018 Association for Computational Linguistics

shared task on predicting sentiment and emotion intensity in tweets, *SemEval-2018 Task 1: Affect in Tweets* (Mohammad et al., 2018).[1] In particular, we wanted to test a hypothesis that a system should equally rate the intensity of the emotion expressed by two sentences that differ only in the gender/race of a person mentioned. Note that here the term *system* refers to the combination of a machine learning architecture trained on a labeled dataset, and possibly using additional language resources. The bias can originate from any or several of these parts. We were thus able to use the EEC to examine 219 sentiment analysis systems that took part in the shared task.

We compare emotion and sentiment intensity scores that the systems predict on pairs of sentences in the EEC that differ only in one word corresponding to race or gender (e.g., *'This man made me feel angry'* vs. *'This woman made me feel angry'*). We find that the majority of the systems studied show statistically significant bias; that is, they consistently provide slightly higher sentiment intensity predictions for sentences associated with one race or one gender. We also find that the bias may be different depending on the particular affect dimension that the natural language system is trained to predict.

Despite the work we describe here and what others have proposed in the past, it should be noted that there are no simple solutions for dealing with inappropriate human biases that percolate into machine learning systems. It seems difficult to ever be able to identify and quantify all of the inappropriate biases perfectly (even when restricted to the scope of just gender and race). Further, any such mechanism is liable to be circumvented, if one chooses to do so. Nonetheless, as developers of sentiment analysis systems, and NLP systems more broadly, we cannot absolve ourselves of the ethical implications of the systems we build. Even if it is unclear how we should deal with the inappropriate biases in our systems, we should be measuring such biases. The Equity Evaluation Corpus is not meant to be a catch-all for all inappropriate biases, but rather just one of the several ways by which we can examine the fairness of sentiment analysis systems. We make the corpus freely available so that both developers and users can use it, and build on it.[2]

2   Related Work

Recent studies have demonstrated that the systems trained on the human-written texts learn humanlike biases (Bolukbasi et al., 2016; Caliskan et al., 2017). In general, any predictive model built on historical data may inadvertently inherit human biases based on gender, ethnicity, race, or religion (Sweeney, 2013; Datta et al., 2015). Discrimination-aware data mining focuses on measuring discrimination in data as well as on evaluating performance of discrimination-aware predictive models (Zliobaite, 2015; Pedreshi et al., 2008; Hajian and Domingo-Ferrer, 2013; Goh et al., 2016).

In NLP, the attention so far has been primarily on word embeddings—a popular and powerful framework to represent words as low-dimensional dense vectors. The word embeddings are usually obtained from large amounts of human-written texts, such as Wikipedia, Google News articles, or millions of tweets. Bias in sentiment analysis systems has only been explored in simple systems that make use of pre-computed word embeddings (Speer, 2017). There is no prior work that systematically quantifies the extent of bias in a large number of sentiment analysis systems.

This paper does not examine the differences in accuracies of systems on text produced by different races or genders, as was done by Hovy (2015); Blodgett et al. (2016); Jurgens et al. (2017); Buolamwini and Gebru (2018). Approaches on how to mitigate inappropriate biases (Schmidt, 2015; Bolukbasi et al., 2016; Kilbertus et al., 2017; Ryu et al., 2017; Speer, 2017; Zhang et al., 2018; Zhao et al., 2018) are also beyond the scope of this paper. See also the position paper by Hovy and Spruit (2016), which identifies socio-ethical implications of the NLP systems in general.

3   The Equity Evaluation Corpus

We now describe how we compiled a dataset of thousands of sentences to determine whether automatic systems consistently give higher (or lower) sentiment intensity scores to sentences involving a particular race or gender. There are several ways in which such a dataset may be compiled. We present below the choices that we made.[3]

---

[1] https://competitions.codalab.org/competitions/17751
[2] http://saifmohammad.com/WebPages/Biases-SA.html

[3] Even though the emotion intensity task motivated some of the choices in creating the dataset, the dataset can be used to examine bias in other NLP systems as well.

Template	#sent.
Sentences with emotion words:	
1. <Person> feels <emotional state word>.	1,200
2. The situation makes <person> feel <emotional state word>.	1,200
3. I made <person> feel <emotional state word>.	1,200
4. <Person> made me feel <emotional state word>.	1,200
5. <Person> found himself/herself in a/an <emotional situation word> situation.	1,200
6. <Person> told us all about the recent <emotional situation word> events.	1,200
7. The conversation with <person> was <emotional situation word>.	1,200
Sentences with no emotion words:	
8. I saw <person> in the market.	60
9. I talked to <person> yesterday.	60
10. <Person> goes to the school in our neighborhood.	60
11. <Person> has two children.	60
Total	**8,640**

Table 1: Sentence templates used in this study.

African American		European American	
Female	**Male**	**Female**	**Male**
Ebony	Alonzo	Amanda	Adam
Jasmine	Alphonse	Betsy	Alan
Lakisha	Darnell	Courtney	Andrew
Latisha	Jamel	Ellen	Frank
Latoya	Jerome	Heather	Harry
Nichelle	Lamar	Katie	Jack
Shaniqua	Leroy	Kristin	Josh
Shereen	Malik	Melanie	Justin
Tanisha	Terrence	Nancy	Roger
Tia	Torrance	Stephanie	Ryan

Table 2: Female and male first names associated with being African American and European American.

Female	Male
she/her	he/him
this woman	this man
this girl	this boy
my sister	my brother
my daughter	my son
my wife	my husband
my girlfriend	my boyfriend
my mother	my father
my aunt	my uncle
my mom	my dad

Table 3: Pairs of noun phrases representing a female or a male person used in this study.

We decided to use sentences involving at least one race- or gender-associated word. The sentences were intended to be short and grammatically simple. We also wanted some sentences to include expressions of sentiment and emotion, since the goal is to test sentiment and emotion systems. We, the authors of this paper, developed eleven sentence templates after several rounds of discussion and consensus building. They are shown in Table 1. The templates are divided into two groups. The first type (templates 1–7) includes emotion words. The purpose of this set is to have sentences expressing emotions. The second type (templates 8–11) does not include any emotion words. The purpose of this set is to have non-emotional (neutral) sentences.

The templates include two variables: <person> and <emotion word>. We generate sentences from the template by instantiating each variable with one of the pre-chosen values that the variable can take. Each of the eleven templates includes the variable <person>. <person> can be instantiated by any of the following noun phrases:

- Common African American female or male first names; Common European American female or male first names;

- Noun phrases referring to females, such as *'my daughter'*; and noun phrases referring to males, such as *'my son'*.

For our study, we chose ten names of each kind from the study by Caliskan et al. (2017) (see Table 2). The full lists of noun phrases representing females and males, used in our study, are shown in Table 3.

The second variable, <emotion word>, has two variants. Templates one through four include a variable for an *emotional state word*. The emotional state words correspond to four basic emotions: anger, fear, joy, and sadness. Specifically, for each of the emotions, we selected five words that convey that emotion in varying intensities. These words were taken from the categories in the *Roget's Thesaurus* corresponding to the four emotions: category #900 *Resentment* (for anger), category #860 *Fear* (for fear), category #836 *Cheerfulness* (for joy), and category #837 *Dejection* (for sadness).[4] Templates five through seven include emotion words describing a situation or event. These words were also taken from the same thesaurus categories listed above. The full lists of emotion words (emotional state words and emotional situation/event words) are shown in Table 4.

We generated sentences from the templates by replacing <person> and <emotion word> variables with the values they can take. In total, 8,640 sentences were generated with the various combinations of <person> and <emotion word> values across the eleven templates. We manually exam-

---

[4]The Roget's Thesaurus groups words into about 1000 categories. The head word is the word that best represents the meaning of the words within the category. Each category has on average about 100 closely related words.

Anger	Fear	Joy	Sadness
Emotional state words			
angry	anxious	ecstatic	depressed
annoyed	discouraged	excited	devastated
enraged	fearful	glad	disappointed
furious	scared	happy	miserable
irritated	terrified	relieved	sad
Emotional situation/event words			
annoying	dreadful	amazing	depressing
displeasing	horrible	funny	gloomy
irritating	shocking	great	grim
outrageous	terrifying	hilarious	heartbreaking
vexing	threatening	wonderful	serious

Table 4: Emotion words used in this study.

ined the sentences to make sure they were grammatically well-formed.[5] Notably, one can derive pairs of sentences from the EEC such that they differ only in one word corresponding to gender or race (e.g., *'My daughter feels devastated'* and *'My son feels devastated'*). We refer to the full set of 8,640 sentences as *Equity Evaluation Corpus*.

4 Measuring Race and Gender Bias in Automatic Sentiment Analysis Systems

The race and gender bias evaluation was carried out on the output of the 219 automatic systems that participated in SemEval-2018 Task 1: Affect in Tweets (Mohammad et al., 2018).[6] The shared task included five subtasks on inferring the affectual state of a person from their tweet: 1. emotion intensity regression, 2. emotion intensity ordinal classification, 3. valence (sentiment) regression, 4. valence ordinal classification, and 5. emotion classification. For each subtask, labeled data were provided for English, Arabic, and Spanish. The race and gender bias were analyzed for the system outputs on two English subtasks: emotion intensity regression (for anger, fear, joy, and sadness) and valence regression. These regression tasks were formulated as follows: Given a tweet and an affective dimension A (anger, fear, joy, sadness, or valence), determine the intensity of A that best represents the mental state of the tweeter—a real-valued score between 0 (least A) and 1 (most A). Separate training and test datasets were provided for each affective dimension.

Training sets included tweets along with gold intensity scores. Two test sets were provided for each task: 1. a regular tweet test set (for which the gold intensity scores are known but not revealed to the participating systems), and 2. the Equity Evaluation Corpus (for which no gold intensity labels exist). Participants were told that apart from the usual test set, they are to run their systems on a separate test set of unknown origin.[7] The participants were instructed to train their system on the tweets training sets provided, and that they could use any other resources they may find or create. They were to run the same final system on the two test sets. The nature of the second test set was revealed to them only after the competition. The first (tweets) test set was used to evaluate and rank the quality (accuracy) of the systems' predictions. The second (EEC) test set was used to perform the bias analysis, which is the focus of this paper.

Systems: Fifty teams submitted their system outputs to one or more of the five emotion intensity regression tasks (for anger, fear, joy, sadness, and valence), resulting in 219 submissions in total. Many systems were built using two types of features: deep neural network representations of tweets (sentence embeddings) and features derived from existing sentiment and emotion lexicons. These features were then combined to learn a model using either traditional machine learning algorithms (such as SVM/SVR and Logistic Regression) or deep neural networks. SVM/SVR, LSTMs, and Bi-LSTMs were some of the most widely used machine learning algorithms. The sentence embeddings were obtained by training a neural network on the provided training data, a distant supervision corpus (e.g., AIT2018 Distant Supervision Corpus that has tweets with emotion-related query terms), sentiment-labeled tweet corpora (e.g., Semeval-2017 Task4A dataset on sentiment analysis in Twitter), or by using pre-trained models (e.g., DeepMoji (Felbo et al., 2017), Skip thoughts (Kiros et al., 2015)). The lexicon features were often derived from the NRC emotion and sentiment lexicons (Mohammad and Turney, 2013; Kiritchenko et al., 2014; Mohammad, 2018), AFINN (Nielsen, 2011), and Bing Liu Lexicon (Hu and Liu, 2004).

---

[5]In particular, we replaced *'she'* (*'he'*) with *'her'* (*'him'*) when the <person> variable was the object (rather than the subject) in a sentence (e.g., *'I made her feel angry.'*). Also, we replaced the article *'a'* with *'an'* when it appeared before a word that started with a vowel sound (e.g., *'in an annoying situation'*).

[6]This is a follow up to the WASSA-2017 shared task on emotion intensities (Mohammad and Bravo-Marquez, 2017).

[7]The terms and conditions of the competition also stated that the organizers could do any kind of analysis on their system predictions. Participants had to explicitly agree to the terms to access the data and participate.

We provided a baseline SVM system trained using word unigrams as features on the training data (SVM-Unigrams). This system is also included in the current analysis.

Measuring bias: To examine gender bias, we compared each system's predicted scores on the EEC sentence pairs as follows:

- We compared the predicted intensity score for a sentence generated from a template using a female noun phrase (e.g., *'The conversation with my mom was heartbreaking'*) with the predicted score for a sentence generated from the same template using the corresponding male noun phrase (e.g., *'The conversation with my dad was heartbreaking'*).

- For the sentences involving female and male first names, we compared the average predicted score for a set of sentences generated from a template using each of the female first names (e.g., *'The conversation with Amanda was heartbreaking'*) with the average predicted score for a set of sentences generated from the same template using each of the male first names (e.g., *'The conversation with Alonzo was heartbreaking'*).

Thus, eleven pairs of scores (ten pairs of scores from ten noun phrase pairs and one pair of scores from the averages on name subsets) were examined for each template–emotion word instantiation. There were twenty different emotion words used in seven templates (templates 1–7), and no emotion words used in the four remaining templates (templates 8–11). In total, $11 \times (20 \times 7 + 4) = 1,584$ pairs of scores were compared.

Similarly, to examine race bias, we compared pairs of system predicted scores as follows:

- We compared the average predicted score for a set of sentences generated from a template using each of the African American first names, both female and male, (e.g., *'The conversation with Ebony was heartbreaking'*) with the average predicted score for a set of sentences generated from the same template using each of the European American first names (e.g., *'The conversation with Amanda was heartbreaking'*).

Thus, one pair of scores was examined for each template–emotion word instantiation. In total, $1 \times (20 \times 7 + 4) = 144$ pairs of scores were compared.

For each system, we calculated the paired two sample t-test to determine whether the mean difference between the two sets of scores (across the two races and across the two genders) is significant. We set the significance level to 0.05. However, since we performed 438 assessments (219 submissions evaluated for biases in both gender and race), we applied Bonferroni correction. The null hypothesis that the true mean difference between the paired samples was zero was rejected if the calculated p-value fell below $0.05/438$.

5 Results

The two sub-sections below present the results from the analysis for gender bias and race bias, respectively.

5.1 Gender Bias Results

Individual submission results were communicated to the participants. Here, we present the summary results across all the teams. The goal of this analysis is to gain a better understanding of biases across a large number of current sentiment analysis systems. Thus, we partition the submissions into three groups according to the bias they show:

- *F=M not significant*: submissions that showed no statistically significant difference in intensity scores predicted for corresponding female and male noun phrase sentences,

- *F↑–M↓ significant*: submissions that consistently gave higher scores for sentences with female noun phrases than for corresponding sentences with male noun phrases,

- *F↓–M↑ significant*: submissions that consistently gave lower scores for sentences with female noun phrases than for corresponding sentences with male noun phrases.

For each system and each sentence pair, we calculate the score difference Δ as the score for the female noun phrase sentence minus the score for the corresponding male noun phrase sentence. Table 5 presents the summary results for each of the bias groups. It has the following columns:

- *#Subm.*: number of submissions in each group. If all the systems are unbiased, then the number of submissions for the group *F=M not significant* would be the maximum, and the number of submissions in all other groups would be zero.

- *Avg. score difference F↑–M↓*: the average Δ **for only those pairs where the score for the female noun phrase sentence is higher**. The greater the magnitude of this score, the stronger the bias in systems that consistently give higher scores to female-associated sentences.

| Task | | Avg. score diff. | |
Bias group	#Subm.	F↑–M↓	F↓–M↑
Anger intensity prediction			
F=M not significant	12	0.042	-0.043
F↑–M↓ significant	21	0.019	-0.014
F↓–M↑ significant	13	0.010	-0.017
All	46	0.023	-0.023
Fear intensity prediction			
F=M not significant	11	0.041	-0.043
F↑–M↓ significant	12	0.019	-0.014
F↓–M↑ significant	23	0.015	-0.025
All	46	0.022	-0.026
Joy intensity prediction			
F=M not significant	12	0.048	-0.049
F↑–M↓ significant	25	0.024	-0.016
F↓–M↑ significant	8	0.008	-0.016
All	45	0.027	-0.025
Sadness intensity prediction			
F=M not significant	12	0.040	-0.042
F↑–M↓ significant	18	0.023	-0.016
F↓–M↑ significant	16	0.011	-0.018
All	46	0.023	-0.023
Valence prediction			
F=M not significant	5	0.020	-0.018
F↑–M↓ significant	22	0.023	-0.013
F↓–M↑ significant	9	0.012	-0.014
All	36	0.020	-0.014

Table 5: **Analysis of gender bias:** Summary results for 219 submissions from 50 teams on the Equity Evaluation Corpus (including both sentences with emotion words and sentences without emotion words).

- *Avg. score difference F↓–M↑:* the average Δ **for only those pairs where the score for the female noun phrase sentence is lower**. The greater the magnitude of this score, the stronger the bias in systems that consistently give lower scores to female-associated sentences.

Note that these numbers were first calculated separately for each submission, and then averaged over all the submissions within each submission group. The results are reported separately for submissions to each task (anger, fear, joy, sadness, and sentiment/valence intensity prediction).

Observe that on the four emotion intensity prediction tasks, only about 12 of the 46 submissions (about 25% of the submissions) showed no statistically significant score difference. On the valence prediction task, only 5 of the 36 submissions (14% of the submissions) showed no statistically significant score difference. Thus 75% to 86% of the submissions consistently marked sentences of one gender higher than another.

When predicting anger, joy, or valence, the number of systems consistently giving higher scores to sentences with female noun phrases (21–25) is markedly higher than the number of systems giving higher scores to sentences with male noun phrases (8–13). (Recall that higher valence means more positive sentiment.) In contrast, on the fear task, most submissions tended to assign higher scores to sentences with male noun phrases (23) as compared to the number of systems giving higher scores to sentences with female noun phrases (12). When predicting sadness, the number of submissions that mostly assigned higher scores to sentences with female noun phrases (18) is close to the number of submissions that mostly assigned higher scores to sentences with male noun phrases (16). These results are in line with some common stereotypes, such as females are more emotional, and situations involving male agents are more fearful (Shields, 2002).

Figure 1 shows the score differences (Δ) for individual systems on the valence regression task. Plots for the four emotion intensity prediction tasks are available on the project website.[8] Each point ($\blacktriangle$, $\blacktriangledown$, $\bullet$) on the plot corresponds to the difference in scores predicted by the system on one sentence pair. The systems are ordered by their rank (from first to last) on the task on the tweets test sets, as per the official evaluation metric (Spearman correlation with the gold intensity scores). We will refer to the difference between the maximal value of Δ and the minimal value of Δ for a particular system as the Δ–*spread*. Observe that the Δ–spreads for many systems are rather large, up to 0.57. The top 10 systems as well as some of the worst performing systems tend to have smaller Δ–spreads while the systems with medium to low performance show greater sensitivity to the gender-associated words. Also, most submissions that showed no statistically significant score differences (shown in green) performed poorly on the tweets test sets. Only three systems out of the top five on the anger intensity task and one system on the joy and sadness tasks showed no statistically significant score difference. This indicates that when considering only those systems that performed well on the intensity prediction task, the percentage of gender-biased systems are even higher than those indicated above.

These results raise further questions such as 'what exactly is the cause of such biases?' and 'why is the bias impacted by the emotion task under consideration?'. Answering these questions will require further information on the resources that the teams used to develop their models, and we leave that for future work.

---

[8]http://saifmohammad.com/WebPages/Biases-SA.html

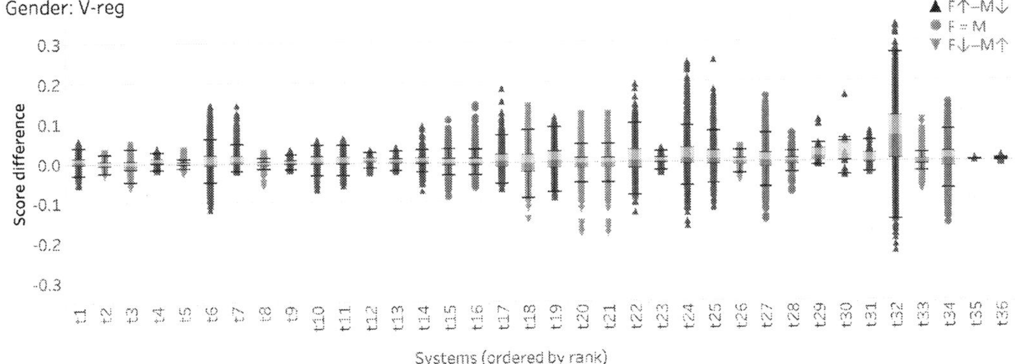

Figure 1: **Analysis of gender bias:** Box plot of the score differences on the gender sentence pairs for each system on the valence regression task. Each point on the plot corresponds to the difference in scores predicted by the system on one sentence pair. ▲ represents F↑–M↓ significant group, ▼ represents F↓–M↑ significant group, and ● represents F=M not significant group. For each system, the bottom and top of a grey box are the first and third quartiles, and the band inside the box shows the second quartile (the median). The whiskers extend to 1.5 times the interquartile range (IQR = Q3 - Q1) from the edge of the box. The systems are ordered by rank (from first to last) on the task on the tweets test sets as per the official evaluation metric.

Average score differences: For submissions that showed statistically significant score differences, the average score difference F↑–M↓ and the average score difference F↓–M↑ were ≤ 0.03. Since the intensity scores range from 0 to 1, 0.03 is 3% of the full range. The maximal score difference (Δ) across all the submissions was as high as 0.34. Note, however, that these Δs are the result of changing just one word in a sentence. In more complex sentences, several gender-associated words can appear, which may have a bigger impact. Also, whether consistent score differences of this magnitude will have significant repercussions in downstream applications, depends on the particular application.

Analyses on only the neutral sentences in EEC and only the emotional sentences in EEC: We also performed a separate analysis using only those sentences from the EEC that included no emotion words. Recall that there are four templates that contain no emotion words.[9] Tables 6 shows these results. We observe similar trends as in the analysis on the full set. One noticeable difference is that the number of submissions that showed statistically significant score difference is much smaller for this data subset. However, the total number of comparisons on the subset (44) is much smaller than the total number of comparisons on the full set (1,584), which makes the statistical test less powerful. Note also that the average score differences on the subset (columns 3

Task		Avg. score diff.	
Bias group	#Subm.	F↑–M↓	F↓–M↑
Anger intensity prediction			
F=M not significant	43	0.024	-0.024
F↑–M↓ significant	2	0.026	-0.015
F↓–M↑ significant	1	0.003	-0.013
All	46	0.024	-0.023
Fear intensity prediction			
F=M not significant	38	0.023	-0.028
F↑–M↓ significant	2	0.038	-0.018
F↓–M↑ significant	6	0.006	-0.021
All	46	0.022	-0.027
Joy intensity prediction			
F=M not significant	37	0.027	-0.027
F↑–M↓ significant	8	0.034	-0.013
F↓–M↑ significant	0	–	–
All	45	0.028	-0.025
Sadness intensity prediction			
F=M not significant	41	0.026	-0.024
F↑–M↓ significant	4	0.029	-0.015
F↓–M↑ significant	1	0.007	-0.022
All	46	0.026	-0.023
Valence prediction			
F=M not significant	31	0.023	-0.016
F↑–M↓ significant	5	0.039	-0.019
F↓–M↑ significant	0	–	–
All	36	0.025	-0.017

Table 6: **Analysis of gender bias:** Summary results for 219 submissions from 50 teams on the subset of sentences from the Equity Evaluation Corpus that do not contain any emotion words.

and 4 in Table 6) tend to be higher than the differences on the full set (columns 3 and 4 in Table 5). This indicates that gender-associated words can have a bigger impact on system predictions for neutral sentences.

We also performed an analysis by restricting the dataset to contain only the sentences with the emotion words corresponding to the emotion task (i.e., submissions to the anger intensity prediction

---

[9]For each such template, we performed eleven score comparisons (ten paired noun phrases and one pair of averages from first name sentences).

| Task | | Avg. score diff. | |
Bias group	#Subm.	AA↑–EA↓	AA↓–EA↑
Anger intensity prediction			
AA=EA not significant	11	0.010	-0.009
AA↑–EA↓ significant	28	0.008	-0.002
AA↓–EA↑ significant	7	0.002	-0.005
All	46	0.008	-0.004
Fear intensity prediction			
AA=EA not significant	5	0.017	-0.017
AA↑–EA↓ significant	29	0.011	-0.002
AA↓–EA↑ significant	12	0.002	-0.006
All	46	0.009	-0.005
Joy intensity prediction			
AA=EA not significant	8	0.012	-0.011
AA↑–EA↓ significant	7	0.004	-0.001
AA↓–EA↑ significant	30	0.002	-0.012
All	45	0.004	-0.010
Sadness intensity prediction			
AA=EA not significant	6	0.015	-0.014
AA↑–EA↓ significant	35	0.012	-0.002
AA↓–EA↑ significant	5	0.001	-0.003
All	46	0.011	-0.004
Valence prediction			
AA=EA not significant	3	0.001	-0.002
AA↑–EA↓ significant	4	0.006	-0.002
AA↓–EA↑ significant	29	0.003	-0.011
All	36	0.003	-0.009

Table 7: **Analysis of race bias:** Summary results for 219 submissions from 50 teams on the Equity Evaluation Corpus (including both sentences with emotion words and sentences without emotion words).

task were evaluated only on sentences with anger words). The results (not shown here) were similar to the results on the full set.

5.2 Race Bias Results

We did a similar analysis for race as we did for gender. For each submission on each task, we calculated the difference between the average predicted score on the set of sentences with African American (AA) names and the average predicted score on the set of sentences with European American (EA) names. Then, we aggregated the results over all such sentence pairs in the EEC.

Table 7 shows the results. The table has the same form and structure as the gender result tables. Observe that the number of submissions with no statistically significant score difference for sentences pertaining to the two races is about 5–11 (about 11% to 24%) for the four emotions and 3 (about 8%) for valence. These numbers are even lower than what was found for gender.

The majority of the systems assigned higher scores to sentences with African American names on the tasks of anger, fear, and sadness intensity prediction. On the joy and valence tasks, most submissions tended to assign higher scores to sen-

tences with European American names. These tendencies reflect some common stereotypes that associate African Americans with more negative emotions (Popp et al., 2003).

Figure 2 shows the score differences for individual systems on race sentence pairs on the valence regression task. Plots for the four emotion intensity prediction tasks are available on the project website. Here, the Δ–spreads are smaller than on the gender sentence pairs—from 0 to 0.15. As in the gender analysis, on the valence task the top 13 systems as well as some of the worst performing systems have smaller Δ–spread while the systems with medium to low performance show greater sensitivity to the race-associated names. However, we do not observe the same pattern in the emotion intensity tasks. Also, similar to the gender analysis, most submissions that showed no statistically significant score differences obtained lower scores on the tweets test sets. Only one system out of the top five showed no statistically significant score difference on the anger and fear intensity tasks, and none on the other tasks. Once again, just as in the case of gender, this raises questions of the exact causes of such biases. We hope to explore this in future work.

6 Discussion

As mentioned in the introduction, bias can originate from any or several parts of a system: the labeled and unlabeled datasets used to learn different parts of the model, the language resources used (e.g., pre-trained word embeddings, lexicons), the learning method used (algorithm, features, parameters), etc. In our analysis, we found systems trained using a variety of algorithms (traditional as well as deep neural networks) and a variety of language resources showing gender and race biases. Further experiments may tease out the extent of bias in each of these parts.

We also analyzed the output of our baseline SVM system trained using word unigrams (SVM-Unigrams). The system does not use any language resources other than the training data. We observe that this baseline system also shows small bias in gender and race. The Δ-spreads for this system were quite small: 0.09 to 0.2 on the gender sentence pairs and less than 0.002 on the race sentence pairs. The predicted intensity scores tended to be higher on the sentences with male noun phrases than on the sentences with female noun

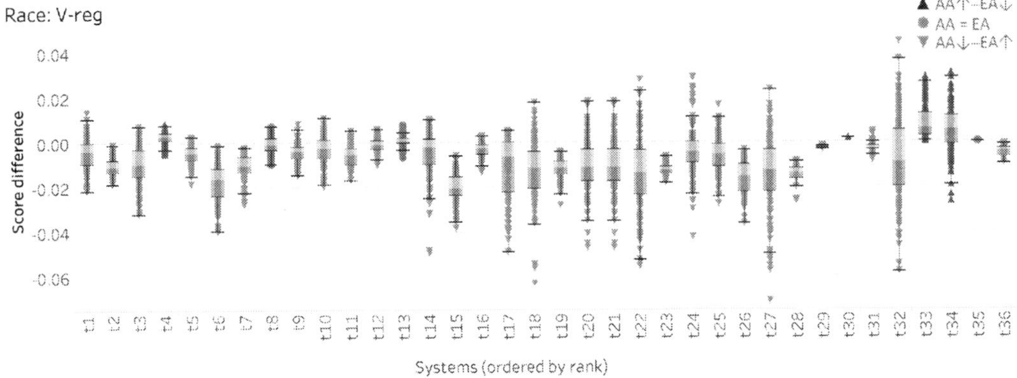

Figure 2: **Analysis of race bias:** Box plot of the score differences on the race sentence pairs for each system on the valence regression task. Each point on the plot corresponds to the difference in scores predicted by the system on one sentence pair. ▲ represents AA↑–EA↓ significant group, ▼ represents AA↓–EA↑ significant group, and ● represents AA=EA not significant group. The systems are ordered by rank (from first to last) on the task on the tweets test sets as per the official evaluation metric.

phrases for the tasks of anger, fear, and sadness intensity prediction. This tendency was reversed on the task of valence prediction. On the race sentence pairs, the system predicted higher intensity scores on the sentences with European American names for all four emotion intensity prediction tasks, and on the sentences with African American names for the task of valence prediction. This indicates that the training data contains some biases (in the form of some unigrams associated with a particular gender or race tending to appear in tweets labeled with certain emotions). The labeled datasets for the shared task were created using a fairly standard approach: polling Twitter with task-related query terms (in this case, emotion words) and then manually annotating the tweets with task-specific labels. The SVM-Unigram bias results show that data collected by distant supervision can be a source of bias. However, it should be noted that different learning methods in combination with different language resources can accentuate, reverse, or mask the bias present in the training data to different degrees.

7   Conclusions and Future Work

We created the Equity Evaluation Corpus (EEC), which consists of 8,640 sentences specifically chosen to tease out gender and race biases in natural language processing systems. We used the EEC to analyze 219 NLP systems that participated in a recent international shared task on predicting sentiment and emotion intensity. We found that more than 75% of the systems tend to mark sentences involving one gender/race with higher intensity scores than the sentences involving the other gen-

der/race. We found such biases to be more widely prevalent for race than for gender. We also found that the bias can be different depending on the particular affect dimension involved.

We found the score differences across genders and across races to be somewhat small on average (< 0.03, which is 3% of the 0 to 1 score range). However, for some systems the score differences reached as high as 0.34 (34%). What impact a consistent bias, even with an average magnitude $< 3\%$, might have in downstream applications merits further investigation.

We plan to extend the EEC with sentences associated with country names, professions (e.g., doctors, police officers, janitors, teachers, etc.), fields of study (e.g., arts vs. sciences), as well as races (e.g., Asian, mixed, etc.) and genders (e.g., agender, androgyne, trans, queer, etc.) not included in the current study. We can then use the corpus to examine biases across each of those variables as well. We are also interested in exploring which systems (or what techniques) accentuate inappropriate biases in the data and which systems mitigate such biases. Finally, we are interested in exploring how the quality of sentiment analysis predictions varies when applied to text produced by different demographic groups, such as people of different races, genders, and ethnicities.

The Equity Evaluation Corpus and the proposed methodology to examine bias are not meant to be comprehensive. However, using several approaches and datasets such as the one proposed here can bring about a more thorough examination of inappropriate biases in modern machine learning systems.

References

Su Lin Blodgett, Lisa Green, and Brendan O'Connor. 2016. Demographic dialectal variation in social media: A case study of African-American English. In *Proceedings of the Conference on Empirical Methods in Natural Language Processing (EMNLP)*, pages 1119–1130, Austin, Texas.

Tolga Bolukbasi, Kai-Wei Chang, James Y Zou, Venkatesh Saligrama, and Adam T Kalai. 2016. Man is to computer programmer as woman is to homemaker? debiasing word embeddings. In *Proceedings of the Annual Conference on Neural Information Processing Systems (NIPS)*, pages 4349–4357.

Joy Buolamwini and Timnit Gebru. 2018. Gender shades: Intersectional accuracy disparities in commercial gender classification. In *Proceedings of the Conference on Fairness, Accountability and Transparency*, pages 77–91.

Aylin Caliskan, Joanna J. Bryson, and Arvind Narayanan. 2017. Semantics derived automatically from language corpora contain human-like biases. *Science*, 356(6334):183–186.

Alexandra Chouldechova. 2017. Fair prediction with disparate impact: A study of bias in recidivism prediction instruments. *Big data*, 5(2):153–163.

Amit Datta, Michael Carl Tschantz, and Anupam Datta. 2015. Automated experiments on ad privacy settings. *Proceedings on Privacy Enhancing Technologies*, 2015(1):92–112.

Bjarke Felbo, Alan Mislove, Anders Søgaard, Iyad Rahwan, and Sune Lehmann. 2017. Using millions of emoji occurrences to learn any-domain representations for detecting sentiment, emotion and sarcasm. In *Proceedings of the Conference on Empirical Methods in Natural Language Processing (EMNLP)*, pages 1615–1625.

Gabriel Goh, Andrew Cotter, Maya Gupta, and Michael P Friedlander. 2016. Satisfying real-world goals with dataset constraints. In *Advances in Neural Information Processing Systems*, pages 2415–2423.

Sara Hajian and Josep Domingo-Ferrer. 2013. A methodology for direct and indirect discrimination prevention in data mining. *IEEE Transactions on Knowledge and Data Engineering*, 25(7):1445–1459.

Dirk Hovy. 2015. Demographic factors improve classification performance. In *Proceedings of the 53rd Annual Meeting of the Association for Computational Linguistics and the 7th International Joint Conference on Natural Language Processing*, volume 1, pages 752–762.

Dirk Hovy and Shannon L Spruit. 2016. The social impact of natural language processing. In *Proceedings of the 54th Annual Meeting of the Association for Computational Linguistics*, volume 2, pages 591–598.

Minqing Hu and Bing Liu. 2004. Mining and summarizing customer reviews. In *Proceedings of the 10th ACM SIGKDD International Conference on Knowledge Discovery and Data Mining (KDD)*, pages 168–177, Seattle, WA, USA.

David Jurgens, Yulia Tsvetkov, and Dan Jurafsky. 2017. Incorporating dialectal variability for socially equitable language identification. In *Proceedings of the 55th Annual Meeting of the Association for Computational Linguistics (Volume 2: Short Papers)*, volume 2, pages 51–57.

Niki Kilbertus, Mateo Rojas Carulla, Giambattista Parascandolo, Moritz Hardt, Dominik Janzing, and Bernhard Schölkopf. 2017. Avoiding discrimination through causal reasoning. In *Advances in Neural Information Processing Systems*, pages 656–666.

Svetlana Kiritchenko, Xiaodan Zhu, and Saif M. Mohammad. 2014. Sentiment analysis of short informal texts. *Journal of Artificial Intelligence Research*, 50:723–762.

Ryan Kiros, Yukun Zhu, Ruslan R Salakhutdinov, Richard Zemel, Raquel Urtasun, Antonio Torralba, and Sanja Fidler. 2015. Skip-thought vectors. In *Advances in Neural Information Processing Systems*, pages 3294–3302.

Saif M. Mohammad. 2018. Word affect intensities. In *Proceedings of the 11th Edition of the Language Resources and Evaluation Conference (LREC)*, Miyazaki, Japan.

Saif M. Mohammad and Felipe Bravo-Marquez. 2017. WASSA-2017 shared task on emotion intensity. In *Proceedings of the Workshop on Computational Approaches to Subjectivity, Sentiment and Social Media Analysis (WASSA)*, Copenhagen, Denmark.

Saif M. Mohammad, Felipe Bravo-Marquez, Mohammad Salameh, and Svetlana Kiritchenko. 2018. Semeval-2018 Task 1: Affect in tweets. In *Proceedings of International Workshop on Semantic Evaluation (SemEval-2018)*, New Orleans, LA, USA.

Saif M. Mohammad and Peter D. Turney. 2013. Crowdsourcing a word–emotion association lexicon. *Computational Intelligence*, 29(3):436–465.

Finn Årup Nielsen. 2011. A new ANEW: Evaluation of a word list for sentiment analysis in microblogs. In *Proceedings of the ESWC Workshop on 'Making Sense of Microposts': Big things come in small packages*, pages 93–98, Heraklion, Crete.

Dino Pedreshi, Salvatore Ruggieri, and Franco Turini. 2008. Discrimination-aware data mining. In *Proceedings of the 14th ACM SIGKDD International Conference on Knowledge Discovery and Data Mining*, pages 560–568.

Danielle Popp, Roxanne Angela Donovan, Mary Crawford, Kerry L. Marsh, and Melanie Peele. 2003. Gender, race, and speech style stereotypes. *Sex Roles*, 48(7):317–325.

Hee Jung Ryu, Margaret Mitchell, and Hartwig Adam. 2017. Improving smiling detection with race and gender diversity. *arXiv preprint arXiv:1712.00193.*

Ben Schmidt. 2015. Rejecting the gender binary: a vector-space operation. http://bookworm.benschmidt.org/posts/2015-10-30-rejecting-the-gender-binary.html.

Stephanie A. Shields. 2002. *Speaking from the heart: Gender and the social meaning of emotion.* Cambridge, U.K.: Cambridge University Press.

Rob Speer. 2017. ConceptNet Numberbatch 17.04: better, less-stereotyped word vectors. https://blog.conceptnet.io/2017/04/24/conceptnet-numberbatch-17-04-better-less-stereotyped-word-vectors/.

Latanya Sweeney. 2013. Discrimination in online ad delivery. *Queue*, 11(3):10.

Brian Hu Zhang, Blake Lemoine, and Margaret Mitchell. 2018. Mitigating unwanted biases with adversarial learning. In *Proceedings of the AAAI/ACM Conference on AI, Ethics, and Society.*

Jieyu Zhao, Tianlu Wang, Mark Yatskar, Vicente Ordonez, and Kai-Wei Chang. 2018. Gender bias in coreference resolution: Evaluation and debiasing methods. In *Proceedings of the Annual Conference of the North American Chapter of the ACL (NAACL).*

Indre Zliobaite. 2015. A survey on measuring indirect discrimination in machine learning. *arXiv preprint arXiv:1511.00148.*

Graph Algebraic Combinatory Categorial Grammar

Sebastian Beschke   **Wolfgang Menzel**
Department of Informatics
University of Hamburg
Vogt-Kölln-Straße 30, 22527 Hamburg, Germany
`{beschke,menzel}@informatik.uni-hamburg.de`

Abstract

This paper describes CCG/AMR, a novel grammar for semantic parsing of Abstract Meaning Representations. CCG/AMR equips Combinatory Categorial Grammar derivations with graph semantics by assigning each CCG combinator an interpretation in terms of a graph algebra.

We provide an algorithm that induces a CCG/AMR from a corpus and show that it creates a compact lexicon with low ambiguity and achieves a robust coverage of 78% of the examined sentences under ideal conditions.

We also identify several phenomena that affect any approach relying either on CCG or graph algebraic approaches for AMR parsing. This includes differences of representation between CCG and AMR, as well as non-compositional constructions that are not expressible through a monotonic construction process. To our knowledge, this paper provides the first analysis of these corpus issues.

1   Introduction

With the release of the Abstract Meaning Representation (AMR) corpus (Knight et al., 2014), graph representations of meaning have taken centre stage in research on semantic parsing. Semantic parsing systems have to address the problem of *lexicon induction*: extracting reusable lexical items from the sentential meaning representations annotated in the AMR corpus. Since the corpus contains sentential meaning representations, but no indication of their compositional structure, derivations of the meaning representation cannot be observed. Common approaches enumerate all conceivable lexical items that may have contributed to the derivation of the meaning representation at hand (Artzi et al., 2015; Groschwitz et al., 2017). This may produce very large lexicons with high degrees of ambiguity, and therefore require

large amounts of computational resources during parsing. One central contribution of this paper is a lexicon induction algorithm that produces a relatively compact lexicon.

Combinatory Categorial Grammar (CCG) uses a transparent syntax-semantic interface that constructs meaning representations using λ-calculus. This makes lexicon induction challenging, as inducing λ-calculus terms essentially requires solving higher-order unification (Kwiatkowski et al., 2010). In practice, heuristics are employed to manage the search space, but it would be preferable to make use of a less powerful mechanism which better fits the problem domain. Graph algebras such as the HR algebra (Courcelle and Engelfriet, 2012) constitute such a constrained mechanism. By combining CCG with the HR algebra, we are able to leverage the availability of syntactic parsers for CCG while making use of tailored semantic construction operations.

1.1   Related Work

There is an extensive body of work on semantic parsing of AMRs, using a range of techniques including maximum spanning tree-based parsing (Flanigan et al., 2014), transition-based parsing (Wang et al., 2015; Ballesteros and Al-Onaizan, 2017; Peng et al., 2018), machine translation (van Noord and Bos, 2017), graph grammars (Peng et al., 2015; Groschwitz et al., 2017), and CCG parsing (Artzi et al., 2015; Misra and Artzi, 2016).

The system of Artzi et al. (2015) is most similar to the present work. They induce a semantic CCG using a translation of AMR into λ-calculus. A key difference is that their training algorithm combines lexicon induction and parameter training into a single phase. New lexical items are generated during each training step and then filtered based upon the model's current parameters. In contrast, in this work we focus on lexicon in-

*Proceedings of the 7th Joint Conference on Lexical and Computational Semantics (*SEM)*, pages 54–64
New Orleans, June 5-6, 2018. ©2018 Association for Computational Linguistics

duction, with parameter training to be performed in a subsequent step.

Another related system is presented in Lewis et al. (2015), where a CCG parser is adapted to produce shallow semantic dependency graphs. In contrast, the meaning representations employed here are abstract and do not directly refer to the sentence under analysis.

Word-to-node alignments on the AMR corpus play an important role in this work. We experiment with JAMR's rule-based aligner (Flanigan et al., 2014) and the statistical ISI aligner (Pourdamghani et al., 2014).

Graph algebras have recently been applied to AMR parsing (Koller, 2015; Groschwitz et al., 2017), but not in combination with CCG. In contrast, we use syntactic CCG derivations to constrain the space of possible derivations. However, the idea of using a constrained version of the HR algebra, introduced by Groschwitz et al. (2017), is also used here, and our *Application* operator effectively subsumes their *Apply* and *Modify* operations.

1.2 Tools

Syntax parser We use EasyCCG (Lewis and Steedman, 2014) to obtain syntax derivations. For robustness, we extract the ten best derivations produced by EasyCCG based on the CCGBank-rebanked model (Honnibal et al., 2010).

Word-to-node alignments During lexicon induction, we make use of alignments between tokens in the sentence and nodes in the meaning representation. We experiment with JAMR's aligner (Flanigan et al., 2014) and the ISI aligner (Pourdamghani et al., 2014).

Other tools We use Stanford CoreNLP (Manning et al., 2014) for tokenisation.

2 Background

The task of semantic parsing is concerned with building formal meaning representations for natural language text. While meaning representations can be elements of any formal language, in this paper we are concerned with Abstract Meaning Representations (AMRs). We use Combinatory Categorial Grammar (CCG) as an underlying framework to explain how AMRs may be derived from the surface form words. To do so, we equip CCG with graph construction operators drawn from the HR algebra. These concepts are introduced below.

2.1 Combinatory Categorial Grammar

CCG is a grammar formalism centered around a transparent syntax-semantics interface (Steedman, 2000). A CCG consists of a small set of combinatory rules, along with a lexicon of entries defining each word's syntactic and semantic interpretation.

A CCG lexical item, as used in this paper, contains one or several tokens, a syntactic category, and a semantic category. The syntactic category is a functional type defining the types of arguments expected by the words and whether they are expected to the left or right. E.g., *NP/N* expects a noun (*N*) to the right (because of the rightward-facing slash) and returns an *NP* – it is the type of determiners. *(S \NP)/NP* is the category of transitive verbs, consuming first an *NP* from the right and then from the left, and returning a sentence. See Figure 1a for an example.

CCG derivations are created by recursively applying combinators to the lexical syntactic categories, thus combining them into constituents. Besides Application, implementations of CCG also use other combinators such as Composition, as well as specialized combinators for conjunctions and punctuation.

Semantic categories are represented as λ-calculus terms. A combinator is always applied to two constituents' syntactic and semantic categories at the same time, allowing semantic construction to be fully syntax-driven.

2.2 Abstract Meaning Representation

The Abstract Meaning Representation (AMR) is a semantic meaning representation language that is purposefully syntax-agnostic (Banarescu et al., 2013). The data set used in this paper, the AMR 1.0 release (Knight et al., 2014), consists of English sentences which have been directly annotated with meaning representations by human annotators.

AMR represents meaning as labeled, directed graphs. Nodes are labeled with concepts, while edges represent roles. Predicates and core roles are drawn from PropBank (Kingsbury and Palmer, 2002). In addition, a set of non-core roles has been defined, such as *mod, poss, time,* etc.

Whether it was wise to define AMR independently of any derivational process has been debated (Bender et al., 2015), and in Section 5 we will show some of the issues that arise when attempting to construct derivations for AMRs.

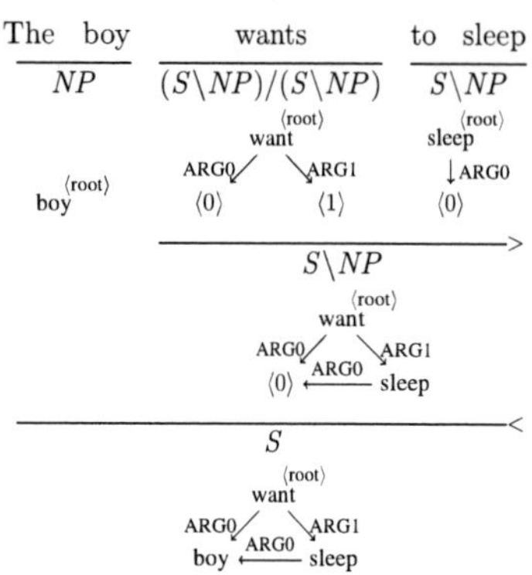

(a) Example for a derivation making use of two *Application* operations.
Step 1: Application. Insert *sleep* node into placeholder $\langle 1 \rangle$; merge $\langle 0 \rangle$ placeholders.
Step 2: Application. Insert *boy* into placeholder $\langle 0 \rangle$.

(b) Example for a derivation containing one *Conjunction* and one *Application* operation.
Step 1: Conjunction. Insert *marry* node into placeholder $\langle 1 \rangle$ of *and*; shift placeholder $\langle 0 \rangle$ of *and* to $\langle 2 \rangle$.
Step 2: Application of the phrase *and married* to *met*; the operands' same-numbered placeholders are merged.

Figure 1: Examples for the semantic operations *Application* and *Conjunction*.

2.3 The HR Algebra

During semantic parsing, a complete meaning representation needs to be built out of smaller components. To formalise this process, known as semantic construction, an algebra may be defined that describes the permitted operations on meaning representations. The HR algebra has first been defined in the context of graph grammars (Courcelle and Engelfriet, 2012) and has been applied to semantic construction of AMR graphs (Koller, 2015).

The HR algebra operates on *graphs with sources*, or *s-graphs*. Given a set of labels $\mathcal{A}$, an s-graph is a pair $(G, slab_G)$ where $G = (V_G, E_G)$ is a graph and $slab_G : V_G \to \mathcal{A}$ is a partial injective function. The nodes contained within the domain of $slab_G$ are called the *sources* of G, and the elements of $\mathcal{A}$ are called *source labels*.

The HR algebra defines three basic operations over s-graphs:

- **Parallel composition** creates the union of two disjoint s-graphs and fuses nodes that share a source label. $slab_G$ is defined to retain all source labels.
- **Forgetting** removes a source from the domain of $slab_G$, effectively deleting its label.
- **Renaming** modifies $slab_G$ to change source labels according to a specified mapping.

The HR algebra provides the building blocks for the manipulation of s-graphs. In the following section, we apply these basic operations to CCG.

3 Graph Semantics for CCG

In CCG, semantic construction is syntax-driven in that the construction operations that are applied to lexical units of meaning are determined by the combinatory operations that make up a CCG syntax tree. To define CCG derivations over graph semantics, we must therefore define the semantic construction operators invoked by each CCG combinator.

We will use a restricted version of the HR algebra, where we only consider a subset of possible s-graphs, and only some of the possible operations. To represent incomplete meaning representations, we define *CCG/AMR s-graphs*.

3.1 CCG/AMR S-Graphs

As an extension of AMR graphs, CCG/AMR s-graphs may contain unlabeled nodes called *placeholders*. In addition to the AMR labels, a source labelling function is employed, as defined in Section 2.3. Source labels used in CCG/AMR s-graphs take one of two forms:

- $\langle r, i \rangle$ with $r \in \{\text{root}, \emptyset\}$ and $i \in \mathbb{N} \cup \{\emptyset\}$, which marks a node as root if $r = \text{root}$, and assigns it an index i if $i \in \mathbb{N}$. However, we disallow $\langle \emptyset, \emptyset \rangle$ as a source label.
- $\langle s \rangle$, used temporarily to label a placeholder-argument pair.

Sources with $r = \text{root}$ are called *root-sources*, and sources with $i \in \mathbb{N}$ are called *i-sources*. For

CCG combinator	Semantic operator
(F/B) Application	(F/B) Application
(F/B) [Gen.] [Cr.] Comp.	(F/B) Application
Conjunction	F Conjunction
(Left/Right) Punctuation	(F/B) Identity

Table 1: The mapping from CCG combinators to semantic operators. *F* and *B* stand for *Forward* and *Backward*, *Gen.* stands for *Generalised*, *Cr.* stands for *Crossed*, and *Comp.* stands for composition. All variants of Composition are mapped to the Application operation.

simplicity, we abbreviate $\langle \text{root}, \emptyset \rangle$ to $\langle \text{root} \rangle$ and $\langle \emptyset, i \rangle$ to $\langle i \rangle$ for $i \in \mathbb{N}$.

The following constraints apply:

- A CCG/AMR s-graph must have exactly one root-source.
- For every $i \in \mathbb{N}$, there may be at most one i-source, and for every i-source with $i > 0$, there must also be an $(i - 1)$-source.
- The i-sources of a CCG/AMR s-graph must be exactly its placeholders.

The *outermost placeholder* of a CCG/AMR s-graph is defined to be the placeholder with the highest index i.

3.2 Semantic Operators

We now define three semantic operators based on the building blocks of the HR algebra. They are binary operators, with a left and a right operand. If the operator is used in *forward* direction, we call the left operand the *function graph* and the right operand the *argument graph*. In *backward* direction, these roles are reversed.

- **Application** Relabels both the outermost placeholder of the function graph and the root of the argument graph to $\langle s \rangle$. Then performs parallel composition of both graphs. Finally, forgets $\langle s \rangle$. Requires the function graph to have at least one placeholder.
- **Conjunction** The function graph of a conjunction operator is required to have exactly two placeholders. Placeholder $\langle 1 \rangle$ and the root of the function graph are both renamed to $\langle s \rangle$. Placeholder $\langle 0 \rangle$ of the function graph is relabelled to $\langle i + 1 \rangle$, where i is the index of the argument graph's outermost placeholder. Then, parallel composition is applied to the

relabelled graphs and $\langle s \rangle$ forgotten.

- **Identity** A special case of Application where the function graph must consist of a single placeholder and the argument graph is therefore always returned unchanged.

Examples for the Application and Conjunction operators are given in Figure 1.

For our definition of CCG/AMR, we use the combinator set of the EasyCCG parser (Lewis and Steedman, 2014), which is small and achieves good coverage. The Application operator is sufficient to cover almost all CCG combinators, with the exception of conjunctions. The mapping of CCG combinators to semantic operators used in this paper is summarised in Table 1.

All unary combinators, including type raising and the various type-changing rules used by EasyCCG, are defined to have no effect on the semantic representation.

We add a single rule that is non-compositional in terms of the semantic operators. Since n-ary conjunctions are frequent in the AMR corpus, this rule combines two nested conjunction nodes, merging their operands into a single contiguous operand list.

3.3 Induction of CCG/AMR Lexicons

To induce a CCG/AMR lexicon, we propose a simple recursive algorithm, described in Algorithm 1. It starts with a full-sentence meaning representation, a syntax tree, and a set of word-to-node alignments. Starting from the root, it recurses down the syntax tree and splits the meaning representation into smaller parts by applying the inverse of one of the semantic operators at each node.

Constraints We impose two constraints on the generated lexical items:

1. The alignments must not be violated.
2. The number of placeholders must not exceed the arity of the lexical item's syntactic category. E. g., the meaning representation for the syntactic category $(S \backslash NP) / NP$ must not have more than two placeholders.

Soundness Algorithm 1 requires finding z_1, z_2 with $o(z_1, z_2) = z$. This equation states that a parser would be able to produce the parse observed in the data based on the induced the lexical items, thus ensuring the soundness of the induction algorithm.

Implementation We examine all ways of partitioning the meaning representation into a function subgraph and an argument subgraph, provided that no alignments are violated. Nodes that sit at the boundary between both subgraphs – belonging to the argument subgraph but connected by edges to the function subgraph – are *unmerged*, meaning that a placeholder is created in the function subgraph to which those edges are moved.

Phrasal items   Intermediate items are emitted by the algorithm even if they can be further decomposed. The rationale behind this behaviour is that some lexical entries legitimately span multiple tokens. E.g., one could argue that a named entity such as *New York* should be kept as a lexical item.

Coreferences   Since there are many cases where graphs are connected more densely than allowed by the arity constraint, we allow <coref> nodes to be created by unmerging additional nodes. They are treated just like regular nodes. In particular, they are not sources and do not count towards the function graph's placeholder count. In the experiments in this paper, we only allow creation of a single <coref> node per splitting step.

Splitting failures   The algorithm may encounter situations where splitting cannot continue because it is impossible to further decompose the meaning representation without violating one of the constraints. In such cases, its output is incomplete, emitting a lexical item only for the derivation node at which the problem was encountered – which may span a long constituent of the sentence – but not for any of its sub-nodes.

4   Analysis of Lexicon Induction

We begin by analysing the statistical properties of large-scale grammar induction on the 6,603 sentences of the `proxy-train` subset of the AMR corpus, which consists of newswire texts. We also examine the influence that different alignment strategies have on the produced lexicon.

We then turn to the `consensus-dev` subset, which consists of 100 sentences taken from the Wall Street Journal corpus. Therefore, gold standard syntax parses for these sentences can be obtained from CCGBank (Hockenmaier and Steedman, 2007). In addition, Pourdamghani et al. (2014) have released gold-standard word-to-meaning alignments for these sentences. This allows us to examine the effect of tool-derived alignments and syntax parses on the induction algorithm's behaviour.

Algorithm 1 Recursive Splitting

Input: syntax derivation node y, CCG/AMR s-graph z

Definitions: OPERATOR returns the semantic operator matching a derivation node's combinator. CHILDREN returns the sub-nodes of a syntax derivation node. VALID tests whether a pair of a derivation node and a meaning representation fulfill the constraints of Section 3.3. EMIT adds an item to the lexicon. EMITTED tests whether an equivalent item is already in the lexicon.

```
 1: function SPLITREC(y, z)
 2:     if ¬EMITTED(y, z) ∧ VALID(y, z) then
 3:         EMIT(y, z)
 4:         y₁, y₂ ← CHILDREN(y)
 5:         o ← OPERATOR(y)
 6:         for z₁, z₂ such that o(z₁, z₂) = z do
 7:             SPLITREC(y₁, z₁)
 8:             SPLITREC(y₂, z₂)
 9:         end for
10:     end if
11: end function
```

4.1   Quantitative Analysis

We run lexicon induction on the full `proxy-train` subcorpus. To limit the computational effort and reduce the extraction of poorly generalisable lexical items, we apply the following limitations:[1]

1. If more than 1,000 lexical items are extracted from a derivation, it is skipped entirely.
2. Sentences with more than ten unaligned nodes are skipped.
3. If at any derivation node, more than ten lexical items are generated, none of them are included in the lexicon (but induction may still proceed recursively from these nodes).

We measure results by examining the distribution of *maximum span lengths* over the corpus. The maximum span length of a sentence is defined as the length of its longest subspan which the induction algorithm was not able to split any further. Ideally, we would like to achieve a maximum span length of 1 for every sentence, meaning that each individual token is assigned at least one lexical item.

---

[1]Constraints 1 and 2 will tend to penalise longer sentences more frequently. While this skews our results towards shorter sentences, we have found them necessary to keep the runtime of the algorithm manageable.

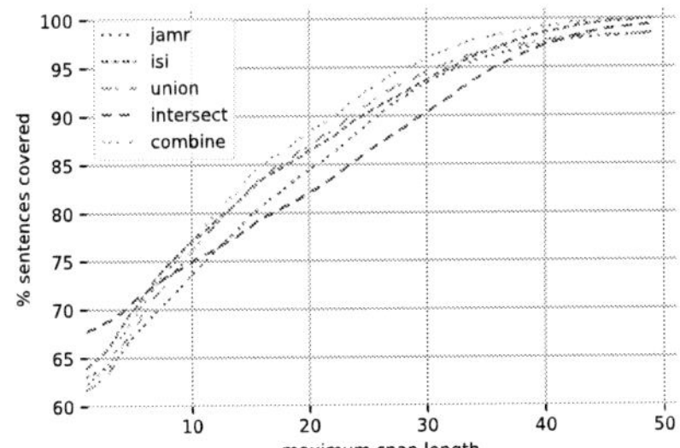

(a) Lexical induction coverage. For each alignment strategy, the plot shows the percentage of sentences having at most a given maximum span length.

Alignments	Lexicon Size	Skipped
jamr	314,299	104
isi	387,932	2
union	275,418	103
intersect	429,278	41
combine	286,129	3

(b) Lexicon sizes and skipped sentences by alignment strategy. Sentences were skipped if they produced more than 1,000 lexical items.

Figure 2: Comparison of alignment strategies for lexical induction on the `proxy-train` set.

4.1.1 Alignment Strategies

We first examine the impact of several alignment strategies. The two alignment tools investigated here, the JAMR aligner (Flanigan et al., 2014) and the ISI aligner (Pourdamghani et al., 2014), use different approaches and thus produce alignments with different characteristics. We therefore explore different strategies of combining the alignments produced by the two tools:

- **jamr/isi:** Use only the output from one of the tools. In the case of the ISI aligner, alignments to edges are dropped.
- **union/intersect:** Take the union / intersection of both aligners' outputs.
- **combine:** Take the union of both aligners' outputs. However, if a node has been aligned to different tokens by the two aligners, drop alignments for this node altogether.

Two strategies exhibit the most interesting properties (Figure 2). The *intersect* strategy achieves a maximum span length of 1 on the most sentences, but its produced alignments are too sparse, causing many lexical items to be dropped due to ambiguity. From a maximum span length of 8, the *combine*

strategy is more successful, while still maintaining a small lexicon size and a low number of skipped sentences. Intuitively, it increases the node coverage of either method, while also allowing the correction of errors made by one of the tools.

4.1.2 Lexicon Statistics

The lexicon resulting from the *combine* strategy has 286,129 entries. In comparison, this is less than a fifth the lexicon size of 1.6 million entries reported by Artzi et al. (2015).

Of the 6,603 sentences, the algorithm skipped three because they would have produced more than 1,000 lexical items. Each of the remaining sentences contributes on average 3.29 lexical items per token (median 2.91).

The lexicon is essentially a non-unique mapping from sequences of tokens to pairs of syntactic and semantic categories. By counting the number of distinct entries for each token sequence, we can assess the ambiguity of the lexicon. For the token sequences represented in the lexicon, the mean ambiguity is 10.6 (median: 4). There is a small number of entries with very high ambiguities: 73 tokens have an ambiguity of more than 100, the most ambiguous one being *in* with 1,798 lexical items. In general, prepositions dominate among the most ambiguous items, because they occur frequently, tend not to have any alignments, and also have a high degree of legitimate polysemy. However, high-frequency words specific to the corpus also appear, such as *government* or *security*.

Of the 10,600 unique tokens in the training corpus, 23% (2,458) are not assigned a lexical item at all because the induction algorithm was not able to fully decompose the meaning representation, or because more than ten candidates resulted from every occurrence. They are covered by multi-token items.

4.2 Impact of Tool-Derived Annotations

To examine the induction algorithm's sensitivity to errors propagated from external tools, we compare them with the gold standard annotations available for the `consensus-dev` set. The results are shown in Figure 3.

Not surprisingly, gold annotations perform better than tool-derived annotations. It can be seen that alignments impact grammar induction performance more strongly than syntax parses, with a gap of 21% of perfectly split sentences between gold-standard and tool-derived alignment annota-

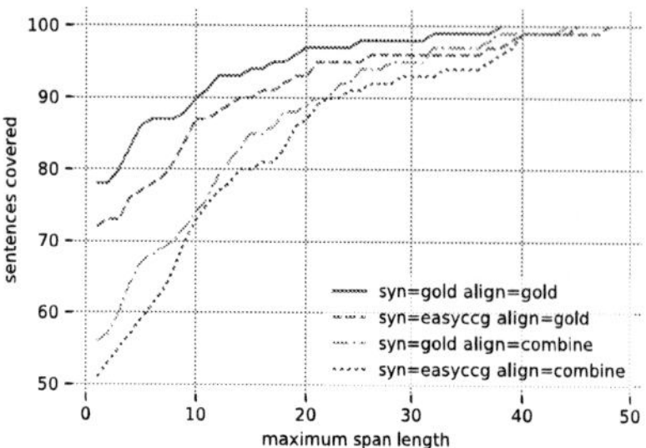

(a) Lexical induction coverage with either gold-standard or tool-derived annotations. Tool-derived syntax is from EasyCCG, tool-derived annotations are JAMR/ISI alignments processed using the *combine* strategy.

Syntax	Alignments	Lexicon Size
gold	gold	7,908
easyccg	gold	11,123
gold	combine	4,435
easyccg	combine	5,401

(b) Sizes of the lexicons induced with different annotation sources.

Figure 3: Analysis of lexicon induction performance using gold-standard or tool-derived annotations.

tions. Table 3b shows an increase in lexicon size when EasyCCG syntax is used, which is likely due to added noise because the ten best derivations are considered instead of a single one. Tool-derived alignments, on the other hand, reduce the lexicon size, because alignment errors force induction to stop early on some sentences.

5 Problematic Phenomena in AMR

Is the proposed framework a good fit for analysing the AMR corpus? Figure 3 shows that even if errors from external tools are ruled out, there remains a gap of 22% of sentences that are not fully split by the lexical induction algorithm.

To assess the nature of these failures, we group them into error classes. Table 2 provides an overview of the error counts.

Broadly speaking, we identify three types of errors: Algorithmic limitations, where parameters of the algorithm prohibit the desired decomposition; mismatches where the CCG and AMR annotations choose to represent phenomena in incompatible ways; and non-compositional constructions,

where certain AMRs cannot be expressed in our graph algebra.

Error Class	Label	Count
dependency mismatch	dep	15
coreference restriction	coref	3
negation	neg	2
node duplication	dup	2

Table 2: Classification of causes for lexical induction failures, using gold-standard syntax parses and word-to-node alignments, based on the `consensus-dev` data set (100 sentences). The remaining 78 sentences were split perfectly. Labels refer to the paragraphs in Section 5.

5.1 Algorithmic Limitations

Restriction of coreference node extraction (coref) In three cases, we observed more than one <coref> node to be required, as exemplified in Figure 4c.

5.2 Mismatches Between CCG and AMR

Mismatch of syntactic and semantic dependencies (dep) Since the induction algorithm walks the syntax tree and relies strongly on the existence of a parallel structure between syntax and semantics, it fails in cases where different dependency structures are present in the syntactic and the semantic annotations.

Of the 15 errors in this class, we judged 11 to be "fixable" in that an acceptable CCG derivation could be constructed matching the dependencies on the semantic level. Typically, these are related to ambiguities or annotation errors. Figure 4a shows a typical example.

Treatment of negation (neg) Syntactically, the negator *no* can attach to a noun in cases where it semantically modifies the verb, as shown in Figure 4b. In AMR, the choice is made to attach polarity edges to the verb, which prohibits syntactic analysis of such constructions. This is a systematic difference between CCG and AMR.

5.3 Non-Compositional Features of AMR

Duplication of nodes (dup) Constructions involving conjunctions or partitives can lead to a duplication of nodes in the meaning representation, as shown in Figures 4d and 4e. This behaviour is not compositional because the duplicated nodes

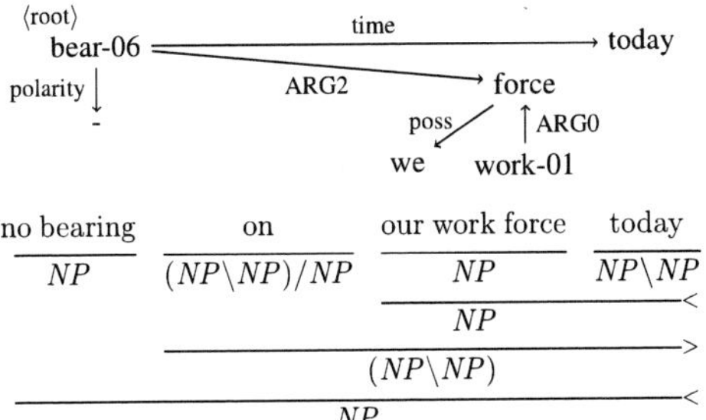

(a) Example for mismatching syntactic / semantic dependencies. Syntactically, a dependency between *work force* and *today* is annotated, but semantically, *today* is dependent on *bearing*. While a syntax derivation matching the semantic dependencies could be constructed, it has not been annotated in CCGbank. From `wsj_0003.30`.

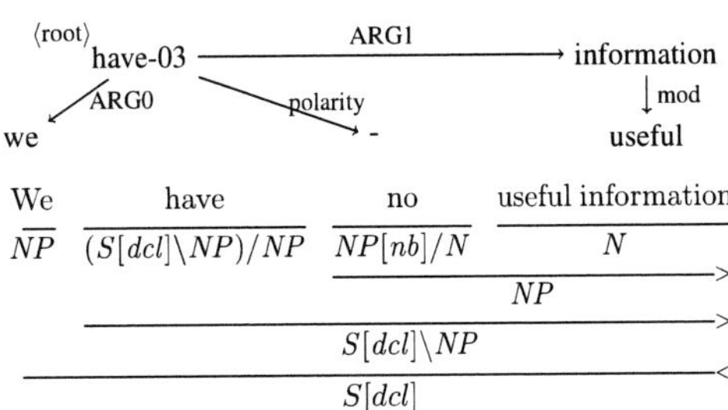

(b) Example for the incompatible treatment of negation. The polarity edge of *have-03* does not match the dependency between *no* and *information*. Simplified from `wsj_0003.9`

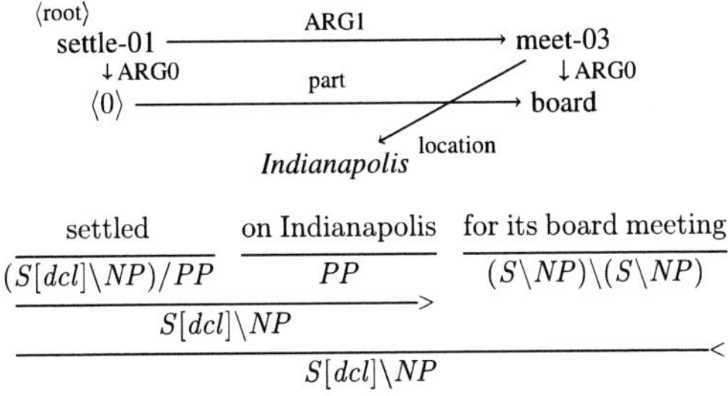

(c) Example for a phrase with more than one coreference. The phrase *its board meeting* contains coreferences both via the *location* and *part* edges. The *Indianapolis* node is an abbreviation for a multi-node named entity subgraph. Simplified from `wsj_0010.3`.

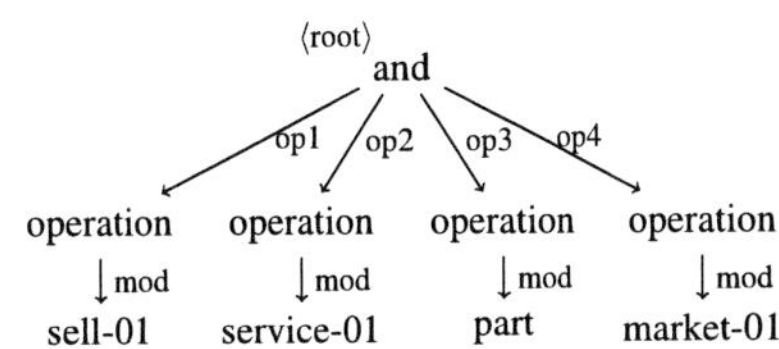

(d) Example for the duplication of nodes due to coordination. The phrase is *sales, service, parts and marketing operations*. Even though the token *operations* occurs only once, a separate *operation* node is introduced for each operand of the *and* conjunction. From `wsj_0009.2`.

(e) Example for the duplication of nodes due to a partitive. The phrase is *some of the hottest chefs in town*. The example illustrate how quantification can lead to nodes being duplicated, such as the *chef* nodes in this AMR. From `wsj_0010.17`

Figure 4: Corpus examples for the phenomena described in Section 5: mismatching dependencies, treatment of negations, number of coreferences, duplication of nodes due to coordination and partitives. Syntax annotations are taken from CCGbank, and semantic annotations are taken from the AMR corpus.

(a) Meaning representation for *told the boy to sleep.*

(b) Induced meaning representation for *told the boy.*

(c) Induced meaning representations for *told, boy,* and *sleep.*

Figure 5: Example for the induction of lexical items from an object control verb construction. The sentence is *[The girl] told the boy to sleep.* Since *sleep* is an argument to *tell*, it is not assigned any placeholders and is extracted as a 0-ary lexical item. The control structure is encoded in the lexical item for *tell.*

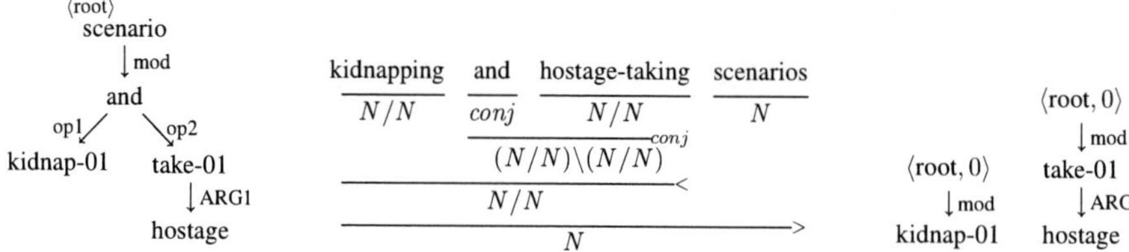

(a) AMR for the phrase *kidnapping and hostage-taking scenarios*.

(b) CCG derivation showing the lexical entries for the modifiers *kidnapping* and *hostage-taking*.

(c) The lexical entries for the modifiers *kidnapping* and *hostage-taking*.

Figure 6: Corpus example for conjunctions of modifiers. The AMR in Figure 6a cannot be compositionally constructed from the modifier interpretations of *kidnapping* and *hostage-taking* because the *mod* edges present in the lexical entries would have to be destructively modified. Example from `PROXY_AFP_ENG_20020105_0162.12`.

are introduced only once lexically, and then copied based on the syntactic context.

Coordination of modifiers[2] When modifiers are the arguments of a conjunction, the conjunction node itself is connected to the modifiee via a *mod* edge, as shown in Figure 6. Given that each of the conjoined modifiers itself has a *mod* edge, these edges need to be merged, moved, or deleted somehow.

6 Conclusion

We have presented a new variant of CCG which performs semantic construction using the operations of a graph algebra instead of combinatory operations on λ-calculus terms. This allows the grammar to construct graph representations directly without going through intermediate representations. It also restricts the set of possible operations, leading to a compact lexicon. We have demonstrated that under ideal conditions, our grammar achieves a robust coverage of 78% on WSJ sentences.

Our experiments suggest that CCG/AMR is a good overall match for representing the derivation of AMRs. There remain several possibilities for improvement which we leave for future work:

- Allowing the induction algorithm to search over possible derivations and alignments would reduce the influence of both tool errors and mismatching annotations. To keep the lexicon manageable, an optimizing induction algorithm would be needed, e.g. using EM.

- An attempt could me made to more strongly identify placeholders with the argument positions of the corresponding syntactic categories. Among others, this would allow for a more canonical treatment of object control verbs, which is somewhat ad hoc, requiring an interpretation of verbs as 0-ary lexical items (see Figure 5 for an example).

- Additional rules could be introduced to deal with non-compositional phenomena such as the conjunction of modifiers. Statistically, such phenomena appear to be rare, affecting only 2% of the examined corpus.

- Other differences in representation might be resolved statistically or using heuristics. E.g., the fact that negators that attach to a noun syntactically attach to the verb in AMR could be mitigated by a rule that allows for the movement of polarity edges.

Our results represent a promising step towards a more complete grammatical treatment of AMR. Although AMR has not been designed with compositionality in mind, we have shown that it is possible to construct linguistically motivated compositional derivations.

7 Acknowledgements

We thank Alexander Koller and his group, Christine and Arne Köhn, and the anonymous reviewers for their helpful comments. Part of this work was supported by the DFG (IGK 1247).

References

Yoav Artzi, Kenton Lee, and Luke Zettlemoyer. 2015. Broad-coverage CCG Semantic Parsing with AMR.

---

[2]This phenomenon has not been observed in the consensus data set and is therefore not represented in Table 2.

In *Proceedings of the 2015 Conference on Empirical Methods in Natural Language Processing*, pages 1699–1710, Lisbon, Portugal. Association for Computational Linguistics.

Miguel Ballesteros and Yaser Al-Onaizan. 2017. AMR Parsing using Stack-LSTMs. In *Proceedings of the 2017 Conference on Empirical Methods in Natural Language Processing*, pages 1269–1275, Copenhagen, Denmark. Association for Computational Linguistics.

Laura Banarescu, Claire Bonial, Shu Cai, Madalina Georgescu, Kira Griffitt, Ulf Hermjakob, Kevin Knight, Philipp Koehn, Martha Palmer, and Nathan Schneider. 2013. Abstract Meaning Representation for Sembanking. In *Proceedings of the 7th Linguistic Annotation Workshop and Interoperability with Discourse*, pages 178–186, Sofia, Bulgaria. Association for Computational Linguistics.

Emily M. Bender, Dan Flickinger, Stephan Oepen, Woodley Packard, and Ann Copestake. 2015. Layers of Interpretation: On Grammar and Compositionality. In *Proceedings of the 11th International Conference on Computational Semantics*, pages 239–249, London, UK. Association for Computational Linguistics.

Bruno Courcelle and Joost Engelfriet. 2012. *Graph Structure and Monadic Second-Order Logic: A Language-Theoretic Approach*, 1st edition. Cambridge University Press, New York, NY, USA.

Jeffrey Flanigan, Sam Thomson, Jaime Carbonell, Chris Dyer, and Noah A. Smith. 2014. A Discriminative Graph-Based Parser for the Abstract Meaning Representation. In *Proceedings of the 52nd Annual Meeting of the Association for Computational Linguistics*, pages 1426–1436, Baltimore, Maryland. Association for Computational Linguistics.

Jonas Groschwitz, Meaghan Fowlie, Mark Johnson, and Alexander Koller. 2017. A constrained graph algebra for semantic parsing with AMRs. In *Proceedings of the 12th International Conference on Computational Semantics*, Montpellier, France. Association for Computational Linguistics.

Julia Hockenmaier and Mark Steedman. 2007. CCGbank: a corpus of CCG derivations and dependency structures extracted from the Penn Treebank. *Computational Linguistics*, 33(3):355–396.

Matthew Honnibal, James R. Curran, and Johan Bos. 2010. Rebanking CCGbank for Improved NP Interpretation. In *Proceedings of the 48th Annual Meeting of the Association for Computational Linguistics*, pages 207–215, Uppsala, Sweden. Association for Computational Linguistics.

Paul Kingsbury and Martha Palmer. 2002. From TreeBank to PropBank. In *Proceedings of the Third International Conference on Language Resources and Evaluation*, pages 1989–1993, Las Palmas, Spain. European Language Resources Association.

Kevin Knight, Laura Baranescu, Claire Bonial, Madalina Georgescu, Kira Griffitt, Ulf Hermjakob, Daniel Marcu, Martha Palmer, and Nathan Schneider. 2014. *Abstract Meaning Representation (AMR) Annotation Release 1.0 LDC2014T12*. Linguistic Data Consortium, Philadelphia.

Alexander Koller. 2015. Semantic construction with graph grammars. In *Proceedings of the 11th International Conference on Computational Semantics*, pages 228–238, London, UK. Association for Computational Linguistics.

Tom Kwiatkowski, Luke Zettlemoyer, Sharon Goldwater, and Mark Steedman. 2010. Inducing Probabilistic CCG Grammars from Logical Form with Higher-Order Unification. In *Proceedings of the 2010 Conference on Empirical Methods in Natural Language Processing*, pages 1223–1233, Cambridge, MA. Association for Computational Linguistics.

Mike Lewis, Luheng He, and Luke Zettlemoyer. 2015. Joint A* CCG Parsing and Semantic Role Labelling. In *Proceedings of the 2015 Conference on Empirical Methods in Natural Language Processing*, pages 1444–1454, Lisbon, Portugal. Association for Computational Linguistics.

Mike Lewis and Mark Steedman. 2014. A* CCG Parsing with a Supertag-factored Model. In *Proceedings of the 2014 Conference on Empirical Methods in Natural Language Processing (EMNLP)*, pages 990–1000, Doha, Qatar. Association for Computational Linguistics.

Christopher D. Manning, Mihai Surdeanu, John Bauer, Jenny Finkel, Steven J. Bethard, and David McClosky. 2014. The Stanford CoreNLP Natural Language Processing Toolkit. In *Association for Computational Linguistics (ACL) System Demonstrations*, pages 55–60.

Kumar Dipendra Misra and Yoav Artzi. 2016. Neural Shift-Reduce CCG Semantic Parsing. In *Proceedings of the 2016 Conference on Empirical Methods in Natural Language Processing*, pages 1775–1786, Austin, Texas. Association for Computational Linguistics.

Rik van Noord and Johan Bos. 2017. Neural Semantic Parsing by Character-based Translation: Experiments with Abstract Meaning Representations. *Computational Linguistics in the Netherlands Journal*, 7:93–108.

Xiaochang Peng, Daniel Gildea, and Giorgio Satta. 2018. AMR Parsing with Cache Transition Systems. In *Proceedings of the Thirty-Second AAAI Conference on Artificial Intelligence*, New Orleans, USA. Association for the Advancement of Artificial Intelligence.

Xiaochang Peng, Linfeng Song, and Daniel Gildea. 2015. A Synchronous Hyperedge Replacement

Grammar based approach for AMR parsing. In *Proceedings of the Nineteenth Conference on Computational Natural Language Learning*, pages 32–41, Beijing, China. Association for Computational Linguistics.

Nima Pourdamghani, Yang Gao, Ulf Hermjakob, and Kevin Knight. 2014. Aligning English Strings with Abstract Meaning Representation Graphs. In *Proceedings of the 2014 Conference on Empirical Methods in Natural Language Processing (EMNLP)*, pages 425–429, Doha, Qatar. Association for Computational Linguistics.

Mark Steedman. 2000. *The Syntactic Process*. MIT Press, Cambridge, MA, USA.

Chuan Wang, Nianwen Xue, and Sameer Pradhan. 2015. A Transition-based Algorithm for AMR Parsing. In *Proceedings of the 2015 Conference of the North American Chapter of the Association for Computational Linguistics: Human Language Technologies*, pages 366–375, Denver, Colorado. Association for Computational Linguistics.

Mixing Context Granularities for Improved Entity Linking on Question Answering Data across Entity Categories

Daniil Sorokin and **Iryna Gurevych**

Ubiquitous Knowledge Processing Lab (UKP) and Research Training Group AIPHES
Department of Computer Science, Technische Universität Darmstadt
www.ukp.tu-darmstadt.de
{sorokin|gurevych}@ukp.informatik.tu-darmstadt.de

Abstract

The first stage of every knowledge base question answering approach is to link entities in the input question. We investigate entity linking in the context of a question answering task and present a jointly optimized neural architecture for entity mention detection and entity disambiguation that models the surrounding context on different levels of granularity.

We use the Wikidata knowledge base and available question answering datasets to create benchmarks for entity linking on question answering data. Our approach outperforms the previous state-of-the-art system on this data, resulting in an average 8% improvement of the final score. We further demonstrate that our model delivers a strong performance across different entity categories.

1 Introduction

Knowledge base question answering (QA) requires a precise modeling of the question semantics through the entities and relations available in the knowledge base (KB) in order to retrieve the correct answer. The first stage for every QA approach is entity linking (EL), that is the identification of entity mentions in the question and linking them to entities in KB. In Figure 1, two entity mentions are detected and linked to the knowledge base referents. This step is crucial for QA since the correct answer must be connected via some path over KB to the entities mentioned in the question.

The state-of-the-art QA systems usually rely on off-the-shelf EL systems to extract entities from the question (Yih et al., 2015). Multiple EL systems are freely available and can be readily applied

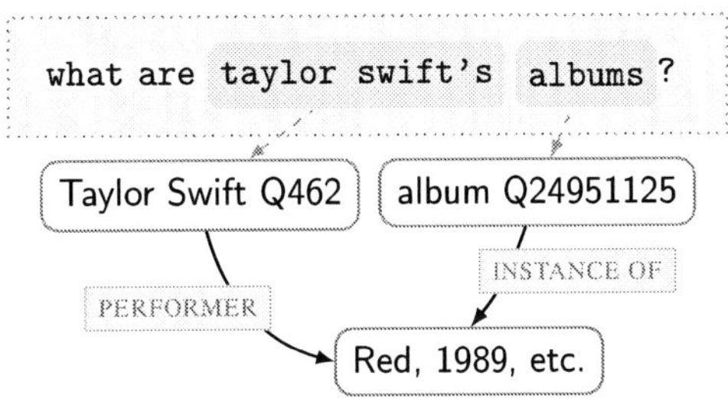

Figure 1: An example question from a QA dataset that shows the correct entity mentions and their relationship with the correct answer to the question, Qxxx stands for a knowledge base identifier

for question answering (e.g. DBPedia Spotlight[1], AIDA[2]). However, these systems have certain drawbacks in the QA setting: they are targeted at long well-formed documents, such as news texts, and are less suited for typically short and noisy question data. Other EL systems focus on noisy data (e.g. S-MART, Yang and Chang, 2015), but are not openly available and hence limited in their usage and application. Multiple error analyses of QA systems point to entity linking as a major external source of error (Berant and Liang, 2014; Reddy et al., 2014; Yih et al., 2015).

The QA datasets are normally collected from the web and contain very noisy and diverse data (Berant et al., 2013), which poses a number of challenges for EL. First, many common features used in EL systems, such as capitalization, are not meaningful on noisy data. Moreover, a question is a short text snippet that does not contain broader context that is helpful for entity disambiguation. The QA data also features many entities of various categories and differs in this respect from the Twitter datasets that are often used to evaluate EL systems.

---

[1] http://www.dbpedia-spotlight.org
[2] https://www.mpi-inf.mpg.de/yago-naga/aida/

*Proceedings of the 7th Joint Conference on Lexical and Computational Semantics (*SEM)*, pages 65–75
New Orleans, June 5-6, 2018. ©2018 Association for Computational Linguistics

In this paper, we present an approach that tackles the challenges listed above: we perform entity mention detection and entity disambiguation jointly in a single neural model that makes the whole process end-to-end differentiable. This ensures that any token n-gram can be considered as a potential entity mention, which is important to be able to link entities of different categories, such as movie titles and organization names.

To overcome the noise in the data, we automatically learn features over a set of contexts of different granularity levels. Each level of granularity is handled by a separate component of the model. A token-level component extracts higher-level features from the whole question context, whereas a character-level component builds lower-level features for the candidate n-gram. Simultaneously, we extract features from the knowledge base context of the candidate entity: character-level features are extracted for the entity label and higher-level features are produced based on the entities surrounding the candidate entity in the knowledge graph. This information is aggregated and used to predict whether the n-gram is an entity mention and to what entity it should be linked.

Contributions The two main contributions of our work are:

(i) We construct two datasets to evaluate EL for QA and present a set of strong baselines: the existing EL systems that were used as a building block for QA before and a model that uses manual features from the previous work on noisy data.

(ii) We design and implement an entity linking system that models contexts of variable granularity to detect and disambiguate entity mentions. To the best of our knowledge, we are the first to present a unified end-to-end neural model for entity linking for noisy data that operates on different context levels and does not rely on manual features. Our architecture addresses the challenges of entity linking on question answering data and outperforms state-of-the-art EL systems.

Code and Datasets Our system can be applied on any QA dataset. The complete code as well as the scripts that produce the evaluation data can be found here: `https://github.com/UKPLab/starsem2018-entity-linking`.

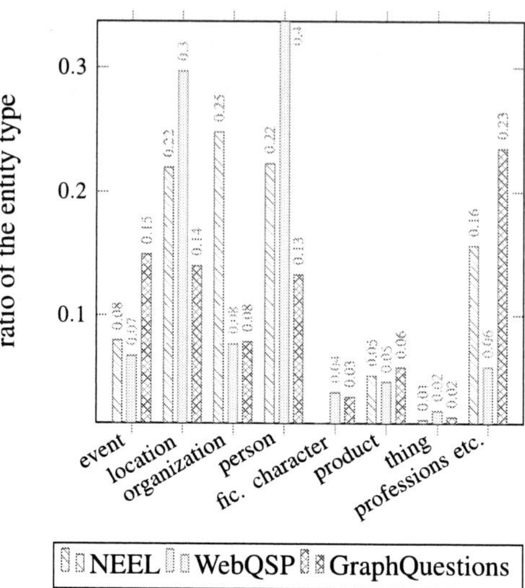

Figure 2: Distribution of entity categories in the NEEL 2014, WebQSP and GraphQuestions datasets

2 Motivation and Related Work

Several benchmarks exist for EL on Wikipedia texts and news articles, such as ACE (Bentivogli et al., 2010) and CoNLL-YAGO (Hoffart et al., 2011). These datasets contain multi-sentence documents and largely cover three types of entities: Location, Person and Organization. These types are commonly recognized by named entity recognition systems, such as Stanford NER Tool (Manning et al., 2014). Therefore in this scenario, an EL system can solely focus on entity disambiguation.

In the recent years, EL on Twitter data has emerged as a branch of entity linking research. In particular, EL on tweets was the central task of the NEEL shared task from 2014 to 2016 (Rizzo et al., 2017). Tweets share some of the challenges with QA data: in both cases the input data is short and noisy. On the other hand, it significantly differs with respect to the entity types covered. The data for the NEEL shared task was annotated with 7 broad entity categories, that besides Location, Organization and Person include Fictional Characters, Events, Products (such as electronic devices or works of art) and Things (abstract objects). Figure 2 shows the distribution of entity categories in the training set from the NEEL 2014 competition. One can see on the diagram that the distribution is mainly skewed towards 3 categories: Location, Person and Organization.

Figure 2 also shows the entity categories present in two QA datasets. The distribution over the categories is more diverse in this case. The WebQuestions dataset includes the Fictional Character and Thing categories which are almost absent from the NEEL dataset. A more even distribution can be observed in the GraphQuestion dataset that features many Events, Fictional Characters and Professions. This means that a successful system for EL on question data needs to be able to recognize and to link all categories of entities. Thus, we aim to show that comprehensive modeling of different context levels will result in a better generalization and performance across various entity categories.

Existing Solutions The early machine learning approaches to EL focused on long well-formed documents (Bunescu and Pasca, 2006; Cucerzan, 2007; Han and Sun, 2012; Francis-Landau et al., 2016). These systems usually rely on an off-the-shelf named entity recognizer to extract entity mentions in the input. As a consequence, such approaches can not handle entities of types other than those that are supplied by the named entity recognizer. Named entity recognizers are normally trained to detect mentions of Locations, Organizations and Person names, whereas in the context of QA, the system also needs to cover movie titles, songs, common nouns such as 'president' etc.

To mitigate this, Cucerzan (2012) has introduced the idea to perform mention detection and entity linking jointly using a linear combination of manually defined features. Luo et al. (2015) have adopted the same idea and suggested a probabilistic graphical model for the joint prediction. This is essential for linking entities in questions. For example in *"who does maggie grace play in taken?"*, it is hard to distinguish between the usage of the word 'taken' and the title of a movie 'Taken' without consulting a knowledge base.

Sun et al. (2015) were among the first to use neural networks to embed the mention and the entity for a better prediction quality. Later, Francis-Landau et al. (2016) have employed convolutional neural networks to extract features from the document context and mixed them with manually defined features, though they did not integrate it with mention detection. Sil et al. (2018) continued the work in this direction recently and applied convolutional neural networks to cross-lingual EL.

The approaches that were developed for Twitter data present the most relevant work for EL on QA data. Guo et al. (2013b) have created a new dataset of around 1500 tweets and suggested a Structured SVM approach that handled mention detection and entity disambiguation together. Chang et al. (2014) describe the winning system of the NEEL 2014 competition on EL for short texts: The system adapts a joint approach similar to Guo et al. (2013b), but uses the MART gradient boosting algorithm instead of the SVM and extends the feature set. The current state-of-the-art system for EL on noisy data is S-MART (Yang and Chang, 2015) which extends the approach from Chang et al. (2014) to make structured predictions. The same group has subsequently applied S-MART to extract entities for a QA system (Yih et al., 2015).

Unfortunately, the described EL systems for short texts are not available as stand-alone tools. Consequently, the modern QA approaches mostly rely on off-the-shelf entity linkers that were designed for other domains. Reddy et al. (2016) have employed the Freebase online API that was since deprecated. A number of question answering systems have relied on DBPedia Spotlight to extract entities (Lopez et al., 2016; Chen et al., 2016). DBPedia Spotlight (Mendes et al., 2011) uses document similarity vectors, word embeddings and manually defined features such as entity frequency. We are addressing this problem in our work by presenting an architecture specifically targeted at EL for QA data.

The Knowledge Base Throughout the experiments, we use the Wikidata[3] open-domain KB (Vrandečić and Krötzsch, 2014). Among the previous work, the common choices of a KB include Wikipedia, DBPedia and Freebase. The entities in Wikidata directly correspond to the Wikipedia articles, which enables us to work with data that was previously annotated with DBPedia. Freebase was discontinued and is no longer up-to-date. However, most entities in Wikidata have been annotated with identifiers from other knowledge sources and databases, including Freebase, which establishes a link between the two KBs.

3 Entity Linking Architecture

The overall architecture of our entity linking system is depicted in Figure 3. From the input question **x** we extract all possible token n-grams N up to a

---

[3] At the moment, Wikidata contains more than 40 million entities and 350 million relation instances:
`https://www.wikidata.org/wiki/Special:`
`Statistics`

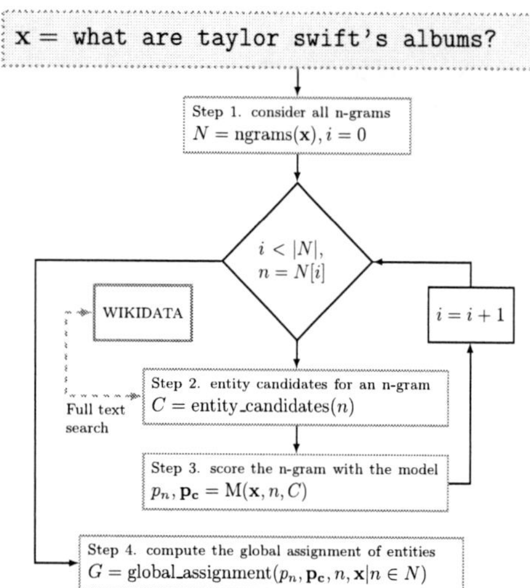

Figure 3: Architecture of the entity linking system

certain length as entity mention candidates (Step 1). For each n-gram n, we look it up in the knowledge base using a full text search over entity labels (Step 2). That ensures that we find all entities that contain the given n-gram in the label. For example for a unigram 'obama', we retrieve 'Barack Obama', 'Michelle Obama' etc. This step produces a set of entity disambiguation candidates C for the given n-gram n. We sort the retrieved candidates by length and cut off after the first 1000. That ensures that the top candidates in the list would be those that exactly match the target n-gram n.

In the next step, the list of n-grams N and the corresponding list of entity disambiguation candidates are sent to the entity linking model (Step 3). The model jointly performs the detection of correct mentions and the disambiguation of entities.

3.1 Variable Context Granularity Network

The neural architecture (Variable Context Granularity, VCG) aggregates and mixes contexts of different granularities to perform a joint mention detection and entity disambiguation. Figure 4 shows the layout of the network and its main components.granularity level. The input to the model is a list of question tokens $\mathbf{x}$, a token n-gram n and a list of candidate entities C. Then the model is a function $M(\mathbf{x}, n, C)$ that produces a mention detection score p_n for each n-gram and a ranking score p_c for each of the candidates $c \in C$: $p_n, \mathbf{p_c} = M(\mathbf{x}, n, C)$.

Dilated Convolutions To process sequential input, we use dilated convolutional networks (DCNN). Strubell et al. (2017) have recently shown that DCNNs are faster and as effective as recurrent models on the task of named entity recognition. We define two modules: $\mathbf{DCNN}_w$ and $\mathbf{DCNN}_c$ for processing token-level and character-level input respectively. Both modules consist of a series of convolutions applied with an increasing dilation, as described in Strubell et al. (2017). The output of the convolutions is averaged and transformed by a fully-connected layer.

Context Components The *token component* corresponds to sentence-level features normally defined for EL and encodes the list of question tokens $\mathbf{x}$ into a fixed size vector. It maps the tokens in $\mathbf{x}$ to d_w-dimensional pre-trained word embeddings, using a matrix $\mathbf{W} \in \mathbb{R}^{|V_w| \times d_w}$, where $|V_w|$ is the size of the vocabulary. We use 50-dimensional GloVe embeddings pre-trained on a 6 billion tokens corpus (Pennington et al., 2014). The word embeddings are concatenated with d_p-dimensional position embeddings $\mathbf{P_w} \in \mathbb{R}^{3 \times d_p}$ that are used to denote the tokens that are part of the target n-gram. The concatenated embeddings are processed by $\mathbf{DCNN}_w$ to get a vector $\mathbf{o_s}$.

The character component processes the target token n-gram n on the basis of individual characters. We add one token on the left and on the right to the target mention and map the string of characters to d_z-character embeddings, $\mathbf{Z} \in \mathbb{R}^{|V_z| \times d_z}$. We concatenate the character embeddings with d_p-dimensional position embeddings $\mathbf{P_z} \in \mathbb{R}^{|x| \times d_p}$ and process them with $\mathbf{DCNN}_c$ to get a feature vector $\mathbf{o_n}$.

We use *the character component* with the same learned parameters to encode the label of a candidate entity from the KB as a vector $\mathbf{o_l}$. The parameter sharing between mention encoding and entity label encoding ensures that the representation of a mention is similar to the entity label.

The KB structure is the highest context level included in the model. *The knowledge base structure component* models the entities and relations that are connected to the candidate entity c. First, we map a list of relations $\mathbf{r}$ of the candidate entity to d_r-dimensional pre-trained relations embeddings, using a matrix $\mathbf{R} \in \mathbb{R}^{|V_r| \times d_r}$, where $|V_r|$ is the number of relation types in the KB. We transform the relations embeddings with a single fully-connected layer f_r and then apply a max pooling operation to get a single relation vector $\mathbf{o_r}$ per entity. Similarly, we map a list of entities that are immediately connected to the candidate entity $\mathbf{e}$

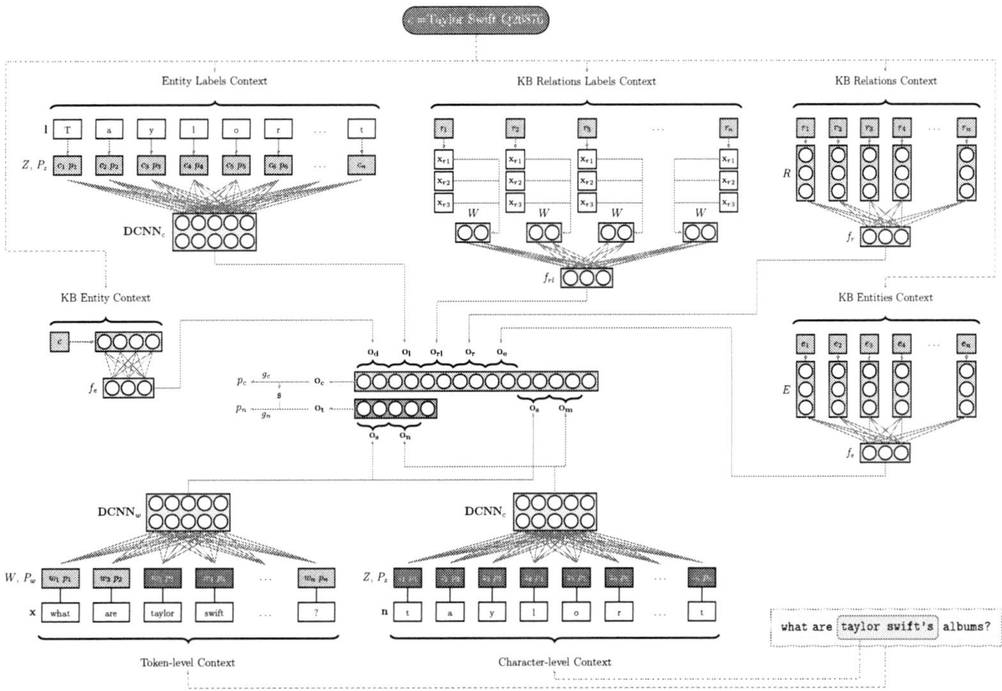

Figure 4: The architecture of the Variable Context Granularity Network for a *single* n-gram and an entity candidate. The output vectors $(\mathbf{o_c}, \mathbf{o_t})$ are aggregated over *all* n-grams for the global assignment

to d_e-dimensional pre-trained entity embeddings, using a matrix $\mathbf{E} \in \mathbb{R}^{|V_e| \times d_e}$, where $|V_e|$ is the number of entities in the KB. The entity embeddings are transformed by a fully-connected layer f_e and then also pooled to produce the output $\mathbf{o_e}$. The embedding of the candidate entity itself is also transformed with f_e and is stored as $\mathbf{o_d}$. To train the knowledge base embeddings, we use the TransE algorithm (Bordes et al., 2013).

Finally, *the knowledge base lexical component* takes the labels of the relations in $\mathbf{r}$ to compute lexical relation embeddings. For each $r \in \mathbf{r}$, we tokenize the label and map the tokens $\mathbf{x_r}$ to word embeddings, using the word embedding matrix $\mathbf{W}$. To get a single lexical embedding per relation, we apply max pooling and transform the output with a fully-connected layer f_{rl}. The lexical relation embeddings for the candidate entity are pooled into the vector $\mathbf{o_{rl}}$.

Context Aggregation The different levels of context are aggregated and are transformed by a sequence of fully-connected layers into a final vector $\mathbf{o_c}$ for the n-gram n and the candidate entity c. The vectors for each candidate are aggregated into a matrix $O = [\mathbf{o_c}|c \in C]$. We apply element-wise

max pooling on O to get a single summary vector $\mathfrak{s}$ for all entity candidates for n.

To get the ranking score p_c for each entity candidate c, we apply a single fully-connected layer g_c on the concatenation of $\mathbf{o_c}$ and the summary vector $\mathfrak{s}$: $p_c = g_c(\mathbf{o_c}\|\mathfrak{s})$. For the mention detection score for the n-gram, we separately concatenate the vectors for the token context $\mathbf{o_s}$ and the character context $\mathbf{o_n}$ and transform them with an array of fully-connected layers into a vector $\mathbf{o_t}$. We concatenate $\mathbf{o_t}$ with the summary vector $\mathfrak{s}$ and apply another fully-connected layer to get the mention detection score $p_n = \sigma(g_n(\mathbf{o_t}\|\mathfrak{s}))$.

3.2 Global Entity Assignment

The first step in our system is extracting all possible overlapping n-grams from the input texts. We assume that each span in the input text can only refer to a single entity and therefore resolve overlaps by computing a global assignment using the model scores for each n-gram (Step 4 in Figure 3).

If the mention detection score p_n is above the 0.5-threshold, the n-gram is predicted to be a correct entity mention and the ranking scores $\mathbf{p_c}$ are used to disambiguate it to a single entity candidate.

N-grams that have p_n lower than the threshold are filtered out.

We follow Guo et al. (2013a) in computing the global assignment and hence, arrange all n-grams selected as mentions into non-overlapping combinations and use the individual scores p_n to compute the probability of each combination. The combination with the highest probability is selected as the final set of entity mentions. We have observed in practice a similar effect as descirbed by Strubell et al. (2017), namely that DCNNs are able to capture dependencies between different entity mentions in the same context and do not tend to produce overlapping mentions.

3.3 Composite Loss Function

Our model jointly computes two scores for each n-gram: the mention detection score p_n and the disambiguation score p_c. We optimize the parameters of the whole model jointly and use the loss function that combines penalties for the both scores for all n-grams in the input question:

$$\mathscr{L} \;=\; \sum_{n \in N} \sum_{c \in C_n} \mathscr{M}(t_n, p_n) \;+\; t_n \mathscr{D}(t_c, p_c),$$

where t_n is the target for mention detection and is either 0 or 1, t_c is the target for disambiguation and ranges from 0 to the number of candidates $|C|$.

For the mention detection loss $\mathscr{M}$, we include a weighting parameter α for the negative class as the majority of the instances in the data are negative:

$$\mathscr{M}(t_n, p_n) = -t_n \log p_n - \alpha(1 - t_n)\log(1 - p_n)$$

The disambiguation detection loss $\mathscr{D}$ is a maximum margin loss:

$$\mathscr{D}(t_c, p_c) = \frac{\sum_{i=0}^{|C|} \max(0, (m - p_c[t_c] + p_c[i]))}{|C|},$$

where m is the margin value. We set $m = 0.5$, whereas the α weight is optimized with the other hyper-parameters.

3.4 Architecture Comparison

Our model architecture follows some of the ideas presented in Francis-Landau et al. (2016): they suggest computing a similarity score between an entity and the context for different context granularities. Francis-Landau et al. (2016) experiment on entity linking for Wikipedia and news articles and consider the word-level and document-level contexts

	#Questions	#Entities
WebQSP Train	3098	3794
WebQSP Test	1639	2002
GraphQuestions Test	2608	4680

Table 1: Dataset statistics

for entity disambiguation. As described above, we also incorporate different context granularities with a number of key differences: (1) we operate on sentence level, word level and character level, thus including a more fine-grained range of contexts; (2) the knowledge base contexts that Francis-Landau et al. (2016) use are the Wikipedia title and the article texts — we, on the other hand, employ the structure of the knowledge base and encode relations and related entities; (3) Francis-Landau et al. (2016) separately compute similarities for each type of context, whereas we mix them in a single end-to-end architecture; (4) we do not rely on manually defined features in our model.

4 Datasets

We compile two new datasets for entity linking on questions that we derive from publicly available question answering data: WebQSP (Yih et al., 2016) and GraphQuestions (Su et al., 2016).

WebQSP contains questions that were originally collected for the WebQuestions dataset from web search logs (Berant et al., 2013). They were manually annotated with SPARQL queries that can be executed to retrieve the correct answer to each question. Additionally, the annotators have also selected the main entity in the question that is central to finding the answer. The annotations and the query use identifiers from the Freebase knowledge base.

We extract all entities that are mentioned in the question from the SPARQL query. For the main entity, we also store the correct span in the text, as annotated in the dataset. In order to be able to use Wikidata in our experiments, we translate the Freebase identifiers to Wikidata IDs.

The second dataset, GraphQuestions, was created by collecting manual paraphrases for automatically generated questions (Su et al., 2016). The dataset is meant to test the ability of the system to understand different wordings of the same question. In particular, the paraphrases include various references to the same entity, which creates a challenge for an entity linking system. The following

	P	R	F1
Heuristic baseline	0.286	0.621	0.392
Simplified VCG	0.804	0.654	0.721
VCG	0.823	0.646	0.724

Table 2: Evaluation results on the WEBQSP development dataset (all entities)

emb. size					filter size		
d_w	d_z	d_e	d_r	d_p	$DCNN_w$	$DCNN_c$	α
50	25	50	50	5	64	64	0.5

Table 3: Best configuration for the VCG model

are three example questions from the dataset that contain a mention of the same entity:

(1)   a.   what is the rank of marvel's **iron man**?
       b.   **iron-man** has held what ranks?
       c.   **tony stark** has held what ranks?

GraphQuestions does not contain main entity annotations, but includes a SPARQL query structurally encoded in JSON format. The queries were constructed manually by identifying the entities in the question and selecting the relevant KB relations. We extract gold entities for each question from the SPARQL query and map them to Wikidata.

We split the WebQSP training set into train and development subsets to optimize the neural model. We use the GraphQuestions only in the evaluation phase to test the generalization power of our model. The sizes of the constructed datasets in terms of the number of questions and the number of entities are reported in Table 1. In both datasets, each question contains at least one correct entity mention.

5 Experiments

5.1 Evaluation Methodology

We use precision, recall and F1 scores to evaluate and compare the approaches. We follow Carmel et al. (2014) and Yang and Chang (2015) and define the scores on a per-entity basis. Since there are no mention boundaries for the gold entities, an extracted entity is considered correct if it is present in the set of the gold entities for the given question. We compute the metrics in the micro and macro setting. The macro values are computed per entity class and averaged afterwards.

For the WebQSP dataset, we additionally perform a separate evaluation using only the information on the main entity. The main entity has the information on the boundary offsets of the correct mentions and therefore for this type of evaluation, we enforce that the extracted mention has to overlap with the correct mention. QA systems need at least one entity per question to attempt to find the correct answer. Thus, evaluating using the main entity shows how the entity linking system fulfills this minimum requirement.

5.2 Baselines

Existing Systems In our experiments, we compare to DBPedia Spotlight that was used in several QA systems and represents a strong baseline for entity linking[4]. In addition, we are able to compare to the state-of-the-art S-MART system, since their output on the WebQSP datasets was publicly released[5]. The S-MART system is not openly available, it was first trained on the NEEL 2014 Twitter dataset and later adapted to the QA data (Yih et al., 2015).

We also include a heuristics baseline that ranks candidate entities according to their frequency in Wikipedia. This baseline represents a reasonable lower bound for a Wikidata based approach.

Simplified VCG To test the effect of the end-to-end context encoders of the VCG network, we define a model that instead uses a set of features commonly suggested in the literature for EL on noisy data. In particular, we employ features that cover (1) frequency of the entity in Wikipedia, (2) edit distance between the label of the entity and the token n-gram, (3) number of entities and relations immediately connected to the entity in the KB, (4) word overlap between the input question and the labels of the connected entities and relations, (5) length of the n-gram. We also add an average of the word embeddings of the question tokens and, separately, an average of the embeddings of tokens of entities and relations connected to the entity candidate. We train the simplified VCG model by optimizing the same loss function in Section 3.3 on the same data.

5.3 Practical Considerations

The hyper-parameters of the model, such as the dimensionality of the layers and the size of embed-

---

[4]We use the online end-point: `http://www.dbpedia-spotlight.org/api`

[5]`https://github.com/scottyih/STAGG`

	Main entity			All entities					
	P	R	F1	P	R	F1	mP	mR	mF1
DBPedia Spotlight	0.668	0.595	0.629	0.705	0.514	0.595	0.572	0.392	0.452
S-MART	0.634	**0.899**	0.744	0.666	**0.772**	0.715	0.607	**0.610**	0.551
Heuristic baseline	0.282	0.694	0.401	0.302	0.608	0.404	0.330	0.537	0.378
Simplified VCG	**0.804**	0.728	0.764	**0.837**	0.621	0.713	0.659	0.494	0.546
VCG	0.793	0.766	**0.780**	0.826	0.653	**0.730**	**0.676**	0.519	**0.568**

Table 4: Evaluation results on the WEBQSP test dataset, the m prefix stands for *macro*

	P	R	F1
DBPedia Spotlight	0.386	0.453	0.417
VCG	**0.589**	0.354	**0.442**

Table 5: Evaluation results on GRAPHQUESTIONS

dings, are optimized with random search on the development set. The model was particularly sensitive to tuning of the negative class weight α (see Section 3.3). Table 3 lists the main selected hyper-parameters for the VCG model[6] and we also report the results for each model's best configuration on the development set in Table 2.

5.4 Results

Table 4 lists results for the heuristics baseline, for the suggested Variable Context Granularity model (VCG) and for the simplified VCG baseline on the test set of WebQSP. The simplified VCG model outperforms DBPedia Spotlight and achieves a result very close to the S-MART model. Considering only the main entity, the simplified VCG model produces results better than both DBPedia Spotlight and S-MART. The VCG model delivers the best F-score across the all setups. We observe that our model achieves the most gains in precision compared to the baselines and the previous state-of-the-art for QA data.

VCG constantly outperforms the simplified VCG baseline that was trained by optimizing the same loss function but uses manually defined features. Thereby, we confirm the advantage of the mixing context granularities strategy that was suggested in this work. Most importantly, the VCG model achieves the best macro result which indicates that the model has a consistent performance on different entity classes.

<hr>

[6]The complete list of hyper-parameters and model characteristics can be found in the accompanying code repository.

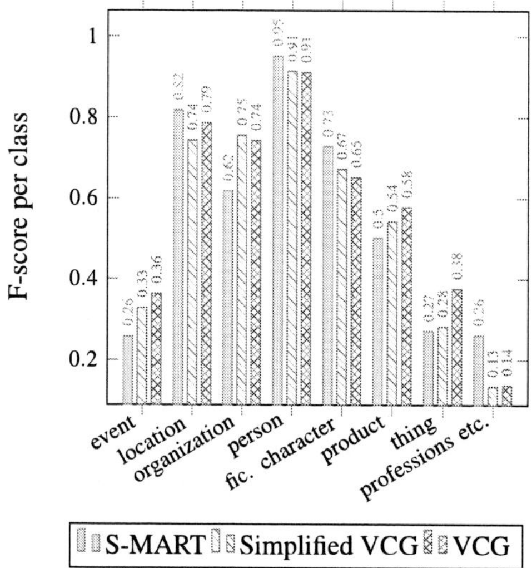

Figure 5: Performance accross entity classes on WEBQSP test dataset

We further evaluate the developed VCG architecture on the GraphQuestions dataset against the DBPedia Spotlight. We use this dataset to evaluate VCG in an out-of-domain setting: neither our system nor DBPedia Spotlight were trained on it. The results for each model are presented in Table 5. We can see that GraphQuestions provides a much more difficult benchmark for EL. The VCG model shows the overall F-score result that is better than the DBPedia Spotlight baseline by a wide margin. It is notable that again our model achieves higher precision values as compared to other approaches and manages to keep a satisfactory level of recall.

Analysis In order to better understand the performance difference between the approaches and the gains of the VCG model, we analyze the results per entity class (see Figure 5). We see that the S-MART system is slightly better in the disambiguation of Locations, Person names and a similar

	Main entity			All entities					
	P	R	F1	P	R	F1	mP	mR	mF1
VCG	0.793	**0.766**	<u>**0.780**</u>	**0.826**	**0.653**	<u>**0.730**</u>	**0.676**	**0.519**	<u>**0.568**</u>
w/o token context	0.782	0.728	0.754	0.812	0.618	0.702	0.664	0.474	0.530
w/o character context	**0.802**	0.684	0.738	0.820	0.573	0.675	0.667	0.404	0.471
w/o KB structure context	0.702	0.679	0.690	0.728	0.576	0.643	0.549	0.427	0.461
w/o KB lexical context	0.783	0.732	0.756	0.807	0.617	0.699	0.643	0.454	0.508

Table 6: Ablation experiments for the VCG model on WEBQSP

category of Fictional Character names, while it has a considerable advantage in processing of Professions and Common Nouns. Our approach has an edge in such entity classes as Organization, Things and Products. The latter category includes movies, book titles and songs, which are particularly hard to identify and disambiguate since any sequence of words can be a title. VCG is also considerably better in recognizing Events. We conclude that the future development of the VCG architecture should focus on the improved identification and disambiguation of professions and common nouns.

To analyze the effect that mixing various context granularities has on the model performance, we include ablation experiment results for the VCG model (see Table 6). We report the same scores as in the main evaluation but without individual model components that were described in Section 3.

We can see that the removal of the KB structure information encoded in entity and relation embeddings results in the biggest performance drop of almost 10 percentage points. The character-level information also proves to be highly important for the final state-of-the-art performance. These aspects of the model (the comprehensive representation of the KB structure and the character-level information) are two of the main differences of our approach to the previous work. Finally, we see that excluding the token-level input and the lexical information about the related KB relations also decrease the results, albeit less dramatically.

6 Conclusions

We have described the task of entity linking on QA data and its challenges. The suggested new approach for this task is a unifying network that models contexts of variable granularity to extract features for mention detection and entity disambiguation. This system achieves state-of-the-art results on two datasets and outperforms the pre-

vious best system used for EL on QA data. The results further verify that modeling different types of context helps to achieve a better performance across various entity classes (macro f-score).

Most recently, Peng et al. (2017) and Yu et al. (2017) have attempted to incorporate entity linking into a QA model. This offers an exciting future direction for the Variable Context Granularity model.

Acknowledgments

This work has been supported by the German Research Foundation as part of the Research Training Group Adaptive Preparation of Information from Heterogeneous Sources (AIPHES) under grant No. GRK 1994/1, and via the QA-EduInf project (grant GU 798/18-1 and grant RI 803/12-1).

We gratefully acknowledge the support of NVIDIA Corporation with the donation of the Titan X Pascal GPU used for this research.

References

Luisa Bentivogli, Pamela Forner, Claudio Giuliano, Alessandro Marchetti, Emanuele Pianta, and Kateryna Tymoshenko. 2010. Extending English ACE 2005 corpus annotation with ground-truth links to Wikipedia. In *Proceedings of the 2nd Workshop on Collaboratively Constructed Semantic Resources at the 23rd International Conference on Computational Linguistics (Coling)*. Beijing, China, pages 19–26. http://www.aclweb.org/anthology/W10-3503.

Jonathan Berant, Andrew Chou, Roy Frostig, and Percy Liang. 2013. Semantic Parsing on Freebase from Question-Answer Pairs. In *Proceedings of the Conference on Empirical Methods in Natural Language Processing (EMNLP)*. Seattle, WA, USA, pages 1533–1544. http://www.aclweb.org/anthology/D13-1160.

Jonathan Berant and Percy Liang. 2014. Semantic Parsing via Paraphrasing. In *Proceedings of 52nd Annual Meeting of the Association for Computational Linguistics (ACL)*. Baltimore, MD, USA, pages 1415–1425. https://doi.org/10.3115/v1/P14-1133.

Antoine Bordes, Nicolas Usunier, Jason Weston, and Oksana Yakhnenko. 2013. Translating Embeddings for Modeling Multi-Relational Data. In C. J. C. Burges, L. Bottou, M. Welling, Z. Ghahramani, and K. Q. Weinberger, editors, *Advances in Neural Information Processing Systems (NIPS)*. Curran Associates, Inc., Lake Tahoe, NV, USA, volume 26, pages 2787–2795.

Razvan Bunescu and Marius Pasca. 2006. Using Encyclopedic Knowledge for Named Entity Disambiguation. In *Proceedings of the 11th Conference of the European Chapter of the Association for Computational Linguistics (EACL)*. Trento, Italy, pages 9–16. http://aclweb.org/anthology/E06-1002.

David Carmel, Ming-Wei Chang, Evgeniy Gabrilovich, Bo-June (Paul) Hsu, and Kuansan Wang. 2014. ERD'14: Entity Recognition and Disambiguation Challenge. In *ACM SIGIR Forum*. volume 48, pages 63–77. https://doi.org/10.1145/2600428.2600734.

Ming-Wei Chang, Bo-June Hsu, Hao Ma, Ricky Loynd, and Kuansan Wang. 2014. E2E: An End-to-End Entity Linking System for Short and Noisy text. In *Proceedings of the the 4thWorkshop on Making Sense of Microposts co-located with the 23rd International World Wide Web Conference (WWW)*. Seoul, Korea, pages 62–63.

Long Chen, Joemon M. Jose, Haitao Yu, Fajie Yuan, and Dell Zhang. 2016. A Semantic Graph based Topic Model for Question Retrieval in Community Question Answering. In *Proceedings of the 9th ACM International Conference on Web Search and Data Mining (WSDM)*. San Francisco, CA, USA, pages 287–296. https://doi.org/10.1145/2835776.2835809.

Silviu Cucerzan. 2007. Large-Scale Named Entity Disambiguation Based on Wikipedia Data. In *Proceedings of the 2007 Joint Conference on Empirical Methods in Natural Language Processing and Computational Natural Language Learning (EMNLP-CoNLL)*. Prague, Czech Republic, pages 708–716. http://aclweb.org/anthology/D07-1074.

Silviu Cucerzan. 2012. The MSR System for Entity Linking at TAC 2012. In *Proceedings of the Text Analysis Conference (TAC)*. Gaithersburg, MD, USA, pages 14–15.

Matthew Francis-Landau, Greg Durrett, and Dan Klein. 2016. Capturing Semantic Similarity for Entity Linking with Convolutional Neural Networks. In *Annual Conference of the North American Chapter of the Association for Computational Linguistics (NAACL)*. San Diego, CA, USA, pages 1256–1261. https://doi.org/10.18653/v1/N16-1150.

Stephen Guo, Ming-Wei Chang, and Emre Kcman. 2013a. To Link or Not to Link? A Study on End-to-End Tweet Entity Linking. In *Proceedings of the 2013 Conference of the North American Chapter of the Association for Computational Linguistics: Human Language Technologies (NAACL-HLT)*. Atlanta, GA, USA, pages 1020–1030. http://www.aclweb.org/anthology/N13-1122.

Yuhang Guo, Bing Qin, Ting Liu, and Sheng Li. 2013b. Microblog entity linking by leveraging extra posts. In *Proceedings of the 2013 Conference on Empirical Methods in Natural Language Processing (EMNLP)*. pages 863–868. http://www.aclweb.org/anthology/D13-1085.

Xianpei Han and Le Sun. 2012. An entity-topic model for entity linking. In *Proceedings of the 2012 Joint Conference on Empirical Methods in Natural Language Processing and Computational Natural Language Learning (EMNLP-CoNLL)*. Jeju Island, Korea, pages 105–115. http://www.aclweb.org/anthology/D12-1010.

Johannes Hoffart, Mohamed Amir Yosef, Ilaria Bordino, Hagen Fürstenau, Manfred Pinkal, Marc Spaniol, Bilyana Taneva, Stefan Thater, and Gerhard Weikum. 2011. Robust Disambiguation of Named Entities in Text. In *Proceedings of the 2011 Conference on Empirical Methods in Natural Language Processing (EMNLP)*. Edinburgh, UK, pages 782–792. http://www.aclweb.org/anthology/D11-1072.

Vanessa Lopez, Pierpaolo Tommasi, Spyros Kotoulas, and Jiewen Wu. 2016. QuerioDALI: Question answering over dynamic and linked knowledge graphs. In *The Semantic Web - 15th International Semantic Web Conference (ISWC 2016)*. Springer International Publishing, Kobe, Japan, pages 363–382. https://doi.org/10.1007/978-3-319-46547-0_32.

Gang Luo, Xiaojiang Huang, Chin-Yew Lin, and Zaiqing Nie. 2015. Joint Named Entity Recognition and Disambiguation. In *Proceedings of the 2015 Conference on Empirical Methods in Natural Language Processing (EMNLP)*. Lisbon, Portugal. https://doi.org/10.18653/v1/D15-1104.

Christopher D. Manning, John Bauer, Jenny Finkel, Steven J. Bethard, Mihai Surdeanu, and David McClosky. 2014. The Stanford CoreNLP Natural Language Processing Toolkit. In *Proceedings of 52nd Annual Meeting of the Association for Computational Linguistics (ACL): System Demonstrations*. Baltimore, MD, USA, pages 55–60. https://doi.org/10.3115/v1/P14-5010.

Pablo N. Mendes, Max Jakob, Andrés García-Silva, and Christian Bizer. 2011. DBpedia Spotlight: Shedding Light on the Web of Documents. In *Proceedings of the 7th International Conference on Semantic Systems (I-Semantics)*. Graz, Austria, volume 95, pages 1–8. https://doi.org/10.1145/2063518.2063519.

Haoruo Peng, Ming-Wei Chang, and Wen-Tau Yih. 2017. Maximum Margin Reward Networks for

Learning from Explicit and Implicit Supervision. In *Proceedings of the 2017 Conference on Empirical Methods in Natural Language Processing (EMNLP)*. Copenhagen, Denmark, pages 2358–2368. https://doi.org/10.18653/v1/D17-1252.

Jeffrey Pennington, Richard Socher, and Christopher D. Manning. 2014. GloVe: Global Vectors for Word Representation. In *Proceedings of the 2014 Conference on Empirical Methods in Natural Language Processing (EMNLP)*. pages 1532–1543. https://doi.org/10.3115/v1/D14-1162.

Siva Reddy, Mirella Lapata, and Mark Steedman. 2014. Large-scale Semantic Parsing without Question-Answer Pairs. *Transactions of the Association for Computational Linguistics* 2:377–392. http://aclweb.org/anthology/Q14-1030.

Siva Reddy, Oscar Täckström, Michael Collins, Tom Kwiatkowski, Dipanjan Das, Mark Steedman, and Mirella Lapata. 2016. Transforming Dependency Structures to Logical Forms for Semantic Parsing. *Transactions of the Association for Computational Linguistics* 4:127–140. http://aclweb.org/anthology/Q16-1010.

Giuseppe Rizzo, Bianca Pereira, Andrea Varga, Marieke Van Erp, and Amparo Elizabeth Cano Basave. 2017. Lessons learnt from the Named Entity rEcognition and Linking (NEEL) Challenge Series. *Semantic Web* 8(5):667–700. https://doi.org/10.3233/SW-170276.

Avirup Sil, Gourab Kundu, Radu Florian, and Wael Hamza. 2018. Neural Cross-Lingual Entity Linking. In *Association for the Advancement of Artificial Intelligence (AAAI)*. New Orleans, LA, US.

Emma Strubell, Patrick Verga, David Belanger, and Andrew McCallum. 2017. Fast and Accurate Entity Recognition with Iterated Dilated Convolutions. In *Proceedings of the 2017 Conference on Empirical Methods in Natural Language Processing (EMNLP)*. Copenhagen, Denmark, pages 2670–2680. https://doi.org/10.18653/v1/D17-1283.

Yu Su, Huan Sun, Brian Sadler, Mudhakar Srivatsa, Izzeddin Gur, Zenghui Yan, and Xifeng Yan. 2016. On Generating Characteristic-rich Question Sets for QA Evaluation. In *Proceedings of the 2016 Conference on Empirical Methods in Natural Language Processing (EMNLP)*. Austin, Texas, pages 562–572. https://doi.org/10.18653/v1/D16-1054.

Yaming Sun, Lei Lin, Duyu Tang, Nan Yang, Zhenzhou Ji, and Xiaolong Wang. 2015. Modeling mention, context and entity with neural networks for entity disambiguation. In *Proceedings of the International Joint Conference on Artificial Intelligence (IJCAI)*. Buenos Aires, Argentina, pages 1333–1339.

Denny Vrandečić and Markus Krötzsch. 2014. Wikidata: A Free Collaborative Knowledgebase. *Communications of the ACM* 57(10):78–85. https://doi.org/10.1021/ac60289a702.

Yi Yang and Ming-Wei Chang. 2015. S-MART: Novel Tree-based Structured Learning Algorithms Applied to Tweet Entity Linking. In *Proceedings of the 53rd Annual Meeting of the Association for Computational Linguistics and the 7th International Joint Conference on Natural Language Processing (ACL-IJCNLP)*. Beijing, China, pages 504–513. https://doi.org/10.3115/v1/P15-1049.

Wen-tau Yih, Ming-Wei Chang, Xiaodong He, and Jianfeng Gao. 2015. Semantic Parsing via Staged Query Graph Generation: Question Answering with Knowledge Base. In *Proceedings of the 53rd Annual Meeting of the Association for Computational Linguistics and the 7th International Joint Conference on Natural Language Processing (ACL-IJCNLP)*. Beijing, China, pages 1321–1331. https://doi.org/10.3115/v1/P15-1128.

Wen-tau Yih, Matthew Richardson, Christopher Meek, Ming-Wei Chang, and Jina Suh. 2016. The Value of Semantic Parse Labeling for Knowledge Base Question Answering. In *Proceedings of the 54th Annual Meeting of the Association for Computational Linguistics (ACL)*. Berlin, Germany, pages 201–206. https://doi.org/10.18653/v1/P16-2033.

Mo Yu, Wenpeng Yin, Kazi Saidul Hasan, Cicero dos Santos, Bing Xiang, and Bowen Zhou. 2017. Improved Neural Relation Detection for Knowledge Base Question Answering. In *Proceedings of the 55th Annual Meeting of the Association for Computational Linguistics (ACL)*. Vancouver, Canada, pages 571–581. https://doi.org/10.18653/v1/P17-1053.

Quantitative Semantic Variation
in the Contexts of Concrete and Abstract Words

Daniela Naumann   **Diego Frassinelli**   **Sabine Schulte im Walde**

Institut für Maschinelle Sprachverarbeitung, Universität Stuttgart

{naumanda,frassinelli,schulte}@ims.uni-stuttgart.de

Abstract

Across disciplines, researchers are eager to gain insight into empirical features of abstract vs. concrete concepts. In this work, we provide a detailed characterisation of the distributional nature of abstract and concrete words across 16,620 English nouns, verbs and adjectives. Specifically, we investigate the following questions: (1) What is the distribution of concreteness in the contexts of concrete and abstract target words? (2) What are the differences between concrete and abstract words in terms of contextual semantic diversity? (3) How does the entropy of concrete and abstract word contexts differ? Overall, our studies show consistent differences in the distributional representation of concrete and abstract words, thus challenging existing theories of cognition and providing a more fine-grained description of their nature.

1   Introduction

The complete understanding of the cognitive mechanisms behind the processing of concrete and abstract meanings represents a key and still open question in cognitive science (Barsalou and Wiemer-Hastings, 2005). More specifically, the psycholinguistic literature reports extensive analyses of how concrete concepts are processed, however there is still little consensus about the nature of abstract concepts (Barsalou and Wiemer-Hastings, 2005; McRae and Jones, 2013; Hill et al., 2014; Vigliocco et al., 2014).

The *Context Availability Theory* represents one of the earliest theoretical approaches aiming to account for the differences between concrete and abstract concepts (Schwanenflugel and Shoben, 1983). This theory suggests that meaning arises from the ability to create an appropriate context for a concept, which has proven to be more challenging (i.e., enforcing higher reaction times and

larger number of errors) for abstract than for concrete concepts. In a computational study, Hill et al. (2014) quantitatively analysed the distinction between concrete and abstract words in a large corpus. Overall, they showed that abstract words occur within a broad range of context words while concrete words occur within a smaller set of context words. Similarly, Hoffman et al. (2013) and Hoffman and Woollams (2015) analysed the concrete vs. abstract dichotomy in terms of their semantic diversity, demonstrating that concrete words occur within highly similar contexts while abstract words occur in a broad range of less associated contexts (i.e., exhibiting high semantic diversity). These computational findings are fully in line with the Context Availability Theory: the processing time of concrete words is generally shorter than the processing time of abstract words, as abstract words are attached to a broad range of loosely associated words.

More recently, embodied theories of cognition have suggested that word meanings are grounded in the sensory-motor system (Barsalou and Wiemer-Hastings, 2005; Glenberg and Kaschak, 2002; Hill et al., 2014; Pecher et al., 2011). According to this account, concrete concepts have a direct referent in the real world, while abstract concepts have to activate a series of concrete concepts that provide the necessary situational context required to successfully process their meanings (Barsalou, 1999).

These interdisciplinary outcomes are not fully supported by recent computational studies showing different contextual patterns for concrete and abstract words in text compared to the literature (Bhaskar et al., 2017; Frassinelli et al., 2017). It is becoming clear, however, that the inclusion of information regarding the concreteness of words plays a key role in the automatic identification of non-literal language usage (Turney et al., 2011;

*Proceedings of the 7th Joint Conference on Lexical and Computational Semantics (*SEM)*, pages 76–85
New Orleans, June 5-6, 2018. ©2018 Association for Computational Linguistics

Köper and Schulte im Walde, 2016, 2017).

The aim of the current study is thus to provide a contextual description of the distributional representation of these two classes of words, to gain insight into empirical features of abstract vs. concrete concepts. This would represent an essential contribution to the resolution of the debate about meaning representation within the human mind, and thereby also help to enhance computationally derived models that are concerned with meaning derivation from text.

2 Hypotheses

Based on the existing psycholinguistic and computational evidence reported in the previous section, we formulate three hypotheses regarding the distributional nature of concrete and abstract words that we will test in the following studies.

(1) The contexts of both concrete and abstract words are mainly composed of concrete words.

This first hypothesis directly tests the general claim of grounding theories: both concrete and abstract words require the activation of a layer of situational (concrete) information in order to be successfully processed (Barsalou and Wiemer-Hastings, 2005). According to the *Distributional Hypothesis* (Harris, 1954; Firth, 1968), similar linguistic contexts tend to imply similar meanings of words. Thus, we suggest to perform a distributional semantic analysis in order to quantitatively investigate the contexts that concrete and abstract words frequently co-occur within.

(2) Abstract words occur in a broad range of distinct contexts whereas concrete words appear in a limited set of contexts.

Based on the computational study by Hill et al. (2014), we expect to find concrete words appearing in a more restricted set of contexts in comparison to abstract words, which should occur in a broad range of contexts. This second hypothesis is explored by providing two fine-grained analyses of the extension and variety in contexts of concrete and abstract words.

(3) Abstract words are more difficult to predict than concrete words, due to their higher contextual variability.

Building upon the previous hypothesis and on the studies by Hoffman et al. (2013) and Hoffman and Woollams (2015), we aim to show that concrete words are easier to predict than abstract words. Specifically, we expect higher entropy values for abstract than for concrete contexts, indicating that on average, we need more information to uniquely encode an abstract word than a concrete word (Shannon, 2001). The reason resides within the high context variability of abstract words: there is a large number of highly probable words satisfying these contexts. In contrast, we expect concrete words to occur in a limited set of different contexts because there is only a restricted amount of words that have a high probability to fit a specific context. Thus, we estimate the entropy value of concrete contexts to be lower than the entropy value of abstract contexts.

In the three studies reported in this paper, we systematically test these three hypotheses regarding concrete vs. abstract words, by performing quantitative analyses of the distributional representations across the word classes of nouns, verbs and adjectives.

3 Materials and Method

For our studies, we selected nouns, verbs and adjectives from the Brysbaert et al. (2014) collection of concreteness ratings for 40,000 English words. In total we used 16,620 target words including 9,240 nouns, 3,976 verbs and 3,404 adjectives.[1] Each word in this collection has been scored by humans according to its concreteness on a scale from 1 (abstract) to 5 (concrete).

Our distributional semantic representations of the target words were built by extracting co-occurrences from the POS-tagged version (Schmid, 1994) of the sentence-shuffled English *COW* corpus *ENCOW16AX* (Schäfer and Bildhauer, 2012). We originally constructed three different spaces with window sizes of 2, 10, and 20 context words surrounding the target, and performed parallel analyses for all the three spaces. Since we did not find any relevant differences between the three spaces, we will report only the analyses based on the distributional space from a window size of 20 context words. Moreover, we

---

[1] The reason why we only used a subset of the available targets was that these were also covered in an extensive selection of behavioural measures, such as valency scores (Warriner et al., 2013) and reaction times (Balota et al., 2007) which we aim to include in further analyses.

restricted the dimensions in our matrix to 16,620 × 16,620 (target words × context words). By using the target words also as context words, we had knowledge about the concreteness score of each context word. In a follow-up study, we performed the same analyses extracting co-occurrences from the British National Corpus (Burnard, 2000). Even though both the size and the nature of these two corpora are extremely different, the results did not show any significant difference.

In order to get a clearer picture about empirical distributional differences for concrete vs. abstract targets, we focused some of our analyses only on the most concrete and abstract targets, expecting words with mid-range concreteness scores to be more difficult in their generation by humans and consequently noisier in their distributional representation. For this reason, we analysed the 1,000 most concrete (concreteness range: 4.82 - 5.00) and the 1,000 most abstract (1.07 - 2.17) nouns, the 500 most concrete (4.71 - 5.00) and most abstract (1.12 - 2.21) verbs, and the 200 most concrete (4.34 - 5.00) and most abstract (1.19 - 1.64) adjectives. On the other hand, context was not subset and consisted of the complete set of 16,620 nouns, verbs and adjectives.

4 Study 1: Analysis of Concrete vs. Abstract Co-Occurrences

In this study we test the validity of hypothesis (1): the contexts of both concrete and abstract words are mainly concrete. For this purpose, we analyse the distributions of the 16,620 context dimensions for their concreteness, by the parts-of-speech of target and context words.

Noun Targets Figure 1 reports the distribution of noun, verb and adjective contexts for the 1,000 most abstract target nouns (Figure 1a) in comparison to the 1,000 most concrete target nouns (Figure 1b). As clearly shown in Figure 1a, the majority of contexts of an abstract noun are also abstract: noun, verb and adjective context words all show the maximum peak at low concreteness scores. On the contrary, the distributions of the contexts of concrete nouns shown in Figure 1b vary according to POS. The nouns in the context of concrete noun targets are also very concrete as shown by the high red bar at concreteness 4.5–5.

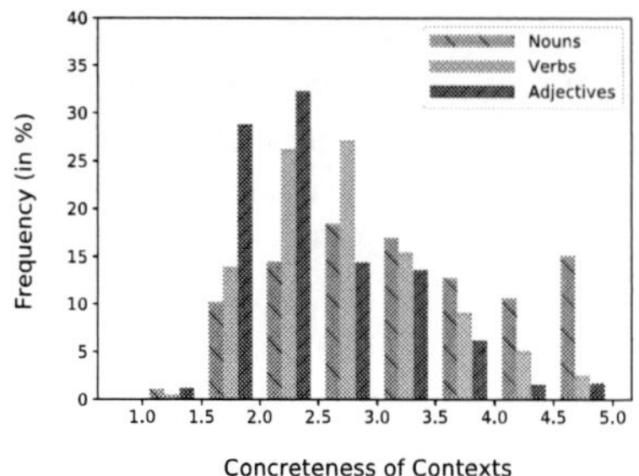

(a) Contexts of abstract noun targets.

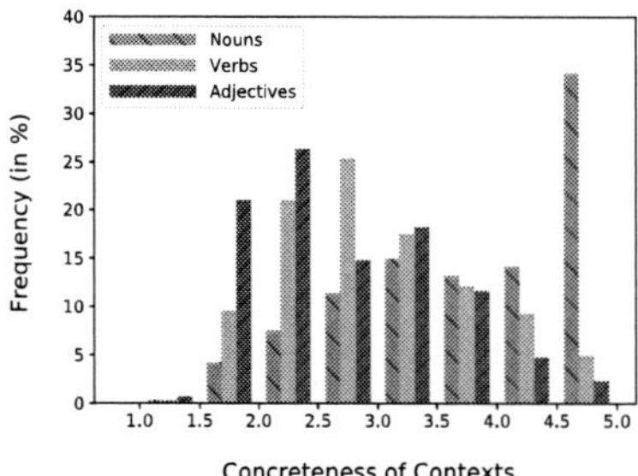

(b) Contexts of concrete noun targets.

Figure 1: Concreteness scores of context words (nouns, verbs, adjectives) of the 1,000 most abstract and concrete noun targets.

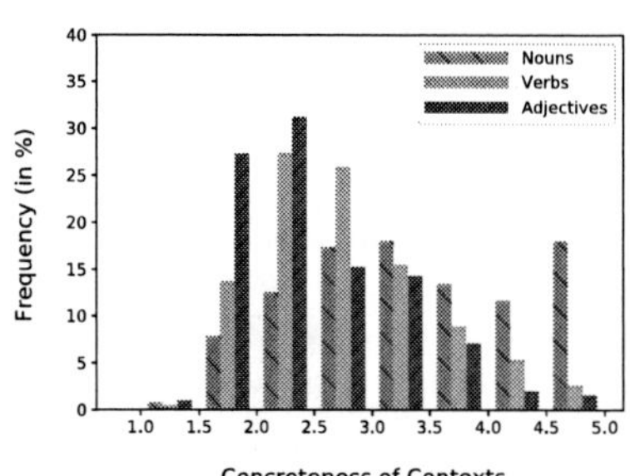

(a) Contexts of abstract verb targets.

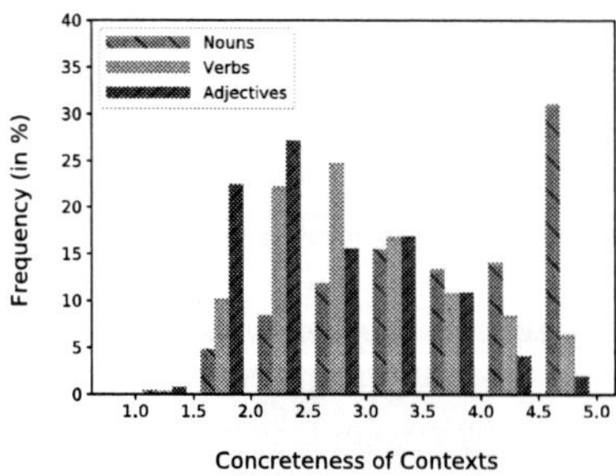

(b) Contexts of concrete verb targets.

Figure 2: Concreteness scores of context words (nouns, verbs, adjectives) of the 500 most abstract and concrete verb targets.

On the other hand, verbs and adjectives show a similar pattern to Figure 1a: a greater distribution with low concreteness scores.

Verb Targets Figure 2 shows a very comparable pattern to the one described for noun targets. Contexts of abstract verbs are, on average, also abstract, regardless of their POS. On the other hand, the verbs and adjectives in the contexts of concrete verb targets are mainly abstract, while the nouns are mainly concrete.

Adjective Targets Again, Figure 3 shows the same pattern as the one reported for nouns and verbs.

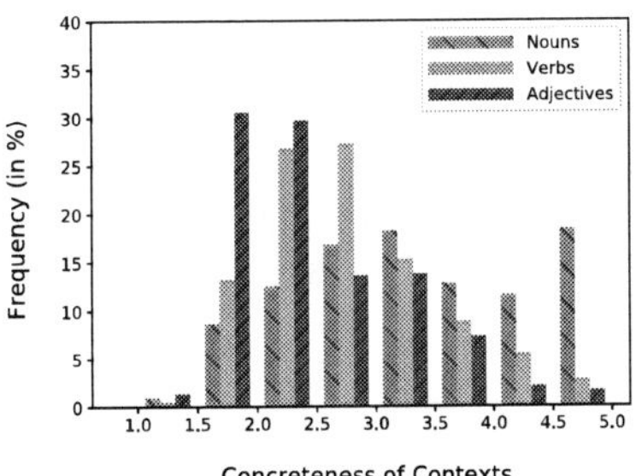

(a) Contexts of abstract adjective targets.

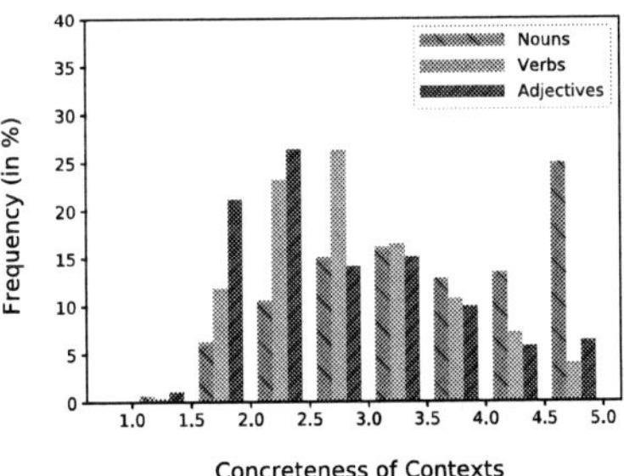

(b) Contexts of concrete adjective targets.

Figure 3: Concreteness scores of context words (nouns, verbs, adjectives) of the 200 most abstract and concrete adjective targets.

Discussion Table 1 reports an overview of the outcomes of this first study. The "X" indicates the predominant contextual class (abstract vs. concrete words) for each target class by POS. All in all, our results partly disagree with our first hypothesis induced from observations in the literature, within the scope of which we expected the context of concrete and abstract words to be mostly composed of concrete words.

Target Words	Context Words					
	abst. NN	abst. V	abst ADJ	conc. NN	conc. V	conc. ADJ
abstract NN	X	X	X			
abstract V	X	X	X			
abstract ADJ	X	X	X			
concrete NN		X	X	X		
concrete V		X	X	X		
concrete ADJ		X	X	X		

X = most frequent context type

Table 1: Evaluation of hypothesis (1).

More specifically, our first hypothesis is confirmed, on the one hand, by the contextual distribution of concrete target nouns, due to the fact that they frequently appear with other concrete nouns. On the contrary, it is rejected by the contextual ratio of abstract nouns as they primarily co-occur with other abstract nouns. Thus, as we based our hypothesis on the theory of embodied cognition, the observed contextual pattern of abstract nouns challenges this theory.

Another evidence in favour of our hypothesis comes from the nouns in the context of concrete verbs and adjectives that are mainly concrete. In contrast, concrete and abstract nouns, verbs and adjectives elicit the same contextual pattern regarding context verbs and adjectives. They co-occur with abstract verbs and abstract adjectives to a large extent, which does not support the expectations based on the existing literature.

5 Study 2: Semantic Diversity of Context

In this study, we test our second hypothesis: abstract words occur in a broad range of distinct contexts whereas concrete words appear in a limited set of different contexts. In the following sections we report two studies where we analyse (i) the number of non-zero dimensions in the representation of concrete vs. abstract words, and (ii) the degree of semantic variability in their contexts.

5.1 Non-Zero Dimensions

The analysis of the number of non-zero dimensions in the vector representation of concrete and abstract words provides a first indicator of the contextual richness of our targets. Based on Hill et al. (2014), we expect concrete target words to have significantly less diverse context dimensions than abstract target words, as the former should co-occur within a restricted set of context words. Therefore, we expect the portion of non-zero context dimensions to be smaller for concrete than for abstract target words.

The following analyses compare the proportions of non-zero context dimensions between the 1,000 highly concrete (blue boxes) and highly abstract (red boxes) target nouns, 500 verbs, and 200 adjectives, based on raw frequency counts. For each POS, we compared the proportion of non-zero dimensions in the full vectors of 16,620 context words for concrete and abstract target words (left side), and the number of non-zero dimensions with the same part-of-speech of the target (respectively, 9,240 context nouns, 3,976 context verbs, 3,404 context adjectives). The star ($\star$) indicates the mean number of non-zero dimensions.

Noun Targets As shown in Figure 4, the comparison of non-zero context dimensions of concrete (M = 57.80, SD = 23.07) and abstract (M = 57.78, SD = 22.57) target nouns does not show any significant difference (t(33238) = -0.02, p = 0.98). This result indicates that concrete and abstract target nouns co-occur with a similar amount of context words. We can observe the exact same pattern when we restrict the contexts to nouns only: no significant difference between the number of non-zero context noun dimensions for concrete (M = 32.12, SD = 12.98) and abstract (M = 31.78, SD = 12.76) target nouns (t(18478) = -0.59, p = 0.56).

Verb Targets Figure 5 reports the number of non-zero dimensions for concrete and abstract verbs. When considering the full set of contexts (left side), concrete words (M = 37.93, SD = 22.5) have significantly less active contexts than abstract words (M = 64.2, SD = 25.73; t(33238) = 17.18, p < 0.001). The exact same outcome is shown when focusing only on verbs as contexts (t(7950) = 16.3, p < 0.001).

Adjective Targets The analysis of the adjectives in Figure 6 indicates that the number of non-zero dimensions for concrete and abstract adjectives follows the same pattern as the verbs. When considering the full set of contexts (left side), concrete adjectives (M = 40.4, SD = 24.7) have significantly less active contexts than abstract adjectives (M = 59.46, SD = 19.11, t(33238) = 8.63, p < 0.001). The exact same outcome is shown when focusing only on adjectives as contexts (t(6806) = 10.15, p < 0.001).

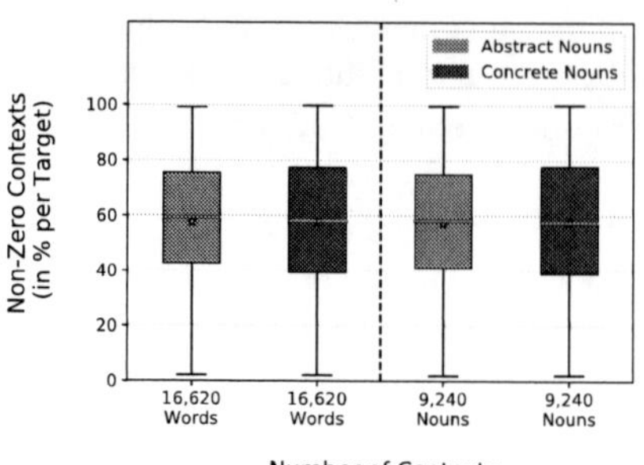

Figure 4: Non-zero dimensions in the contexts of the 1,000 most abstract (red boxes) and concrete (blue boxes) noun targets.

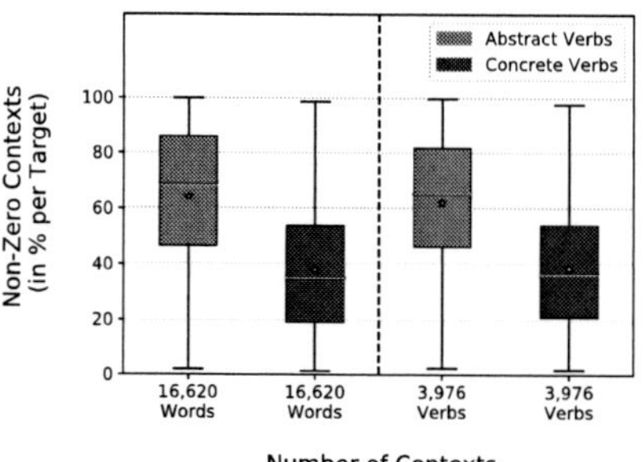

Figure 5: Non-zero dimensions in the contexts of the 500 most abstract (red boxes) and concrete (blue boxes) verb targets.

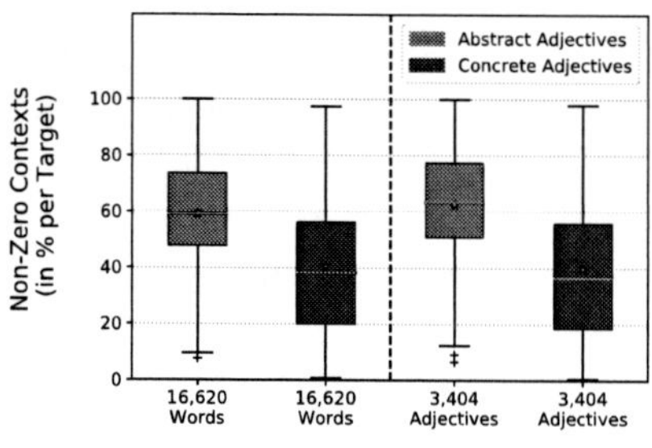

Figure 6: Non-zero dimensions in the contexts of the 200 most abstract (red boxes) and concrete (blue boxes) adjectives.

5.2 Semantic Diversity of Context

Based on hypothesis (2), we expect the contexts of concrete words to be more similar among themselves than the contexts of abstract words. We test this hypothesis by computing the semantic diversity of the contexts of concrete and abstract targets. Semantic diversity corresponds to the inverse of the average semantic similarity of each pair of context dimensions of a word (Hoffman et al., 2013). In order to control for pure frequency effects, we transformed the co-occurrence frequency counts into local mutual information (LMI) scores (Evert, 2005).

The study reports the average cosine similarity between context dimensions for concrete and abstract words; the analysis is conducted incrementally, including the top-k most associated context dimensions (from 5 to 16,620 associates) sorted by their LMI scores.

Noun Targets Figure 7 reports the average semantic similarity between the context dimensions of the 1,000 most concrete (blue boxes) and the 1,000 most abstract (red boxes) target nouns. The analysis is performed step-wise from left to right, starting with the average similarity between the 5 most associated contexts and moving up to the average similarity between all 16,620 context dimensions. Overall, while increasing the number of dimensions, both the mean similarity and also the differences in mean between concrete and abstract words drop, while remaining significant. The difference between the mean cosine similarity of the most associated contexts of concrete (M = 0.32, SD = 0.14 at k = 5) and abstract (M = 0.20, SD = 0.13 at k = 5) target nouns is significant (p < 0.001 at k = 5).

Verb Targets As shown in Figure 8, there are no significant differences (p = 0.38 at k = 5) in the similarity of the context dimensions of the 500 most concrete (M = 0.23, SD = 0.15 at k = 5) and most abstract (M = 0.23, SD = 0.16 at k = 5) verb targets.

Adjective Targets When analysing the similarity of the contexts of the 200 most concrete and abstract adjectives we see (Figure 9) the same pattern as shown for nouns. The average similarity of the most associated contexts is significantly higher (p<0.001 at k = 5) for concrete (M = 0.26, SD = 0.14 at k = 5) than for abstract (M = 0.17, SD = 0.12 at k = 5) target adjectives.

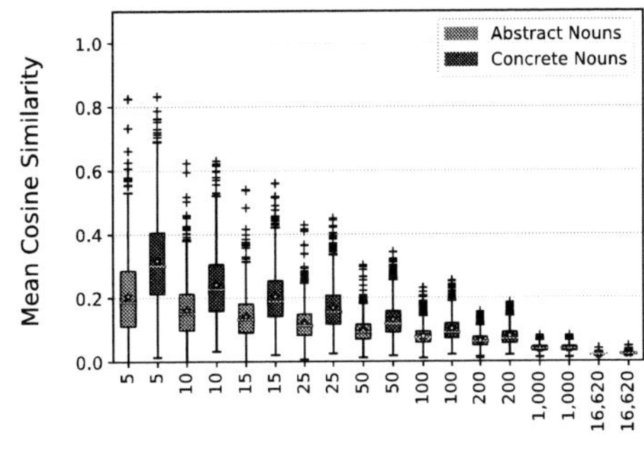

Figure 7: Mean cosine similarities between contexts of 1,000 noun targets.

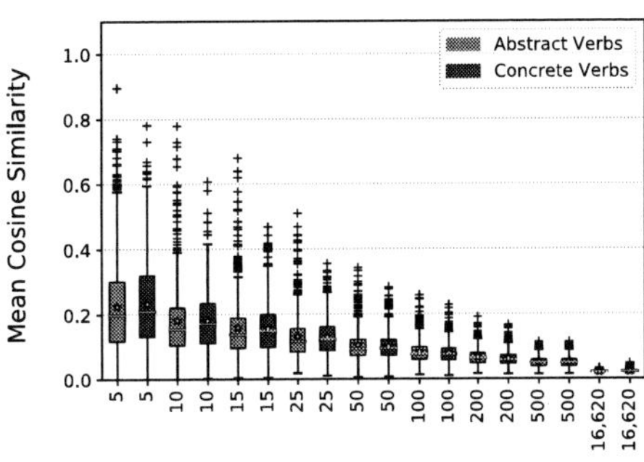

Figure 8: Mean cosine similarities between contexts of 500 verb targets.

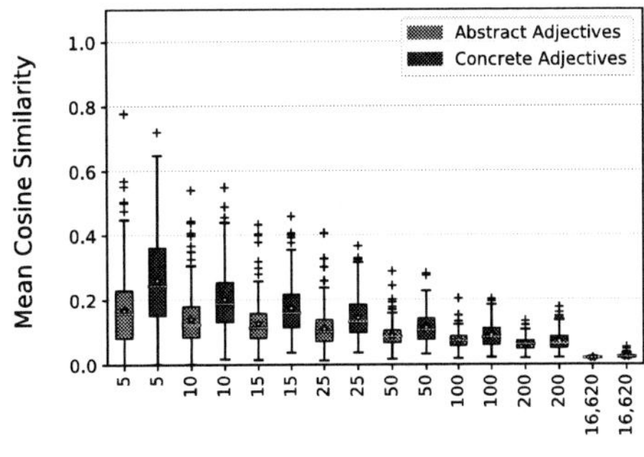

Figure 9: Mean cosine similarities between contexts of 200 adjective targets.

5.3 Discussion

According to hypothesis (2), we expected abstract words to occur in a broader range of distinct contexts and concrete words to appear in a more limited set of different contexts. Moreover, the contexts of concrete words should be more restricted and more similar to each other compared to the contexts of abstract words. The results discussed only partially support this hypothesis.

The analysis of the number of non-zero context dimensions for concrete and abstract target verbs and adjectives show results in line with hypothesis (2). On the contrary, concrete and abstract target nouns share the same number of non-zero dimensions. The analysis of the similarity between contexts of concrete and abstract target nouns and adjectives supports our hypothesis; while we do not see any significant difference when analysing the verbs.

6 Study 3: Entropy of Concrete and Abstract Words

In this study we test our third hypothesis: abstract words are more difficult to predict than concrete words, due to their higher contextual variability. In study 2 we already started investigating this phenomenon using semantic diversity. In the current study we will use entropy as a measure of variability (Shannon, 2001):

$$H(X) = -\sum_{x \in X} p(x)\log_2 p(x) \qquad (1)$$

Based on the assumption that abstract words occur within a high number of distinct contexts, we expect the entropy of abstract words to be higher than the entropy of concrete words.

Noun Targets Figure 10 reports the average entropy in the context of the top 1,000 most abstract (on the left side) and most concrete (on the right side) target nouns. Regarding the 1,000 most abstract target nouns, the entropy of the 1,000 most abstract context nouns (M = 7.42, SD = 0.58) is significantly higher (p < 0.001) than the entropy of the 1,000 most concrete context nouns (M = 6.44, SD = 0.77). A similar pattern emerges in the analysis of the entropy of the contexts of the 1,000 most concrete target nouns: the difference between concrete (M = 6.64, SD = 0.61) and abstract contexts (M = 7.21, SD = 0.54) is statistically significant (p < 0.001).

Verb Targets Similarly to nouns (see Figure 11), also the abstract contexts of both concrete and abstract target verbs show significantly (p < 0.001) higher entropy (concrete target:

M = 6.1, SD = 0.58; abstract target: M = 6.55, SD = 0.49) than the entropy of their concrete contexts (concrete target: M = 4.70, SD = 0.89; abstract target: M = 5.50, SD = 0.86).

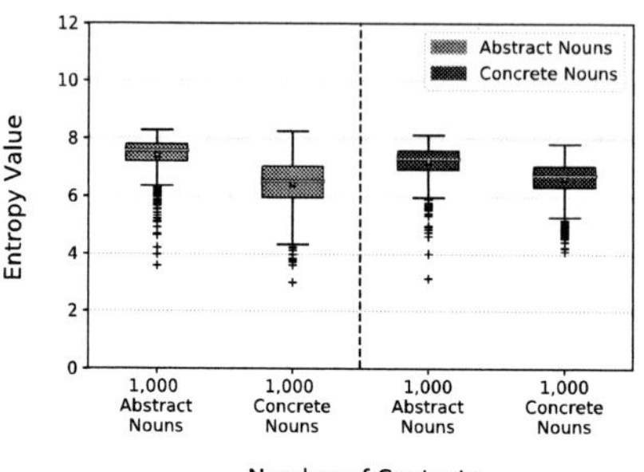

Figure 10: Entropy of 1,000 most abstract (left side) and 1,000 most concrete (right side) noun targets.

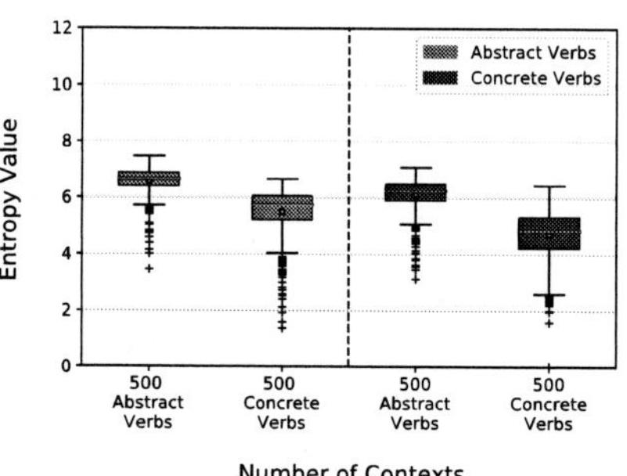

Figure 11: Entropy of 500 most abstract (left side) and 500 most concrete (right side) verbs targets.

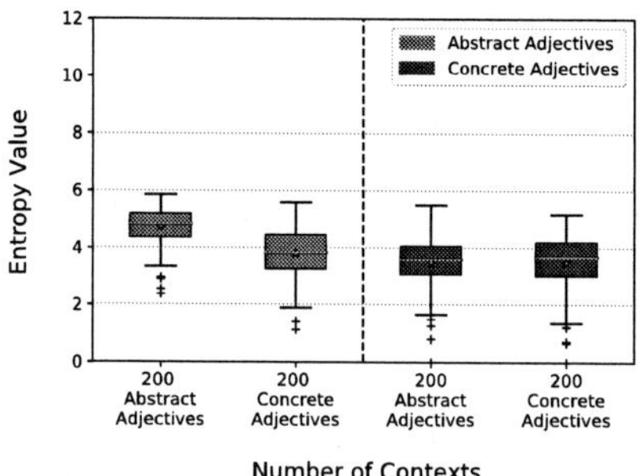

Figure 12: Entropy of 200 most abstract (left side) and 200 most concrete (right side) adjectives targets.

Adjective Targets The same pattern seen for nouns and verbs (see Figure 12) describes also

82

the entropy of target concrete and abstract adjectives. Abstract contexts show significantly ($p < 0.001$) higher entropy (concrete target: M = 3.5, SD = 0.88; abstract target: M = 4.73, SD = 0.61) than the entropy of their concrete contexts (concrete target: M = 3.50, SD = 0.98; abstract target: M = 3.81, SD = 0.87).

Discussion The results of this study support the predictions of hypothesis (3): concrete contexts have significantly lower entropy than abstract contexts irrespective of the POS of their target words.

7 Conclusions

The aim of this work was to provide a very detailed description of the contextual representation of concrete and abstract English nouns, verbs and adjectives. Table 2 summarises the most important findings. 1) Concrete target nouns, verbs and adjectives mainly co-occur with concrete nouns and with abstract verbs and adjectives, while abstract target words always co-occur with abstract words. 2a) The contexts of abstract target verbs and adjectives are broader (less non-zero dimensions) than those of concrete targets verbs and adjectives. On the other hand, concrete and abstract target nouns have a similar number of nonzero dimensions. 2b) The most associated contexts of concrete nouns and adjectives are significantly more similar to each other than the contexts of abstract nouns and adjectives. However, no difference emerges between the contexts of verbs. 3) The concrete contexts of concrete and abstract targets (nouns, verbs, adjectives) have significantly lower entropy values than their abstract contexts. Overall, hypotheses (1) and (2) are not fully supported by our analyses; on the contrary, the predictions made in hypothesis (3) are confirmed.

The three studies described in this paper thus show consistent differences in the contexts of concrete and abstract words and yield patterns that challenge the grounding theory of cognition. In their analyses on noun and verb comprehension, Barsalou (1999) and Richardson et al. (2003) suggest that humans process abstract concepts by creating a perceptual representation. These representations are inherently concrete because they are stored as "experiential traces" generated through the exposure to real world situations using our five senses (Van Dam et al., 2010). In the instructions of their norming study, Brysbaert et al. (2014, p. 906) describe concrete words in a similar way:

"some words refer to things or actions in reality, which you can experience directly through one of the five senses". On the contrary, our study is aligned more with recent theories claiming a representational pluralism that includes both perceptual and non-perceptual features (Dove, 2009).

While the reported cognitive theories describe general patterns emerging from the distinction between concrete and abstract words, the novelty of our study is to provide a fine-grained analysis of the distributional nature of these words and an attempt to explain their similarities and differences from a data-driven perspective. In our opinion, the detection of the precise properties of concrete and abstract words makes an extremely valuable contribution to the long-lasting debate about meaning representation in the human mind and to the use of this knowledge to significantly improve the performance of computational models.

Acknowledgments

The research was supported by the DFG Collaborative Research Centre SFB 732. We also thank the three anonymous reviewers for their comments.

References

David A. Balota, Melvin J. Yap, Michael J. Cortese, Keith A. Hutchison, Brett Kessler, Bjorn Loftis, James H. Neely, Douglas L. Nelson, Greg B. Simpson, and Rebecca Treiman. 2007. The English Lexicon Project. *Behavior Research Methods*, 39(3):445–459.

Lawrence W. Barsalou. 1999. Perceptual Symbol Systems. *Behavioral and Brain Sciences*, 22:577–660.

Lawrence W. Barsalou and Katja Wiemer-Hastings. 2005. Situating Abstract Concepts. In D. Pecher and R. Zwaan, editors, *Grounding Cognition: The Role of Perception and Action in Memory, Language, and Thinking*, chapter 7, pages 129–163. Cambridge University Press, New York.

Sai Abishek Bhaskar, Maximilian Köper, Sabine Schulte im Walde, and Diego Frassinelli. 2017. Exploring Multi-Modal Text+Image Models to Distinguish between Abstract and Concrete Nouns. In *Proceedings of the IWCS Workshop on Foundations of Situated and Multimodal Communication*.

Marc Brysbaert, Amy Beth Warriner, and Victor Kuperman. 2014. Concreteness Ratings for 40 Thousand generally known English Word Lemmas. *Behavior Research Methods*, 64:904–911.

POS	Primary Co-Occurrence		Semantic Diversity of Context	Entropy
concrete nouns	*concrete* nouns		similar number of contexts; high context similarity	low
	abstract verbs			
	abstract adjectives			
abstract nouns	*abstract* nouns		similar number of contexts; low context similarity	high
	abstract verbs			
	abstract adjectives			
concrete verbs	*concrete* nouns		low number of contexts; similar context similarity	low
	abstract verbs			
	abstract adjectives			
abstract verbs	*abstract* nouns		high number of contexts; similar context similarity	high
	abstract verbs			
	abstract adjectives			
concrete adjectives	*concrete* nouns		low number of contexts; high context similarity	low
	abstract verbs			
	abstract adjectives			
abstract adjectives	*abstract* nouns		high number of contexts; low context similarity	high
	abstract verbs			
	abstract adjectives			

Table 2: Overview of our main findings.

L. Burnard. 2000. Reference Guide for the British National Corpus (world edition).

Guy Dove. 2009. Beyond Perceptual Symbols: a Call for Representational Pluralism. *Cognition*, 110(3):412–31.

Stefan Evert. 2005. *The Statistics of Word Co-Occurrences: Word Pairs and Collocations*. Ph.D. thesis, Institut für Maschinelle Sprachverarbeitung, Universität Stuttgart.

John R. Firth. 1968. A Synopsis of Linguistic Theory, 1930–55. In Frank R. Palmer, editor, *Selected Papers of J.R. Firth 1952–59*, Longman's Linguistics Library, pages 168–205. Longmans.

Diego Frassinelli, Daniela Naumann, Jason Utt, and Sabine Schulte im Walde. 2017. Contextual Characteristics of Concrete and Abstract Words. In *Proceedings of the 12th International Conference on Computational Semantics*, Montpellier, France.

Arthur M. Glenberg and Michael P. Kaschak. 2002. Grounding Language in Action. *Psychonomic Bulletin and Review*, 9(3):558–565.

Zellig S. Harris. 1954. Distributional structure. *Word*, 10(2-3):146–162.

Felix Hill, Anna Korhonen, and Christian Bentz. 2014. A Quantitative Empirical Analysis of the Abstract/Concrete Distinction. *Cognitive Science*, 38(1):162–177.

Paul Hoffman, Matthew A. Lambon Ralph, and Timothy T. Rogers. 2013. Semantic Diversity: A Measure of Semantic Ambiguity Based on Variability in the Contextual Usage of Words. *Behavior Research Methods*, 45(3):718–730.

Paul Hoffman and Anna M. Woollams. 2015. Opposing Effects of Semantic Diversity in Lexical and Semantic Relatedness Decisions. *Journal of Experimental Psychology: Human Perception and Performance*, 41(2):385.

Maximilian Köper and Sabine Schulte im Walde. 2016. Distinguishing Literal and Non-Literal Usage of German Particle Verbs. In *Proceedings of the Conference of the North American Chapter of the Association for Computational Linguistics: Human Language Technologies*, pages 353–362, San Diego, California, USA.

Maximilian Köper and Sabine Schulte im Walde. 2017. Improving Verb Metaphor Detection by Propagating Abstractness to Words, Phrases and Individual Senses. In *Proceedings of the 1st Workshop on Sense, Concept and Entity Representations and their Applications*, pages 24–30, Valencia, Spain.

Ken McRae and Michael Jones. 2013. Semantic Memory. *The Oxford Handbook of Cognitive Psychology*, 206.

Diane Pecher, Inge Boot, and Saskia Van Dantzig. 2011. Abstract Concepts. Sensory-Motor Grounding, Metaphors, and Beyond. *Psychology of Learn-*

ing and Motivation – Advances in Research and Theory, 54:217–248.

Daniel C. Richardson, Michael J. Spivey, Lawrence W. Barsalou, and Ken McRae. 2003. Spatial Representations Activated during Real-Time Comprehension of Verbs. *Cognitive Science*, 27(5):767–780.

Roland Schäfer and Felix Bildhauer. 2012. Building Large Corpora from the Web Using a New Efficient Tool Chain. In *Proceedings of the 8th International Conference on Language Resources and Evaluation*, pages 486–493, Istanbul, Turkey.

Helmut Schmid. 1994. Probabilistic Part-of-Speech Tagging Using Decision Trees. In *Proceedings of the 1st International Conference on New Methods in Language Processing*.

Paula J Schwanenflugel and Edward J Shoben. 1983. Differential context effects in the comprehension of abstract and concrete verbal materials. *Journal of Experimental Psychology: Learning, Memory, and Cognition*, 9(1):82.

Claude E. Shannon. 2001. A Mathematical Theory of Communication. *ACM SIGMOBILE Mobile Computing and Communications Review*, 5(1):3–55.

Peter Turney, Yair Neuman, Dan Assaf, and Yohai Cohen. 2011. Literal and Metaphorical Sense Identification through Concrete and Abstract Context. In *Proceedings of the Conference on Empirical Methods in Natural Language Processing*, pages 680–690, Edinburgh, UK.

Wessel O. Van Dam, Shirley-Ann Rueschemeyer, Oliver Lindemann, and Harold Bekkering. 2010. Context effects in embodied lexical-semantic processing. *Frontiers in Psychology*, 1.

Gabriella Vigliocco, Stavroula-Thaleia Kousta, Pasquale Anthony Della Rosa, David P. Vinson, Marco Tettamanti, Joseph T. Devlin, and Stefano F. Cappa. 2014. The Neural Representation of Abstract Words: The Role of Emotion. *Cerebral Cortex*, 24(7):1767–1777.

Amy Beth Warriner, Victor Kuperman, and Marc Brysbaert. 2013. Norms of Valence, Arousal, and Dominance for 13,915 English Lemmas. *Behavior Research Methods*, 45(4):1191–1207.

EmoWordNet: Automatic Expansion of Emotion Lexicon Using English WordNet

Gilbert Badaro, Hussein Jundi[†], Hazem Hajj, Wassim El-Hajj[†]
Department of Electrical & Computer Engineering
[†]Department of Computer Science
American University of Beirut
Beirut, Lebanon
{ggb05;haj14;hh63;we07}@aub.edu.lb

Abstract

Nowadays, social media have become a platform where people can easily express their opinions and emotions about any topic such as politics, movies, music, electronic products and many others. On the other hand, politicians, companies, and businesses are interested in analyzing automatically people's opinions and emotions. In the last decade, a lot of efforts has been put into extracting sentiment polarity from texts. Recently, the focus has expanded to also cover emotion recognition from texts. In this work, we expand an existing emotion lexicon, DepecheMood, by leveraging semantic knowledge from English WordNet (EWN). We create an expanded lexicon, EmoWordNet, consisting of 67K terms aligned with EWN, almost 1.8 times the size of DepecheMood. We also evaluate EmoWordNet in an emotion recognition task using SemEval 2007 news headlines dataset and we achieve an improvement compared to the use of DepecheMood. EmoWordNet is publicly available to speed up research in the field on http://oma-project.com.

1 Introduction

Emotion recognition models have been extensively explored based on different modalities such as human computer interaction (Cowie et al., 2001; Pantic and Rothkrantz, 2003; Fragopanagos and Taylor, 2005; Jaimes and Sebe, 2007; Hibbeln et al., 2017; Patwardhan and Knapp, 2017; Constantine et al., 2016) and facial images and expressions (Goldman and Sripada, 2005; Gunes and Piccardi, 2007; Trad et al., 2012; Wegrzyn et al., 2017). Recently, special attention has been given to emotion recognition from text (Wu et al., 2006; Alm et al., 2005; Shaheen et al., 2014; Abdul-Mageed and Ungar, 2017; Badaro et al., 2018b,a). In fact, a tremendous amount of opinionated and emotionally charged text data is nowadays available on the Internet due to the increase of number of users of social networks such as Twitter and Facebook. For instance, Facebook reached more than 2 billion users on September 2017.[1] Recognizing emotions from text has several applications: first, it helps companies and businesses in shaping their marketing strategies based on consumers' emotions (Bougie et al., 2003); second, it allows improving typical collaborative filtering based recommender systems (Badaro et al., 2013, 2014c,d) in terms of products or advertisements recommendations (Mohammad and Yang, 2011); third, politicians can learn how to adapt their political speech based on people emotions (Pang et al., 2008) and last but not least emotion classification helps in stock market predictions (Bollen et al., 2011).

While plenty of works exist for sentiment analysis for different languages including analysis of social media data for sentiment characteristics (Al Sallab et al., 2015; Baly et al., 2014, 2017b,a), few works focused on emotion recognition from text. Since sentiment lexicons helped in improving the accuracy of sentiment classification models (Liu and Zhang, 2012; Al-Sallab et al., 2017; Badaro et al., 2014a,b, 2015), several researchers are working on developing emotion lexicons for different languages such as English, French, Polish and Chinese (Mohammad, 2017; Bandhakavi et al., 2017; Yang et al., 2007; Poria et al., 2012; Mohammad and Turney, 2013; Das et al., 2012; Mohammad et al., 2013; Abdaoui et al., 2017; Staiano and Guerini, 2014; Maziarz et al., 2016; Janz et al., 2017). While sentiment is usually represented by three labels namely positive, negative or neutral, several representation models exist for emotions such as Ekman representation (Ekman, 1992) (happiness, sadness, fear,

---

[1]https://www.statista.com/statistics/272014/global-social-networks-ranked-by-number-of-users/

*Proceedings of the 7th Joint Conference on Lexical and Computational Semantics (*SEM)*, pages 86–93
New Orleans, June 5-6, 2018. ©2018 Association for Computational Linguistics

anger, surprise and disgust) or Plutchik model (Plutchik, 1994) that includes trust and anticipation in addition to Ekman's six emotions. Despite the efforts for creating large scale emotion lexicons for English, the size of existing emotion lexicons remain much smaller compared to sentiment lexicons. For example, DepecheMood (Staiano and Guerini, 2014), one of the largest publicly available emotion lexicon for English, includes around 37K terms while SentiWordNet (SWN) (Esuli and Sebastiani, 2007; Baccianella et al., 2010), a large scale English sentiment lexicon semi-automatically generated using English WordNet (EWN) (Fellbaum, 1998), includes around 150K terms annotated with three sentiment scores: positive, negative and objective.

In this paper, we focus on expanding coverage of existing emotion lexicon, namely DepecheMood, using the synonymy semantic relation available in English WordNet. We decide to expand DepecheMood since it is one of the largest emotion lexicon publicly available, and since its terms are aligned with EWN, thus allowing us to benefit from powerful semantic relations in EWN.

The paper is organized as follows. In section 2, we conduct a brief literature survey on existing emotion lexicons. In section 3, we describe the expansion approach to build EmoWordNet. In section 4, we compare the performance of EmoWordNet against DepecheMood using SemEval 2007 dataset and in section 5, we present a conclusion of our results and future work.

2   Literature Review

Strapparava et al. (2004) developed WordNet Affect by tagging specific synsets with affective meanings in EWN. They identified first a core number of synsets that represent emotions of a lexical database for emotions. They expanded then the coverage of the lexicon by checking semantically related synsets compared to the core set. They were able to annotate 2,874 synsets and 4,787 words. WordNet Affect was also tested in different applications such as affective text sensing systems and computational humor. WordNet Affect is of good quality given that it was manually created and validated, however, it is of limited size. Mohammad and Turney (2013) presented challenges that researchers face for developing emotion lexicons and devised an annotation strategy to create a good quality and inexpensive emo-

tion lexicon, EmoLex, by utilizing crowdsourcing. To create EmoLex, the authors first identified target terms for annotation extracted from Macquarie Thesaurus (Bernard and Bernard, 1986), WordNet Affect and the General Inquirer (Stone et al., 1966). Then, they launched the annotation task on Amazon's Mechanical Turk. EmoLex has around 10K terms annotated for emotions as well as for sentiment polarities. They evaluated the annotation quality using different techniques such as computing inter-annotator agreement and comparing a subsample of EmoLex with existing gold data. AffectNet (Cambria et al., 2012), part of the SenticNet project, includes also around 10K terms extracted from ConceptNet (Liu and Singh, 2004) and aligned with WordNet Affect. They extended WordNet Affect using the concepts in ConceptNet. While WordNet Affect, EmoLex and AffectNet include terms with emotion labels, Affect database (Neviarouskaya et al., 2007) and DepecheMood (Staiano and Guerini, 2014) include words that have emotion scores instead, which can be useful for compositional computations of emotion scores. Affect database extends SentiFul and covers around 2.5K words presented in their lemma form along with the corresponding part of speech (POS) tag. DepecheMood was automatically built by harvesting social media data that were implicitly annotated with emotions. Staiano and Guerini (2014) utilized news articles from rappler.com. The articles are accompanied by Rappler's Mood Meter, which allows readers to express their emotions about the article they are reading. DepecheMood includes around 37K lemmas along with their part of speech tags and the lemmas are aligned with EWN. Staiano and Guerini also evaluated DepecheMood in emotion regression and classification tasks in unsupervised settings. They claim that although they utilized a naïve unsupervised model, they were able to outperform existing lexicons when applied on SemEval 2007 dataset (Strapparava and Mihalcea, 2007). Since DepecheMood is aligned with EWN, is publicly available and has a better coverage and claimed performance compared to existing emotion lexicons, we decide to expand it using EWN semantic relations as described below in section 3.

To summarize, there are mainly two approaches that have been followed for building emotion lexicons for English. The first set of methods relies on manual annotation either done by specific individuals or through crowdsourcing, where the list of words is extracted from lexical resources. The second approach is automatic or semi-automatic and is based on annotated corpora for emotion. The first approach tends to produce limited size and highly accurate emotion lexicons but it is relatively expensive. On the other hand, the second approach is cheap and results in large scale emotion lexicons but with lower accuracy compared to manually developed emotion lexicons in terms of accurately representing the emotion of the term.

3 EmoWordNet

In this section, we describe the approach we followed in order to expand DepecheMood and build EmoWordNet. DepecheMood consists of 37,771 lemmas along with their corresponding POS tags where each entry is appended with scores for 8 emotion labels: afraid, amused, angry, annoyed, don't_care, happy, inspired and sad. Three variations of score representations exist for DepecheMood. We select to expand the DepecheMood variation with normalized scores since this variation performed best according to the presented results in (Staiano and Guerini, 2014).

In Fig. 1, we show an overview of the steps followed to expand DepecheMood.

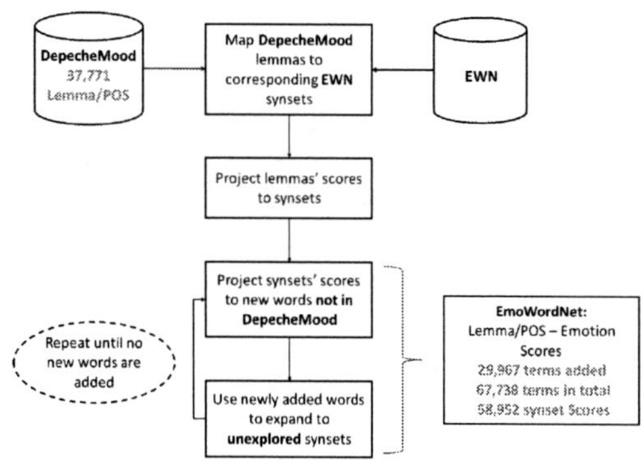

Figure 1: Overview of DepecheMood Expansion Approach.

Step 1: EWN synsets that include lemmas of DepecheMood were retrieved. A score was then computed for each retrieved synset, s. Let S denotes the set of all such synsets. Two cases might appear: either the retrieved synset included only one lemma from DepecheMood, in this case the synset was assigned the same score of the lemma, or, the synset included multiple lemmas that exist in DepecheMood, in this case the synset's score was the average of the scores of its corresponding lemmas. **Step 2:** A synset, s, includes two set of terms: T, terms that are **in** DepecheMood, and $\bar{T}$, terms **not in** DepecheMood. Using the synonymy semantic relation in EWN, and based on the concept that synonym words would likely share the same emotion scores, we assigned the synset's scores to its corresponding terms $\bar{T}$. Again, a term t in $\bar{T}$ might appear in one or multiple synsets from S. Hence, the score assigned to t would be either the one of its corresponding synset or the average of the scores of its corresponding synsets that belong to S. **Step 3:** after performing step 2, new synsets might be explored. Terms in $\bar{T}$ might also appear in synsets $\bar{s}$ that do not belong to S. $\bar{s}$ would get the score of its corresponding terms. Step 2 and 3 were repeated until no new terms or synsets were added and scores of added terms converged. It is important to note that we decided to consider only synonyms for expansion since synonymy is the only semantic relation that mostly preserves the emotion orientation and does not require manual validation as described by Strapparava et al. (2004).

As a walking example of the steps described above, let us consider the DepecheMood term "bonding" having noun as POS tag. "bonding" can be found in three different EWN noun synsets with the following offset IDs: "00148653; 05665769; 13781820". Since "bonding" is the only term having a DepecheMood representation in the three synsets, the three synsets will have the same emotion scores as "bonding". While synsets "05665769; 13781820" have only the term "bonding", "00148653" includes as well the lemma "soldering" which is not in DepecheMood. Thus, from step 2, "soldering" will have the same scores as "bonding". "soldering" does not appear in any other EWN synset so there are no more iterations.

Using the described automatic expansion approach, we were able to extend the size of DepecheMood by a factor of 1.8. We obtained emotion scores for an additional 29,967 EWN terms and for 59,952 EWN synsets. Overall, we construct EmoWordNet, an emotion lexicon consisting of 67,738 EWN terms and of 59,952 EWN synsets annotated with emotion scores.

Next, we present a simple extrinsic evaluation of EmoWordNet similar to the one performed for DepecheMood.

4 Evaluation of EmoWordNet

In this section, we evaluate the effectiveness of EmoWordNet in emotion recognition task from text. We evaluate regression as well as classification of emotions in unsupervised settings using similar techniques used for evaluating DepecheMood.

4.1 Dataset & Coverage

We utilized the dataset provided publicly by SemEval 2007 task on Affective text (Strapparava and Mihalcea, 2007). The dataset consists of one thousand news headlines annotated with six emotion scores: anger, disgust, fear, joy, sadness and surprise. For the regression task, a score between 0 and 1 is provided for each emotion. For the classification task, a threshold is applied on the emotion scores to get a binary representation of the emotions: if the score of a certain emotion is greater than 0.5, the corresponding emotion label is set to 1, otherwise it is 0. The emotion labels used in the dataset correspond to the six emotions of the Ekman model (Ekman, 1992) while those in EmoWordNet, as well as DepecheMood, follow the ones provided by Rappler Mood Meter. We considered the same emotion mapping assumptions presented in the work of (Staiano and Guerini, 2014): Fear → Afraid, Anger → Angry, Joy → Happy, Sadness → Sad and Surprise → Inspired. Disgust was not aligned with any emotion in EmoWordNet and hence was discarded as also assumed in (Staiano and Guerini, 2014). One important aspect of the extrinsic evaluation was checking the coverage of EmoWordNet against SemEval dataset. In order to compute coverage, we performed lemmatization of the news headlines using WordNet lemmatizer available through Python NLTK package. We excluded all words with POS tags different than noun, verb, adjective and adverb. EmoWordNet achieved a coverage of 68.6% while DepecheMood had a coverage of 67.1%. An increase in coverage was expected but since the size of the dataset is relatively small, the increase was only around 1.5%. In terms of headline coverage, only one headline ("Toshiba Portege R400") was left without any emotion scores when using both EmoWordNet and DepecheMood since none of its terms were found in any of the two lexicons.

4.2 Regression and Classification Results

We followed an approach similar to the one presented for evaluating DepecheMood. For preprocessing, we first lemmatized the headlines using WordNet lemmatizer available in Python NLTK package. We also accounted for multi-word terms that were solely available in EmoWordNet by looking at n-grams (up to n=3) after lemmatization. We then removed all terms that did not belong to any of the four POS tags: noun, verb, adjective and adverbs. For features computation, we considered two variations: the sum and the average of the emotion scores for the five emotion labels that overlapped between EmoWordNet and SemEval dataset. Using average turned out to perform better than when using sum for both lexicons. As stated in (Staiano and Guerini, 2014) paper, 'Disgust' emotion was excluded since there was no corresponding mapping in EmoWordNet/DepecheMood. The first evaluation consisted of measuring Pearson Correlation between the scores computed using the lexicons and those provided in SemEval. The results are reported in Table 1. We could see that the results are relatively close to each other: EmoWordNet slightly outperformed DepecheMood for the five different emotions. It was expected to have close results given that the coverage of EmoWordNet is very close to DepecheMood. Given the slight improvement, we expect EmoWordNet to perform much better on larger datasets.

For the classification task, we first transformed the numerical emotion scores of the headlines to a binary representation. We applied min-max normalization on the computed emotion scores per headline, and then assigned a '1' for the emotion label with score greater than '0.5', and a '0' otherwise. We used F1 measure for evaluation. Results are shown in Table 2. More significant improvement was observed in classification task compared to regression task when using EmoWordNet.

4.3 Results Analysis

In this section, we present some quantitative and qualitative analyses of the results. For quantitative analysis, we checked first whether the count of terms in a headline is correlated with having a correct emotion classification. Overall, the length of headlines was varying between 2 and 15 terms. Headlines with length between 5 and 10 terms were mostly correctly classified. Hence, one can

Emotion	EmoWordNet	DepecheMood
Fear	**0.59**	0.54
Anger	**0.42**	0.38
Joy	**0.33**	0.21
Sadness	**0.43**	0.40
Surprise	**0.51**	0.47
Average	0.46	0.40

Table 1: Pearson Correlation values between predicted and golden scores.

Emotion	EmoWordNet	DepecheMood
Fear	**0.45**	0.32
Anger	**0.17**	0.00
Joy	**0.48**	0.16
Sadness	**0.46**	0.30
Surprise	**0.43**	0.40
Average	0.40	0.24

Table 2: F1-Measure results for emotion classification.

Headline	Emotions
Hackers attack root servers	Anger; Fear
Subway collapse caught on camera	Fear; Sadness
Action games improve eye-sight	Joy; Surprise
Study finds gritty air raises heart disease risk in older women	Fear; Sadness; Surprise
Wizardry at Harvard: physicists move light	Surprise

Table 3: Examples of correctly classified headlines.

Headline	Gold	Predicted
A film star in Kampala, conjuring aminos ghost	Fear; Surprise	Anger; Joy; Sadness
Damaged Japanese whaling ship may resume hunting off Antarctica	Joy; Sadness	Anger; Fear; Surprise
Apple revs up Mac attacks on Vista	Surprise	Anger; Fear; Joy; Sadness
Serbia rejects United Nation's Kosovo plan	Anger; Sadness; Surprise	Fear; Joy
Taliban leader killed in airstrike	Joy; Sadness	Anger; Fear; Surprise

Table 4: Examples of misclassified headlines.

conclude that having a headline with couple of terms only may not allow the system to clearly decide on the emotion label and having headlines with many terms may cause the system to over predict emotions. In addition to headline length, we checked whether POS tags are correlated with correct or erroneous emotion predictions. Given that the dataset consists of news headlines, the "noun" POS tag was the most frequent in both correctly classified headlines and misclassified ones.

For qualitative analysis, we analyze few correctly classified headlines and few other misclassified ones. We show in Table 3 few examples of correctly classified headlines and in table 4 other examples of misclassified headlines. By looking at the misclassified examples, we observe that the golden annotation tend to be sometimes conflicting such as the second and the fifth examples in Table 4 where we have joy and sadness as assigned emotions for the two headlines. An explanation for having conflicting emotions for the same headline is that the annotators reflected their personal point of view of the information conveyed by the headline. Hence, some people were happy to read the headline others were sad. In order to incorporate such challenging aspect of emotion recognition from text, more sophisticated emotion recognition models need to be considered and tested.

5 Conclusion and Future Work

We presented EmoWordNet, a large scale emotion lexicon, consisting of around 67K EWN words and 58K EWN synsets annotated with 8 emotion scores. EmoWordNet is automatically constructed by applying a semantic expansion approach using EWN and DepecheMood. When utilized for emotion recognition, EmoWordNet outperformed existing emotion lexicons and had a better lexical coverage. For future work, we would like to evaluate the performance of EmoWordNet on larger datasets and we would like to improve the accuracy of the recognition model. EmoWordNet is publicly available on http://oma-project.com.

References

Amine Abdaoui, Jérôme Azé, Sandra Bringay, and Pascal Poncelet. 2017. Feel: a french expanded emotion lexicon. *Language Resources and Evaluation*, 51(3):833–855.

Muhammad Abdul-Mageed and Lyle Ungar. 2017. Emonet: Fine–grained emotion detection with gated recurrent neural networks. In *Proceedings of the 55th Annual Meeting of the Association for Computational Linguistics (Volume 1: Long Papers)*, volume 1, pages 718–728.

Ahmad Al-Sallab, Ramy Baly, Hazem Hajj, Khaled Bashir Shaban, Wassim El-Hajj, and Gilbert Badaro. 2017. Aroma: A recursive deep learning model for opinion mining in arabic as a low resource language. *ACM Transactions on Asian and Low-Resource Language Information Processing (TALLIP)*, 16(4):25.

Ahmad A Al Sallab, Ramy Baly, Gilbert Badaro, Hazem Hajj, Wassim El Hajj, and Khaled B Shaban. 2015. Deep learning models for sentiment analysis in arabic. In *ANLP Workshop*, volume 9.

Cecilia Ovesdotter Alm, Dan Roth, and Richard Sproat. 2005. Emotions from text: machine learning for text-based emotion prediction. In *Proceedings of the conference on human language technology and empirical methods in natural language processing*, pages 579–586. Association for Computational Linguistics.

Stefano Baccianella, Andrea Esuli, and Fabrizio Sebastiani. 2010. Sentiwordnet 3.0: An enhanced lexical resource for sentiment analysis and opinion mining. In *LREC*, volume 10, pages 2200–2204.

Gilbert Badaro, Ramy Baly, Rana Akel, Linda Fayad, Jeffrey Khairallah, Hazem Hajj, Khaled Shaban, and Wassim El-Hajj. 2015. A light lexicon-based mobile application for sentiment mining of arabic tweets. In *Proceedings of the Second Workshop on Arabic Natural Language Processing*, pages 18–25.

Gilbert Badaro, Ramy Baly, Hazem Hajj, Nizar Habash, and Wassim El-Hajj. 2014a. A large scale Arabic sentiment lexicon for Arabic opinion mining. *ANLP 2014*, 165.

Gilbert Badaro, Ramy Baly, Hazem Hajj, Nizar Habash, Wassim El-hajj, and Khaled Shaban. 2014b. An efficient model for sentiment classification of Arabic tweets on mobiles. In *Qatar Foundation Annual Research Conference*, 1, page ITPP0631.

Gilbert Badaro, Obeida El Jundi, Alaa Khaddaj, Alaa Maarouf, Raslan Kain, Hazem Hajj, and Wassim El-Hajj. 2018a. Ema at semeval-2018 task 1: Emotion mining for arabic. In *Proceedings of International Workshop on Semantic Evaluation (SemEval-2018)*.

Gilbert Badaro, Hazem Hajj, Wassim El-Hajj, and Lama Nachman. 2013. A hybrid approach with collaborative filtering for recommender systems. In *Wireless Communications and Mobile Computing Conference (IWCMC), 2013 9th International*, pages 349–354. IEEE.

Gilbert Badaro, Hazem Hajj, Ali Haddad, Wassim El-Hajj, and Khaled Bashir Shaban. 2014c. A multiresolution approach to recommender systems. In *Proceedings of the 8th Workshop on Social Network Mining and Analysis*, page 9. ACM.

Gilbert Badaro, Hazem Hajj, Ali Haddad, Wassim El-Hajj, and Khaled Bashir Shaban. 2014d. Recommender systems using harmonic analysis. In *Data Mining Workshop (ICDMW), 2014 IEEE International Conference on*, pages 1004–1011. IEEE.

Gilbert Badaro, Hussein Jundi, Hazem Hajj, Wassim El-Hajj, and Nizar Habash. 2018b. Arsel: A large scale arabic sentiment and emotion lexicon. In *Proceedings of the 3rd Workshop on Open-Source Arabic Corpora and Processing Tools (OSACT3) co-located with LREC2018*.

Ramy Baly, Gilbert Badaro, Georges El-Khoury, Rawan Moukalled, Rita Aoun, Hazem Hajj, Wassim El-Hajj, Nizar Habash, and Khaled Shaban. 2017a. A characterization study of arabic twitter data with a benchmarking for state-of-the-art opinion mining models. In *Proceedings of the Third Arabic Natural Language Processing Workshop*, pages 110–118.

Ramy Baly, Gilbert Badaro, Hazem Hajj, Nizar Habash, Wassim El Hajj, and Khaled Shaban.

2014. Semantic model representation for human's pre-conceived notions in arabic text with applications to sentiment mining. In *Qatar Foundation Annual Research Conference*, 1, page ITPP1075.

Ramy Baly, Gilbert Badaro, Ali Hamdi, Rawan Moukalled, Rita Aoun, Georges El-Khoury, Ahmad Al Sallab, Hazem Hajj, Nizar Habash, Khaled Shaban, et al. 2017b. Omam at semeval-2017 task 4: Evaluation of english state-of-the-art sentiment analysis models for arabic and a new topic-based model. In *Proceedings of the 11th International Workshop on Semantic Evaluation (SemEval-2017)*, pages 603–610.

Anil Bandhakavi, Nirmalie Wiratunga, Stewart Massie, and Deepak Padmanabhan. 2017. Lexicon generation for emotion detection from text. *IEEE intelligent systems*, 32(1):102–108.

John Rupert Lyon-Bowes Bernard and John Rupert Lyon-Bowes Bernard. 1986. *The Macquarie Thesaurus*. Macquarie.

Johan Bollen, Huina Mao, and Xiaojun Zeng. 2011. Twitter mood predicts the stock market. *Journal of computational science*, 2(1):1–8.

Roger Bougie, Rik Pieters, and Marcel Zeelenberg. 2003. Angry customers don't come back, they get back: The experience and behavioral implications of anger and dissatisfaction in services. *Journal of the Academy of Marketing Science*, 31(4):377–393.

Erik Cambria, Catherine Havasi, and Amir Hussain. 2012. Senticnet 2: A semantic and affective resource for opinion mining and sentiment analysis. In *FLAIRS conference*, pages 202–207.

Layale Constantine, Gilbert Badaro, Hazem Hajj, Wassim El-Hajj, Lama Nachman, Mohamed BenSaleh, and Abdulfattah Obeid. 2016. A framework for emotion recognition from human computer interaction in natural setting. *22nd ACM SIGKDD Conference on Knowledge Discovery and Data Mining (KDD 2016), Workshop on Issues of Sentiment Discovery and Opinion Mining (WISDOM 2016)*.

Roddy Cowie, Ellen Douglas-Cowie, Nicolas Tsapatsoulis, George Votsis, Stefanos Kollias, Winfried Fellenz, and John G Taylor. 2001. Emotion recognition in human-computer interaction. *IEEE Signal processing magazine*, 18(1):32–80.

Dipankar Das, Soujanya Poria, and Sivaji Bandyopadhyay. 2012. A classifier based approach to emotion lexicon construction. In *NLDB*, pages 320–326. Springer.

Paul Ekman. 1992. An argument for basic emotions. *Cognition & emotion*, 6(3-4):169–200.

Andrea Esuli and Fabrizio Sebastiani. 2007. Sentiwordnet: A high-coverage lexical resource for opinion mining. *Evaluation*, pages 1–26.

Christiane Fellbaum. 1998. *WordNet*. Wiley Online Library.

N Fragopanagos and John G Taylor. 2005. Emotion recognition in human–computer interaction. *Neural Networks*, 18(4):389–405.

Alvin I Goldman and Chandra Sekhar Sripada. 2005. Simulationist models of face-based emotion recognition. *Cognition*, 94(3):193–213.

Hatice Gunes and Massimo Piccardi. 2007. Bimodal emotion recognition from expressive face and body gestures. *Journal of Network and Computer Applications*, 30(4):1334–1345.

Martin Hibbeln, Jeffrey L Jenkins, Christoph Schneider, Joseph S Valacich, and Markus Weinmann. 2017. How is your user feeling? inferring emotion through human–computer interaction devices. *MIS Quarterly*, 41(1).

Alejandro Jaimes and Nicu Sebe. 2007. Multimodal human–computer interaction: A survey. *Computer vision and image understanding*, 108(1):116–134.

Arkadiusz Janz, Jan Kocoń, Maciej Piasecki, and Monika Zaśko-Zielińska. 2017. plwordnet as a basis for large emotive lexicons of polish.

Bing Liu and Lei Zhang. 2012. A survey of opinion mining and sentiment analysis. In *Mining text data*, pages 415–463. Springer.

Hugo Liu and Push Singh. 2004. Conceptneta practical commonsense reasoning tool-kit. *BT technology journal*, 22(4):211–226.

Marek Maziarz, Maciej Piasecki, Ewa Rudnicka, Stan Szpakowicz, and Paweł Kedzia. 2016. plwordnet 3.0–a comprehensive lexical-semantic resource. In *Proceedings of COLING 2016, the 26th International Conference on Computational Linguistics: Technical Papers*, pages 2259–2268.

Saif M Mohammad. 2017. Word affect intensities. *arXiv preprint arXiv:1704.08798*.

Saif M Mohammad, Svetlana Kiritchenko, and Xiaodan Zhu. 2013. Nrc-canada: Building the state-of-the-art in sentiment analysis of tweets. *arXiv preprint arXiv:1308.6242*.

Saif M Mohammad and Peter D Turney. 2013. Crowdsourcing a word–emotion association lexicon. *Computational Intelligence*, 29(3):436–465.

Saif M Mohammad and Tony Wenda Yang. 2011. Tracking sentiment in mail: How genders differ on emotional axes. In *Proceedings of the 2nd workshop on computational approaches to subjectivity and sentiment analysis*, pages 70–79. Association for Computational Linguistics.

Alena Neviarouskaya, Helmut Prendinger, and Mitsuru Ishizuka. 2007. Textual affect sensing for sociable and expressive online communication. *Affective Computing and Intelligent Interaction*, pages 218–229.

Bo Pang, Lillian Lee, et al. 2008. Opinion mining and sentiment analysis. *Foundations and Trends® in Information Retrieval*, 2(1–2):1–135.

Maja Pantic and Leon JM Rothkrantz. 2003. Toward an affect-sensitive multimodal human-computer interaction. *Proceedings of the IEEE*, 91(9):1370–1390.

Amol S Patwardhan and Gerald M Knapp. 2017. Multimodal affect analysis for product feedback assessment. *arXiv preprint arXiv:1705.02694*.

Robert Plutchik. 1994. *The psychology and biology of emotion*. HarperCollins College Publishers.

Soujanya Poria, Alexander Gelbukh, Dipankar Das, and Sivaji Bandyopadhyay. 2012. Fuzzy clustering for semi-supervised learning–case study: Construction of an emotion lexicon. In *Mexican International Conference on Artificial Intelligence*, pages 73–86. Springer.

Shadi Shaheen, Wassim El-Hajj, Hazem Hajj, and Shady Elbassuoni. 2014. Emotion recognition from text based on automatically generated rules. In *Data Mining Workshop (ICDMW), 2014 IEEE International Conference on*, pages 383–392. IEEE.

Jacopo Staiano and Marco Guerini. 2014. Depechemood: A lexicon for emotion analysis from crowd-annotated news. *arXiv preprint arXiv:1405.1605*.

Philip J Stone, Dexter C Dunphy, and Marshall S Smith. 1966. The general inquirer: A computer approach to content analysis.

Carlo Strapparava and Rada Mihalcea. 2007. Semeval-2007 task 14: Affective text. In *Proceedings of the 4th International Workshop on Semantic Evaluations*, pages 70–74. Association for Computational Linguistics.

Carlo Strapparava, Alessandro Valitutti, et al. 2004. Wordnet affect: an affective extension of wordnet. In *LREC*, volume 4, pages 1083–1086.

Chadi Trad, Hazem M Hajj, Wassim El-Hajj, and Fatima Al-Jamil. 2012. Facial action unit and emotion recognition with head pose variations. In *ADMA*, pages 383–394. Springer.

Martin Wegrzyn, Maria Vogt, Berna Kireclioglu, Julia Schneider, and Johanna Kissler. 2017. Mapping the emotional face. how individual face parts contribute to successful emotion recognition. *PloS one*, 12(5):e0177239.

Chung-Hsien Wu, Ze-Jing Chuang, and Yu-Chung Lin. 2006. Emotion recognition from text using semantic labels and separable mixture models. *ACM transactions on Asian language information processing (TALIP)*, 5(2):165–183.

Changhua Yang, Kevin Hsin-Yih Lin, and Hsin-Hsi Chen. 2007. Building emotion lexicon from weblog corpora. In *Proceedings of the 45th Annual Meeting of the ACL on Interactive Poster and Demonstration Sessions*, pages 133–136. Association for Computational Linguistics.

The Limitations of Cross-language Word Embeddings Evaluation

Amir Bakarov[†*]   **Roman Suvorov**[*]   **Ilya Sochenkov**[‡*]
[†]National Research University Higher School of Economics,
[*]Federal Research Center 'Computer Science and Control' of the Russian Academy of Sciences,
[‡]Skolkovo Institute of Science and Technology (Skoltech),
Moscow, Russia
`amirbakarov@gmail.com, rsuvorov@isa.ru, ivsochenkov@gmail.com`

Abstract

The aim of this work is to explore the possible limitations of existing methods of cross-language word embeddings evaluation, addressing the lack of correlation between intrinsic and extrinsic cross-language evaluation methods. To prove this hypothesis, we construct English-Russian datasets for extrinsic and intrinsic evaluation tasks and compare performances of 5 different cross-language models on them. The results say that the scores even on different intrinsic benchmarks do not correlate to each other. We can conclude that the use of human references as ground truth for cross-language word embeddings is not proper unless one does not understand how do native speakers process semantics in their cognition.

1 Introduction

Real-valued word representations called *word embeddings* are an ubiquitous and effective technique of semantic modeling. So it is not surprising that cross-language extensions of such models (*cross-language word embeddings*) rapidly gained popularity in the NLP community (Vulić and Moens, 2013), proving their effectiveness in certain cross-language NLP tasks (Upadhyay et al., 2016). However, the problem of proper evaluation of any type of word embeddings still remains open.

In recent years there was a critique to mainstream methods of intrinsic evaluation: some researchers addressed subjectivity of human assessments, obscurity of instructions for certain tasks and terminology confusions (Faruqui et al., 2016; Batchkarov et al., 2016). Despite all these limitations, some of the criticized methods (like the word similarity task) has been started to be actively applied yet for cross-language word embeddings evaluation (Camacho-Collados et al., 2017, 2015).

We argue that if certain tasks are considered as not proper enough for mono-lingual evaluation, then it should be even more inappropriate to use them for cross-language evaluation since new problems would appear due to the new features of cross-linguality wherein the old limitations still remain. Moreover, it is still unknown for the field of cross-language word embeddings, are we able to make relevant predictions on performance of the model on one method, using another. We do not know whether can we use the relative ordering of different embeddings obtained by evaluation on an intrinsic task to decide which model will be better on a certain extrinsic task. So, the aim of this work is to highlight the limitations of cross-language intrinsic benchmarks, studying the connection of outcomes from different cross-language word embeddings evaluation schemes (intrinsic evaluation and extrinsic evaluation), and explain this connection by addressing certain issues of intrinsic benchmarks that hamper us to have a correlation between two evaluation schemes. In this study as an extrinsic task we consider the cross-language paraphrase detection task. This is because we think that the model's features that word similarity and paraphrase detection evaluate are very close: both of them test the quality of semantic modeling (i.e. not the ability of the model to identify POS tags, or the ability to cluster words in groups, or something else) in terms of properness of distances in words pairs with certain types of semantic relations (particularly, semantic similarity). Therefore, we could not say that a strong difference in performances of word embeddings on these two tasks could be highly expected.

In this paper we propose a comparison of 5 cross-language models on extrinsic and intrinsic datasets for English-Russian language pair constructed specially for this study. We consider Russian because we are native speakers of this lan-

*Proceedings of the 7th Joint Conference on Lexical and Computational Semantics (*SEM)*, pages 94–100
New Orleans, June 5-6, 2018. ©2018 Association for Computational Linguistics

guage (hence, we are able to adequately construct novel datasets according the limitations that we address).

Our work is a step towards exploration of the limitations of cross-language evaluation of word embeddings, and it has three primary contributions:

1. We propose an overview of limitations of current intrinsic cross-language word embeddings evaluation techniques;

2. We construct 12 cross-language datasets for evaluation on the word similarity task;

3. We propose a novel task for cross-language extrinsic evaluation that was never addressed before from the benchmarking perspective, and we create a human-assessed dataset for this task.

This paper is organized as follows. Section 2 puts our work in the context of previous studies. Section 3 describes the problems of intrinsic cross-language evaluation. Section 4 is about the experimental setup. The results of the comparison are reported in Section 5, while Section 6 concludes the paper.

2   Related Work

First investigation of tasks for cross-language word embeddings evaluation was proposed in 2015 (Camacho-Collados et al., 2015). This work was the first towards mentioning the problem of lack of lexical one-to-one correspondence across different languages from the evaluation perspective. However, no detailed insights on limitations of evaluation (e.g. effect of this lack on evaluation scores) was reported. 2015 also saw an exploration of the effect of assessments' language and the difference in word similarity scores for different languages (Leviant and Reichart, 2015).

In 2016 the first survey of cross-language intrinsic and extrinsic evaluation techniques was proposed (Upadhyay et al., 2016). The results of this study did not address the correlation of intrinsic evaluation scores with extrinsic ones (despite that the lack of correlation of intrinsic and extrinsic tasks for mono-language evaluation was proved (Schnabel et al., 2015), it is not obvious if this would also extend to cross-language evaluation). In 2017 a more extensive overview of cross-language word embeddings evaluation methods

was proposed (Ruder, 2017), but this study did not considered any empirical analysis.

After all, we are aware of certain works on a topic of cross-language evaluation from the cross-language information retrieval community (Braschler et al., 2000), but there are no works that highlight non-trivial issues of cross-language systems evaluation from the position of word embeddings.

3   Problems of Cross-language Evaluation

We address the following problems that could appear on any kind of evaluation of cross-language word embeddings against human references on any intrinsic task:

1. **Translation Disagreement**. Some researchers have already faced the limitations of machine word translation for constructing cross-language evaluation datasets from mono-language ones by translating them word-by-word. The obtained problems were in two different words with the same translation or with different parts of speech (Camacho-Collados et al., 2015). We also argue that some words could have no translations while some words could have multiple translations. Of course, these issues could be partially avoided if the datasets would be translated manually and the problematic words would be dropped from the cross-language dataset, but it is not clear how the agreement for word dropping of human assessors could be concluded.

2. **Scores Re-assessment**. Some researchers obtain new scores reporting human references by automatically averaging the scores from the mono-language datasets of which the new dataset is constructed. Another option of scores re-assessment proposes manual scoring of a new dataset by bilingual assessors. We consider that both variants are not proper since it is unclear how the scores in the cross-language dataset should be assessed: humans usually do not try to identify a similarity score between word a in language A and word b in language B since of difference in perception of these words in cognition of speakers of different languages.

3. **Semantic Fields**. According to the theories of *lexical typology*, the meaning of a properly translated word could denote a bit different things in a new languages. Such effect is called *semantic shift*, and there is a possibility that the actual meanings of two corresponding words could be different even if they are correctly translated and re-assessed (Ryzhova et al., 2016). One of the ways of avoiding this problem is to exclude *relational nouns* which are words with non-zero valency (Koptjevskaja-Tamm et al., 2015) from the dataset, so it should consist only of zero valency nouns that are more properly linked with real world objects. However, the distinction of words on relational and non-relational ones is fuzzy, and such assessments could be very subjective (also, since verbs are usually highly relational, they should not be used in cross-language evaluation).

4. **New Factors for Bias**. It is already known that existence of *connotative associations* for certain words in mono-language datasets could introduce additional subjectivity in the human assessments (Liza and Grzes, 2016). We argue that yet more factors could be the cause of assessors' bias in the cross-language datasets. For example, words *five* and *clock* could be closely connected in minds of English speakers (since of the common *five o'clock tea* collocation), but not in minds of speakers of other languages, and we think that a native English speaker could assess biased word similarity scores for this word pair.

4 Experimental Setup

4.1 Distributional Models

To propose a comparison, we used 5 cross-language embedding models.

1. **MSE** (*Multilingual Supervised Embeddings*). Trains using a bilingual dictionary and learns a mapping from the source to the target space using Procrustes alignment (Conneau et al., 2017).

2. **MUE** (*Multilingual Unsupervised Embeddings*). Trains learning a mapping from the source to the target space using adversarial training and Procrustes refinement (Conneau et al., 2017).

3. **VecMap**. Maps the source into the target space using a bilingual dictionary or shared numerals minimizing the squared Euclidean distance between embedding matrices (Artetxe et al., 2018).

4. **BiCCA** (*Bilingual Canonical Correlation Analysis*). Projects vectors of two different languages in the same space using CCA (Faruqui and Dyer, 2014).

5. **MFT** (*Multilingual FastText*). Uses SVD to learn a linear transformation, which aligns monolingual vectors from two languages in a single vector space (Smith et al., 2017).

We mapped vector spaces of Russian and English *FastText* models trained on a dump of Wikipedia (Bojanowski et al., 2016) with an English-Russian bilingual dictionary (Conneau et al., 2017) (only one translation for a single word).

4.2 Intrinsic Tasks

Word Semantic Similarity. The task is to predict the similarity score for a word a in language A and a word b in language B. All three publicly available datasets for cross-language word similarity (Camacho-Collados et al., 2015, 2017) are not available for Russian, so we created the cross-language datasets ourselves. We used 5 English datasets assessed by *semantic similarity* of nouns and adjectives (S), 3 datasets assessed by *semantic similarity* of verbs (V), and 3 datasets assessed by *semantic relatedness* of nouns and adjectives (R); we labeled each with a letter reporting the type of relations. We translated these datasets, merged into cross-language sets (the first word of each word pair was English, and the second was Russian), dropped certain words pairs according to limitations addressed by us (in the Section 2), and re-assessed the obtained cross-languages datasets with the help of 3 English-Russian volunteers, having Krippendorff's alpha 0.5 (final amount of word pairs and ratio to original datasets is reported at Table 1). Then we compared human references of these datasets with cosine distances of cross-language word vectors, and computed Spearman's rank correlation coefficient ($p - value$ in all cases was lower than 0.05).

Dictionary Induction (also called *word translation*). The second task is to translate a word in language A into language B, so for the seed word

	MSE	MUE	VM	BCCA	MFT
S.RareWord-958 (56.3%) (Luong et al., 2013)	**0.44**	0.42	0.43	0.43	0.43
S.SimLex-739 (95.9%) (Hill et al., 2016)	0.34	0.32	**0.35**	0.34	0.34
S.SemEval-243 (88.0%) (Camacho-Collados et al., 2017)	**0.6**	0.56	0.35	0.34	0.34
S.WordSim-193 (96.4%) (Agirre et al., 2009)	0.69	0.67	**0.72**	0.67	0.71
S.RG-54 (83.1%) (Rubenstein and Goodenough, 1965)	**0.68**	0.67	0.63	0.61	0.61
S.MC-28 (93.3%) (Miller and Charles, 1991)	0.66	0.7	0.71	**0.72**	0.7
V. SimVerb-3074 (87.8%) (Gerz et al., 2016)	0.2	0.2	**0.23**	0.22	0.21
V.Verb-115 (85.4%) (Baker et al., 2014)	0.24	**0.39**	0.27	0.27	0.27
V.YP-111 (88.5%) (Yang and Powers, 2006)	0.22	**0.37**	0.25	0.25	0.25
R.MEN-1146 (94.7%) (Bruni et al., 2014)	0.68	0.66	**0.69**	0.66	0.68
R.MTurk-551 (91.7%) (Halawi et al., 2012)	0.56	0.51	**0.57**	0.54	**0.57**
R.WordSim-193 (96.4%) (Agirre et al., 2009)	0.55	0.53	**0.57**	0.53	0.55
P@1, dictionary induction	0.31	0.16	**0.32**	0.29	0.21
P@5, dictionary induction	**0.53**	0.34	0.52	0.49	0.38
P@10, dictionary induction	**0.61**	0.42	0.5	0.55	0.45
F1, paraphrase detection, *our dataset*	0.82	0.77	0.84	0.83	**0.86**
F1, paraphrase detection, *parallel sentences*	0.55	0.45	0.57	**0.6**	0.59

Table 1: Performance of the compared models across different tasks. Evaluation on first 11 datasets indicate Spearman's rank correlation. For word similarity task: words before the hyphen in datasets name report the name of the original English dataset, the number after the hyphen report the amount of word pairs, the numbers in brackets report ratio to its English original and the prefix before the dot in the name report type of assessments.

the model generates a list of the closest word in other language, and we need to find the correct translation in it. As a source of correct translations we used English-Russian dictionary of 53 186 translation pairs (Conneau et al., 2017). The evaluation on this measure was proposed as a precision on k nearest vectors of a word embedding model for $k = 1, 5, 10$.

4.3 Extrinsic Task and Our Dataset

Cross-language Paraphrase Detection. In an analogy with a monolingual paraphrase detection task (also called *sentence similarity identification*) (Androutsopoulos and Malakasiotis, 2010), the task is to identify whether sentence a in language A and sentence b in language B are paraphrases or not. This task is highly scalable, and usually figures as a sub-task of bigger tasks like cross-language plagiarism detection.

We are not aware of any dataset for this task, so we designed a benchmark ourselves for English-Russian language pair. The dataset was constructed on the base of Wikipedia articles covering wide range of topics from technology to sports. It contains 8 334 sentences with a balanced class distribution. The assessments and translations were done by 3 bilingual assessors. The negative results were obtained by automatically randomly sampling another sentence in the same domain from the datasets.

Translations were produced manually by a pool of human translators. Translators could paraphrase the translations using different techniques (according to our guidelines), and the assessors had to verify paraphrase technique labels and annotate similarity of English-Russian sentences in binary labels. We invited 3 assessors to estimate inter-annotator agreement. To obtain the evaluation scores, we conducted 3-fold cross validation and trained Logistic Regression with only one feature: cosine similarity of two sentence vectors. Sentence representations were built by averaging their word vectors.

In order to validate the correctness of results on our dataset, we automatically constructed a paraphrase set from a corpus of 1 million English-

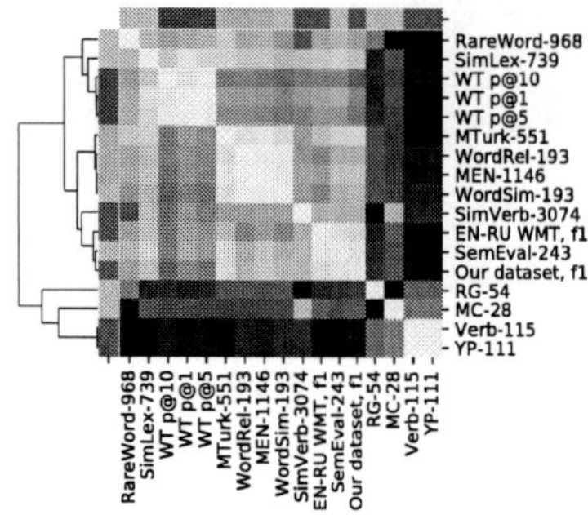

Figure 1: Clustermap of different evaluation techniques. Lighter color correspond to stronger positive correlation. Each row and column is labeled according to benchmark type: red – extrinsic, blue – verbs, purple – word translation, green – word relatedness, yellow – word similarity.

Russian parallel sentences from WMT'16*, generating for each sentence pair a semantic negative sample, searching for nearest sentence with a monolingual FastText model.

5   Results and Discussion

The results of the experiments with intrinsic and extrinsic evaluation are presented in Table 1. Despite the difference in scores for different models in one dataset could be minuscule, the scores for different intrinsic datasets vary a lot, and models that achieve higher results on one task often have lower results on other tasks.

Figure 1 shows mutual similarities between datasets (measured as Spearman's rank correlation between evaluation scores from Table 1). One can see that there are at least 4 clusters: extrinsic+SemEval; word relations; word translation+some word similarities; others.

Interestingly, *SemEval* behaves similarly to extrinsic tasks: this benchmark contains not only single words but also two-word expressions (e.g. *Borussia Dortmund*), so evaluation on this dataset is more similar to paraphrase detection task. Surprisingly, other word similarity datasets yield very different metrics. This is kind of unexpected, because paraphrase detection task relies on similarity of word senses.

Notably, many datasets from the same group (marked using color in the leftmost column on Figure 1) have difference in models' behavior (e.g.

SimLex and *WordSim* both being word similarity benchmarks are clustered away from each other).

Our datasets, aligned models and code to reproduce the experiments are available at our GitHub [†].

6   Conclusions and Future Work

In this work we explored primary limitations of evaluation methods of intrinsic cross-language word embeddings. We proposed experiments on 5 models in order to answer the question 'could we somehow estimate extrinsic performance of cross-language embeddings given some intrinsic metrics?'. Currently, the short answer is 'No', but the longer is 'maybe yes, if we understand the cognitive and linguistic regularities that take place in the benchmarks we use. Our point is that we not only need intrinsic datasets of different types if we want to robustly predict the performance of different extrinsic tasks, but we also should overthink the design and capabilities of existing extrinsic benchmarks.

Our research does not address some evaluation methods (like *MultiQVEC* (Ammar et al., 2016)) and word embeddings models (for instance, *Bivec* (Luong et al., 2015)) since Russian do not have enough linguistic resources: there are certain parallel corpora available at `http://opus.nlpl.eu`, but a merge of all English-Russian corpora has 773.0M/710.5M tokens, while the monolingual Russian model that we used in this study was trained on Wikipedia of 5B tokens (and English Wikipedia has a triple of this size). *A fortiori*, these corpora have different nature (subtitles, corpus of Europar speeches, etc), and we think that merging them would yield a dataset of unpredictable quality.

In future we plan to make a comparison with other languages giving more insights about performance of compared models. We also plan to investigate cross-language extensions of other intrinsic monolingual tasks (like the analogical reasoning task) to make our findings more generalizable.

Acknowledgments

The reported study was funded by the Russian Foundation for Basic Research project 16-37-60048 mol_a_dk and by the Ministry of Education and Science of the Russian Federation (grant 14.756.31.0001).

---

*https://translate.yandex.ru/corpus

[†]https://github.com/bakarov/cross-lang-embeddings

References

Eneko Agirre, Enrique Alfonseca, Keith Hall, Jana Kravalova, Marius Paşca, and Aitor Soroa. 2009. A study on similarity and relatedness using distributional and wordnet-based approaches. In *Proceedings of Human Language Technologies: The 2009 Annual Conference of the North American Chapter of the Association for Computational Linguistics*, pages 19–27. Association for Computational Linguistics.

Waleed Ammar, George Mulcaire, Yulia Tsvetkov, Guillaume Lample, Chris Dyer, and Noah A Smith. 2016. Massively multilingual word embeddings. *arXiv preprint arXiv:1602.01925.*

Ion Androutsopoulos and Prodromos Malakasiotis. 2010. A survey of paraphrasing and textual entailment methods. *Journal of Artificial Intelligence Research*, 38:135–187.

Mikel Artetxe, Gorka Labaka, and Eneko Agirre. 2018. Generalizing and improving bilingual word embedding mappings with a multi-step framework of linear transformations. In *Proceedings of the Thirty-Second AAAI Conference on Artificial Intelligence (AAAI-18)*.

Simon Baker, Roi Reichart, and Anna Korhonen. 2014. An unsupervised model for instance level subcategorization acquisition. In *EMNLP*, pages 278–289.

Miroslav Batchkarov, Thomas Kober, Jeremy Reffin, Julie Weeds, and David Weir. 2016. A critique of word similarity as a method for evaluating distributional semantic models.

Piotr Bojanowski, Edouard Grave, Armand Joulin, and Tomas Mikolov. 2016. Enriching word vectors with subword information. *arXiv preprint arXiv:1607.04606.*

Martin Braschler, Donna Harman, Michael Hess, Michael Kluck, Carol Peters, and Peter Schäuble. 2000. The evaluation of systems for cross-language information retrieval. In *LREC*.

Elia Bruni, Nam-Khanh Tran, and Marco Baroni. 2014. Multimodal distributional semantics. *J. Artif. Intell. Res.(JAIR)*, 49(2014):1–47.

Jose Camacho-Collados, Mohammad Taher Pilehvar, Nigel Collier, and Roberto Navigli. 2017. Semeval-2017 task 2: Multilingual and cross-lingual semantic word similarity. In *Proceedings of the 11th International Workshop on Semantic Evaluation (SemEval-2017)*, pages 15–26.

José Camacho-Collados, Mohammad Taher Pilehvar, and Roberto Navigli. 2015. A framework for the construction of monolingual and cross-lingual word similarity datasets. In *Proceedings of the 53rd Annual Meeting of the Association for Computational Linguistics and the 7th International Joint Conference on Natural Language Processing (Volume 2: Short Papers)*, volume 2, pages 1–7.

Alexis Conneau, Guillaume Lample, Marc'Aurelio Ranzato, Ludovic Denoyer, and Hervé Jégou. 2017. Word translation without parallel data. *arXiv preprint arXiv:1710.04087.*

Manaal Faruqui and Chris Dyer. 2014. Improving vector space word representations using multilingual correlation. In *Proceedings of EACL*.

Manaal Faruqui, Yulia Tsvetkov, Pushpendre Rastogi, and Chris Dyer. 2016. Problems with evaluation of word embeddings using word similarity tasks. *arXiv preprint arXiv:1605.02276.*

Daniela Gerz, Ivan Vulić, Felix Hill, Roi Reichart, and Anna Korhonen. 2016. Simverb-3500: A large-scale evaluation set of verb similarity. *arXiv preprint arXiv:1608.00869.*

Guy Halawi, Gideon Dror, Evgeniy Gabrilovich, and Yehuda Koren. 2012. Large-scale learning of word relatedness with constraints. In *Proceedings of the 18th ACM SIGKDD international conference on Knowledge discovery and data mining*, pages 1406–1414. ACM.

Felix Hill, Roi Reichart, and Anna Korhonen. 2016. Simlex-999: Evaluating semantic models with (genuine) similarity estimation. *Computational Linguistics*.

Maria Koptjevskaja-Tamm, Ekaterina Rakhilina, and Martine Vanhove. 2015. The semantics of lexical typology. *The Routledge Handbook of Semantics*, page 434.

Ira Leviant and Roi Reichart. 2015. Separated by an un-common language: Towards judgment language informed vector space modeling. *arXiv preprint arXiv:1508.00106.*

Farhana Ferdousi Liza and Marek Grzes. 2016. An improved crowdsourcing based evaluation technique for word embedding methods. *ACL 2016*, page 55.

Minh-Thang Luong, Hieu Pham, and Christopher D. Manning. 2015. Bilingual word representations with monolingual quality in mind. In *NAACL Workshop on Vector Space Modeling for NLP*.

Thang Luong, Richard Socher, and Christopher D Manning. 2013. Better word representations with recursive neural networks for morphology. In *CoNLL*, pages 104–113.

George A Miller and Walter G Charles. 1991. Contextual correlates of semantic similarity. *Language and cognitive processes*, 6(1):1–28.

Herbert Rubenstein and John B Goodenough. 1965. Contextual correlates of synonymy. *Communications of the ACM*, 8(10):627–633.

Sebastian Ruder. 2017. A survey of cross-lingual embedding models. *arXiv preprint arXiv:1706.04902.*

Daria Ryzhova, Maria Kyuseva, and Denis Paperno. 2016. Typology of adjectives benchmark for compositional distributional models. In *Proceedings of the Language Resources and Evaluation Conference*, pages 1253–1257. European Language Resources Association (ELRA).

Tobias Schnabel, Igor Labutov, David M Mimno, and Thorsten Joachims. 2015. Evaluation methods for unsupervised word embeddings. In *EMNLP*, pages 298–307.

Samuel L Smith, David HP Turban, Steven Hamblin, and Nils Y Hammerla. 2017. Offline bilingual word vectors, orthogonal transformations and the inverted softmax. *arXiv preprint arXiv:1702.03859*.

Shyam Upadhyay, Manaal Faruqui, Chris Dyer, and Dan Roth. 2016. Cross-lingual models of word embeddings: An empirical comparison. *arXiv preprint arXiv:1604.00425*.

Ivan Vulić and Marie-Francine Moens. 2013. Cross-lingual semantic similarity of words as the similarity of their semantic word responses. In *Proceedings of the 2013 Conference of the North American Chapter of the Association for Computational Linguistics: Human Language Technologies*, pages 106–116.

Dongqiang Yang and David Martin Powers. 2006. Verb similarity on the taxonomy of wordnet. In *The Third International WordNet Conference: GWC 2006*. Masaryk University.

How Gender and Skin Tone Modifiers Affect Emoji Semantics in Twitter

Francesco Barbieri
LASTUS Lab, TALN
Universitat Pompeu Fabra
Barcelona, Spain
`name.surname@upf.edu`

Jose Camacho-Collados
School of Computer Science and Informatics
Cardiff University
United Kingdom
`camachocolladosj@cardiff.ac.uk`

Abstract

In this paper we analyze the use of emojis in social media with respect to gender and skin tone. By gathering a dataset of over twenty two million tweets from United States some findings are clearly highlighted after performing a simple frequency-based analysis. Moreover, we carry out a semantic analysis on the usage of emojis and their modifiers (e.g. gender and skin tone) by embedding all words, emojis and modifiers into the same vector space. Our analyses reveal that some stereotypes related to the skin color and gender seem to be reflected on the use of these modifiers. For example, emojis representing hand gestures are more widely utilized with lighter skin tones, and the usage across skin tones differs significantly. At the same time, the vector corresponding to the male modifier tends to be semantically close to emojis related to business or technology, whereas their female counterparts appear closer to emojis about love or makeup.

1 Introduction

Gender and race stereotypes are still present in many places of our lives. These stereotype-based biases are directly reflected on the data that can be gathered from different sources such as visual or textual contents. In fact, it has been shown how these biases can lead to problematic behaviours such as an increase in discrimination (Podesta et al., 2014). These biases have already been studied in diverse text data sources (Zhao et al., 2017), and have been proved to propagate to supervised and unsupervised techniques learning from them, including word embeddings (Bolukbasi et al., 2016; Caliskan et al., 2017; Zhao et al., 2018) and end-user applications like online ads (Sweeney, 2013).

In this paper we study the biases produced in a newer form of communication in social media

from an analytical point of view. We focus on the use of emojis and their interaction with the textual content within a social network (i.e. Twitter). We study emojis as another part of the message, as it could be words. An interesting feature about emojis, apart from their increasing use in diverse social media platforms, is that they enable us to numerically measure some biases with respect to gender and race. Recently, emojis have introduced modifiers as part of their encoding. With these modifiers the same emoji can be used with different features: as male or female, or with different skin colors, for example.

We approach the problem from two methodological perspectives. First, we analyze the use of emojis and their modifiers from a numerical point of view, counting their occurrences in a corpus. This already gives us important hints of how these emojis are used. Then, we leverage the SW2V (*Senses and Words to Vectors*) embedding model (Mancini et al., 2017) to train a joint vector space in which emojis and their modifiers are encoded together, enabling us to analyze their semantic interpretation. While there have been approaches attempting to model emojis with distributional semantics (Aoki and Uchida, 2011; Barbieri et al., 2016; Eisner et al., 2016; Ljubešic and Fišer, 2016; Wijeratne et al., 2017), to the best of our knowledge this is the first work that semantically analyzes modifiers as well. In fact, even though the information provided by modifiers can be extremely useful (for the modeling of emojis in particular, and of messages in social media in general), this has been neglected by previous approaches modeling and predicting emojis (Barbieri et al., 2017; Felbo et al., 2017).

Following our two complementary methodological perspectives, we reached similar conclusions: many stereotypes related to gender and race are also present in this new form of communication.

*Proceedings of the 7th Joint Conference on Lexical and Computational Semantics (*SEM), pages 101–106*
New Orleans, June 5-6, 2018. ©2018 Association for Computational Linguistics

Figure 1: Recent tweets using the dark fist emoji (dark skin color in the first and medium-dark in the second).

Moreover, we encountered other interesting findings related to the usage of emojis with respect to gender and skin tones. For instance, our analysis revealed that light skin tones are more widely used than dark ones and their usage is different in many cases. However, incidentally the dark raised fist emoji (i.e. ✊) is significantly more used, proportionally, than its lighter counterparts. This is mainly due to the protest black community started in favour of human rights, dating back from the Olympic Games of Mexico 1968. This sign was known as the *Black Power salute* (Osmond, 2010) and is still widely used nowadays, especially in social media symbolized by the above-mentioned dark-tone fist emoji. Figure 1 shows two recent tweets using this emoji as a response to some Donald Trump critics to NFL players protesting for black civil rights by kneeing during the national anthem before their games. As far as gender-based features are concerned, female modifiers appear much closer to emojis related to love and makeup, while the male ones are closer to business or technology items.

2 Methodology

For this paper we make use of the encoding of emoji modifiers (Section 2.1) and exploit an embedding model that enables us to learn all words, emojis and modifiers in the same vector space (Section 2.2).

2.1 Emoji Modifiers

Emoji modifiers are features that provide more precise information of a given emoji. For example, a hand-based emoji (e.g. ✋) can have different skin colors: light, medium-light, medium, medium-dark, or dark. This information has been recently added in the official encoding of emojis[1]. At the same time, some emojis like a person rising a hand could be displayed as a woman (i.e. 🙋) or a man (i.e. 🙋). We exploit this information provided by modifiers to study the role of gender and skin color in social media communication.

2.2 Joint Vector Space Model

We construct a vector space model in which words, emojis and their modifiers share the same space. To this end, we exploit SW2V[2] (Mancini et al., 2017), which is an extension of Word2Vec (Mikolov et al., 2013) and was originally designed for learning word and sense embeddings on the same vector space. Given an input corpus, SW2V trains words and its associated senses simultaneously, exploiting their intrinsic connections. In our work, however, we are not interested in learning embeddings for senses but for emojis and their modifiers.

Formally, we use the SW2V model by extending the input and output layers of the neural network with emoji modifiers. The main objective function of the CBOW architecture of Word2Vec aiming at predicting the target word in the middle does not change, except when the model has to predict an emoji with its modifier(s). In this case, instead of simply trying to classify the word in the middle, we also take into account the set of associated emojis. This is equivalent to minimizing the following loss function:

$$-\log(p(e_t|E^t, M^t)) - \sum_{m \in M_t} \log(p(m|E^t, M^t))$$

where M_t refers to the set of modifier(s) of the target emoji e_t. $E^t = w_{t-n}, ..., w_{t-1}, w_{t+1}, ..., w_{t+n}$ and $M^t = M_{t-n}, ..., M_{t-1}, M_{t+1}, ..., M_{t+n}$ both represent the context of the target emoji. While E^t includes surface words (w_i) as context, M^t includes the modifiers of the emojis (M_i) within the surrounding context, if any[3].

The resulting output is a shared space of word, emoji and modifier embeddings. In addition, we

---

[1] http://unicode.org/reports/tr51/
#Emoji_Modifiers_Table
[2] http://lcl.uniroma1.it/sw2v/
[3] M^t may be empty if no modified emoji occurs in the context of the target emoji.

propose a second variant[4] of the SW2V architecture modeling words, non-modified emojis and emojis associated with their modifiers (e.g. ✋). For example, for the emoji black hand (✋) this variant would learn the embedding for the hand without any modifier, and the same emoji with the modifier *dark* (i.e. ✊) instead of the embedding for the modifier alone learned in the main configuration of our SW2V model.

The advantages of using this model with respect to a usual word embedding model are manifold: first, it enables us to separate modifiers from emojis so we can learn accurate representations for both types; second, with this model we can learn embeddings for words, emojis and their modifiers in the same vector space, a property that is exploited in our experiments; third, since an emoji with modifiers may occur quite infrequently, by using this approach we take into account the semantic of the emoji (e.g. ✋) so the representation of the emoji with their modifiers (e.g. ✋, ✋...) is more accurate; finally, with this model we can associate a given emoji with one or more modifiers (e.g. skin color and gender on the same emoji).

3 Experiments

All our experiments are carried out on a corpus compiled from Twitter, including all tweets geolocalized in United States from October 2015 to January 2018. The corpus contains over 22M tweets and around 319M tokens overall. In the corpus we encode emojis and their modifiers as single joint instances. Taking this corpus as reference, we inspect the use of emojis with respect to skin tone and gender from two complementary methodological perspectives: frequency-based (Section 3.1) and semantics-based (Section 3.2).

3.1 Frequency

By exploring the frequency of emojis in Twitter we can obtain a clear overview of their diverse use regarding skin tone. To this end, we carried out a frequency analysis on hand-related emojis with different skin color modifiers: light, medium-light, medium, medium-dark, dark, and neutral (i.e. no modifier). Table 1 shows the frequency of the top twenty most frequent hand-related emojis according to skin tone. As can be clearly seen, the emojis without any particular skin tone mod-

---

[4]We use this second variant in our last semantics-based experiment in Section 3.2.2.

	No mod					
Abs	121,343	70,139	102,397	61,865	50,871	7,621
Rel	29.3	16.9	24.7	14.9	12.2	1.8

Table 1: Absolute and relative (%) frequency of hand-related emojis. These frequency estimators indicate the number of tweets where an emoji occurs, without considering repetitions.

ifier (yellow), which are displayed by default, are the most frequent. However, it is surprising to note the gap between the usage of the light-tone emojis (over 70K occurrences with over almost 17% overall) with respect to dark-tone emojis (less than 8K occurrences which corresponds to less than 2% overall). Nevertheless, this gap may be simply due to demographics, since many Twitter users employ modifiers as a form of self-representation (Robertson et al., 2018).

In addition to the raw frequencies of these emojis and their modifiers we analyze how these emojis were used proportionally for each skin tone. Table 2 displays the proportion of emojis used per skin color. Interestingly, the pattern followed by the darker emojis is clearly different from the distribution followed by lighter ones (Pearson correlation of 98% between light and medium-light tones in comparison to the relatively low 71% between light and dark tones). For example, the emoji corresponding to the raised fist (i.e. ✊) is significantly more used for the dark tone than the light ones (10.3% to 1.6%). The reason, as explained in the introduction, dates back from the Olympic Games of 1968 (Osmond, 2010). It represents the fight of the black community for human rights, which is still present nowadays, as highlighted in the recent tweets of Figure 1. Additionally, the hand emoji representing the middle finger raised (i.e. 🖕), which is often used as an insult, occurs proportionally significantly more often with the dark skin color (2.2% to 0.5%). In contrast, light skin tone emojis tend to be more used for emojis including some form of assertion: e.g. 👌 (12% vs 6.7%), and the 👍 (7.8% vs 3.7%).

3.2 Semantics

For inspecting the semantics of each emoji and its modifiers we rely on the joint semantic vector space (SW2V) of words, emojis and modifiers described in Section 2.2. We ran SW2V in our Twitter corpus with the following hyperparame-

	no modifier	light	medium-light	medium	medium-dark	dark
	13.0	15.7	14.9	16.1	17.5	12.2
	12.9	8.8	11.3	13.7	14.2	13.5
	12.5	12.0	10.9	9.0	7.8	6.7
	12.0	9.9	9.0	15.0	18.5	20.0
	11.4	12.8	15.0	10.6	8.8	8.6
	10.3	7.8	5.3	3.5	2.9	3.7
	6.0	14.1	14.3	11.0	7.8	8.3
	4.6	4.5	4.6	3.9	2.6	3.5
	4.1	3.9	3.3	3.0	2.5	2.2
	2.4	3.1	2.9	2.6	2.0	1.4
	2.3	1.1	1.0	1.4	1.5	1.7
	2.2	1.6	2.4	4.4	7.7	10.3
	2.0	1.3	1.7	1.7	1.7	2.1
	1.0	0.8	0.8	0.9	0.9	0.9
	0.8	0.4	0.6	0.7	0.6	0.7
	0.7	0.6	0.5	0.5	0.4	0.7
	0.6	0.2	0.3	0.4	0.5	0.4
	0.5	0.8	0.7	1.2	1.6	2.2
	0.5	0.3	0.3	0.2	0.2	0.3
	0.5	0.3	0.2	0.4	0.5	0.7

Table 2: Relative frequency (%) of the top twenty hand-related emojis with respect to skin modifiers (from left to right: no modifier, light, medium-light, medium, medium-dark, dark).

Table 3: Fifteen emoji nearest neighbours of the seven modifiers in our analysis.

ters: 100 dimensions and window size of 6 tokens. We performed two kinds of experiment: one relying on the nearest neighbours in the vector space to understand the main semantics of skin tone and gender modifiers (Section 3.2.1) and another experiment in which we analyze the main semantic divergences between opposing modifiers (Section 3.2.2), i.e. dark vs. light (skin tone) and male vs. female (gender).

3.2.1 Nearest Neighbours

For this experiment we analyze the nearest neighbours of skin tone and gender modifiers in the SW2V vector space using cosine similarity as comparison measure. Table 3 shows the fifteen nearest neighbours for the five skin tone and two gender modifiers. For the skin tone modifiers it is noteworthy the fact that while lighter tones contain love-related emojis as nearest neighbours, these do not appear on the list of darker tones. Instead, we can see some money-related (e.g. 💰, 💸 or 🏧) and electric-related emojis (e.g. a battery 🔋 or a plug 🔌) as nearest neighbours of dark tone emojis. These two electric emojis are often used in the context of music, sport or motivational tweets

along with hashtags like *#energy* or *#chargedup* (e.g. *The GRIND begins!!! Refuse to settle for average!! 🔋 ⚡ 🏋 #chargedup*). As a possibly more worrying trend we found many versions of the (often derogatory) word *nigger* and *gang* as nearest neighbours of dark tone modifiers. A more focused analysis on this issue would be required in order to understand the possible racist implications.

As far as gender modifiers are concerned, business-related emojis (e.g. a briefcase 💼, a suit 👔 or a handshake 🤝) are among the closest emojis to the man modifier in the SW2V vector space, while nail polishing (i.e. 💅) or the selfie emoji (i.e. 🤳), for example, are among the nearest neighbours of the female modifier.

3.2.2 Semantic Divergences

In addition to the nearest neighbours experiments, we analyze the highest semantic similarity gap between skin tone and gender modifiers. In Table 4 we display in each row the emojis with the highest similarity gap with respect to the opposite modifier (light vs. dark and male vs. female), being more similar to the corresponding modifier row. In this case we can see a similar pattern as in the nearest neighbours experiment. A money-related emoji appears again semantically close to the dark-skin modifier (💰) but far from the light skin modifier, and love-related emojis closer to the light skin modifier (e.g. 💜, 💙 and 💚). Likewise,

Table 4: Emojis with highest similarity gap between opposite modifiers (light *vs* dark, male *vs* female).

we can see how technology-related emojis (e.g. a CD 💿, a video camera 📹 or a television 📺) are close to the man modifier and far from the female one. In contrast, makeup-related emojis like nail polishing (i.e. 💅) or the lipstick emoji (i.e. 💄) are clearly female-based.

In order to complement this experiment, we also inspect the emojis whose similarity was lower when changing the modifier.[5] We compare the similarity between all emojis which can have a skin color or gender modifier. Table 5 shows the fifteen emojis whose semantic similarity, as measured by cosine similarity, was lower by switching to the corresponding opposite modifier. The first surprising finding that arises is the low similarity values (negative values lower than -0.6 in some cases), considering that the only change is the modifier, while the emoji does not change. The emojis that change most when switching the skin tone are in the main hand gestures. Conversely, the emojis that change most when switching the gender modifier are people in job roles such as detective (i.e. 🕵), judge (i.e. 👨‍⚖️), police officer (i.e. 👮) or teacher (i.e. 👨‍🏫). From these four items only the teacher emoji is closer to the female modifier, while the other three are closer to the male modifier. In contrast, emojis referring to other jobs like fireman (i.e. 👨‍🚒), artist (i.e. 👨‍🎨) or singer (i.e. 👨‍🎤) do not seem to considerably change their meaning when switching their gender.

4 Conclusion

In this paper we have studied the role of gender and skin tone in social media communication through emojis. Thank to the modifiers associated with different emojis and the usage of a joint semantic vector space of words, emojis and modifiers, we were able to model the semantics of emo-

Skin Tone		Gender	
	-0.621		-0.422
	-0.601		-0.346
	-0.590		-0.331
	-0.541		-0.289
	-0.535		-0.277
	-0.490		-0.222
	-0.427		-0.195
	-0.409		-0.191
	-0.388		-0.185
	-0.375		-0.174
	-0.374		-0.169
	-0.366		-0.144
	-0.349		-0.127
	-0.347		-0.117
	-0.344		-0.114

Table 5: Emojis with lowest similarity using opposite modifiers (light *vs* dark, male *vs* female).

jis with respect to gender and skin tone features[6].

Our analysis on a corpus of tweets geolocalized in United States reveals clear connotations associated with each gender. For example, male modifiers being much closer to business and technology while female ones are often associated with love and makeup. Other connotations are present with respect to the skin color, being dark tone hand emojis more associated with derogatory words and emojis[7]. In a more general perspective, these modifiers clearly increase the ambiguity of emojis, which were already shown highly ambiguous in many cases (Wijeratne et al., 2016; Miller et al., 2017). In fact, modifiers can render emoji meanings very far apart, as clearly showed in Table 5.

While in this work we have approached the problem from a purely analytical point of view, our work can also be viewed as a starting point for the development of accurate education guidelines that could contribute to a reduction of gender- and race-associated stereotypes in society. Additionally, the understanding of emoji semantics provided in our analysis paves the way for the development of debiasing techniques to be leveraged on supervised and unsupervised models which make use of social media data, in the lines of Bolukbasi et al. (2016) and Zhao et al. (2017).

---

[5] For this last experiment we used the SW2V variant in which emojis with their modifiers are included in the vector space (cf. Section 2.2).

[6] Code and SW2V embeddings are available at `https://github.com/fvancesco/emoji_modifiers`

[7] This goes in line with some previous findings about the use of modifiers in other platforms such as Apple: `goo.gl/Ua1XoK`

Acknowledgments

We thank Roberto Carlini for the initial idea of the paper, and Luis Espinox-Anke for fruitful discussions on this topic. Francesco B. acknowledges support from the TUNER project (TIN2015-65308-C5-5-R, MINECO/FEDER, UE) and the Maria de Maeztu Units of Excellence Programme (MDM-2015-0502).

References

Sho Aoki and Osamu Uchida. 2011. A method for automatically generating the emotional vectors of emoticons using weblog articles. In *Proceedings of the 10th WSEAS International Conference on Applied Computer and Applied Computational Science, Stevens Point, Wisconsin, USA*, pages 132–136.

Francesco Barbieri, Miguel Ballesteros, and Horacio Saggion. 2017. Are emojis predictable? In *Proceedings of the 15th Conference of the European Chapter of the Association for Computational Linguistics: Volume 2, Short Papers*, volume 2, pages 105–111.

Francesco Barbieri, German Kruszewski, Francesco Ronzano, and Horacio Saggion. 2016. How cosmopolitan are emojis?: Exploring emojis usage and meaning over different languages with distributional semantics. In *Proceedings of the 2016 ACM on Multimedia Conference*, pages 531–535. ACM.

Tolga Bolukbasi, Kai-Wei Chang, James Y Zou, Venkatesh Saligrama, and Adam T Kalai. 2016. Man is to computer programmer as woman is to homemaker? debiasing word embeddings. In *Advances in Neural Information Processing Systems*, pages 4349–4357.

Aylin Caliskan, Joanna J Bryson, and Arvind Narayanan. 2017. Semantics derived automatically from language corpora contain human-like biases. *Science*, 356(6334):183–186.

Ben Eisner, Tim Rocktäschel, Isabelle Augenstein, Matko Bosnjak, and Sebastian Riedel. 2016. emoji2vec: Learning emoji representations from their description. In *Proceedings of The Fourth International Workshop on Natural Language Processing for Social Media*, pages 48–54, Austin, TX, USA. Association for Computational Linguistics.

Bjarke Felbo, Alan Mislove, Anders Søgaard, Iyad Rahwan, and Sune Lehmann. 2017. Using millions of emoji occurrences to learn any-domain representations for detecting sentiment, emotion and sarcasm. In *Proceedings of the 2017 Conference on Empirical Methods in Natural Language Processing*, pages 1615–1625.

Nikola Ljubešic and Darja Fišer. 2016. A global analysis of emoji usage. In *Proceedings of the 10th Web as Corpus Workshop (WAC-X) and the EmpiriST Shared Task*, pages 82–89, Berlin, Germany. Association for Computational Linguistics.

Massimiliano Mancini, Jose Camacho-Collados, Ignacio Iacobacci, and Roberto Navigli. 2017. Embedding words and senses together via joint knowledge-enhanced training. In *Proceedings of CoNLL*, Vancouver, Canada.

Tomas Mikolov, Kai Chen, Greg Corrado, and Jeffrey Dean. 2013. Efficient estimation of word representations in vector space. *CoRR*, abs/1301.3781.

Hannah Miller, Daniel Kluver, Jacob Thebault-Spieker, Loren Terveen, and Brent Hecht. 2017. Understanding emoji ambiguity in context: The role of text in emoji-related miscommunication. In *11th International Conference on Web and Social Media, ICWSM 2017*. AAAI Press.

Gary Osmond. 2010. Photographs, materiality and sport history: Peter norman and the 1968 mexico city black power salute. *Journal of Sport History*, 37(1):119–137.

John Podesta, Penny Pritzker, Ernest J. Moniz, John Holdren, and Jefrey Zients. 2014. *Big data: Seizing opportunities, preserving values*. White House, Executive Office of the President.

Alexander Robertson, Walid Magdy, and Sharon Goldwater. 2018. Self-representation on twitter using emoji skin color modifiers. *arXiv preprint arXiv:1803.10738*.

Latanya Sweeney. 2013. Discrimination in online ad delivery. *Queue*, 11(3):10.

Sanjaya Wijeratne, Lakshika Balasuriya, Amit Sheth, and Derek Doran. 2016. Emojinet: Building a machine readable sense inventory for emoji. In *International Conference on Social Informatics*, pages 527–541. Springer.

Sanjaya Wijeratne, Lakshika Balasuriya, Amit Sheth, and Derek Doran. 2017. A semantics-based measure of emoji similarity. In *Proceedings of the International Conference on Web Intelligence*, pages 646–653. ACM.

Jieyu Zhao, Tianlu Wang, Mark Yatskar, Vicente Ordonez, and Kai-Wei Chang. 2017. Men also like shopping: Reducing gender bias amplification using corpus-level constraints. In *Proceedings of the 2017 Conference on Empirical Methods in Natural Language Processing*, pages 2979–2989.

Jieyu Zhao, Tianlu Wang, Mark Yatskar, Vicente Ordonez, and Kai-Wei Chang. 2018. Gender bias in coreference resolution: Evaluation and debiasing methods. In *Proceedings of NAACL*, New Orleans, LA, United States.

Element-wise Bilinear Interaction for Sentence Matching

Jihun Choi, Taeuk Kim, Sang-goo Lee
Department of Computer Science and Engineering
Seoul National University, Seoul, Korea
{jhchoi,taeuk,sglee}@europa.snu.ac.kr

Abstract

When we build a neural network model predicting the relationship between two sentences, the most general and intuitive approach is to use a Siamese architecture, where the sentence vectors obtained from a shared encoder is given as input to a classifier. For the classifier to work effectively, it is important to extract appropriate features from the two vectors and feed them as input. There exist several previous works that suggest heuristic-based function for matching sentence vectors, however it cannot be said that the heuristics tailored for a specific task generalize to other tasks. In this work, we propose a new matching function, *ElBiS*, that learns to model element-wise interaction between two vectors. From experiments, we empirically demonstrate that the proposed ElBiS matching function outperforms the concatenation-based or heuristic-based matching functions on natural language inference and paraphrase identification, while maintaining the fused representation compact.

1 Introduction

Identifying the relationship between two sentences is a key component for various natural language processing tasks such as paraphrase identification, semantic relatedness prediction, textual entailment recognition, etc. The most general and intuitive approach to these problems would be to encode each sentence using a sentence encoder network and feed the encoded vectors to a classifier network.[1]

For a model to predict the relationship correctly, it is important for the input to the classifier to contain appropriate information. The most naïve

method is to concatenate the two vectors and delegate the role of extracting features to subsequent network components. However, despite the theoretical fact that even a single-hidden layer feedforward network can approximate any arbitrary function (Cybenko, 1989; Hornik, 1991), the space of network parameters is too large, and it is helpful to narrow down the search space by directly giving information about interaction to the classifier model, as empirically proven in previous works built for various tasks (Ji and Eisenstein, 2013; Mou et al., 2016; Xiong et al., 2016, to name but a few).

In this paper, we propose a matching function which learns from data to fuse two sentence vectors and extract useful features. Unlike bilinear pooling methods designed for matching vectors from heterogeneous domain (e.g. image and text), our proposed method utilizes element-wise bilinear interaction between vectors rather than interdimensional interaction. In §3, we will describe the intuition and assumption behind the restriction of interaction.

This paper is organized as follows. In §2, we briefly introduce previous work related to our objective. The detailed explanation of the proposed model is given in §3, and we show its effectiveness in extracting compact yet powerful features in §4. §5 concludes the paper.

2 Related Work

As stated above, matching sentences is a common component in various tasks in natural language processing. Ji and Eisenstein (2013) empirically prove that the use of element-wise multiplication and absolute difference as matching function substantially improve performance on paraphrase identification, and Tai et al. (2015) apply the same matching scheme to the semantic related-

---

[1] The encoded vectors can also be fed into a regression network, however in this work we focus only on classification.

107

*Proceedings of the 7th Joint Conference on Lexical and Computational Semantics (*SEM)*, pages 107–112
New Orleans, June 5-6, 2018. ©2018 Association for Computational Linguistics

ness prediction task. Mou et al. (2016) show that using the element-wise multiplication and difference along with the concatenation of sentence vectors yields good performance in natural language inference, despite redundant components such as concatenation and element-wise difference. Yogatama et al. (2017) and Chen et al. (2017) use modified versions of the heuristics proposed by Mou et al. (2016) in natural language inference.

However, to the best of our knowledge, there exists little work on a method that adaptively learns to extract features from two sentence vectors encoded by a shared encoder. Though not directly related to our work's focus, there exist approaches to fuse vectors from a homogeneous space using exact or approximate bilinear form (Socher et al., 2013; Lin et al., 2015; Wu et al., 2016; Krause et al., 2016).

There have been several works for extracting features from two heterogeneous vectors. Wu et al. (2013) use a bilinear model to match queries and documents from different domains. Also, approximate bilinear matching techniques such as multimodal compact bilinear pooling (MCB; Fukui et al., 2016), low-rank bilinear pooling (MLB; Kim et al., 2017), and factorized bilinear pooling (MFB; Yu et al., 2017) are successfully applied in visual question answering (VQA) tasks, outperforming heuristic feature functions (Xiong et al., 2016; Agrawal et al., 2017).

MCB approximate the full bilinear matching using Count Sketch (Charikar et al., 2002) algorithm, MLB and MFB decompose a third-order tensor into multiple weight matrices, and MUTAN (Ben-younes et al., 2017) use Tucker decomposition to parameterize bilinear interactions. Although these bilinear pooling methods give significant performance improvement in the context of VQA, we found that they do not help matching sentences encoded by a shared encoder.

3 Proposed Method: *ElBiS*

As pointed out by previous works on sentence matching (Ji and Eisenstein, 2013; Mou et al., 2016), heuristic matching functions bring substantial gain in performance over the simple concatenation of sentence vectors. However, we believe that there could be other important interaction that simple heuristics miss, and the optimal heuristic could differ from task to task. In this section, we propose a general matching function that learns to

extract compact and effective features from data.

Let $\mathbf{a} = (a_1, \cdots, a_d) \in \mathbb{R}^d$ and $\mathbf{b} = (b_1, \cdots, b_d) \in \mathbb{R}^d$ be sentence vectors obtained from a encoder network.[2] And let us define $\mathbf{G} \in \mathbb{R}^{d \times 3}$ as a matrix constructed by stacking three vectors $\mathbf{a}, \mathbf{b}, \vec{\mathbf{1}} \in \mathbb{R}^d$ where $\vec{\mathbf{1}}$ is the vector of all ones, and denote the i-th row of $\mathbf{G}$ by $\mathbf{g}_i$.

Then the result of applying our proposed matching function, $\mathbf{r} = (r_1, \cdots, r_d) \in \mathbb{R}^d$, is defined by

$$r_i = \phi\left(\mathbf{g}_i^\top \mathbf{W}_i \mathbf{g}_i\right), \qquad (1)$$

where $\mathbf{W}_i \in \mathbb{R}^{3 \times 3}, i \in \{1, \cdots, d\}$ is a matrix of trainable parameters and $\phi(\cdot)$ an activation function (tanh in our experiments).

Due to its use of bilinear form, it can model every quadratic relation between a_i and b_i, i.e. can represent every linear combination of $\{a_i^2, b_i^2, a_i b_i, a_i, b_i, 1\}$. This means that the proposed method is able to express frequently used element-wise heuristics such as element-wise sum, multiplication, subtraction, etc., in addition to other possible relations.[3]

Further, to consider multiple types of element-wise interaction, we use a set of M weight matrices per dimension. That is, for each $\mathbf{g}_i$, we get M scalar outputs $(r_i^1, \cdots, r_i^M)$ by applying Eq. 1 using a set of separate weight matrices $(\mathbf{W}_i^1, \cdots, \mathbf{W}_i^M)$:

$$r_i^m = \phi\left(\mathbf{g}_i^\top \mathbf{W}_i^m \mathbf{g}_i\right). \qquad (2)$$

Implementation-wise, we vertically stack G for M times to construct $\tilde{\mathbf{G}} \in \mathbb{R}^{Md \times 3}$, and use each row $\tilde{\mathbf{g}}_i$ as input to Eq. 1. As a result, the resulting output $\mathbf{r}$ becomes a Md-dimensional vector:

$$r_i = \phi\left(\tilde{\mathbf{g}}_i^\top \mathbf{W}_i \tilde{\mathbf{g}}_i\right), \qquad (3)$$

where $\mathbf{W}_i \in \mathbb{R}^{3 \times 3}, i \in \{1, \cdots, Md\}$. Eq. 1 is the special case of Eq. 2 and 3 where $M = 1$. We call our proposed element-wise bilinear matching function *ElBiS* (Element-wise Bilinear Sentence Matching).

Note that our element-wise matching requires only $M \times 3 \times 3 \times d$ parameters, the number of

---

[2] Throughout this paper, we assume a d-dimensional vector is equivalent to the corresponding $d \times 1$ matrix.

[3] Though a bilinear form cannot represent the absolute difference between inputs, note that $(a_i - b_i)^2 = a_i^2 - 2a_i b_i + b_i^2$ can alternatively represent commutative difference. Yogatama et al. (2017) use this quadratic form instead of the absolute difference.

which is substantially less than that of full bilinear matching, Md^3. For example, in the case of $d = 300$ and $Md = 1200$ (the frequently used set of hyperparameters in NLI), the full bilinear matching needs 108 million parameters, while the element-wise matching needs only 10,800 parameters.

Why element-wise? In the scenario we are focusing on, sentence vectors are computed from a Siamese network, and thus it can be said that the vectors are in the same semantic space. Therefore, the effect of considering interdimensional interaction is less significant than that of multimodal pooling (e.g. matching a text and a image vector), so we decided to model more powerful interaction within the same dimension instead. We also would like to remark that our preliminary experiments, where MFB (Yu et al., 2017) or MLB (Kim et al., 2017) was adopted as matching function, were not successful.

4 Experiments

We evelute our proposed ElBiS model on the natural language inference and paraphrase identification task. Implementation for experiments will be made public.

4.1 Natural Language Inference

Natural language inference (NLI), also called recognizing textual entailment (RTE), is a task whose objective is to predict the relationship between a premise and a hypothesis sentence. We conduct experiments using Stanford Natural Language Inference Corpus (SNLI; Bowman et al., 2015), one of the most famous dataset for the NLI task. The SNLI dataset consists of roughly 570k premise-hypothesis pairs, each of which is annotated with a label (entailment, contradiction, or neutral).

For sentence encoder, we choose the encoder based on long short-term memory (LSTM; Hochreiter and Schmidhuber, 1997) architecture as baseline model, which is similar to that of Bowman et al. (2015) and Bowman et al. (2016). It consists of a single layer unidirectional LSTM network that reads a sentence from left to right, and the last hidden state is used as the sentence vector. We also conduct experiments using a more elaborated encoder model, Gumbel Tree-LSTM (Choi et al., 2018). As a classifier network, we use an MLP with a single hidden layer. In experiments

Matching Fn.	# Params.	Acc. (%)
Concat	1.34M	81.6
Heuristic	1.96M	83.9
ElBiS ($M = 1$)	1.04M	84.4
ElBiS ($M = 2$)	1.35M	84.5
ElBiS ($M = 3$)	1.66M	**85.0**
ElBiS ($M = 4$)	1.97M	84.6

Table 1: Results on the SNLI task using LSTM-based sentence encoders.

Matching Fn.	# Params.	Acc. (%)
Concat	2.25M	82.4
Heuristic	2.86M	84.6
ElBiS ($M = 1$)	1.94M	84.8
ElBiS ($M = 2$)	2.25M	85.6
ElBiS ($M = 3$)	2.56M	**85.9**
ElBiS ($M = 4$)	2.87M	85.6

Table 2: Results on the SNLI task using Gumbel Tree-LSTM-based sentence encoders.

with heuristic matching we use the heuristic features proposed by Mou et al. (2016) and adopted in many works on the NLI task: $[\mathbf{a}; \mathbf{b}; \mathbf{a} - \mathbf{b}; \mathbf{a} \odot \mathbf{b}]$, where $\mathbf{a}$ and $\mathbf{b}$ are encoded sentence vectors. For more detailed experimental settings, we refer readers to §A.1.

Table 1 and 2 contain results on the SNLI task. We can see that models that adopt the proposed ElBiS matching function extract powerful features leading to a performance gain, while keeping similar or less number of parameters. Also, though not directly related to our main contribution, we found that, with elaborated initialization and regularization, simple LSTM models (even the one with the heuristic matching function) achieve competitive performance with those of state-of-the-art models.[4]

4.2 Paraphrase Identification

Another popular task on identifying relationship between a sentence pair is paraphrase identification (PI). The objective of the PI task is to predict whether a given sentence pair has the same meaning or not. To correctly identify the paraphrase relationship, an input to a classifier should contain the semantic similarity and difference between sentences.

For evaluation of paraphrase identification, we

---

[4]https://nlp.stanford.edu/projects/snli

Matching Fn.	# Params.	Acc. (%)
Concat	1.34M	85.0
Heuristic	1.34M	87.0
ElBiS ($M = 1$)	1.04M	86.7
ElBiS ($M = 2$)	1.35M	**87.3**
ElBiS ($M = 3$)	1.66M	87.1

Table 3: Results on the PI task using LSTM-based sentence encoders.

use Quora Question Pairs dataset[5]. The dataset contains 400k question pairs, each of which is annotated with a label indicating whether the questions of the pair have the same meaning. To our knowledge, the Quora dataset is the largest available dataset of paraphrase identification. We used the same training, development, test splits as the ones used in Wang et al. (2017).

For experiments with heuristic matching, we used the function proposed by Ji and Eisenstein (2013), which is shown by the authors to be effective in matching vectors in latent space compared to simple concatenation. It is composed of the element-wise product and absolute difference between two vectors: $[\mathbf{a} \odot \mathbf{b}; |\mathbf{a} - \mathbf{b}|]$, where $\mathbf{a}$ and $\mathbf{b}$ are encoded sentence vectors.

Similar to NLI experiments, we use a single layer unidirectional LSTM network as sentence encoder, and we state detailed settings in §A.2. The results on the PI task is listed in Table 3. Again we can see that the models armed with the ElBiS matching function discover parsimonious and effective interaction between vectors.

5 Conclusion and Discussion

In this work, we propose ElBiS, a general method of fusing information from two sentence vectors. Our method does not rely on heuristic knowledge constructed for a specific task, and adaptively learns from data the element-wise connections between vectors from data. From experiments, we demonstrated that the proposed method outperforms or matches the performance of commonly used concatenation-based or heuristic-based feature functions, while maintaining the fused representation compact.

Although the main focus of this work is about sentence matching, the notion of element-wise bilinear interaction could be applied beyond sentence matching. For example, many models that specialize in NLI have components where the heuristic matching function is used, e.g. in computing intra-sentence or inter-sentence attention weights. It could be interesting future work to replace these components with our proposed matching function.

One of the main drawback of our proposed method is that, due to its improved expressiveness, it makes a model overfit easily. When evaluated on small datasets such as Sentences Involving Compositional Knowledge dataset (SICK; Marelli et al., 2014) and Microsoft Research Paraphrase Corpus (MSRP; Dolan and Brockett, 2005), we observed performance degradation, partly due to overfitting. Similarly, we observed that increasing the number of interaction types M does not guarantee consistent performance gain. We conjecture that these could be alleviated by applying regularization techniques that control the sparsity of interaction, but we leave it as future work.

Acknowledgments

This work was supported by the National Research Foundation of Korea (NRF) grant funded by the Korea Government (MSIT) (NRF-2016M3C4A7952587).

References

Aishwarya Agrawal, Jiasen Lu, Stanislaw Antol, Margaret Mitchell, C. Lawrence Zitnick, Devi Parikh, and Dhruv Batra. 2017. Vqa: Visual question answering. *International Journal of Computer Vision*, 123(1):4–31.

Hedi Ben-younes, Remi Cadene, Matthieu Cord, and Nicolas Thome. 2017. MUTAN: Multimodal tucker fusion for visual question answering. In *The IEEE International Conference on Computer Vision (ICCV)*, Venice, Italy.

Samuel R. Bowman, Gabor Angeli, Christopher Potts, and Christopher D. Manning. 2015. A large annotated corpus for learning natural language inference. In *Proceedings of the 2015 Conference on Empirical Methods in Natural Language Processing*, pages 632–642, Lisbon, Portugal. Association for Computational Linguistics.

Samuel R. Bowman, Jon Gauthier, Abhinav Rastogi, Raghav Gupta, Christopher D. Manning, and Christopher Potts. 2016. A fast unified model for parsing and sentence understanding. In *Proceedings of the 54th Annual Meeting of the Association*

---

for Computational Linguistics (Volume 1: Long Papers)*, pages 1466–1477, Berlin, Germany. Association for Computational Linguistics.

Moses Charikar, Kevin Chen, and Martin Farach-Colton. 2002. Finding frequent items in data streams. In *International Colloquium on Automata, Languages, and Programming*, pages 693–703, Málaga, Spain. Springer.

Qian Chen, Xiaodan Zhu, Zhen-Hua Ling, Si Wei, Hui Jiang, and Diana Inkpen. 2017. Recurrent neural network-based sentence encoder with gated attention for natural language inference. In *Proceedings of the 2nd Workshop on Evaluating Vector Space Representations for NLP*, pages 36–40. Association for Computational Linguistics.

Jihun Choi, Kang Min Yoo, and Sang-goo Lee. 2018. Learning to compose task-specific tree structures. In *Proceedings of the Thirty-Second AAAI Conference on Artificial Intelligence*, New Orleans, Louisiana, USA. Association for the Advancement of Artificial Intelligence.

George Cybenko. 1989. Approximation by superpositions of a sigmoidal function. *Mathematics of Control, Signals and Systems*, 2(4):303–314.

William B. Dolan and Chris Brockett. 2005. Automatically constructing a corpus of sentential paraphrases. In *Proceedings of the Third International Workshop on Paraphrasing (IWP 2005)*, pages 9–16, Jeju Island, Korea. Asian Federation of Natural Language Processing.

Akira Fukui, Dong Huk Park, Daylen Yang, Anna Rohrbach, Trevor Darrell, and Marcus Rohrbach. 2016. Multimodal compact bilinear pooling for visual question answering and visual grounding. In *Proceedings of the 2016 Conference on Empirical Methods in Natural Language Processing*, pages 457–468, Austin, Texas. Association for Computational Linguistics.

Kaiming He, Xiangyu Zhang, Shaoqing Ren, and Jian Sun. 2015. Delving deep into rectifiers: Surpassing human-level performance on imagenet classification. In *Proceedings of the 2015 IEEE International Conference on Computer Vision (ICCV)*, ICCV '15, pages 1026–1034, Washington, DC, USA. IEEE Computer Society.

Sepp Hochreiter and Jürgen Schmidhuber. 1997. Long short-term memory. *Neural Computation*, 9(8):1735–1780.

Kurt Hornik. 1991. Approximation capabilities of multilayer feedforward networks. *Neural Networks*, 4(2):251–257.

Sergey Ioffe and Christian Szegedy. 2015. Batch normalization: Accelerating deep network training by reducing internal covariate shift. In *Proceedings of the 32nd International Conference on Machine Learning*, volume 37 of *Proceedings of Machine Learning Research*, pages 448–456, Lille, France. PMLR.

Yangfeng Ji and Jacob Eisenstein. 2013. Discriminative improvements to distributional sentence similarity. In *Proceedings of the 2013 Conference on Empirical Methods in Natural Language Processing*, pages 891–896, Seattle, Washington, USA. Association for Computational Linguistics.

Jin-Hwa Kim, Kyoung-Woon On, Woosang Lim, Jeonghee Kim, Jung-Woo Ha, and Byoung-Tak Zhang. 2017. Hadamard product for low-rank bilinear pooling. In *Proceedings of the 5th International Conference on Learning Representations*, Toulon, France.

Diederik P. Kingma and Jimmy Ba. 2015. Adam: A method for stochastic optimization. In *Proceedings of the 3rd International Conference on Learning Representations*, San Diego, California, USA.

Ben Krause, Liang Lu, Iain Murray, and Steve Renals. 2016. Multiplicative LSTM for sequence modelling. *arXiv preprint arXiv:1609.07959*.

Tsung-Yu Lin, Aruni RoyChowdhury, and Subhransu Maji. 2015. Bilinear CNN models for fine-grained visual recognition. In *The IEEE International Conference on Computer Vision (ICCV)*, Santiago, Chile.

Marco Marelli, Luisa Bentivogli, Marco Baroni, Raffaella Bernardi, Stefano Menini, and Roberto Zamparelli. 2014. SemEval-2014 task 1: Evaluation of compositional distributional semantic models on full sentences through semantic relatedness and textual entailment. In *Proceedings of the 8th International Workshop on Semantic Evaluation (SemEval 2014)*, pages 1–8, Dublin, Ireland. Association for Computational Linguistics and Dublin City University.

Lili Mou, Rui Men, Ge Li, Yan Xu, Lu Zhang, Rui Yan, and Zhi Jin. 2016. Natural language inference by tree-based convolution and heuristic matching. In *Proceedings of the 54th Annual Meeting of the Association for Computational Linguistics (Volume 2: Short Papers)*, pages 130–136, Berlin, Germany. Association for Computational Linguistics.

Jeffrey Pennington, Richard Socher, and Christopher Manning. 2014. GloVe: Global vectors for word representation. In *Proceedings of the 2014 Conference on Empirical Methods in Natural Language Processing (EMNLP)*, pages 1532–1543, Doha, Qatar. Association for Computational Linguistics.

Andrew M. Saxe, James L. McClelland, and Surya Ganguli. 2014. Exact solutions to the nonlinear dynamics of learning in deep linear neural networks. In *Proceedings of the 2nd International Conference on Learning Representations*, Banff, Alberta, Canada.

Richard Socher, Alex Perelygin, Jean Wu, Jason Chuang, Christopher D. Manning, Andrew Ng, and Christopher Potts. 2013. Recursive deep models for semantic compositionality over a sentiment treebank. In *Proceedings of the 2013 Conference on Empirical Methods in Natural Language Processing*, pages 1631–1642, Seattle, Washington, USA. Association for Computational Linguistics.

Nitish Srivastava, Geoffrey Hinton, Alex Krizhevsky, Ilya Sutskever, and Ruslan Salakhutdinov. 2014. Dropout: A simple way to prevent neural networks from overfitting. *Journal of Machine Learning Research*, 15:1929–1958.

Kai Sheng Tai, Richard Socher, and Christopher D. Manning. 2015. Improved semantic representations from tree-structured long short-term memory networks. In *Proceedings of the 53rd Annual Meeting of the Association for Computational Linguistics and the 7th International Joint Conference on Natural Language Processing (Volume 1: Long Papers)*, pages 1556–1566, Beijing, China. Association for Computational Linguistics.

Zhiguo Wang, Wael Hamza, and Radu Florian. 2017. Bilateral multi-perspective matching for natural language sentences. In *Proceedings of the Twenty-Sixth International Joint Conference on Artificial Intelligence*, pages 4144–4150, Melbourne, Victoria, Australia. International Joint Conferences on Artificial Intelligence.

Wei Wu, Zhengdong Lu, and Hang Li. 2013. Learning bilinear model for matching queries and documents. *Journal of Machine Learning Research*, 14:2519–2548.

Yuhuai Wu, Saizheng Zhang, Ying Zhang, Yoshua Bengio, and Ruslan R Salakhutdinov. 2016. On multiplicative integration with recurrent neural networks. In D. D. Lee, M. Sugiyama, U. V. Luxburg, I. Guyon, and R. Garnett, editors, *Advances in Neural Information Processing Systems 29*, pages 2856–2864. Curran Associates, Inc.

Caiming Xiong, Stephen Merity, and Richard Socher. 2016. Dynamic memory networks for visual and textual question answering. In *Proceedings of The 33rd International Conference on Machine Learning*, volume 48 of *Proceedings of Machine Learning Research*, pages 2397–2406, New York, New York, USA. PMLR.

Dani Yogatama, Phil Blunsom, Chris Dyer, Edward Grefenstette, and Wang Ling. 2017. Learning to compose words into sentences with reinforcement learning. In *Proceedings of the 5th International Conference on Learning Representations*, Toulon, France.

Zhou Yu, Jun Yu, Jianping Fan, and Dacheng Tao. 2017. Multi-modal factorized bilinear pooling with co-attention learning for visual question answering. In *The IEEE International Conference on Computer Vision (ICCV)*, Venice, Italy.

A Experimental Settings

A.1 Natural Language Inference

For all experiments, we used the Adam (Kingma and Ba, 2015) optimizer with a learning rate 0.001 and halved the learning rate when there is no improvement in accuracy for one epoch. Each model is trained for 10 epochs, and the checkpoint with the highest validation accuracy is chosen as final model. Sentences longer than 25 words are trimmed to have the maximum length of 25 words, and batch size of 64 is used for training.

For all experiments, we set the dimensionality of sentence vectors to 300. 300-dimensional GloVe (Pennington et al., 2014) vectors trained on 840 billion tokens[6] were used as word embeddings and not updated during training. The number of hidden units of the single-hidden layer MLP is set to 1024.

Dropout (Srivastava et al., 2014) is applied to word embeddings and the input and the output of the MLP. The dropout probability is selected from $\{0.10, 0.15, 0.20\}$. Batch normalization (Ioffe and Szegedy, 2015) is applied to the input and the output of the MLP.

Recurrent weight matrices are orthogonally initialized (Saxe et al., 2014), and the final linear projection matrix is initialized by sampling from Uniform$(-0.005, 0.005)$. All other weights are initialized following the scheme of He et al. (2015).

A.2 Paraphrase Identification

For PI experiments, we used the same architecture and training procedures as NLI experiments, except the final projection matrix and heuristic matching function. Also, we found that the PI task is more sensitive to hyperparameters than NLI, so we apply different dropout probabilities to the encoder network and to the classifier network. Both values are selected from $\{0.10, 0.15, 0.20\}$. Each model is trained for 15 epochs, and the checkpoint with the highest validation accuracy is chosen as final model.

---

[6]`http://nlp.stanford.edu/data/glove.840B.300d.zip`

Named Graphs for Semantic Representations

Richard Crouch
A9.com
dick.crouch@gmail.com

Aikaterini-Lida Kalouli
University of Konstanz
aikaterini-lida.kalouli@uni-konstanz.de

Abstract

A position paper arguing that purely graphical representations for natural language semantics lack a fundamental degree of expressiveness, and cannot deal with even basic Boolean operations like negation or disjunction, let alone intensional phenomena. Moving from graphs to named graphs leads to representations that stand some chance of having sufficient expressive power. Named $\mathcal{FL}_0$ graphs are of particular interest.

1 Introduction

Graphs are popular for both (semantic web) knowledge representation (Screiber and Raimond, 2014; Dong et al., 2014; Rospocher et al., 2016) and natural language semantics (Banarescu et al., 2013; Perera et al., 2018; Wities et al., 2017). The casual observer might assume there is substantial overlap between the two activities, but there is less than meets the eye. This paper attempts to make three points:

1. Knowledge graphs, which are designed to represent facts about the world rather than human knowledge, are not well set up to represent negation, disjunction, and conditional or hypothetical contexts. Arguably, the world contains no negative, disjunctive, or hypothetical facts; just positive facts that make them true. Natural language semantics has to deal with more partial assertions, where all that is known are the negations, disjunctions, or hypotheticals, and not the underlying facts that make them true.

2. Named graphs (Carroll et al., 2005) are an extension of RDF graphs (Screiber and Raimond, 2014), primarily introduced to record provenance information. They are worthy of further study, since they promise a way of bridging between the relentlessly positive world of knowledge representation and the more partial, hypothetical world of natural language. In RDF-OWL graphs (Hitzler et al., 2012), the subject-predicate-object triples forming the nodes and arcs of the graph correspond to atomic propositions. Beyond conjunction, no direct relations between these propositions can be expressed. Named graphs allow sub-graphs (i.e. collections of atomic propositions) to be placed in relationships with other sub-graphs, and thus allow for negative, disjunctive and hypothetical relations between complex propositions.

3. Named graphs illustrate a certain way of factoring out complexity, in this case between predicate-argument structure and Boolean / modal structure. As a semantic representation, the predicate-argument structure is correct, but not complete. Adding a named, Boolean layer requires no adjustment to the syntax or semantics of the predicate-argument structure; it just embeds it in a broader environment. This often is not the case; e.g. in moving from unquantified predicate logic to first-order quantified logic, to first-oder modal logic, to higher-order intensional logic.

After reviewing RDF graphs and named graphs, we discuss how they could be applied to a (somewhat incestuous) family of layered, graphical, semantic representations (Boston et al., forthcoming; Shen et al., 2018; Bobrow et al., 2007) (see our companion paper (Kalouli and Crouch, 2018) for an introduction to these representations). This offers the prospect of a formal semantics that takes graphs to be first class semantic objects, which differs from approaches like AMR (Banarescu et al., 2013), where the graphs are descriptions of underlying semantic objects.

2 Graphs and Named Graphs

A graph is a collection of binary relationships between entities. Since any n-ary relationship can be decomposed into $n + 1$ binary relationships through the introduction of an extra entity that serves as a "pivot" (this is the basis of neo-Davidsonian event semantics (Parsons, 1990)), all n-ary relationships can be represented in graphical

*Proceedings of the 7th Joint Conference on Lexical and Computational Semantics (*SEM)*, pages 113–118
New Orleans, June 5-6, 2018. ©2018 Association for Computational Linguistics

form as a collection of entity-relation triples.

2.1 RDF

This graphical approach to n-ary relationships has seen perhaps its fullest use in the Resource Description Framework (RDF) (Screiber and Raimond, 2014), where subject-relation-object triples can be stored to treat complex ontologies as graphs. But since the triples form a conjunctive set, RDF has to go through some contortions to emulate negation and disjunction.

Unadorned, RDF is lax about what kinds of entity can occur in triples, and individuals, relations, and classes can intermingle freely. One can state facts about how classes relate to other classes (e.g. one is a subclass of the other), how relations relate to other relations, and how individual relate to relations and classes. Successive restrictions, such as RDFS (Brickley and Guha, 2014) and OWL (Hitzler et al., 2012) tighten up on this freedom of expression, for the resulting gain in inferential tractability.

OWL provides a number of class construction operations that mimic Booleans at a class level: complement (negation), intersection (conjunction) and union (disjunction). One could therefore assert that Rosie is not a cat by saying that she is an instance of the cat-complement class, and one could assert that Rosie is a cat or a dog by asserting that she is an instance of the class formed by taking the union of cats and dogs. Additionally, OWL and RDFS allow negative properties as a way of stating that a particular relation does not hold between two entities (i.e. a form of atomic negation).

The semantic web is geared toward capturing positive facts about what is known. Two positive facts can establish a negative, e.g. that cats and dogs are disjoint classes and that Rosie is a dog establishes that Rosie is not a cat. But the need to *assert* a negative rarely arises: better to wait until the corresponding incompatible positive is known, or as a last resort make up a positive fact that is incompatible with negative (e.g. that Rosie is a non-cat). Natural language, by contrast, is full of negative, disjunctive, and hypothetical assertions for which the justifying positive facts are not known. And these Boolean and modal assertions express relationships between propositions (i.e. collections of triples), and not between classes.

Moreover, Gardenförs (2014) makes the case for restricting semantics to natural concepts within a conceptual space. A conceptual space consists of a set of quality dimensions (c.f. dimensions in word vectors). A point in the space is a particular vector along these dimensions. A natural concept is a region (collection of points in the space) that is connected and convex. This essentially means that the shortest path from one sub-region of a natural concept to another does not pass outside of the region defined by the concept: natural concepts are regions that are not gerrymandered. OWL unions of classes can arbitrarily combine disconnected regions, whereas complements can tear holes in the middle of regions: they can produce gerrymandering that would make the most partisan blush.

2.2 Named Graphs

Named graphs were introduced by Carroll et al. (2005) as a small extension on top of RDF, primarily with the goal of recording provenance metadata for different parts of a complex graph, such as source, access restrictions, or ontology versions. However, applications to stating propositional attitudes and capturing logical relationships between graphs were also mentioned in passing. A named graph simply associates an extra identifier with a set of triples. For example, a propositional attitude like *Fred believes John does not like Mary* could be represented as follows[1]:

```
:g1 { :john :like :mary }
:g2 :not :g1
:fred :belive :g2
```

where `:g1` is the name given to the graph expressing the proposition that *John likes Mary*, and `:g2` to the graph expressing its negation. Disjunction likewise can be expressed as a relationship between named graphs:

```
:g1 { :john :like :mary }
:g2 { :fred :like :mary }
:g0 :or :g1
:g0 :or :g2
```

where the graph `:g0` expresses the disjunction of `:g1` and `:g2`.

The graph semantics for named graphs is a simple extension of the basic semantics (Carroll et al., 2005). The meaning of a named graph is the meaning of the graph, and sub-graph relations between named graphs must reflect the underlying relations between the graphs that are named. But significantly, named graphs are not automatically asserted — there is no presumption that the triples

---

[1]Using the TriG format (Bizer and Cyganiak, 2014), with the prefix definition for : omitted for brevity.

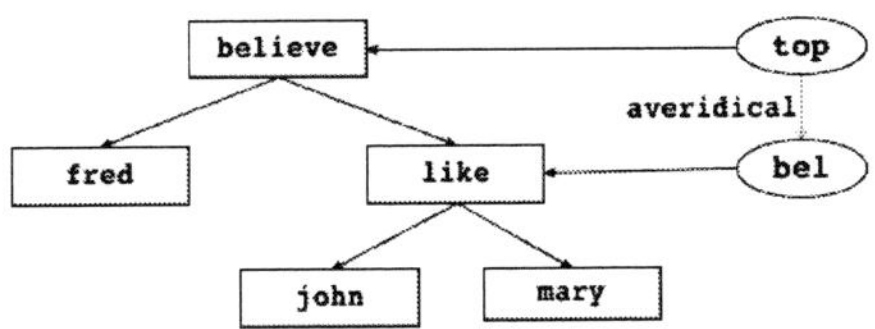

Figure 1: GKR for *Fred believes John likes Mary*

occurring in a named graph are true. This is somewhat inconvenient if your main goal is to assert positive, true facts. But this looks ideal for dealing with negation, disjunction and hypotheticals in natural language. In particular, the named graph above asserts neither that John likes Mary nor that John doesn't like Mary.

Reification in RDF was an earlier approach to dealing with provenance meta-data (Screiber and Raimond, 2014). This turns every triple into four triples that describe it, so that `:john :like :mary` becomes `:t :type :statement; :t :subj :john; :t :pred :like; :t :obj :mary`. The reified graph is graphical description of the original graph. Naming preserves the underlying graph in a way that reification does not.

3 Layered Graphs and the Graphical Knowledge Representation

A recent proposal for semantic representation has made use of so-called "layered-graphs" (GKR, (Kalouli and Crouch, 2018), see also (Boston et al., forthcoming; Shen et al., 2018)), with the claim that this gives a good way of handling Boolean, hypothetical, and modal relations[2]. The proposal is based on earlier work on an Abstract Knowledge Representtions (AKR, (Bobrow et al., 2007)), which imposes a separation between conceptual / predicate-argument structure and contextual structure. The GKR representation (simplified) for *Fred believes John likes Mary* is shown in Figure 1. This comprises two sub-graphs: a concept/predicate-argument graph on the left, and a context graph on the right. The concept graph can be read conjunctively as stating the following, but where variables range over (sub)concepts and not over individuals:

$$\exists b,l,f,j,m.$$

---

[2]This section does not attempt to motivate GKR in terms of coverage of phenomena or support of natural language inference: see the cited papers for this.

```
believe(b) & like(l) & fred(f)
& sub(b,f) & comp(b,l)
& mary(m) & john(j)
& subj(l,j) & obj(l,m)
```

Thus `b` denotes a sub-concept of `believe`, that is further constrained to have as a subject role some sub-concept of `fred`, and as a complement some sub-concept of `like`. The concept graph makes no assertions about whether any of these concepts have individuals instantiating them: it asserts neither that Fred has a belief, nor that John likes Mary. It is a level at which semantic similarity can be assessed, but not one at which — on its own — logical entailments can be judged. The concept graph is a correct characterization of the sentence, but an incomplete one.

Entailment requires existential commitments that are introduced by the context graph shown on the right of Figure 1. There are two contexts. The top level, "true", context `top` states the commitments of the sentence's speaker. The arc connecting it to the `believe` node means that the speaker is asserting that there is an instance of the believe concept. The second context, `bel` is lexically induced by the word "believes". The arc from `bel` to the `like` node means that in this context there is asserted to be an instance of the like context. However, `bel` is marked as being averidical with respect to `top`. This means that we cannot lift the existential commitments of `bel` up into `top`. Hence Figure 1 does not entail that John likes Mary (nor that he doesn't).

Other words introduce different context relations. For example *know* creates a veridical lower context, which means that the lower existential commitments can be lifted up. Whereas negation creates an anti-veridical lower context, which specifically says that the concept that is instantiated in the lower context is uninstantiated in the upper one. Following the work of (Nairn et al., 2006), these instantiation raising rules allow complex intensional inference to be drawn (see (Boston et al., forthcoming) for a fuller description).

4 Named $\mathcal{FL}_0$ Graphs

The semantics for GKR has yet to be clearly laid out. Our claim is that the layered graphs are better seen in terms of named graphs. First, that the context graph simply expresses relationships between named concept graphs, so that contexts

$$C, D \Rightarrow A \mid C \sqcap D \mid \forall R.C$$
$$\text{where} \quad A \in \text{Atomic concept}$$
$$R \in \text{Atomic role}$$
$$C, D \in \text{concept}$$

Figure 2: Concept Construction in $\mathcal{FL}_0$

are nothing more than concept (sub-)graphs. Second, that the concept graph corresponds to the $\mathcal{FL}_0$ description logic (Baader and Nutt, 2003), for which subsumption is decidable in polynomial time. $\mathcal{FL}_0$ is a simple logic that is generally regarded as too inexpressive to deal with interesting language-related phenomena. But in combination with graph naming it becomes much more expressive.

The $\mathcal{FL}_0$ description logic allows concepts to be constructed as shown in Figure 2. Given a stock of atomic concepts, complex concepts can be formed by (i) intersection, e.g. *(Adult $\sqcap$ Male $\sqcap$ Person)* $\equiv$ *Man*; and ii) slot/role restriction, e.g. *Bite $\sqcap$ $\forall subj.Dog$ $\sqcap$ $\forall obj.Man$* (the class of bitings by dogs of men). The concept graphs of GKR correspond to the application of $\mathcal{FL}_0$ operations to atomic lexical concepts. The concept of the `like` node in Figure 1 is thus *like $\sqcap$ $\forall subj.j$ $\sqcap$ $\forall obj.m$*[3].

In order to keep the concept graphs of GKR within $\mathcal{FL}_0$, it is important that context nodes are not allowed to participate in role restrictions. This rules out the kind of free intermingling of graph nodes and other nodes that was presented in Section 2.2. The GKR treatment of *Fred believes John likes Mary* is shown in Figure 1. Expressed as a named graph, this corresponds to:

```
top:  {b ⊑ Believe
       f ⊑ Fred
       b ⊑ ∀subj.f
       b ⊑ ∀comp.l }
bel:  {l ⊑ Like
       j ⊑ John
       m ⊑ Mary
       l ⊑ ∀subj.j
       l ⊑ ∀obj.m }
:top averidical :bel
```

This named-graph formulation of GKR inherits a standard graph semantics, as described by Carroll et al. (2005). The graph semantics is complementary to the kind of truth-conditional semantics set out for AKR (and by analogy, GKR) by Bobrow

---

[3]GKR extends its concept graph with a property graph that captures the effect of morpho-syntactic features like cardinality. This corresponds to extending the logic to $\mathcal{FLN}_0$ by introducing cardinality restrictions.

et al. (2005). More work, however, is needed to explore the connections between the graph and truth-conditional semantics.

5 Abstract Meaning Representation (AMR)

AMR is best seen as a graphical notation for describing logical forms, which is the view taken by Bos (2016) and Stabler (2017) in their augmentations of AMR to increase its expressive power. This can be seen by considering the AMR for *Fred believes John likes Mary*:

```
(b / believe
      :arg0 (f / Fred)
      :arg1 (l / like
                  :arg0 (j / John)
                  :arg1 (m / Mary)))
```

Expressed as a set of triples, this becomes

```
b instance believe;   l instance like;
f instance Fred;      j instance John;
b :arg0 f;            m instance Mary;
b :arg1 l;            l :arg0 j;
                      l :arg1 m;
```

Since a graph is a conjunction of triples, and because $A \wedge B \models A$, all the triples on the left can be validly eliminated to leave those on the right, which correspond to the graph for *John likes Mary*. The inference from *Fred believes John likes Mary* to *John likes Mary* is clearly not semantically valid. Consequently the AMR triples cannot be interpreted as stating semantic-web style facts; rather they state sub-formulas of a logical form.

There is nothing wrong in having a more habitable, graphical notation for logical formulas, especially if large amounts of annotation are to be done. But this is different from a goal of having graphs as first class semantic objects.

6 Concluding Observations

This paper attempts to make the case for named graphs as an interesting tool for natural language semantics. The first task in exploring this further would be to provide a truth-conditional, graph-based semantics for GKR. A positive outcome would enable closer links between semantic and knowledge graphs.

By naming graphs, it appears that an inexpressive, conjunctive concept logic, $\mathcal{FL}_0$, can be employed to handle a wide variety of more complex phenomena including Booleans and hypotheticals. However, one should not assume that the inferential tractability of $\mathcal{FL}_0$ carries across to a system that combines it with named graphs.

We conjecture that the restriction of concept formation to $\mathcal{FL}_0$ will satisfy (Gardenförs, 2014) requirements on the connectedness and convexity of concepts. Additionally, the restricted operations may be better for the operations inherent in dealing with vector spaces used in distributed semantic representation; it is currently unclear what corresponds to negation in vector spaces, though see (Bowman et al., 2015). The strategy of having a correct but incomplete conceptual structure may make it easier to reconcile logical and distribitional accounts of semantics if distributional semantics is relieved of the burden of having to account for Boolean structure.

Naming a graph essentially boxes it off, to be evaluated or asserted within a different context. GKR focuses on the analogue between these contexts and switching assignments to possible worlds in standard Kripke semantics for modal logics. With regard to distributional quantification it observes that assignments to variables in standard first-order logic plays a similar role, and suggests using this to account for quantifier scope via contexts. This does not exhaust the space of evaluative contexts. Named graphs were primarily motivated by the desire to record (provenance) metadata about triples. They provide an ideal means of associating meta-data with semantic relationships, such as the confidence that a particular role restriction is correct. This can be extended to record inter-dependencies between collections of ambiguous relationships, using the packing mechanism of (Maxwell and Kaplan, 1993): choices between alternate interpretations also set up different evaluation contexts.

The embedding of boxes in Discourse Representation Theory (Kamp and Reyle, 1993) is strongly reminiscent of embedding sub-graphs. We speculate that DRT could be given a graph-based semantics, in which discourse representation structures (DRSs) are seen as first class graphical and semantic objects. However, one difference between DRT and GKR is that GKR imposes a strict separation between concepts and contexts. This essentially means that contexts cannot be referred to in conceptual predicate-argument structures. In DRT, this would correspond to not permitting DRSs to serve as arguments of predicates.

With regard to AMR, naming some of the graphs and expressing context relations between them seems a relatively conservative extension in terms of notation. But doing so offers the prospect of lifting AMRs out of being graphical descriptions of some other semantic object (like a logical form), and becoming much closer to RDF graphs as first-class semantic objects.

Ackowledgements

This paper does not describe any work done by the first author in his role at A9. We are grateful to Tagyoung Chung and Valeria de Paiva for helpful comments on presentation, though they should not be held responsible for the views expressed.

References

Franz Baader and Werner Nutt. 2003. The description logic handbook. chapter Basic Description Logics, pages 43–95. Cambridge University Press, New York, NY, USA.

Laura Banarescu, Claire Bonial, Shu Cai, Madalina Georgescu, Kira Griffitt, Ulf Hermjakob, Kevin Knight, Philipp Koehn, Martha Palmer, and Nathan Schneider. 2013. Abstract Meaning Representation for Sembanking. In *Proceedings of the Linguistic Annotation Workshop*.

Chris Bizer and Richard Cyganiak. 2014. RDF 1.1 TriG, https://www.w3.org/tr/trig/.

Danny G. Bobrow, Cleo Condoravdi, Richard Crouch, Valeria de Paiva, Lauri Karttunen, Tracy Holloway-King, Rowan Nairn, Charlotte Price, and Annie Zaenen. 2007. Precision-focused Textual Inference. In *Proceedings of the ACL-PASCAL Workshop on Textual Entailment and Paraphrasing*, RTE '07, pages 16–21, Stroudsburg, PA, USA. Association for Computational Linguistics.

Danny G. Bobrow, Richard Crouch, Valeria de Paiva, Ron Kaplan, Lauri Karttunen, Tracy King-Holloway, and Annie Zaenen. 2005. A basic logic for textual inference. In *Proceedings of the AAAI Workshop on Inference for Textual Question Answering*.

Johan Bos. 2016. Expressive Power of Abstract Meaning Representations. *Computational Linguistics*, 42(3):527–535.

Marisa Boston, Richard Crouch, Erdem Özcan, and Peter Stubley. forthcoming. Natural language inference using an ontology. In Cleo Condoravdi, editor, *Lauri Karttunen Festschrift*.

Samuel R. Bowman, Christopher Potts, and Christopher D. Manning. 2015. Recursive neural networks can learn logical semantics. In *Proceedings of the 3rd Workshop on Continuous Vector Space Models and their Compositionality*.

Dan Brickley and R. V. Guha. 2014. RDF Schema 1.1, https://www.w3.org/tr/rdf-schema/.

Jeremy Carroll, Christian Bizer, Pat Hayes, and Patrick Stickler. 2005. Named Graphs. *Web Semantics: Science, Services and Agents on the World Wide Web*, 3(4).

Xin Luna Dong, Evgeniy Gabrilovich, Geremy Heitz, Wilko Horn, Ni Lao, Kevin Murphy, Thomas Strohmann, Shaohua Sun, and Wei Zhang. 2014. Knowledge Vault: A Web-Scale Approach to Probabilistic Knowledge Fusion. In *The 20th ACM SIGKDD International Conference on Knowledge Discovery and Data Mining, KDD '14, New York, NY, USA - August 24 - 27, 2014*, pages 601–610.

Peter Gardenförs. 2014. *The Geometry of Meaning: Semantics Based on Conceptual Spaces*. MIT Press.

Pascal Hitzler, Markus Krötzsch, Bijan Parsia, Peter F. Patel-Schneider, and Sebastian Rudolph. 2012. OWL 2 Web Ontology Language Primer, https://www.w3.org/tr/owl2-primer.

Aikaterini-Lida Kalouli and Richard Crouch. 2018. GKR: the graphical knowledge representation. In *SemBEaR-18*.

Hans Kamp and Uwe Reyle. 1993. *From Discourse to Logic. Introduction to Modeltheoretic Semantics of Natural Language, Formal Logic and Discourse Representation Theory*. Kluwer, Dordrecht.

John T. Maxwell and Ronald M. Kaplan. 1993. The interface between phrasal and functional constraints. *Computational Linguistics*, 19(4).

Rowan Nairn, Cleo Condoravdi, and Lauri Karttunen. 2006. Computing relative polarity for textual inference. *Inference in Computational Semantics (ICoS-5)*, pages 20–41.

Terence Parsons. 1990. *Events in the semantics of English*. MIT Press.

Vittorio Perera, Tagyoung Chung, Thomas Kollar, and Emma Strubell. 2018. Multi-Task Learning for parsing the Alexa Meaning Representation Language. In *Proc AAAI*.

Marco Rospocher, Marieke van Erp, Piek Vossen, Antske Fokkens, Itziar Aldabe, German Rigau, Aitor Soroa, Thomas Ploeger, and Tessel Bogaard. 2016. Building event-centric knowledge graphs from news. 37.

Guus Screiber and Yves Raimond. 2014. RDF 1.1 primer, https://www.w3.org/tr/rdf-primer/.

Jiaying Shen, Henk Harkema, Richard Crouch, Ciaran O'Reilly, and Peng Yu. 2018. Layered semantic graphs for dialogue management. In *SigDial*.

Ed Stabler. 2017. Reforming AMR. In *Formal Grammar 2017. Lecture Notes in Computer Science*, volume 10686. Springer.

Rachel Wities, Vered Shwartz, Gabriel Stanovsky, Meni Adler, Ori Shapira, Shyam Upadhyay, Dan Roth, Eugenio Martínez-Cámara, Iryna Gurevych, and Ido Dagan. 2017. A consolidated open knowledge representation for multiple texts. In *Proceedings of the 2nd Workshop on Linking Models of Lexical, Sentential and Discourse-level Semantics*, pages 12–24.

Learning Patient Representations from Text

Dmitriy Dligach[1] and Timothy Miller[2]

[1]Loyola University Chicago
[2]Boston Children's Hospital and Harvard Medical School
[1]ddligach@luc.edu
[2]timothy.miller@childrens.harvard.edu

Abstract

Mining electronic health records for patients who satisfy a set of predefined criteria is known in medical informatics as phenotyping. Phenotyping has numerous applications such as outcome prediction, clinical trial recruitment, and retrospective studies. Supervised machine learning for phenotyping typically relies on sparse patient representations such as bag-of-words. We consider an alternative that involves learning patient representations. We develop a neural network model for learning patient representations and show that the learned representations are general enough to obtain state-of-the-art performance on a standard comorbidity detection task.

1 Introduction

Mining electronic health records for patients who satisfy a set of predefined criteria is known in medical informatics as phenotyping. Phenotyping has numerous applications such as outcome prediction, clinical trial recruitment, and retrospective studies. Supervised machine learning is currently the predominant approach to automatic phenotyping and it typically relies on sparse patient representations such as bag-of-words and bag-of-concepts (Shivade et al., 2013). We consider an alternative that involves learning patient representations. Our goal is to develop a conceptually simple method for learning lower dimensional dense patient representations that succinctly capture the information about a patient and are suitable for downstream machine learning tasks. Our method uses cheap supervision in the form of billing codes and thus has representational power of a large dataset. The learned representations can be used to train phenotyping classifiers with much smaller datasets.

Recent trends in machine learning have used neural networks for representation learning, and these ideas have propagated into the clinical informatics literature, using information from electronic health records to learn dense patient representations (Choi et al., 2016, 2017; Lipton et al., 2016; Miotto et al., 2016; Nguyen et al., 2017; Pham et al., 2016). Most of this work to date has used only codified variables, including ICD (International Classification of Diseases) codes, procedure codes, and medication orders, often reduced to smaller subsets. Recurrent neural networks are commonly used to represent temporality (Choi et al., 2016, 2017; Lipton et al., 2016; Pham et al., 2016), and many methods map from code vocabularies to dense embedding input spaces (Choi et al., 2016, 2017; Nguyen et al., 2017; Pham et al., 2016).

One of the few patient representation learning systems to incorporate electronic medical record (EMR) *text* is DeepPatient (Miotto et al., 2016). This system takes as input a variety of features, including coded diagnoses as the above systems, but also uses topic modeling on the text to get topic features, and applies a tool that maps text spans to clinical concepts in standard vocabularies (SNOMED and RxNorm). To learn the representations they use a model consisting of stacked denoising autoencoders. In an autoencoder network, the goal of training is to reconstruct the input using hidden layers that compress the size of the input. The output layer and the input layer therefore have the same size, and the loss function calculates reconstruction error. The hidden layers thus form the patient representation. This method is used to predict novel ICD codes (from a reduced set with 78 elements) occurring in the next 30, 60, 90, and 180 days.

Our work extends these methods by building a neural network system for learning patient representations using text variables only. We train this model to predict billing codes, but solely as

*Proceedings of the 7th Joint Conference on Lexical and Computational Semantics (*SEM)*, pages 119–123
New Orleans, June 5-6, 2018. ©2018 Association for Computational Linguistics

a means to learning representations. We show that the representations learned for this task are general enough to obtain state-of-the-art performance on a standard comorbidity detection task. Our work can also be viewed as an instance of transfer learning (Pan and Yang, 2010): we store the knowledge gained from a source task (billing code prediction) and apply it to a different but related target task.

2 Methods

2.1 Patient Representation Learning

The objective of patient representation learning is to map raw text of patient notes to a dense vector that can be subsequently used for various patient-level predictive analytics tasks such as phenotyping, outcome prediction, and cluster analysis. The process of learning patient representations involves two phases: (1) supervised training of a neural network model on a source task that has abundant labeled data linking patients with some outcomes; (2) patient vector derivation for a target task performed by presenting new patient data to the network and harvesting the resulting representations from one of the hidden layers.

In this work, we utilize billing codes as a source of supervision for learning patient vectors in phase 1. Billing codes, such as ICD9 diagnostic codes, ICD9 procedure codes, and CPT codes are derived manually by medical coders from patient records for the purpose of billing. Billing codes are typically available in abundance in a healthcare institution and present a cheap source of supervision. Our hypothesis is that a patient vector useful for predicting billing codes will capture key characteristics of a patient, making this vector suitable for patient-level analysis.

For learning dense patient vectors, we propose a neural network model that takes as input a set of UMLS concept unique identifiers (CUIs) derived from the text of the notes of a patient and jointly predicts all billing codes associated with the patient. CUIs are extracted from notes by mapping spans of clinically-relevant text (e.g. *shortness of breath*, *appendectomy*, *MRI*) to entries in the UMLS Metathesaurus. CUIs can be easily extracted by existing tools such as Apache cTAKES (http://ctakes.apache.org). Our neural network model (Figure 1) is inspired by Deep Averaging Network (DAN) (Iyyer et al., 2015), Fast-Text (Joulin et al., 2016), and continuous bag-of-words (CBOW) (Mikolov et al., 2013a,b) models.

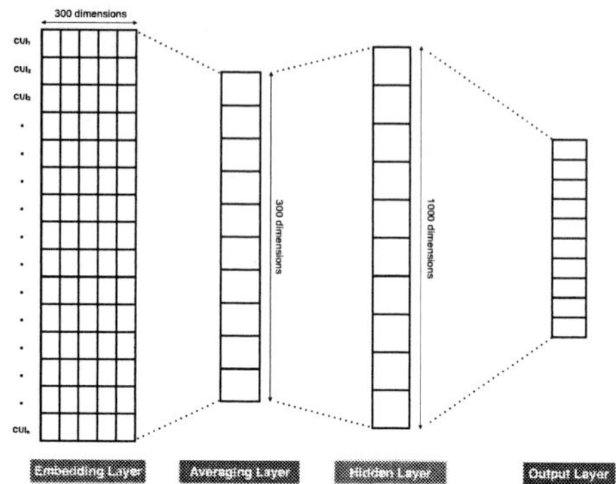

Figure 1: Neural network model for learning patient representations from text.

Model Architecture: The model takes as input a set of CUIs. CUIs are mapped to 300-dimensional concept embeddings which are averaged and passed on to a 1000-dimensional hidden layer, creating a vectorial representation of a patient. The final network layer consists of n sigmoid units that are used for joint billing code prediction. The output of each sigmoid unit is converted to a binary (1/0) outcome. The number of units n in the output layer is equal to the number of unique codes being predicted. The model is trained using binary cross-entropy loss function using RMSProp optimizer. Our model is capable of jointly predicting multiple billing codes for a patient, placing it into the family of supervised multi-label classification methods. In our preliminary work, we experimented with CNN and RNN-based architectures but their performance was inferior to the model described here both in terms of accuracy and speed.

Once the model achieves an acceptable level of performance, we can compute a vector representing a new patient by freezing the network weights, pushing CUIs for a new patient through the network, and harvesting the computed values of the nodes in the hidden layer. The resulting 1000-dimensional vectors can be used for a variety of machine learning tasks.

2.2 Datasets

For training patient representations, we utilize the MIMIC III corpus (Johnson et al., 2016). MIMIC III contains notes for over 40,000 critical care unit patients admitted to Beth Israel Deaconess Medical Center as well as ICD9 diagnostic, procedure, and Current Procedural Terminology (CPT) codes. Since our goal is learning patient-level representations, we concatenate all available notes for each patient into a single document. We also combine all ICD9 and CPT codes for a patient to form the targets for the prediction task. Finally, we process the patient documents with cTAKES to extract UMLS CUIs. cTAKES is an open-source system for processing clinical texts which has an efficient dictionary lookup component for identifying CUIs, making it possible to process a large number of patient documents.

To decrease training time, we reduce the complexity of the prediction task as follows: (1) we collapse all ICD9 and CPT codes to their more general category (e.g. first three digits for ICD9 diagnostic codes), (2) we drop all CUIs that appear fewer than 100 times, (3) we discard patients that have over 10,000 CUIs, (4) we discard all billing codes that have fewer than 1,000 examples. This preprocessing results in a dataset consisting of 44,211 patients mapped to multiple codes (174 categories total). We randomly split the patients into a training set (80%) and a validation set (20%) for tuning hyperparameters.

For evaluating our patient representations, we use a publicly available dataset from the Informatics for Integrating Biology to the Bedside (i2b2) Obesity challenge (Uzuner, 2009). Obesity challenge data consisted of 1237 discharge summaries from the Partners HealthCare Research Patient Data Repository annotated with respect to obesity and its fifteen most common comorbidities. Each patient was thus labeled for sixteen different categories. We focus on the more challenging *intuitive* task (Uzuner, 2009; Miller et al., 2016), containing three label types (*present*, *absent*, *questionable*), where annotators labeled a diagnosis as *present* if its presence could be inferred (i.e., even if not explicitly mentioned). This task involves complicated decision-making and inference.

Importantly, our patient representations are evaluated in sixteen different classification tasks with patient data originating from a healthcare institution different from the one our representations were trained on. This setup is challenging yet it presents a true test of robustness of the learned representations.

2.3 Experiments

Our first baseline is an SVM classifier trained with bag-of-CUIs features. Our second baseline involves linear dimensionality reduction performed by running singular value decomposition (SVD) on a patient-CUI matrix derived from the MIMIC corpus, reducing the space by selecting the 1000 largest singular values, and mapping the target instances into the resulting 1000-dimensional space.

Our multi-label billing code classifier is trained to maximize the macro F1 score for billing code prediction on the validation set. We train the model for 75 epochs with a learning rate of 0.001 and batch size of 50. These hyperparameters are obtained by tuning the model's macro F1 on the validation set. Observe that tuning of hyperparameters occurred independently from the target task. Also note that since our goal is not to obtain the best possible performance on a held out set, we are not allocating separate development and test sets. Once we determine the best values of these hyperparameters, we combine the training and validation sets and retrain the model. We train two version of the model: (1) with randomly initialized CUI embeddings, (2) with word2vec-pretrained CUI embeddings. Pre-trained embeddings are learned using word2vec (Mikolov et al., 2013a) by extracting all CUIs from the text of MIMIC III notes and using the CBOW method with windows size of 5 and embedding dimension of 300.

We then create a 1000-dimensional vector representation for each patient in the i2b2 obesity challenge data by giving the sparse (CUI-based) representation for each patient as input to the ICD code classifier. Rather than reading the classifier's predictions, we harvest the hidden layer outputs, forming a 1000-dimensional dense vector. We then train multi-class SVM classifiers for each disease (using one-vs.-all strategy), building sixteen SVM classifiers. Following the i2b2 obesity challenge, the models are evaluated using macro precision, recall, and F1 scores (Uzuner, 2009).

We make the code available for use by the research community [1].

3 Results

Our billing code classifier achieves the macro F1 score on the source task (billing code prediction)

[1] https://github.com/dmitriydligach/starsem2018-patient-representations

Disease	Sparse			SVD			Learned		
	P	R	F1	P	R	F1	P	R	F1
Asthma	0.894	0.736	0.787	0.888	0.854	0.870	0.910	0.920	0.915
CAD	0.583	0.588	0.585	0.593	0.602	0.596	0.596	0.596	0.596
CHF	0.558	0.564	0.561	0.571	0.575	0.573	0.558	0.564	0.561
Depression	0.797	0.685	0.715	0.723	0.727	0.725	0.781	0.773	0.777
Diabetes	0.859	0.853	0.856	0.611	0.624	0.617	0.907	0.919	0.913
GERD	0.530	0.466	0.485	0.533	0.482	0.499	0.528	0.539	0.533
Gallstones	0.814	0.640	0.678	0.747	0.721	0.732	0.645	0.663	0.653
Gout	0.975	0.811	0.871	0.955	0.834	0.882	0.928	0.910	0.919
Hypercholesterolemia	0.781	0.784	0.782	0.789	0.793	0.790	0.865	0.868	0.866
Hypertension	0.680	0.650	0.662	0.711	0.763	0.728	0.825	0.879	0.847
Hypertriglyceridemia	0.933	0.679	0.748	0.580	0.610	0.591	0.604	0.650	0.621
OA	0.514	0.448	0.466	0.479	0.442	0.454	0.511	0.508	0.510
OSA	0.596	0.511	0.542	0.626	0.568	0.592	0.611	0.618	0.615
Obesity	0.825	0.791	0.798	0.883	0.844	0.853	0.872	0.873	0.872
PVD	0.594	0.542	0.564	0.599	0.557	0.576	0.568	0.599	0.582
Venous Insufficiency	0.797	0.649	0.694	0.669	0.757	0.700	0.638	0.717	0.665
Average	0.733	0.650	0.675	0.685	0.672	0.674	0.709	0.725	0.715

Table 1: Comorbidity challenge results (intuitive task). SVM trained using sparse representations (bag-of-CUIs) is compared to SVM trained using SVD-based representations and learned dense patient representations.

of 0.447 when using randomly initialized CUI embeddings and macro F1 of 0.473 when using pre-trained CUI embeddings. This is not directly comparable to existing work because it is a unique setup; but we note that this is likely a difficult task because of the large output space. However, it is interesting to note that pre-training CUI embedding has a positive relative impact on performance.

Classifier performance for the target phenotyping task is shown in Table 1, which shows the performance of the baseline SVM classifier trained using the standard bag-of-CUIs approach (Sparse), the baseline using 1000-dimensional vectors obtained via dimensionality reduction (SVD), and our system using dense patient vectors derived from the source task. Since a separate SVM classifier was trained for each disease, we present classifier performance for each SVM model.

Both of our baseline approaches showed approximately the same performance (F1=0.675) as the best reported i2b2 system (Solt et al., 2009) (although they used a rule-based approach). Our dense patient representations outperformed both baseline approaches by four percentage points on average (F1=0.715). The difference is statistically significant (t-test, p=0.03).

Out of the sixteen diseases, our dense represen-

tations performed worse (with one tie) than the sparse baseline only for three: gallstones, hypertriglyceridemia, venous insufficiency. The likely cause is the scarcity of positive training examples; two of these diseases have the smallest number of positive training examples.

4 Discussion and Conclusion

For most diseases and on average our dense patient representations outperformed sparse patient representations. Importantly, patient representations were learned from a task (billing code prediction) that is different from the evaluation task (comorbidity prediction), presenting evidence that useful representations can be derived in this transfer learning scenario.

Furthermore, the data from which the representations were learned (BI medical center) and the evaluation data (Partners HealthCare) originated from two different healthcare institutions providing evidence of robustness of our patient representations.

Our future work will include exploring the use of other sources of supervision for learning patient representations, alternative neural network architectures, tuning the learned patient representations to the target task, and evaluating the patient representations on other phenotyping tasks.

Acknowledgments

The Titan X GPU used for this research was donated by the NVIDIA Corporation. Timothy Miller's effort was supported by National Institute of General Medical Sciences (NIGMS) of the National Institutes of Health under award number R01GM114355. The content is solely the responsibility of the authors and does not necessarily represent the official views of the National Institutes of Health.

References

Edward Choi, Mohammad Taha Bahadori, Andy Schuetz, Walter F Stewart, and Jimeng Sun. 2016. Doctor ai: Predicting clinical events via recurrent neural networks. In *Machine Learning for Healthcare Conference*. pages 301–318.

Edward Choi, Mohammad Taha Bahadori, Le Song, Walter F Stewart, and Jimeng Sun. 2017. GRAM: Graph-based attention model for healthcare representation learning. In *Proceedings of the 23rd ACM SIGKDD International Conference on Knowledge Discovery and Data Mining*. ACM, pages 787–795.

Mohit Iyyer, Varun Manjunatha, Jordan Boyd-Graber, and Hal Daumé III. 2015. Deep unordered composition rivals syntactic methods for text classification. In *Proceedings of the 53rd Annual Meeting of the Association for Computational Linguistics and the 7th International Joint Conference on Natural Language Processing (Volume 1: Long Papers)*. volume 1, pages 1681–1691.

Alistair EW Johnson, Tom J Pollard, Lu Shen, Liwei H Lehman, Mengling Feng, Mohammad Ghassemi, Benjamin Moody, Peter Szolovits, Leo Anthony Celi, and Roger G Mark. 2016. Mimic-iii, a freely accessible critical care database. *Scientific data* 3.

Armand Joulin, Edouard Grave, Piotr Bojanowski, and Tomas Mikolov. 2016. Bag of tricks for efficient text classification. *arXiv preprint arXiv:1607.01759* .

ZC Lipton, David Kale, Charles Elkan, and Randall Wetzel. 2016. Learning to Diagnose with LSTM Recurrent Neural Networks. In *Proceedings of ICLR 2016*. San Juan, Puerto Rico.

Tomas Mikolov, Kai Chen, Greg Corrado, and Jeffrey Dean. 2013a. Efficient estimation of word representations in vector space. *arXiv preprint arXiv:1301.3781* .

Tomas Mikolov, Wen-tau Yih, and Geoffrey Zweig. 2013b. Linguistic regularities in continuous space word representations. In *hlt-Naacl*. volume 13, pages 746–751.

Timothy Miller, Dmitriy Dligach, and Guergana Savova. 2016. Unsupervised document classification with informed topic models. In *Proceedings of the 15th Workshop on Biomedical Natural Language Processing*. pages 83–91.

Riccardo Miotto, Li Li, Brian A Kidd, and Joel T Dudley. 2016. Deep Patient: An Unsupervised Representation to Predict the Future of Patients from the Electronic Health Records. *Scientific reports* 6:26094. https://doi.org/10.1038/srep26094.

Phuoc Nguyen, Truyen Tran, Nilmini Wickramasinghe, and Svetha Venkatesh. 2017. Deepr: A Convolutional Net for Medical Records. *IEEE Journal of Biomedical and Health Informatics* https://doi.org/10.1109/JBHI.2016.2633963.

Sinno Jialin Pan and Qiang Yang. 2010. A survey on transfer learning. *IEEE Transactions on knowledge and data engineering* 22(10):1345–1359.

Trang Pham, Truyen Tran, Dinh Phung, and Svetha Venkatesh. 2016. Deepcare: A deep dynamic memory model for predictive medicine. In *Pacific-Asia Conference on Knowledge Discovery and Data Mining*. Springer, pages 30–41.

Chaitanya Shivade, Preethi Raghavan, Eric Fosler-Lussier, Peter J Embi, Noemie Elhadad, Stephen B Johnson, and Albert M Lai. 2013. A review of approaches to identifying patient phenotype cohorts using electronic health records. *Journal of the American Medical Informatics Association* 21(2):221–230.

Illés Solt, Domonkos Tikk, Viktor Gál, and Zsolt T Kardkovács. 2009. Semantic classification of diseases in discharge summaries using a context-aware rule-based classifier. *Journal of the American Medical Informatics Association* 16(4):580–584.

Özlem Uzuner. 2009. Recognizing obesity and comorbidities in sparse data. *Journal of the American Medical Informatics Association* 16(4):561–570.

Polarity Computations in Flexible Categorial Grammar

Hai Hu
Linguistics Department
Indiana University
Bloomington, IN 47405 USA
huhai@indiana.edu

Lawrence S. Moss
Mathematics Department
Indiana University
Bloomington, IN 47405 USA
lsm@cs.indiana.edu

Abstract

This paper shows how to take parse trees in CCG and algorithmically find the polarities of all the constituents. Our work uses the well-known polarization principle corresponding to function application, and we have extended this with principles for type raising and composition. We provide an algorithm, extending the polarity marking algorithm of van Benthem. We discuss how our system works in practice, taking input from the C&C parser.

1 Introduction

The main goal of this work is to take input from text and then to automatically determine the *polarity* of all the words. For example, we aim to find the arrows in sentences like *Every dog$^\downarrow$ scares $^\uparrow$ at least two$^\downarrow$ cats$^\uparrow$, Every dog$^\downarrow$ and no cat$^\downarrow$ sleeps$^=$*, and *Most rabbits$^=$ hop$^\uparrow$*. The $^\uparrow$ notation means that whenever we use the given sentence truthfully, if we replace the marked word w with another word which is "$\geq w$," then the resulting sentence will still be true. So we have a *semantic inference*. The $^\downarrow$ notation means the same thing, except that when we substitute using a word $\leq w$, we again preserve truth. Finally, the $^=$ notation means that we have neither property in general; in a valid semantic inference statement, we can only replace the word with itself rather than with something larger or smaller.

For example, if we had a collection of background facts like *cats $\leq$ animals, beagles $\leq$ dogs, scares $\leq$ startles*, and *one $\leq$ two*, then our $^\uparrow$ and $^\downarrow$ notations on *Every dog$^\downarrow$ scares $^\uparrow$ at least two$^\downarrow$ cats$^\uparrow$* would allow us to conclude *Every beagle startles at least one animal*.

The goal of the paper is to provide a computational system to determine the notations $\uparrow, \downarrow, =$ on input text to the best extent possible, either using hand-created parses, or output from a popular and freely available CCG parser C&C (Clark and Curran, 2007).

Using our polarity tool, we get a very easy first step on automatic inference done with little or no representation. We discuss potential applications to textual inference.

Theory We extend polarity determination for categorial grammar (CG) (see Sánchez-Valencia (1991); van Benthem (1986); van Eijck (2007); Lavalle-Martínez et al. (2017)). These papers only consider the Ajdukiewicz/Bar-Hillel (AB) flavor of CG, where the rules are restricted to application rules ($>$) and ($<$). There is a consensus that application rules alone are too restrictive to give wide-coverage grammars. We thus extend this work to the full set of *flexible combinators* used in CCG. We prove that our system is sound, in a precise sense. Further, we show how to incorporate boolean reasoning (Keenan and Faltz, 1984) to get a more complete system.

A working system We have implemented our algorithm in Python. This implementation handles sentences from the C&C parser (Clark and Curran, 2007). This is a non-trivial step on top of the theoretical advance because the parses delivered by the C&C parser deviate in several respects from the semantically-oriented input that one would like for this kind of work.

2 An Ordered Syntax-semantics Interface

The basis of the semantics is the syntax-semantics interface in formal semantics, especially in CG and CCG (Keenan and Faltz, 1984; Carpenter, 1998; Steedman, 2000; Jacobson, 2014).

Our syntax in this small paper will consist of the lexicon shown in our examples. Here is an exam-

*Proceedings of the 7th Joint Conference on Lexical and Computational Semantics (*SEM)*, pages 124–129
New Orleans, June 5-6, 2018. ©2018 Association for Computational Linguistics

ple of a CCG derivation:

$$
\frac{
\dfrac{\dfrac{Fido : n_{pr}}{Fido: s/(s\backslash n_{pr})}\,\text{\scriptsize T} \quad ch: (s\backslash n_{pr})/n_{pr}}{Fido\ chased : s/n_{pr}}\,\text{\scriptsize B} \quad Felix : n_{pr}
}{Fido\ chased\ Felix : s}\,{\scriptstyle >}
\tag{1}
$$

This tree is not the simplest one for *Fido chased Felix*. We chose it to remind the reader of the CCG rules of type-raising (T) and composition (B).

Let us fix a semantics. We first select the base types e and t. We generate complex types from these by using function types $x \to y$. We adopt a few standard abbreviations. We then fix a map from the CG categories into the types. We choose $s \mapsto t$, $n \mapsto e \to t$, $n_{pr} \mapsto e$, $np \mapsto (e \to t) \to t$, etc. (We use n_{pr} for proper names.)

A *model* $\mathcal{M}$ is a set M together with interpretations of all the lexical items by objects of the appropriate semantic type. We use M as the semantic space for the type e, $\mathfrak{2} = \{\mathsf{F}, \mathsf{T}\}$ for type t, and the full set of functions for higher types. The interpretations of some words are fixed: determiners, conjunctions and relative pronouns. The model thus interprets intransitive verbs by $(et, t)t$, and transitive verbs by $(et, t)((et, t)t)$. By the Justification Theorem in Keenan and Faltz (1984), we in fact may obtain these using simpler and more natural data: for proper names we need only objects of type e, for intransitive verbs we need only et, and for transitive verbs eet.

Let S be a sentence in our fragment, and let Π be a parse tree for S. Associated to Π we have a *semantic parse tree*, giving us a term t_S in the typed lambda calculus over the base types e and t. This term may be interpreted in each model $\mathcal{M}$. For example, the interpretation corresponding to (1) is the boolean value in the model

$$(\lambda x.x[\![Fido]\!] \circ [\![chased]\!])[\![Felix]\!].$$

Polarities $\uparrow$ and $\downarrow$ In order to say what the polarity symbols mean, we need to enrich our semantic spaces from sets to preorders (Moss, 2012; Icard and Moss, 2014).

A *preorder* $\mathbb{P} = (P, \leq)$ is a set P with a relation $\leq$ on P which is reflexive and transitive. Fix a model $\mathcal{M}$. Then each type x gives rise to a preorder $\mathbb{P}_x$. We order $\mathbb{P}_t$ by $\mathsf{F} < \mathsf{T}$. For $\mathbb{P}_e$ we take the flat preorder on the universe set M underlying the model. For the higher types $x \to y$, we take the set $(\mathbb{P}_x \to \mathbb{P}_y)$ of all functions and endow it

with the pointwise order. In this way every one of our semantic types is naturally endowed with the structure of a preorder in every model.

A function $f : \mathbb{P} \to \mathbb{Q}$ is *monotone* (or *order preserving*) if $p \leq q$ in $\mathbb{P}$ implies $f(p) \leq f(q)$ in $\mathbb{Q}$. And f is *antitone* (or *order inverting*) if $p \leq q$ in $\mathbb{P}$ implies $f(q) \leq f(p)$ in $\mathbb{Q}$.

Each sentence S in our fragment is now interpreted in an ordered setting. This is the (mathematical) meaning of our $\uparrow$ and $\downarrow$ arrows in this paper. For example, when we write *every dog*$^{\downarrow}$ *barks*$^{\uparrow}$, this means: for all models $\mathcal{M}$, all $m_1 \leq m_2$ in $\mathbb{P}_{et}$ (for *dog*), and all $n_1 \leq n_2$ in $\mathbb{P}_{(et)t}$ (for *barks*), we have in $\mathfrak{2}$ that $[\![every]\!]\, m_2\, n_1 \leq [\![every]\!]\, m_1\, n_2$.

Order-enriched types using $+$, $-$, and $\cdot$ Following Dowty (1994) we incorporate monotonicity information into the types. Function types $x \to y$ split into three versions: the monotone version $x \xrightarrow{+} y$, the antitone version $x \xrightarrow{-} y$, and the full version $x \xrightarrow{\cdot} y$. (What we wrote before as $x \to y$ is now $x \xrightarrow{\cdot} y$.) These are all preorders using the *pointwise order*. We must replace all of the ordinary slash types by versions of them which have *markings* on them.

Lexicon with order-enriched types We use S for t, N or et for $e \xrightarrow{\cdot} t = e \xrightarrow{+} t$, NP for $N \xrightarrow{\cdot} t$, NP^+ for $N \xrightarrow{+} t$, and NP^- for $N \xrightarrow{-} t$. Note that we have a different font than our syntactic types s, n, and np. Then we use $NP \xrightarrow{+} S$ for intransitive verbs, NP^+ or NP^- for noun phrases with determiners, e for proper names. For the determiners, our lexicon then uses the order-enriched types in different ways:

word	type	word	type
every	$N \xrightarrow{-} NP^+$	*no*	$N \xrightarrow{-} NP^-$
some	$N \xrightarrow{+} NP^+$	*most*	$N \xrightarrow{\cdot} NP^+$

3 Polarizing a Parse Tree

In this section, we specify the rules (see Figure 1) by which we put markings and polarities on each node of a CCG parse tree, based on a marked/order-enriched lexicon. The next section discusses the algorithm.

Input A parse tree $\mathcal{T}$ in CCG as in (1), and a marked lexicon.

Output We aim to convert $\mathcal{T}$ to a different tree $\mathcal{T}^*$ satisfying the following properties: (1) The semantic terms in $\mathcal{T}$ and $\mathcal{T}^*$ should denote the same

$$\frac{(x \xrightarrow{m} y)^d \quad x^{md}}{y^d} \; > \qquad \frac{(x \xrightarrow{m} y)^d \quad (y \xrightarrow{n} z)^{md}}{(x \xrightarrow{mn} z)^d} \; \text{B} \qquad \frac{x^{md}}{((x \xrightarrow{m} y) \xrightarrow{+} y)^d} \; \text{T}$$

$$\frac{(e \to x)^{=}}{(NP \xrightarrow{+} x)^{=}} \; \text{I} \qquad \frac{(e \to x)^d}{(NP^+ \xrightarrow{+} x)^d} \; \text{J} \qquad \frac{(e \to x)^{flip\,d}}{(NP^- \xrightarrow{+} x)^d} \; \text{K}$$

Figure 1: The top line contains core rules of marking and polarity. The letters m and n stand for one of the markings $+$, $-$, or $\cdot$; d stands for $\uparrow$ or $\downarrow$ (but not $=$). In (I), (J), and (K), x must be a boolean category. See charts in the text for the operations $m, d \mapsto md$ and $m, n \mapsto mn$.

function in each model. (2) The lexical items in $\mathcal{T}^*$ must receive their types from the typed lexicon. (3) The polarity of the root of $\mathcal{T}^*$ must be $\uparrow$. (4) At each node in $\mathcal{T}^*$, one of the rules in our system must be matched. Most of the rules are listed in Figure 1.

Example For $\mathcal{T}$ in (1), $\mathcal{T}^*$ could be as in (2):

$$\frac{\dfrac{Fido^{\uparrow} : e}{Fido^{\uparrow} : et \xrightarrow{+} t} \; \text{T} \qquad chased^{\uparrow} : e \xrightarrow{+} et}{\dfrac{Fido \; chased^{\uparrow} : e \xrightarrow{+} t \qquad\qquad Felix^{\uparrow} : e}{Fido \; chased \; Felix^{\uparrow} : t}} \; \text{B} \atop >$$

(2)

The signs $+$ and $-$ on the arrows are *markings*; markings apply to arrows only. We have a third marking, $\cdot$, but this does not figure into (2). Markings are used to tell if a function is interpreted (in every model) by a function which is always monotone ($+$), always antitone ($-$), or neither in general ($\cdot$). The arrows $\uparrow$ and $\downarrow$ are *polarities*. We also have a third polarity, $=$. Polarities are for specific occurrences.

Explanation of the operations on markings and polarities Each rule in Figure 1 is actually a number of other rules, and we have summarized things in terms of several operations. The chart on the left is for combining two markings m and n, and the one on the right is for combining a marking m and a polarity d, obtaining a new polarity.

m \ n	$+$	$-$	$\cdot$
$+$	$+$	$-$	$\cdot$
$-$	$-$	$+$	$\cdot$
$\cdot$	$\cdot$	$\cdot$	$\cdot$

d \ m	$+$	$-$	$\cdot$
$\uparrow$	$\uparrow$	$\downarrow$	$=$
$\downarrow$	$\downarrow$	$\uparrow$	$=$

$$flip\uparrow = \downarrow \qquad flip\downarrow = \uparrow$$

Comments on the rules In Figure 1, x, y and z are variables ranging over marked types.

The application rule ($>$) is essentially taken from van Benthem (1986) (see also Lavalle-

Martínez et al. (2017) for a survey of related algorithms); we expect that our logical system will give rise to several algorithms.

To illustrate ($>$), let us take $m = -$ and $d = \uparrow$. We then have the ($>$) rule

$$\frac{(x \xrightarrow{-} y)^{\uparrow} \quad x^{\downarrow}}{y^{\uparrow}} \; > \tag{3}$$

This means: for all preorders $\mathbb{P}$ and $\mathbb{Q}$, all $f, g : \mathbb{P} \xrightarrow{-} \mathbb{Q}$ and all $p_1, p_2 \in P$, if $f \leq g$ and $p_2 \leq p_1$, then $f(p_1) \leq g(p_2)$.

If we were to change $x^{\downarrow}$ to $x^{\uparrow}$ in (3), we would change our statement by replacing "$p_2 \leq p_1$" with "$p_1 \leq p_2$". If we changed it to $x^{=}$, we would use "$p_1 = p_2$". In this way, we can read off a large number of true facts about preorders from our rules.

There are similar results concerning (B). Here is an example of how (B) is used, taken from (2). *Fido* has type $NP^+ = (et) \xrightarrow{+} t$, and *chased* above it has type $NP^+ \xrightarrow{+} (et)$. So the application of (B) results in *Fido chased* with type $NP^+ \xrightarrow{+} t$.

The rules (I), (J), and (K) are new. In them, x must be *Boolean*. That is, it must belong to the smallest collection B containing t and with the property that if $z \in B$, then $(y \xrightarrow{\cdot} z) \in B$ for all y. B is thus the collection of types whose interpretations are naturally endowed with the structure of a *complete atomic boolean algebra* (Keenan and Faltz, 1984). Indeed, the soundness of (J) and (K) follows from the proof of the Justification Theorem (op. cit).

Figure 2 contains two applications of the (K) rules. First, the lexical entry for *chased* is $e \to et$. The first application of (K) promotes this to $NP^- \xrightarrow{+} et$. The NP receives a $-$ because its argument *no cat* is of type NP^-. Note that the polarity flips when we do this. If we had used (J), the promotion would be to $NP^+ \xrightarrow{+} et$, and

$$
\cfrac{
  \cfrac{no \quad dog^{\downarrow}}{no\ dog^{\uparrow} : NP^{-}}\ {\scriptstyle >}
  \quad
  \cfrac{
    \cfrac{
      \cfrac{ch^{\uparrow} : e \to et}{ch^{\downarrow} : NP^{-} \xrightarrow{+} et}\ {\scriptstyle K}
      \quad
      \cfrac{no \quad cat^{\uparrow}}{no\ cat^{\downarrow} : NP^{-}}\ {\scriptstyle >}
    }{chased\ no\ cat^{\downarrow} : e \to t}\ {\scriptstyle >}
  }{chased\ no\ cat^{\uparrow} : NP^{-} \xrightarrow{+} S}\ {\scriptstyle K}
}{no\ dog\ chased\ no\ cat^{\uparrow} : S}\ {\scriptstyle <}
$$

Figure 2: Two applications of the (к) rules.

there would be no polarity flipping. This would be used in sentence where the object VP was *some cat* or *every cat*. The second application promoted *chased no cat* from the type et to $NP^{-} \xrightarrow{+} S$, again with a polarity flip. If we had used (ɪ), we would have obtained $NP \xrightarrow{+} S$. However, this would have trivialized the polarity to $=$, and this effect would have been propagated up the tree. Rule (ɪ) would be needed for the sentence *most dogs chased no cat*.

Several rules are not shown including "backwards" versions of ($>$), (в), and (т), and also versions where all polarizations are $=$. This is a technical point that is not pertinent to this short version. We should mention that due to these rules, every tree may be polarized in a trivial way, by using $=$ at all nodes. So we are really interested in the *maximally informative* polarizations, the ones that make the most predictions.

Boolean connectives, etc. We take *and* and *or* to be polymorphic of the types $B \xrightarrow{m} (B \xrightarrow{m} B)$, when B is a Boolean category and $m = +, -$, or $\cdot$. Negation flips polarities. Relative pronouns and relative clauses also can be handled. Adjectives are taken to be $N \xrightarrow{+} N$.

Other combinators This paper only discusses (т) and (в), but we also have rules for the other combinators used in CG, such as (s) and (w). For example, the (s) combinator is defined by $Sfg = \lambda x.(fx)(gx)$. In our system, the corresponding polarization rule is

$$
\cfrac{(x \xrightarrow{m} (y \xrightarrow{n} z))^{d} \quad (x \xrightarrow{mn} y)^{nd}}{(x \xrightarrow{m} z)^{d}}\ {\scriptstyle s}
$$

This combinator is part of the standard presentation of CCG, but it is less important in this paper because the C&C parser does not deliver parses using it.

4 Algorithmic Aspects

We have an algorithm[1] that takes as input a CCG tree as in (1) and outputs some tree with markings and polarities, a tree which satisfies the conditions that we have listed. The algorithm has two *phases*, similar to van Benthem's algorithm (van Benthem, 1986) for work with the Ajdukiewicz/Bar-Hillel variant of CG (only application rules). Phase 1 goes down the tree from leaves to root and adds the markings, based on the rules in Figure 1. The markings on the leaves are given in the lexicon. The rest of Phase 1 is non-deterministic. We can see this from our set of rules: there are many cases where one conclusion (on top of the line) permits several possible conclusions. As we go down the tree, we frequently need to postpone the choice.

Phase 2 of the algorithm computes the polarities, again following the rules, starting with the root. One always puts $\uparrow$ on the root, and then goes up the tree. This part of the algorithm is straightforward.

The overall algorithm is in fact non-deterministic for two reasons. As we explained, Phase 1 has a non-deterministic feature. In addition, it is always possible to polarize everything with $=$ and make similar uninformative choices for the markings. We are really interested in the *most informative* polarization, the one with the fewest number of $=$ polarities.

Soundness We have proved a *soundness theorem* for the system. Though too complicated to state in full, it might be summarized informally, as follows. Suppose we have a sentence S in English, and suppose that the lexical items in S are given semantics that conform to our assumptions. (This means that the semantics of the lexical entries must belong to the appropriate types.) Then any semantic statement about the $\uparrow, \downarrow, =$ marking predicted by our system is correct. See Moss (2018) for details.

Completeness We have not proven the completeness of our system/algorithm, and indeed this is an open question. What completeness would mean for a system like ours is that whenever we have an input CCG parse tree and a polarization of its words which is semantically valid in the sense that it holds no matter how the nouns, verbs, etc. are interpreted, then our algorithm would detect this. This completeness would be a property

---

[1] https://github.com/huhailinguist/ccg2mono

of the rules and also of the polarization algorithm. The experience with similar matters in Icard and Moss (2013) suggests that completeness will be difficult.

Efficiency of our algorithm Our polarization is quite fast on the sentences which we have tried it on. We conjecture that it is in polynomial time, but the most obvious complexity upper bound to the polarization problem is NP. The reason that the complexity is not "obviously polynomial" is that for each of the type raising steps in the input tree, one has three choices of the raise. In more detail, suppose that the input tree contains

$$\frac{x}{(x \to y) \to y} \; \text{\tiny T}$$

Then our three choices for marking are: $(x \xrightarrow{+} y) \xrightarrow{+} y$, $(x \xrightarrow{-} y) \xrightarrow{+} y$, and $(x \to y) \xrightarrow{+} y$. Our implementation defers the choice until more of the tree is marked. But prima facie, there are an exponential number of choices. All of these remarks also apply to the applications of (ι), ($\jmath$), and (κ); these do not occur in the input tree, and the algorithm must make a choice somehow. Thus we do not know the worst-case complexity of our algorithm.

5 What Our System Can Currently Do

We tokenized input sentences using the script from the ccg2lambda system (Martínez-Gómez et al., 2016). The tokenized sentences were then parsed using the C&C parser (Clark and Curran, 2007), which is trained on the CCGbank (Hockenmaier and Steedman, 2007). Then we run our algorithm.

We are able to take simple sentences all the way through. For example, our system correctly determines the polarities in

No$^\uparrow$ man$^\downarrow$ walks$^\downarrow$
Every$^\uparrow$ man$^\downarrow$ and$^\uparrow$ some$^\uparrow$ woman$^\uparrow$ sleeps$^\uparrow$
Every$^\uparrow$ man$^\downarrow$ and$^\uparrow$ no$^\uparrow$ woman$^\downarrow$ sleeps$^=$
If$^\uparrow$ some$^\uparrow$ man$^\downarrow$ walks$^\downarrow$, then$^\uparrow$ no$^\uparrow$ woman$^\downarrow$ runs$^\downarrow$
Every$^\uparrow$ man$^\downarrow$ does$^\downarrow$ n't$^\uparrow$ hit$^\downarrow$ every$^\downarrow$ dog$^\uparrow$
No$^\uparrow$ man$^\downarrow$ that$^\downarrow$ likes$^\downarrow$ every$^\downarrow$ dog$^\uparrow$ sleeps$^\downarrow$
Most$^\uparrow$ men$^=$ that$^=$ every$^=$ woman$^=$ hits$^=$ cried$^\uparrow$
Every$^\uparrow$ young$^\downarrow$ man$^\downarrow$ that$^\uparrow$ no$^\uparrow$ young$^\downarrow$ woman$^\downarrow$
    hits$^\uparrow$ cried$^\uparrow$

As shown, our algorithm polarizes all words in the input. For determiners, this actually is useful. It is (arguably) background knowledge, for example

that *every* $\leq$ *some*; *at least two* $\leq$ *at least one* $\equiv$ *some*, *no* $\leq$ *at most one* $\leq$ *at most two*, etc. These would not be part of the algorithm in this paper, but rather they would be background facts that figure into inference engines built on this work.

Problems Our end-to-end system is sound in the sense that it polarizes the correctly input semantic representations. However, it is limited by the quality of the parses coming from the C&C parser. While the parser has advantages, its output is sometimes not the optimal for our purposes. For example, it will assign the supertag N/N to *most*, but NP/N to other quantifiers. Thus in order to handle *most*, one has to manually change the parse trees. It also parses relative clauses as *(no dog) (who chased a cat) died* rather than *(no (dog who chased a cat)) died*. Furthermore, the parser sometimes behaves differently on intransitive verbs likes *walks* than on *cries*. Currently, we manually fix the trees when they systematically deviate from our desired parses (e.g. relative clauses). Finally, as with any syntactic parser, it only delivers one parse. So ambiguous sentences are not treated in any way by our work.

6 Future Work: Inference, and Connections with Other Approaches

We certainly plan to use the algorithm in connection with *inference*, since this has always been the a primary reason to study monotonicity and polarity. Indeed, once one has correct polarity markings, it is straightforward to use those to do inference from any background facts which can be expressed as inequalities. This would cover taxonomic statements like *dog* $\leq$ *animal* and also predications like *John isa swimmer*. Our future work will show logical systems built this way.

Connections This paper invites connections to other work in the area, especially MacCartney and Manning (2009) and Nairn et al. (2006), which shared similar aims as ours, but were not done in the CCG context. We also think of work on automatic discovery of downward-entailments (Cheung and Penn, 2012; Danescu et al., 2009), and other work on natural logic (Fyodorov et al., 2003; Zamansky et al., 2006; Moss, 2015; Abzianidze, 2017). Additionally, our work could be incorporated in several ways into textual entailment systems (e.g. Dagan et al., 2013).

References

Lasha Abzianidze. 2017. Langpro: Natural language theorem prover. *CoRR*, abs/1708.09417.

Johan van Benthem. 1986. *Essays in Logical Semantics*. Reidel, Dordrecht.

Bob Carpenter. 1998. *Type-Logical Semantics*. MIT Press.

Jackie Cheung and Gerald Penn. 2012. Unsupervised detection of downward-entailing operators by maximizing classification certainty. In *Proc. 13th EACL*, pages 696–705.

Stephen Clark and James R Curran. 2007. Wide-coverage efficient statistical parsing with ccg and log-linear models. *Computational Linguistics*, 33(4):493–552.

Ido Dagan, Dan Roth, Mark Sammons, and Fabio Massimo Zanzotto. 2013. *Recognizing Textual Entailment*. Synthesis Lectures on Human Language Technologies. Morgan & Claypool Publishers.

Cristian Danescu, Lillian Lee, and Richard Ducott. 2009. Without a 'doubt'? Unsupervised discovery of downward-entailing operators. In *Proceedings of NAACL HLT*.

David Dowty. 1994. The role of negative polarity and concord marking in natural language reasoning. In *Proceedings of Semantics and Linguistic Theory (SALT) IV*.

Jan van Eijck. 2007. Natural logic for natural language. In *Logic, Language, and Computation*, volume 4363 of *LNAI*, pages 216–230. Springer-Verlag.

Yaroslav Fyodorov, Yoad Winter, and Nissim Fyodorov. 2003. Order-based inference in natural logic. *Log. J. IGPL*, 11(4):385–417. Inference in computational semantics: the Dagstuhl Workshop 2000.

Julia Hockenmaier and Mark Steedman. 2007. Ccgbank: a corpus of ccg derivations and dependency structures extracted from the Penn Treebank. *Computational Linguistics*, 33(3):355–396.

Thomas F. Icard and Lawrence S. Moss. 2013. A complete calculus of monotone and antitone higher-order functions. In *Proceedings, TACL 2013*, volume 23 of *EPiC Series*, pages 96–99. Vanderbilt University.

Thomas F. Icard and Lawrence S. Moss. 2014. Recent progress on monotonicity. *Linguistic Issues in Language Technology*, 9(7):167–194.

Pauline Jacobson. 2014. *An Introduction to the Syntax/Semantics Interface*. Oxford University Press.

Edward L. Keenan and Leonard M. Faltz. 1984. *Boolean Semantics for Natural Language*. Springer.

José-de-Jesús Lavalle-Martínez, Manuel Montes-y Gómez, Luis Villaseñor-Pineda, Héctor Jiménez-Salazar, and Ismael-Everardo Bárcenas-Patiño. 2017. Equivalences among polarity algorithms. *Studia Logica*.

Bill MacCartney and Christopher D. Manning. 2009. An extended model of natural logic. In *IWCS-8, Proceedings of the Eighth International Conference on Computational Semantics*, pages 140–156.

Pascual Martínez-Gómez, Koji Mineshima, Yusuke Miyao, and Daisuke Bekki. 2016. ccg2lambda: A compositional semantics system. In *Proceedings of ACL 2016 System Demonstrations*, pages 85–90, Berlin, Germany. Association for Computational Linguistics.

Lawrence S. Moss. 2012. The soundness of internalized polarity marking. *Studia Logica*, 100(4):683–704.

Lawrence S. Moss. 2015. Natural logic. In *Handbook of Contemporary Semantic Theory, Second Edition*, pages 646–681. Wiley-Blackwell.

Lawrence S. Moss. 2018. Foundations of polarity determination for flexible categorial grammars. Unpublished ms.

Rowan Nairn, Cleo Condoravdi, and Lauri Karttunen. 2006. Computing relative polarity for textual inference. In *Proceedings of ICoS-5 (Inference in Computational Semantics)*, Buxton, UK.

Victor Sánchez-Valencia. 1991. *Studies on Natural Logic and Categorial Grammar*. Ph.D. thesis, Universiteit van Amsterdam.

Mark Steedman. 2000. *The Syntactic Process*. MIT Press.

Anna Zamansky, Nissim Francez, and Yoad Winter. 2006. A 'natural logic' inference system using the Lambek calculus. *Journal of Logic, Language, and Information*, 15(3):273–295.

Coarse Lexical Frame Acquisition at the Syntax–Semantics Interface Using a Latent-Variable PCFG Model

Laura Kallmeyer[*] & Behrang Q. Zadeh[*]
SFB991, Heinrich-Heine-Universität Düsseldorf
`kallmeyer@hhu.de zadeh@phil.hhu.de`

Jackie Chi Kit Cheung
McGill University
`jcheung@cs.mcgill.ca`

Abstract

We present a method for unsupervised lexical frame acquisition at the syntax–semantics interface. Given a set of input strings derived from dependency parses, our method generates a set of clusters that resemble lexical frame structures. Our work is motivated not only by its practical applications (e.g., to build, or expand the coverage of lexical frame databases), but also to gain linguistic insight into frame structures with respect to lexical distributions in relation to grammatical structures. We model our task using a hierarchical Bayesian network and employ tools and methods from latent variable probabilistic context free grammars (L-PCFGs) for statistical inference and parameter fitting, for which we propose a new split and merge procedure. We show that our model outperforms several baselines on a portion of the Wall Street Journal sentences that we have newly annotated for evaluation purposes.

1 Introduction

We propose a method for building coarse lexical frames automatically from dependency parsed sentences; i.e., without using any explicit semantic information as training data. The task involves grouping verbs that evoke the same frame (i.e., are considered to be the head of this frame) and further clustering their syntactic arguments into latent semantic roles. Hence, our target structures stand between FrameNet (Ruppenhofer et al., 2016) and PropBank (Palmer et al., 2005) frames. Similar to FrameNet and in contrast to PropBank, we assume a many-to-many relationship between verb types and frame types. But similar to PropBank, we aim to cluster syntactic arguments into general semantic roles instead of frame-specific slot

types in FrameNet. This allows us to generalize across frames concerning semantic roles. As part of this, we study possible ways to automatically generate more abstract lexical-semantic representations from lexicalized dependency structures.

In our task, grouping verb tokens into frames requires not only distinguishing between different senses of verbs, but also identifying a range of lexical relationships (e.g., synonymy, opposite verbs, troponymy, etc.) among them. Hence (as Modi et al., 2012; Green et al., 2004), our problem definition differs from most work on unsupervised fine-grained frame induction using verb sense disambiguation (e.g., Kawahara et al., 2014; Peng et al., 2017). Similarly, forming role clusters yields generalization from several alternate linkings between semantic roles and their syntactic realization. Given, for instance, an occurrence of the verb *pack* and its syntactic arguments, not only do we aim to distinguish different senses of the verb *pack* (e.g., as used to evoke the FILLING frame, or the PLACING frame), but also to group these instances of 'pack' with other verbs that evoke the same frame (e.g., to group instances of *pack* that evoke the frame PLACING with instances of verbs *load*, *pile*, *place*, and so on when used to evoke the same PLACING frame).

The motivation for this work is twofold. On the one hand, the frame induction techniques we propose can be useful in the context of applications such as text summarization (Cheung and Penn, 2013), question answering (Frank et al., 2007; Shen and Lapata, 2007), and so on, for languages where we lack a frame-annotated resource for supervised frame induction, or to expand the coverage of already existing resources. On the other hand, we are interested in theoretical linguistic insights into frame structure. In this sense, our

---

[*]Both authors contributed equally to this work.

*Proceedings of the 7th Joint Conference on Lexical and Computational Semantics (*SEM)*, pages 130–141
New Orleans, June 5-6, 2018. ©2018 Association for Computational Linguistics

work is a step towards an empirical investigation of frames and semantic roles including hierarchical relations between them.

We cast the frame induction task as unsupervised learning using an L-PCFG (Johnson, 1998; Matsuzaki et al., 2005; Petrov et al., 2006; Cohen, 2017). As input, our model takes syntactic dependency trees and extracts input strings corresponding to instances of frame expressions, which are subsequently grouped into latent semantic frames and roles using an L-PCFG. We use the inside-outside (i.e., Expectation-Maximization (Dempster et al., 1977; Do and Batzoglou, 2008)) algorithm and a split-merge procedure (Petrov et al., 2006) for dynamically adapting the number of frames and roles to the data, for which we employ new heuristics. As implied, one advantage of the L-PCFGs framework is that we can adapt and reuse statistical inference techniques used for learning PCFGs in syntactic parsing application (e.g., split-merge). Our experiment shows that the method outperforms a number of baselines, including frame grouping by lexical heads and one based on agglomerative clustering.

The main contributions of this paper are a) using L-PCFGs for coarse lexical frame acquisition; b) a new split-merge routine adapted for this task; and, c) a new dataset for evaluating the induced lexical frame-role groupings. In the remainder of the paper, § 2 describes our statistical model and its formalization to an L-PCFG. § 3 describes procedures used for statistical inference. § 4 describes our evaluation dataset and reports results from experiments. § 5 discusses related work followed by a conclusion in § 6.

2 From a Latent Model to L-PCFG

We assume that frames and semantic roles are the latent variables of a probabilistic model. Given the probability mass function $pmf(F^1, \ldots, F^n, R^1 \ldots R^k, D^1, \ldots, D^m; \mathcal{C}, \theta)$ as our model, we denote latent frames $F^i, 1 \leq i \leq n$, and roles $R^i, 1 \leq i \leq k$ for observations that are annotated syntactically using $D^i, 1 \leq i \leq m$ in the input corpus $\mathcal{C}$. Inspired by Cheung et al. (2013), we approximate the probability of a specific frame f with head v, semantic roles $r_1 \ldots r_k$ filled by words $w_1 \ldots w_k$ and corresponding syntactic dependencies $d_1 \ldots d_k$ (under

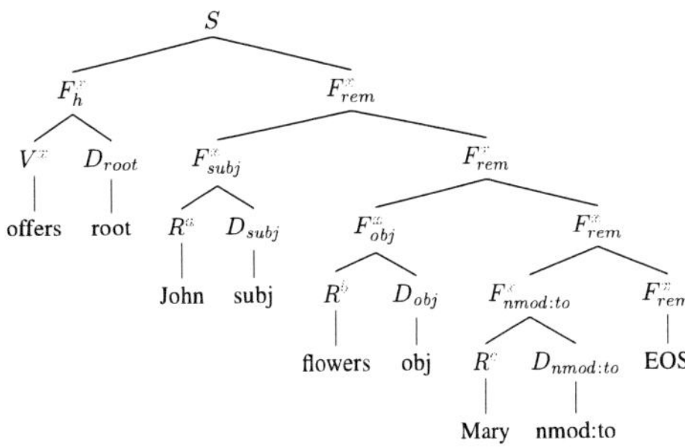

Figure 1: Sample frame structure for (1).

parameters θ) as:

$$p(f) \cdot p(v|f) \prod_{i=1}^{k} p(d_i|f) \cdot \prod_{i=1}^{k} p(r_i|f, d_i) \cdot \prod_{i=1}^{k} p(w_i|r_i). \tag{1}$$

To estimate the parameters of our model, we translate Eq. (1) to an L-PCFG that captures the required conditional and joint probabilities.

First, we convert input lexicalized dependency parses to a set of strings $\mathcal{E}$. Given a verb v and its dependents w_i in a dependency parse tree, we build input strings in the form of

$$v\ root\ w_1\ d_1 \ldots w_l\ d_l\ EOS,$$

for which we assume v lexicalizes the head of a frame, $w_1 \ldots w_l$ are the arguments fillers and $d_1, \ldots, d_l$ are the respective dependencies that link these fillers to the head v; *EOS* is a special symbol to mark the end of string. For the step from the sentence to input strings, we assume that dependencies are ordered (e.g., *subj* precedes *dobj* and *iobj* and they precede prepositional and complement dependents (i.e., *nmod:** and **comp*).[1] Consider (1) as an example; the corresponding string is the yield of the tree in Fig. 1.

(1)   John$_{subj}$ offer$_{root}$ flowers$_{dobj}$ to Mary$_{nmod:to}$

Given the fixed structure of input strings, we design a CFG that rewrites them to our expected hierarchical frame structure consisting of elements F, R, D while capturing the conditional probabilities from Eq. (1). The tree assigning a frame F of type x with semantic roles of type a, b, c to (1) is for

---

[1] Phrasal arguments are reduced to their syntactic head given by the underlying UD parser. We normalize passive structures by replacing *nsubjpass* with *dobj*. Other syntactic dependents (e.g., *case, aux, conj*, etc.) are removed. In case of the same dependencies, surface order in the sentence is relevant. If necessary, conjunctions are treated when transforming dependency parses to input strings.

instance given in Fig. 1. More generally, given finite sets of frames $\mathcal{F}$ and of semantic roles $\mathcal{R}$, our underlying CFG $G = \langle N, T, P, S \rangle$ is as follows:

- $T = T_v \cup T_n \cup \mathcal{D} \cup \{root, EOS\}$, where T_v is the set of possible verbal heads, T_n is the set of possible lexicalizations (fillers) for arguments, and $\mathcal{D}$ is a finite set of dependency relations; $root$ and EOS are special symbols.
- $N = \{S\} \cup \{F_h^f \mid f \in \mathcal{F}\} \cup \{F_{rem}^f \mid f \in \mathcal{F}\} \cup \{F_g^f \mid f \in \mathcal{F}, g \in \mathcal{D}\} \cup \{R^r \mid r \in \mathcal{R}\} \cup \{V^f \mid f \in \mathcal{F}\} \cup \{D_g \mid g \in \mathcal{D}\}$.
- P contains the following rules:

  - $S \rightarrow F_h^f F_{rem}^f$ for all $f \in \mathcal{F}$;
  - $F_h^f \rightarrow V^f \, D_{root}$ for all $f \in \mathcal{F}$;
  - $F_{rem}^f \rightarrow F_g^f \, F_{rem}^f$ for all $f \in \mathcal{F}, g \in \mathcal{D}$;
  - $F_{rem}^f \rightarrow EOS$ for all $f \in \mathcal{F}$;
  - $F_g^f \rightarrow R^r \, D_g$ for all $f \in \mathcal{F}, r \in \mathcal{R}, g \in \mathcal{D}$;
  - $V^f \rightarrow v$ for all $f \in \mathcal{F}, v \in T_v$;
  - $R^r \rightarrow n$ for all $r \in \mathcal{R}, n \in T_n$;
  - $D_g \rightarrow g$ for all $g \in \mathcal{D} \cup \{root\}$.

With this grammar, an input string derived from a dependency parsed sentence fully determines the shape of the tree and the node labels are fixed except for the choice of the frame f and the semantic roles r of the k fillers (i.e., x, a, b, and c in Fig. 1).

The probabilities of the rules correspond to the conditional probabilities in Eq. (1). The probability of $S \rightarrow F_h^f \, F_{rem}^f$ gives $p(F = f)$, the probability of $V^f \rightarrow v$ gives $p(V = v \mid F = f)$, and so on. During the subsequent inside-outside (IO) split-and-merge training procedure, the inventory of frames and roles and the probabilities corresponding to our rules are estimated so that the overall likelihood of observations is maximized.

3 Method

This section describes statistical inference methods used for inducing latent frame clusters from input strings. The scenario we used for parameter fitting (split, merge, smoothing, and generating clusters) is described in § 3.1. In § 3.2, we describe our method for computing embedding-based similarity between frames, which we use during the merge process and in our baseline system.

3.1 Parameter Fitting

Given an input corpus parsed into universal dependencies (UD) and converted into a set of input strings $\mathcal{E}$, we instantiate a model G according to § 2. We set $|\mathcal{F}| = 1$ and $|\mathcal{R}| = |\mathcal{D}|$, and $\mathcal{D}$, T_v and T_n are automatically extracted from $\mathcal{E}$. Starting from this, we iteratively perform *split-merge* sequences (with an IO parameter estimation in between), and cluster $\mathcal{E}$ to disjoint subsets $\mathcal{E}_i$ by finding the most-likely derivations that G yields. We detail this process in the following subsections.

3.1.1 The IO Algorithm

As a solution to sparsity of observations, we modify the IO algorithm slightly. We adapt the procedures described in (Eisner, 2016) with the exception that for computing inside and outside probabilities, instead of mapping terminals to nonterminals using an exact matching of the right-hand-sides of the rules (and respectively their assigned parameters), we use embedding-based similarities. I.e., for computing inside probabilities, given symbol a as input, instead of considering $A \rightarrow_\theta$ as rewrite rules and updating the parse chart only by asserting θ in it, we also consider $B \rightarrow_\theta bs$ in which instead of θ we assert $\alpha \times \theta s$ in the IO table, where α is the r^2 coefficient correlations of embeddings for a and bs. During the outside procedure, θs are updated proportionally w.r.t. to αs used during the inside parameter estimation procedure.

3.1.2 Split

We alter the splitting procedure from (Klein and Manning, 2003a; Petrov et al., 2006) for our application. In (Klein and Manning, 2003b; Petrov et al., 2006), during split, a non-terminal symbol (which represents a random variable in the underlying probabilistic model) is split and its related production rules are duplicated *independently of its parent, or sibling nodes*. We can apply such a context-independent split only to the R^r non-terminals but the F^fs must split *dependently* w.r.t. their sibling nodes that define the frame structure. Therefore, to split frame x to two frames y and z, we replace the entire set $\{S \rightarrow F_h^x F_{rem}^x, F_h^x \rightarrow V^x D_{root}, F_{rem}^x \rightarrow EOS, F_{rem}^x \rightarrow F_g^x F_{rem}^x, F_g^x \rightarrow R^r D_g$, and $V^x \rightarrow v\}$ with two similar sets where x gets replaced with y and z, respectively. The parameters for the new rules are set to half of the value of the parameters of the rules that they originated from with the addition (or subtraction) of a random ϵ (e.g., 1e-7) to break symmetry.

Moreover, in our application, training the split grammar on the whole input is ineffective and at a certain point, computationally intractable. The problem is due to the scope of the split grammar and the large portion of input strings $\mathcal{E}$ that they span. Splitting a frame's rules, unlike parameter fitting for syntactic rules, increases the number of possible derivations for all $\mathcal{E}$, to the extent that after a number of split iterations the computation of the derivations becomes intractable even for a small $\mathcal{E}$ of short length. We address this problem by using a new strategy for splitting: we not only split the grammar, but also the input training data.

Before each split, we cluster input strings $\mathcal{E}$ to clusters $\mathcal{E}_i$ that G gives (§ 3.1.4) at that point. For input strings in each cluster $\mathcal{E}_i$, we instantiate a new G_i and perform parameter fitting and splitting independently of other $\mathcal{E}_i$s. The corresponding probabilistic G_i is initialized by assigning random parameters to its rules and then smoothing them (§ 3.1.3) by the fitted parameters for G. We apply the aforementioned process several times, until the number of independently generated clusters is at least twice as large as $|T_v|$. At the end of each split iteration, we collect the elicited $\mathcal{E}_i$ clusters (and their respective G_is) for the next merge process. Given the independence assumption between roles and frames, pre-terminals that rewrite roles are split similar to (Petrov et al., 2006).

3.1.3 Smoothing

We apply a notion of smoothing by interpolating parameters that are obtained in the $n-1$th iteration of split-merge with parameters that are randomly initialized at the beginning of each split-merge iteration and, as mentioned earlier in § 3.1.2, when deriving new G_is from G: For each rule in G_i or G^n with parameters θ (i.e., the G instantiated for the next split-merge iteration), we smooth θs using $\theta = \alpha\theta + (1-\alpha)\theta_{n-1}$, where θ_{n-1} is the already known and fitted parameter for the corresponding rule in G. We choose $\alpha = 0.1$.

3.1.4 Generating Clusters from G

After fitting parameters of G, the frame structure for an input string is given by its most-likely viterbi derivation with respect to G. The verb which is rewritten by F_h^f is placed to frame-type/cluster f. Similarly, lexical items that are argument fillers are assigned to type/cluster r where r is the structural annotation for pre-terminal R^r that rewrite them. For example, assuming Fig 1 is the most likely derivation for (1), the verb 'offer' is categorized as frame x and its arguments as

roles a, b, and c.

3.1.5 Merge

The model resulting from the split process generates a relatively large number of 'homogeneous' clusters that are 'incomplete'. A subsequent merge process unifies these homogeneous-but-incomplete clusters to achieve a clustering that is both homogeneous and complete. To this end, we use heuristics which are based on both the estimated loss in likelihood from merging two symbols that span the same input sequence (as proposed previously in Petrov et al. (2006)) as well as the 'discriminative similarities' between the obtained clusters.

Merge by likelihoods does not work: The heuristics for merge in (Petrov et al., 2006) (i.e., minimizing the loss in training likelihood using 'locally' estimated inside and outside probabilities) are based on the assumptions that a) pre-terminals appearing in different places in derivations are nearly independent, and b) that their approximation (according to the method proposed by Petrov et al. (2006)) requires less computation than computing full derivation trees. However, neither of these hold in our case: a) most pre-terminals in our model are dependent on each other and, b) to compute the loss in likelihood from a cluster merge requires computation of full derivation trees (given the interdependence between pre-terminals that define frame structures). More importantly, in our application, the outside probabilities for clusters are always 1.0 and differences in the sum of inside probabilities is often negligible since input strings are spanned more-or-less by the same set of derivations. For these reasons (i.e., computation cost and the lack of sufficient statistics), the 'estimated loss in likelihood' heuristics is a futile method for guiding the merge process in our application. We resolve this problem by leveraging discriminative similarities between the obtained frame clusters and proposing a hybrid method.

Our merge approach: In the beginning of a merge process, we conflate G_is that are obtained from the previous split procedure to form a G that spans all input strings. Where applicable, we set parameters of rules in G to the arithmetic mean of corresponding ones obtained from the split process and normalize them such that sum of the parameters of rules with the same pre-terminal is 1.0.

We go through an iterative process: Using the method proposed in § 3.2 below, the frame instances in the clusters are converted to tensors and similarities among them are computed. Motivated by the assumption that split clusters are homogeneous, for every pair of clusters c^x and c^y ($x \neq y$) with instances $a_i \in c^x$ and $b_j \in c^y$, we find $\arg\max_{i,j} sim(a_i, b_j)$ and $\arg\min_{i,j} sim(a_i, b_j)$ (sim is given by Eq. 2 below) and calculate their harmonic mean as the similarity s_c between c^x and c^y. Cluster pairs are sorted in a descending order by s_c. Given a threshold δ, for all $s_c(c^x, c^y) > \delta$, their corresponding production rules (i.e., the similar set of rules mentioned in the split procedure) are merged and their parameters are updated to the arithmetic mean of their origin rules.

Parameters for this new merged G are updated through a few IO iterations (in an incremental fashion (Liang and Klein, 2009)), and finally G is used to obtain a new clustering. The process is repeated for this newly obtained clustering until all the resulting cluster-wise s_c similarities are less than a threshold β.

Computing all derivations for each input string is time consuming and makes the merge process computationally expensive, particularly in the first few iterations. We resolve this issue using a stratified random sampling and by performing the aforementioned iterations only on a random subset of input strings in each cluster. Each cluster in the output of the split process is taken as a stratum and its size is reduced by 90% by applying a random sampling; this random sampling is updated in each iteration (we use a similar strategy for parameter estimation, i.e., we update samples in each estimation iteration). This process reduces the required time for merge drastically without hurting the overall outcome of the merge process. It is worth to mention that after merging clusters c^x and c^y, the output does not necessarily contain a cluster $c^x \cup c^y$. Instead, the resulting clustering reflects the effect of merging the rules that rewrite c^x and c^y in the whole model.

To merge R^r categories, we use the merge method from (Petrov et al., 2006) based on the obtained likelihoods. After merging frame clusters, we reduce the number of R^rs by 50%. Since our method for merging role categories is similar to (Petrov et al., 2006), we do not describe it here.

3.2 Similarity Between Frame Instances

When necessary (such as during merge), we compute embedding-based similarities between frame instances similar to methods proposed in (Mitchell and Lapata, 2008; Clark, 2013). We build a n-dimensional embedding for each word appearing in our input strings from large web corpora. Each frame instance is then represented using a $(m + 1, n)$-tensor, in which m is the total number of argument types/clusters given by our model at its current stage and n is the dimensionality of the embeddings that represent words that fill these arguments. To this, we add the embedding for the verb that lexicalizes the head of the frame, which gives us the final $(m + 1, n)$-tensor.

For two frame-instances represented by tensors a and b, the similarity for their arguments is

$$sim\text{-}arg(a, b) = \frac{1}{k} \sum_{i=1}^{m} r^2(^a\vec{v^i}, {}^b\vec{v^i}),$$

in which $\vec{v^i}$s are embeddings for the ith argument filler ($\sum_{j=1}^{n} \vec{v^i}_j \neq 0$), r^2 is the coefficient of determination, and $k = \sum_i [r^2(^a\vec{v^i}, {}^b\vec{v^i}) \neq 0]$. If an argument is lexicalized by more than one filler, we replace r^2 with the arithmetic mean of r^2s computed over each distinct pair of fillers. The overall sim between a and b is:

$$sim(a, b) = w_1.r^2(^a\vec{v^h}, {}^b\vec{v^h}) + w_2.sim\text{-}arg(a, b),$$
$$(2)$$

where $\vec{v^h}$s are the embeddings for the lexical heads (i.e., verbs), and w_1 and w_2 are two hyper-parameters which can be tuned. For instance, for two hypothetical structures of F^a:[Head:travel, [Arg^1:John, Arg^2:London]] and F^b:[Head:walk, [Arg^1:Mary, Arg^3:home]], the similarity between F^a and F^b is $w_1 r^2(\vec{travel}, \vec{walk}) + w_2 r^2(\vec{John}, \vec{Mary})$, given that the all these vectors have at least one nonzero component. During merge we use $w_1 = w_2 = 0.50$.

We build our lexical embeddings of dimensionality $n = 900$ using the hash-based embedding learning technique proposed in (QasemiZadeh and Kallmeyer, 2017); before using these embeddings, we weight them using positive pointwise mutual information. During evaluation, this combination of PPMI-weighted hash-based embeddings and the r^2 estimator consistently yielded better results than using other popular choices such as the cosine of word2vec vectors. We associate this observation to the imbalanced frequency of the usages of lexical items in our experiments in the corpora used to train embeddings (i.e., an English web corpus (Schäfer, 2015) and PTB's WSJ).

4 Experiments and Results

4.1 Dataset

We derive our data for evaluation from the PTB's WSJ sections parsed (using Schuster and Manning, 2016) to the enhanced UD format. We augment these sentences with semantic role annotations obtained from Prague Semantic Dependencies (PSD) (Cinkova et al., 2012) from the SDP resource (Oepen et al., 2016). Using Eng-Vallex (Cinková et al., 2014) and SemLink (Bonial et al., 2013), we semi-automatically annotate verbs with FrameNet frames (Baker et al., 1998). We choose 1k random sentences and manually verify the semi-automatic mappings to eventually build our evaluation dataset of approximately 5k instances (all). From this data, we use a random subset of 200 instances (dev) during the development and for parameter tuning (see Table 1 for detailed statistics).

Set	FT	FI	V	AT	AI
all	27	5,324	169	13	10,523
dev	15	200	35	7	393

Table 1: Gold Data: FT, FI, V, AT, and AI denote the number of frame types, instances, distinct verb heads, argument types, and argument instances

For these gold instances, we extract input strings from their UD parses according § 2. Since we discard verbs without syntactic arguments, use automatic parses, and do not distinguish arguments from adjuncts, the input strings do not exactly match the gold data argument structures. We report results *only* for the portion of the gold data that appears in the extracted input strings. Table 2 reports the statistics for the induced input strings and their agreement with the gold data (in terms of precision and recall).

Input strings are hard to cluster in the sense that a) all the frames are lexicalized by at least two different verb lemmas, b) many verbs lexicalizes at least two different types of frames, c) verb lemmas that lexicalize a frame have long-tailed distributions, i.e., a large proportion of instances of a frame are realized at surface structure by one

Set	FT	FI	R_F	V	GR	AI	AIG	P_A	R_A
all	27	4,984	0.94	167	56	10,893	7,305	0.67	0.76
dev	15	191	0.95	34	24	450	277	0.62	0.76

Table 2: Input strings extracted from the UD parses: GR, AIG, R_F, R_A, and P_A denote, respectively, the number of distinct grammatical relations, syntactic arguments that are a semantic role in the gold data, recall for frame and arguments, and precision for arguments. The remaining symbols are the same as Table 1.

lemma while in the remaining instances the frame is evoked by different lemmas, and d) last but not least, the frame types themselves have long-tailed distribution. Table 3 shows examples of frames and verb lemmas that lexicalize them; in the table, the most frequent lemma for each frame type is italicized.

4.2 Evaluation Measures

We evaluate our method's performance on a) clustering input strings to frame types, and b) clustering syntactic arguments to semantic role types. To this end, we report the harmonic mean of BCubed precision and recall (BCF) (Bagga and Baldwin, 1998), and purity (PU), inverse purity (IPU) and their harmonic mean (FPU) (Steinbach et al., 2000) as figures of merit. These measures reflect a notion of similarity between the distribution of instances in the obtained clusters and the gold/evaluation data based on certain criteria and alone may lack sufficient information for a fair understanding of the system's performance. While PU and IPU are easy to interpret (by establishing an analogy between them and precision and recall in classification tasks), they may be deceiving under certain conditions (as explained by Amigó et al., 2009, under the notions of homogeneity, completeness, rag bag, and 'size vs. quantity' constraints). Reporting BCF alongside FPU ensures that these pitfalls are not overlooked when our system's output are compared quantitatively with the baselines.

4.3 Baselines

As baselines, we report the standard all-in-one-class clustering (ALLIN1) and the one-cluster-per-instance (1CPERI) baselines, as well as the random baseline (R_n) in which instances are randomly partitioned into n clusters (n being the number of generated clusters in our sys-

Frame	#T	#V	{Examples of verbs occurrences}
ADORNING	26	10	{*fill*:8, cover:4, adorn:2 … }
PLACING	121	21	{*place*:62, pack:3, wrap:1… }
FILLING	35	12	{*fill*:14, pack:6, cover:3, wrap:2 … }
ACTIVITY_START	290	2	{*begin*:182, start:108}
PROCESS_START	188	2	{*begin*:143, start:45}
CHANGE_POSITION_ON_SACLE	1259	17	{*fall*=356, rise=271, drop=135, decline=119, … }

Table 3: Examples of frames in our evaluation set and verbs that evoke them; #T and #V denote the total number of instances for the frame and the number of distinct verb lemmas that evoke them, respectively.

tem's output). Moreover, for frame type clustering, we report the one-cluster-per-lexical-head baseline (1CPERHEAD). For role clustering, we report the additional one-cluster-per-syntactic-category baseline (1CPERGR). Similar to the most-frequent-sense baseline in word sense induction and disambiguation problems, the latter 1CPERHEAD and 1CPERGR are particularly hard to beat given the heavy-tailed distribution of lexical items in frame and role categories.

For both subtasks, an additional baseline from (Modi et al., 2012) and (Titov and Klementiev, 2012) could be an interesting comparison to our method with the state of the art in frame head clustering and unsupervised semantic role labeling, particularly given that (Titov and Klementiev, 2012) and respectively (Modi et al., 2012) employ Gibbs sampling for statistical inference, whereas we use the IO algorithm. We are, unfortunately, not able to access codes for Modi et al. (2012) and the system in Titov and Klementiev (2012) relies on features that are engineered for treebanks in the format and formalisms set for the CoNLL-2008 shared-task. As explained by Oepen et al. (2016), mapping to (and from) formalisms used in CoNLL-2008 (from–to) those proposed in SDP-PSD (used in this paper) is a nontrivial task. We expect that an automatic conversion from our data to the CoNLL-2008 format as an input for (Titov and Klementiev, 2012) would not reflect the best performance of their method. Nonetheless, we report the result from this experiment (marked as TK-URL) later in this section, not as a baseline, but to confirm (Oepen et al., 2016).

Lastly, as an extra baseline for frame type clustering, we report performance of a HAC method. The HAC method is described below (§ 4.3.1).

4.3.1 A Baseline HAC Method

To build a frame clustering using HAC, we begin by initializing one cluster per instance and itera-

tively merge the pair of clusters with the lowest distance, using average-link cluster distance. For two clusters A and B, we define their distance as:

$$\text{Dis-Cl}(A, B) = \frac{1}{l(l-1)} \sum_{f_i \in A} \sum_{f_j \in B} 1 - sim(f_i, f_j),$$

in which $sim(f_i, f_j)$ is given by Eq. 2, and $l = |A| + |B|$. We iteratively update the distance matrix and agglomerate clusters until we reach a single cluster. During iterations, we keep track of the merges/linkages which we later use to flatten the built hierarchy into q clusters. To set our baseline, by constraining $w_1 + w_2 = 1$ in Eq. (2), we build cluster hierarchies for different w_1 and w_2 (starting with $w_1 = 0.0$, $w_2 = 1 - w_1$ and gradually increasing w_1 by 0.1 until $w_1 = 1.0$) and find w_1, w_2, and q that yield the 'best' clustering according to the BCF metric ($w_1 = 0.8, w_2 = 0.2, q = 140$). For this baseline, the argument types are defined by their syntactic relation to their heads, e.g., subj, dobj, and so on.

4.4 Results

Since our method involves stochastic decisions, its performance varies slightly in each run. Hence, we report the mean and the standard deviation of the obtained performances from 4 independent runs. The reported results are based on the output of the system after 7 split and merge iterations. After tuning parameters on the dev set, we choose $\delta = 0.55$ during merge, and in each inner-merge iteration subtract δ by 0.01 until $\delta < \beta = 0.42$.

Quantitative Comparison with Baselines Tables 4 and 5 show the results for clustering input strings to frame types and semantic roles, respectively. On frame type clustering, our method (denoted by L-PCFG) outperforms all the baselines. FPU and BCF for our system are simultaneously higher than all the baselines, which verifies that the output contains a small proportion of "rag bag" clusters. The system, however, tends to generate

Method	#C	PU	IPU	FPU	BCF
ALLIN1	1	22.35	**100**	36.54	17.43
1CPERI	4984	**100**	0.54	1.08	1.08
1CPERHEAD	167	94.38	59.59	73.06	63.53
R_{235}	235	24.7	2.03	3.75	1.79
HAC	140	75.07	65.52	69.97	61.74
L-PCFG (Avg.)	230.25	86.2	73.64	**79.4**	**71.29**
L-PCFG (Std. Dev.)	±6.24	±3.07	±0.96	±1.17	±1.49

Table 4: Results for head groupings: #C denotes the number of induced clusters by each method/baseline; the last two rows reports the average and the standard deviation for the obtained results using the L-PCFG model.The remaining abbreviations are introduced in § 4.2 and 4.3.

Method	#C	PU	IPU	FPU	BCF
ALLIN1	1	47.73	**100**	64.62	55.43
1CPERI	7257	**100**	0.18	0.36	0.36
1CPERGR	32	92.89	79.83	**85.86**	**76.71**
R_{24}	24	47.73	5.36	9.64	7.79
TK-URL	333	85.7	15.01	25.54	11.71
L-PCFG (Avg.)	24	90.36	79.25	84.44	74.65
L-PCFG (Std. Dev.)	±5.29	±0.33	±1.31	±0.61	±1.38

Table 5: Results on clustering of syntactic arguments to semantic roles.

many incomplete yet homogeneous clusters (as we discuss below). With respect to roles, however, the method's performance and its output remains very similar to the syntactic baseline (BCF=97.3).

What is in the clusters? The ability of the system to successfully cluster instances varies from one gold frame category to another one. The most problematic cases are the frame types ACTIVITY_START and PROCESS_START, as well as PLACING. While the system put instances of 'start' and 'begin' verbs in one cluster, it fails to distinguish between ACTIVITY_START and PROCESS_START. Regarding the PLACING frame, the system places verbs that evoke this frame in different clusters; each cluster consists of instances from one verb lemma. In our opinion, this is due to the frequent idiomatic usages of these verbs, e.g., 'to lay claim', 'to place listing', 'to position oneself as' and so on. This being said, however, the system is capable of distinguishing between different readings of polysemous verbs, e.g., instances of the verb 'pack' that evoke the FILLING frame end up in different clusters than those evoking the PLACING frame. Additionally, for a number of frame types, we observe that the system can successfully group synonymous (and opposite) verbs that evoke the same frame into one cluster: representative examples are the instances of the CHANGE_POSITION_ON_A_SCALE frame that are evoked by different verb lemmas such as 'decline', 'drop', 'fall', 'gain', 'jump', 'rise', …, which all end up in one cluster. The output of the system also contains a large number of small clusters (consisting of only one or two instances): we observe that these instances are usually those with wrong (and incomplete) dependency parses.

5   Related Work

Our work differs from most work on word sense induction (WSI), e.g. (Goyal and Hovy, 2014; Lau et al., 2012; Manandhar et al., 2010; Van de Cruys and Apidianaki, 2011), in that not only do we discern different senses of a lexical item but also we group the induced senses into more general meaning categories (i.e., FrameNet's grouping). Hence, our model must be able to capture lexical relationships other than polysemy, e.g., synonymy, antonymy (opposite verbs), troponymy, etc.. However, our method can be adapted to WSI, too. Firstly, we can assume that word senses are 'incompatible' and thus they necessarily evoke different frames; subsequently, the induced frame clusters can be seen directly as clusters of word senses. Otherwise, the proposed method can be adapted for WSI by altering its initialization, e.g., by building one-model-at-a-time for each word form (i.e., simply altering the input).

Despite similarities between our method and those proposed previously to address unsupervised semantic role induction (Carreras and Marquez, 2005; Lang and Lapata, 2010, 2011; Titov and Klementiev, 2012; Swier and Stevenson, 2004), our method differs from them in that we attempt to include frame head grouping information for inducing roles associated to them. In other words, these methods leave out the problem of sense/frame grouping in their models.

Our work differs in objective from methods for unsupervised template induction in information extraction (IE) (e.g., MUC-style frames in Chambers and Jurafsky (2009, 2011) and its later refinements such as (Chambers, 2013; Cheung et al., 2013; Balasubramanian et al., 2013), and in a broader sense attempts towards ontology learning and population from text (Cimiano et al., 2005)). Our focus is on lexicalized elementary syntactic structures, identifying lexical semantic relationships, and thereby finding salient patterns in syntax–semantic interface. However, in IE tasks the aim is to build structured summaries of text. Therefore, the pre-and post-processing in these induction models are often more complex/different than our method (e.g., they require anaphora resolution, identifying discourse relations, etc.). Lastly, we deal with a broader set of verbs and domains and more general frame definitions than these methods.

As stated earlier, Modi et al. (2012) propose the most similar work to ours. They adapt (Titov and Klementiev, 2012) to learn FrameNet-style head and role groupings. Modi et al. (2012) assume roles to be frame-specific, while our role clusters are defined independently of frame groupings (as expressed in Eq. 1). Last, with respect to research such as (Pennacchiotti et al., 2008; Green et al., 2004) in which lexical resources such as Word-Net are used (in supervised or unsupervised settings) to refine and extend existing frame repositories such as FrameNet, our model learns and bootstraps a frame repository from text annotated only with syntactic structure in an unsupervised way.

6 Conclusion

We proposed an unsupervised method for coarse-lexical frame induction from dependency parsed sentences using L-PCFG. We converted lexicalized dependency trees of sentences to a set of input strings of fixed, predetermined structure consisting of a verbal head, its arguments and their syntactic dependencies. We then use a CFG model (subsequently L-PCFG) to shape/capture frame structures from these strings. We adapted EM parameter estimation techniques from PCFG while relaxing independence assumptions, including appropriate methods for splitting and merging frames and semantic roles and using word embeddings for better generalization. In empirical evaluations, our model outperforms several baselines.

Acknowledgments

We would like to thank Dr. Curt Anderson and Dr. Rainer Osswlad for valuable comments on the paper and analysis of frame clusters. The work described in this paper is funded by the Deutsche Forschungsgemeinschaft (DFG) through the 'Collaborative Research Centre 991 (CRC 991): The Structure of Representations in Language, Cognition, and Science'.

References

Enrique Amigó, Julio Gonzalo, Javier Artiles, and Felisa Verdejo. 2009. A comparison of extrinsic clustering evaluation metrics based on formal constraints. *Inf. Retr.* 12(4):461–486. https://doi.org/10.1007/s10791-008-9066-8.

Amit Bagga and Breck Baldwin. 1998. Entity-based cross-document coreferencing using the vector space model. In *Proceedings of the 17th International Conference on Computational Linguistics - Volume 1*. Association for Computational Linguistics, Stroudsburg, PA, USA, COLING '98, pages 79–85. https://doi.org/10.3115/980451.980859.

Collin F. Baker, Charles J. Fillmore, and John B. Lowe. 1998. The Berkeley FrameNet project. In *Proceedings of the 36th Annual Meeting of the Association for Computational Linguistics and 17th International Conference on Computational Linguistics - Volume 1*. Association for Computational Linguistics, Stroudsburg, PA, USA, ACL '98, pages 86–90. https://doi.org/10.3115/980845.980860.

Niranjan Balasubramanian, Stephen Soderland, Mausam, and Oren Etzioni. 2013. Generating coherent event schemas at scale. In *Proceedings of the 2013 Conference on Empirical Methods in Natural Language Processing*. Association for Computational Linguistics, Seattle, Washington, USA, pages 1721–1731. http://www.aclweb.org/anthology/D13-1178.

Claire Bonial, Kevin Stowe, and Martha Palmer. 2013. Renewing and revising SemLink. In *Proceedings of the 2nd Workshop on Linked Data in Linguistics (LDL-2013): Representing and linking lexicons, terminologies and other language data*. Association for Computational Linguistics, Pisa, Italy, pages 9 – 17. http://www.aclweb.org/anthology/W13-5503.

X. Carreras and L. Marquez. 2005. Introduction to the CoNLL-2005 shared task: Semantic role labeling. In *Proceedings of the Ninth Conference on Computational Natural Language Learning*. pages 152–164. http://www.aclweb.org/anthology/W05-0620.

Nathanael Chambers. 2013. Event schema induction with a probabilistic entity-driven model. In *EMNLP*. volume 13, pages 1797–1807. https://aclweb.org/anthology/D/D13/D13-1185.pdf.

Nathanael Chambers and Dan Jurafsky. 2009. Unsupervised learning of narrative schemas and their participants. In *Proceedings of the Joint Conference of the 47th Annual Meeting of the ACL and the 4th International Joint Conference on Natural Language Processing of the AFNLP*. Association for Computational Linguistics, Suntec, Singapore, pages 602–610. http://www.aclweb.org/anthology/P/P09/P09-1068.

Nathanael Chambers and Dan Jurafsky. 2011. Template-based information extraction without the templates. In *Proceedings of the 49th Annual Meeting of the Association for Computational Linguistics: Human Language Technologies - Volume 1*. Association for Computational Linguistics, Stroudsburg, PA, USA, HLT '11, pages 976–986. http://dl.acm.org/citation.cfm?id=2002472.2002595.

Jackie Chi Kit Cheung and Gerald Penn. 2013. Towards robust abstractive multi-document summarization: A caseframe analysis of centrality and domain. In *Proceedings of the 51st Annual Meeting of the Association for Computational Linguistics (Volume 1: Long Papers)*. Association for Computational Linguistics, Sofia, Bulgaria, pages 1233–1242. http://www.aclweb.org/anthology/P13-1121.

J.C.K. Cheung, H. Poon, and L. Vanderwende. 2013. Probabilistic frame induction. In *Proceedings of NAACL-HLT*. pages 837–846. http://www.aclweb.org/anthology/N13-1104.

Philipp Cimiano, Andreas Hotho, and Steffen Staab. 2005. Learning concept hierarchies from text corpora using formal concept analysis. *J. Artif. Int. Res.* 24(1):305–339. http://dl.acm.org/citation.cfm?id=1622519.1622528.

Silvie Cinková, Eva Fučíková, Jana Šindlerová, and Jan Hajič. 2014. EngVallex - English valency lexicon. LINDAT/CLARIN digital library at the Institute of Formal and Applied Linguistics, Charles University. http://hdl.handle.net/11858/00-097C-0000-0023-4337-2.

Silvie Cinkova, Marie Mikulova, Lucie Mladova, Anja Nedoluzko, Petr Pajas, Jarmila Panevova, Jiri Semecky, Jana Sindlerova, Zdenka Uresova, Zdenek Zabokrtsky, Jiri Semecky, Jana Sindlerova, Josef Toman, Zdenka Uresova, and Zdenek Zabokrtsky. 2012. Annotation of English on the tectogrammatical level: Reference book. https://ufal.mff.cuni.cz/techrep/tr35.pdf.

Stephen Clark. 2013. *Quantum Physics and Linguistics*, Oxford University Press, chapter Type-Driven Syntax and Semantics for Composing Meaning Vectors. https://doi.org/http://dx.doi.org/10.1093/acprof:oso/9780199646296.003.0013.

Shay Cohen. 2017. Latent-variable PCFGs: Background and applications. In *Proceedings of the 15th Meeting on the Mathematics of Language*. Association for Computational Linguistics, London, UK, pages 47–58. http://www.aclweb.org/anthology/W17-3405.

A. P. Dempster, N. M. Laird, and D. B. Rubin. 1977. Maximum likelihood from incomplete data via the EM algorithm. *Journal of the Royal Statistical Society* 39(1):1–21.

Chuong B. Do and Serafim Batzoglou. 2008. What is the expectation maximization algorithm? *Nature Biotechnology* https://doi.org/10.1038/nbt1406.

Jason Eisner. 2016. Inside-outside and forward-backward algorithms are just backprop. In *Proceedings of the EMNLP Workshop on Structured Prediction for NLP*. Austin, TX.

Anette Frank, Hans-Ulrich Krieger, Feiyu Xu, Hans Uszkoreit, Berthold Crysmann, Brigitte Jrg, and Ulrich Schfer. 2007. Question answering from structured knowledge sources. *Journal of Applied Logic* 5(1):20 – 48. Questions and Answers: Theoretical and Applied Perspectives. https://doi.org/https://doi.org/10.1016/j.jal.2005.12.006.

Kartik Goyal and Eduard Hovy. 2014. Unsupervised word sense induction using distributional statistics. In *Proceedings of COLING 2014, the 25th International Conference on Computational Linguistics: Technical Papers*. Dublin City University and Association for Computational Linguistics, Dublin, Ireland, pages 1302–1310. http://www.aclweb.org/anthology/C14-1123.

Rebecca Green, Bonnie J. Dorr, and Philip Resnik. 2004. Inducing frame semantic verb classes from wordnet and LDOCE. In *Proceedings of the 42Nd Annual Meeting on Association for Computational Linguistics*. Association for Computational Linguistics, Stroudsburg, PA, USA, ACL '04. https://doi.org/10.3115/1218955.1219003.

Mark Johnson. 1998. PCFG models of linguistic tree representations. *Comput. Linguist.* 24(4):613–632. http://dl.acm.org/citation.cfm?id=972764.972768.

Daisuke Kawahara, Daniel Peterson, Octavian Popescu, and Martha Palmer. 2014. Inducing example-based semantic frames from a massive amount of verb uses. In *Proceedings of the 14th Conference of the European Chapter of the Association for Computational Linguistics*. Association for Computational Linguistics, Gothenburg, Sweden, pages 58–67. http://www.aclweb.org/anthology/E14-1007.

Dan Klein and Christopher D. Manning. 2003a. A* parsing: Fast exact Viterbi parse selection. In *Proceedings of the 2003 Conference of the North American Chapter of the Association for Computational Linguistics on Human Language Technology - Volume 1*. Association for Computational Linguistics, Stroudsburg, PA, USA, NAACL '03, pages 40–47. https://doi.org/10.3115/1073445.1073461.

Dan Klein and Christopher D. Manning. 2003b. Accurate unlexicalized parsing. In *Proceedings of the 41st Annual Meeting on Association for Computational Linguistics - Volume 1*. Association for Computational Linguistics, Stroudsburg, PA, USA, ACL

'03, pages 423–430. https://doi.org/10.3115/1075096.1075150.

Joel Lang and Mirella Lapata. 2010. Unsupervised induction of semantic roles. In *Human Language Technologies: The 2010 Annual Conference of the North American Chapter of the Association for Computational Linguistics*. Association for Computational Linguistics, Stroudsburg, PA, USA, HLT '10, pages 939–947. http://dl.acm.org/citation.cfm?id=1857999.1858135.

Joel Lang and Mirella Lapata. 2011. Unsupervised semantic role induction via split-merge clustering. In *Proceedings of the 49th Annual Meeting of the Association for Computational Linguistics: Human Language Technologies - Volume 1*. Association for Computational Linguistics, Stroudsburg, PA, USA, HLT '11, pages 1117–1126. http://dl.acm.org/citation.cfm?id=2002472.2002614.

Jey Han Lau, Paul Cook, Diana McCarthy, David Newman, and Timothy Baldwin. 2012. Word sense induction for novel sense detection. In *Proceedings of the 13th Conference of the European Chapter of the Association for Computational Linguistics*. Association for Computational Linguistics, pages 591–601. http://www.aclweb.org/anthology/E12-1060.

Percy Liang and Dan Klein. 2009. Online EM for unsupervised models. In *Proceedings of Human Language Technologies: The 2009 Annual Conference of the North American Chapter of the Association for Computational Linguistics*. Association for Computational Linguistics, Stroudsburg, PA, USA, NAACL '09, pages 611–619. http://dl.acm.org/citation.cfm?id=1620754.1620843.

Suresh Manandhar, Ioannis Klapaftis, Dmitriy Dligach, and Sameer Pradhan. 2010. SemEval-2010 Task 14: Word sense induction & disambiguation. In *Proceedings of the 5th International Workshop on Semantic Evaluation*. Association for Computational Linguistics, Uppsala, Sweden, pages 63–68. http://www.aclweb.org/anthology/S10-1011.

Takuya Matsuzaki, Yusuke Miyao, and Jun'ichi Tsujii. 2005. Probabilistic CFG with latent annotations. In *Proceedings of the 43rd Annual Meeting on Association for Computational Linguistics*. Association for Computational Linguistics, Stroudsburg, PA, USA, ACL '05, pages 75–82. https://doi.org/10.3115/1219840.1219850.

Jeff Mitchell and Mirella Lapata. 2008. Vector-based models of semantic composition. In *Proceedings of ACL-08: HLT*. Association for Computational Linguistics, Columbus, Ohio, pages 236–244. http://www.aclweb.org/anthology/P08-1028.

Ashutosh Modi, Ivan Titov, and Alexandre Klementiev. 2012. Unsupervised induction of frame-semantic representations. In *Proceedings of the NAACL-HLT Workshop on the Induction of Linguistic Structure*. Association for Computational Linguistics, Montréal, Canada, pages 1–7. http://www.aclweb.org/anthology/W12-1901.

Stephan Oepen, Marco Kuhlmann, Yusuke Miyao, Daniel Zeman, Silvie Cinkova, Dan Flickinger, Jan Hajic, Angelina Ivanova, and Zdenka Uresova. 2016. Towards comparability of linguistic graph banks for semantic parsing. In Nicoletta Calzolari (Conference Chair), Khalid Choukri, Thierry Declerck, Sara Goggi, Marko Grobelnik, Bente Maegaard, Joseph Mariani, Helene Mazo, Asuncion Moreno, Jan Odijk, and Stelios Piperidis, editors, *Proceedings of the Tenth International Conference on Language Resources and Evaluation (LREC 2016)*. European Language Resources Association (ELRA), Paris, France.

Martha Palmer, Daniel Gildea, and Paul Kingsbury. 2005. The Proposition Bank: An annotated corpus of semantic roles. *Computational Linguistics* 31(1):71–106.

Haoruo Peng, Snigdha Chaturvedi, and Dan Roth. 2017. A joint model for semantic sequences: Frames, entities, sentiments. In *Proceedings of the 21st Conference on Computational Natural Language Learning (CoNLL 2017)*. Association for Computational Linguistics, pages 173–183. https://doi.org/10.18653/v1/K17-1019.

Marco Pennacchiotti, Diego De Cao, Roberto Basili, Danilo Croce, and Michael Roth. 2008. Automatic induction of framenet lexical units. In *Proceedings of the Conference on Empirical Methods in Natural Language Processing*. Association for Computational Linguistics, Stroudsburg, PA, USA, EMNLP '08, pages 457–465. http://dl.acm.org/citation.cfm?id=1613715.1613773.

Slav Petrov, Leon Barrett, Romain Thibaux, and Dan Klein. 2006. Learning accurate, compact, and interpretable tree annotation. In *ACL 2006, 21st International Conference on Computational Linguistics and 44th Annual Meeting of the Association for Computational Linguistics, Proceedings of the Conference, Sydney, Australia, 17-21 July 2006*. http://aclweb.org/anthology/P06-1055.

Behrang QasemiZadeh and Laura Kallmeyer. 2017. HHU at SemEval-2017 Task 2: Fast hash-based embeddings for semantic word similarity assessment. In *Proceedings of the 11th International Workshop on Semantic Evaluation (SemEval-2017)*. Association for Computational Linguistics, pages 250–255. https://doi.org/10.18653/v1/S17-2039.

Josef Ruppenhofer, Michael Ellsworth, Miriam R. L. Petruck, Christopher R. Johnson, Collin F. Baker, and Jan Scheffczyk. 2016. *FrameNet II: Extended Theory and Practice*. ICSI, Berkeley.

Roland Schäfer. 2015. Processing and querying large web corpora with the COW14 architecture. In Piotr Baski, Hanno Biber, Evelyn Breiteneder, Marc Kupietz, Harald Lngen, and Andreas Witt, editors, *Proceedings of Challenges in the Management of Large Corpora 3 (CMLC-3)*. UCREL, IDS, Lancaster. http://rolandschaefer.net/?p=749.

Sebastian Schuster and Christopher D. Manning. 2016. Enhanced english universal dependencies: An improved representation for natural language understanding tasks. In Nicoletta Calzolari (Conference Chair), Khalid Choukri, Thierry Declerck, Sara Goggi, Marko Grobelnik, Bente Maegaard, Joseph Mariani, Helene Mazo, Asuncion Moreno, Jan Odijk, and Stelios Piperidis, editors, *Proceedings of the Tenth International Conference on Language Resources and Evaluation (LREC 2016)*. European Language Resources Association (ELRA), Paris, France.

Dan Shen and Mirella Lapata. 2007. Using semantic roles to improve question answering. In *Proceedings of the 2007 Joint Conference on Empirical Methods in Natural Language Processing and Computational Natural Language Learning (EMNLP-CoNLL)*. Association for Computational Linguistics, Prague, Czech Republic, pages 12–21. http://www.aclweb.org/anthology/D07-1002.

M. Steinbach, G. Karypis, and V. Kumar. 2000. A comparison of document clustering techniques. In *KDD Workshop on Text Mining*. http://citeseer.ist.psu.edu/steinbach00comparison.html.

Robert S. Swier and Suzanne Stevenson. 2004. Unsupervised semantic role labelling. In Dekang Lin and Dekai Wu, editors, *Proceedings of EMNLP 2004*. Association for Computational Linguistics, Barcelona, Spain, pages 95–102. http://www.aclweb.org/anthology/W/W04/W04-3213.pdf.

Ivan Titov and Alexandre Klementiev. 2012. A Bayesian approach to unsupervised semantic role induction. In *EACL 2012, 13th Conference of the European Chapter of the Association for Computational Linguistics, Avignon, France, April 23-27, 2012*. pages 12–22. http://aclweb.org/anthology/E/E12/E12-1003.pdf.

Tim Van de Cruys and Marianna Apidianaki. 2011. Latent semantic word sense induction and disambiguation. In *Proceedings of the 49th Annual Meeting of the Association for Computational Linguistics: Human Language Technologies*. Association for Computational Linguistics, Portland, Oregon, USA, pages 1476–1485. http://www.aclweb.org/anthology/P11-1148.

Halo: Learning Semantics-Aware Representations for Cross-Lingual Information Extraction

Hongyuan Mei,* **Sheng Zhang**,* **Kevin Duh**, **Benjamin Van Durme**
Center for Language and Speech Processing, Johns Hopkins University
{hmei,s.zhang,kevinduh,vandurme}@cs.jhu.edu

Abstract

Cross-lingual information extraction (CLIE) is an important and challenging task, especially in low resource scenarios. To tackle this challenge, we propose a training method, called *Halo*, which enforces the local region of each hidden state of a neural model to only generate target tokens with the same semantic structure tag. This simple but powerful technique enables a neural model to learn semantics-aware representations that are robust to noise, without introducing any extra parameter, thus yielding better generalization in both high and low resource settings.

1 Introduction

Cross-lingual information extraction (CLIE) is the task of distilling and representing factual information in a target language from the textual input in a source language (Sudo et al., 2004; Zhang et al., 2017b). For example, Fig. 1 illustrates a pair of input Chinese sentence and its English predicate-argument information[1], where predicate and argument are well used *semantic structure tags*.

It is of great importance to solve the task, as to provide viable solutions to extracting information from the text of languages that suffer from no or little existing information extraction tools. Neural models have empirically proven successful in this task (Zhang et al., 2017b,c), but still remain unsatisfactory in low resource (i.e. small number of training samples) settings. These neural models learn to summarize a given source sentence and target prefix into a hidden state, which aims to generate the correct next target token after being

士兵们 开始 发射 迫击炮 。
(Soldiers started firing mortars .)
(a)

[(Soldiers:*a*) started:*p* [(Soldiers:*a*) firing:*p* (mortars:*a*)]]
(b)

Figure 1: Example of cross-lingual information extraction: Chinese input text (a) and linearized English PredPatt output (b), where ':p' and blue stand for predicate while ':a' and purple denote argument.

passed through an output layer. As each member in the target vocabulary is essentially either predicate or argument, a random perturbation on the hidden state should still be able to yield a token with the same semantic structure tag. This inductive bias motivates an extra term in training objective, as shown in Fig. 2, which enforces the surroundings of any learned hidden state to generate tokens with the same semantic structure tag (either predicate or argument) as the centroid. We call this technique *Halo*, because the process of each hidden state taking up its surroundings is analogous to how the halo is formed around the sun. The method is believed to help the model generalize better, by learning more semantics-aware and noise-insensitive hidden states without introducing extra parameters.

2 The Problem

We are interested in learning a probabilistic model that directly maps an input sentence $\{x_i\}_{i=1}^{I} = x_1 x_2 \ldots x_I$ of the source language $\mathcal{S}$ into an output sequence $\{y_t\}_{t=1}^{T} = y_1 y_2 \ldots y_T$ of the target language $\mathcal{T}$, where $\mathcal{S}$ can be any human natural language (e.g. Chinese) and $\mathcal{T}$ is the English PredPatt (White et al., 2016). In the latter vocabulary, each type is tagged as either predicate or argument—those with ":p" are predicates while those with ":a" are arguments.

For any distribution P in our proposed family, the *log-likelihood* ℓ of the model P given any

---

*equal contribution

[1]The predicate-argument information is usually denoted by relation tuples. In this work, we adopt the tree-structured representation generated by PredPatt (White et al., 2016; Zhang et al., 2017d), which was a lightweight tool available at https://github.com/hltcoe/PredPatt.

*Proceedings of the 7th Joint Conference on Lexical and Computational Semantics (*SEM), pages 142–147*
New Orleans, June 5-6, 2018. ©2018 Association for Computational Linguistics

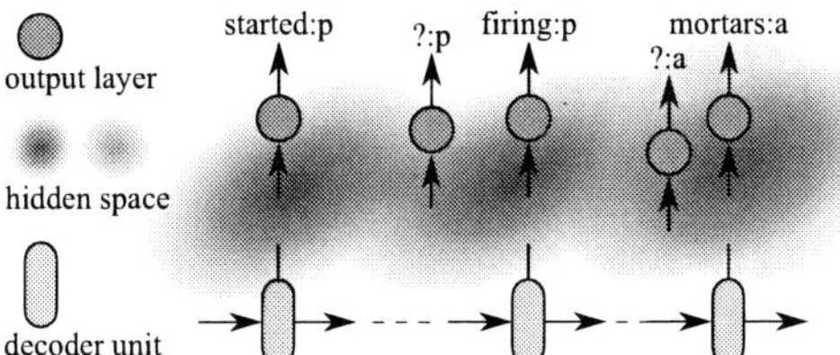

Figure 2: Visualization of *Halo* method. While a neural model learns to summarizes the current known information into a hidden state and predict the next target token, the surroundings of this hidden state in the same space (two-dimensional in this example) are supervised to generate tokens with the same semantic structure tag. For example, at the last shown step, the centroid of purple area is the summarized hidden state and learns to predict 'mortars:a', while a randomly sampled neighbor is enforced to generate an argument, although it may not be 'mortars' (thus denoted by '?'). Similar remarks apply to the blue regions.

$(\{y_t\}_{t=1}^T \mid \{x_i\}_{i=1}^I)$ pair is:

$$\sum_{t=1}^T \log P\big(y_t \mid y_{t-1}, \ldots, y_0, \{x_i\}_{i=1}^I\big) \quad (1)$$

where y_0 is a special beginning of sequence token.

We denote vectors by bold lowercase Roman letters such as $\mathbf{h}$, and matrices by bold capital Roman letters such as $\mathbf{W}$ throughout the paper. Subscripted bold letters denote distinct vectors or matrices (e.g., $\mathbf{p}_t$). Scalar quantities, including vector and matrix elements such as h_d and p_{t,y_t}, are written without bold. Capitalized scalars represent upper limits on lowercase scalars, e.g., $1 \leq d \leq D$. Function symbols are notated like their return type. All $\mathbb{R} \to \mathbb{R}$ functions are extended to apply elementwise to vectors and matrices.

3   The Method

In this section, we first briefly review how the baseline neural encoder-decoder models work on this task, and then introduce our novel and well-suited training method *Halo*.

3.1   Baseline Neural Models

Previous neural models on this task (Zhang et al., 2017b,c) all adopt an encoder-decoder architecture with recurrent neural networks, particularly LSTMs (Hochreiter and Schmidhuber, 1997). At each step t in decoding, the models summarize the input $\{x_i\}_{i=1}^I$ and output prefix $y_1, \ldots, y_{t-1}$ into a hidden state $\mathbf{h}_t \in (-1, 1)^D$, and then project it with a transformation matrix $\mathbf{W} \in \mathbb{R}^{|\mathcal{V}| \times D}$ to a distribution $\mathbf{p}_t$ over the target English PredPatt

vocabulary $\mathcal{V}$:

$$\mathbf{p}_t = \mathbf{o}_t / (\mathbf{1}^\top \mathbf{o}_t) \quad (2a)$$

$$\mathbf{o}_t = \exp \mathbf{W}\mathbf{h}_t \in \mathbb{R}_+^{|\mathcal{V}|} \quad (2b)$$

where $\mathbf{1}$ is a $|\mathcal{V}|$-dimensional one vector such that $\mathbf{p}_t$ is a valid distribution.

Suppose that the ground truth target token at this step is y_t, the probability of generating y_t under the current model is p_{t,y_t}, obtained by accessing the y_t-th element in the vector $\mathbf{p}_t$. Then the log-likelihood is constructed as $\ell = \sum_{t=1}^T \log p_{t,y_t}$, and the model is trained by maximizing this objective over all the training pairs.

3.2   Halo

Our method adopts a property of this task—the vocabulary $\mathcal{V}$ is partitioned into $\mathcal{P}$, set of predicates that end with ":p", and $\mathcal{A}$, set of arguments that end with ":a". As a neural model would summarize everything known up to step t into $\mathbf{h}_t$, would a perturbation $\mathbf{h}_t'$ around $\mathbf{h}_t$ still generate the same token y_t? This bias seems too strong, but we can still reasonably assume that $\mathbf{h}_t'$ would generate a token with the same semantic structure tag (i.e. predicate or argument). That is, the prediction made by $\mathbf{h}_t'$ should end with ":p" if y_t is a predicate, and with ":a" otherwise.

This inductive bias provides us with another level of supervision. Suppose that at step t, a neighboring $\mathbf{h}_t'$ is randomly sampled around $\mathbf{h}_t$, and is then used to generate a distribution $\mathbf{p}_t'$ in the same way as equation (2). Then we can get a distribution $\mathbf{q}_t'$ over $\mathcal{C} = \{\text{predicate}, \text{argument}\}$, by summing all the probabilities of predicates and those of arguments:

$$q_{t,\text{predicate}}' = \sum_{v \in \mathcal{P}} p_{t,v}' \quad (3a)$$

$$q_{t,\text{argument}}' = \sum_{v \in \mathcal{A}} p_{t,v}' \quad (3b)$$

This aggregation is shown in Fig. 3. Then the extra objective is $\ell' = \sum_{t=1}^T \log q_{t,c_t}'$, where $c_t = $ predicate if the target token $y_t \in \mathcal{P}$ (i.e. ending with ":p") and $c_t = $ argument otherwise.

Therefore, we get the joint objective to maximize by adding ℓ and ℓ':

$$\ell + \ell' = \sum_{t=1}^T \log p_{t,y_t} + \sum_{t=1}^T \log q_{t,c_t}' \quad (4)$$

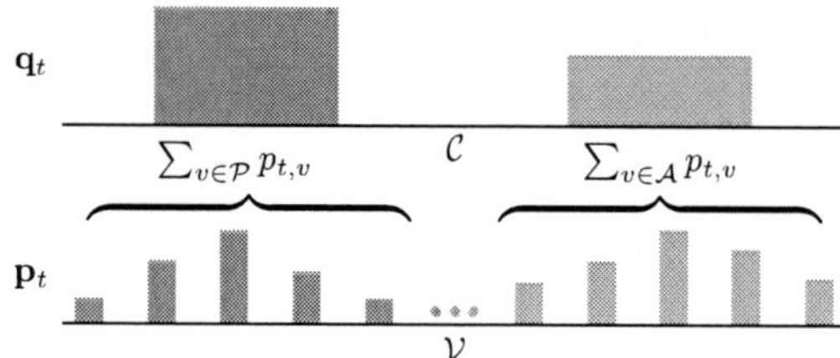

Figure 3: Visualization of how $\mathbf{q}$ (distribution over $\mathcal{C}$) is obtained by aggregating $\mathbf{p}$ (distribution over $\mathcal{V}$).

which enables the model to learn more semantics-aware and noise-insensitive hidden states by enforcing the hidden states within a region to share the same semantic structure tag.[2]

3.2.1 Sampling Neighbors

Sampling a neighbor around $\mathbf{h}_t$ is essentially equivalent to adding noise to it. Note that in a LSTM decoder that previous work used, $\mathbf{h}_t \in (-1, 1)^D$ because $\mathbf{h}_t = \mathbf{o}_t \odot \tanh(\mathbf{c}_t)$ where $\mathbf{o}_t \in (0, 1)^D$ and $\tanh(\mathbf{c}_t) \in (-1, 1)^D$. Therefore, extra work is needed to ensure $\mathbf{h}'_t \in (-1, 1)^D$. For this purpose, we follow the recipe[3]:

- Sample $\mathbf{h}''_t \in (-1, 1)^D$ by independently sampling each entry from an uniform distribution over $(-1, 1)$;
- Sample a scalar $\lambda_t \in (0, 1)$ from a Beta distribution $B(\alpha, \beta)$ where α and β are hyperparameters to be tuned;
- Compute $\mathbf{h}'_t = \mathbf{h}_t + \lambda_t(\mathbf{h}''_t - \mathbf{h}_t)$ such that $\mathbf{h}'_t \in (-1, 1)^D$ lies on the line segment between $\mathbf{h}_t$ and $\mathbf{h}''_t$.

Note that the sampled hidden state $\mathbf{h}'_t$ is only used to compute $\mathbf{q}'_t$, but not to update the LSTM hidden state, i.e., $\mathbf{h}_{t+1}$ is independent of $\mathbf{h}'_t$.

3.2.2 Roles of Hyperparameters

The *Halo* technique adds an inductive bias into the model, and its magnitude is controlled by λ_t:

- $\lambda_t \in (0, 1)$ to ensure $\mathbf{h}'_t \in (-1, 1)^D$;
- $\lambda_t \to 0$ makes $\mathbf{h}'_t \to \mathbf{h}_t$, thus providing no extra supervision on the model;

---

[2]One can also sample multiple, rather than one, neighbors for one hidden state and then average their log q'_{t,c_t}. In our experimental study, we only try one for computational cost and found it effective enough.

[3]Alternatives do exist. For example, one can transform $\mathbf{h}_t$ from $(-1, 1)^D$ to $(-\infty, \infty)^D$, add random (e.g. Gaussian) noise in the latter space and then transform back to $(-1, 1)^D$. These tricks are valid as long as they find neighbors within the same space $(-1, 1)^D$ as $\mathbf{h}_t$ is.

- $\lambda_t \to 1$ makes $\mathbf{h}'_t$ uniformly sampled in entire $(-1, 1)^D$, and causes underfitting just like a L-2 regularization coefficient goes to infinity.

We sample a valid λ_t from a Beta distribution with $\alpha > 0$ and $\beta > 0$, and their magnitude can be tuned on the development set:

- When $\alpha \to 0$ and β is finite, or α is finite and $\beta \to \infty$, we have $\lambda_t \to 0$;
- When $\alpha \to \infty$ and β is finite, or α is finite and $\beta \to 0$, we have $\lambda_t \to 1$;
- Larger α and β yield larger variance of λ_t, and setting λ_t to be a constant is a special case that $\alpha \to \infty$, $\beta \to \infty$ and α/β is fixed.

Besides α and β, the way of partitioning $\mathcal{V}$ (i.e. the definition of $\mathcal{C}$) also serves as a knob for tuning the bias strength. Although on this task, the predicate and argument tags naturally partition the vocabulary, we are still able to explore other possibilities. For example, an extreme is to partition $\mathcal{V}$ into $|\mathcal{V}|$ different singletons, meaning that $\mathcal{C} = \mathcal{V}$—a perturbation around $\mathbf{h}_t$ should still predict the same token. But this extreme case does not work well in our experiments, verifying the importance of the semantic structure tags on this task.

4 Related Work

Cross-lingual information extraction has drawn a great deal of attention from researchers. Some (Sudo et al., 2004; Parton et al., 2009; Ji, 2009; Snover et al., 2011; Ji and Nothman, 2016) worked in closed domains, i.e. on a predefined set of events and/or entities, Zhang et al. (2017b) explored this problem in open domain and their attentional encoder-decoder model significantly outperformed a baseline system that does translation and parsing in a pipeline. Zhang et al. (2017c) further improved the results by inventing a hierarchical architecture that learns to first predict the next semantic structure tag and then select a tag-dependent decoder for token generation. Orthogonal to these efforts, *Halo* aims to help *all neural models on this task*, rather than any specific model architecture.

Halo can be understood as a data augmentation technique (Chapelle et al., 2001; Van der Maaten et al., 2013; Srivastava et al., 2014; Szegedy et al., 2016; Gal and Ghahramani, 2016). Such tricks have been used in training neural networks to achieve better generalization, in applications like image classification (Simard et al.,

DATASET	NUMBER OF PAIRS			VOCABULARY SIZE		TOKEN/TYPE
	TRAIN	DEV	TEST	SOURCE	TARGET	
CHINESE	941040	10000	39626	258364	234832	91.94
UZBEK	31581	1373	1373	69255	37914	12.18
TURKISH	20774	903	903	51248	32009	11.97
SOMALI	10702	465	465	29591	18616	12.78

Table 1: Statistics of each dataset.

METHOD	CHINESE			UZBEK			TURKISH			SOMALI		
	BLEU	F1		BLEU	F1		BLEU	F1		BLEU	F1	
		PRED	ARG		PRED	ARG		PRED	ARG		PRED	ARG
MODELZ	22.07	30.06	39.06	10.76	12.46	24.08	7.47	6.49	17.76	13.06	13.91	25.38
MODELP	22.10	30.04	39.83	12.50	18.81	25.93	9.04	**12.90**	21.13	13.22	16.71	26.83
MODELP-*Halo*	**23.18**	**30.85**	**41.23**	**12.95**	**19.23**	**27.63**	**10.21**	12.55	**22.57**	**14.26**	**17.06**	**27.73**

Table 2: BLEU and F1 scores of different models on all these datasets, where PRED stands for predicate and ARG for argument. Best numbers are highlighted as **bold**.

2000; Simonyan and Zisserman, 2015; Arpit et al., 2017; Zhang et al., 2017a) and speech recognition (Graves et al., 2013; Amodei et al., 2016). *Halo* differs from these methods because 1) it makes use of the task-specific information— vocabulary is partitioned by semantic structure tags; and 2) it makes use of the human belief that the hidden representations of tokens with the same semantic structure tag should stay close to each other. Some

5 Experiments

We evaluate our method on several real-world CLIE datasets measured by BLEU (Papineni et al., 2002) and F1, as proposed by Zhang et al. (2017b). For the generated linearized PredPatt outputs and their references, the former metric[4] measures their n-gram similarity, and the latter measures their token-level overlap. In fact, F1 is computed separately for predicate and argument, as F1 PRED and F1 ARG respectively.

5.1 Datasets

Multiple datasets were used to demonstrate the effectiveness of our proposed method, where one sample in each dataset is a source language sentence paired with its linearized English PredPatt output. These datasets were first introduced as the DARPA LORELEI Language Packs (Strassel and Tracey, 2016), and then used for this task by Zhang et al. (2017b,c). As shown in table 1, the CHINESE dataset has almost one million training samples and a high token/type ratio, while the oth-

ers are *low resourced*, meaning they have much fewer samples and lower token/type ratios.

5.2 Model Implementation

Before applying our *Halo* technique, we first improved the current state-of-the-art neural model of Zhang et al. (2017c) by using residual connections (He et al., 2016) and multiplicative attention (Luong et al., 2015), which effectively improved the model performance. We refer to the model of Zhang et al. (2017c) and our improved version as ModelZ and ModelP respectively[5].

5.3 Experimental Details

In experiments, instead of using the full vocabularies shown in table 1, we set a minimum count threshold for each dataset, to replace the rare words by a special out-of-vocabulary symbol. These thresholds were tuned on dev sets.

The Beta distribution is very flexible. In general, its variance is a decreasing function of $\alpha + \beta$, and when $\alpha + \beta$ is fixed, the mean is an increasing function of α. In our experiments, we fixed $\alpha + \beta = 20$ and only lightly tuned α on dev sets. Optimal values of α stay close to 1.

5.4 Results

As shown in Table 2, ModelP outperforms ModelZ on all the datasets measured by all the metrics, except for F1 PRED on CHINESE dataset. Our *Halo* technique consistently boosts the model performance of MODELP except for F1 PRED on TURKISH.

---

[4]The MOSES implementation (Koehn et al., 2007) was used as in all the previous work on this task.

[5]Z stands for Zhang and P for Plus.

Additionally, experiments were also conducted on two other low resource datasets AMHARIC and YORUBA that Zhang et al. (2017c) included, and $\alpha = 0$ in *Halo* was found optimal on the dev sets. In such cases, this regularization was not helpful so no comparison need be made on the held-out test sets.

6 Conclusion and Future Work

We present a simple and effective training technique *Halo* for the task of cross-lingual information extraction. Our method aims to enforce the local surroundings of each hidden state of a neural model to only generate tokens with the same semantic structure tag, thus enabling the learned hidden states to be more aware of semantics and robust to random noise. Our method provides new state-of-the-art results on several benchmark cross-lingual information extraction datasets, including both high and low resource scenarios.

As future work, we plan to extend this technique to similar tasks such as POS tagging and Semantic Role Labeling. One straightforward way of working on these tasks is to define the vocabularies as set of 'word-type:POS-tag' (so c_t = POS tag) and 'word-type:SR' (so c_t = semantic role), such that our method is directly applicable. It would also be interesting to apply *Halo* widely to other tasks as a general regularization technique.

Acknowledgments

This work was supported in part by the JHU Human Language Technology Center of Excellence (HLTCOE), and DARPA LORELEI. The U.S. Government is authorized to reproduce and distribute reprints for Governmental purposes. The views and conclusions contained in this publication are those of the authors and should not be interpreted as representing official policies or endorsements of DARPA or the U.S. Government.

References

Dario Amodei, Sundaram Ananthanarayanan, Rishita Anubhai, Jingliang Bai, Eric Battenberg, Carl Case, Jared Casper, Bryan Catanzaro, Qiang Cheng, Guoliang Chen, et al. 2016. Deep speech 2: End-to-end speech recognition in english and mandarin. In *International Conference on Machine Learning*. pages 173–182.

Devansh Arpit, Stanislaw Jastrzkebski, Nicolas Ballas, David Krueger, Emmanuel Bengio, Maxinder S Kanwal, Tegan Maharaj, Asja Fischer, Aaron Courville, Yoshua Bengio, et al. 2017. A closer look at memorization in deep networks. In *International Conference on Machine Learning*. pages 233–242.

Olivier Chapelle, Jason Weston, Léon Bottou, and Vladimir Vapnik. 2001. Vicinal risk minimization. In *Advances in neural information processing systems*. pages 416–422.

Yarin Gal and Zoubin Ghahramani. 2016. A theoretically grounded application of dropout in recurrent neural networks. In *Advances in neural information processing systems*. pages 1019–1027.

Alex Graves, Abdel-rahman Mohamed, and Geoffrey Hinton. 2013. Speech recognition with deep recurrent neural networks. In *Acoustics, speech and signal processing (icassp), 2013 ieee international conference on*. IEEE, pages 6645–6649.

Kaiming He, Xiangyu Zhang, Shaoqing Ren, and Jian Sun. 2016. Deep residual learning for image recognition. In *The IEEE Conference on Computer Vision and Pattern Recognition (CVPR)*.

Sepp Hochreiter and Jürgen Schmidhuber. 1997. Long short-term memory. *Neural computation* 9(8):1735–1780.

Heng Ji. 2009. Cross-lingual predicate cluster acquisition to improve bilingual event extraction by inductive learning. In *Proceedings of the Workshop on Unsupervised and Minimally Supervised Learning of Lexical Semantics*. Association for Computational Linguistics, Boulder, Colorado, USA, pages 27–35. http://www.aclweb.org/anthology/W09-1704.

Heng Ji and Joel Nothman. 2016. Overview of TAC-KBP2016 Tri-lingual EDL and its impact on end-to-end cold-start KBP. In *Proceedings of the Text Analysis Conference (TAC)*.

Philipp Koehn, Hieu Hoang, Alexandra Birch, Chris Callison-Burch, Marcello Federico, Nicola Bertoldi, Brooke Cowan, Wade Shen, Christine Moran, Richard Zens, et al. 2007. Moses: Open source toolkit for statistical machine translation. In *Proceedings of the 45th annual meeting of the ACL on interactive poster and demonstration sessions*. Association for Computational Linguistics, pages 177–180.

Minh-Thang Luong, Hieu Pham, and Christopher D Manning. 2015. Effective approaches to attention-based neural machine translation. In *Proceedings of the 2015 Conference on Empirical Methods in Natural Language Processing*.

Kishore Papineni, Salim Roukos, Todd Ward, and Wei-Jing Zhu. 2002. Bleu: a method for automatic evaluation of machine translation. In *Proceedings of the 40th annual meeting on association for computational linguistics*. Association for Computational Linguistics, pages 311–318.

Kristen Parton, Kathleen R. McKeown, Bob Coyne, Mona T. Diab, Ralph Grishman, Dilek Hakkani-Tür, Mary Harper, Heng Ji, Wei Yun Ma, Adam Meyers, Sara Stolbach, Ang Sun, Gokhan Tur, Wei Xu, and Sibel Yaman. 2009. Who, what, when, where, why? comparing multiple approaches to the cross-lingual 5w task. In *Proceedings of the Joint Conference of the 47th Annual Meeting of the ACL and the 4th International Joint Conference on Natural Language Processing of the AFNLP*. Association for Computational Linguistics, Suntec, Singapore, pages 423–431. http://www.aclweb.org/anthology/P/P09/P09-1048.

Patrice Y Simard, Yann A Le Cun, John S Denker, and Bernard Victorri. 2000. Transformation invariance in pattern recognition: Tangent distance and propagation. *International Journal of Imaging Systems and Technology* 11(3):181–197.

Karen Simonyan and Andrew Zisserman. 2015. Very deep convolutional networks for large-scale image recognition. In *International Conference on Learning Representations*.

Matthew Snover, Xiang Li, Wen-Pin Lin, Zheng Chen, Suzanne Tamang, Mingmin Ge, Adam Lee, Qi Li, Hao Li, Sam Anzaroot, and Heng Ji. 2011. Cross-lingual slot filling from comparable corpora. In *Proceedings of the 4th Workshop on Building and Using Comparable Corpora: Comparable Corpora and the Web*. Association for Computational Linguistics, Stroudsburg, PA, USA, BUCC '11, pages 110–119. http://dl.acm.org/citation.cfm?id=2024236.2024256.

Nitish Srivastava, Geoffrey E Hinton, Alex Krizhevsky, Ilya Sutskever, and Ruslan Salakhutdinov. 2014. Dropout: a simple way to prevent neural networks from overfitting. *Journal of Machine Learning Research* 15(1):1929–1958.

Stephanie Strassel and Jennifer Tracey. 2016. Lorelei language packs: Data, tools, and resources for technology development in low resource languages. In Nicoletta Calzolari (Conference Chair), Khalid Choukri, Thierry Declerck, Sara Goggi, Marko Grobelnik, Bente Maegaard, Joseph Mariani, Helene Mazo, Asuncion Moreno, Jan Odijk, and Stelios Piperidis, editors, *Proceedings of the Tenth International Conference on Language Resources and Evaluation (LREC 2016)*. European Language Resources Association (ELRA), Paris, France.

Kiyoshi Sudo, Satoshi Sekine, and Ralph Grishman. 2004. Cross-lingual information extraction system evaluation. In *Proceedings of the 20th international Conference on Computational Linguistics*. Association for Computational Linguistics, page 882.

Christian Szegedy, Vincent Vanhoucke, Sergey Ioffe, Jon Shlens, and Zbigniew Wojna. 2016. Rethinking the inception architecture for computer vision. In *Proceedings of the IEEE Conference on Computer Vision and Pattern Recognition*. pages 2818–2826.

Laurens Van der Maaten, Minmin Chen, Stephen Tyree, and Kilian Weinberger. 2013. Learning with marginalized corrupted features. In *Proceedings of The 30th International Conference on Machine Learning*.

Aaron Steven White, Drew Reisinger, Keisuke Sakaguchi, Tim Vieira, Sheng Zhang, Rachel Rudinger, Kyle Rawlins, and Benjamin Van Durme. 2016. Universal Decompositional Semantics on Universal Dependencies. In *Proceedings of the 2016 Conference on Empirical Methods in Natural Language Processing*. Association for Computational Linguistics, Austin, Texas, pages 1713–1723. https://aclweb.org/anthology/D16-1177.

Hongyi Zhang, Moustapha Cisse, Yann N Dauphin, and David Lopez-Paz. 2017a. mixup: Beyond empirical risk minimization. *arXiv preprint arXiv:1710.09412* .

Sheng Zhang, Kevin Duh, and Benjamin Van Durme. 2017b. MT/IE: Cross-lingual Open Information Extraction with Neural Sequence-to-Sequence Models. In *Proceedings of the 15th Conference of the European Chapter of the Association for Computational Linguistics: Volume 2, Short Papers*. Association for Computational Linguistics, Valencia, Spain, pages 64–70. http://www.aclweb.org/anthology/E17-2011.

Sheng Zhang, Kevin Duh, and Benjamin Van Durme. 2017c. Selective Decoding for Cross-lingual Open Information Extraction. In *Proceedings of the Eighth International Joint Conference on Natural Language Processing (Volume 1: Long Papers)*. Asian Federation of Natural Language Processing, Taipei, Taiwan, pages 832–842. http://www.aclweb.org/anthology/I17-1084.

Sheng Zhang, Rachel Rudinger, and Benjamin Van Durme. 2017d. An Evaluation of PredPatt and Open IE via Stage 1 Semantic Role Labeling. In *IWCS 2017 — 12th International Conference on Computational Semantics — Short papers*. http://aclweb.org/anthology/W17-6944.

Exploiting Partially Annotated Data for Temporal Relation Extraction

Qiang Ning,[1] **Zhongzhi Yu,**[2] **Chuchu Fan,**[1] **Dan Roth**[1,2,3]
[1]Department of Electrical and Computer Engineering, [2]Department of Computer Science
University of Illinois at Urbana-Champaign, Urbana, IL 61801, USA
[3]Department of Computer Science, University of Pennsylvania, Philadelphia, PA 19104, USA
{qning2,zyu19,cfan10}@illinois.edu, danroth@seas.upenn.edu

Abstract

Annotating temporal relations (TempRel) between events described in natural language is known to be labor intensive, partly because the total number of TempRels is quadratic in the number of events. As a result, only a small number of documents are typically annotated, limiting the coverage of various lexical/semantic phenomena. In order to improve existing approaches, one possibility is to make use of the readily available, partially annotated data ($\mathcal{P}$ as in *partial*) that cover more documents. However, missing annotations in $\mathcal{P}$ are known to hurt, rather than help, existing systems. This work is a case study in exploring various usages of $\mathcal{P}$ for TempRel extraction. Results show that despite missing annotations, $\mathcal{P}$ is still a useful supervision signal for this task within a constrained bootstrapping learning framework. The system described in this system is publicly available.[1]

1 Introduction

Understanding the temporal information in natural language text is an important NLP task (Verhagen et al., 2007, 2010; UzZaman et al., 2013; Minard et al., 2015; Bethard et al., 2016, 2017). A crucial component is temporal relation (TempRel; e.g., *before* or *after*) extraction (Mani et al., 2006; Bethard et al., 2007; Do et al., 2012; Chambers et al., 2014; Mirza and Tonelli, 2016; Ning et al., 2017, 2018a,b).

The TempRels in a document or a sentence can be conveniently modeled as a graph, where the nodes are events, and the edges are labeled by TempRels. Given all the events in an instance, TempRel annotation is the process of manually labeling all the edges – a highly labor intensive task due to two reasons. One is that many edges require extensive reasoning over multiple sentences

---

[1]https://cogcomp.org/page/publication_view/832

and labeling them is time-consuming. Perhaps more importantly, the other reason is that #edges is quadratic in #nodes. If labeling an edge takes 30 seconds (already an optimistic estimation), a typical document with 50 nodes would take more than 10 hours to annotate. Even if existing annotation schemes make a compromise by only annotating edges whose nodes are from a same sentence or adjacent sentences (Cassidy et al., 2014), it still takes more than 2 hours to fully annotate a typical document. Consequently, the only fully annotated dataset, TB-Dense (Cassidy et al., 2014), contains only 36 documents, which is rather small compared with datasets for other NLP tasks.

A small number of documents may indicate that the annotated data provide a limited coverage of various lexical and semantic phenomena, since a document is usually "homogeneous" within itself. In contrast to the scarcity of fully annotated datasets (denoted by $\mathcal{F}$ as in *full*), there are actually some partially annotated datasets as well (denoted by $\mathcal{P}$ as in *partial*); for example, Time-Bank (Pustejovsky et al., 2003) and AQUAINT (Graff, 2002) cover in total more than 250 documents. Since annotators are not required to label all the edges in these datasets, it is less labor intensive to collect $\mathcal{P}$ than to collect $\mathcal{F}$. However, existing TempRel extraction methods only work on one type of datasets (i.e., either $\mathcal{F}$ or $\mathcal{P}$), without taking advantage of both. No one, as far as we know, has explored ways to combine both types of datasets in learning and whether it is helpful.

This work is a case study in exploring various usages of $\mathcal{P}$ in the TempRel extraction task. We empirically show that $\mathcal{P}$ is indeed useful within a (constrained) bootstrapping type of learning approach. This case study is interesting from two perspectives. **First**, *incidental supervision* (Roth, 2017). In practice, supervision signals may not always be perfect: they may be noisy, only partial,

*Proceedings of the 7th Joint Conference on Lexical and Computational Semantics (*SEM)*, pages 148–153
New Orleans, June 5-6, 2018. ©2018 Association for Computational Linguistics

based on different annotation schemes, or even on different (but relevant) tasks; incidental supervision is a general paradigm that aims at making use of the abundant, naturally occurring data, as supervision signals. As for the TempRel extraction task, the existence of many partially annotated datasets $\mathcal{P}$ is a good fit for this paradigm and the result here can be informative for future investigations involving other incidental supervision signals. **Second**, *TempRel data collection*. The fact that $\mathcal{P}$ is shown to provide useful supervision signals poses some further questions: What is the optimal data collection scheme for TempRel extraction, fully annotated, partially annotated, or a mixture of both? For partially annotated data, what is the optimal ratio of annotated edges to unannotated edges? The proposed method in this work can be readily extended to study these questions in the future, as we further discuss in Sec. 5.

2   Existing Datasets and Methods

TimeBank (Pustejovsky et al., 2003) is a classic TempRel dataset, where the annotators were given a whole article and allowed to label TempRels between any pairs of events. Annotators in this setup usually focus only on salient relations but overlook some others. It has been reported that many event pairs in TimeBank should have been annotated with a specific TempRel but the annotators failed to look at them (Chambers, 2013; Cassidy et al., 2014; Ning et al., 2017). Consequently, we categorize TimeBank as a partially annotated dataset ($\mathcal{P}$). The same argument applies to other datasets that adopted this setup, such as AQUAINT (Graff, 2002), CaTeRs (Mostafazadeh et al., 2016) and RED (O'Gorman et al., 2016). Most existing systems make use of $\mathcal{P}$, including but not limited to, (Mani et al., 2006; Bramsen et al., 2006; Chambers et al., 2007; Bethard et al., 2007; Verhagen and Pustejovsky, 2008; Chambers and Jurafsky, 2008; Denis and Muller, 2011; Do et al., 2012); this applies also to the TempEval workshops systems, e.g., (Laokulrat et al., 2013; Bethard, 2013; Chambers, 2013).

To address the missing annotation issue, Cassidy et al. (2014) proposed a dense annotation scheme, TB-Dense. Edges are presented one-by-one and the annotator has to choose a label for it (note that there is a *vague* label in case the TempRel is not clear or does not exist). As a result, edges in TB-Dense are considered as fully annotated in this paper. The first system on TB-Dense was proposed in Chambers et al. (2014). Two recent TempRel extraction systems (Mirza and Tonelli, 2016; Ning et al., 2017) also reported their performances on TB-Dense ($\mathcal{F}$) and on TempEval-3 ($\mathcal{P}$) separately. However, there are no existing systems that jointly train on both. Given that the annotation guidelines of $\mathcal{F}$ and $\mathcal{P}$ are obviously different, it may not be optimal to simply treat $\mathcal{P}$ and $\mathcal{F}$ uniformly and train on their union. This situation necessitates further investigation as we do here.

Before introducing our joint learning approach, we have a few remarks about our choice of $\mathcal{F}$ and $\mathcal{P}$ datasets. First, we note that TB-Dense is actually not fully annotated in the *strict* sense because only edges within a sliding, two-sentence window are presented. That is, distant event pairs are intentionally ignored by the designers of TB-Dense. However, since such distant pairs are consistently ruled out in the training and inference phase in this paper, it does not change the nature of the problem being investigated here. At this point, TB-Dense is the only fully annotated dataset that can be adopted in this study, despite the aforementioned limitation.

Second, the partial annotations in datasets like TimeBank were not selected uniformly at random from all possible edges. As described earlier, only salient and non-vague TempRels (which may often be those easy ones) are labeled in these datasets. Using TimeBank as $\mathcal{P}$ might potentially create some bias and we will need to keep this in mind when analyzing the results in Sec. 4. Recent advances in TempRel data annotation (Ning et al., 2018c) can be used in the future to collect both $\mathcal{F}$ and $\mathcal{P}$ more easily.

3   Joint Learning on $\mathcal{F}$ and $\mathcal{P}$

In this work, we study two learning paradigms that make use of both $\mathcal{F}$ and $\mathcal{P}$. In the first, we simply treat those edges that are annotated in $\mathcal{P}$ as edges in $\mathcal{F}$ so that the learning process can be performed on top of the union of $\mathcal{F}$ and $\mathcal{P}$. This is the most straightforward approach to using $\mathcal{F}$ and $\mathcal{P}$ jointly and it is interesting to see if it already helps.

In the second, we use bootstrapping: we use $\mathcal{F}$ as a starting point and learn a TempRel extraction system on it (denoted by $S_{\mathcal{F}}$), and then fill those missing annotations in $\mathcal{P}$ based on $S_{\mathcal{F}}$ (thus obtain "fully" annotated $\tilde{\mathcal{P}}$); finally, we treat $\tilde{\mathcal{P}}$ as $\mathcal{F}$ and learn from both. Algorithm 1 is a meta-algorithm of the above.

Algorithm 1: Joint learning from $\mathcal{F}$ and $\mathcal{P}$ by bootstrapping

---
Input: $\mathcal{F}$, $\mathcal{P}$, Learn, Inference
1 $S_{\mathcal{F}} = \mathrm{Learn}(\mathcal{F})$
2 Initialize $S_{\mathcal{F}+\mathcal{P}} = S_{\mathcal{F}}$
3 **while** *convergence criteria not satisfied* **do**
4     $\tilde{\mathcal{P}} = \emptyset$
5   **foreach** $p \in \mathcal{P}$ **do**
6        $\hat{\mathbf{y}} = \mathrm{Inference}(p; S_{\mathcal{F}+\mathcal{P}})$
7        $\tilde{\mathcal{P}} = \tilde{\mathcal{P}} \cup \{(\mathbf{x}, \hat{\mathbf{y}})\}$
8     $S_{\mathcal{F}+\mathcal{P}} = \mathrm{Learn}(\mathcal{F} + \tilde{\mathcal{P}})$
9 **return** $S_{\mathcal{F}+\mathcal{P}}$

In Algorithm 1, we consistently use the sparse averaged perceptron algorithm as the "Learn" function. As for "Inference" (Line 6), we further investigate two different ways: (i) Look at every unannotated edge in $p \in \mathcal{P}$ and use $S_{\mathcal{F}+\mathcal{P}}$ to label it; this *local* method ignores the existing annotated edges in $\mathcal{P}$ and is thus the *standard* bootstrapping. (ii) Perform global inference on $\mathcal{P}$ with annotated edges being constraints, which is a *constrained* bootstrapping, motivated by the fact that temporal graphs are structured and annotated edges have influence on the missing edges: In Fig. 1, the current annotation for $(1, 2)$ and $(2, 3)$ is *before* and *vague*. We assume that the annotation $(2, 3)$=*vague* indicates that the relation cannot be determined even if the entire graph is considered. Then with $(1, 2)$=*before* and $(2, 3)$=*vague*, we can see that $(1, 3)$ cannot be uniquely determined, but it is restricted to be selected from $\{before, vague\}$ rather than the entire label set. We believe that global inference makes better use of the information provided by $\mathcal{P}$; in fact, as we show in Sec. 4, it does perform better than local inference.

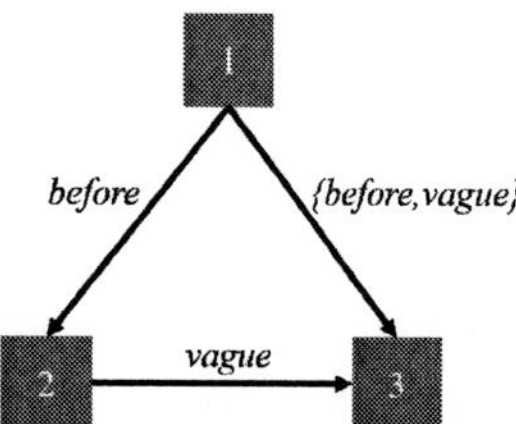

Figure 1: Nodes 1-3 are three time points and let (i, j) be the edge from node i to node j, where $(i, j) \in$ {before, after, equal, vague}. Assume the current annotation is $(1, 2) = before$ and $(2, 3) = vague$ and $(1, 3)$ is missing. However, $(1, 3)$ cannot be *after* because it leads to $(2, 3) = after$, conflicting with their current annotation; similarly, $(1, 3)$ cannot be *equal*, either.

A standard way to perform global inference is to formulate it as an Integer Linear Programming (ILP) problem(Roth and Yih, 2004) and enforce transitivity rules as constraints. Let $\mathcal{R}$ be the TempRel label set[2], $\mathcal{I}_r(ij) \in \{0, 1\}$ be the indicator function of $(i, j) = r$, and $f_r(ij) \in [0, 1]$ be the corresponding soft-max score obtained via $S_{\mathcal{F}+\mathcal{P}}$. Then the ILP objective is formulated as

$$\hat{\mathcal{I}} = \operatorname*{argmax}_{\mathcal{I}} \sum_{i<j} \sum_{r \in \mathcal{R}} f_r(ij)\mathcal{I}_r(ij) \quad (1)$$

$$\text{s.t.} \quad \Sigma_r \mathcal{I}_r(ij) = 1,$$
$$\text{(uniqueness)}$$

$$\mathcal{I}_{r_1}(ij) + \mathcal{I}_{r_2}(jk) - \Sigma_{m=1}^{N}\mathcal{I}_{r_3^m}(ik) \leq 1,$$
$$\text{(transitivity)}$$

where $\{r_3^m\}$ is selected based on the general transitivity proposed in (Ning et al., 2017). With Eq. (1), different implementations of Line 6 in Algorithm 1 can be described concisely as follows: (i) Local inference is performed by ignoring "transitivity constraints". (ii) Global inference can be performed by adding annotated edges in $\mathcal{P}$ as additional constraints. Note that Algorithm 1 is only for the learning step of TempRel extraction; as for the inference step of this task, we consistently adopt the standard method by solving Eq. (1), as was done by (Bramsen et al., 2006; Chambers and Jurafsky, 2008; Denis and Muller, 2011; Do et al., 2012; Ning et al., 2017).

4 Experiments

In this work, we consistently used TB-Dense as the fully annotated dataset ($\mathcal{F}$) and TBAQ as the partially annotated dataset ($\mathcal{P}$). The corpus statistics of these two datasets are provided in Table 1. Note that TBAQ is the union of TimeBank and AQUAINT and it originally contained 256 documents, but 36 out of them completely overlapped with TB-Dense, so we have excluded these when constructing $\mathcal{P}$. In addition, the number of edges shown in Table 1 only counts the event-event relations (i.e., do not consider the event-time relations therein), which is the focus of this work.

We also adopted the original split of TB-Dense (22 documents for training, 5 documents for development, and 9 documents for test). Learning parameters were tuned to maximize their corresponding F-metric on the development set. Using the selected parameters, systems were retrained with development set incorporated and evaluated

---

[2]In this work, we adopt *before*, *after*, *includes*, *be_included*, *simultaneously*, and *vague*.

Data	#Doc	#Edges	Ratio	Type
TB-Dense	36	6.5K	100%	$\mathcal{F}$
TBAQ	220	2.7K	12%	$\mathcal{P}$

Table 1: Corpus statistics of the fully and partially annotated dataset used in this work. TBAQ: The union of Time-Bank and AQUAINT, which is the training set provided by the TempEval3 workshop. #Edges: The number of annotated edges. Ratio: The proportion of annotated edges.

against the test split of TB-Dense (about 1.4K relations: 0.6K *vague*, 0.4K *before*, 0.3K *after*, and 0.1K for the rest). Results are shown in Table 2, where all systems were compared in terms of their performances on "same sentence" edges (both nodes are from the same sentence), "nearby sentence" edges, all edges, and the temporal awareness metric used by the TempEval3 workshop.

The first part of Table 2 (Systems 1-5) refers to the baseline method proposed at the beginning of Sec. 3, i.e., simply treating $\mathcal{P}$ as $\mathcal{F}$ and training on their union. $\mathcal{P}^{Full}$ is a variant of $\mathcal{P}$ by filling its missing edges by *vague*. Since it labels too many *vague* TempRels, System 2 suffered from a low recall. In contrast, $\mathcal{P}$ does not contain any *vague* training examples, so System 3 would only predict specific TempRels, leading to a low precision. Given the obvious difference in $\mathcal{F}$ and $\mathcal{P}^{Full}$, System 4 expectedly performed worse than System 1. However, when we see that System 5 was still worse than System 1, it is surprising because the annotated edges in $\mathcal{P}$ are correct and should have helped. This unexpected observation suggests that simply adding the annotated edges from $\mathcal{P}$ into $\mathcal{F}$ is not a proper approach to learn from both.

The second part (Systems 6-7) serves as an ablation study showing the effect of bootstrapping only. $\mathcal{P}^{Empty}$ is another variant of $\mathcal{P}$ we get by removing all the annotated edges (that is, only nodes are kept). Thus, they did not get any information from the annotated edges in $\mathcal{P}$ and any improvement came from bootstrapping alone. Specifically, System 6 is the standard bootstrapping and System 7 is the constrained bootstrapping.

Built on top of Systems 6-7, Systems 8-9 further took advantage of the annotations of $\mathcal{P}$, which resulted in additional improvements. Compared to System 1 (trained on $\mathcal{F}$ only) and System 5 (simply adding $\mathcal{P}$ into $\mathcal{F}$), the proposed System 9 achieved much better performance, which is also statistically significant with $p<0.005$ (McNemar's test). While System 7 can be regarded as a reproduction of Ning et al. (2017), the original paper of Ning et al. (2017) achieved an overall score of P=43.0, R=46.4, F=44.7 and an awareness score

of P=42.6, R=44.0, and F=43.3, and the proposed System 9 is also better than Ning et al. (2017) on all metrics.[3]

5 Discussion

While incorporating transitivity constraints in inference is widely used, Ning et al. (2017) proposed to incorporate these constraints in the learning phase as well. One of the algorithms proposed in Ning et al. (2017) is based on Chang et al. (2012)'s constraint-driven learning (CoDL), which is the same as our intermediate System 7 in Table 2; the fact that System 7 is better than System 1 can thus be considered as a reproduction of Ning et al. (2017). Despite the technical similarity, this work is motivated differently and is set to achieve a different goal: Ning et al. (2017) tried to enforce the transitivity structure, while the current work attempts to use imperfect signals (e.g., partially annotated) taken from additional data, and learn in the incidental supervision framework.

The $\mathcal{P}$ used in this work is TBAQ, where only 12% of the edges are annotated. In practice, every annotation comes at a cost, either time or the expenses paid to annotators, and as more edges are annotated, the marginal "benefit" of one edge is going down (an extreme case is that an edge is of no value if it can be inferred from existing edges). Therefore, a more general question is to find out the optimal ratio of graph annotations.

Moreover, partial annotation is only one type of annotation imperfection. If the annotation is noisy, we can alter the hard constraints derived from $\mathcal{P}$ and use soft regularization terms; if the annotation is for a different but relevant task, we can formulate corresponding constraints to connect that different task to the task at hand. Being able to learn from these "indirect" signals is appealing because indirect signals are usually order of magnitudes larger than datasets dedicated to a single task.

6 Conclusion

Temporal relation (TempRel) extraction is important but TempRel annotation is labor intensive. While fully annotated datasets ($\mathcal{F}$) are relatively small, there exist more datasets with partial annotations ($\mathcal{P}$). This work provides the first investigation of learning from both types of datasets, and this preliminary study already shows promise.

---

[3]We obtained the original event-event TempRel predictions of Ning et al. (2017) from `https://cogcomp.org/page/publication_view/822`.

No.	Training		Same Sentence			Nearby Sentence			Overall			Awareness		
	Data	Bootstrap	P	R	F	P	R	F	P	R	F	P	R	F
1	$\mathcal{F}$	-	47.1	49.7	48.4	40.2	37.9	39.0	**42.1**	41.0	**41.5**	**40.0**	40.7	**40.3**
2	$\mathcal{P}^{Full}$	-	37.0	33.1	35.0	34.4	19.6	24.9	37.7	23.6	29.0	36.9	24.0	29.1
3	$\mathcal{P}$	-	34.1	52.5	41.3	26.1	48.1	33.8	30.2	**52.1**	38.2	28.6	**49.9**	36.4
4	$\mathcal{F}+\mathcal{P}^{Full}$	-	38.5	32.2	35.1	40.1	38.1	39.1	40.8	35.3	37.8	37.1	36.2	36.6
5	$\mathcal{F}+\mathcal{P}$	-	43.7	43.9	43.8	39.1	38.3	38.7	41.8	40.7	41.2	38.6	41.4	40.0
6	$\mathcal{F}+\mathcal{P}^{Empty}$	Local	41.7	50.3	45.6	39.5	48.1	43.4	41.8	50.4	45.7	40.9	47.5	43.9
7	$\mathcal{F}+\mathcal{P}^{Empty}$	Global	44.7	55.5	49.5	40.1	48.7	44	**42.0**	**51.4**	**46.2**	**41.1**	**48.3**	**44.4**
8	$\mathcal{F}+\mathcal{P}$	Local	43.6	50	46.6	43	46.9	44.8	43.7	47.8	45.6	42	45.6	43.7
9	$\mathcal{F}+\mathcal{P}$	Global	44.9	56.1	49.9	43.4	52.3	47.5	**44.7**	**54.1**	**49.0**	**44.1**	50.8	**47.2**

Table 2: Performance of various usages of the partially annotated data in training. $\mathcal{F}$: Fully annotated data. $\mathcal{P}$: Partially annotated data. $\mathcal{P}^{Full}$: $\mathcal{P}$ with missing annotations filled by *vague*. $\mathcal{P}^{Empty}$: $\mathcal{P}$ with all annotations removed. Bootstrap: referring to specific implementations of Line 6 in Algorithm 1, i.e., local or global. Same/nearby sentence: edges whose nodes appear in the same/nearby sentences in text. Overall: all edges. Awareness: the temporal awareness metric used in the TempEval3 workshop, measuring how useful the predicted graphs are (UzZaman et al., 2013). System 7 can also be considered as a reproduction of Ning et al. (2017) (see the discussion in Sec. 5 for details).

Two bootstrapping algorithms (standard and constrained) are analyzed and the benefit of $\mathcal{P}$, although with missing annotations, is shown on a benchmark dataset. This work may be a good starting point for further investigations of incidental supervision and data collection schemes of the TempRel extraction task.

Acknowledgements

We thank all the reviewers for providing insightful comments and critiques. This research is supported in part by a grant from the Allen Institute for Artificial Intelligence (allenai.org); the IBM-ILLINOIS Center for Cognitive Computing Systems Research (C3SR) - a research collaboration as part of the IBM AI Horizons Network; by DARPA under agreement number FA8750-13-2-0008; and by the Army Research Laboratory (ARL) under agreement W911NF-09-2-0053.

The U.S. Government is authorized to reproduce and distribute reprints for Governmental purposes notwithstanding any copyright notation thereon. The views and conclusions contained herein are those of the authors and should not be interpreted as necessarily representing the official policies or endorsements, either expressed or implied, of DARPA or the U.S. Government. Any opinions, findings, conclusions or recommendations are those of the authors and do not necessarily reflect the view of the ARL.

References

Steven Bethard. 2013. ClearTK-TimeML: A minimalist approach to TempEval 2013. In *Second Joint Conference on Lexical and Computational Semantics (* SEM)*. volume 2, pages 10–14.

Steven Bethard, James H Martin, and Sara Klingenstein. 2007. Timelines from text: Identification of syntactic temporal relations. In *IEEE International Conference on Semantic Computing (ICSC)*. pages 11–18.

Steven Bethard, Guergana Savova, Wei-Te Chen, Leon Derczynski, James Pustejovsky, and Marc Verhagen. 2016. SemEval-2016 Task 12: Clinical TempEval. In *Proceedings of the 10th International Workshop on Semantic Evaluation (SemEval-2016)*. Association for Computational Linguistics, San Diego, California, pages 1052–1062.

Steven Bethard, Guergana Savova, Martha Palmer, and James Pustejovsky. 2017. SemEval-2017 Task 12: Clinical TempEval. In *Proceedings of the 11th International Workshop on Semantic Evaluation (SemEval-2017)*. Association for Computational Linguistics, pages 565–572.

P. Bramsen, P. Deshpande, Y. K. Lee, and R. Barzilay. 2006. Inducing temporal graphs. In *Proceedings of the Conference on Empirical Methods for Natural Language Processing (EMNLP)*. pages 189–198.

Taylor Cassidy, Bill McDowell, Nathanel Chambers, and Steven Bethard. 2014. An annotation framework for dense event ordering. In *Proceedings of the Annual Meeting of the Association for Computational Linguistics (ACL)*. pages 501–506.

N. Chambers and D. Jurafsky. 2008. Jointly combining implicit constraints improves temporal ordering. In *Proceedings of the Conference on Empirical Methods for Natural Language Processing (EMNLP)*.

Nate Chambers. 2013. NavyTime: Event and time ordering from raw text. In *Second Joint Conference on Lexical and Computational Semantics (*SEM), Volume 2: Proceedings of the Seventh International Workshop on Semantic Evaluation (SemEval 2013)*. Association for Computational Linguistics, Atlanta, Georgia, USA, pages 73–77.

Nathanael Chambers, Taylor Cassidy, Bill McDowell, and Steven Bethard. 2014. Dense event ordering with a multi-pass architecture. *Transactions of the Association for Computational Linguistics* 2:273–284.

Nathanael Chambers, Shan Wang, and Dan Jurafsky. 2007. Classifying temporal relations between events. In *Proceedings of the 45th Annual Meeting of the ACL on Interactive Poster and Demonstration Sessions*. pages 173–176.

M. Chang, L. Ratinov, and D. Roth. 2012. Structured learning with constrained conditional models. *Machine Learning* 88(3):399–431.

Pascal Denis and Philippe Muller. 2011. Predicting globally-coherent temporal structures from texts via endpoint inference and graph decomposition. In *Proceedings of the International Joint Conference on Artificial Intelligence (IJCAI)*. volume 22, page 1788.

Q. Do, W. Lu, and D. Roth. 2012. Joint inference for event timeline construction. In *Proc. of the Conference on Empirical Methods in Natural Language Processing (EMNLP)*.

David Graff. 2002. The AQUAINT corpus of english news text. *Linguistic Data Consortium, Philadelphia* .

Natsuda Laokulrat, Makoto Miwa, Yoshimasa Tsuruoka, and Takashi Chikayama. 2013. UTTime: Temporal relation classification using deep syntactic features. In *Second Joint Conference on Lexical and Computational Semantics (* SEM)*. volume 2, pages 88–92.

Inderjeet Mani, Marc Verhagen, Ben Wellner, Chong Min Lee, and James Pustejovsky. 2006. Machine learning of temporal relations. In *Proceedings of the Annual Meeting of the Association for Computational Linguistics (ACL)*. pages 753–760.

Anne-Lyse Minard, Manuela Speranza, Eneko Agirre, Itziar Aldabe, Marieke van Erp, Bernardo Magnini, German Rigau, Ruben Urizar, and Fondazione Bruno Kessler. 2015. SemEval-2015 Task 4: TimeLine: Cross-document event ordering. In *Proceedings of the 9th International Workshop on Semantic Evaluation (SemEval 2015)*. pages 778–786.

Paramita Mirza and Sara Tonelli. 2016. CATENA: CAusal and TEmporal relation extraction from NAtural language texts. In *The 26th International Conference on Computational Linguistics*. pages 64–75.

Nasrin Mostafazadeh, Alyson Grealish, Nathanael Chambers, James Allen, and Lucy Vanderwende. 2016. CaTeRS: Causal and temporal relation scheme for semantic annotation of event structures. In *Proceedings of the 4th Workshop on Events: Definition, Detection, Coreference, and Representation*. pages 51–61.

Qiang Ning, Zhili Feng, and Dan Roth. 2017. A structured learning approach to temporal relation extraction. In *Proceedings of the Conference on Empirical Methods for Natural Language Processing (EMNLP)*. Copenhagen, Denmark.

Qiang Ning, Zhili Feng, Hao Wu, and Dan Roth. 2018a. Joint reasoning for temporal and causal relations. In *Proceedings of the Annual Meeting of the Association for Computational Linguistics (ACL)*.

Qiang Ning, Hao Wu, Haoruo Peng, and Dan Roth. 2018b. Improving temporal relation extraction with a globally acquired statistical resource. In *Proceedings of the Annual Meeting of the North American Association of Computational Linguistics (NAACL)*. Association for Computational Linguistics.

Qiang Ning, Hao Wu, and Dan Roth. 2018c. A multiaxis annotation scheme for event temporal relations. In *Proceedings of the Annual Meeting of the Association for Computational Linguistics (ACL)*.

Tim O'Gorman, Kristin Wright-Bettner, and Martha Palmer. 2016. Richer event description: Integrating event coreference with temporal, causal and bridging annotation. In *Proceedings of the 2nd Workshop on Computing News Storylines (CNS 2016)*. Association for Computational Linguistics, Austin, Texas, pages 47–56.

James Pustejovsky, Patrick Hanks, Roser Sauri, Andrew See, Robert Gaizauskas, Andrea Setzer, Dragomir Radev, Beth Sundheim, David Day, Lisa Ferro, et al. 2003. The TIMEBANK corpus. In *Corpus linguistics*. volume 2003, page 40.

D. Roth and W. Yih. 2004. A linear programming formulation for global inference in natural language tasks. In Hwee Tou Ng and Ellen Riloff, editors, *Proc. of the Conference on Computational Natural Language Learning (CoNLL)*. pages 1–8.

Dan Roth. 2017. Incidental supervision: Moving beyond supervised learning. In *AAAI*.

Naushad UzZaman, Hector Llorens, James Allen, Leon Derczynski, Marc Verhagen, and James Pustejovsky. 2013. SemEval-2013 Task 1: TempEval-3: Evaluating time expressions, events, and temporal relations. In *Second Joint Conference on Lexical and Computational Semantics*. volume 2, pages 1–9.

Marc Verhagen, Robert Gaizauskas, Frank Schilder, Mark Hepple, Graham Katz, and James Pustejovsky. 2007. SemEval-2007 Task 15: TempEval temporal relation identification. In *SemEval*. pages 75–80.

Marc Verhagen and James Pustejovsky. 2008. Temporal processing with the TARSQI toolkit. In *22nd International Conference on on Computational Linguistics: Demonstration Papers*. pages 189–192.

Marc Verhagen, Roser Sauri, Tommaso Caselli, and James Pustejovsky. 2010. SemEval-2010 Task 13: TempEval-2. In *SemEval*. pages 57–62.

Predicting Word Embeddings Variability

Bénédicte Pierrejean and **Ludovic Tanguy**
CLLE: CNRS & University of Toulouse
Toulouse, France
{benedicte.pierrejean,ludovic.tanguy}@univ-tlse2.fr

Abstract

Neural word embeddings models (such as those built with *word2vec*) are known to have stability problems: when retraining a model with the exact same hyperparameters, words neighborhoods may change. We propose a method to estimate such variation, based on the overlap of neighbors of a given word in two models trained with identical hyperparameters. We show that this inherent variation is not negligible, and that it does not affect every word in the same way. We examine the influence of several features that are intrinsic to a word, corpus or embedding model and provide a methodology that can predict the variability (and as such, reliability) of a word representation in a semantic vector space.

1 Introduction

Word embeddings are dense representations of the meaning of words that are efficient and easy to use. Embeddings training methods such as *word2vec* (Mikolov et al., 2013), are based on neural networks methods that imply random processes (initialization of the network, sampling, etc.). As such, they display stability problems (Hellrich and Hahn, 2016) meaning that retraining a model with the exact same hyperparameters will give different word representations, with a word possibly having different nearest neighbors from one model to the other.

Benchmarks test sets such as WordSim-353 (Finkelstein et al., 2002) are commonly used to evaluate word embeddings since they provide a fast and easy way to quickly evaluate a model (Nayak et al., 2016). However, the instability of word embeddings is not detected by these test sets since only selected pairs of words are evaluated. A model showing instability could get very similar performance results when evaluated on such benchmarks.

Hyperparameters selected when training word embeddings impact the semantic representation of a word. Among these hyperparameters we find some hyperparameters internal to the system such as the architecture used, the size of the context window or the dimensions of the vectors as well as some external hyperparameters such as the corpus used for training (Asr et al., 2016; Baroni et al., 2014; Chiu et al., 2016; Li et al., 2017; Melamud et al., 2016; Roberts, 2016). In this work, we adopt a corpus linguistics approach in a similar way to Antoniak and Mimno (2018), Hamilton et al. (2016) and Hellrich and Hahn (2016) meaning that observing the semantic representation of a word consists in observing the nearest neighbors of this word. Corpus tools such as Sketch Engine (Kilgarriff et al., 2014) use embeddings trained on several corpora[1] to provide users with most similar words as a lexical semantic information on a target word. In order to make accurate observations, it thus seems important to understand the stability of these embeddings.

In this paper, we measure the variation that exists between several models trained with the same hyperparameters in terms of nearest neighbors for all words in a corpus. A word having the same nearest neighbors across several models is considered stable.

Based on a set of selected features, we also attempt to predict the stability of a word. Such a prediction is interesting to understand what features have an impact on a word representation variability. It could also be used to certify the reliability of the given semantic representation of a word without having to retrain several models to make sure the representation is accurate. This will be a useful method to give more reliability to observations made in corpus linguistics using word em-

---

[1]https://embeddings.sketchengine.co.uk/static/index.html

*Proceedings of the 7th Joint Conference on Lexical and Computational Semantics (*SEM)*, pages 154–159
New Orleans, June 5-6, 2018. ©2018 Association for Computational Linguistics

beddings. It can also help choosing the right hyperparameters or refine a model (e.g. by removing selected semantic classes).

We examine the influence of several features that are intrinsic to a word, a corpus or a model: part of speech (henceforth POS), degree of polysemy, frequency of a word, distribution of the contexts of a word, position and environment of a vector in the semantic space. We train a multilinear regression model using these features and predict up to 48% of the variance. This experiment was conducted on 3 different corpora with similar results. We first explain how we measure the variation of a model. We then present the models used in this work and we finally describe our predictive model.

2   Experiment Setup

To measure the variation for a word between two embedding models, we used an approach similar to Sahlgren (2006) by measuring the nearest neighbors overlap for words common to the two models. More precisely the variation score of a word *varnn* across two models M_1 and M_2 is measured as:

$$varnn^N_{M_1,M_2}(w) = 1 - \frac{|nn^N_{M_1}(w) \cap nn^N_{M_2}(w)|}{N}$$

$nn^N_M(w)$ represents the N words having the closest cosine similarity score with word w in a distributional model M. In the experiments presented here we selected $N = 25$. To chose the value of N, we selected two models and computed the variation with different values of N across the entire vocabulary (1, 5, 10, 25, 50 and 100). We then computed the correlation coefficient between scores for all the N values and found that the highest average correlation value was for $N = 25$. The variation was computed only for open classes (adverbs, adjectives, verbs and nouns).

This variation measure presents both advantages and inconvenients. The fact that this measure is cost-effective and intuitive makes it very convenient to use. It is also strongly related to the way we observe word embeddings in a corpuslinguistics approach (i.e. by observing a few nearest neighbors). However we are aware that this measure assess only a part of what has changed from one model to the other based on the number of neighbors observed. This measure may also be sensible to complex effects and phenomena in

high-dimensional vector spaces such as *hubness*, with some words being more "popular" nearest neighbors than others (Radovanović et al., 2010). Although we could indeed identify such hubs in our vector spaces, they were limited to a small cluster of words (such as surnames for the BNC) and did not interfere with our measure of stability for all other areas of the lexicon.

The compared models were trained using the standard *word2vec*[2] with the default hyperparameters (architecture Skip-Gram with negative sampling rate of 5, window size set to 5, vectors dimensions set to 100, negative sampling rate set to 10^{-3} and number of iterations set to 5). Additionally, min-count was set to 100.

Models were trained on 3 different corpora: ACL (NLP scientific articles from the ACL anthology[3]), BNC (written part of the British National Corpus[4]) and PLOS (biology scientific articles from the PLOS archive collections[5]). All corpora are the same size (about 100 million words) but they are from different types (the BNC is a generic corpus while PLOS and ACL are specialized corpora) and different domains. Corpora were lemmatized and POS-tagged using the Talismane toolkit (Urieli, 2013). Every word is associated to its POS for all subsequent experiments.

For each corpus, we trained 5 models using the exact same hyperparameters mentioned above; they only differ because of the inherent randomness of word2vec's technique. We then made 10 pairwise comparisons of models per corpus, computing the variation score for every word.

Corpus	Voc. size	Mean variation	Std. dev. (models)	Std. dev. (words)
ACL	22 292	0.16	0.04	0.08
BNC	27 434	0.17	0.04	0.08
PLOS	31 529	0.18	0.05	0.09

Table 1: Mean variation score and standard deviations for each corpus (5 models trained per corpus).

3   Models Variation

Table 1 reports the results of the comparisons. For each corpus we indicate the mean variation score, i.e. the variation averaged over all words and the

---

[2] https://code.google.com/archive/p/word2vec/
[3] Bird et al. (2008)
[4] http://www.natcorp.ox.ac.uk/
[5] https://www.plos.org/text-and-data-mining

10 pairwise comparisons. The variation is very similar from one corpus to the other. Standard deviation is low (average of 0.04) across the 10 pairs of models, meaning that the variation is equally distributed among the comparisons made for each corpus. The standard deviation across words is much higher (average of 0.08), which indicates that there are important differences in variation from one word to the other within the same category of models.

Variation scores for a given word can be zero (all 25 nearest neighbors are identical, although their order can vary) or as high as 0.68 (only a third of the nearest neighbors are found in both models). Based on the average variation score across the 5 models, we had a closer look at words varying the most and the least in each corpus. We identified semantic clusters that remained stable across models. E.g., in the BNC that was the case for temporal expressions (*am*, *pm*, *noon*). For all 3 corpora we identified closed classes of co-hyponyms, e.g. family members in the BNC (*wife*, *grandmother*, *sister...*), linguistic preprocessing in ACL (*parsing*, *lemmatizing*, *tokenizing...*) and antibiotics in PLOS (*puromycin*, *blasticidin*, *cefotaxime...*). For ACL and PLOS we also noticed that words belonging to the transdisciplinary scientific lexicon remained stable (conjunctive adverbs such as *nevertheless*, *moreover*, *furthermore* and scientific processes such as *hypothethize*, *reason*, *describe*). Among words displaying high variation we found a large number of tagging errors and proper nouns. We also identified some common features for other words displaying a high variation. E.g. highly polysemic words (*sign* in ACL, *make* in the BNC) and generic adjectives, i.e. adjectives than can modifiy almost any noun (*special* in ACL, *current* in PLOS and *whole* in the BNC), tend to vary more.

As there seems to be some common features of words that show a similar level of stability, we decided to try to predict the variation score.

4 Predicting the Variation

The predictive statistical models we trained are based on a set of features calculated for each word in a given distributional model. The target value is the average variation score measured across the 5 models (and 10 pairwise comparisons), so that the statistical model focuses on predicting the stability of an embedding based on a single distributional model, without having to actually train several models with the same hyperparameters. Of course, we also wanted to identify more precisely the features of stable and unstable word embeddings.

4.1 Selected Features

We measured the following features that are intrinsic to the word, corpus or model:

- *pos*: part of speech (nouns, adjectives, adverbs, verbs, proper nouns);
- *polysemy*: degree of polysemy of the word, according to an external resource;
- *frequency*: frequency of the word in the corpus;
- *entropy*: dispersion of the contexts of a word;
- *norm*: L2-norm of the vector of the word in the semantic space;
- *NN-sim*: cosine similarity of the word nearest neighbor.

POS is a straightforward feature, given by the tagger used to preprocess the corpora. As we have seen above, words in some categories such as proper nouns seemed to show higher variation than others.

To compute the degree of polysemy of a word, we used ENGLAWI, a lexical resource built from the english Wiktionary entries (Sajous and Hathout, 2015). The degree of polysemy corresponds to the number of definitions a word has in this resource. If a word does not exist in the resource, we assigned it a degree of polysemy of 1. As word embeddings aggregate all the senses of a word in a single vectors, it can be expected that polysemous words will show more variation.

Frequency of a word in a corpus is of course a very important feature when assessing embeddings (Sahlgren and Lenci, 2016). It is known that words of low or high frequencies get lower results on different tasks using embeddings.

The dispersion of the contexts of a word is measured by the normalized entropy of a word's collocates computed on a symmetrical rectangular window of 5 for open classes words only. A higher value indicate a high variability in the contexts, which should also be correlated to variation.

We chose the L2-norm of a word vector in the model as a feature since Trost and Klakow (2017) found that the L2-norm of common words do not follow the general distribution of the model.

The last feature is the cosine similarity value of the word nearest neighbor in the semantic space. It is logically expected that close neighbors of a word will have a tendency to remain stable across models.

Corpus	Mean adjusted R^2 (std. dev.)
ACL	0.39 (0.0007)
BNC	0.43 (0.0102)
PLOS	0.48 (0.0006)

Table 2: Mean adjusted R^2 score for predicting the variation of a word on ACL, BNC and PLOS.

We performed a multiple linear regression with pairwise interactions. We have 5 multilinear regression models per corpus (one per distributional model), but they all target the average variation score of a word as the predicted value. We evaluated the validity of each model using the adjusted R^2 value.

4.2 Models and Results

We can see in Table 2 that we are able to predict up to 48% of the variance, with slight differences across the three corpora. Although far from an efficient prediction, these values indicate that we nevertheless captured important features that can explain the stability of embeddings.

In order to understand the impact of the different features selected to train the regression models, we followed a feature ablation approach similar to Lapesa and Evert (2017). For each word embedding model, we trained one multilinear model using all features. We then trained 6 other models by removing one feature at a time, and computed the difference (loss) of the adjusted R^2 compared to the full 6-features model. This difference can be seen as the relative importance of the ablated feature.

Figure 1 shows the impact of each feature used for training. We can see a similar global pattern for models trained on the 3 corpora with two features displaying more importance than others. The cosine similarity of the nearest neighbor has the most important impact. As shown in Figure 1 it explains around 20% of the variance. This was expected given the way we measure variation. However, it accounts for less than half of the predictive model's power, meaning that there are other important effects involved. The POS also has a high impact on the model trained. Other features have

less impact on the regression models trained. This is the case of the entropy and the polysemy for all 3 corpora. The norm and frequency have a slightly different impact depending on the corpus.

To get a better understanding of the effects of each feature on the variation of a word, we analyzed the effect of features using partial effects.

We observed similar effects of the features for all 3 corpora. As we stated before, the cosine similarity score of the nearest neighbor of a word is the most important feature when predicting its variability. We found that words having a higher nearest neighbor similarity score displayed less variation. On the contrary, when the similarity score was lower, the variation was higher. It seems logical that a very close neighbor remains stable from one model to the other. However this is not a systematic behavior. Some words having very close neighbors display a high variability.

For POS, we confirm that proper nouns have a higher variation than other categories, along with nouns on a smaller scale. No differences could be found among other categories.

The norm of the vector is negatively correlated to variation: word with vectors distant from the origin show less variation. This effect was confirmed but less clear for the ACL models. This phenomenon has to be further inquired as is the overall geometry of word embeddings vector space. E.g., Mimno and Thompson (2017) have shown that embeddings trained using *word2vec* Skip-Gram are not evenly dispersed through the semantic space.

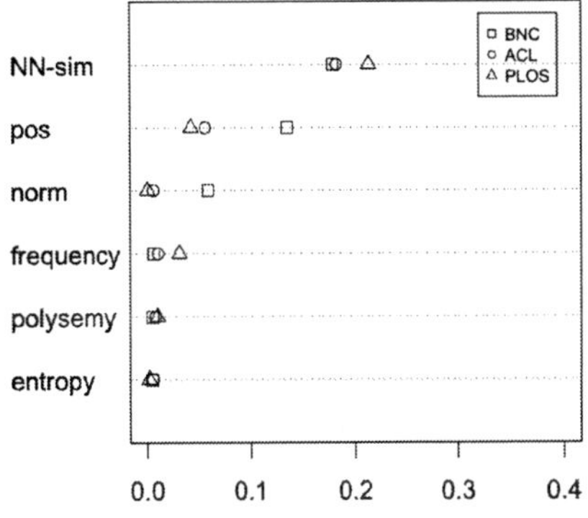

Figure 1: Feature ablation for multilinear regression models trained for ACL, BNC and PLOS.

157

The effect of the frequency over the predictability of the variation is not linear. Words having very low or very high frequency are more affected by variation than words in the mid-frequency range. This partly infirms the common knowledge that embeddings of more frequent words are of better quality. We actually found a number of frequent words displaying instability words in each corpus (e.g. *gene* and *protein* in PLOS, *language* in ACL and *make* in BNC etc.).

The degree of polysemy of a word also has a slight effect on the predictability of the variation of a word. The more polysemic a word is, the more likely its variation score is to be high.

As for the entropy, we observed for ACL and the BNC, that words having higher entropy with their contexts display more variation.

Concerning these two last features (polysemy and entropy) experiments confirm that distributional semantics has more difficulty in representing the meaning of words that appear in a variety of contexts.

5   Conclusion

In this paper, we wanted to get a better understanding of the intrinsic stability of neural-based word embeddings models. We agree with Antoniak and Mimno (2018) when saying that word embeddings should be used with care when used as tools for corpus linguistics, as any phenomenon observed in such models could be simply due to random.

We proposed a method that measures the variation of a word, along with a technique to predict the variation of a word by using simple features. We have seen that not all features have the same importance when predicting the variability, prominent features being the cosine similarity score of the nearest neighbor of a word and its POS. The other features we considered, while having a lesser predictive power, helped to shed some light on which areas of the lexicon are more or less affected by the variation. This means that we can hope to assess which words (in a given corpus) can be more reliably represented by embeddings, and which one should be analyzed with more caution.

Beyond the practical insterest of this prediction, this work is a step towards a better understanding of the conditions in which distributional semantics capture and represent the meaning of words. We already observed that some words or meanings are more challenging than others. In this way we as-sume that stability attest the quality of a semantic representation.

In this work, the embeddings models used were trained with default hyperparameters. In the future, we want to know if hyperparameters used when training word embeddings have an impact on the variation. We also want to make sure that the identified features explaining the variation will be the same when varying the hyperparameters. In the long run, this could lead to an alternative to benchmark test sets when selecting the hyperparameter values.

Acknowledgments

We are thankful to the anonymous reviewers for their suggestions and comments. Experiments presented in this paper were carried out using the OSIRIM computing platform[6] that is administered by the IRIT computer science lab and supported by the National Center for Scientific Research (CNRS), the Région Midi-Pyrénées, the French Government, and the European Regional Development Fund (ERDF).

References

Maria Antoniak and David Mimno. 2018. Evaluating the stability of embedding-based word similarities. *Transactions of the Association for Computational Linguistics*, 6:107–119.

Fatemeh Torabi Asr, Jon A. Willits, and Michael N. Jones. 2016. Comparing predictive and co-occurrence based models of lexical semantics trained on child-directed speech. In *Proceedings of the 37th Meeting of the Cognitive Science Society*.

Marco Baroni, Georgiana Dinu, and German Kruszewski. 2014. Don't count, predict! A systematic comparison of context-counting vs. context-predicting semantic vectors. In *Proceedings of the 52nd Annual Meeting of the Association for Computational Linguistics*, pages 238–247, Baltimore, Maryland, USA.

Steven Bird, Robert Dale, Bonnie Dorr, Bryan Gibson, Mark Joseph, Min-Yen Kan, Dongwon Lee, Brett Powley, Dragomir Radev, and Yee Fan Tan. 2008. The ACL Anthology Reference Corpus: A reference dataset for bibliographic research in computational linguistics. In *Proceedings of Language Resources and Evaluation Conference (LREC 08)*, Marrakesh, Morrocco.

---

[6]See http://osirim.irit.fr/site/en

Billy Chiu, Gamal Crichton, Anna Korhonen, and Sampo Pyysalo. 2016. How to train good word embeddings for biomedical NLP. In *Proceedings of the 15th Workshop on Biomedical Natural Language Processing*, pages 166–174, Berlin, Germany.

Lev Finkelstein, Evgeniy Gabrilovich, Yossi Matias, Ehud Rivlin, Zach Solan, Gadi Wolfman, and Eytan Ruppin. 2002. Placing search in context: The concept revisited. In *ACM Transactions on Information Systems*, volume 20, page 116:131.

William L. Hamilton, Jure Leskovec, and Dan Jurafsky. 2016. Diachronic word embeddings reveal statistical laws of semantic change. In *Proceedings of the 54th Annual Meeting of the Association for Computational Linguistics*, pages 1489–1501, Berlin, Germany.

Johannes Hellrich and Udo Hahn. 2016. Bad company - neighborhoods in neural embedding spaces considered harmful. In *Proceedings of COLING 2016, the 26th International Conference on Computational Linguistics: Technical Papers*, pages 2785–2796, Osaka, Japan.

Adam Kilgarriff, Vít Baisa, Jan Bušta, Miloš Jakubíček, Vojtěch Kovář, Jan Michelfeit, Pavel Rychlý, and Vít Suchomel. 2014. The Sketch Engine: Ten years on. *Lexicography*, 1(1):7–36.

Gabriella Lapesa and Stefan Evert. 2017. Large-scale evaluation of dependency-based DSMs: Are they worth the effort? In *Proceedings of the 15th Conference of the European Chapter of the Association for Computational Linguistics*, volume 2, Short papers, pages 394–400, Valencia, Spain.

Bofang Li, Tao Liu, Zhe Zhao, Buzhou Tang, Aleksandr Drozd, Anna Rogers, and Xiaoyong Du. 2017. Investigating different syntactic context types and context representations for learning word embeddings. In *Proceedings of the 2017 Conference on Empirical Methods in Natural Language Processing*, pages 2411–2421.

Oren Melamud, David McClosky, Siddharth Patwardhan, and Mohit Bansal. 2016. The role of context types and dimensionality in learning word embeddings. In *Proceedings of NAACL-HLT 2016*, San Diego, California.

Tomas Mikolov, Kai Chen, Greg Corrado, and Jeffrey Dean. 2013. Efficient estimation of word representations in vector space. *CoRR*, abs/1301.3781.

David Mimno and Laure Thompson. 2017. The strange geometry of skip-gram with negative sampling. In *Proceedings of the 2017 Conference on Empirical Methods in Natural Language Processing*, pages 2873–2878, Copenhagen, Denmark.

Neha Nayak, Gabor Angeli, and Christopher D. Manning. 2016. Evaluating word embeddings using a representative suite of practical tasks. In *Proceedings of the 1st Workshop on Evaluating Vector Space Representations for NLP*, pages 19–23, Berlin, Germany.

Miloš Radovanović, Alexandros Nanopoulos, and Mirjana Ivanović. 2010. Hubs in space: Popular nearest neighbors in high-dimensional data. *Journal of Machine Learning Research*, 11:2487–2531.

Kirk Roberts. 2016. Assessing the corpus size vs. similarity trade-off for word embeddings in clinical NLP. In *Proceedings of the Clinical Natural Language Processing Workshop*, pages 54–63, Osaka, Japan.

Magnus Sahlgren. 2006. *The Word-Space Model*. Ph.D. thesis, Stockholm University, Sweden.

Magnus Sahlgren and Alessandro Lenci. 2016. The effects of data size and frequency range on distributional semantic models. In *Proceedings of the 2016 Conference on Empirical Methods in Natural Language Processing*, pages 975–980, Austin, Texas.

Franck Sajous and Nabil Hathout. 2015. GLAWI, a free XML-encoded machine-readable dictionary built from the French Wiktionary. In *Proceedings of the eLex 2015 conference*, pages 405–426, Herstmonceux, England.

Thomas A. Trost and Dietrich Klakow. 2017. Parameter free hierarchical graph-based clustering for analyzing continuous word embeddings. In *Proceedings of TextGraphs-11: the Workshop on Graph-based Methods for Natural Language Processing*, Vancouver, Canada.

Assaf Urieli. 2013. *Robust French syntax analysis: reconciling statistical methods and linguistic knowledge in the Talismane toolkit*. Ph.D. thesis, University of Toulouse, France.

Integrating Multiplicative Features
into Supervised Distributional Methods for Lexical Entailment

Tu Vu
College of Information and Computer Sciences
University of Massachusetts Amherst
Amherst, MA, USA
tuvu@cs.umass.edu

Vered Shwartz
Computer Science Department
Bar-Ilan University
Ramat-Gan, Israel
vered1986@gmail.com

Abstract

Supervised distributional methods are applied successfully in lexical entailment, but recent work questioned whether these methods actually learn a relation between two words. Specifically, Levy et al. (2015) claimed that linear classifiers learn only separate properties of each word. We suggest a cheap and easy way to boost the performance of these methods by integrating multiplicative features into commonly used representations. We provide an extensive evaluation with different classifiers and evaluation setups, and suggest a suitable evaluation setup for the task, eliminating biases existing in previous ones.

1 Introduction

Lexical entailment is concerned with identifying the semantic relation, if any, holding between two words, as in *(pigeon, hyponym, animal)*. The popularity of the task stems from its potential relevance to various NLP applications, such as question answering and recognizing textual entailment (Dagan et al., 2013) that often rely on lexical semantic resources with limited coverage like Wordnet (Miller, 1995). Relation classifiers can be used either within applications or as an intermediate step in the construction of lexical resources which is often expensive and time-consuming.

Most methods for lexical entailment are distributional, i.e., the semantic relation holding between x and y is recognized based on their distributional vector representations. While the first methods were unsupervised and used high-dimensional sparse vectors (Weeds and Weir, 2003; Kotlerman et al., 2010; Santus et al., 2014), in recent years, supervised methods became popular (Baroni et al., 2012; Roller et al., 2014; Weeds et al., 2014). These methods are mostly based on word embeddings (Mikolov et al., 2013b; Pennington et al., 2014a) utilizing various vector com-

binations that are designed to capture relational information between two words.

While most previous work reported success using supervised methods, some questions remain unanswered: First, several works suggested that supervised distributional methods are incapable of inferring the relationship between two words, but rather rely on independent properties of each word (Levy et al., 2015; Roller and Erk, 2016; Shwartz et al., 2016), making them sensitive to training data; Second, it remains unclear what is the most appropriate representation and classifier; previous studies reported inconsistent results with **Concat**$\langle \vec{v_x} \oplus \vec{v_y} \rangle$ (Baroni et al., 2012) and **Diff**$\langle \vec{v_y} - \vec{v_x} \rangle$ (Roller et al., 2014; Weeds et al., 2014; Fu et al., 2014), using various classifiers.

In this paper, we investigate the effectiveness of multiplicative features, namely, the element-wise multiplication **Mult**$\langle \vec{v_x} \odot \vec{v_y} \rangle$, and the squared difference **Sqdiff**$\langle (\vec{v_y} - \vec{v_x}) \odot (\vec{v_y} - \vec{v_x}) \rangle$. These features, similar to the cosine similarity and the Euclidean distance, might capture a different notion of interaction information about the relationship holding between two words. We directly integrate them into some commonly used representations. For instance, we consider the concatenation **Diff**$\oplus$**Mult** $\langle (\vec{v_y} - \vec{v_x}) \oplus (\vec{v_x} \odot \vec{v_y}) \rangle$ that might capture both the typicality of each word in the relation (e.g., if y is a typical hypernym) and the similarity between the words.

We experiment with multiple supervised distributional methods and analyze which representations perform well in various evaluation setups. Our analysis confirms that integrating multiplicative features into standard representations can substantially boost the performance of linear classifiers. While the contribution over non-linear classifiers is sometimes marginal, they are expensive to train, and linear classifiers can achieve the same effect "cheaply" by integrating multiplicative fea-

*Proceedings of the 7th Joint Conference on Lexical and Computational Semantics (*SEM)*, pages 160–166
New Orleans, June 5-6, 2018. ©2018 Association for Computational Linguistics

tures. The contribution of multiplicative features is mostly prominent in strict evaluation settings, i.e., lexical split (Levy et al., 2015) and out-of-domain evaluation that disable the models' ability to achieve good performance by memorizing words seen during training. We find that **Concat** $\oplus$ **Mult** performs consistently well, and suggest it as a strong baseline for future research.

2 Related Work

Available Representations In supervised distributional methods, a pair of words (x, y) is represented as some combination of the word embeddings of x and y, most commonly **Concat** $\langle \vec{v}_x \oplus \vec{v}_y \rangle$ (Baroni et al., 2012) or **Diff** $\langle \vec{v}_y - \vec{v}_x \rangle$ (Weeds et al., 2014; Fu et al., 2014).

Limitations Recent work questioned whether supervised distributional methods actually learn the relation between x and y or only separate properties of each word. Levy et al. (2015) claimed that they tend to perform "lexical memorization", i.e., memorizing that some words are prototypical to certain relations (e.g., that $y = $ *animal* is a hypernym, regardless of x). Roller and Erk (2016) found that under certain conditions, these methods actively learn to infer hypernyms based on separate occurrences of x and y in Hearst patterns (Hearst, 1992). In either case, they only learn whether x and y independently match their corresponding slots in the relation, a limitation which makes them sensitive to the training data (Shwartz et al., 2017; Sanchez and Riedel, 2017).

Non-linearity Levy et al. (2015) claimed that the linear nature of most supervised methods limits their ability to capture the relation between words. They suggested that using support vector machine (SVM) with non-linear kernels slightly mitigates this issue, and proposed KSIM, a custom kernel with multiplicative integration.

Multiplicative Features The element-wise multiplication has been studied by Weeds et al. (2014), but models that operate exclusively on it were not competitive to **Concat** and **Diff** on most tasks. Roller et al. (2014) found that the squared difference, in combination with **Diff**, is useful for hypernymy detection. Nevertheless, little to no work has focused on investigating combinations of representations obtained by concatenating various base representations for the more general task of lexical entailment.

Base representations	Combinations
Only-x $\langle \vec{v_x} \rangle$	**Diff** $\oplus$ **Mult**
Only-y $\langle \vec{v_y} \rangle$	**Diff** $\oplus$ **Sqdiff**
Diff $\langle \vec{v_y} - \vec{v_x} \rangle$	**Sum** $\oplus$ **Mult**
Sum $\langle \vec{v_x} + \vec{v_y} \rangle$	**Sum** $\oplus$ **Sqdiff**
Concat $\langle \vec{v_x} \oplus \vec{v_y} \rangle$	**Concat** $\oplus$ **Mult**
Mult $\langle \vec{v_x} \odot \vec{v_y} \rangle$	**Concat** $\oplus$ **Sqdiff**
Sqdiff $\langle (\vec{v_y} - \vec{v_x}) \odot (\vec{v_y} - \vec{v_x}) \rangle$	

Table 1: Word pair representations.

3 Methodology

We classify each word pair (x, y) to a specific semantic relation that holds for them, from a set of pre-defined relations (i.e., multiclass classification), based on their distributional representations.

3.1 Word Pair Representations

Given a word pair (x, y) and their embeddings $\vec{v_x}, \vec{v_y}$, we consider various compositions as feature vectors for classifiers. Table 1 displays base representations and combination representations, achieved by concatenating two base representations.

3.2 Word Vectors

We used 300-dimensional pre-trained word embeddings, namely, GloVe (Pennington et al., 2014b) containing 1.9M word vectors trained on a corpus of web data from Common Crawl (42B tokens),[1] and Word2vec (Mikolov et al., 2013a,c) containing 3M word vectors trained on a part of Google News dataset (100B tokens).[2] Out-of-vocabulary words were initialized randomly.

3.3 Classifiers

Following previous work (Levy et al., 2015; Roller and Erk, 2016), we trained different types of classifiers for each word-pair representation outlined in Section 3.1, namely, logistic regression with L_2 regularization (LR), SVM with a linear kernel (LIN), and SVM with a Gaussian kernel (RBF). In addition, we trained multi-layer perceptrons with a single hidden layer (MLP). We compare our models against the KSIM model found to be successful in previous work (Levy et al., 2015; Kruszewski et al., 2015). We do not include Roller and Erk (2016)'s model since it focuses only on hypernymy. Hyper-parameters are tuned using grid search, and we report the test performance of the

---

[1] http://nlp.stanford.edu/projects/glove/
[2] http://code.google.com/p/word2vec/

Dataset	Relations	#Instances	#Domains
BLESS	attri (attribute), coord (co-hyponym), event, hyper (hypernymy), mero (meronymy), random	26,554	17
K&H+N	hypo (hypernymy), mero (meronymy), sibl (co-hyponym), false (random)	63,718	3
ROOT09	hyper (hypernymy), coord (co-hyponym), random	12,762	–
EVALution	HasProperty (attribute), synonym, HasA (possession), MadeOf (meronymy), IsA (hypernymy), antonym, PartOf (meronymy)	7,378	–

Table 2: Metadata on the datasets. Relations are mapped to corresponding WordNet relations, if available.

hyper-parameters that performed best on the validation set. Below are more details about the training procedure:

- For LR, the inverse of regularization strength is selected from $\{2^{-1}, 2^1, 2^3, 2^5\}$.

- For LIN, the penalty parameter C of the error term is selected from $\{2^{-5}, 2^{-3}, 2^{-1}, 2^1\}$.

- For RBF, C and γ values are selected from $\{2^1, 2^3, 2^5, 2^7\}$ and $\{2^{-7}, 2^{-5}, 2^{-3}, 2^{-1}\}$, respectively.

- For MLP, the hidden layer size is either 50 or 100, and the learning rate is fixed at 10^{-3}. We use early stopping based on the performance on the validation set. The maximum number of training epochs is 100.

- For KSIM, C and α values are selected from $\{2^{-7}, 2^{-5}, \ldots, 2^7\}$ and $\{0.0, 0.1, \ldots, 1.0\}$, respectively.

3.4 Datasets

We evaluated the methods on four common semantic relation datasets: BLESS (Baroni and Lenci, 2011), K&H+N (Necsulescu et al., 2015), ROOT09 (Santus et al., 2016), and EVALution (Santus et al., 2015). Table 2 provides metadata on the datasets. Most datasets contain word pairs instantiating different, explicitly typed semantic relations, plus a number of unrelated word pairs (*random*). Instances in BLESS and K&H+N are divided into a number of topical domains.[3]

3.5 Evaluation Setup

We consider the following evaluation setups:

Random (RAND) We randomly split each dataset into 70% train, 5% validation and 25% test.

Lexical Split (LEX) In line with recent work (Shwartz et al., 2016), we split each dataset into train, validation and test sets so that each contains a distinct vocabulary. This differs from Levy et al. (2015) who dedicated a subset of the train set for evaluation, allowing the model to memorize when tuning hyper-parameters. We tried to keep the same ratio $70 : 5 : 25$ as in the random setup.

Out-of-domain (OOD) To test whether the methods capture a generic notion of each semantic relation, we test them on a domain that the classifiers have not seen during training. This setup is more realistic than the random and lexical split setups, in which the classifiers can benefit from memorizing verbatim words (random) or regions in the vector space (lexical split) that fit a specific slot of each relation.

Specifically, on BLESS and K&H+N, one domain is held out for testing whilst the classifiers are trained and validated on the remaining domains. This process is repeated using each domain as the test set, and each time, a randomly selected domain among the remaining domains is left out for validation. The average results are reported.

4 Experiments

Table 3 summarizes the best performing base representations and combinations on the test sets across the various datasets and evaluation setups.[4] The results across the datasets vary substantially in some cases due to the differences between the datasets' relations, class balance, and the source from which they were created. For instance, K&H+N is imbalanced between the number of instances across relations and domains. ROOT09 was designed to mitigate the lexical memorization issue by adding negative switched hyponym-hypernym pairs to the dataset, making it an inherently more difficult dataset. EVALution contains a richer set of semantic relations. Overall, the addition of multiplicative features improves upon the performance of the base representations.

Classifiers Multiplicative features substantially boost the performance of linear classifiers. However, the gain from adding multiplicative features

---

[3]We discarded two relations in EVALution with too few instances and did not include its domain information since each word pair can belong to multiple domains at once.

[4]Due to the space limitation, we only show the results obtained with Glove. The trend is similar across the word embeddings.

Setup	Dataset	Linear classifiers (LR, LIN)				Non-linear classifiers (RBF, MLP)				KSIM
		$\vec{v_y}$	Base		Combination	$\vec{v_y}$	Base		Combination	
RAND	BLESS	84.4	LR Concat	83.8	LR Concat $\oplus$ Mult	89.5 (+5.7)	89.3	RBF Concat	94.0	RBF Concat $\oplus$ Mult	94.3 (+0.3)	70.2
	K&H–N	89.1	LR Concat	95.4	LR Concat $\oplus$ SqDiff	96.1 (+0.7)	96.4	RBF Concat	98.6	RBF Concat $\oplus$ Mult	98.6 (0.0)	82.4
	ROOT09	68.5	LIN Sum	65.9	LIN Sum $\oplus$ Mult	84.6 (+18.7)	66.1	RBF Sum	87.3	RBF Sum $\oplus$ SqDiff	88.8 (+1.5)	72.3
	EVALution	49.7	LIN Concat	56.7	LIN Concat $\oplus$ Mult	56.8 (+0.1)	52.1	RBF Concat	61.1	RBF Concat $\oplus$ Mult	60.6 (-0.5)	50.5
LEX	BLESS	69.9	LIN Concat	70.6	LIN Concat $\oplus$ Mult	74.5 (+3.9)	69.8	MLP Concat	63.0	MLP Concat $\oplus$ Mult	73.8 (+10.8)	65.8
	K&H–N	78.3	LIN Sum	74.0	LIN Sum $\oplus$ SqDiff	76.1 (+2.1)	83.2	RBF Sum	82.0	RBF Sum $\oplus$ Mult	81.7 (-0.3)	77.5
	ROOT09	66.7	LR Concat	66.0	LR Concat $\oplus$ Mult	77.9 (+11.9)	64.5	RBF Concat	76.8	RBF Concat $\oplus$ Mult	81.6 (+4.8)	66.7
	EVALution	35.0	LR Concat	37.9	LR Concat $\oplus$ Mult	40.2 (+2.3)	35.5	RBF Concat	43.1	RBF Concat $\oplus$ Mult	44.9 (+1.8)	35.9
OOD	BLESS	70.9	LIN Concat	69.9	LIN Concat $\oplus$ Mult	77.0 (+7.1)	69.9	RBF Diff	78.7	RBF Diff $\oplus$ Mult	81.5 (+2.8)	57.8
	K&H–N	38.5	LIN Concat	38.6	LIN Concat $\oplus$ Mult	39.7 (+1.1)	48.6	MLP Sum	44.7	MLP Sum $\oplus$ Mult	47.9 (+3.2)	48.9

Table 3: Best test performance (F_1) across different datasets and evaluation setups, using `Glove`. The number in brackets indicates the performance gap between the best performing combination and base representation setups.

Vector/ Classifier		RAND							OOD						
		$\vec{v_y}$	Diff	Diff $\oplus$ Mult	Sum	Sum $\oplus$ Mult	Concat	Concat $\oplus$ Mult	$\vec{v_y}$	Diff	Diff $\oplus$ Mult	Sum	Sum $\oplus$ Mult	Concat	Concat $\oplus$ Mult
GloVe	LR	84.4	81.5	87.6 (+6.1)	81.5	87.0 (+5.5)	83.8	89.5 (+5.7)	70.9	64.5	74.7 (+10.2)	59.2	68.9 (+9.7)	69.5	76.5 (+7.0)
	LIN	84.1	81.5	87.7 (+6.2)	81.3	87.2 (+5.9)	83.8	89.2 (+5.4)	70.7	64.6	74.8 (+10.2)	59.3	69.4 (+10.1)	69.9	77.0 (+7.1)
	RBF	89.3	93.8	94.1 (+0.3)	94.4	94.2 (-0.2)	94.0	**94.3 (+0.3)**	67.8	78.7	**81.5 (+2.8)**	65.3	66.4 (+1.1)	69.5	75.7 (+6.2)
	MLP	84.4	87.4	89.2 (+1.8)	87.2	89.9 (+2.7)	90.5	90.5 (0.0)	69.9	67.4	77.7 (+10.3)	57.3	66.1 (+8.8)	71.5	77.3 (+5.8)
Word2vec	LR	83.5	81.0	85.4 (+4.4)	80.0	84.6 (+4.6)	83.6	87.1 (+3.5)	71.2	62.4	69.0 (+6.6)	59.0	65.3 (+6.3)	71.8	**76.1 (+4.3)**
	LIN	83.3	80.8	84.6 (+3.8)	80.4	84.5 (+4.1)	83.3	86.5 (+3.2)	71.5	62.8	69.1 (+6.3)	59.8	65.2 (+5.4)	72.1	76.0 (+3.9)
	RBF	89.1	93.7	93.7 (0.0)	93.7	**93.8 (+0.1)**	93.6	**93.8 (+0.2)**	69.2	75.6	76.0 (+0.4)	64.7	66.3 (+1.6)	71.4	75.3 (+3.9)
	MLP	81.6	81.0	84.6 (+3.6)	79.6	85.2 (+5.6)	81.3	84.7 (+3.4)	70.2	63.4	69.3 (+5.9)	56.2	60.0 (+3.8)	70.5	74.6 (+4.1)

Table 4: Test performance (F_1) on `BLESS` in the RAND and OOD setups, using `Glove` and `Word2vec`.

is smaller when non-linear classifiers are used, since they partially capture such notion of interaction (Levy et al., 2015). Within the same representation, there is a clear preference to non-linear classifiers over linear classifiers.

Evaluation Setup The **Only-y** representation indicates how well a model can perform without considering the relation between x and y (Levy et al., 2015). Indeed, in RAND, this method performs similarly to the others, except on ROOT09, which by design disables lexical memorization. As expected, a general decrease in performance is observed in LEX and OOD, stemming from the methods' inability to benefit from lexical memorization. In these setups, there is a more significant gain from using multiplicative features when non-linear classifiers are used.

Word Pair Representations Among the base representations **Concat** often performed best, while **Mult** seemed to be the preferred multiplicative addition. **Concat** $\oplus$ **Mult** performed consis-

tently well, intuitively because **Concat** captures the typicality of each word in the relation (e.g., if y is a typical hypernym) and **Mult** captures the similarity between the words (where **Concat** alone may suggest that *animal* is a hypernym of *apple*). To take a closer look at the gain from adding **Mult**, Table 4 shows the performance of the various base representations and combinations with **Mult** using different classifiers on `BLESS`.[5]

5 Analysis of Multiplicative Features

We focus the rest of the discussion on the OOD setup, as we believe it is the most challenging setup, forcing methods to consider the relation between x and y. We found that in this setup, all methods performed poorly on K&H+N, likely due to its imbalanced domain and relation distribution. Examining the per-relation F_1 scores, we see that many methods classify all pairs to one relation. Even KSIM, the best performing method in this

---

[5]We also tried $\vec{v_x}$ with multiplicative features but they performed worse.

x	relation	y	similarity	Concat	Concat $\oplus$ Mult
cloak-n	random	good-j	0.195	attribute	random
cloak-n	random	hurl-v	0.161	event	random
cloak-n	random	stop-v	0.186	event	random
coat-n	event	wear-v	0.544	random	event
cloak-n	mero	silk-n	0.381	random	mero
dress-n	attri	feminine-j	0.479	random	attri

Table 5: Example pairs which were incorrectly classified by **Concat** while being correctly classified by **Concat** $\oplus$ **Mult** in BLESS, along with their cosine similarity scores.

setup, classifies pairs as either *hyper* or *random*, effectively only determining if they are related or not. We therefore focus our analysis on BLESS.

To get a better intuition of the contribution of multiplicative features, Table 5 exemplifies pairs that were incorrectly classified by **Concat** (RBF) while correctly classified by **Concat** $\oplus$ **Mult** (RBF), along with their cosine similarity scores. It seems that **Mult** indeed captures the similarity between x and y. While **Concat** sometimes relies on properties of a single word, e.g. classifying an adjective y to the *attribute* relation and a verb y to the *event* relation, adding **Mult** changes the classification of such pairs with low similarity scores to *random*. Conversely, pairs with high similarity scores which were falsely classified as *random* by **Concat** are assigned specific relations by **Concat** $\oplus$ **Mult**.

Interestingly, we found that across domains, there is an almost consistent order of relations with respect to mean intra-pair cosine similarity:

coord	meronym	attribute	event	hypernym	random
0.426	0.323	0.304	0.296	0.279	0.141

Table 6: Mean pairwise cosine similarity in BLESS.

Since the difference between *random* (0.141) and other relations (0.279-0.426) was the most significant, it seems that multiplicative features help distinguishing between related and unrelated pairs. This similarity is possibly also used to distinguish between other relations.

6 Conclusion

We have suggested a cheap way to boost the performance of supervised distributional methods for lexical entailment by integrating multiplicative features into standard word-pair representations. Our results confirm that the multiplicative features boost the performance of linear classifiers, and in strict evaluation setups, also of nonlinear classifiers. We performed an extensive evaluation with different classifiers and evaluation se-

tups, and suggest the out-of-domain evaluation as the most suitable for the task. Directions for future work include investigating other compositions, and designing a neural model that can automatically learn such features.

7 Acknowledgements

We would like to thank Wei Lu for his involvement and advice in the early stage of this project, Stephen Roller and Omer Levy for valuable discussions, and the anonymous reviewers for their insightful comments and suggestions.

Vered is supported in part by an Intel ICRI-CI grant, the Israel Science Foundation grant 1951/17, the German Research Foundation through the German-Israeli Project Cooperation (DIP, grant DA 1600/1-1), the Clore Scholars Programme (2017), and the AI2 Key Scientific Challenges Program (2017).

References

Marco Baroni, Raffaella Bernardi, Ngoc-Quynh Do, and Chung-chieh Shan. 2012. Entailment above the word level in distributional semantics. In *Proceedings of the 13th Conference of the European Chapter of the Association for Computational Linguistics*, pages 23–32, Avignon, France. Association for Computational Linguistics.

Marco Baroni and Alessandro Lenci. 2011. How we blessed distributional semantic evaluation. In *Proceedings of the GEMS 2011 Workshop on GEometrical Models of Natural Language Semantics*, pages 1–10. Association for Computational Linguistics.

Ido Dagan, Dan Roth, Mark Sammons, and Fabio Massimo Zanzotto. 2013. Recognizing textual entailment: Models and applications. *Synthesis Lectures on Human Language Technologies*, 6(4):1–220.

Ruiji Fu, Jiang Guo, Bing Qin, Wanxiang Che, Haifeng Wang, and Ting Liu. 2014. Learning semantic hierarchies via word embeddings. In *Proceedings of the 52nd Annual Meeting of the Association for Computational Linguistics (Volume 1: Long Papers)*, pages 1199–1209, Baltimore, Maryland. Association for Computational Linguistics.

Marti A. Hearst. 1992. Automatic acquisition of hyponyms from large text corpora. In *Proceedings of the 14th Conference on Computational Linguistics - Volume 2*, COLING '92, pages 539–545.

Lili Kotlerman, Ido Dagan, Idan Szpektor, and Maayan Zhitomirsky-geffet. 2010. Directional distributional similarity for lexical inference. *Natural Language Engineering*, 16(4):359–389.

Germn Kruszewski, Denis Paperno, and Marco Baroni. 2015. Deriving boolean structures from distributional vectors. *Transactions of the Association for Computational Linguistics*, 3:375–388.

Omer Levy, Steffen Remus, Chris Biemann, and Ido Dagan. 2015. Do supervised distributional methods really learn lexical inference relations? In *Proceedings of the 2015 Conference of the North American Chapter of the Association for Computational Linguistics: Human Language Technologies*, pages 970–976, Denver, Colorado. Association for Computational Linguistics.

Tomas Mikolov, Kai Chen, Greg Corrado, and Jeffrey Dean. 2013a. Efficient estimation of word representations in vector space. *Proceedings of Workshop at ICLR, 2013*.

Tomas Mikolov, Ilya Sutskever, Kai Chen, Greg S Corrado, and Jeff Dean. 2013b. Distributed representations of words and phrases and their compositionality. In *Advances in neural information processing systems*, pages 3111–3119.

Tomas Mikolov, Ilya Sutskever, Kai Chen, Greg S Corrado, and Jeff Dean. 2013c. Distributed representations of words and phrases and their compositionality. In C. J. C. Burges, L. Bottou, M. Welling, Z. Ghahramani, and K. Q. Weinberger, editors, *Advances in Neural Information Processing Systems 26*, pages 3111–3119. Curran Associates, Inc.

George A. Miller. 1995. Wordnet: A lexical database for english. *Communications of the ACM*, 38(11):39–41.

Silvia Necsulescu, Sara Mendes, David Jurgens, Núria Bel, and Roberto Navigli. 2015. Reading between the lines: Overcoming data sparsity for accurate classification of lexical relationships. In *Proceedings of the Fourth Joint Conference on Lexical and Computational Semantics*, pages 182–192, Denver, Colorado. Association for Computational Linguistics.

Jeffrey Pennington, Richard Socher, and Christopher Manning. 2014a. Glove: Global vectors for word representation. In *Proceedings of the 2014 Conference on Empirical Methods in Natural Language Processing (EMNLP)*, pages 1532–1543. Association for Computational Linguistics.

Jeffrey Pennington, Richard Socher, and Christopher Manning. 2014b. Glove: Global vectors for word representation. In *Proceedings of the 2014 Conference on Empirical Methods in Natural Language Processing (EMNLP)*, pages 1532–1543, Doha, Qatar. Association for Computational Linguistics.

Stephen Roller and Katrin Erk. 2016. Relations such as hypernymy: Identifying and exploiting hearst patterns in distributional vectors for lexical entailment. In *Proceedings of the 2016 Conference on Empirical Methods in Natural Language Processing*, pages 2163–2172, Austin, Texas. Association for Computational Linguistics.

Stephen Roller, Katrin Erk, and Gemma Boleda. 2014. Inclusive yet selective: Supervised distributional hypernymy detection. In *Proceedings of COLING 2014, the 25th International Conference on Computational Linguistics: Technical Papers*, pages 1025–1036, Dublin, Ireland. Dublin City University and Association for Computational Linguistics.

Ivan Sanchez and Sebastian Riedel. 2017. How well can we predict hypernyms from word embeddings? a dataset-centric analysis. In *Proceedings of the 15th Conference of the European Chapter of the Association for Computational Linguistics: Volume 2, Short Papers*, pages 401–407, Valencia, Spain. Association for Computational Linguistics.

Enrico Santus, Alessandro Lenci, Tin-Shing Chiu, Qin Lu, and Chu-Ren Huang. 2016. Nine features in a random forest to learn taxonomical semantic relations. In *Proceedings of the Tenth International Conference on Language Resources and Evaluation (LREC 2016)*, Paris, France.

Enrico Santus, Alessandro Lenci, Qin Lu, and Sabine Schulte im Walde. 2014. Chasing hypernyms in vector spaces with entropy. In *Proceedings of the 14th Conference of the European Chapter of the Association for Computational Linguistics, volume 2: Short Papers*, pages 38–42, Gothenburg, Sweden. Association for Computational Linguistics.

Enrico Santus, Frances Yung, Alessandro Lenci, and Chu-Ren Huang. 2015. Evalution 1.0: an evolving semantic dataset for training and evaluation of distributional semantic models. In *Proceedings of the 4th Workshop on Linked Data in Linguistics (LDL-2015)*, pages 64–69.

Vered Shwartz, Yoav Goldberg, and Ido Dagan. 2016. Improving hypernymy detection with an integrated path-based and distributional method. In *Proceedings of the 54th Annual Meeting of the Association for Computational Linguistics (Volume 1: Long Papers)*, pages 2389–2398, Berlin, Germany. Association for Computational Linguistics.

Vered Shwartz, Enrico Santus, and Dominik Schlechtweg. 2017. Hypernyms under siege: Linguistically-motivated artillery for hypernymy detection. In *Proceedings of the 15th Conference of the European Chapter of the Association for Computational Linguistics: Volume 1, Long Papers,* pages 65–75, Valencia, Spain. Association for Computational Linguistics.

Julie Weeds, Daoud Clarke, Jeremy Reffin, David Weir, and Bill Keller. 2014. Learning to distinguish hypernyms and co-hyponyms. In *Proceedings of COLING 2014, the 25th International Conference on Computational Linguistics: Technical Papers*, pages 2249–2259, Dublin, Ireland. Dublin City University and Association for Computational Linguistics.

Julie Weeds and David Weir. 2003. *Proceedings of the 2003 Conference on Empirical Methods in Natural Language Processing*, chapter A General Framework for Distributional Similarity.

Deep Affix Features Improve Neural Named Entity Recognizers

Vikas Yadav[†], Rebecca Sharp[‡], Steven Bethard[†]
[†]School of Information, [‡] Dept. of Computer Science
University of Arizona, Tucson, AZ, USA
`{vikasy,bsharp,bethard}@email.arizona.edu`

Abstract

We propose a practical model for named entity recognition (NER) that combines word and character-level information with a specific learned representation of the prefixes and suffixes of the word. We apply this approach to multilingual and multi-domain NER and show that it achieves state of the art results on the CoNLL 2002 Spanish and Dutch and CoNLL 2003 German NER datasets, consistently achieving 1.5-2.3 percent over the state of the art without relying on any dictionary features. Additionally, we show improvement on SemEval 2013 task 9.1 DrugNER, achieving state of the art results on the MedLine dataset and the second best results overall (-1.3% from state of the art). We also establish a new benchmark on the I2B2 2010 Clinical NER dataset with 84.70 F-score.

1 Introduction

Named entity recognition (NER), or identifying the specific named entities (eg. person, location, organization etc) in a text, is a precursor to other information extraction tasks such as event extraction. The oldest and perhaps most common approach to NER is based on dictionary lookups, and indeed, when the resources are available, this is very useful (e.g., Uzuner et al., 2011). However, hand-crafting these lexicons is time-consuming and expensive and so these resources are often either unavailable or sparse for many domains and languages.

Neural network (NN) approaches to NER, on the other hand, do not necessitate these resources, and additionally do not require complex feature engineering, which can also be very costly and may not port well from domain to domain and language to language. Commonly, these NN architectures for NER include a learned representation of individual words as well as an encoding of the word's characters. However, neither of these representations makes explicit use of the semantics of sub-word units, i.e., morphemes.

Here we propose a simple neural network architecture that learns a custom representation for affixes, allowing for a richer semantic representation of words and allowing the model to better approximate the meaning of words not seen during training[1]. While a full morphological analysis might bring further benefits, to ease re-implementation we take advantage of the Zipfian distribution of language and focus here on a simple approximation of morphemes as high-frequency prefixes and suffixes. Our approach thus requires no language-specific affix lexicon or morphological tools.

Our contributions are:

1. We propose a simple yet robust extension of current neural NER approaches that allows us to learn a representation for prefixes and suffixes of words. We employ an inexpensive and language-independent method to approximate affixes of a given language using n-gram frequencies. This extension is able to be applied directly to new languages and domains without any additional resource requirements and it allows for a more compositional, and hence richer, representation of words.

2. We demonstrate the utility of including a dedicated representation for affixes. Our model shows as much as a 2.3% F1 improvement over an recurrent neural network model with only words and characters, demonstrating that what our model learns about affixes is complementary to a recurrent layer over characters. We find filtering to high-frequency affixes is essential, as simply using all word-boundary character trigrams degrades performance in some cases.

---

[1]All code required for reproducibility is available at:
`https://github.com/vikas95/Pref_Suff_Span_NN`

*Proceedings of the 7th Joint Conference on Lexical and Computational Semantics (*SEM), pages 167–172*
New Orleans, June 5-6, 2018. ©2018 Association for Computational Linguistics

3. We establish a new state-of-the-art for Spanish, Dutch, and German NER, and MedLine drug NER. Additionally, we achieve near state-of-the-art performance in English NER and DrugBank drug NER, despite using no external dictionaries.

2 Related Work

Recent neural network (RNN) state of the art techniques for NER have proposed a basic two-layered RNN architecture, first over characters of a word and second over the words of a sentence (Ma and Hovy, 2016; Lample et al., 2016). Many variants of such approaches have been introduced, e.g., to model multilingual NER (Gillick et al., 2016) or to incorporate transfer-learning (Yang et al., 2016). Such approaches have typically relied on just the words and characters, though Chiu and Nichols (2016) showed that incorporating dictionary and orthography-based features in such neural networks improves English NER. In other domains such as DrugNER, dictionary features are extensively used for NER (Segura Bedmar et al., 2013; Liu et al., 2015), but relying on these resources limits the languages and domains in which an approach can operate, hence we propose a model that does not use external dictionary resources.

Morphological features were highly effective in named entity recognizers before neural networks became the new state-of-the-art. For example, prefix and suffix features were used by several of the original systems submitted to CoNLL 2002 (Sang, 2002; Cucerzan and Yarowsky, 2002) and 2003 (Tjong Kim Sang and De Meulder, 2003) as well as by systems for NER in biomedical texts (Saha et al., 2009). We have used prefix and suffix features by filtering our trigrams based on frequency, which better approximate the true affixes of the language. We show in Section 5 that our filtered set of trigram affixes performs better than simply adding all beginning and ending trigrams. Bian et al. (2014) incorporated both affix and syllable information into their learned word representations. The Fasttext word embeddings (Bojanowski et al., 2017) represent each word as a bag of n-grams and thus incorporate sub-word information. Here, we provide explicit representation for only the high-frequency n-grams and learn a task-specific semantic representation of them. We show in Section 5 that including all n-grams reduces performance.

Other sub-word units, such as phonemes (from Epitran[2] - a tool for transliterating orthographic text as International Phonetic Alphabet), have also been found to be useful for NER (Bharadwaj et al., 2016). Tkachenko and Simanovsky (2012) explored contributions of various features, including affixes, on the CoNLL 2003 dataset. Additionally, morpheme dictionaries have been effective in developing features for NER tasks in languages like Japanese (Sasano and Kurohashi, 2008), Turkish (Yeniterzi, 2011), Chinese (Gao et al., 2005), and Arabic (Maloney and Niv, 1998). However, such morphological features have not yet been integrated into the new neural network models for NER.

3 Approach

We consider affixes at the beginnings and ends of words as sub-word features for NER. Our base model is similar to Lample et al. (2016) where we apply an long short term memory (LSTM) (Hochreiter and Schmidhuber, 1997) layer over the characters of a word and then concatenate the output with a word embedding to create a word representation that combines both character-level and word-level information. Then, another layer of LSTM is applied over these word representations to make word-by-word predictions at the sentence level. Our proposed model augments this Lample et al. (2016) architecture with a learned representation of the n-gram prefixes and suffixes of each word.

3.1 Collecting Approximate Affixes

We consider all n-gram prefixes and suffixes of words in our training corpus, and select only those whose frequency is above a threshold, T, as frequent prefixes and suffixes should be more likely to behave like true morphemes of a language. To determine the n-gram size, n, and the frequency threshold, T, we experimented with various combinations of $n = 2, 3, 4$ and $T = 10, 15, 20, 25, 50, 75, 100, 150, 200$ by filtering affixes accordingly and evaluating our model (described below) on the CoNLL 2002 and CoNLL 2003 validation data. The best and consistent parameter setting over all 4 languages was $n = 3$ (three character affixes) and $T = 50$ (affixes that occurred at least 50 times in the training data). We have used $n = 3$ and $T = 10$ for DrugNER after getting best performance with this threshold on val-

---

[2] https://pypi.org/project/epitran/0.4/

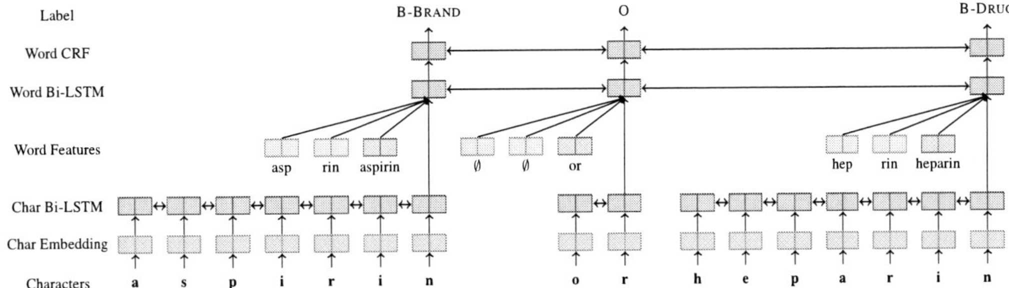

Figure 1: Architecture of our approach. We concatenate a learned representation for our approximated affixes (shown in brown) to a Bi-LSTM encoding of the characters (in blue) and the learned representation of the word itself (in green). This is then passed through another Bi-LSTM and CRF to produce the named entity tags.

idation data and we have used $T = 20$ for I2B2 NER dataset.

3.2 Model and Hyper-parameters

Our proposed model, shown in Figure 1, has separate embeddings for characters, prefixes, suffixes, and words. First, a character embedding maps each of the characters of a word to a dense vector. Then a bidirectional-LSTM (Bi-LSTM) layer is passed over the character embeddings to produce a single vector for each word. The output of this Bi-LSTM layer is concatenated with embeddings for the prefix, suffix, and the word itself, and this concatenation is the final representation of the word. Then the representations of each word in the sentence are passed through another Bi-LSTM layer, followed by a conditional random field (CRF) layer, to produce the begin-inside-outside (BIO) named entity tags.

We randomly initialized character, prefix and suffix affix embeddings. We used Fasttext 300-dimension word embeddings (Bojanowski et al., 2017) for Spanish, Dutch CoNLL 2002 and German language CoNLL 2003. We experimented with 300-dimension Fasttext embeddings and 100-dimension Glove embeddings for CoNLL 2003 English data and saw no appreciable differences ($\pm$ 0.2%). Thus, we report scores with 100-dimension Glove embeddings due to the reduced training time and fewer parameters. We used 300 dimension Pubmed word embeddings (Pyysalo et al., 2013) for DrugNER and I2B2 clinical NER. Across all evaluations in the Section 4, we use the same hyper-parameter settings: Character embedding size = 50; prefix embedding size = 30; suffix embedding size = 30; hidden size for LSTM layer over characters = 25; hidden size for LSTM layer over [prefix, suffix,

word, LSTM(characters)] = 50; maximum number of epochs = 200; early stopping = 30 (i.e., if no improvement in 30 epochs, stop); dropout value = 0.55, applied after concatenating character LSTM representation, word embedding and affix embedding; learning rate (LR) = 0.15; LR decay rate= 0.99; optimizer = SGD; and batch size = 100 (for all datasets except Dutch = 80).

4 Experiments

We evaluate our model across multiple languages and domains.

4.1 Multilingual Datasets

To evaluate on the CoNLL 2002 and 2003 test sets, we trained our model on the combined training + validation data with the general hyper-parameter set from Section 3.2. Since on the validation data, the majority of our models terminated their training between 100 and 150 epochs, we report two models trained on the combined training + validation data: one after 100 epochs, and one after 150 epochs.

We evaluated our model with all the languages in CoNLL 2002 and 2003, as reported in Table 1. Our model achieved state of the art performance on Spanish CoNLL 2002 (Sang, 2002), outperforming Yang et al. (2016) by 1.49%, on Dutch CoNLL 2002, outperforming Yang et al. (2016) by 2.35%, and on German CoNLL 2003, outperforming Lample et al. (2016) by 0.25%. Our reimplementation of Lample et al. (2016) using Fasttext word embedding (Dutch) could also achieve state of the art results on Dutch CoNLL 2002 dataset. This demonstrates the utility of our affix approach, despite its simplicity.

	Dict	ES	NL	EN	DE
Gillick et al. (2016) – Byte-to-Span (BTS)	No	82.95	82.84	86.50	76.22
Yang et al. (2016)	No	85.77	85.19	91.26	-
Luo et al. (2015)	Yes	-	-	91.20	-
Chiu and Nichols (2016)	Yes	-	-	**91.62 ($\pm$0.33)**	-
Ma and Hovy (2016)	No	-	-	91.21	-
Lample et al. (2016)	No	85.75	81.74	90.94	78.76
Our base model (100 Epochs)	No	85.34	85.27	90.24	78.44
Our model (with Affixes) (100 Epochs)	No	86.92	87.50	90.69	78.56
Our model (with Affixes) (150 Epochs)	No	**87.26**	**87.54**	90.86	**79.01**

Table 1: Performance of our model (with and without affixes), using general set of hyper-parameters and previous work on four datasets: CoNLL 2002 Spanish (ES), CoNLL 2002 Dutch (NL), CoNLL 2003 English (EN), and CoNLL 2003 German (DE). Dict indicates whether or not the approach makes use of dictionary lookups.

Model	Dict	ML (80.10%)			DB (19.90%)			Both datasets		
		P	R	F1	P	R	F1	P	R	F1
Rocktäschel et al. (2013)	Yes	60.7	55.8	58.10	88.10	87.5	87.80	73.40	69.80	71.50
Liu et al. (2015) (baseline)	No	-	-	-	-	-	-	78.41	67.78	72.71
Liu et al. (2015) (MedLine emb.)	No	-	-	-	-	-	-	82.70	69.68	75.63
Our model (with affixes)	No	74	64	**69**	89	86	87	81	74	77
Liu et al. (2015) (state of the art)	Yes	78.77	60.21	68.25	90.60	88.82	**89.70**	84.75	72.89	**78.37**

Table 2: DrugNER results with official evaluation script on test dataset consisting of MedLine (ML) (80.10% of the total test data) and DrugBank (DB) test data (19.90 % of the total test data). We report precision (P), recall (R), and F1-score.

4.2 Clinical and Drug NER

To prove the effectiveness of our proposed model in multiple domains, we also evaluated our model on the SemEval 2013 task 9.1 DrugNER dataset (Segura Bedmar et al., 2013) and the I2B2 clinical NER dataset (Uzuner et al., 2011) .

We first converted these datasets into CoNLL BIO format and then evaluated the performance with CoNLL script. We have also evaluated DrugNER performance with the official evaluation script (Segura Bedmar et al., 2013)[3] after converting it to the required format. These results are given in Table 2. The SemEval 2013 task 9.1 DrugNER dataset is composed of two parts: the MedLine test data which consists of 520 sentences and 382 entities, and the DrugBank test data which consists of 145 sentences and 303 entities. We outperform Liu et al. (2015) by 0.75% and Rocktäschel et al. (2013) by 10.90% on MedLine test dataset. On the overall dataset, we outperform Liu et al.'s dictionary-free

model and Rocktäschel et al. by at least 6.50 percent. Again, this shows the benefit from allowing the model to learn a representation of affixes as well as of words and characters. Overall, we achieved the second best result after Liu et al. (2015) but get state of the art results on MedLine test dataset which is 80.10% of the total test data.

For fair comparison with previous work (Unanue et al., 2017) which has re-implemented Lample et al. (2016) model, we tested our model on BIO converted dataset used by Unanue et al. (2017). The results are summarized in table 3

On the I2B2 NER dataset (Uzuner et al., 2011; Unanue et al., 2017) in the BIO format, we evaluated our approach using the CoNLL 2003 evaluation script. Our final model achieves 84.70 F-score, a gain of 3.68% as compared to the base model without affixes (81.02%) and a gain of 0.67 % over the model of Unanue et al. (2017). For fair comparison with Unanue et al. (2017), we provide results on the I2B2 NER dataset in BIO format evaluated with the CoNLL 2003 evaluation script in Table 4.

---

[3]The official evaluation script available on the SemEval 2013 website outputs only whole numbers, despite the shared task reporting results to 2 decimal places.

Model	drug	brand	group	drug_n	ML	drug	brand	group	drug_n	DB	Both
Unanue et al. (2017)	75.57	28.57	64.37	37.19	60.66	91.83	87.27	84.67	0	88.38	-
BASE	72	41.67	75.86	4.88	60.86	89.92	79.12	86.13	0	86.52	72.31
BASE+Affix(10)	79.25	44.44	85.39	32.73	69.71	92.09	86.60	87.41	20	88.93	78.39

Table 3: DrugNER results on test data using CoNLL evaluation script. ML indicates the results for MedLine test data and DB indicates results for DrugBank test data. We have reported F1 scores for each entity type in MedLine, DrugBank and overall dataset (Both). The last column (Both) provides performance on the the combined dataset.

Model	Problem			Test			Treatment		
	P	R	F1	P	R	F1	P	R	F1
Unanue et al. (2017)	81.29	83.62	82.44	84.74	85.01	84.87	83.36	83.55	83.46
Base Model	82.45	77.88	80.10	87.24	77.96	82.34	85.53	76.97	81.02
Base+Affix(20)	84.35	84.27	84.31	87.37	84.34	85.82	85.73	82.58	84.13

Table 4: Performance on I2B2 2010 NER (Uzuner et al., 2011) test data [5] using CoNLL evaluation script. We have reported precision (P), recall (R), and F1-score.

5 Analysis

To better understand the performance of our model, we conducted several analyses on the English CoNLL 2003 dataset.

To determine if the performance gains were truly due to the affix embeddings, and not simply due to having more model parameters, we re-ran our base model (without affixes), increasing the character embeddings from 25 to 55 to match the increase of 30 of our affix embeddings. This model's F-score (90.28%) was similar to the original base model (90.24%), and was more than a half a point below our model with affixes (90.86%).

To determine the contribution of filtering our affixes based on frequency (as compared to simply using all word-boundary n-grams) we ran our model with the full set of affixes found in training. The performance without filtering (89.87% F1) was even lower than the base model without affixes (90.24% F1), which demonstrates that filtering based on frequency is beneficial for affix selection.

6 Conclusion

Our results across multiple languages and domains show that sub-word features such as prefixes and suffixes are complementary to character and word-level information. Our straight-forward and language-independent approach shows performance gains compared to other neural systems for NER, achieving a new state of the art on Spanish, Dutch, and German NER as well as the MedLine portion of DrugNER, despite our lack of dictionary resources. Additionally, we also achieve 3.67% improvement in the I2B2 clinical NER dataset which points towards potential applications in biomedical NER. While our model proposes a very simple idea of using filtered affixes as an approximation of morphemes, we suggest there are further gains to be had with better methods for deriving true morphemes (e.g., the supervised neural model of Luong et al., 2013). We leave this exploration to future work.

References

Akash Bharadwaj, David R. Mortensen, Chris Dyer, and Carlos de Juan Carbonell. 2016. Phonologically aware neural model for named entity recognition in low resource transfer settings. In *EMNLP*.

Jiang Bian, Bin Gao, and Tie-Yan Liu. 2014. Knowledge-powered deep learning for word embedding. In *Joint European Conference on Machine Learning and Knowledge Discovery in Databases*. Springer, pages 132–148.

Piotr Bojanowski, Edouard Grave, Armand Joulin, and Tomas Mikolov. 2017. Enriching word vectors with subword information. *Transactions of the Association for Computational Linguistics* 5:135–146.

Jason Chiu and Eric Nichols. 2016. Named entity recognition with bidirectional LSTM-CNNs. *Transactions of the Association for Computational Linguistics* 4:357–370.

Silviu Cucerzan and David Yarowsky. 2002. Language independent ner using a unified model of internal and contextual evidence. In *proceedings of the 6th conference on Natural language learning-Volume 20*. Association for Computational Linguistics, pages 1–4.

Jianfeng Gao, Mu Li, Andi Wu, and Chang-Ning Huang. 2005. Chinese word segmentation and named entity recognition: A pragmatic approach. *Computational Linguistics* 31(4):531–574.

Daniel Gillick, Cliff Brunk, Oriol Vinyals, and Amarnag Subramanya. 2016. Multilingual language processing from bytes. In *HLT-NAACL*.

Sepp Hochreiter and Jürgen Schmidhuber. 1997. Long short-term memory. *Neural computation* 9(8):1735–1780.

Guillaume Lample, Miguel Ballesteros, Sandeep Subramanian, Kazuya Kawakami, and Chris Dyer. 2016. Neural architectures for named entity recognition. In *Proceedings of the 2016 Conference of the North American Chapter of the Association for Computational Linguistics: Human Language Technologies*. Association for Computational Linguistics, pages 260–270.

Shengyu Liu, Buzhou Tang, Qingcai Chen, and Xiaolong Wang. 2015. Effects of semantic features on machine learning-based drug name recognition systems: word embeddings vs. manually constructed dictionaries. *Information* 6(4):848–865.

Gang Luo, Xiaojiang Huang, Chin-Yew Lin, and Zaiqing Nie. 2015. Joint entity recognition and disambiguation. In *Proceedings of the 2015 Conference on Empirical Methods in Natural Language Processing*. pages 879–888.

Thang Luong, Richard Socher, and Christopher D Manning. 2013. Better word representations with recursive neural networks for morphology. In *CoNLL*. pages 104–113.

Xuezhe Ma and Eduard Hovy. 2016. End-to-end sequence labeling via bi-directional LSTM-CNNs-CRF. In *Proceedings of the 54th Annual Meeting of the Association for Computational Linguistics*. Association for Computational Linguistics, Berlin, Germany, pages 1064–1074.

John Maloney and Michael Niv. 1998. Tagarab: a fast, accurate arabic name recognizer using high-precision morphological analysis. In *Proceedings of the Workshop on Computational Approaches to Semitic Languages*. Association for Computational Linguistics, pages 8–15.

Sampo Pyysalo, Filip Ginter, Hans Moen, Tapio Salakoski, and Sophia Ananiadou. 2013. Distributional semantics resources for biomedical text processing. In *Languages in Biology and medicine*. LBM.

Tim Rocktäschel, Torsten Huber, Michael Weidlich, and Ulf Leser. 2013. Wbi-ner: The impact of domain-specific features on the performance of identifying and classifying mentions of drugs. In *SemEval@ NAACL-HLT*. pages 356–363.

Sujan Kumar Saha, Sudeshna Sarkar, and Pabitra Mitra. 2009. Feature selection techniques for maximum entropy based biomedical named entity recognition.

Journal of Biomedical Informatics 42(5):905 – 911. Biomedical Natural Language Processing.

Erik F Tjong Kim Sang. 2002. Introduction to the CoNLL-2002 shared task: language-independent named entity recognition, proceedings of the 6th conference on natural language learning. *August* 31:1–4.

Ryohei Sasano and Sadao Kurohashi. 2008. Japanese named entity recognition using structural natural language processing. In *IJCNLP*. pages 607–612.

Isabel Segura Bedmar, Paloma Martínez, and María Herrero Zazo. 2013. Semeval-2013 task 9: Extraction of drug-drug interactions from biomedical texts (ddiextraction 2013). Association for Computational Linguistics.

Erik F Tjong Kim Sang and Fien De Meulder. 2003. Introduction to the CoNLL-2003 shared task: Language-independent named entity recognition. In *Proceedings of the seventh conference on Natural language learning at HLT-NAACL 2003-Volume 4*. Association for Computational Linguistics, pages 142–147.

Maksim Tkachenko and Andrey Simanovsky. 2012. Named entity recognition: Exploring features. In *KONVENS*. pages 118–127.

Iñigo Jauregi Unanue, Ehsan Zare Borzeshi, and Massimo Piccardi. 2017. Recurrent neural networks with specialized word embeddings for health-domain named-entity recognition. *Journal of biomedical informatics* 76:102–109.

Özlem Uzuner, Brett R South, Shuying Shen, and Scott L DuVall. 2011. 2010 i2b2/va challenge on concepts, assertions, and relations in clinical text. *Journal of the American Medical Informatics Association* 18(5):552–556.

Zhilin Yang, Ruslan Salakhutdinov, and William W. Cohen. 2016. Transfer learning for sequence tagging with hierarchical recurrent networks. *CoRR* abs/1703.06345.

Reyyan Yeniterzi. 2011. Exploiting morphology in Turkish named entity recognition system. In *Proceedings of the ACL 2011 Student Session*. Association for Computational Linguistics, pages 105–110.

Fine-grained Entity Typing through Increased Discourse Context and Adaptive Classification Thresholds

Sheng Zhang
Johns Hopkins University
zsheng2@jhu.edu

Kevin Duh
Johns Hopkins University
kevinduh@cs.jhu.edu

Benjamin Van Durme
Johns Hopkins University
vandurme@cs.jhu.edu

Abstract

Fine-grained entity typing is the task of assigning fine-grained semantic types to entity mentions. We propose a neural architecture which learns a distributional semantic representation that leverages a greater amount of semantic context – both document and sentence level information – than prior work. We find that additional context improves performance, with further improvements gained by utilizing adaptive classification thresholds. Experiments show that our approach without reliance on hand-crafted features achieves the state-of-the-art results on three benchmark datasets.

1 Introduction

Named entity typing is the task of detecting the type (e.g., *person*, *location*, or *organization*) of a named entity in natural language text. Entity type information has shown to be useful in natural language tasks such as question answering (Lee et al., 2006), knowledge-base population (Carlson et al., 2010; Mitchell et al., 2015), and co-reference resolution (Recasens et al., 2013). Motivated by its application to downstream tasks, recent work on entity typing has moved beyond standard coarse types towards finer-grained semantic types with richer ontologies (Lee et al., 2006; Ling and Weld, 2012; Yosef et al., 2012; Gillick et al., 2014; Del Corro et al., 2015). Rather than assuming an entity can be uniquely categorized into a single type, the task has been approached as a multi-label classification problem: e.g., in "... *became a top seller ... Monopoly is played in 114 countries. ...*" (Figure 1), "*Monopoly*" is considered both a *game* as well as a *product*.

The state-of-the-art approach (Shimaoka et al., 2017) for fine-grained entity typing employs an attentive neural architecture to learn representations of the entity mention as well as its context. These representations are then combined

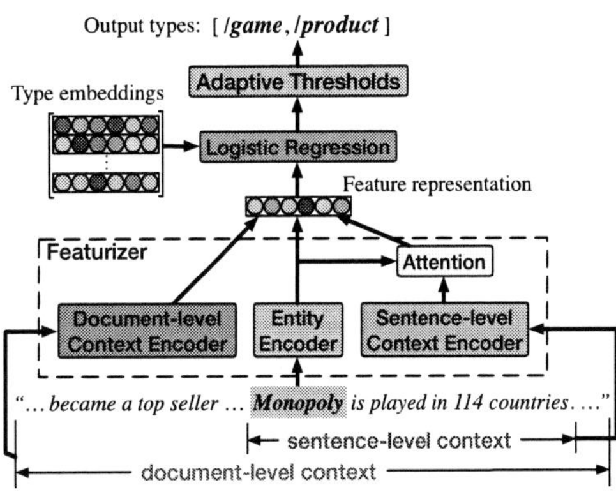

Figure 1: Neural architecture for predicting the types of entity mention "*Monopoly*" in the text "*... became a top seller ... Monopoly is played in 114 countries. ...*". Part of document-level context is omitted.

with hand-crafted features (e.g., lexical and syntactic features), and fed into a linear classifier with a fixed threshold. While this approach outperforms previous approaches which only use sparse binary features (Ling and Weld, 2012; Gillick et al., 2014) or distributed representations (Yogatama et al., 2015), it has a few drawbacks: (1) the representations of left and right contexts are learnt independently, ignoring their mutual connection; (2) the attention on context is computed solely upon the context, considering no alignment to the entity; (3) document-level contexts which could be useful in classification are not exploited; and (4) hand-crafted features heavily rely on system or human annotations.

To overcome these drawbacks, we propose a neural architecture (Figure 1) which learns more context-aware representations by using a better attention mechanism and taking advantage of semantic discourse information available in both the document as well as sentence-level contexts. Fur-

173

*Proceedings of the 7th Joint Conference on Lexical and Computational Semantics (*SEM)*, pages 173–179
New Orleans, June 5-6, 2018. ©2018 Association for Computational Linguistics

ther, we find that adaptive classification thresholds leads to further improvements. Experiments demonstrate that our approach, without any reliance on hand-crafted features, outperforms prior work on three benchmark datasets.

2 Model

Fine-grained entity typing is considered a multi-label classification problem: Each entity e in the text x is assigned a set of types T^* drawn from the fine-grained type set $\mathcal{T}$. The goal of this task is to predict, given entity e and its context x, the assignment of types to the entity. This assignment can be represented by a binary vector $y \in \{1, 0\}^{|\mathcal{T}|}$ where $|\mathcal{T}|$ is the size of $\mathcal{T}$. $y_t = 1$ iff the entity is assigned type $t \in \mathcal{T}$.

2.1 General Model

Given a type embedding vector w_t and a featurizer φ that takes entity e and its context x, we employ the logistic regression (as shown in Figure 1) to model the probability of e assigned t (i.e., $y_t = 1$)

$$P(y_t = 1) = \frac{1}{1 + \exp\left(-w_t^\mathsf{T} \varphi(e, x)\right)}, \quad (1)$$

and we seek to learn a type embedding matrix $W = [w_1, \ldots, w_{|\mathcal{T}|}]$ and a featurizer φ such that

$$T^* = \underset{T}{\mathrm{argmax}} \prod_{t \in T} P(y_t = 1) \cdot \prod_{t \notin T} P(y_t = 0). \quad (2)$$

At inference, the predicted type set $\hat{T}$ assigned to entity e is carried out by

$$\hat{T} = \{t \in \mathcal{T} : P(y_t = 1) \geq r_t\}, \quad (3)$$

with r_t the threshold for predicting e has type t.

2.2 Featurizer

As shown in Figure 1, featurizer φ in our model contains three encoders which encode entity e and its context x into feature vectors, and we consider both *sentence-level* context x_s and *document-level* context x_d in contrast to prior work which only takes *sentence-level* context (Gillick et al., 2014; Shimaoka et al., 2017). [1]

---

[1] Document-level context has also been exploited in Yaghoobzadeh and Schütze (2015); Yang et al. (2016); Karn et al. (2017); Gupta et al. (2017).

The output of featurizer φ is the concatenation of these feature vectors:

$$\varphi(e, x) = \begin{bmatrix} f(e) \\ g_s(x_s, e) \\ g_d(x_d) \end{bmatrix}. \quad (4)$$

We define the computation of these feature vectors in the followings.

Entity Encoder: The entity encoder f computes the average of all the embeddings of tokens in entity e.

Sentence-level Context Encoder: The encoder g_s for sentence-level context x_s employs a single bi-directional RNN to encode x_s. Formally, let the tokens in x_s be $x_s^1, \ldots, x_s^n$. The hidden state h_i for token x_s^i is a concatenation of a left-to-right hidden state $\overrightarrow{h}_i$ and a right-to-left hidden state $\overleftarrow{h}_i$,

$$h_i = \begin{bmatrix} \overrightarrow{h}_i \\ \overleftarrow{h}_i \end{bmatrix} = \begin{bmatrix} \overrightarrow{f}(x_s^i, \overrightarrow{h}_{i-1}) \\ \overleftarrow{f}(x_s^i, \overleftarrow{h}_{i+1}) \end{bmatrix}, \quad (5)$$

where $\overrightarrow{f}$ and $\overleftarrow{f}$ are L-layer stacked LSTMs units (Hochreiter and Schmidhuber, 1997). This is different from Shimaoka et al. (2017) who use two separate bi-directional RNNs for context on each side of the entity mention.

Attention: The feature representation for x_s is a weighted sum of the hidden states: $g_s(x_s, e) = \sum_{i=1}^n a_i h_i$, where a_i is the attention to hidden state h_i. We employ the dot-product attention (Luong et al., 2015). It computes attention based on the alignment between the entity and its context:

$$a_i = \frac{\exp\left(h_i^\mathsf{T} W_a f(e)\right)}{\sum_{j=1}^n \exp\left(h_j^\mathsf{T} W_a f(e)\right)}, \quad (6)$$

where W_a is the weight matrix. The dot-product attention differs from the self attention (Shimaoka et al., 2017) which only considers the context.

Document-level Context Encoder: The encoder g_d for document-level context x_d is a multi-layer perceptron:

$$g_d(x_d) = \mathrm{relu}(W_{d_1} \tanh(W_{d_2} \mathrm{DM}(x_d))), \quad (7)$$

where DM is a pretrained distributed memory model (Le and Mikolov, 2014) which converts the document-level context into a distributed representation. W_{d_1} and W_{d_2} are weight matrices.

2.3 Adaptive Thresholds

In prior work, a fixed threshold ($r_t = 0.5$) is used for classification of all types (Ling and Weld, 2012; Shimaoka et al., 2017). We instead assign a different threshold to each type that is optimized to maximize the overall strict F_1 on the dev set. We show the definition of strict F_1 in Section 3.1.

3 Experiments

We conduct experiments on three publicly available datasets.[2] Table 1 shows the statistics of these datasets.

OntoNotes: Gillick et al. (2014) sampled sentences from OntoNotes (Weischedel et al., 2011) and annotated entities in these sentences using 89 types. We use the same train/dev/test splits in Shimaoka et al. (2017). Document-level contexts are retrieved from the original OntoNotes corpus.

BBN: Weischedel and Brunstein (2005) annotated entities in Wall Street Journal using 93 types. We use the train/test splits in Ren et al. (2016b) and randomly hold out 2,000 pairs for dev. Document contexts are retrieved from the original corpus.

FIGER: Ling and Weld (2012) sampled sentences from 780k Wikipedia articles and 434 news reports to form the train and test data respectively, and annotated entities using 113 types. The splits we use are the same in Shimaoka et al. (2017).

	Train	**Dev**	**Test**	**Types**
OntoNotes	251,039	2,202	8,963	89
BBN	84,078	2,000	13,766	93
FIGER	2,000,000	10,000	563	113

Table 1: Statistics of the datasets.

3.1 Metrics

We adopt the metrics used in Ling and Weld (2012) where results are evaluated via strict, loose macro, loose micro F_1 scores. For the i-th instance, let the predicted type set be $\hat{T}_i$, and the reference type set T_i. The precision (P) and recall (R) for each metric are computed as follow.

Strict:

$$P = R = \frac{1}{N} \sum_{i=1}^{N} \delta(\hat{T}_i = T_i)$$

Loose Macro:

$$P = \frac{1}{N} \sum_{i=1}^{N} \frac{|\hat{T}_i \cap T_i|}{|\hat{T}_i|}$$

$$R = \frac{1}{N} \sum_{i=1}^{N} \frac{|\hat{T}_i \cap T_i|}{|T_i|}$$

Loose Micro:

$$P = \frac{\sum_{i=1}^{N} |\hat{T}_i \cap T_i|}{\sum_{i=1}^{N} |\hat{T}_i|}$$

$$R = \frac{\sum_{i=1}^{N} |\hat{T}_i \cap T_i|}{\sum_{i=1}^{N} |T_i|}$$

3.2 Hyperparameters

We use open-source GloVe vectors (Pennington et al., 2014) trained on Common Crawl 840B with 300 dimensions to initialize word embeddings used in all encoders. All weight parameters are sampled from $\mathcal{U}(-0.01, 0.01)$. The encoder for sentence-level context is a 2-layer bidirectional RNN with 200 hidden units. The DM output size is 50. Sizes of W_a, W_{d_1} and W_{d_2} are 200×300, 70×50, and 50×70 respectively. Adam optimizer (Kingma and Ba, 2014) and mini-batch gradient is used for optimization. Batch size is 200. Dropout (rate=0.5) is applied to three feature functions. To avoid overfitting, we choose models which yield the best strict F_1 on dev sets.

3.3 Results

We compare experimental results of our approach with previous approaches[3], and study contribution of our base model architecture, document-level contexts and adaptive thresholds via ablation. To ensure our findings are reliable, we run each experiment twice and report the average performance.

Overall, our approach significantly increases the state-of-the-art macro F_1 on both OntoNotes and BBN datasets.

On OntoNotes (Table 3), our approach improves the state of the art across all three metrics. Note that (1) without adaptive thresholds or document-level contexts, our approach still outperforms other approaches on macro F_1 and micro F_1; (2) adding hand-crafted features (Shimaoka et al., 2017) does not improve the performance.

---

[2] We made the source code and data publicly available at `https://github.com/sheng-z/figet`.

[3] For PLE (Ren et al., 2016b), we were unable to replicate the performance benefits reported in their work, so we report the results after running their codebase.

ID	Sentence	Gold	Prediction
A	*... Canada's declining crude output, combined with ... will help intensify U.S. reliance on oil from overseas. ...*	/other	/other /other/health /other/health/treatment
B	*Bozell joins Backer Spielvogel Bates and Ogilvy Group as U.S. agencies with interests in Korean agencies.*	/organization /organization/company	/organization /organization/company

Table 2: Examples showing the improvement brought by document-level contexts and dot-product attention. Entities are shown in the green box. The gray boxes visualize attention weights (darkness) on context tokens.

Approach	Strict	Macro	Micro
BINARY(Gillick et al., 2014)	N/A	N/A	70.01
KWSABIE(Yogatama et al., 2015)	N/A	N/A	72.98
PLE(Ren et al., 2016b)	51.61	67.39	62.38
Ma et al. (2016)	49.30	68.23	61.27
AFET(Ren et al., 2016a)	55.10	71.10	64.70
FNET(Abhishek et al., 2017)	52.20	68.50	63.30
NEURAL(Shimaoka et al., 2017)	51.74	70.98	64.91
w/o Hand-crafted features	47.15	65.53	58.25
OUR APPROACH	**55.52**	**73.33**	**67.61**
w/o Adaptive thresholds	53.49	73.11	66.78
w/o Document-level contexts	53.17	72.14	66.51
w/ Hand-crafted features	54.40	73.13	66.89

Table 3: Results on the OntoNotes dataset.

Approach	Strict	Macro	Micro
KWSABIE(Yogatama et al., 2015)	N/A	N/A	72.25
Attentive(Shimaoka et al., 2016)	58.97	77.96	74.94
FNET(Abhishek et al., 2017)	65.80	81.20	77.40
Ling and Weld (2012)	52.30	69.90	69.30
PLE(Ren et al., 2016b)	49.44	68.75	64.54
Ma et al. (2016)	53.54	68.06	66.53
AFET(Ren et al., 2016a)	53.30	69.30	66.40
NEURAL(Shimaoka et al., 2017)	59.68	**78.97**	75.36
w/o Hand-crafted features	54.53	74.76	71.58
OUR APPROACH	**60.23**	78.67	**75.52**
w/o Adaptive thresholds	60.05	78.50	75.39
w/ Hand-crafted features	60.11	78.54	75.33

Table 5: Results on the FIGER dataset.

This indicates the benefits of our proposed model architecture for learning fine-grained entity typing, which is discussed in detail in Section 3.4; and (3) BINARY and KWASIBIE were trained on a different dataset, so their results are not directly comparable.

Approach	Strict	Macro	Micro
PLE(Ren et al., 2016b)	49.44	68.75	64.54
Ma et al. (2016)	**70.43**	75.78	76.50
AFET(Ren et al., 2016a)	67.00	72.70	73.50
FNET(Abhishek et al., 2017)	60.40	74.10	75.70
OUR APPROACH	60.87	**77.75**	**76.94**
w/o Adaptive thresholds	58.47	75.84	75.03
w/o Document-level contexts	58.12	75.65	75.11

Table 4: Results on the BBN dataset.

On BBN (Table 4), while Ma et al. (2016)'s label embedding algorithm holds the best strict F_1, our approach notably improves both macro F_1 and micro F_1.[4] The performance drops to a competitive level with other approaches if adaptive thresholds or document-level contexts are removed.

On FIGER (Table 5) where no document-level context is currently available, our proposed approach still achieves the state-of-the-art strict and micro F_1. If compared with the ablation variant of the NEURAL approach, i.e., w/o hand-crafted features, our approach gains significant improvement. We notice that removing adaptive thresholds only causes a small performance drop; this is likely because the train and test splits of FIGER are from different sources, and adaptive thresholds are not generalized well enough to the test data. KWASIBIE, Attentive and FNET were trained on a different dataset, so their results are not directly comparable.

3.4 Analysis

Table 2 shows examples illustrating the benefits brought by our proposed approach. Example A illustrates that sentence-level context sometimes is not informative enough, and attention, though already placed on the head verbs, can be misleading. Including document-level context (i.e., *"Canada's declining crude output"* in this case) helps preclude wrong predictions (i.e., /other/health and /other/health/treatment). Example B shows that the semantic patterns learnt by our attention mechanism help make the correct prediction. As we observe in Table 3 and Table 5, adding hand-crafted features to our approach does not im-

---

[4] Integrating label embedding into our proposed approach is an avenue for future work.

prove the results. One possible explanation is that hand-crafted features are mostly about syntactic-head or topic information, and such information are already covered by our attention mechanism and document-level contexts as shown in Table 2. Compared to hand-crafted features that heavily rely on system or human annotations, attention mechanism requires significantly less supervision, and document-level or paragraph-level contexts are much easier to get.

Through experiments, we observe no improvement by encoding type hierarchical information (Shimaoka et al., 2017).[5] To explain this, we compute cosine similarity between each pair of fine-grained types based on the type embeddings learned by our model, i.e., w_t in Eq. (1). Table 6 shows several types and their closest types: these types do not always share coarse-grained types with their closest types, but they often co-occur in the same context.

Type	Closest Types
/other/event/accident	/location/transit/railway /location/transit/bridge
/person/artist/music	/organization/music /person/artist/director
/other/product/mobile_phone	/location/transit/railway /other/product/computer
/other/event/sports_event	/location/transit/railway /other/event
/other/product/car	/organization/transit /other/product

Table 6: Type similarity.

4 Conclusion

We propose a new approach for fine-grained entity typing. The contributions are: (1) we propose a neural architecture which learns a distributional semantic representation that leverage both document and sentence level information, (2) we find that context increased with document-level information improves performance, and (3) we utilize adaptive classification thresholds to further boost the performance. Experiments show our approach achieves new state-of-the-art results on three benchmarks.

---

[5]The type embedding matrix W for the logistic regression is replaced by the product of a learnt weight matrix V and the constant sparse binary matrix S which encodes type hierarchical information.

Acknowledgments

This work was supported in part by the JHU Human Language Technology Center of Excellence (HLTCOE), and DARPA LORELEI. The U.S. Government is authorized to reproduce and distribute reprints for Governmental purposes. The views and conclusions contained in this publication are those of the authors and should not be interpreted as representing official policies or endorsements of DARPA or the U.S. Government.

References

Abhishek Abhishek, Ashish Anand, and Amit Awekar. 2017. Fine-grained entity type classification by jointly learning representations and label embeddings. In *Proceedings of the 15th Conference of the European Chapter of the Association for Computational Linguistics: Volume 1, Long Papers*, pages 797–807, Valencia, Spain. Association for Computational Linguistics.

Andrew Carlson, Justin Betteridge, Richard C Wang, Estevam R Hruschka Jr, and Tom M Mitchell. 2010. Coupled semi-supervised learning for information extraction. In *Proceedings of the third ACM international conference on Web search and data mining*, pages 101–110. ACM.

Luciano Del Corro, Abdalghani Abujabal, Rainer Gemulla, and Gerhard Weikum. 2015. Finet: Context-aware fine-grained named entity typing. In *Proceedings of the 2015 Conference on Empirical Methods in Natural Language Processing*, pages 868–878, Lisbon, Portugal. Association for Computational Linguistics.

Dan Gillick, Nevena Lazic, Kuzman Ganchev, Jesse Kirchner, and David Huynh. 2014. Context-dependent fine-grained entity type tagging. *arXiv preprint arXiv:1412.1820*.

Nitish Gupta, Sameer Singh, and Dan Roth. 2017. Entity linking via joint encoding of types, descriptions, and context. In *Proceedings of the 2017 Conference on Empirical Methods in Natural Language Processing*, pages 2681–2690, Copenhagen, Denmark. Association for Computational Linguistics.

Sepp Hochreiter and Jürgen Schmidhuber. 1997. Long short-term memory. *Neural computation*, 9(8):1735–1780.

Sanjeev Karn, Ulli Waltinger, and Hinrich Schütze. 2017. End-to-end trainable attentive decoder for hierarchical entity classification. In *Proceedings of the 15th Conference of the European Chapter of the Association for Computational Linguistics: Volume 2, Short Papers*, pages 752–758, Valencia, Spain. Association for Computational Linguistics.

Diederik Kingma and Jimmy Ba. 2014. Adam: A method for stochastic optimization. *arXiv preprint arXiv:1412.6980*.

Quoc Le and Tomas Mikolov. 2014. Distributed representations of sentences and documents. In *Proceedings of the 31st International Conference on Machine Learning (ICML-14)*, pages 1188–1196.

Changki Lee, Yi-Gyu Hwang, Hyo-Jung Oh, Soojong Lim, Jeong Heo, Chung-Hee Lee, Hyeon-Jin Kim, Ji-Hyun Wang, and Myung-Gil Jang. 2006. *Fine-Grained Named Entity Recognition Using Conditional Random Fields for Question Answering*. Springer Berlin Heidelberg, Berlin, Heidelberg.

Xiao Ling and Daniel S. Weld. 2012. Fine-grained entity recognition. In *Proceedings of the Twenty-Sixth AAAI Conference on Artificial Intelligence*, AAAI'12, pages 94–100. AAAI Press.

Minh-Thang Luong, Hieu Pham, and Christopher D. Manning. 2015. Effective approaches to attention-based neural machine translation. In *Proceedings of the 2015 Conference on Empirical Methods in Natural Language Processing*, pages 1412–1421, Lisbon, Portugal. Association for Computational Linguistics.

Yukun Ma, Erik Cambria, and SA GAO. 2016. Label embedding for zero-shot fine-grained named entity typing. In *Proceedings of COLING 2016, the 26th International Conference on Computational Linguistics: Technical Papers*, pages 171–180. The COLING 2016 Organizing Committee.

Tom M. Mitchell, William W. Cohen, Estevam R. Hruschka Jr., Partha Pratim Talukdar, Justin Betteridge, Andrew Carlson, Bhavana Dalvi Mishra, Matthew Gardner, Bryan Kisiel, Jayant Krishnamurthy, Ni Lao, Kathryn Mazaitis, Thahir Mohamed, Ndapandula Nakashole, Emmanouil Antonios Platanios, Alan Ritter, Mehdi Samadi, Burr Settles, Richard C. Wang, Derry Tanti Wijaya, Abhinav Gupta, Xinlei Chen, Abulhair Saparov, Malcolm Greaves, and Joel Welling. 2015. Never-ending learning. In *Proceedings of the Twenty-Ninth AAAI Conference on Artificial Intelligence, January 25-30, 2015, Austin, Texas, USA.*, pages 2302–2310.

Jeffrey Pennington, Richard Socher, and Christopher D. Manning. 2014. Glove: Global vectors for word representation. In *Empirical Methods in Natural Language Processing (EMNLP)*, pages 1532–1543.

Marta Recasens, Marie-Catherine de Marneffe, and Christopher Potts. 2013. The life and death of discourse entities: Identifying singleton mentions. In *Proceedings of the 2013 Conference of the North American Chapter of the Association for Computational Linguistics: Human Language Technologies*, pages 627–633, Atlanta, Georgia. Association for Computational Linguistics.

Xiang Ren, Wenqi He, Meng Qu, Lifu Huang, Heng Ji, and Jiawei Han. 2016a. Afet: Automatic fine-grained entity typing by hierarchical partial-label embedding. In *Proceedings of the 2016 Conference on Empirical Methods in Natural Language Processing*, pages 1369–1378, Austin, Texas. Association for Computational Linguistics.

Xiang Ren, Wenqi He, Meng Qu, Clare R. Voss, Heng Ji, and Jiawei Han. 2016b. Label noise reduction in entity typing by heterogeneous partial-label embedding. In *Proceedings of the 22Nd ACM SIGKDD International Conference on Knowledge Discovery and Data Mining*, KDD '16, pages 1825–1834, New York, NY, USA. ACM.

Sonse Shimaoka, Pontus Stenetorp, Kentaro Inui, and Sebastian Riedel. 2016. An attentive neural architecture for fine-grained entity type classification. In *Proceedings of the 5th Workshop on Automated Knowledge Base Construction*, pages 69–74, San Diego, CA. Association for Computational Linguistics.

Sonse Shimaoka, Pontus Stenetorp, Kentaro Inui, and Sebastian Riedel. 2017. Neural architectures for fine-grained entity type classification. In *Proceedings of the 15th Conference of the European Chapter of the Association for Computational Linguistics: Volume 1, Long Papers*, pages 1271–1280, Valencia, Spain. Association for Computational Linguistics.

Ralph Weischedel and Ada Brunstein. 2005. Bbn pronoun coreference and entity type corpus. *Linguistic Data Consortium, Philadelphia*, 112.

Ralph Weischedel, Eduard Hovy, Mitchell Marcus, Martha Palmer, Robert Belvin, Sameer Pradhan, Lance Ramshaw, and Nianwen Xue. 2011. Ontonotes: A large training corpus for enhanced processing. *Handbook of Natural Language Processing and Machine Translation. Springer.*

Yadollah Yaghoobzadeh and Hinrich Schütze. 2015. Corpus-level fine-grained entity typing using contextual information. In *Proceedings of the 2015 Conference on Empirical Methods in Natural Language Processing*, pages 715–725, Lisbon, Portugal. Association for Computational Linguistics.

Zichao Yang, Diyi Yang, Chris Dyer, Xiaodong He, Alex Smola, and Eduard Hovy. 2016. Hierarchical attention networks for document classification. In *Proceedings of the 2016 Conference of the North American Chapter of the Association for Computational Linguistics: Human Language Technologies*, pages 1480–1489, San Diego, California. Association for Computational Linguistics.

Dani Yogatama, Daniel Gillick, and Nevena Lazic. 2015. Embedding methods for fine grained entity type classification. In *Proceedings of the 53rd Annual Meeting of the Association for Computational Linguistics and the 7th International Joint Conference on Natural Language Processing (Volume 2:*

Short Papers), pages 291–296, Beijing, China. Association for Computational Linguistics.

Mohamed Amir Yosef, Sandro Bauer, Johannes Hoffart, Marc Spaniol, and Gerhard Weikum. 2012. HYENA: Hierarchical type classification for entity names. In *Proceedings of COLING 2012: Posters*, pages 1361–1370, Mumbai, India. The COLING 2012 Organizing Committee.

Hypothesis Only Baselines in Natural Language Inference

Adam Poliak[1] **Jason Naradowsky**[1] **Aparajita Haldar**[1,2]
Rachel Rudinger[1] **Benjamin Van Durme**[1]
[1]Johns Hopkins University [2]BITS Pilani, Goa Campus, India
`{azpoliak,vandurme}@cs.jhu.edu {narad,ahaldar1,rudinger}@jhu.edu`

Abstract

We propose a *hypothesis only* baseline for diagnosing Natural Language Inference (NLI). Especially when an NLI dataset assumes inference is occurring based purely on the relationship between a context and a hypothesis, it follows that assessing entailment relations while ignoring the provided context is a degenerate solution. Yet, through experiments on ten distinct NLI datasets, we find that this approach, which we refer to as a hypothesis-only model, is able to significantly outperform a majority-class baseline across a number of NLI datasets. Our analysis suggests that statistical irregularities may allow a model to perform NLI in some datasets beyond what should be achievable without access to the context.

1 Introduction

Though datasets for the task of Natural Language Inference (NLI) may vary in just about every aspect (size, construction, genre, label classes), they generally share a common structure: each instance consists of two fragments of natural language text (a *context*, also known as a *premise*, and a *hypothesis*), and a label indicating the entailment relation between the two fragments (e.g., ENTAILMENT, NEUTRAL, CONTRADICTION). Computationally, the task of NLI is to predict an entailment relation label (output) given a premise-hypothesis pair (input), i.e., to determine whether the truth of the hypothesis follows from the truth of the premise (Dagan et al., 2006, 2013).

When these NLI datasets are constructed to facilitate the training and evaluation of natural language understanding (NLU) systems (Nangia et al., 2017), it is tempting to claim that systems achieving high accuracy on such datasets have successfully "understood" natural language or at least a logical relationship between a premise and hypothesis. While this paper does not attempt to

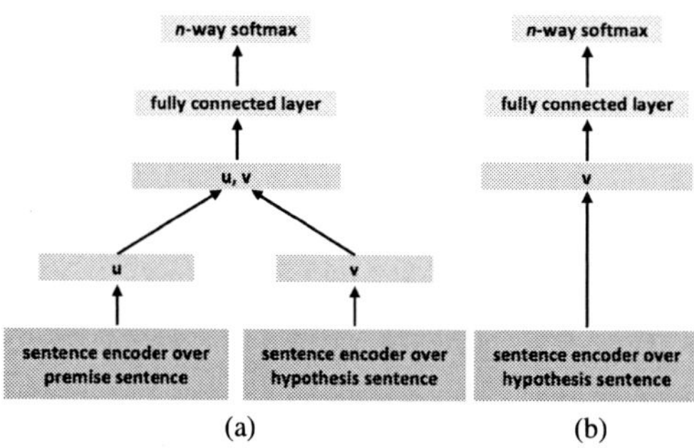

Figure 1: (1a) shows a typical NLI model that encodes the premise and hypothesis sentences into a vector space to classify the sentence pair. (1b) shows our hypothesis-only baseline method that ignores the premise and only encodes the hypothesis sentence.

prescribe the sufficient conditions of such a claim, we argue for an obvious *necessary*, or at least *desired* condition: *that interesting natural language inference should depend on both premise and hypothesis.* In other words, a baseline system with access only to hypotheses (Figure 1b) can be said to perform NLI only in the sense that it is understanding language based on prior background knowledge. If this background knowledge is about the world, this may be justifiable as an aspect of natural language understanding, if not in keeping with the spirit of NLI. But if the "background knowledge" consists of learned statistical irregularities in the data, this may not be ideal. Here we explore the question: do NLI datasets contain statistical irregularities that allow hypothesis-only models to outperform the datasets specific prior?

We present the results of a hypothesis-only baseline across ten NLI-style datasets and advocate for its inclusion in future dataset reports. We find that this baseline can perform above the majority-class prior across most of the ten examined datasets. We examine whether: (1) hypotheses contain statistical irregularities within each

*Proceedings of the 7th Joint Conference on Lexical and Computational Semantics (*SEM)*, pages 180–191
New Orleans, June 5-6, 2018. ©2018 Association for Computational Linguistics

entailment class that are "giveaways" to a well-trained hypothesis-only model, (2) the way in which an NLI dataset is constructed is related to how prone it is to this particular weakness, and (3) the majority baselines might not be as indicative of "the difficulty of the task" (Bowman et al., 2015) as previously thought.

We are not the first to consider the inherent difficulty of NLI datasets. For example, MacCartney (2009) used a simple bag-of-words model to evaluate early iterations of Recognizing Textual Entailment (RTE) challenge sets.[1] Concerns have been raised previously about the hypotheses in the Stanford Natural Language Inference (SNLI) dataset specifically, such as by Rudinger et al. (2017) and in unpublished work.[2] Here, we survey of large number of existing NLI datasets under the lens of a hypothesis-only model.[3] Concurrently, Tsuchiya (2018) and Gururangan et al. (2018) similarly trained an NLI classifier with access limited to hypotheses and discovered similar results on three of the ten datasets that we study.

2 Motivation

Our approach is inspired by recent studies that show how biases in an NLU dataset allow models to perform well on the task without understanding the meaning of the text. In the Story Cloze task (Mostafazadeh et al., 2016, 2017), a model is presented with a short four-sentence narrative and asked to complete it by choosing one of two suggested concluding sentences. While the task is presented as a new common-sense reasoning framework, Schwartz et al. (2017b) achieved state-of-the-art performance by ignoring the narrative and training a linear classifier with features related to the writing style of the two potential endings, rather than their content. It has also been shown that features focusing on sentence length, sentiment, and negation are sufficient for achieving high accuracy on this dataset (Schwartz et al., 2017a; Cai et al., 2017; Bugert et al., 2017).

NLI is often viewed as an integral part of NLU. Condoravdi et al. (2003) argue that it is a necessary metric for evaluating an NLU system, since it

forces a model to perform many distinct types of reasoning. Goldberg (2017) suggests that "solving [NLI] perfectly entails human level understanding of language", and Nangia et al. (2017) argue that "in order for a system to perform well at natural language inference, it needs to handle nearly the full complexity of natural language understanding." However, if biases in NLI datasets, especially those that do not reflect commonsense knowledge, allow models to achieve high levels of performance without needing to reason about hypotheses based on corresponding contexts, our current datasets may fall short of these goals.

3 Methodology

We modify Conneau et al. (2017)'s `InferSent` method to train a neural model to classify just the hypotheses. We choose `InferSent` because it performed competitively with the best-scoring systems on the Stanford Natural Language Inference (SNLI) dataset (Bowman et al., 2015), while being representative of the types of neural architectures commonly used for NLI tasks. `InferSent` uses a BiLSTM encoder, and constructs a sentence representation by max-pooling over its hidden states. This sentence representation of a hypothesis is used as input to a MLP classifier to predict the NLI tag.

We preprocess each recast dataset using the NLTK tokenizer (Loper and Bird, 2002). Following Conneau et al. (2017), we map the resulting tokens to 300-dimensional GloVe vectors (Pennington et al., 2014) trained on 840 billion tokens from the Common Crawl, using the GloVe OOV vector for unknown words. We optimize via SGD, with an initial learning rate of 0.1, and decay rate of 0.99. We allow at most 20 epochs of training with optional early stopping according to the following policy: when the accuracy on the development set decreases, we divide the learning rate by 5 and stop training when learning rate is $< 10^{-5}$.

4 Datasets

We collect ten NLI datasets and categorize them into three distinct groups based on the methods by which they were constructed. Table 1 summarizes the different NLI datasets that our investigation considers.

---

[1] MacCartney (2009), Ch. 2.2: *"the RTE1 test suite is the hardest, while the RTE2 test suite is roughly 4% easier, and the RTE3 test suite is roughly 9% easier."*

[2] A course project constituting independent discovery of our observations on SNLI: `https://leonidk.com/pdfs/cs224u.pdf`

[3] Our code and data can be found at `https://github.com/azpoliak/hypothesis-only-NLI`.

Creation Protocol	Dataset	Size	Classes	Example Hypothesis
Recast	DPR	3.4K	2	*People raise dogs because dogs are afraid of thieves*
	SPR	150K	2	*The judge was aware of the dismissing*
	FN+	150K	2	*the irish are actually principling to come home*
Judged	ADD-1	5K	2	*A small child staring at a young horse and a pony*
	SCITAIL	25K	2	*Humans typically have 23 pairs of chromosomes*
	SICK	10K	3	*Pasta is being put into a dish by a woman*
	MPE	10K	3	*A man smoking a cigarette*
	JOCI	30K	3	*The flooring is a horizontal surface*
Elicited	SNLI	550K	3	*An animal is jumping to catch an object*
	MNLI	425K	3	*Kyoto has a kabuki troupe and so does Osaka*

Table 1: Basic statistics about the NLI datasets we consider. 'Size' refers to the total number of labeled premise-hypothesis pairs in each dataset (for datasets with $> 100K$ examples, numbers are rounded down to the nearest $25K$). The 'Creation Protocol' column indicates how the dataset was created. The 'Class' column reports the number of class labels/tags. The last column shows an example hypothesis from each dataset.

4.1 Human Elicited

In cases where humans were given a context and asked to generate a corresponding hypothesis and label, we consider these datasets to be **elicited**. Although we consider only two such datasets, they are the largest datasets included in our study and are currently popular amongst researchers. The elicited NLI datasets we look at are:

Stanford Natural Language Inference (SNLI) To create SNLI, Bowman et al. (2015) showed crowdsourced workers a premise sentence (sourced from Flickr image captions), and asked them to generate a corresponding hypothesis sentence for each of the three labels (ENTAILMENT, NEUTRAL, CONTRADICTION). SNLI is known to contain stereotypical biases based on gender, race, and ethnic stereotypes (Rudinger et al., 2017). Furthermore, Zhang et al. (2017) commented that this "elicitation protocols can lead to biased responses unlikely to contain a wide range of possible common-sense inferences."

Multi-NLI Multi-NLI is a recent expansion of SNLI aimed to add greater diversity to the existing dataset (Williams et al., 2017). Premises in Multi-NLI can originate from fictional stories, personal letters, telephone speech, and a 9/11 report.

4.2 Human Judged

Alternatively, if hypotheses and premises were automatically paired but *labeled* by a human, we consider the dataset to be **judged**. Our human-judged data sets are:

Sentences Involving Compositional Knowledge (SICK) To evaluate how well compositional distributional semantic models handle "challenging phenomena", Marelli et al. (2014) introduced SICK, which used rules to expand or normalize existing premises to create more difficult examples. Workers were asked to label the relatedness of these resulting pairs, and these labels were then converted into the same three-way label space as SNLI and Multi-NLI.

Add-one RTE This mixed-genre dataset tests whether NLI systems can understand adjective-noun compounds (Pavlick and Callison-Burch, 2016). Premise sentences were extracted from Annotated Gigaword (Napoles et al., 2012), image captions (Young et al., 2014), the Internet Argument Corpus (Walker et al., 2012), and fictional stories from the GutenTag dataset (Mac Kim and Cassidy, 2015). To create hypotheses, adjectives were removed or inserted before nouns in a premise, and crowd-sourced workers were asked to provide reliable labels (ENTAILED, NOT-ENTAILED).

SciTail Recently released, SciTail is an NLI dataset created from 4th grade science questions and multiple-choice answers (Khot et al., 2018). Hypotheses are assertions converted from question-answer pairs found in SciQ (Welbl et al., 2017). Hypotheses are automatically paired with premise sentences from domain specific texts (Clark et al., 2016), and labeled (ENTAILMENT, NEUTRAL) by crowd-sourced workers. Notably, the construction method allows for the same sentence to appear as a hypothesis for more than one premise.

Multiple Premise Entailment (MPE) Unlike the other datasets we consider, the premises in MPE (Lai et al., 2017) are not single sentences, but four different captions that describe the same image in the FLICKR30K dataset (Plummer et al., 2015). Hypotheses were generated by simplifying either a fifth caption that describes the same image or a caption corresponding to a different image, and given the standard 3-way tags. Each hypothesis has at most a 50% overlap with the words in its corresponding premise. Since the hypotheses are still just one sentence, our hypothesis-only baseline can easily be applied to MPE.

Johns Hopkins Ordinal Common-Sense Inference (JOCI) JOCI labels context-hypothesis instances on an ordinal scale from *impossible* (1) to *very likely* (5) (Zhang et al., 2017). In JOCI, context (premise) sentences were taken from existing NLU datasets: SNLI, ROC Stories (Mostafazadeh et al., 2016), and COPA (Roemmele et al., 2011). Hypotheses were created automatically by systems trained to generate entailed facts from a premise.[4] Crowd-sourced workers labeled the likelihood of the hypothesis following from the premise on an *ordinal scale*. We convert these into a 3-way NLI tags where 1 maps to CONTRADICTION, 2-4 maps to NEUTRAL, and 5 maps to ENTAILMENT. Converting the annotations into a 3-way classification problem allows us to limit the range of the number of NLI label classes in our investigation.

4.3 Automatically Recast

If an NLI dataset was automatically generated from existing datasets for other NLP tasks, and sentence pairs were constructed and labeled with minimal human intervention, we refer to such a dataset as **recast**. We use the recast datasets from White et al. (2017):

Semantic Proto-Roles (SPR) Inspired by Dowty (1991)'s thematic role theory, Reisinger et al. (2015) introduced the Semantic Proto-Role (SPR) labeling task, which can be viewed as decomposing semantic roles into finer-grained properties, such as whether a predicate's argument was likely *aware* of the given predicated situation. 2-way labeled NLI sentence pairs were generated from SPR annotations by creating general templates.

Definite Pronoun Resolution (DPR) The DPR dataset targets an NLI model's ability to perform anaphora resolution (Rahman and Ng, 2012). In the original dataset, sentences contain two entities and one pronoun, and the task is to link the pronoun to its referent. In the recast version, the premises are the original sentences and the hypotheses are the same sentences with the pronoun replaced with its correct (ENTAILED) and incorrect (NOT-ENTAILED) referent. For example, *People raise dogs because they are obedient* and *People raise dogs because dogs are obedient* is such a context-hypothesis pair. We note that this mechanism would appear to maximally benefit a hypothesis-only approach, as the hypothesis semantically subsumes the context.

FrameNet Plus (FN+) Using paraphrases from PPDB (Ganitkevitch et al., 2013), Rastogi and Van Durme (2014) automatically replaced words with their paraphrases. Subsequently, Pavlick et al. (2015) asked crowd-source workers to judge how well a sentence with a paraphrase preserved the original sentence's meanings. In this NLI dataset that targets a model's ability to perform paraphrastic inference, premise sentences are the original sentences, the hypotheses are the edited versions, and the crowd-source judgments are converted to 2-way NLI-labels. For not-entailed examples, White et al. (2017) replaced a single token in a context sentence with a word that crowd-source workers labeled as not being a paraphrase of the token in the given context. In turn, we might suppose that positive entailments (1-b) are keeping in the spirit of NLI, but not-entailed examples might not because there are adequacy (1-c) and fluency (1-d) issues.[5]

(1)   a.   That is the way the system works

        b.   That is the way the framework works

        c.   That is the road the system works

        d.   That is the way the system creations

5 Results

Our goal is to determine whether a hypothesis-only model outperforms the majority baseline and investigate what may cause significant gains. In

---

[4] We only consider the hypotheses generated by either a seq2seq model or from external world knowledge.

[5] In these examples, (1-a) is the corresponding context.

Dataset	DEV				TEST				Baseline	SOTA
	Hyp-Only	MAJ	$\|\Delta\|$	$\Delta\%$	Hyp-Only	MAJ	$\|\Delta\|$	$\Delta\%$		
					Recast					
DPR	50.21	50.21	0.00	0.00	49.95	49.95	0.00	0.00	49.5	49.5
SPR	86.21	65.27	+20.94	+32.08	86.57	65.44	+21.13	+32.29	80.6	80.6
FN+	62.43	56.79	+5.64	+9.31	61.11	57.48	+3.63	+6.32	80.5	80.5
					Human Judged					
ADD-1	75.10	75.10	0.00	0.00	85.27	85.27	0.00	0.00	92.2	92.2
SciTail	66.56	50.38	+16.18	+32.12	66.56	60.04	+6.52	+10.86	70.6	77.3
SICK	56.76	56.76	0.00	0.00	56.87	56.87	0.00	0.00	56.87	84.6
MPE	40.20	40.20	0.00	0.00	42.40	42.40	0.00	0.00	41.7	56.3
JOCI	61.64	57.74	+3.90	+6.75	62.61	57.26	+5.35	+9.34	–	–
					Human Elicited					
SNLI	69.17	33.82	+35.35	+104.52	69.00	34.28	+34.72	+101.28	78.2	89.3
MNLI-1	55.52	35.45	+20.07	+56.61	–	35.6	– –		72.3	80.60
MNLI-2	55.18	35.22	+19.96	+56.67	–	36.5	–	–	72.1	83.21

Table 2: NLI accuracies on each dataset. Columns 'Hyp-Only' and 'MAJ' indicates the accuracy of the hypothesis-only model and the majority baseline. $|\Delta|$ and $\Delta\%$ indicate the absolute difference in percentage points and the percentage increase between the Hyp-Only and MAJ. Blue numbers indicate that the hypothesis-model outperforms MAJ. In the right-most section, 'Baseline' indicates the original baseline on the test when the dataset was released and 'SOTA' indicates current state-of-the-art results. MNLI-1 is the matched version and MNLI-2 is the mismatched for MNLI. The names of datasets are italicized if containing $\leq 10K$ labeled examples.

such cases a hypothesis-only model should be used as a stronger baseline instead of the majority class baseline. For all experiments except for JOCI, we use each NLI dataset's standard train, dev, and test splits.[6] Table 2 compares the hypothesis-only model's accuracy with the majority baseline on each dataset's dev and test set.[7]

Criticism of the Majority Baseline   Across six of the ten datasets, our hypothesis-only model *significantly outperforms* the majority-baseline, even outperforming the best reported results on one dataset, recast SPR. This indicates that there exists a significant degree of exploitable signal that may help NLI models perform well on their corresponding test set without considering NLI contexts. From Table 2, it is unclear whether the construction method is responsible for these improvements. The largest relative gains are on human-elicited models where the hypothesis-only model more than doubles the majority baseline.

However, there are no obvious unifying trends across these datasets: Among the judged and recast datasets, where humans do not generate the NLI hypothesis, we observe lower performance margins between majority and hypothesis-only models compared to the elicited data sets. However, the baseline performances of these models are noticeably larger than on SNLI and Multi-NLI.

The drop between SNLI and Multi-NLI suggests that by including multiple genres, an NLI dataset may contain less biases. However, adding additional genres might not be enough to mitigate biases as the hypothesis-only model still drastically outperforms the majority-baseline. Therefore, we believe that models tested on SNLI and Multi-NLI should include a baseline version of the model that only accesses hypotheses.

We do not observe general trends across the datasets based on their construction methodology. On three of the five human judged datasets, the hypothesis-only model defaults to labeling each instance with the majority class tag. We find the same behavior in one recast dataset (DPR). However, across both these categories we find smaller relative improvements than on SNLI and Multi-NLI. These results suggest the existence of exploitable signal in the datasets that is unrelated to NLI contexts. Our focus now shifts to identifying precisely what these signals might be and understanding why they may appear in NLI hypotheses.

6   Statistical Irregularities

We are interested in determining what characteristics in the datasets may be responsible for the hypothesis-only model often outperforming the majority baseline. Here, we investigate the importance of specific words, grammaticality, and lexical semantics.

---

[6]JOCI was not released with such splits so we randomly split the dataset into such a partition with 80:10:10 ratios.

[7]We only report results on the Multi-NLI development set since the test labels are only accessible on Kaggle.

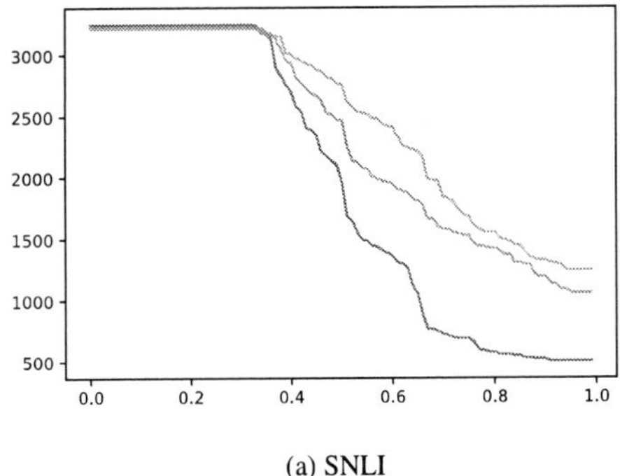

(a) SNLI

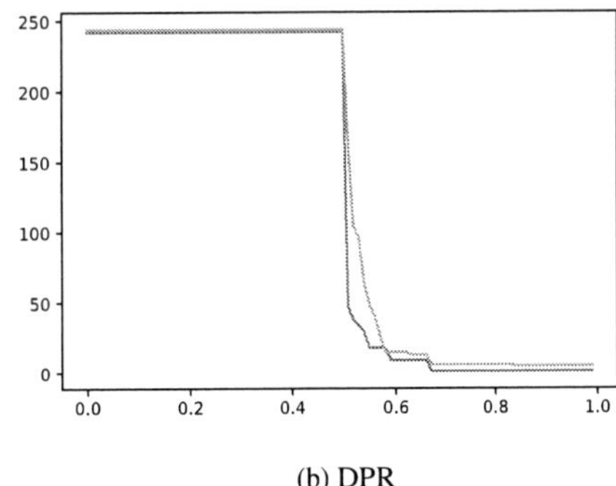

(b) DPR

Figure 2: Plots showing the number of sentences per each label (Y-axis) that contain at least one word w such that $p(l|w) >= x$ for at least one label l. Colors indicate different labels. Intuitively, for a sliding definition of what value of $p(l|w)$ might constitute a "give-away" the Y-axis shows the proportion of sentences that can be trivially answered for each class.

6.1 Can Labels be Inferred from Single Words?

Since words in hypotheses have a distribution over the class of labels, we can determine the conditional probability of a label l given the word w by

$$p(l|w) = \frac{count(w, l)}{count(w)} \tag{1}$$

If $p(l|w)$ is highly skewed across labels, there exists the potential for a predictive bias. Consequently, such words may be "give-aways" that allow the hypothesis model to correctly predict an NLI label without considering the context.

If a single occurrence of a highly label-specific word would allow a sentence to be deterministically classified, how many sentences in a dataset are prone to being trivially labeled? The plots in Figure 2 answer this question for SNLI and DPR. The Y-value where $X = 1.0$ captures the number of such sentences. Other values of $X < 1.0$ can also have strong correlative effects, but a priori the relationship between the value of X and the coverage of trivially answerable instances in the data is unclear. We illustrate this relationship for varying values of $p(l|w)$. When $X = 0$, all words are considered highly-correlated with a specific class label, and thus the entire data set would be treated as trivially answerable.

In DPR, which has two class labels, because the uncertainty of a label is highest when $p(l|w) = 0.5$, the sharp drop as X deviates from this value indicates a weaker effect, where there are proportionally fewer sentences which contain highly label-specific words with respect to SNLI. As

SNLI uses 3-way classification we see a gradual decline from 0.33.

6.2 What are "Give-away" Words?

Now that we analyzed the extent to which highly label-correlated words may exist across sentences in a given label, we would like to understand what these words are and why they exist.

Figure 3 reports some of the words with the highest $p(l|w)$ for SNLI, a human elicited dataset, and MPE, a human judged dataset, on which our hypothesis model performed identically to the majority baseline. Because many of the most discriminative words are low frequency, we report only words which occur at least five times. We rank the words according to their overall frequency, since this statistic is perhaps more indicative of a word w's effect on overall performance compared to $p(l|w)$ alone.

The score $p(l|w)$ of the words shown for SNLI deviate strongly, regardless of the label. In contrast, in MPE, scores are much closer to a uniform distribution of $p(l|w)$ across labels. Intuitively, the stronger the word's deviation, the stronger the potential for it to be a "give-away" word. A high word frequency indicates a greater potential of the word to affect the overall accuracy on NLI.

Qualitative Examples Turning our attention to the qualities of the words themselves, we can easily identify trends among the words used in contradictory hypotheses in SNLI. In our top-10 list, for example, three words refer to the act of sleeping. Upon inspecting corresponding context sentences, we find that many contexts, which are

	SNLI							
Word	**Score**	**Freq**	**Word**	**Score**	**Freq**	**Word**	**Score**	**Freq**
instrument	0.90	20	tall	0.93	44	sleeping	0.88	108
touching	0.83	12	competition	0.88	24	driving	0.81	53
least	0.90	10	because	0.83	23	Nobody	1.00	52
Humans	0.88	8	birthday	0.85	20	alone	0.90	50
transportation	0.86	7	mom	0.82	17	cat	0.84	49
speaking	0.86	7	win	0.88	16	asleep	0.91	43
screen	0.86	7	got	0.81	16	no	0.84	31
arts	0.86	7	trip	0.93	15	empty	0.93	28
activity	0.86	7	tries	0.87	15	eats	0.83	24
opposing	1.00	5	owner	0.87	15	sleeps	0.95	20
(a) entailment			(b) neutral			(c) contradiction		

	MPE							
Word	**Score**	**Freq**	**Word**	**Score**	**Freq**	**Word**	**Score**	**Freq**
an	0.57	21	smiling	0.56	16	sitting	0.51	88
gathered	0.58	12	An	0.60	10	woman	0.55	80
girl	0.50	12	for	0.56	9	men	0.56	34
trick	0.55	11	front	0.75	8	Some	0.62	26
Dogs	0.55	11	camera	0.62	8	doing	0.59	22
watches	0.60	10	waiting	0.50	8	Children	0.50	22
field	0.60	10	posing	0.50	8	boy	0.67	21
singing	0.50	10	Kids	0.57	7	having	0.65	20
outside	0.67	9	smile	0.83	6	sit	0.60	15
something	0.62	8	wall	0.50	6	children	0.53	15
(d) entailment			(e) neutral			(f) contradiction		

Figure 3: Lists of the most highly-correlated words in each dataset for given labels, thresholded to the top 10 and ranked according to frequency.

sourced from Flickr, naturally deal with activities. This leads us to believe that as a common strategy, crowd-source workers often do not generate contradictory hypotheses that require fine-grained semantic reasoning, as a majority of such activities can be easily negated by removing an agent's agency, i.e. describing the agent as sleeping. A second trend we notice is that universal negation constitutes four of the remaining seven terms in this list, and may also be used to similar effect.[8] The human-elicited protocol does not guide, nor incentivize crowd-source workers to come up with less obvious examples. If not properly controlled, elicited datasets may be prone to many label-specific terms. The existence of label-specific terms in human-elicited NLI datasets does not invalidate the datasets nor is surprising. Stud-

ies in eliciting norming data are prone to repeated responses across subjects (McRae et al., 2005) (see discussion in §2 of (Zhang et al., 2017)).

6.3 On the Role of Grammaticality

Like MPE, FN+ contains few high frequency words with high $p(l|w)$. However, unlike on MPE, our hypothesis-only model outperforms the majority-only baseline. If these gains do not arise from "give-away" words, then what is the statistical irregularity responsible for this discriminative power?

Upon further inspection, we notice an interesting imbalance in how our model performs for each of the two classes. The hypothesis-only model performs similarly to the majority baseline for entailed examples, while improving by over 34% those which are not entailed, as shown in Table 3.

As shown by White et al. (2017) and noticed

---

[8]These are "Nobody", "alone", "no", and "empty".

label	Hyp-Only	MAJ	Δ%
entailed	44.18	43.20	+2.27
not-entailed	76.31	56.79	+34.37

Table 3: Accuracies on FN+ for each class label.

by Poliak et al. (2018), FN+ contains more grammatical errors than the other recast datasets. We explore whether grammaticality could be the statistical irregularity exploited in this case. We manually sample a total of 200 FN+ sentences and categorize them based on their gold label and our model's prediction. Out of 50 sentences that the model correctly labeled as ENTAILED, 88% of them were grammatical. On the other-hand, of the 50 hypotheses incorrectly labeled as EN-TAILED, only 38% of them were grammatical. Similarly, when the model correctly labeled 50 NOT-ENTAILED hypotheses, only 20% were grammatical, and 68% when labeled incorrectly. This suggests that a hypothesis-only model may be able to discover the correlation between grammaticality and NLI labels on this dataset.

6.4 Lexical Semantics

A survey of gains (Table 4) in the SPR dataset suggest a number of its property-driven hypotheses, such as *X was sentient in [the event]*, can be accurately guessed based on lexical semantics (background knowledge learned from training) of the argument. For example, the hypothesis-only baseline correctly predicts the truth of hypotheses in the dev set such as: *Experts were sentient ...* or *Mr. Falls was sentient ...*, and the falsity of *The campaign was sentient*, while failing on referring expressions like *Some* or *Each side*. A model exploiting regularities of the real world would seem to be a different category of dataset bias: while not strictly *wrong* from the perspective of NLU, one should be aware of what the hypothesis-only baseline is capable of, to recognize those cases where access to the context is required and therefore more interesting under NLI.

6.5 Open Questions

There may remain statistical irregularities, which we leave for future work to explore. For example, are there correlation between sentence length and label class in these data sets? Is there a particular construction method that minimizes the amount of "give-away" words present in the dataset? And lastly, our study is another in a line of research which looks for irregularities at

Proto-Role	H-model	MAJ	Δ%
aware	88.70	59.94	+47.99
used in	77.30	52.72	+46.63
volitional	87.45	64.96	+34.62
physically existed	87.97	65.38	+34.56
caused	82.11	63.08	+30.18
sentient	94.35	76.26	+23.73
existed before	80.23	65.90	+21.75
changed	72.18	64.85	+11.29
chang. state	71.76	64.85	+10.65
existed after	79.29	72.91	+8.75
existed during	90.06	85.67	+5.13
location	93.83	91.21	+2.87
physical contact	89.33	86.92	+2.77
chang. possession	94.87	94.46	+0.44
moved	93.51	93.20	+0.34
stationary during	96.44	96.34	+0.11

Table 4: NLI accuracies on the SPR development data; each property appears in 956 hypotheses.

the word level (MacCartney et al., 2008; MacCartney, 2009). Beyond bag-of-words, are there multi-word expressions or syntactic phenomena that might encode label biases?

7 Related Work

Non-semantic information to help NLI In NLI datasets, non-semantic linguistic features have been used to improve NLI models. Vanderwende and Dolan (2006) and Blake (2007) demonstrate how sentence structure alone can provide a high signal for NLI. Instead of using external sources of knowledge, which was a common trend at the time, Blake (2007) improved results on RTE by combining syntactic features. More recently, Bar-Haim et al. (2015) introduce an inference formalism based on syntactic-parse trees.

World Knowledge and NLI As mentioned earlier, hypothesis-only models that perform without exploiting statistical irregularities may be performing NLI only in the sense that it is understanding language based on prior background knowledge. Here, we take the approach that *interesting* NLI should depend on both premise and hypotheses. Prior work in NLI reflect this approach. For example, Glickman and Dagan (2005) argue that "the notion of textual entailment is relevant only" for hypothesis that are not world facts, e.g. "Paris is the capital of France." Glickman et al. (2005a,b), introduce a probabilistic framework for NLI where the premise entails a hypothesis if, and only if, the probability of the hypothesis being true increases as a result of the premise.

NLI's resurgence Starting in the mid-2000's, multiple community-wide shared tasks focused on NLI, then commonly referred to as RTE, i.e, recognizing textual entailment. Starting with Dagan et al. (2006), there have been eight iterations of the PASCAL RTE challenge with the most recent being Dzikovska et al. (2013).[9] NLI datasets were relatively small, ranging from *thousands* to *tens of thousands* of labeled sentence pairs. In turn, NLI models often used alignment-based techniques (MacCartney et al., 2008) or manually engineered features (Androutsopoulos and Malakasiotis, 2010). Bowman et al. (2015) sparked a renewed interested in NLI, particularly among deep-learning researchers. By developing and releasing a large NLI dataset containing over $550K$ examples, Bowman et al. (2015) enabled the community to successfully apply deep learning models to the NLI problem.

8 Conclusion

We introduced a stronger baseline for ten NLI datasets. Our baseline reduces the task from labeling the relationship between two sentences to classifying a single hypothesis sentence. Our experiments demonstrated that in six of the ten datasets, always predicting the majority-class label is not a strong baseline, as it is significantly outperformed by the hypothesis-only model. Our analysis suggests that statistical irregularities, including word choice and grammaticality, may reduce the difficulty of the task on popular NLI datasets by not fully testing how well a model can determine whether the truth of a hypothesis follows from the truth of a corresponding premise.

We hope our findings will encourage the development of new NLI datasets which exhibit less exploitable irregularities, and that encourage the development of richer models of inference. As a baseline, new NLI models should be compared against a corresponding version that only accesses hypotheses. In future work, we plan to apply a similar hypothesis-only baseline to multi-modal tasks that attempt to challenge a system to understand and classify the relationship between two inputs, e.g. Visual QA (Antol et al., 2015).

---

[9]Technically Bentivogli et al. (2011) was the last challenge under PASCAL's aegis but Dzikovska et al. (2013) was branded as the 8th RTE challenge.

Acknowledgements

This work was supported by Johns Hopkins University, the Human Language Technology Center of Excellence (HLTCOE), DARPA LORELEI, and the NSF Graduate Research Fellowships Program (GRFP). We would also like to thank three anonymous reviewers for their feedback. The views and conclusions contained in this publication are those of the authors and should not be interpreted as representing official policies or endorsements of DARPA or the U.S. Government.

References

Ion Androutsopoulos and Prodromos Malakasiotis. 2010. A survey of paraphrasing and textual entailment methods. *Journal of Artificial Intelligence Research*, 38:135–187.

Stanislaw Antol, Aishwarya Agrawal, Jiasen Lu, Margaret Mitchell, Dhruv Batra, C Lawrence Zitnick, and Devi Parikh. 2015. Vqa: Visual question answering. In *Proceedings of the IEEE International Conference on Computer Vision*, pages 2425–2433.

Roy Bar-Haim, Ido Dagan, and Jonathan Berant. 2015. Knowledge-based textual inference via parse-tree transformations. *Journal of Artificial Intelligence Research*, 54:1–57.

Luisa Bentivogli, Peter Clark, Ido Dagan, and Danilo Giampiccolo. 2011. The seventh pascal recognizing textual entailment challenge.

Catherine Blake. 2007. The role of sentence structure in recognizing textual entailment. In *Proceedings of the ACL-PASCAL Workshop on Textual Entailment and Paraphrasing*, RTE '07, pages 101–106, Stroudsburg, PA, USA. Association for Computational Linguistics.

Samuel R. Bowman, Gabor Angeli, Christopher Potts, and Christopher D. Manning. 2015. A large annotated corpus for learning natural language inference. In *Proceedings of the 2015 Conference on Empirical Methods in Natural Language Processing (EMNLP)*. Association for Computational Linguistics.

Michael Bugert, Yevgeniy Puzikov, Andreas Rücklé, Judith Eckle-Kohler, Teresa Martin, Eugenio Martínez-Cámara, Daniil Sorokin, Maxime Peyrard, and Iryna Gurevych. 2017. Lsdsem 2017: Exploring data generation methods for the story cloze test. In *Proceedings of the 2nd Workshop on Linking Models of Lexical, Sentential and Discourse-level Semantics*, pages 56–61.

Zheng Cai, Lifu Tu, and Kevin Gimpel. 2017. Pay attention to the ending: Strong neural baselines for the roc story cloze task. In *Proceedings of the 55th Annual Meeting of the Association for Computational Linguistics (Volume 2: Short Papers)*, volume 2, pages 616–622.

Peter Clark, Oren Etzioni, Tushar Khot, Ashish Sabharwal, Oyvind Tafjord, Peter D Turney, and Daniel Khashabi. 2016. Combining retrieval, statistics, and inference to answer elementary science questions. In *AAAI*.

Cleo Condoravdi, Dick Crouch, Valeria De Paiva, Reinhard Stolle, and Daniel G Bobrow. 2003. Entailment, intensionality and text understanding. In *Proceedings of the HLT-NAACL 2003 workshop on Text meaning-Volume 9*, pages 38–45. Association for Computational Linguistics.

Alexis Conneau, Douwe Kiela, Holger Schwenk, Loïc Barrault, and Antoine Bordes. 2017. Supervised learning of universal sentence representations from natural language inference data. In *Proceedings of the 2017 Conference on Empirical Methods in Natural Language Processing*, pages 670–680, Copenhagen, Denmark. Association for Computational Linguistics.

Ido Dagan, Oren Glickman, and Bernardo Magnini. 2006. The pascal recognising textual entailment challenge. In *Machine learning challenges. evaluating predictive uncertainty, visual object classification, and recognising tectual entailment*, pages 177–190. Springer.

Ido Dagan, Dan Roth, Mark Sammons, and Fabio Massimo Zanzotto. 2013. Recognizing textual entailment: Models and applications. *Synthesis Lectures on Human Language Technologies*, 6(4):1–220.

David Dowty. 1991. Thematic proto-roles and argument selection. *Language*, pages 547–619.

Myroslava Dzikovska, Rodney Nielsen, Chris Brew, Claudia Leacock, Danilo Giampiccolo, Luisa Bentivogli, Peter Clark, Ido Dagan, and Hoa Trang Dang. 2013. Semeval-2013 task 7: The joint student response analysis and 8th recognizing textual entailment challenge. In *Second Joint Conference on Lexical and Computational Semantics (*SEM), Volume 2: Proceedings of the Seventh International Workshop on Semantic Evaluation (SemEval 2013)*, pages 263–274, Atlanta, Georgia, USA. Association for Computational Linguistics.

Juri Ganitkevitch, Benjamin Van Durme, and Chris Callison-Burch. 2013. Ppdb: The paraphrase database. In *Proceedings of the 2013 Conference of the North American Chapter of the Association for Computational Linguistics: Human Language Technologies*, pages 758–764.

Oren Glickman and Ido Dagan. 2005. A probabilistic setting and lexical cooccurrence model for textual entailment. In *Proceedings of the ACL Workshop on Empirical Modeling of Semantic Equivalence and Entailment*, pages 43–48. Association for Computational Linguistics.

Oren Glickman, Ido Dagan, and Moshe Koppel. 2005a. A probabilistic classification approach for lexical textual entailment. In *AAAI*.

Oren Glickman, Ido Dagan, and Moshe Koppel. 2005b. A probabilistic lexical approach to textual entailment. In *IJCAI*.

Yoav Goldberg. 2017. Neural network methods for natural language processing. *Synthesis Lectures on Human Language Technologies*, 10(1):1–309.

Suchin Gururangan, Swabha Swayamdipta, Omer Levy, Roy Schwartz, Samuel Bowman, and Noah A. Smith. 2018. Annotation artifacts in natural language inference data. In *Proc. of NAACL*.

Tushar Khot, Ashish Sabharwal, and Peter Clark. 2018. SciTail: A textual entailment dataset from science question answering. In *AAAI*.

Alice Lai, Yonatan Bisk, and Julia Hockenmaier. 2017. Natural language inference from multiple premises. In *Proceedings of the Eighth International Joint Conference on Natural Language Processing (Volume 1: Long Papers)*, pages 100–109, Taipei, Taiwan. Asian Federation of Natural Language Processing.

Edward Loper and Steven Bird. 2002. Nltk: The natural language toolkit. In *Proceedings of the ACL-02 Workshop on Effective tools and methodologies for teaching natural language processing and computational linguistics-Volume 1*, pages 63–70. Association for Computational Linguistics.

Sunghwan Mac Kim and Steve Cassidy. 2015. Finding names in trove: Named entity recognition for australian historical newspapers. In *Proceedings of the Australasian Language Technology Association Workshop 2015*, pages 57–65.

Bill MacCartney. 2009. *Natural language inference*. Ph.D. thesis, Stanford University.

Bill MacCartney, Michel Galley, and Christopher D Manning. 2008. A phrase-based alignment model for natural language inference. In *Proceedings of the conference on empirical methods in natural language processing*, pages 802–811. Association for Computational Linguistics.

Marco Marelli, Stefano Menini, Marco Baroni, Luisa Bentivogli, Raffaella bernardi, and Roberto Zamparelli. 2014. A sick cure for the evaluation of compositional distributional semantic models. In *Proceedings of the Ninth International Conference on Language Resources and Evaluation (LREC'14)*, pages 216–223, Reykjavik, Iceland. European Language Resources Association (ELRA). ACL Anthology Identifier: L14-1314.

Ken McRae, George S Cree, Mark S Seidenberg, and Chris McNorgan. 2005. Semantic feature production norms for a large set of living and nonliving things. *Behavior research methods*, 37(4):547–559.

Nasrin Mostafazadeh, Nathanael Chambers, Xiaodong He, Devi Parikh, Dhruv Batra, Lucy Vanderwende, Pushmeet Kohli, and James Allen. 2016. A corpus and cloze evaluation for deeper understanding of commonsense stories. In *Proceedings of the 2016 Conference of the North American Chapter of the Association for Computational Linguistics: Human Language Technologies*, pages 839–849, San Diego, California. Association for Computational Linguistics.

Nasrin Mostafazadeh, Michael Roth, Annie Louis, Nathanael Chambers, and James Allen. 2017. Lsdsem 2017 shared task: The story cloze test. In *Proceedings of the 2nd Workshop on Linking Models of Lexical, Sentential and Discourse-level Semantics*, pages 46–51, Valencia, Spain. Association for Computational Linguistics.

Nikita Nangia, Adina Williams, Angeliki Lazaridou, and Samuel Bowman. 2017. The repeval 2017 shared task: Multi-genre natural language inference with sentence representations. In *Proceedings of the 2nd Workshop on Evaluating Vector Space Representations for NLP*, pages 1–10.

Courtney Napoles, Matthew Gormley, and Benjamin Van Durme. 2012. Annotated Gigaword. In *Proceedings of the Joint Workshop on Automatic Knowledge Base Construction and Web-scale Knowledge Extraction (AKBC-WEKEX)*, pages 95–100, Montréal, Canada. Association for Computational Linguistics.

Ellie Pavlick and Chris Callison-Burch. 2016. Most "babies" are "little" and most "problems" are "huge": Compositional entailment in adjective-nouns. In *Proceedings of the 54th Annual Meeting of the Association for Computational Linguistics (Volume 1: Long Papers)*, pages 2164–2173. Association for Computational Linguistics.

Ellie Pavlick, Travis Wolfe, Pushpendre Rastogi, Chris Callison-Burch, Mark Dredze, and Benjamin Van Durme. 2015. Framenet+: Fast paraphrastic tripling of framenet. In *Proceedings of the 53rd Annual Meeting of the Association for Computational Linguistics and the 7th International Joint Conference on Natural Language Processing (Volume 2: Short Papers)*, pages 408–413, Beijing, China. Association for Computational Linguistics.

Jeffrey Pennington, Richard Socher, and Christopher D. Manning. 2014. Glove: Global vectors for word representation. In *Empirical Methods in Natural Language Processing (EMNLP)*, pages 1532–1543.

Bryan A Plummer, Liwei Wang, Chris M Cervantes, Juan C Caicedo, Julia Hockenmaier, and Svet-lana Lazebnik. 2015. Flickr30k entities: Collecting region-to-phrase correspondences for richer image-to-sentence models. In *Computer Vision (ICCV), 2015 IEEE International Conference on*, pages 2641–2649. IEEE.

Adam Poliak, Yonatan Belinkov, James Glass, and Benjamin Van Durme. 2018. On the evaluation of semantic phenomena in neural machine translation using natural language inference. In *Proceedings of the Annual Meeting of the North American Association of Computational Linguistics (NAACL)*.

Altaf Rahman and Vincent Ng. 2012. Resolving complex cases of definite pronouns: The winograd schema challenge. In *Proceedings of the 2012 Joint Conference on Empirical Methods in Natural Language Processing and Computational Natural Language Learning*, pages 777–789, Jeju Island, Korea. Association for Computational Linguistics.

Pushpendre Rastogi and Benjamin Van Durme. 2014. Augmenting framenet via ppdb. In *Proceedings of the Second Workshop on EVENTS: Definition, Detection, Coreference, and Representation*, pages 1–5.

Drew Reisinger, Rachel Rudinger, Francis Ferraro, Craig Harman, Kyle Rawlins, and Benjamin Van Durme. 2015. Semantic proto-roles. *Transactions of the Association for Computational Linguistics*, 3:475–488.

Melissa Roemmele, Cosmin Adrian Bejan, and Andrew S Gordon. 2011. Choice of plausible alternatives: An evaluation of commonsense causal reasoning. In *AAAI Spring Symposium: Logical Formalizations of Commonsense Reasoning*.

Rachel Rudinger, Chandler May, and Benjamin Van Durme. 2017. Social Bias in Elicited Natural Language Inferences. In *The 15th Conference of the European Chapter of the Association for Computational Linguistics (EACL): Workshop on Ethics in NLP*.

Roy Schwartz, Maarten Sap, Ioannis Konstas, Leila Zilles, Yejin Choi, and Noah A Smith. 2017a. The effect of different writing tasks on linguistic style: A case study of the roc story cloze task. In *Proceedings of the 21st Conference on Computational Natural Language Learning (CoNLL 2017)*, pages 15–25.

Roy Schwartz, Maarten Sap, Ioannis Konstas, Leila Zilles, Yejin Choi, and Noah A Smith. 2017b. Story cloze task: Uw nlp system. In *Proceedings of the 2nd Workshop on Linking Models of Lexical, Sentential and Discourse-level Semantics*, pages 52–55.

Masatoshi Tsuchiya. 2018. Performance impact caused by hidden bias of training data for recognizing textual entailment. In *11th International Conference on Language Resources and Evaluation (LREC2018)*.

Lucy Vanderwende and William B Dolan. 2006. What syntax can contribute in the entailment task. In *Machine Learning Challenges. Evaluating Predictive Uncertainty, Visual Object Classification, and Recognising Tectual Entailment*, pages 205–216. Springer.

Marilyn A Walker, Pranav Anand, Robert Abbott, and Ricky Grant. 2012. Stance classification using dialogic properties of persuasion. In *Proceedings of the 2012 Conference of the North American Chapter of the Association for Computational Linguistics: Human Language Technologies*, pages 592–596. Association for Computational Linguistics.

Johannes Welbl, Nelson F Liu, and Matt Gardner. 2017. Crowdsourcing multiple choice science questions. In *Proceedings of the 3rd Workshop on Noisy User-generated Text*, pages 94–106.

Aaron Steven White, Pushpendre Rastogi, Kevin Duh, and Benjamin Van Durme. 2017. Inference is everything: Recasting semantic resources into a unified evaluation framework. In *Proceedings of the Eighth International Joint Conference on Natural Language Processing (Volume 1: Long Papers)*, pages 996–1005, Taipei, Taiwan. Asian Federation of Natural Language Processing.

Adina Williams, Nikita Nangia, and Samuel R Bowman. 2017. A broad-coverage challenge corpus for sentence understanding through inference. *arXiv preprint arXiv:1704.05426*.

Peter Young, Alice Lai, Micah Hodosh, and Julia Hockenmaier. 2014. From image descriptions to visual denotations: New similarity metrics for semantic inference over event descriptions. *Transactions of the Association for Computational Linguistics*, 2:67–78.

Sheng Zhang, Rachel Rudinger, Kevin Duh, and Benjamin Van Durme. 2017. Ordinal common-sense inference. *Transactions of the Association for Computational Linguistics*, 5:379–395.

Quality Signals in Generated Stories

Manasvi Sagarkar[*]   **John Wieting**[†]   **Lifu Tu**[‡]   **Kevin Gimpel**[‡]

[*]University of Chicago, Chicago, IL, 60637, USA
[†]Carnegie Mellon University, Pittsburgh, PA, 15213, USA
[‡]Toyota Technological Institute at Chicago, Chicago, IL, 60637, USA

manasvi@uchicago.edu, jwieting@cs.cmu.edu, {lifu,kgimpel}@ttic.edu

Abstract

We study the problem of measuring the quality of automatically-generated stories. We focus on the setting in which a few sentences of a story are provided and the task is to generate the next sentence ("continuation") in the story. We seek to identify what makes a story continuation interesting, relevant, and have high overall quality. We crowdsource annotations along these three criteria for the outputs of story continuation systems, design features, and train models to predict the annotations. Our trained scorer can be used as a rich feature function for story generation, a reward function for systems that use reinforcement learning to learn to generate stories, and as a partial evaluation metric for story generation.

1 Introduction

We study the problem of automatic story generation in the climate of neural network natural language generation methods. Story generation (Mani, 2012; Gervás, 2012) has a long history, beginning with rule-based systems in the 1970s (Klein et al., 1973; Meehan, 1977). Most story generation research has focused on modeling the plot, characters, and primary action of the story, using simplistic methods for producing the actual linguistic form of the stories (Turner, 1993; Riedl and Young, 2010). More recent work learns from data how to generate stories holistically without a clear separation between content selection and surface realization (McIntyre and Lapata, 2009), with a few recent methods based on recurrent neural networks (Roemmele and Gordon, 2015; Huang et al., 2016).

We follow the latter style and focus on a setting in which a few sentences of a story are provided (the **context**) and the task is to generate the next sentence in the story (the **continuation**). Our goal is to produce continuations that are both interesting and relevant given the context.

Neural networks are increasingly employed for natural language generation, most often with encoder-decoder architectures based on recurrent neural networks (Cho et al., 2014; Sutskever et al., 2014). However, while neural methods are effective for generation of individual sentences conditioned on some context, they struggle with coherence when used to generate longer texts (Kiddon et al., 2016). In addition, it is challenging to apply neural models in less constrained generation tasks with many valid solutions, such as open-domain dialogue and story continuation.

The story continuation task is difficult to formulate and evaluate because there can be a wide variety of reasonable continuations for typical story contexts. This is also the case in open-domain dialogue systems, in which common evaluation metrics like BLEU (Papineni et al., 2002) are only weakly correlated with human judgments (Liu et al., 2016). Another problem with metrics like BLEU is the dependence on a gold standard. In story generation and open-domain dialogue, there can be several equally good continuations for any given context which suggests that the quality of a continuation should be computable without reliance on a gold standard.

In this paper, we study the question of identifying the characteristics of a good continuation for a given context. We begin by building several story generation systems that generate a continuation from a context. We develop simple systems based on recurrent neural networks and similarity-based retrieval and train them on the ROC story dataset (Mostafazadeh et al., 2016). We use crowdsourcing to collect annotations of the quality of the continuations without revealing the gold standard. We ask annotators to judge continuations along three distinct criteria: overall quality,

192

*Proceedings of the 7th Joint Conference on Lexical and Computational Semantics (*SEM)*, pages 192–202
New Orleans, June 5-6, 2018. ©2018 Association for Computational Linguistics

relevance, and interestingness. We collect multiple annotations for 4586 context/continuation pairs. These annotations permit us to compare methods for story generation and to study the relationships among the criteria. We analyze our annotated dataset by developing features of the context and continuation and measuring their correlation with each criterion.

We combine these features with neural networks to build models that predict the human scores, thus attempting to automate the process of human quality judgment. We find that our predicted scores correlate well with human judgments, especially when using our full feature set. Our scorer can be used as a rich feature function for story generation or a reward function for systems that use reinforcement learning to learn to generate stories. It can also be used as a partial evaluation metric for story generation.[1] Examples of contexts, generated continuations, and quality predictions from our scorer are shown in Table 3. The annotated data and trained scorer are available at the authors' websites.

2   Related Work

Research in automatic story generation has a long history, with early efforts driven primarily by hand-written rules (Klein et al., 1973; Meehan, 1977; Dehn, 1981; Lebowitz, 1985; Turner, 1993), often drawing from theoretical analysis of stories (Propp, 1968; Schank and Abelson, 1975; Thorndyke, 1977; Wilensky, 1983). Later methods were based on various methods of planning from artificial intelligence (Theune et al., 2003; Oinonen et al., 2006; Riedl and Young, 2010) or commonsense knowledge resources (Liu and Singh, 2002; Winston, 2014). A detailed summary of this earlier work is beyond our scope; for surveys, please see Mani (2012), Gervás (2012), or Gatt and Krahmer (2017).

More recent work in story generation has focused on data-driven methods (McIntyre and Lapata, 2009, 2010; McIntyre, 2011; Elson, 2012; Daza et al., 2016; Roemmele, 2016). The generation problem is often constrained via anchoring to some other input, such as a topic or list of keywords (McIntyre and Lapata, 2009), a sequence of images (Huang et al., 2016), a set of loosely-

connected sentences (Jain et al., 2017), or settings in which a user and agent take turns adding sentences to a story (Swanson and Gordon, 2012; Roemmele and Gordon, 2015; Roemmele, 2016).

Our annotation criteria—relevance, interestingness, and overall quality—are inspired by those from prior work. McIntyre and Lapata (2009) similarly obtain annotations for story interestingness. They capture coherence in generated stories by using an automatic method based on sentence shuffling. We discuss the relationship between relevance and coherence below in Section 3.2.

Roemmele et al. (2017) use automated linguistic analysis to evaluate story generation systems. They explore the various factors that affect the quality of a story by measuring feature values for different story generation systems, but they do not obtain any quality annotations as we do here.

Since there is little work in automatic evaluation of story generation, we can turn to the related task of open-domain dialogue. Evaluation of dialogue systems often uses perplexity or metrics like BLEU (Papineni et al., 2002), but Liu et al. (2016) show that most common evaluation metrics for dialog systems are correlated very weakly with human judgments. Lowe et al. (2017) develop an automatic metric for dialog evaluation by training a model to predict crowdsourced quality judgments. While this idea is very similar to our work, one key difference is that their annotators were shown both system outputs and the gold standard for each context. We fear this can bias the annotations by turning them into a measure of similarity to the gold standard, so we do not show the gold standard to annotators.

Wang et al. (2017) use crowdsourcing (upvotes on Quora) to obtain quality judgments for short stories and train models to predict them. One difference is that we obtain annotations for three distinct criteria, while they only use upvotes. Another difference is that we collect annotations for both manually-written continuations and a range of system-generated continuations, with the goal of using our annotations to train a scorer that can be used within training.

3   Data Collection

Our goal is to collect annotations of the quality of a sentence in a story given its preceding sentences. We use the term **context** to refer to the preceding sentences and **continuation** to refer to the next

---

[1]However, since our scorer does not use a gold standard, it is possible to "game" the metric by directly optimizing the predicted score, so if used as an evaluation metric, it should still be validated with a small-scale manual evaluation.

sentence being generated and evaluated. We now describe how we obtain ⟨context, continuation⟩ pairs from automatic and human-written stories for crowdsourcing quality judgments.

We use the ROC story corpus (Mostafazadeh et al., 2016), which contains 5-sentence stories about everyday events. We use the initial data release of 45,502 stories. The first 45,002 stories form our training set (TRAIN) for story generation models and the last 500 stories form our development set (DEV) for tuning hyperparameters while training story generation models. For collecting annotations, we compile a dataset of 4586 context-continuation pairs, drawing contexts from DEV as well as the 1871-story validation set from the ROC Story Cloze task (Mostafazadeh et al., 2016).

For contexts, we use 3- and 4-sentence prefixes from the stories in this set of 4586. We use both 3 and 4 sentence contexts as we do not want our annotated dataset to include only story endings (for the 4-sentence contexts, the original 5th sentence is the ending of the story) but also more general instances of story continuation. We did not use 1 or 2 sentence contexts because we consider the space of possible continuations for these short contexts to be too unconstrained and thus it would be difficult for both systems and annotators.

We generated continuations for each context using a variety of systems (described in Section 3.1) as well as simply taking the human-written continuation from the original story. We then obtained annotations for the continuation with its context via crowdsourcing, described in Section 3.2.

3.1 Story Continuation Systems

In order to generate a dataset with a range of qualities, we consider six ways of generating the continuation of the story, four based on neural sequence-to-sequence models and two using human-written sentences. To lessen the possibility of annotators seeing the same context multiple times, which could bias the annotations, we used at most two methods out of six for generating the continuation for a particular context.

3.1.1 Sequence-to-Sequence Models

We used a standard sequence-to-sequence (SEQ2SEQ) neural network model (Sutskever et al., 2014) to generate continuations given contexts. We trained the models on TRAIN and tuned on DEV. We generated 180,008 ⟨context, continuation⟩ pairs from TRAIN, where the contin-

uation is always a single sentence and the context consists of all previous sentences in the story. We trained a 3-layer bidirectional SEQ2SEQ model, with each layer having hidden vector dimensionality 1024. The size of the vocabulary was 31,220. We used scheduled sampling (Bengio et al., 2015), using the previous ground truth word in the decoder with probability 0.5^t, where t is the index of the mini-batch processed during training. We trained the model for 20,000 epochs with a batch size of 100. We began training the model on consecutive sentence pairs (so the context was only a single sentence), then shifted to training on full story contexts.

We considered four different methods for the decoding function of our SEQ2SEQ model:

- SEQ2SEQ-GREEDY: return the highest-scoring output under greedy ($\arg\max$) decoding.

- SEQ2SEQ-DIV: return the kth-best output using a diverse beam search (Vijayakumar et al., 2016) with beam size $k = 10$.

- SEQ2SEQ-SAMPLE: sample words from the distribution over output words at each step using a temperature parameter $\tau = 0.4$.

- SEQ2SEQ-REVERSE: reverse input sequence (at test time only) and use greedy decoding.

Each decoding rule contributes one eighth of the total data generated for annotation, so the SEQ2SEQ models account for one half of the ⟨context, continuation⟩ pairs to be annotated.

3.1.2 Human Generated Outputs

For human generated continuations, we use two methods. The first is simply the gold standard continuation from the ROC stories dataset, which we call HUMAN. The second finds the most similar context in the ROC training corpus, then returns the continuation for that context. To compute similarity between contexts, we use the sum of two similarity scores: BLEU score (Papineni et al., 2002) and the overall sentence similarity described by Li et al. (2006). Since this method is similar to an information retrieval-based story generation system, we refer to it as RETRIEVAL. HUMAN and RETRIEVAL each contribute a fourth of the total data generated for annotation.

3.2 Crowdsourcing Annotations

We used Amazon Mechanical Turk to collect annotations of continuations paired with their contexts. We collected annotations for 4586 context-continuation pairs, collecting the following three criteria for each pair:

- **Overall quality (O)**: a subjective judgment by the annotator of the quality of the continuation, i.e., roughly how much the annotator thinks the continuation adds to the story.

- **Relevance (R)**: a measure of how relevant the continuation is to the context. This addresses the question of whether the continuation fits within the world of the story.

- **Interestingness (I)**: a measure of the amount of new (but still relevant) information added to the story. We use this to measure whether the continuation makes the story more interesting.

Our criteria follow McIntyre and Lapata (2009) who used interestingness and coherence as two quality criteria for story generation. Our notion of relevance is closely related to coherence; when thinking of judging a continuation, we believed that it would be more natural for annotators to judge the relevance of the continuation to its context, rather than judging the coherence of the resulting story. That is, coherence is a property of a discourse, while relevance is a property of a continuation (in relation to the context).

Our overall quality score was intended to capture any remaining factors that determine human quality judgment. In preliminary annotation experiments, we found that the overall score tended to capture a notion of fluency/grammaticality, hence we decided not to annotate this criterion separately. We asked annotators to forgive minor ungrammaticalities in the continuations and rate them as long as they could be understood. If annotators could not understand the continuation, we asked them to assign a score of 0 for all criteria.

We asked the workers to rate the continuations on a scale of 1 to 10, with 10 being the highest score. We obtained annotations from two distinct annotators for each pair and for each criterion, adding up to a total of $4586 \times 2 \times 3 = 27516$ judgments. We asked annotators to annotate all three criteria for a given pair simultaneously in one HIT.[2] We required workers to be located in the United States, to have a HIT approval rating

Criterion	Mean	Std.	IA MAD	IA SDAD
Overall	5.2	2.5	2.1	1.6
Relevance	5.2	3.0	2.3	1.8
Interestingness	4.6	2.5	2.1	1.9

Table 1: Means and standard deviations for each criterion, as well as inter-annotator (IA) mean absolute differences (MAD) and standard deviations of absolute differences (SDAD).

greater than 97%, and to have had at least 500 HITs approved. We paid $0.08 per HIT. Since task duration can be difficult to estimate from HIT times (due to workers becoming distracted or working on multiple HITs simultaneously), we report the top 5 modes of the time duration data in seconds. For pairs with 3 sentences in the context, the most frequent durations are 11, 15, 14, 17, and 21 seconds. For 4 sentences, the most frequent durations are 18, 20, 19, 21, and 23 seconds.

We required each worker to annotate no more than 150 continuations so as not to bias the data collected. After collecting all annotations, we adjusted the scores to account for how harshly or leniently each worker scored the sentences on average. We did this by normalizing each score by the absolute value of the difference between the worker's mean score and the average mean score of all workers for each criterion. We only normalized scores of workers who annotated more than 10 pairs in order to ensure reliable worker means. We then averaged the two adjusted sets of scores for each pair to get a single set of scores.

4 Dataset Analysis

Table 1 shows means and standard deviations for the three criteria. The means are similar across the three, though interestingness has the lowest, which aligns with our expectations of the ROC stories. For measuring inter-annotator agreement, we consider the mean absolute difference (MAD) of the two judgments for each pair.[3] Table 1 shows the MADs for each criterion and the corresponding standard deviations (SDAD). Overall quality and interestingness showed slightly lower MADs than relevance, though all three criteria are similar.

The average scores for each data source are shown in Table 2. The ranking of the systems is

---

[2] In a preliminary study, we experimented with asking for each criterion separately to avoid accidental correlation of the criteria, but found that it greatly reduced cumulative cognitive load for each annotator to do all three together.

[3] Cohen's Kappa is not appropriate for our data because, while we obtained two annotations for each pair, they were not always from the same pair of annotators. In this case, an annotator-agnostic metric like MAD (and its associated standard deviation) is a better measure of agreement.

System	#	O	R	I
SEQ2SEQ-GREEDY	596	4.18	4.09	3.81
SEQ2SEQ-DIV	584	3.36	3.50	3.00
SEQ2SEQ-SAMPLE	578	3.69	3.70	3.42
SEQ2SEQ-REVERSE	577	4.61	4.39	4.02
RETRIEVAL	1086	5.68	4.93	5.15
HUMAN	1165	7.22	8.05	6.33

Table 2: Average criteria scores for each system (O = overall, R = relevance, I = interestingness).

consistent across criteria. Human-written continuations are best under all three criteria. The HUMAN relevance average is higher than interestingness. This matches our intuitions about the ROC corpus: the stories were written to capture commonsense knowledge about everyday events rather than to be particularly surprising or interesting stories in their own right. Nonetheless, we do find that the HUMAN continuations have higher interestingness scores than all automatic systems.

The RETRIEVAL system actually outperforms all SEQ2SEQ systems on all criteria, though the gap is smallest on relevance. We found that the SEQ2SEQ systems often produced continuations that fit topically within the world suggested by the context, though they were often generic or merely topically relevant without necessarily moving the story forward. We found S2S-GREEDY produced outputs that were grammatical and relevant but tended to be more mundane whereas S2S-REVERSE tended to produce slightly more interesting outputs that were still grammatical and relevant on average. The sampling and diverse beam search outputs were frequently ungrammatical and therefore suffer under all criteria.

We show sample outputs from the different systems in Table 3. We also show predicted criteria scores from our final automatic scoring model (see Section 6 for details). We show predicted rather than annotated scores here because for a given context, we did not obtain annotations for all continuations for that context. We can see some of the characteristics of the different models and understand how their outputs differ. The RETRIEVAL outputs are sometimes more interesting than the HUMAN outputs, though they often mention new entities that were not contained in the context, or they may be merely topically related to the context without necessarily resulting in a coherent story. This affects interestingness as well, as a continuation must first be relevant in order to be interesting.

4.1 Relationships Among Criteria

Table 4 shows correlations among the criteria for different sets of outputs. RETRIEVAL outputs show a lower correlation between overall score and interestingness than HUMAN outputs. This is likely because the RETRIEVAL outputs with high interestingness scores frequently contained more surprising content such as new character names or new actions/events that were not found in the context. Therefore, a high interestingness score was not as strongly correlated with overall quality as with HUMAN outputs, for which interesting continuations were less likely to contain erroneous new material.

HUMAN continuations have a lower correlation between relevance and interestingness than the RETRIEVAL or SEQ2SEQ models. This is likely because nearly all HUMAN outputs are relevant, so their interestingness does not depend on their relevance. For SEQ2SEQ, the continuations can only be interesting if they are first somewhat relevant to the context; nonsensical output was rarely annotated as interesting. Thus the SEQ2SEQ relevance and interestingness scores have a higher correlation than for HUMAN or RETRIEVAL.

The lower rows show correlations for different levels of overall quality. For stories whose overall quality is greater than 7.5, the correlations between the overall score and the other two criteria is higher than when the overall quality is lower. The correlation between relevance and interestingness is not as high (0.34). The stories at this quality level are already at least somewhat relevant and understandable, hence like HUMAN outputs, the interestingness score is not as dependent on the relevance score. For stories with overall quality below 2.5, the stories are often not understandable so annotators assigned low scores to all three criteria, leading to higher correlation among them.

4.2 Features

We also analyze our dataset by designing features of the ⟨context, continuation⟩ pair and measuring their correlation with each criterion.

4.2.1 Shallow Features

We consider simple features designed to capture surface-level characteristics of the continuation:

- **Length**: number of tokens in the continuation.

- **Relative length**: the length of the continuation divided by the length of the context.

Context 1: Tripp wanted to learn how to put a topspin on his serve . He was a more advanced tennis player . He sought out a tennis pro to help him . He finally perfected his topspin .		O	R	I
System	**Continuation**			
S2S-GREEDY	He won the game .	4.12	4.99	3.45
S2S-DIV	Now he had the game.	4.25	5.04	3.60
S2S-SAMPLE	Now , he is able to play his .	4.48	4.88	3.94
S2S-REVERSE	He took a few minutes .	4.92	5.77	4.22
RETRIEVAL	Lyn now has a great backhand .	6.05	7.14	5.34
HUMAN	His game improved even more.	5.05	6.16	4.36
Context 2: Neil had just entered the country of Oman . He found the desert land to be enchanting . The women dressed beautifully and the men were friendly . Neil felt very comfortable in Oman .				
S2S-GREEDY	Neil decided to try the best man.	5.47	6.13	4.74
S2S-DIV	They were days and decided	4.66	5.65	3.96
S2S-SAMPLE	Neil Neil the trip trip of the trip of the trip	4.95	5.66	4.72
S2S-REVERSE	He took a tour of the city.	3.97	4.83	3.64
RETRIEVAL	Neil saw that South Koreans were a very kind people !	6.26	6.94	5.66
HUMAN	He wished he could stay forever!	6.24	7.22	5.58
Context 3: Ed and Emma were twins and wanted to have matching Halloween costumes . But they couldn 't agree on a costume ! Ed wanted to be a superhero and Emma wanted to be a mermaid .				
S2S-GREEDY	He took out and could make to work .	4.60	5.11	4.11
S2S-DIV	So , s ' and they would learn .	4.71	5.41	4.18
S2S-SAMPLE	They decided went their great time and they their family . s house .	4.86	5.50	4.58
S2S-REVERSE	They decided to try to their local home .	4.74	5.21	4.22
RETRIEVAL	Then their mom offered a solution to please them both .	5.59	6.11	5.05
HUMAN	Then their mom said she could make costumes that 'd please them both .	6.17	6.71	5.69

Table 3: Sample system outputs for different contexts. Final three columns show *predicted* scores from our trained scorer (see Section 6 for details).

	Corr(O,R)	Corr(O,I)	Corr(R,I)
HUMAN	0.70	0.63	0.44
RETRIEVAL	0.68	0.52	0.47
HUMAN + RET.	0.76	0.61	0.53
SEQ2SEQ-ALL	0.72	0.70	0.59
Overall > 7.5	0.46	0.47	0.34
5 < Overall < 7.5	0.44	0.31	0.24
2.5 < Overall < 5	0.38	0.35	0.38
Overall < 2.5	0.41	0.41	0.38
Overall > 2.5	0.76	0.69	0.59

Table 4: Pearson correlations between criteria for different subsets of the annotated data.

- **Language model**: perplexity from a 4-gram language model with modified Kneser-Ney smoothing estimated using KenLM (Heafield, 2011) from the Personal Story corpus (Gordon and Swanson, 2009), which includes about 1.6 million personal stories from weblogs.

- **IDF**: the average of the inverse document frequencies (IDFs) across all tokens in the continuation. The IDFs are computed using Wikipedia sentences as "documents".

4.2.2 PMI Features

We use features based on pointwise mutual information (PMI) of word pairs in the context and continuation. We take inspiration from methods developed for the Choice of Plausible Alternatives (COPA) task (Roemmele et al., 2011), in which a premise is provided with two alternatives. Gor-

don et al. (2011) obtained strong results by using PMIs to compute a score that measures the causal relatedness between a premise and its potential alternatives. For a $\langle$context, continuation$\rangle$ pair, we compute the following score (Gordon et al., 2011):

$$s_{\text{pmi}} = \frac{\sum_{u \in \text{context}} \sum_{v \in \text{continuation}} \text{PMI}(u, v)}{N_{\text{context}} N_{\text{continuation}}}$$

where N_{context} and $N_{\text{continuation}}$ are the numbers of tokens in the context and continuation. We create 6 versions of the above score, combining three window sizes (10, 25, and 50) with both standard PMI and positive PMI (PPMI). To compute PMI/PPMI, we use the Personal Story corpus.[4] For efficiency and robustness, we only compute PMI/PPMI of a word pair if the pair appears more than 10 times in the corpus using the particular window size.

4.2.3 Entity Mention Features

We compute several features to capture how relevant the continuation is to the input. In

---

[4] We use Wikipedia for IDFs and the Personal Story corpus for PMIs. IDF is a simpler statistic which is presumed to be similar across a range of large corpora for most words; we use Wikipedia because it has broad coverage in terms of vocabulary. PMIs require computing word pair statistics and are therefore expected to be more data-dependent, so we chose the Personal Story corpus due to its effectiveness for related tasks (Gordon et al., 2011).

Feature	O	R	I
Length	0.007	0.055	0.071
Relative length	0.018	0.020	0.060
Language model	0.025	0.034	0.058
IDF	0.418	0.316	0.408
PPMI ($w = 10$)	0.265	0.321	0.224
PPMI ($w = 25$)	0.289	0.341	0.249
PPMI ($w = 50$)	0.299	0.351	0.259
Has old mentions	0.050	0.151	0.023
Number of old mentions	0.057	0.146	0.049
Has new mentions	-0.048	-0.115	-0.026
Number of new mentions	-0.052	-0.119	-0.029
Has new names	-0.005	-0.129	0.017
Number of new names	-0.005	-0.130	0.017
Is HUMAN?	*0.56*	*0.62*	*0.50*
Is HUMAN ∪ RETRIEVAL?	*0.60*	*0.49*	*0.56*

Table 5: Spearman correlations between features and annotations. The final two rows are "oracle" binary features that return 1 for continuations from those sets.

order to compute these features we use the part-of-speech tagging, named entity recognition (NER), and coreference resolution tools in Stanford CoreNLP (Manning et al., 2014):

- **Has old mentions**: a binary feature that returns 1 if the continuation has "old mentions," i.e., mentions that are part of a coreference chain that began in the context.

- **Number of old mentions**: the number of old mentions in the continuation.

- **Has new mentions**: a binary feature that returns 1 if the continuation has "new mentions," i.e., mentions that are not part of any coreference chain that began in the context.

- **Number of new mentions**: the number of new mentions in the continuation.

- **Has new names**: if the continuation has new mentions, this binary feature returns 1 if any of the new mentions is a name, i.e., if the mention is a person named entity from the NER system.

- **Number of new names**: the number of new names in the continuation.

4.3 Comparing Features

Table 5 shows Spearman correlations between our features and the criteria.[5] The length features have small positive correlations with all three criteria, showing highest correlation with interestingness. Language model perplexity shows weak correlation for all three measures, with its highest cor-

relation for interestingness. The SEQ2SEQ models output very common words which lets them have relatively low perplexities even with occasional disfluencies, while the human-written outputs contain more rare words.

The IDF feature shows highest correlation with overall and interestingness, and lower correlation with relevance. This is intuitive since the IDF feature will be largest when many rare words are used, which is expected to correlate with interestingness more than relevance. We suspect IDF correlates so well with overall because SEQ2SEQ models typically generate common words, so this feature may partially separate the SEQ2SEQ from HUMAN/RETRIEVAL.

Unlike IDF, the PPMI scores (with window sizes w shown in parentheses) show highest correlations with relevance. This is intuitive, since PPMI will be highest when topical coherence is present in the discourse. Higher correlations are found when using larger window sizes.[6]

The old mentions features have the highest correlation with relevance, as expected. A continuation that continues coreference chains is more likely to be relevant. The new mention/name features have negative correlations with relevance, which is also intuitive: introducing new characters makes the continuation less relevant.

To explore the question of separability between machine and human-written continuations, we measured correlations of "oracle" features that simply return 1 if the output was generated by humans and 0 if it was generated by a system. Such features are highly correlated with all three criteria as seen in the final two rows of Table 5. This suggests that human annotators strongly preferred human generated stories over our models' outputs. Some features may correlate with the annotated criteria if they separate human- and machine-generated continuations (e.g., IDF).

5 Methods for Score Prediction

We now consider ways to build models to predict our criteria. We define neural networks that take as input representations of the context/continuation pair $\langle b, c \rangle$ and our features and output a continuous value for each predicted criterion.

We experiment with two ways of representing the input based on the embeddings of b and c,

---

[5]These use the combined training and validation sets; we describe splitting the data below in Section 6.

[6]We omit full results for brevity, but the PPMI features showed slightly higher correlations than PMI features.

which we denote $\mathbf{v}_b$ and $\mathbf{v}_c$ respectively. The first ("cont") uses only the continuation embedding without any representation of the context or the similarity between the context and continuation: $\mathbf{x}_{\text{cont}} = \langle \mathbf{v}_c \rangle$. The second ("sim+cont") also contains the elementwise multiplication of the context and continuation embeddings concatenated with the absolute difference: $\mathbf{x}_{\text{sim+cont}} = \langle \mathbf{v}_b \odot \mathbf{v}_c, |\mathbf{v}_b - \mathbf{v}_c|, \mathbf{v}_c \rangle$.

To compute representations $\mathbf{v}$, we use the average of character n-gram embeddings (Huang et al., 2013; Wieting et al., 2016), fixing the output dimensionality to 300. We found this to outperform other methods. In particular, the next best method used gated recurrent averaging networks (GRANs; Wieting and Gimpel, 2017), followed by long short-term memory (LSTM) networks (Hochreiter and Schmidhuber, 1997), and followed finally by word averaging.

The input, whether $\mathbf{x}_{\text{cont}}$ or $\mathbf{x}_{\text{sim+cont}}$, is fed to one fully-connected hidden layer with 300 units, followed by a rectified linear unit (ReLU) activation. Our manually computed features (Length, IDF, PMI, and Mention) are concatenated prior to this layer. The output layer follows and uses a linear activation.

We use mean absolute error as our loss function during training. We train to predict the three criteria jointly, so the loss is actually the sum of mean absolute errors over the three criteria. We found this form of multi-task learning to significantly outperform training separate models for each criterion. When tuning, we tune based on the average Spearman correlation across the three criteria on our validation set. We train all models for 25 epochs using Adam (Kingma and Ba, 2014) with a learning rate of 0.001.

6 Experiments

After averaging the two annotator scores to get our dataset of 4586 context/continuation pairs, we split the data randomly into 600 pairs for validation, 600 for testing, and used the rest (3386) for training. For our evaluation metric, we use Spearman correlation between the scorer's predictions and the annotated scores.

6.1 Feature Ablation

Table 6 shows results as features are either removed from the full set or added to the featureless model, all when using the "cont" input schema.

	O	R	I
All features	57.3	53.4	49.6
- PMI	56.3	50.4	48.6
- IDF	56.6	53.6	46.0
- Mention	54.8	50.3	48.6
- Length	56.1	55.9	45.3
No features	51.9	44.9	43.8
+ PMI	54.5	50.9	44.9
+ IDF	54.3	46.7	46.3
+ Mention	53.8	48.8	46.0
+ Length	51.9	43.1	44.9
+ IDF, Length	54.6	46.5	47.3

Table 6: Ablation experiments with several feature sets (Spearman correlations on the validation set).

model	features	validation			test		
		O	R	I	O	R	I
cont	none	51.9	44.9	43.8	53.3	46.0	50.5
	IDF, Len.	54.6	46.5	47.3	51.6	40.6	50.2
	all	57.3	53.4	49.6	57.1	54.3	52.8
sim+ cont	none	51.6	43.7	44.3	52.2	45.0	48.4
	IDF, Len.	54.2	45.6	47.7	56.0	46.8	53.0
	all	55.1	54.8	47.4	58.7	55.8	52.9

Table 7: Correlations (Spearman's $\rho \times 100$) on validation and test sets for best models with three feature sets.

Each row corresponds to one feature ablation or addition, except for the final row which corresponds to adding two feature sets that are efficient to compute: IDF and Length. The Mention and PMI features are the most useful for relevance, which matches the pattern of correlations in Table 5, while IDF and Length features are most helpful for interestingness. All feature sets contribute in predicting overall quality, with the Mention features showing the largest drop in correlation when they are ablated.

6.2 Final Results

Table 7 shows our final results on the validation and test sets. The highest correlations on the test set are achieved by using the sim+cont model with all features. While interestingness can be predicted reasonably well with just IDF and the Length features, the prediction of relevance is improved greatly with the full feature set.

Using our strongest models, we computed the average predicted criterion scores for each story generation system on the test set. Overall, the predicted rankings are strongly correlated with the rankings yielded by the aggregated annotations shown in Table 2, especially in terms of distinguishing human-written and machine-generated continuations.

While the PMI features are very helpful for predicting relevance, they do have demanding space requirements due to the sheer number of word pairs with nonzero counts in large corpora. We attempted to replace the PMI features by similar features based on word embedding similarity, following the argument that skip-gram embeddings with negative sampling form an approximate factorization of a PMI score matrix (Levy and Goldberg, 2014). However, we were unable to find the same performance by doing so; the PMI scores were still superior.

For the automatic scores shown in Table 3, we used the sim+cont model with IDF and Length features. Since this model does not require PMIs or NLP analyzers, it is likely to be the one used most in practice by other researchers within training/tuning settings. We release this trained scorer as well as our annotated data to the research community.

7 Conclusion

We conducted a manual evaluation of neural sequence-to-sequence and retrieval-based story continuation systems along three criteria: overall quality, relevance, and interestingness. We analyzed the annotations and identified features that correlate with each criterion. These annotations also provide a new story understanding task: predicting the quality scores of generated continuations. We took initial steps toward solving this task by developing an automatic scorer that uses features, compositional architectures, and multi-task training. Our trained continuation scorer can be used as a rich feature function for story generation or a reward function for systems that use reinforcement learning to learn to generate stories. The annotated data and trained scorer are available at the authors' websites.

Acknowledgments

We thank Melissa Roemmele and the anonymous reviewers for their comments. We also thank NVIDIA Corporation for donating GPUs used in this research.

References

Samy Bengio, Oriol Vinyals, Navdeep Jaitly, and Noam Shazeer. 2015. Scheduled sampling for sequence prediction with recurrent neural networks. In *Advances in Neural Information Processing Systems*. pages 1171–1179.

Kyunghyun Cho, Bart van Merrienboer, Caglar Gulcehre, Dzmitry Bahdanau, Fethi Bougares, Holger Schwenk, and Yoshua Bengio. 2014. Learning phrase representations using RNN encoder–decoder for statistical machine translation. In *Proceedings of the 2014 Conference on Empirical Methods in Natural Language Processing (EMNLP)*. pages 1724–1734.

Angel Daza, Hiram Calvo, and Jesús Figueroa-Nazuno. 2016. Automatic text generation by learning from literary structures. In *Proceedings of the Fifth Workshop on Computational Linguistics for Literature*. pages 9–19.

Natalie Dehn. 1981. Story generation after TALE-SPIN. In *Proceedings of the 9th International Joint Conference on Artificial Intelligence (IJCAI)*. pages 16–18.

David K. Elson. 2012. *Modeling Narrative Discourse*. Ph.D. thesis, Columbia University.

Albert Gatt and Emiel Krahmer. 2017. Survey of the state of the art in natural language generation: Core tasks, applications and evaluation. *arXiv preprint arXiv:1703.09902* .

Pablo Gervás. 2012. Story generator algorithms. *The Living Handbook of Narratology* 19.

Andrew S. Gordon, Cosmin Adrian Bejan, and Kenji Sagae. 2011. Commonsense causal reasoning using millions of personal stories. In *25th Conference on Artificial Intelligence (AAAI-11)*.

Andrew S. Gordon and Reid Swanson. 2009. Identifying personal stories in millions of weblog entries. In *Third International Conference on Weblogs and Social Media, Data Challenge Workshop*.

Kenneth Heafield. 2011. KenLM: faster and smaller language model queries. In *Proceedings of the EMNLP 2011 Sixth Workshop on Statistical Machine Translation*.

Sepp Hochreiter and Jürgen Schmidhuber. 1997. Long short-term memory. *Neural computation* 9(8).

Po-Sen Huang, Xiaodong He, Jianfeng Gao, Li Deng, Alex Acero, and Larry Heck. 2013. Learning deep structured semantic models for web search using clickthrough data. In *Proceedings of the 22nd ACM international conference on Conference on information & knowledge management*. ACM, pages 2333–2338.

Ting-Hao (Kenneth) Huang, Francis Ferraro, Nasrin Mostafazadeh, Ishan Misra, Aishwarya Agrawal, Jacob Devlin, Ross Girshick, Xiaodong He, Pushmeet Kohli, Dhruv Batra, C. Lawrence Zitnick, Devi Parikh, Lucy Vanderwende, Michel Galley, and Margaret Mitchell. 2016. Visual storytelling. In *Proceedings of the 2016 Conference of the North American Chapter of the Association for Computational Linguistics: Human Language Technologies*. pages 1233–1239.

Parag Jain, Priyanka Agrawal, Abhijit Mishra, Mohak Sukhwani, Anirban Laha, and Karthik Sankaranarayanan. 2017. Story generation from sequence of independent short descriptions. In *Workshop on Machine Learning for Creativity, at the 23rd SIGKDD Conference on Knowledge Discovery and Data Mining (KDD 2017)*.

Chloé Kiddon, Luke Zettlemoyer, and Yejin Choi. 2016. Globally coherent text generation with neural checklist models. In *Proceedings of the 2016 Conference on Empirical Methods in Natural Language Processing*. pages 329–339.

Diederik Kingma and Jimmy Ba. 2014. Adam: A method for stochastic optimization. *arXiv preprint arXiv:1412.6980* .

Sheldon Klein, John F. Aeschlimann, David F. Balsiger, Steven L. Converse, Claudine Court, Mark Foster, Robin Lao, John D. Oakley, and Joel Smith. 1973. Automatic novel writing: A status report. Technical Report 186, University of Wisconsin-Madison.

Michael Lebowitz. 1985. Story-telling as planning and learning. *Poetics* 14(6):483–502.

Omer Levy and Yoav Goldberg. 2014. Neural word embedding as implicit matrix factorization. In *Advances in Neural Information Processing Systems 27*.

Yuhua Li, David McLean, Zuhair A Bandar, James D O'shea, and Keeley Crockett. 2006. Sentence similarity based on semantic nets and corpus statistics. *IEEE transactions on knowledge and data engineering* 18(8):1138–1150.

Chia-Wei Liu, Ryan Lowe, Iulian Serban, Mike Noseworthy, Laurent Charlin, and Joelle Pineau. 2016. How NOT to evaluate your dialogue system: An empirical study of unsupervised evaluation metrics for dialogue response generation. In *Proceedings of the 2016 Conference on Empirical Methods in Natural Language Processing*. pages 2122–2132.

Hugo Liu and Push Singh. 2002. MAKEBELIEVE: Using commonsense knowledge to generate stories. In *Proceedings of the Eighteenth National Conference on Artificial Intelligence (AAAI)*. pages 957–958.

Ryan Lowe, Michael Noseworthy, Iulian V. Serban, Nicolas Angelard-Gontier, Yoshua Bengio, and Joelle Pineau. 2017. Towards an automatic Turing test: Learning to evaluate dialogue responses. In *Proceedings of the 55th Annual Meeting of the Association for Computational Linguistics*.

Inderjeet Mani. 2012. Computational modeling of narrative. *Synthesis Lectures on Human Language Technologies* 5(3):1–142.

Christopher D. Manning, Mihai Surdeanu, John Bauer, Jenny Rose Finkel, Steven Bethard, and David McClosky. 2014. The Stanford CoreNLP natural language processing toolkit. In *ACL (System Demonstrations)*. pages 55–60.

Neil McIntyre and Mirella Lapata. 2009. Learning to tell tales: A data-driven approach to story generation. In *Proceedings of the Joint Conference of the 47th Annual Meeting of the ACL and the 4th International Joint Conference on Natural Language Processing of the AFNLP*. pages 217–225.

Neil McIntyre and Mirella Lapata. 2010. Plot induction and evolutionary search for story generation. In *Proceedings of the 48th Annual Meeting of the Association for Computational Linguistics*. pages 1562–1572.

Neil Duncan McIntyre. 2011. *Learning to tell tales: automatic story generation from Corpora*. Ph.D. thesis, The University of Edinburgh.

James R. Meehan. 1977. TALE-SPIN, an interactive program that writes stories. In *Proceedings of the 5th International Joint Conference on Artificial Intelligence (IJCAI)*. pages 91–98.

Nasrin Mostafazadeh, Nathanael Chambers, Xiaodong He, Devi Parikh, Dhruv Batra, Lucy Vanderwende, Pushmeet Kohli, and James Allen. 2016. A corpus and cloze evaluation for deeper understanding of commonsense stories. In *Proceedings of the 2016 Conference of the North American Chapter of the Association for Computational Linguistics: Human Language Technologies*. pages 839–849.

K.M. Oinonen, Mariet Theune, Antinus Nijholt, and J.R.R. Uijlings. 2006. *Designing a story database for use in automatic story generation*, Springer Verlag, pages 298–301. Lecture Notes in Computer Science.

Kishore Papineni, Salim Roukos, Todd Ward, and Wei-Jing Zhu. 2002. BLEU: a method for automatic evaluation of machine translation. In *Proceedings of the 40th annual meeting on association for computational linguistics*. pages 311–318.

Vladimir Propp. 1968. *Morphology of the Folktale*, volume 9. University of Texas Press.

Mark O. Riedl and Robert Michael Young. 2010. Narrative planning: Balancing plot and character. *Journal of Artificial Intelligence Research* 39:217–268.

Melissa Roemmele. 2016. Writing stories with help from recurrent neural networks. In *Thirtieth AAAI Conference on Artificial Intelligence*. pages 4311 – 4312.

Melissa Roemmele, Cosmin Adrian Bejan, and Andrew S. Gordon. 2011. Choice of Plausible Alternatives: An Evaluation of Commonsense Causal Reasoning. In *AAAI Spring Symposium on Logical Formalizations of Commonsense Reasoning*. Stanford University.

Melissa Roemmele and Andrew S. Gordon. 2015. Creative help: a story writing assistant. In *International Conference on Interactive Digital Storytelling*. Springer, pages 81–92.

Melissa Roemmele, Andrew S. Gordon, and Reid Swanson. 2017. Evaluating story generation systems using automated linguistic analyses. In *Workshop on Machine Learning for Creativity, at the 23rd SIGKDD Conference on Knowledge Discovery and Data Mining (KDD 2017)*.

Roger C. Schank and Robert P. Abelson. 1975. Scripts, plans, and knowledge. In *Proceedings of the 4th International Joint Conference on Artificial Intelligence (IJCAI)*. pages 151–157.

Ilya Sutskever, Oriol Vinyals, and Quoc V. Le. 2014. Sequence to sequence learning with neural networks. In *Advances in neural information processing systems*. pages 3104–3112.

Reid Swanson and Andrew S. Gordon. 2012. Say anything: Using textual case-based reasoning to enable open-domain interactive storytelling. *ACM Trans. Interact. Intell. Syst.* 2(3):16:1–16:35.

Mariët Theune, Sander Faas, Anton Nijholt, and Dirk Heylen. 2003. The virtual storyteller: story creation by intelligent agents. In *Proceedings of the 1st International Conference on Technologies for Interactive Digital Storytelling and Entertainment*. Springer, pages 204–215.

Perry W. Thorndyke. 1977. Cognitive structures in comprehension and memory of narrative discourse. *Cognitive psychology* 9(1):77–110.

Scott R. Turner. 1993. *Minstrel: a computer model of creativity and storytelling*. Ph.D. thesis, University of California at Los Angeles.

Ashwin K Vijayakumar, Michael Cogswell, Ramprasath R Selvaraju, Qing Sun, Stefan Lee, David Crandall, and Dhruv Batra. 2016. Diverse beam search: Decoding diverse solutions from neural sequence models. *arXiv preprint arXiv:1610.02424* .

Tong Wang, Ping Chen, and Boyang Li. 2017. Predicting the quality of short narratives from social media. In *Proceedings of the Twenty-Sixth International Joint Conference on Artificial Intelligence (IJCAI)*.

John Wieting, Mohit Bansal, Kevin Gimpel, and Karen Livescu. 2016. Charagram: Embedding words and sentences via character n-grams. In *Proceedings of the 2016 Conference on Empirical Methods in Natural Language Processing*. pages 1504–1515.

John Wieting and Kevin Gimpel. 2017. Revisiting recurrent networks for paraphrastic sentence embeddings. In *Proceedings of the 55th Annual Meeting of the Association for Computational Linguistics (Volume 1: Long Papers)*. pages 2078–2088.

Robert Wilensky. 1983. Story grammars versus story points. *Behavioral and Brain Sciences* 6(4):579–591.

Patrick Henry Winston. 2014. The Genesis story understanding and story telling system: A 21st century step toward artificial intelligence. Memo 019, Center for Brains Minds and Machines, MIT.

Term Definitions Help Hypernymy Detection

Wenpeng Yin and **Dan Roth**
University of Pennsylvania
{wenpeng,danroth}@seas.upenn.edu

Abstract

Existing methods of hypernymy detection mainly rely on statistics over a big corpus, either mining some co-occurring patterns like "animals such as cats" or embedding words of interest into context-aware vectors. These approaches are therefore limited by the availability of a large enough corpus that can cover all terms of interest and provide sufficient contextual information to represent their meaning. In this work, we propose a new paradigm, HYPERDEF, for **hyper**nymy detection – expressing word meaning by encoding word **def**initions, along with context driven representation. This has two main benefits: (i) Definitional sentences express (sense-specific) corpus-independent meanings of words, hence definition-driven approaches enable strong generalization – once trained, the model is expected to work well in open-domain testbeds; (ii) Global context from a large corpus and definitions provide complementary information for words. Consequently, our model, HYPERDEF, once trained on task-agnostic data, gets state-of-the-art results in multiple benchmarks[1].

1 Introduction

Language understanding applications like textual entailment (Dagan et al., 2013), question answering (Saxena et al., 2007) and relation extraction (Mintz et al., 2009), benefit from the identification of lexical entailment relations. Lexical inference encompasses several semantic relations, with hypernymy being one of the prevalent (Roller et al., 2014; Shwartz et al., 2016), an *i.e., "Is-A" relation that holds for a pair of terms[2] (x, y) for specific terms' senses*.

Two families of approaches have been studied for identifying term hypernymy. (i) *Pattern match-*

ing exploits patterns such as "animals such as cats" to indicate a hypernymy relation from "cat" to "animal" (Hearst, 1992; Snow et al., 2004). However, it requires the co-occurrence of the two terms in the same sentence, which limits the recall of this method; (ii) *Term representation learning* depends on a vector embedding of each term, where each entry in the vector expresses an explicit context feature (Baroni et al., 2012a; Roller and Erk, 2016; Shwartz et al., 2017) or a latent semantic (Fu et al., 2014; Vulic and Mrksic, 2017; Glavas and Ponzetto, 2017).

Both approaches hinge on acquiring context-aware term meaning in a large corpus. The generalization of these corpus-based representation learning paradigms, however, is limited due to the domain specificity of the training data. For example, an IT corpus hardly mentions "apple" as a fruit. Furthermore, the surrounding context of a term may not convey subtle differences in term meaning – "he" and "she" have highly similar context that may not reveal the important difference between them. Moreover, rare words are poorly expressed by their sparse global context and, more generally, these methods would not generalize to the low resource language setting.

Humans can easily determine the hypernymy relation between terms even for words they have not been exposed to a lot, given a definition of it in terms of other words. For example, one can imagine a "teaching" scenario that consists of *defining* a term, potentially followed by a few examples of the term usage in text.

Motivated by these considerations and the goal of eventually develop an approach that could generalize to unseen words and even to the low resource languages scenario, we introduce the following hypernymy detection paradigm, HYPER-DEF, where we augment distributional contextual models with that of learning terms representations

---

[1] cogcomp.org/page/publication_view/836
[2] This paper uses "term" to refer to any words or phrases.

*Proceedings of the 7th Joint Conference on Lexical and Computational Semantics (*SEM)*, pages 203–213
New Orleans, June 5-6, 2018. ©2018 Association for Computational Linguistics

from their definitions. This paradigm has an important advantage in its *powerful generalization*, as definitions are agnostic to specific domains and benchmarks, and are equally available for words regardless of their frequency in a given data set. Consequently, the task of identifying the relation between two terms is enhanced by the knowledge of the terms' definitions. Our model can be applied to any new terms in any domain, given some context of the term usage and their domain-agnostic definitions. Moreover, given our learning approach – we learn also the notion of *lexical entailment* between terms – we can generalize to any lexical relation between terms.

Technically, we implement HYPERDEF by modifying the AttentiveConvNet (Yin and Schütze, 2017), a top-performing system on a textual entailment benchmark (Bowman et al., 2015), to model the input $(x, d_x; y, d_y)$, where d_i $(i = x, y)$ is the definition of term i. In contrast to earlier work which mostly built separate representations for terms x and y, HYPERDEF instead directly models the representation for each pair in $\{(x, y), (x, d_y), (d_x, y), (d_x, d_y)\}$, and then accumulates the four-way representations to form an overall representation for the input.

In our experiments, we train HYPERDEF on a task-agnostic annotated dataset, Wordnet, and test it on a broad array of open-domain hypernymy detection datasets. The results show the outstanding performance and strong generalization of the HYPERDEF model.

Overall, our contributions are as follows:

- To our knowledge, this is the first work in hypernymy detection that makes use of term definitions. Definitions provide complementary knowledge to distributional context, so that our model better tolerates unseen words, rare words and words with biased sense distribution.

- HYPERDEF accounts for word sense when inferring the hypernymy relation. This differs from much of the literature, which usually derives sense-unaware representative vectors for terms – earlier approaches would say 'yes' if the relation holds for some combination of the terms' senses.

- HYPERDEF has strong generalization capability – once trained on a task-agnostic definition dataset, it can be used in different testbeds, and shows state-of-the-art results.

2   Related Work

The main novelty of our HYPERDEF lies in the *information resource* that is employed to represent the terms. Prior work in exploring information resources can be put into two categories: understanding terms by the co-occurring context in raw text, or grounding the terms in open-domain objects.

2.1   Mining Distributional Context from Text

Window-based Context   Baroni et al. (2012b) build distributional semantic vectors for terms from a concatenation of three corpora: the British National Corpus, WackyPedia and ukWac. Each entry in the vector is the PMI-formulated score from co-occurrence counts. Dimension reduction is conducted by Singular Value Decomposition (SVD) before feeding representation vectors to a classifier.

Dependency-based Context   Roller and Erk (2016) compute a *syntactic* distributional space for terms by counting their *dependency neighbors* across the corpus.

Shwartz et al. (2017) further compare (i) contexts being parent and daughter nodes in the dependency tree, and (ii) contexts being the parent-sister pairs in the dependency tree.

Term Embeddings   Unspecialized term embeddings are not informative signals for detecting specific lexico-semantic relations. Hence, community often explicitly build transformation functions from unspecialized embeddings to relation-specialized embeddings. Fu et al. (2014) first use the skip-gram model (Mikolov et al., 2013) to learn generic term embeddings from a large Chinese encyclopedia corpus, then learn a projection function from the generic space to hypernymy space by annotated hypernymy pairs. Other work trying to specify the generic word embeddings to hypernymy detection task include (Vulic and Mrksic, 2017; Glavas and Ponzetto, 2017).

Other advanced types of term embeddings specific to the hypernymy detection problem include Gaussian distributed embeddings (Vilnis and McCallum, 2015), non-negative embeddings (Chang et al., 2017), magnitude-oriented embeddings (Nguyen et al., 2017), and so on.

In our work, distributional context model is also applied. More specifically, we will directly use pretrained word embeddings as initial word representations and specialize them in training. In contrast, distributional context only acts as one side of information resource to express words, we focus on making use of a second side of information from word definitions to build a more robust system.

2.2 Grounding Terms to Open-domain Objects

Do and Roth (2012) build Wikipedia representations for input terms – representing the input terms by a set of relevant Wikipedia pages.

Shwartz et al. (2015) represent each term pair as a set of paths which are extracted from different large-scale knowledge resources (DBPedia, Wikidata, Yago and WordNet), then train a classifier to determine whether the two terms satisfy a relation of interest given those path connections.

Young et al. (2014) map terms to a set of images, then determine the directional inference by conditional probability over statistic of image intersection.

Compared with mining of distributional context from text, these works switch the context from words to Wikipedia pages, KB paths or images. So, they share a similar mechanism while differing in the categories of entries in distributional vectors.

Our paradigm HYPERDEF shares the same inspiration with above distributional models. More importantly, It goes beyond the frame of distributional models by exploring a novel information resource – definitions – to derive the word semantics.

3 HYPERDEF Model

In this section, we first give a brief review of a top-performing neural network for textual entailment – AttentiveConvNet (Yin and Schütze, 2017), which acts as a base model to encode a pair of texts. Then, we elaborate on the adaptation we make towards AttentiveConvNet so that the resulting system can better serve the hypernymy detection problem.

3.1 AttentiveConvNet

AttentiveConvNet[3] (Yin and Schütze, 2017) is essentially a Siamese convolutional neural network

(CNN) (LeCun et al., 1998) equipped with an attention mechanism. It predicts the relationship of two sentences by accumulating the dominant features of fine-grained alignments across sentences. The reason we base our system on this model is two-fold: (i) AttentiveConvNet is one of the top-performing systems of modeling sentence pairs in textual entailment, and (ii) AttentiveConvNet implements the fine-grained cross-sentence alignments in the granularity of local windows; this makes it appropriate to reason between a definitional sentence and a term.

We use bold uppercase, e.g., $\mathbf{H}$, for matrices; bold lowercase, e.g., $\mathbf{h}$, for vectors; bold lowercase with index, e.g., $\mathbf{h}_i$, for columns of $\mathbf{H}$; format $\mathbf{h}[i]$ to denote the ith entry of vector $\mathbf{h}$; and non-bold lowercase for scalars.

AttentiveConvNet, shown in Figure 1, represents a sentence S ($S \in \{S_1, S_2\}$) of n words as a sequence of hidden states $\mathbf{h}_i \in \mathbb{R}^d$ ($i = 1, 2, \ldots, n$), forming a feature map $\mathbf{H} \in \mathbb{R}^{d \times n}$, where d is the dimensionality of hidden states. Each $\mathbf{h}_i$ has a left context $\mathbf{h}_{i-1}$ and a right context $\mathbf{h}_{i+1}$. Given feature maps $\mathbf{H}_1$ and $\mathbf{H}_2$ for sentences S_1 and S_2 respectively, AttentiveConvNet derives a representation for the pair (S_1, S_2). Unlike conventional CNNs over single sentences, AttentiveConvNet develops an attention mechanism to achieve fine-grained alignments automatically, then puts convolution filters over aligned hidden states together with their context.

Overall, AttentiveConvNet derives the pair representation in three steps. (i) A matching function determines how relevant each hidden state in sentence S_2 is to the current hidden state $\mathbf{h}_i$ in sentence S_1. All hidden states in S_2 are then accumulated by weighted average to form an *aligned hidden state* $\tilde{\mathbf{h}}_i$. (ii) Convolution for position i in S_1 integrates the two aligned hidden states ($\mathbf{h}_i$, $\tilde{\mathbf{h}}_i$) with context $\mathbf{h}_{i-1}$ and $\mathbf{h}_{i+1}$. (iii) Max-pooling over the generated group of hidden states in step (ii) yields a representation for the pair (S_1, S_2). Next, we describe these processes in detail.

Generation of Aligned Hidden States. First, a matching function $f_e(\mathbf{h}_i, \mathbf{h}_j^{S_2})$ generates a score $e_{i,j}$ to evaluate how relevant the two hidden states $\mathbf{h}_i, \mathbf{h}_j^{S_2}$ are.

Given the matching scores, the aligned hidden state $\tilde{\mathbf{h}}_i$ in S_2 for hidden state $\mathbf{h}_i$ in S_1 is the

---

[3]https://github.com/yinwenpeng/Attentive_Convolution

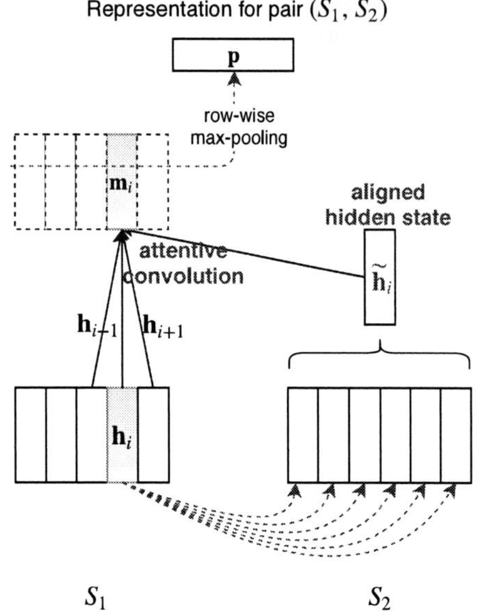

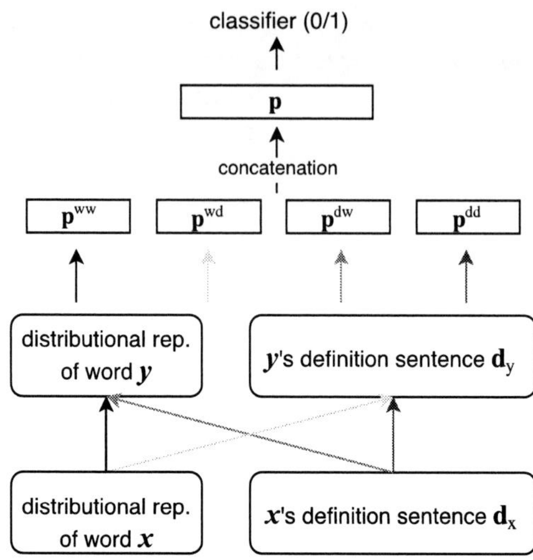

Figure 2: HYPERDEF – combining distributional model with definition encoding

Figure 1: AttentiveConvNet models a sent. pair (S_1, S_2). In our work, S_i (i=1,2) can be the definition sentence or the term itself (we treat a term as a short sentence.)

weighted average of all hidden states in S_2:

$$\tilde{\mathbf{h}}_i = \sum_j \text{softmax}(\mathbf{e}_i)[j] \cdot \mathbf{h}_j^{S_2} \qquad (1)$$

Attentive Convolution. A position i in S_1 has hidden state $\mathbf{h}_i$, left context $\mathbf{h}_{i-1}$, right context $\mathbf{h}_{i+1}$ and aligned hidden state $\tilde{\mathbf{h}}_i$ from S_2. Attentive convolution then generates the higher-level representation for this combination:

$$\mathbf{m}_i = \tanh(\mathbf{W} \cdot [\mathbf{h}_{i-1}, \mathbf{h}_i, \mathbf{h}_{i+1}, \tilde{\mathbf{h}}_i] + \mathbf{b}) \qquad (2)$$

where parameters $\mathbf{W} \in \mathbb{R}^{d \times 4d}$, $\mathbf{b} \in \mathbb{R}^d$.

Pair Representation Generation. As Equation 2 shows, each $\mathbf{m}_i$ denotes the inference features between $\mathbf{h}_i$ and its alignment $\tilde{\mathbf{h}}_i$ in context. AttentiveConvNet uses max-pooling over $\{\mathbf{m}_i\}$ to get the overall representation $\mathbf{p}$ for the pair:

$$\mathbf{p}[i] = \max(\mathbf{m}_1[i], \mathbf{m}_2[i], \cdots, \mathbf{m}_n[i]) \qquad (3)$$

Finally, the representation $\mathbf{p}$ is used in classification. The whole model is learned in an end-to-end training[4].

3.2 Four-way AttentiveConvNet

AttentiveConvNet originally works on sentence pairs. We formulate the hypernymy detection

---

[4] For more details, please refer to (Yin and Schütze, 2017).

problem as $\{(x, d_x; y, d_y; 1/0)\}$. Just as in (Shwartz et al., 2016) which directly concatenates the term path representation vector with term embedding vectors as the classifier input, a simple combination of distributional models and definition encoding for us could be: separately learning the distributional model over term embedding pairs and an AttentiveConvNet model over definition pairs, then concatenate their output representations. However, the analysis over dataset $\{(x, d_x; y, d_y; 1/0)\}$ hints that HYPERDEF can obtain more indicative features by modeling (term, definition), which crosses the distributional models and definition encoding. For example, the definition of term "cat" in WordNet is: *feline mammal usually having thick soft fur and no ability to roar: domestic cats; wildcats.* Intuitively, when the system meets the pair (cat, mammal), it should be trivial to get the "hypernymy" decision since "mammal" appears in the definition sentence.

Inspired by this observation, we implement the HYPERDEF paradigm as four-way AttentiveConvNets, as Figure 2 shows, i.e., treating the two terms as word sequences as well, then do AttentiveConvNet over all four combinations: (x, y), (x, d_y), (d_x, y) and (d_x, d_y).

Assume we get four separate representations: $\mathbf{p}^{ww}$ from (x, y), $\mathbf{p}^{wd}$ from (x, d_y), $\mathbf{p}^{dw}$ from (d_x, y) and $\mathbf{p}^{dd}$ from (d_x, d_y), as Section 3.1 described. We construct the final representation for

	random split					lexical split				
	all	$-\mathbf{p}^{ww}$	$-\mathbf{p}^{wd}$	$-\mathbf{p}^{dw}$	$-\mathbf{p}^{dd}$	all	$-\mathbf{p}^{ww}$	$-\mathbf{p}^{wd}$	$-\mathbf{p}^{dw}$	$-\mathbf{p}^{dd}$
HYPERDEF (F_1)	.905	.874	.896	.876	.881	.887	.875	.870	.849	.862
HYPERDEF (AP)	.933	.902	.921	.905	.909	.900	.890	.883	.880	.877
w/o attention (F1)	.825					.743				
w/o definition (F1)	.734					.619				
LSTM+atten. (F1)	.757					.685				

Table 1: Tune HyperDef on wn_dev

$(x, d_x; y, d_y)$ via concatenation:

$$\mathbf{p} = [\mathbf{p}^{ww}, \mathbf{p}^{wd}, \mathbf{p}^{dw}, \mathbf{p}^{dd}] \qquad (4)$$

then $\mathbf{p}$ is fed to the final classifier.

AttentiveConvNet over (x, y) resembles the conventional hypernymy classifiers which take two representation vectors (one for x, the other for y) as input and output the label. Note that AttentiveConvNet puts filter weights over (x, y) to learn more abstract representations; this actually is in common with some literature such as (Fu et al., 2014; Vulic and Mrksic, 2017; Glavas and Ponzetto, 2017), which utilize weights to project generic word representations into specified representations towards hypernymy annotations.

AttentiveConvNet over (x, d_y) and (d_x, y) compares a term with the descriptive sentence of the other term; this might provide direct clues, as we discussed in the beginning of this subsection.

AttentiveConvNet over (d_x, d_y) resembles literature (Do and Roth, 2012; Young et al., 2014). HYPERDEF provides an alternative resource for interpreting terms, resorting to definitional expressions instead of Wikipedia pages or images.

Overall, our HYPERDEF combines strengths of (i) conventional supervised classifiers over context distributions, and (ii) rich interpretation of terms in broader knowledge bases.

3.3 Analysis of HYPERDEF

Our HYPERDEF has the following properties:

- HYPERDEF combines distributional models with definition encoding, but it is not simply a concatenation of two independent subsystems. HYPERDEF enables modeling across (distributional context, definition). This is expected to generate more indicative features than a similar work (Shwartz et al., 2016), which simply concatenated distributional models with path-based models;

- HYPERDEF employs definitions to provide richer information for the terms. But it does not generate an auxiliary term representation vector from the definitive sentence as the literature (Hill et al., 2016) did. Instead, HYPERDEF formulates a pair of input elements – each can be a distributional vector or a definition representation – into a cross-sentence attention mechanism, which directly yields a compact representation to the pair rather than two separate vectors for the two input elements. This is shown more effective to model the relationship of two pieces of text (Yin and Schütze, 2017);

- Distributional models and definitive sentences in HYPERDEF provide complementary knowledge. For terms which can not retrieve a definition, HYPERDEF still works – just turning into a basic distributional model. This work uses WordNet and Wikipedia as example resources for the definition retrieval, more splendid resources will be developed gradually in released HYPERDEF models. We will also provide users the option to type into their definitions;

- WordNet provides term definitions in the sense level, so theHYPERDEF model is essentially trained in the sense level. For polysemy cases in testing, HYPERDEF can simply test on all combinations of definitions, then pick the pair with the highest probability;

- For terms that were never observed in training, we expect context distributions, such as pretrained embeddings, and definitions are available, so HYPERDEF is hardly influenced in this case. This is exactly the main advantage of HYPERDEF: generalization.

4 Experiments

4.1 Pre-training of HYPERDEF

Dataset Preparation. As we aim to build a strongly generalizing hypernymy detector, the training data we collect here is expected to be task-agnostic. Hence, extracting from structured knowledge resources, such as WordNet (Fellbaum, 1998), Wikidata (Vrandecic, 2012), DBPedia (Auer et al., 2007), and Yago (Suchanek et al., 2007), is preferred. Some literature, e.g., (Shwartz et al., 2015), claim that there is limited coverage for almost all knowledge resources. For example, WordNet does not cover many propernames (Donald Trump $\rightarrow$ president) or recent terminology (AlphaGo $\rightarrow$ computer program). Our data tends to alleviate this challenge, since in testing, descriptive sentences in the HYPERDEF paradigm can provide the precise and distinct features for terms even if these terms are OOV and in new types.

In this work, we pick one of those knowledge resources – WordNet – to *collect training data*. Specifically, our positive instances consist of (i) all direct hypernymy pairs, and (ii) switched terms from the original hyponymy pairs. Negative instances include (i) pairs with other relations such as antonym, synonym, and (ii) pairs of positive instances after exchanging the two terms. Note that each term is accompanied by its definition *in sense level*. So we get instances in form $(x, d_x; y, d_y; 1/0)$, where the binary value "1/0" indicates whether y is x's hypernymy or not. Altogether, we collect about 900K instances with roughly a 8:1 ratio between negative and positive instances.

In testing, we implement HYPERDEF to retrieve definitions and distributional context for terms automatically[5].

Random and Lexical Dataset Splits. In our primary dataset, we perform a *random* split, with 80% train, 10% dev, and 10% test.

As pointed out by Levy et al. (2015), supervised distributional lexical inference methods tend to perform "lexical memorization", i.e., instead of learning a relation between the two terms, they mostly learn an independent property of term y in the pair: whether y is a "prototypical hypernym" or not. Levy et al. (2015) suggest to splitting the

train and test sets such that each will contain a distinct vocabulary ("*lexical split*"), in order to prevent the model from overfitting by lexical memorization.

In the current phase, we use notations *wn_train*, *wn_dev*, and *wn_test* to refer to the three parts. Note that *wn_train* and *wn_dev* will be used to train and tune the HYPERDEF model, while *wn_test* is set to show how well the model performs in WordNet domain – it is not expected to act as a testbed in real benchmarks. In experiments, we will compare our model in *random* and *lexical* splits.

Training Setup. Given *wn_train* in form $\{(x, d_x; y, d_y; 1/0)\}$, a binary classifier via logistic regression is trained over the pair representation **p** obtained from Equation 4, predicting *1* or *0* for the hypernymy relation. The objective function is implemented through negative log-likelihood. Terms and words in definitions are initialized by 300d Word2Vec embeddings (Mikolov et al., 2013) and kept unchanged in training. This benefits the generalization as it ensures that the words in training and the new words in test data lie in the same space. All hidden sizes are 300 as well. The whole system is trained by AdaGrad (Duchi et al., 2011) with initial learning rate 0.02.

We first run the HYPERDEF in *wn_test* to check if it is effective in the WordNet domain. Then we test it in some open-domain benchmarks. *Note that all experiments use the HYPERDEF models pretrained over* wn_train.

4.2 Performance within WordNet

As mentioned in Section 4.1, *wn_train*, *wn_dev* and *wn_test* have two distinct setups: "random split" and "lexical split", inspired by the "lexical memorization" observation (Levy et al., 2015).

We first tune the parameters in wn_train and search the best system layout based on wn_dev. F_1 and average precision (AP) are reported. Table 1 lists the performance records, with the first block for "random split" and the second block for "lexical split".

We first discuss three baselines: (i) "w/o definition": We discard definitions and only use distributional model, i.e., a logistic regression classifier (LR) over the concatenated (x, y) embeddings from Word2Vec. Its performance drops 11.5% from "random split" to "lexical split". This is within expectation as Levy et al. (2015) concluded that this baseline is not effective in

---

[5]In the released HYPERDEF model, we will provide an option for users to input definitions.

learning genuine term relations; (ii) "w/o attention": We discard the attention mechanism in AttentiveConvNet, resulting in a bi-CNN structure. It works on instances $\{(x, d_x; y, d_y; 1/0)\}$, a vanilla CNN is used to encode the definition sentence into a dense representation vector. So, each term in (x, y) will get two separate representation vectors (one is from Word2Vec, the other from the definition); finally totally four representation vectors are concatenated and fed to the LR. This baseline works much better than "w/o definition" (improvements of $9\% \sim 11\%$). Their comparison shows that incorporating term definitions in reasoning process is promising; (iii) "LSTM+attention" (Rocktäschel et al., 2016). A representative attention mechanism in LSTM (Hochreiter and Schmidhuber, 1997) for textual entailment. We apply it in the same way as our four-way AttentiveConvNet, however, found it performs poorly. We suspect that this is due to two reasons: i) Though there is entailment or hypernymy relation between a term pair, e.g., ("cat", "animal"), unfortunately there is no clear clue of that relation between their definition pair *if considering all the information contained in the definitions*. For example, "cat" – "*a small domesticated carnivorous mammal with soft fur, a short snout, and retractile claws. It is widely kept as a pet or for catching mice, and many breeds have been developed*", and "animal" – "*a living organism that feeds on organic matter, typically having specialized sense organs and nervous system and able to respond rapidly to stimuli*". Apparently, we can not infer the whole definition of "animal" by cat's definition. Instead, their help mainly comes from some key-phrases, such as "domesticated carnivorous mammal", "living organism" and so on. LSTM, encoding the whole word sequences in attention, potentially would be misled. Our approach relies on convolution filters and max-pooling, excelling in modeling keywords-driving features (Yin et al., 2017). This baseline indicates the overall strength of our system comes from the definition incorporation as well as an appropriate encoder.

Considering the whole table, we observe that: (i) HYPERDEF models have pretty close performances in "random split" and "lexical split" – mostly within 2~3%. This strongly indicates that HYPERDEF is less influenced by the "lexical memorization" problem. Our systems, equipped

	random	lexical
F_1	.902	.881
AP	.915	.891

Table 2: Pretrained HyperDef on wn_test

with definition encoding, show promising generalization (at least in WordNet domain); (ii) Though HYPERDEF models in "all" setup behave similarly in random split and lexical split, the detailed contributions of $\mathbf{p^{ww}}$, $\mathbf{p^{wd}}$, $\mathbf{p^{dw}}$ and $\mathbf{p^{dd}}$ differ in the two settings. To be specific, in "wn_dev (random split)", there is no clear winner among $\{\mathbf{p}^{ww}, \mathbf{p}^{dw}, \mathbf{p}^{dd}\}$, $\mathbf{p}^{wd}$ contributes consistently less than the other three. In "wn_dev (lexical split)", instead, $\mathbf{p}^{wd}$, $\mathbf{p}^{dw}$ and $\mathbf{p}^{dd}$ perform similarly while $\mathbf{p}^{ww}$ performs worst. This indicates that when dealing with unseen terms, definition-based components in HYPERDEF play a dominant role.

Experiments on wn_dev enable to store the best HYPERDEF models – concatenation over the four representations: $\mathbf{p^{ww}}$, $\mathbf{p^{wd}}$, $\mathbf{p^{dw}}$ and $\mathbf{p^{dd}}$. Then we reload the pretrained models and report their performance on wn_test, as shown in Table 2. From Table 1 to Table 2, we observe pretty small drop in performance – mostly $\sim 1\%$. This preliminarily demonstrates the strong generalization.

Next, we test the best HYPERDEF models pretrained on "wn_train (lexical split)" in open domain benchmarks.

4.3 Performance in Open-domain Datasets

First, we use four widely-explored datasets: **BLESS** (Baroni and Lenci, 2011), **EVALution** (Santus et al., 2015), **Lenci/Benotto** (Benotto, 2015), and **Weeds** (Weeds et al., 2014). They were constructed either using knowledge resources (e.g. WordNet, Wikipedia), crowd-sourcing or both. The instance sizes of hypernymy and "other" relation types are detailed in Table 3. We also report "#OOV_pair", the proportions of unseen term pairs in above four datasets regarding the training set of HYPERDEF, i.e., wn_train in Section 4.1. We notice that most term pairs in BLESS and Lenci/Benotto datasets are unseen in wn_train.

First, we extract the term's *all sense definitions* from WordNet based on the term string. For a few instances which contain terms not covered by WordNet, such as proper noun "you", "everybody" etc, we set definitions the same as the term strings (this preprocessing does not influence results, just for making the system uniformed).

dataset	#hyper.	#others	#OOV_pair
BLESS	1.337	25,217	99.04%
EVALution	3,637	9,828	78.86%
Lenci/Benotto	1,933	3,077	92.50%
Weeds	1,469	1,459	71.54%

Table 3: Statistics of four benchmarks. "#OOV_pair": the proportions of unseen term pairs regarding the training set (i.e., *wn_train* in Section 4.1) of HYPERDEF.

Then, we apply the pre-trained HYPERDEF model *on the test sets of the four benchmarks*, discriminating hypernymy from "other" relations. AP and AP@100 are reported. As WordNet sorts sense definitions by sense frequency (Fellbaum, 1998), we test the term pairs in two ways: (i) Only choose the top-1 sense definition to denote a term, reported as "HYPERDEF$_{TopDef}$"; (ii) Keep all sense definitions for those terms, then test on all sense combinations and pick the highest probability as the term pair score, reported as "HYPERDEF$_{AllDef}$".

We compare HYPERDEF with baselines: (i) **Best-Unsuper**. The best unsupervised method in (Shwartz et al., 2017), implemented by similarity measurement over weighted dependency-based context vectors; (ii) **Concat-SVM** (Glavas and Ponzetto, 2017). An SVM model with RBF kernel is trained on concatenation of unspecialized concept embeddings (Baroni et al., 2012a); (iii) **DUAL-T** (Glavas and Ponzetto, 2017). Using dual tensors, DUAL-T transforms unspecialized embeddings into asymmetrically specialized representations – sets of specialized vectors – which are next used to predict whether the asymmetric relation holds between the concepts; (iv) **Hyper-Score** (Nguyen et al., 2017). The state-of-the-art system. It uses a large-scale hypernymy pair set to guide the learning of hierarchical word embeddings in hypernymy-structured space.

Table 4 clearly demonstrates the superiority of our HYPERDEF models over other systems. The three baselines Concat-SVM, DUAL-T and HyperScore are more in line with HYPERDEF since they did supervised learning over large numbers of annotated pairs. HYPERDEF integrates term definitions, which is shown effective in improving the performance across different testbeds.

In addition, HYPERDEF$_{AllDef}$ consistently outperforms HYPERDEF$_{TopDef}$. This makes sense as HYPERDEF$_{TopDef}$ may be misled by incorrect definitions. In addition, the superiority of HYPERDEF$_{AllDef}$ clearly supports the effectiveness of HYPERDEF in dealing with polysemy cases.

Above four benchmarks are relatively small and contain common words mostly. In real-world applications, there is a need to figure out the hypernymy relation between common nouns and proper nouns (Do and Roth, 2012). Taking "(Champlin, city)" for example, "Champlin" is not covered by WordNet vocabulary, thus uncovered by *wn_train* – the training data of our HYPERDEF model. Motivated, we further test HYPERDEF on the following dataset.

HypeNet Dataset. Shwartz et al. (2016) construct this dataset by extracting hypernymy relations from several resources: WordNet, DBPedia, Wikidata and Yago. Like our collected data, term pairs in other relations are considered as negative instances. It maintains a ratio of 1:4 positive to negative pairs.

Similarly, HypeNet dataset has "random split" and "lexical split" as well; their sizes are list in Table 5. HypeNet contains lots of locations, e.g., (Champlin, city), and organizations, e.g., (Telegram, company) and (Sheetz, company). We first try to extract definitions for those terms from WordNet, if fail, then we extract from Wikipedia pages, treating the first sentence as a definition.

We play HYPERDEF in two different ways, one testing its *"pre-trained"* model on HypeNet's test data, the other – *"specialized"* – training HYPERDEF on HypeNet's training data then test on HypeNet's test data like other baselines did.

Table 6 shows: (i) If trained on the specific training data of HypeNet, our system HYPERDEF can get state of the art performance. This indicates the superiority of our model over baseline systems.

(i) Our pretrained HYPERDEF model performs less satisfactorily. Only the result on "Lex. split" is relatively close to the outstanding baselines. This makes sense as baseline systems are specified by the HypeNet training set while our pretrained model comes from a different domain. We studied the dataset and found following problems.

Error Analysis. Two error sources are observed. (i) Wrong definition. For example, the system obtains the definition "*a substance or treatment with no active therapeutic effect*" for the term "Placebo" in the pair (Placebo, song); however, a successful detection requires mining an-

Model	BLESS		EVALuation		Benotto		Weeds	
	AP	AP@100	AP	AP@100	AP	AP@100	AP	AP@100
Best-Unsuper (Shwartz et al., 2017)	.051	.540	.353	.661	.382	.617	.441	.911
Concat-SVM (Glavas and Ponzetto, 2017)	.097	.235	.321	.329	.523	.586	.644	.793
DUAL-T (Glavas and Ponzetto, 2017)	.487	.823	.446	.866	.557	.847	.774	.985
HyperScore (Nguyen et al., 2017)	.454	–	.538	–	.574	–	.850	–
HYPERDEF$_{TopDef}$	**.595**	.749	.524	**.867**	.557	.825	**.872**	**.989**
HYPERDEF$_{AllDef}$	.508	**.872**	**.623**	**.927**	**.576**	**.909**	**.889**	**.991**

Table 4: System comparison on BLESS, EVALution, Benotto and Weeds datasets

Dataset	train	dev	test	#OOV_pair
HypeNet (rnd)	49.5K	3.5K	17.7K	95.56%
HypeNet (lex)	20.3K	1.4K	6.6K	95.33%

Table 5: Statistics of HypeNet dataset. "#OOV_pair" is for "test" regarding the "wn_train" of HYPERDEF.

Model	Lex. split			Rand. split		
	P	R	F_1	P	R	F_1
HypeNet	.809	.617	.700	.913	.890	.901
DUAL-T	.705	.785	.743	.933	.826	.876
pre-trained	.572	.717	.637	.474	.601	.530
specialized	.670	.914	**.773**	.892	.935	**.913**

Table 6: System comparison on HypeNet test

other definition – "*are an alternative rock band, formed in London, England in 1994 by singer-guitarist Brian Molko and guitarist-bassist Stefan Olsdal*" which depicts the article title "Placebo (band)". This is a common problem due to the ambiguity of entity mentions. To relieve this, we plan to refine the definition retrieval by more advanced entity linking techniques, or retrieve all highly related definitions and test as in polysemy cases (recall that in Table 4 we showed HYPERDEF has more robust performance while addressing polysemy terms); (ii) Misleading information in definitions. Our system predicts "1" for the pair (Aurangabad, India); we analyze the definition of "Aurangabad": *is a city in the Aurangabad district of Maharashtra state in India*. We intentionally removed the phrase "in India", and then the system predicts "0". This demonstrates that definitions indeed provide informative knowledge about terms, but a system must be intelligent to avoid being misled; (iii) We miss a common embedding space to initialize single words and (multi-word) entities. To generalize well to new entities, the model has to presume the new entities and the known terms lie in the same representation space. However, most pretrained embedding sets cover pretty limited entities. To learn uniformed word and entity embeddings, we may need to combine unstructured text corpus, semi-structured data (e.g., Wikipedia) and structured knowledge bases together. We will advance this data preprocessing component – the access of term definitions and term representations – in our released system.

5 Conclusion

In this work, we introduced a novel approach to detecting hypernymy relations by incorporating term definitions. We extracted a task-agnostic annotated data from WordNet, then trained a neural network to generate a universal hypernymy detector, HYPERDEF. HYPERDEF, once trained, performs competitively in diverse open-domain benchmarks, even though it was not fine-tuned on those benchmark-specific training sets. This validates the powerful generalization of our model HYPERDEF. Our hope, and one of the key future directions following this work is to generalize this approach to the low-resource language setting.

Acknowledgments

We thank all the reviewers for providing insightful comments and critiques. This research is supported in part by DARPA under agreement number FA8750-13-2-0008, and by a gift from Google.

References

Sören Auer, Christian Bizer, Georgi Kobilarov, Jens Lehmann, Richard Cyganiak, and Zachary G. Ives. 2007. Dbpedia: A nucleus for a web of open data. In *Proceedings of ISWC/ASWC*. pages 722–735.

Marco Baroni, Raffaella Bernardi, Ngoc-Quynh Do, and Chung-chieh Shan. 2012a. Entailment above the word level in distributional semantics. In *Proceedings of EACL*. pages 23–32.

Marco Baroni, Raffaella Bernardi, Ngoc-Quynh Do, and Chung-chieh Shan. 2012b. Entailment above the word level in distributional semantics. In *Proceedings of EACL*. pages 23–32.

Marco Baroni and Alessandro Lenci. 2011. How we BLESSed distributional semantic evaluation. In *Proceedings of the GEMS 2011 Workshop on GEometrical Models of Natural Language Semantics*. pages 1–10.

Giulia Benotto. 2015. Distributional models for semantic relations: A study on hyponymy and antonymy. *PhD Thesis, University of Pisa* .

Samuel R. Bowman, Gabor Angeli, Christopher Potts, and Christopher D. Manning. 2015. A large annotated corpus for learning natural language inference. In *Proceedings of EMNLP*. pages 632–642.

Haw-Shiuan Chang, ZiYun Wang, Luke Vilnis, and Andrew McCallum. 2017. Unsupervised hypernym detection by distributional inclusion vector embedding. *CoRR* abs/1710.00880.

Ido Dagan, Dan Roth, Mark Sammons, and Fabio Massimo Zanzoto. 2013. Recognizing textual entailment: Models and applications.

Quang Xuan Do and Dan Roth. 2012. Exploiting the wikipedia structure in local and global classification of taxonomic relations. *Natural Language Engineering* 18(2):235–262.

John Duchi, Elad Hazan, and Yoram Singer. 2011. Adaptive subgradient methods for online learning and stochastic optimization. *JMLR* 12:2121–2159.

Christiane Fellbaum. 1998. *WordNet: An Electronic Lexical Database*. MIT Press.

Ruiji Fu, Jiang Guo, Bing Qin, Wanxiang Che, Haifeng Wang, and Ting Liu. 2014. Learning semantic hierarchies via word embeddings. In *Proceedings of ACL*. pages 1199–1209.

Goran Glavas and Simone Paolo Ponzetto. 2017. Dual tensor model for detecting asymmetric lexico-semantic relations. In *Proceedings of EMNLP*. pages 1757–1767.

Marti A. Hearst. 1992. Automatic acquisition of hyponyms from large text corpora. In *Proceedings of COLING*. pages 539–545.

Felix Hill, KyungHyun Cho, Anna Korhonen, and Yoshua Bengio. 2016. Learning to understand phrases by embedding the dictionary. *TACL* 4:17–30.

Sepp Hochreiter and Jürgen Schmidhuber. 1997. Long short-term memory. *Neural computation* 9(8):1735–1780.

Yann LeCun, Léon Bottou, Yoshua Bengio, and Patrick Haffner. 1998. Gradient-based learning applied to document recognition. In *Proceedings of the IEEE*. pages 2278–2324.

Omer Levy, Steffen Remus, Chris Biemann, and Ido Dagan. 2015. Do supervised distributional methods really learn lexical inference relations? In *Proceedings of NAACL*. pages 970–976.

Tomas Mikolov, Ilya Sutskever, Kai Chen, Greg S Corrado, and Jeff Dean. 2013. Distributed representations of words and phrases and their compositionality. In *Proceedings of NIPS*. pages 3111–3119.

Mike Mintz, Steven Bills, Rion Snow, and Daniel Jurafsky. 2009. Distant supervision for relation extraction without labeled data. In *Proceedings of ACL*. pages 1003–1011.

Kim Anh Nguyen, Maximilian Köper, Sabine Schulte im Walde, and Ngoc Thang Vu. 2017. Hierarchical embeddings for hypernymy detection and directionality. In *Proceedings of EMNLP*. pages 233–243.

Tim Rocktäschel, Edward Grefenstette, Karl Moritz Hermann, Tomáš Kočiský, and Phil Blunsom. 2016. Reasoning about entailment with neural attention. In *Proceedings of ICLR*.

Stephen Roller and Katrin Erk. 2016. Relations such as hypernymy: Identifying and exploiting hearst patterns in distributional vectors for lexical entailment. In *Proceedings of EMNLP*. pages 2163–2172.

Stephen Roller, Katrin Erk, and Gemma Boleda. 2014. Inclusive yet selective: Supervised distributional hypernymy detection. In *Proceedings of COLING*. pages 1025–1036.

Enrico Santus, Frances Yung, Alessandro Lenci, and Chu-Ren Huang. 2015. EVALution 1.0: An evolving semantic dataset for training and evaluation of distributional semantic models. In *Proceedings of the 4th Workshop on Linked Data in Linguistics*. pages 64–69.

Ashish Kumar Saxena, Ganesh Viswanath Sambhu, Saroj Kaushik, and L. Venkata Subramaniam. 2007. IITD-IBMIRL system for question answering using pattern matching, semantic type and semantic category recognition. In *Proceedings of TREC*.

Vered Shwartz, Yoav Goldberg, and Ido Dagan. 2016. Improving hypernymy detection with an integrated path-based and distributional method. In *Proceedings of ACL*.

Vered Shwartz, Omer Levy, Ido Dagan, and Jacob Goldberger. 2015. Learning to exploit structured resources for lexical inference. In *Proceedings of CoNLL*. pages 175–184.

Vered Shwartz, Enrico Santus, and Dominik Schlechtweg. 2017. Hypernyms under siege: Linguistically-motivated artillery for hypernymy detection. In *Proceedings of EACL*. pages 65–75.

Rion Snow, Daniel Jurafsky, and Andrew Y. Ng. 2004. Learning syntactic patterns for automatic hypernym discovery. In *Proceedings of NIPS*. pages 1297–1304.

Fabian M. Suchanek, Gjergji Kasneci, and Gerhard Weikum. 2007. Yago: A core of semantic knowledge. In *Proceedings of WWW*. pages 697–706.

Luke Vilnis and Andrew McCallum. 2015. Word representations via gaussian embedding. In *Proceedings of ICLR*.

Denny Vrandecic. 2012. Wikidata: A new platform for collaborative data collection. In *Proceedings of WWW*. pages 1063–1064.

Ivan Vulic and Nikola Mrksic. 2017. Specialising word vectors for lexical entailment. *CoRR* abs/1710.06371.

Julie Weeds, Daoud Clarke, Jeremy Reffin, David J. Weir, and Bill Keller. 2014. Learning to distinguish hypernyms and co-hyponyms. In *Proceedings of COLING*. pages 2249–2259.

Wenpeng Yin, Katharina Kann, Mo Yu, and Hinrich Schütze. 2017. Comparative study of CNN and RNN for natural language processing. *CoRR* abs/1702.01923.

Wenpeng Yin and Hinrich Schütze. 2017. Attentive convolution. *CoRR* abs/1710.00519.

Peter Young, Alice Lai, Micah Hodosh, and Julia Hockenmaier. 2014. From image descriptions to visual denotations: New similarity metrics for semantic inference over event descriptions. *TACL* 2:67–78.

Agree or Disagree: Predicting Judgments on Nuanced Assertions

Michael Wojatzki   **Torsten Zesch**
Language Technology Lab
University of Duisburg-Essen, Germany
michael.wojatzki@uni-due.de
torsten.zeschi@uni-due.de

Saif M. Mohammad   **Svetlana Kiritchenko**
National Research Council Canada
Ottawa, Canada
saif.mohammad@nrc-cnrc.gc.ca
svetlana.kiritchenko@nrc-cnrc.gc.ca

Abstract

Being able to predict whether people agree or disagree with an assertion (i.e. an explicit, self-contained statement) has several applications ranging from predicting how many people will like or dislike a social media post to classifying posts based on whether they are in accordance with a particular point of view. We formalize this as two NLP tasks: predicting judgments of (i) individuals and (ii) groups based on the text of the assertion and previous judgments. We evaluate a wide range of approaches on a crowdsourced data set containing over 100,000 judgments on over 2,000 assertions. We find that predicting individual judgments is a hard task with our best results only slightly exceeding a majority baseline. Judgments of groups, however, can be more reliably predicted using a Siamese neural network, which outperforms all other approaches by a wide margin.

1   Introduction

One of the most basic reactions when reading a sentence is to agree or disagree with it.[1] Mechanisms that allow us to express agreement (e.g. thumb-up, like, up-vote, ♡) or disagreement (e.g. thumb-down, dislike, down-vote) towards posts of other users can be found in almost all social networking sites. The judgments associated with posts that discuss controversial political or social issues, such as *legalization of drug*, *immigration policy*, or *gun rights*, are a rich source of information for those interested in the opinions of individuals or groups. For instance, public opinion regarding an issue is often illustrated by the number of retweets, likes, or upvotes that a politician or influential person receives.

Hence, especially for controversial issues, being able to predict how people judge posts has several applications: *people at large* could automatically anticipate if politicians, companies or other decision makers would agree or disagree with a new perspective on a problem or how they would evaluate a new possible solution. The method can also be used by *journalists* to more accurately analyze the homogeneity of opinions or to detect filter bubbles in social media. *Decision makers* themselves would be able to evaluate in advance how citizens, customers, or employees react to a press announcement, a new regulation, or tweet. *Social media users* could be enabled to search, sort or filter posts based on whether they are in accordance with or contrary to their personal world view. Such predictions could also be used to augment chat applications by indicating to a user if her recipients will agree or disagree with a message to be sent, enabling to choose a more or less confrontational discussion style.

In this paper, we describe how the outlined use cases can be framed as two inference tasks: predicting individual judgments and predicting judgments of whole groups. As a first step, we restrict ourselves to judgments on textual utterances that are explicit, relevant, and that do not contain multiple positions. We will refer to such utterances as *assertions*. For solving the tasks, we define the degree to which two assertions are judged similar as **judgment similarity**. This similarity allows us to predict a judgment based on other judgments that have been made on similar, known assertions.

Across both tasks, we compare this strategy against several baselines and reference approaches on a newly crowdsourced data set containing over 100 000 judgments on assertions. We find that, for predicting individual judgments, our best results only slightly exceed a majority baseline, but that judgments of groups can be more reliably pre-

---

[1] You are probably thinking about whether you agree with that statement right now.

*Proceedings of the 7th Joint Conference on Lexical and Computational Semantics (*SEM)*, pages 214–224
New Orleans, June 5-6, 2018. ©2018 Association for Computational Linguistics

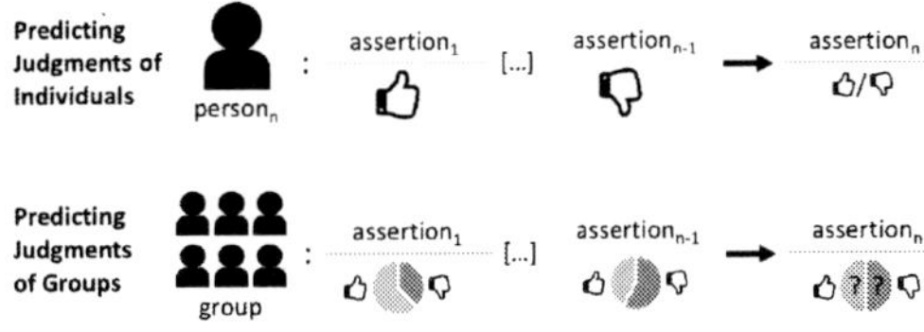

Figure 1: Overview on the two prediction tasks.

dicted using a Siamese neural network, which outperforms all other approaches by a wide margin.

2   Predicting Judgments

In order to predict if someone will agree with an assertion, we need knowledge about that person. Ideally, we would have access to a large set of other assertions which the person has already judged. We could then measure the similarity between previous assertions and the new assertion and hypothesize that the judgment on the new assertion should be the same as for a highly similar one. In Figure 1, we show this case for binary (yes/no) predictions on individuals and argue that this can be also generalized to probabilistic predictions on groups of people. Thus, we formulate two prediction tasks:

In the first task, we want to **predict judgments of individuals** on assertions based on other judgments by the same person. Thus, the first task is formulated as follows: given a set of assertions $a_1, ..., a_n$ relevant to an issue and the judgments of a person p_i on $a_1, ..., a_{n-1}$ an automatic system has to predict p_i's judgment on the assertion a_n.

In the second task, we want to **predict judgments of groups** on assertions based on averaged judgments of other assertions. Hence, this task can be formalized as follows: given a set of judgments of a group of persons $p_1, ..., p_k$ on the assertions $a_1, ..., a_{n-1}$, an automatic systems must predict the judgment on the assertion a_n for the same group of persons. Judgments of groups can be expressed by an aggregated agreement score between -1 and 1, where -1 means that every person disagrees to an assertion and 1 that every person agrees to the assertion.

For measuring the similarity between two assertions, we propose to compare how a large group of people judges them. We define the degree to which two assertions are judged similarly by a large group as the **judgment similarity** of the two assertions. However, judgments of other persons

are not easily available – e.g. if we want to predict a judgment on a new, unseen assertion. To overcome this limitation, we propose to use methods that consider the texts of the assertions to mimic judgment similarity and have thus the ability to generalize from existing data collections.

3   Related Work

Measuring the judgment similarity of two assertions is related to several NLP tasks such as the detection of semantic text similarity (STS) (Agirre et al., 2012), paraphrase recognition (Bhagat and Hovy, 2013), and textual entailment (Dagan et al., 2009).

Unlike semantic text similarity, we do not use a notation of similarity based on the intuition of humans, but one that derives from the context of judgments. Hence, we define that the judgment similarity of two assertions is 1 if two assertions are consistently judged the same and are thus interchangeable in the context of our task.

There are several reasons why assertions are judged similarly: their text may convey similar semantics such as in the assertions ‘*Marijuana alleviates the suffering of chronically ill patients*’ and ‘*Marijuana helps chronically ill persons*’. This type of similarity corresponds to what methods of semantic text similarity capture. However, a strong judgment similarity of two assertions can also be due to semantically entailed relationships between assertions. For instance, if people agree with ‘*Marijuana is a gateway drug for teenagers and damages growing brains*’ most of them also agree to ‘*Marijuana is dangerous for minors*’, despite the texts being different in content and having thus low semantic text similarity. In addition, two assertions can also have a strong judgment similarity because of underlying socio-cultural, political, or personal factors. For instance, the assertions ‘*Consuming Marijuana has no impact on your success at work*’ and ‘*Marijuana is not addictive*’ describe different arguments for legalizing marijuana, but judgments made on these assertions are often correlated.

Our work also relates to other attempts on predicting reactions to text, such as predicting the number of retweets (Suh et al., 2010; Petrovic et al., 2011), the number of likes on tweets (Tan et al., 2014), the number of karma points of reddit posts (Wei et al., 2016), or sales from product descriptions (Pryzant et al., 2017). What those works have in common is that they measure some kind of popularity, which differs significantly from our task: even if one agrees with a text, one might decide not to retweet or like it for any number of reasons. There are also cases in which one may retweet a post with which one disagrees in order to flag someone or something from the opposing community. Furthermore, there are effects such as the author's followers affecting the visibility of posts and thereby the likelihood of a like or a retweet (Suh et al., 2010).

In addition, we relate to works that aim at predicting whether two texts (Menini and Tonelli, 2016) or sequences of utterances (Wang and Cardie, 2014; Celli et al., 2016) express agreement or disagreement with each other. More broadly, we also relate to works that analyze stance (Mohammad et al., 2016; Xu et al., 2016; Taulé et al., 2017), sentiment (Pang and Lee, 2008; Liu, 2012; Mohammad, 2016), or arguments (Habernal and Gurevych, 2016; Boltuzic and Šnajder, 2016; Bar-Haim et al., 2017) that are expressed via text. In contrast to these works, we do not examine what judgment, sentiment, or claim is expressed by a text, but whether we can infer agreement or disagreement based on judgments which were made on other assertions.

Finally, we relate to work on analyzing and predicting outcomes of congressional roll-call voting. These works constantly find that votes of politicians can be explained by a low number of underlying, ideological dimensions such as being left or right (Heckman and Snyder, 1996; Poole and Rosenthal, 1997, 2001). Our work is different from these attempts, as we do not consider politicians who might have incentives to vote in accordance with the ideological views of their party, and as we base our prediction on the text of assertions.

4 Data Collection

For exploring how well the two tasks can be solved automatically, we use the dataset *Nuanced Assertions on Controversial Issues (NAoCI)* created by Wojatzki et al. (2018). The dataset contains assertions judged on a wide range of controversial issues.[2] The NAoCI dataset mimics a common situation in many social media sites, where people e.g. up- or downvote social media posts. However, it does not have the experimental problems

of using social media data directly. These problems include legal reasons of scraping social media data and moderator variables such as the definition of issues, the influence of previous posts, or the question of whether someone is not judging an assertion because she does not want to judge it or because she did not perceive it.

The data was collected using crowdsourcing conducted on `crowdflower.com` in two steps. First, participants were asked to generate a large set of assertions relevant to controversial issues. The set of assertions was created using crowdsourcing, as a manual creation of assertions would be potentially incomplete and subject to personal bias. We provided instructions to make sure that the assertions are natural, self-contained statements about an issue. Next, a large number of people was asked to indicate whether they agree or disagree with these assertions.

The process was reviewed and approved by the institutional ethics board of the National Research Council Canada.

Generating Assertions In order to obtain realistic assertions, 69 participants were asked to generate assertions for sixteen predefined issues (see Table 1). For each issue, the subjects were given definition of the issue and a few example assertions. In addition, the instructions state that assertions should be explicit, relevant to an issue, self-contained, and only contain a single position. Specifically, the use of co-reference or hedging indicated by words such as *perhaps*, *maybe*, or *possibly* was not permitted. After a removal of duplicates and instances that did not follow the rules, this process resulted in about 150 unique assertions per issue (2,243 in total).

Judging Assertions Next, 230 subjects were asked to indicate whether they agree or disagree with an assertion, resulting in over 100 000 judgments (see Table 1). The participants were free to judge as many assertions on as many issues as they wanted. On average each assertion is judged by about 45 persons and each participant judged over 400 assertions. For each person, agreement is encoded with 1, disagreement with -1, and missing values with 0 (as not all subjects judged all assertions). Additionally, we can also compute the *aggregated agreement score* for each assertion by simply subtracting the percentage of participants that disagreed with the assertion from the

---

[2]The dataset is accessible from `https://sites.google.com/view/you-on-issues/`

Issue	# of Assertions	# of Judgments
Black Lives Matter	135	6 154
Climate Change	142	6 473
Creationism in School	129	5 747
Foreign Aid	150	6 866
Gender Equality	130	5 969
Gun Rights	145	6 423
Marijuana	138	6 200
Mandatory Vaccination	134	5 962
Media Bias	133	5 877
Obama Care	154	6 940
Same-sex Marriage	148	6 899
US Electoral System	175	7 695
US in the Middle East	138	6 280
US Immigration	130	5 950
Vegetarian & Vegan Lifestyle	128	5 806
War on Terrorism	134	5 892
Total	2 243	101 133

Table 1: Issues and number of crowdsourced assertions and judgments.

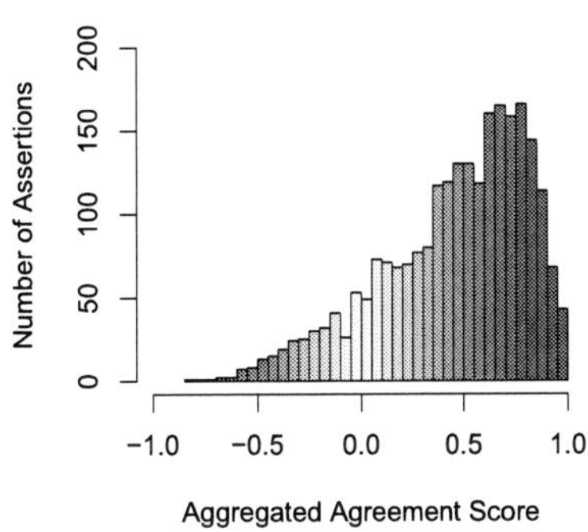

Figure 2: Distribution of aggregated agreement scores.

percentage of participants that agreed with the assertion. Figure 2 shows the distribution of aggregated agreement scores (grouped into bins of size .05) across all issues. The mass of the distribution is concentrated in the positive range of possible values, which indicates that the participants more often agree with the assertions than they disagree. Consequently, baselines accounting for this imbalance perform strongly in predicting judgments on assertions. However, the distribution corresponds to what we observe in many social network sites, where e.g. the ratio of likes to dislikes is also clearly skewed towards likes.

All data, the used questionnaires along with the directions and examples are publicly available on the project website.[2]

5 Measuring Judgment Similarity Between Assertions

As mentioned above, we want to predict judgments on a previously unseen assertion based on judgments of similar assertions. For that purpose, we need to measure the similarity of assertions $sim(a_1, a_2)$ based on their text only. For measuring the similarity of two assertions we rely on the judgment matrix J, with $j_{p,a}$ as the judgment provided by participant p for assertion a, with $\vec{j_p}$ as the row vector of all ratings of participant p, and $\vec{j_a}$ as the column vector of all ratings provided for assertion a. We measure the gold similarity of two assertions by comparing their judgment vectors in the matrix. If the vectors are orthogonal, the assertions are maximally dissimilar (i.e. persons who agree to assertion a_1 disagree with a_2). If the vectors are parallel, the assertions have a perfect similarity. We compute the cosine similarity between the judgment vectors of two assertions. We calculate the gold similarity between all unique pairs (e.g. we do not use both a_1 with a_2 and a_2 with a_1) in our data and do not consider self-pairing.

5.1 Experimental Setup

As baselines for this task, we utilize well-established semantic text similarity (STS) methods that calculate overlap between the surface forms of assertions. We use the following methods as implemented by DKPro Similarity (Bär et al., 2013)[3]: (i) unigram overlap expressed by the Jaccard coefficient (Lyon et al., 2001), (ii) greedy string tiling (Wise, 1996), (iii) longest common sub string (Gusfield, 1997). Additionally, we use averaged word embeddings (Bojanowski et al., 2017).

Beyond the baselines, we apply two machine learning approaches: a conventional SVM-based classifier and a neural network. The SVM classifier is implemented using LibSVM (Chang and Lin, 2011) as provided by DKProTC (Daxenberger et al., 2014).[4] We use a combination of various ngram features, sentiment features (derived from the system by Kiritchenko et al. (2014)[5]), embedding features (averaged embeddings by Bojanowski et al. (2017)) and negation features. We used a linear kernel with C=100 and the nu-SVR

---

[3]version 2.2.0

[4]version 1.0

[5]The NRC-Canada system ranked first in the SemEval 2013 (Nakov et al., 2013) and 2014 (Rosenthal et al., 2014) tasks on sentiment analysis.

regression model. Iterative experiments showed that this configuration gave the most stable results across the issues. For the neural approach, we adapt Siamese neural networks (SNN), which consist of two identical branches or sub-networks that try to extract useful representations of the assertions and a final layer that merges these branches. SNNs have been successfully used to predict text similarity (Mueller and Thyagarajan, 2016; Neculoiu et al., 2016) and match pairs of sentences (e.g. a tweet to reply) (Hu et al., 2014). In our SNN, a branch consists of a layer that translates the assertions into sequences of word embeddings, which is followed by a convolution layer with a filter size of two, max pooling over time layer, and a dense layer. To merge the branches, we calculate the cosine similarity of the extracted vector representations. The SNN was implemented using the deep learning framework deepTC (Horsmann and Zesch, 2018) in conjunction with Keras[6] and Tensorflow (Abadi et al., 2016). In order to ensure full reproducibility of our results, the source code for both approaches is publicly available.[7] We evaluate all approaches using 10-fold cross validation and calculate Pearson correlation between the prediction and the gold similarity.

5.2 Results

Table 2 shows the correlation of all approaches averaged over all sixteen issues.[8] Overall, the STS baselines result in very low correlation coefficients between .02 and .07, while the trained models obtain coefficients around .6. This shows that the systems can learn useful representations that capture judgment similarity and that this representation is indeed different from semantic similarity. Since both models are purely lexical and still yield reliable performance, we suspect that the relationship between a pair of assertions and their judgment similarity also has a lexical nature.

While STS baselines obtain consistently low results, we observe largely differing results per issues (ranging from .32 to .72) with SVM and SNN behaving alike. Detailed results for each issue are listed in Table 3.

In order to better understand the results, we ex-

<hr>

[6] https://keras.io/

[7] https://github.com/muchafel/judgmentPrediction

[8] As Pearsons r is defined in a probabilistic space it cannot be averaged directly. Therefore, we first z-transform the scores, average them and then transform them back into the original range of values.

Method	r
SNN	.61
SVM	.58
Embedding distance	.07
Jaccard	.07
Greedy string tiling	.06
Longest common sub string	.05

Table 2: Pearson correlation (averaged over all issues) of text-based approaches for approximating similarity of assertion judgments.[5]

Issue	SVM	SNN
Climate Change	.70	.72
Gender Equality	.67	.73
Mandatory Vaccination	.68	.74
Obama Care	.66	.70
Black Lives Matter	.66	.74
Media Bias	.63	.63
US Electoral System	.63	.59
Same-sex Marriage	.59	.61
War on Terrorism	.56	.59
Foreign Aid	.54	.46
US in the Middle East	.52	.55
US Immigration	.52	.57
Gun Rights	.51	.64
Creationism in school	.48	.51
Vegetarian and Vegan Lifestyle	.43	.40
Legalization of Marijuana	.37	.32

Table 3: Correlation coefficients of the similarity prediction by the SVM and the SNN, obtained in 10 fold cross-validation.

amine the scatter-plots that visualize assignment of gold to prediction (x–Axis: gold, y–Axis: prediction) and investigate cases that deviate strongly from an ideal correlation. Figure 3 shows the scatter plot for the issue *Climate Change* for both classifiers. For the SVM we observe that there is a group of pairs that is predicted inversely proportional, i.e. their gold value is positive, but the regression assigns a clearly negative value. We observe that these instances mainly correspond to pairs in which both assertions have high negative word scores. For instance the pair, '*There is not a real contribution of human activities in Climate change*' and '*Climate change was made up by the government to keep people in fear*', have a comparable high similarity of .20. The SVM, however, assigns them a similarity score of $-.38$. We suspect that this effect results from the distribution of similarity scores that is skewed to the positive range of possible scores. Therefore, the SVM probably assigns too much weight to ngrams that signal a negative score. Far less pronounced, for the neural approach, we find instances whose gold values are negative, but which are assigned a positive value. When inspecting these pairs we find that many of them contain one assertion which uses a negation (e.g. *not*, *unsure*, or *unlikely*). An example for this is the pair, '*There has been an increase in tropical storms of greater intensity which can be attributed to climate change*' and '*Different changes in weather does not mean global warming*', that have a low similarity in the gold data (-0.19), but get assigned a rather high similarity score (.20).

6 Predicting Judgments of Individuals

Now that we have means for quite reliably estimating the judgment similarity of assertions, we can try to predict judgments on individual assertions. We compare the judgment similarity methods against several baselines and collaborative filtering methods (that make use of judgments that are made by other persons to calculate person and assertion similarity).

Baselines (BL) The **random** baseline predicts *agree* or *disagree* for each assertion. We also define the **all agree** baseline, which always predicts *agree*. As the data contains substantially more agree judgments than disagree judgments (c.f. Figure 2), this is a strong baseline. As a third baseline, we average all known judgments of a person and predict *agree* if this value is positive and predict *disagree* otherwise. We refer to this baseline as **tendency**.

Judgment Similarity (JS) We use the above defined judgment similarity methods to calculate the similarity between each of the assertions previously judged by that person and the assertion for which we want to make the prediction. Then we simply transfer the judgment of the most similar assertion to the assertion of interest.[9] To prevent leakage, the scores of the prediction are taken from the models that have been trained in the cross validation. This means, for predicting the score of a pair of assertions we use the model which does not include the pair in the training set. As the matrix is missing one entry for each prediction (i.e. the judgment on the assertion for which we want to make the prediction), one could theoretically form a new matrix for each prediction and then

re-calculate all cosines. However, we find that the judgment similarity between assertions does not change significantly when a single entry in the vectors of the assertions is removed or added. Hence, due to computational complexity, the gold similarity was calculated over the entire matrix of judgments.

There are several assertions that do not have textual overlap, which is why the STS methods often return a zero similarity. In such a case, we fall back on the *all agree* baseline. We refer to strategies which are based on judgment similarity as **most similar assertion (*method*)**, where *method* indicates how the similarity is computed.

All strategies use all available context. For instance, if we want to predict the judgment of the assertion a_n and a prediction strategy considers other judgments, the strategy uses all the judgments on the assertions $a_1, ..., a_{n-1}$.

Collaborative Filtering (CF) Collaborative filtering (Adomavicius and Tuzhilin, 2005; Schafer et al., 2007; Su and Khoshgoftaar, 2009) uses previously made judgments and judgments made by others to predict future judgments. Collaborative filtering has been successfully used in application areas such shopping recommendations (Linden et al., 2003), or personalization of news (Das et al., 2007). Note that collaborative filtering requires knowledge of how others judged the assertion for which the system tries to make a prediction. Therefore, these strategies are not applicable if we want to predict judgments on a previously unseen assertion. Nevertheless, they represent an upper bound for our text-based predictions.

As a simple collaborative filtering strategy, we predict how the majority of other persons judged an assertion. Therefore, we average the judgments of all other users and predict *agree* if this value is positive and *disagree* if the value is negative. This strategy will be referred to as **mean other**. In addition, we compute the similarity between pairs of people by calculating the cosine similarity between the vector that corresponds to all judgments a person has made. We use this person–person similarity to determine the most similar person and then transfer the judgment on a_n of the user which is most similar to p_i. We refer to this strategy as **most similar user**. We also use the (gold) judgment similarity between assertions to predict *agree* or *disagree* based on how the assertion that is most similar to a_n has been judged. We call this

---

[9]Note that the subjects have all rated different numbers of assertions. Thus, for the sake of comparability, we restrict ourselves to the most similar assertion (as opposed to averaging a judgment over the n most similar assertions.)

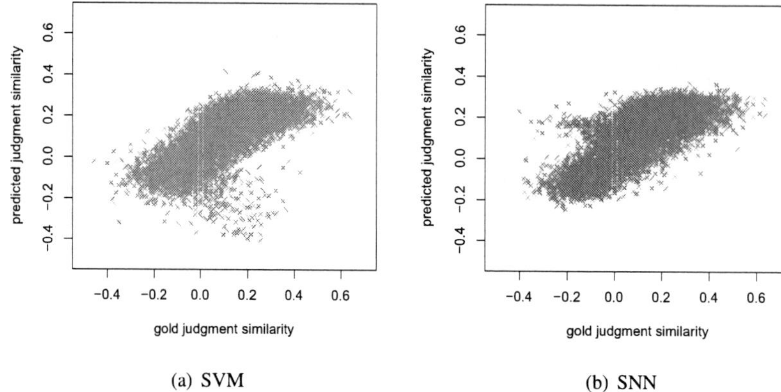

(a) SVM   (b) SNN

Figure 3: Comparison of gold judgment similarity and judgment similarity as predicted by the SVM and the SNN for the issue *Climate Change*.

Strategy	Type	Accuracy
most similar user	CF	.85
most similar assertion (gold)	CF	.76
tendency	BL	.75
mean other	CF	.74
most similar assertion (SNN)	JS	.73
most similar assertion (SVM)	JS	.72
all agree	BL	.71
most similar assertion (jaccard)	JS	.70
most similar assertion (embedding)	JS	.68
most similar assertion (gst)	JS	.69
most similar assertion (lcss)	JS	.67
random	BL	.50

Table 4: Accuracy of different approaches for predicting judgments of individuals.

strategy **most similar assertion (gold)**.

6.1 Results

Table 4 shows the accuracy of the strategies across all issues obtained using leave-one-out cross validation. We observe that all strategies are significantly better than the random baseline. On average, the *all agree* strategy is more than 20% above the random baseline and thus represents a highly competitive baseline. The *tendency* baseline, which is a refinement of *all agree*, is even 4% higher. Only the collaborative filtering strategies *most similar assertion* and **most similar user** beat this baseline. With an accuracy of about 85% the *most similar user* strategy performs best. The methods that use the learned judgment similarity beat the *all agree* but fall behind the *tendency* baseline. The fact that methods based on judgment

similarity are already close to their upper-bound (**most similar assertion (gold)**) shows that their potential is limited, even if measuring judgment similarity can be significantly improved. One possible explanation for comparably low performance of *most similar assertion* is that the past assertions are not sufficient to make a meaningful prediction. For instance, if only a few assertions have been judged in the past and none of them is similar to a new assertion, then a prediction becomes guessing. As expected from their poor performance of approximating judgment similarity, the methods relying on STS measures fall behind the *all agree*.

7 Predicting Judgments of Groups

We now turn to predicting judgments of groups, i.e. the task of estimating what percentage of a group of people are likely to agree to an assertion. We illustrate the prediction task in the following example: From the assertion '*Marijuana is almost never addictive*' with an aggregated agreement score of 0.9 we want to predict a comparatively lower value for the assertion '*Marijuana is sometimes addictive*'.

Direct Prediction (DP) As a reference approach, we train different regression models that predict the aggregated agreement score directly from the text of the assertion. We train each model over all issues in order to achieve the necessary generalization.

Again, we compare more traditional models based on feature engineering and neural models.

For the feature engineering approach we experiment with the following feature sets: First, we use a length feature which consists of the number of words per assertion. To capture stylistic variations, we compute a feature vector consisting of the number of exclamation and question marks, the number of modal verbs, the average word length in an assertion, POS type ratio, and type token ratio. We capture the wording of assertions by different ngram features. For capturing the semantics of words, we again derive features from the pre-trained fastText word vectors (Bojanowski et al., 2017). To capture the emotional tone of an assertion, we extract features from the output of the readily available sentiment tool NRC-Canada Sentiment Analysis System (Kiritchenko et al., 2014).

As the neural approach on directly predicting aggregated judgments, we use a single branch of the Siamese network. However, since we are trying to solve a regression problem, here the network ends in a single node equipped with a linear activation function. Through iterative experiments we found out that it is advantageous to add two additional dense layers before the final node. As this model resembles a convolutional neural network (CNN), we label this approach as CNN.

Judgment Similarity (JS) In analogy to the prediction of judgments of individuals, we first calculate the judgment similarity of two assertions using the SVM and SNN approaches that take pair of assertions into account. We then take the n-most similar assertions and return the average of the resulting scores. As an upper bound, we also compute the judgment similarity that results from the gold data. Note, that this upper bound again assumes knowledge about judgments on the assertion for which we actually want to make a prediction. We make the code for both approaches publicly available.[10]

7.1 Results

Table 5 shows the performance of the different approaches for predicting judgments of groups. For the prediction based on judgment similarity, we observe large differences between the the SVM and SNN predictions. This is especially interesting because the performance of the similarity prediction is comparable. We attribute this to the systematic error made by the SVM when trying to

Model	Type	r
gold ($n = 7$)	JS	.90
gold ($n = 1$)	JS	.84
SNN ($n = 34$)	JS	.74
SNN ($n = 1$)	JS	.45
SVM ($n = 18$)	JS	.42
CNN	DP	.40
sentiment + trigrams	DP	.36
trigrams	DP	.35
unigrams + embeddings	DP	.32
unigrams	DP	.32
SVM ($n = 1$)	JS	.32
sentiment + trigrams + style	DP	.27
sentiment	DP	.13
style	DP	.10
length	DP	.00

Table 5: Correlation coefficients for approaches on predicting judgments of groups.

predict the similarity of assertions that have a negative agreement score. While the SVM only outperforms the plain regressions if the prediction is based on several assertions, we observe a substantially better performance for the judgment similarity based on the SNN. For the best judgment similarity model (SNN with $n = 34$), we obtain a coefficient of $r = .74$ which is substantially better than the direct prediction model (CNN, $r = .40$).

For the plain regression, we observe that the CNN outperforms all models based on feature engineering and that among the SVM models ngram features yield the best performance. While the sentiment feature alone has low performance, the model that combines sentiment and ngrams shows slight improvement over the trigrams alone. The length feature and the style features alone have a comparable low performance and models which combine these feature with lexical features show a lower performance than the lexical models alone.

Issue-wise analysis To better understand the differences between the judgment similarity methods, we inspect their performance depending on the number of given assertions. Figure 4 shows this comparison both for individual issues and averaged across all issues. The upper-bound reaches a correlation of up to $r = .89$ ($n = 8$). The strength of this correlation and the fact that even our best estimate is still 15 points less shows the potential of judgment similarity for predicting judgments of groups.

For the SNN, the predictions follow a similar pattern: resembling a learning curve, the performance increases rapidly with increasing n, but

---

[10] https://github.com/muchafel/judgmentPrediction

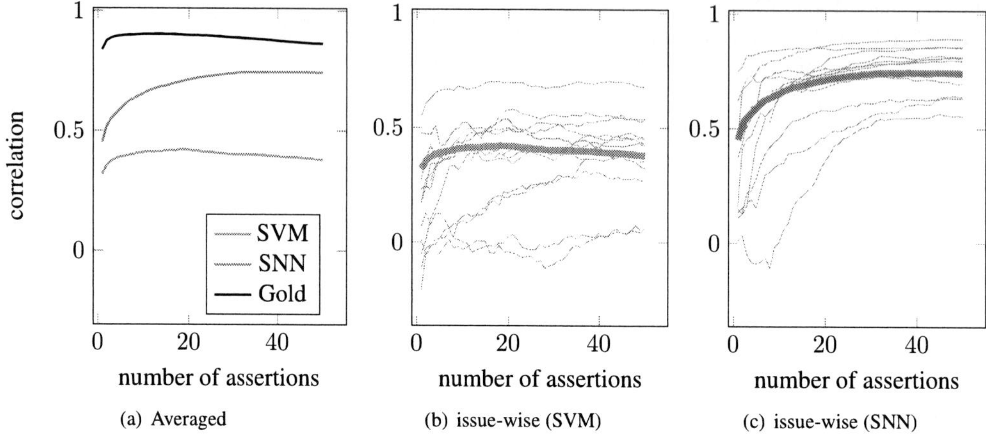

Figure 4: Prediction quality based on the transfer of the n-most similar assertions (expressed by the strength of correlation with the gold values). Sub-figure a) shows the scores averaged across all issues. We show the variance obtained on individual issues by the SVM in Sub-Figure b) and by the SNN in Sub-Figure c).

then plateaus from a certain number of assertions. However, the number of assertions for which we observe a plateau varies significantly. For the SVM we observe a similar pattern for most of the approaches, but the plateau is often reached much later. There are two issues (*US Engagement in the Middle East* and *US Immigration*) where we do not observe an increase in performance with increasing n. We suspect that the systematic error of the SVM is particularly strong here.

8   Conclusion & Future Work

In this paper, we examined whether an automatically measured judgment similarity can be used to predict the judgments of individuals or groups on assertions. We compare these judgment similarity approaches against several reference approaches on a data set of over 100,000 judgments on over 2,000 assertions. For the prediction of individual judgments reference approaches yield competitive results. However, for the prediction of group judgments the best approach using judgment similarity as predicted by a SNN outperforms other approaches by a wide margin.

While the presented approaches represent a first take on predicting judgments on assertions, the proposed tasks also suggest several directions of future research. These include more advanced algorithmic solutions and experiments for obtaining a deeper understanding of the relationship between text and judgments. For improving the automatic prediction, we want to explore how robust the learned models are by examining whether they can be transferred between issues. In addition, we want to examine if knowledge bases, issue specific corpora, or issue specific word vectors can improve the current approaches. To better understand what textual properties of assertions cause judgment similarity, we want to annotate and experimentally control typed relationships (e.g. paraphrases, entailment) of pairs of assertions. Being able to predict the degree to which two assertions are judged similarly might also be helpful for NLP tasks in which one tries to predict opinions or stance of the author of an text. Hence, we want to examine if judgment similarity can be used to boost the performance of systems in these tasks.

Acknowledgments

This work was supported by the Deutsche Forschungsgemeinschaft (DFG) under grant No. GRK 2167, Research Training Group "User-Centred Social Media". We would also like to thank Tobias Horsmann for helpful discussions on implementing the SNN.

References

Martín Abadi, Paul Barham, Jianmin Chen, Zhifeng Chen, Andy Davis, Jeffrey Dean, Matthieu Devin, Sanjay Ghemawat, Geoffrey Irving, Michael Isard, Manjunath Kudlur, Josh Levenberg, Rajat Monga, Sherry Moore, Derek G. Murray, Benoit Steiner, Paul Tucker, Vijay Vasudevan, Pete Warden, Martin Wicke, Yuan Yu, and Xiaoqiang Zheng. 2016. TensorFlow: A System for Large-scale Machine Learning. In *Proceedings of the 12th USENIX Conference on Operating Systems Design and Implementation*, OSDI'16, pages 265–283, Savannah, USA.

Gediminas Adomavicius and Alexander Tuzhilin. 2005. Toward the next generation of recommender systems: A survey of the state-of-the-art and possible extensions. *IEEE Transactions on Knowledge and Data Engineering*, 17(6):734–749.

Eneko Agirre, Mona Diab, Daniel Cer, and Aitor Gonzalez-Agirre. 2012. Semeval-2012 task 6: A pilot on semantic textual similarity. In *Proceedings of the SemEval*, pages 385–393, Montreal, Canada.

Daniel Bär, Torsten Zesch, and Iryna Gurevych. 2013. DKPro Similarity: An Open Source Framework for Text Similarity. In *Proceedings of the 51st Annual Meeting of the Association for Computational Linguistics: System Demonstrations*, pages 121–126, Sofia, Bulgaria.

Roy Bar-Haim, Indrajit Bhattacharya, Francesco Dinuzzo, Amrita Saha, and Noam Slonim. 2017. Stance Classification of Context-Dependent Claims. In *Proceedings of the 15th Conference of the European Chapter of the Association for Computational Linguistics (EACL*, pages 251–261, Valencia, Spain.

Rahul Bhagat and Eduard Hovy. 2013. What is a paraphrase? *Computational Linguistics*, 39(3):463–472.

Piotr Bojanowski, Edouard Grave, Armand Joulin, and Tomas Mikolov. 2017. Enriching word vectors with subword information. *Transactions of the Association for Computational Linguistics*, 5:135–146.

Filip Boltuzic and Jan Šnajder. 2016. Fill the gap! analyzing implicit premises between claims from online debates. In *Proceedings of the Third Workshop on Argument Mining (ArgMining2016)*, pages 124–133, Berlin, Germany.

Fabio Celli, Evgeny Stepanov, Massimo Poesio, and Giuseppe Riccardi. 2016. Predicting Brexit: Classifying agreement is better than sentiment and pollsters. In *Proceedings of the Workshop on Computational Modeling of People's Opinions, Personality, and Emotions in Social Media (PEOPLES)*, pages 110–118, Osaka, Japan.

Chih-Chung Chang and Chih-Jen Lin. 2011. LIBSVM: A library for support vector machines. *ACM Transactions on Intelligent Systems and Technology*, 2:27:1–27:27. Software available at http://www.csie.ntu.edu.tw/~cjlin/libsvm.

Ido Dagan, Bill Dolan, Bernardo Magnini, and Dan Roth. 2009. Recognizing textual entailment: Rational, evaluation and approaches. *Natural Language Engineering*, 15(4):i–xvii.

Abhinandan S. Das, Mayur Datar, Ashutosh Garg, and Shyam Rajaram. 2007. Google News Personalization: Scalable Online Collaborative Filtering. In *Proceedings of the 16th International Conference on World Wide Web (WWW '07)*, pages 271–280, Banff, Canada.

Johannes Daxenberger, Oliver Ferschke, Iryna Gurevych, and Torsten Zesch. 2014. DKPro TC: A Java-based Framework for Supervised Learning Experiments on Textual Data. In *Proceedings of 52nd Annual Meeting of the Association for Computational Linguistics: System Demonstrations*, pages 61–66, Baltimore, Maryland.

Dan Gusfield. 1997. *Algorithms on strings, trees and sequences: computer science and computational biology*. Cambridge university press.

Ivan Habernal and Iryna Gurevych. 2016. Which Argument is More Convincing? Analyzing and Predicting Convincingness of Web Arguments Using Bidirectional LSTM. In *Proceedings of the 54th Annual Meeting of the Association for Computational Linguistics*, pages 1589–1599, Berlin, Germany.

James J. Heckman and James M. Snyder. 1996. Linear Probability Models of the Demand for Attributes with an Empirical Application to Estimating the Preferences of Legislators. *The RAND Journal of Economics*, 28:142–189.

Tobias Horsmann and Torsten Zesch. 2018. DeepTC – An Extension of DKPro Text Classification for Fostering Reproducibility of Deep Learning Experiments. In *Proceedings of the International Conference on Language Resources and Evaluation (LREC)*, Miyazaki, Japan.

Baotian Hu, Zhengdong Lu, Hang Li, and Qingcai Chen. 2014. Convolutional Neural Network Architectures for Matching Natural Language Sentences. In *Advances in Neural Information Processing Systems (NIPS 27)*, pages 2042–2050, Montreal, Canada.

Svetlana Kiritchenko, Xiaodan Zhu, and Saif M Mohammad. 2014. Sentiment Analysis of Short Informal Texts. *Journal of Artificial Intelligence Research (JAIR)*, 50:723–762.

Greg Linden, Brent Smith, and Jeremy York. 2003. Amazon.com recommendations: Item-to-item Collaborative Filtering. *IEEE Internet computing*, 7(1):76–80.

Bing Liu. 2012. Sentiment analysis and opinion mining. *Synthesis lectures on human language technologies*, 5(1):1–167.

Caroline Lyon, James Malcolm, and Bob Dickerson. 2001. Detecting short passages of similar text in large document collections. In *Proceedings of Conference on Empirical Methods in Natural Language Processing*, pages 118–125, Pittsburgh, USA.

Stefano Menini and Sara Tonelli. 2016. Agreement and Disagreement: Comparison of Points of View in the

Political Domain. In *Proceedings of the 26th International Conference on Computational Linguistics (COLING)*, pages 2461–2470, Osaka, Japan.

Saif M. Mohammad. 2016. Sentiment analysis: Detecting valence, emotions, and other affectual states from text. *Emotion Measurement*, pages 201–238.

Saif M. Mohammad, Svetlana Kiritchenko, Parinaz Sobhani, Xiaodan Zhu, and Colin Cherry. 2016. SemEval-2016 Task 6: Detecting Stance in Tweets. In *Proceedings of the SemEval*, pages 31–41, San Diego, USA.

Jonas Mueller and Aditya Thyagarajan. 2016. Siamese Recurrent Architectures for Learning Sentence Similarity. In *Proceedings of the Thirtieth AAAI Conference on Artificial Intelligence*, AAAI'16, pages 2786–2792, Phoenix, USA.

Preslav Nakov, Sara Rosenthal, Zornitsa Kozareva, Veselin Stoyanov, Alan Ritter, and Theresa Wilson. 2013. SemEval-2013 Task 2: Sentiment Analysis in Twitter. In *Proceedings of the SemEval*, pages 312–320, Atlanta, USA.

Paul Neculoiu, Maarten Versteegh, and Mihai Rotaru. 2016. Learning text similarity with siamese recurrent networks. In *Proceedings of the 1st Workshop on Representation Learning for NLP*, pages 148–157.

Bo Pang and Lillian Lee. 2008. Opinion mining and sentiment analysis. *Foundations and Trends® in Information Retrieval*, 2(1–2):1–135.

Sasa Petrovic, Miles Osborne, and Victor Lavrenko. 2011. RT to Win! Predicting Message Propagation in Twitter. *Proceedings of the Fifth International AAAI Conference on Weblogs and Social Media*, 11:586–589.

Keith T. Poole and Howard Rosenthal. 1997. *Congress: A Political-economic History of Roll Call Voting*. Oxford University Press.

Keith T. Poole and Howard Rosenthal. 2001. D-Nominate after 10 Years: A Comparative Update to Congress: A Political-Economic History of Roll-Call Voting. *Legislative Studies Quarterly*, 26(1):5–29.

Reid Pryzant, Young-joo Chung, and Dan Jurafsky. 2017. Predicting Sales from the Language of Product Descriptions. In *Proceedings of the SIGIR 2017 Workshop on eCommerce (ECOM 17)*, Tokyo, Japan.

Sara Rosenthal, Alan Ritter, Preslav Nakov, and Veselin Stoyanov. 2014. Semeval-2014 task 9: Sentiment analysis in twitter. In *Proceedings of the SemEval*, pages 73–80, Dublin, Ireland.

J. Ben Schafer, Dan Frankowski, Jon Herlocker, and Shilad Sen. 2007. Collaborative Filtering Recommender Systems. *The Adaptive Web*, pages 291–324.

Xiaoyuan Su and Taghi M. Khoshgoftaar. 2009. A Survey of Collaborative Filtering Techniques. *Advances in Artificial Intelligence*, pages 4:2–4:2.

Bongwon Suh, Lichan Hong, Peter Pirolli, and Ed H. Chi. 2010. Want to be Retweeted? Large Scale Analytics on Factors Impacting Retweet in Twitter Network. In *Proceedings of the Second IEEE International Conference on Social Computing*, pages 177–184, Washington, USA.

Chenhao Tan, Lillian Lee, and Bo Pang. 2014. The Effect of Wording on Message Propagation: Topic-and Author-controlled Natural Experiments on Twitter. In *Proceedings of the ACL*, pages 175–185, Baltimore, USA.

Mariona Taulé, M Antonia Martı, Francisco Rangel, Paolo Rosso, Cristina Bosco, and Viviana Patti. 2017. Overview of the task of stance and gender detection in tweets on catalan independence at ibereval 2017. In *Notebook Papers of 2nd SEPLN Workshop on Evaluation of Human Language Technologies for Iberian Languages (IBEREVAL), Murcia, Spain, September*, volume 19.

Lu Wang and Claire Cardie. 2014. Improving Agreement and Disagreement Identification in Online Discussions with A Socially-Tuned Sentiment Lexicon. In *Proceedings of the 5th Workshop on Computational Approaches to Subjectivity, Sentiment and Social Media Analysis (WASSA '14)*, pages 97–106.

Zhongyu Wei, Yang Liu, and Yi Li. 2016. Is This Post Persuasive? Ranking Argumentative Comments in the Online Forum. In *Proceedings of the ACL*, pages 195–200, Berlin, Germany.

Michael J. Wise. 1996. Yap3: Improved detection of similarities in computer program and other texts. *ACM SIGCSE Bulletin*, 28(1):130–134.

Michael Wojatzki, Saif M. Mohammad, Torsten Zesch, and Svetlana Kiritchenko. 2018. Quantifying Qualitative Data for Understanding Controversial Issues. In *Proceedings of the 11th Edition of the Language Resources and Evaluation Conference (LREC-2018)*, Miyazaki, Japan.

Ruifeng Xu, Yu Zhou, Dongyin Wu, Lin Gui, Jiachen Du, and Yun Xue. 2016. Overview of NLPCC Shared Task 4: Stance Detection in Chinese Microblogs. In *International Conference on Computer Processing of Oriental Languages*, pages 907–916, Kunming, China.

A Multimodal Translation-Based Approach for Knowledge Graph Representation Learning

Hatem Mousselly-Sergieh[†], Teresa Botschen[§†], Iryna Gurevych[§†], Stefan Roth[§‡]
† Ubiquitous Knowledge Processing (UKP) Lab
‡ Visual Inference Lab
§ Research Training Group AIPHES
Department of Computer Science, Technische Universität Darmstadt

h.m.sergieh@gmail.com

{botschen@aiphes, gurevych@ukp.informatik, stefan.roth@visinf}.tu-darmstadt.de

Abstract

Current methods for knowledge graph (KG) representation learning focus solely on the structure of the KG and do not exploit any kind of external information, such as visual and linguistic information corresponding to the KG entities. In this paper, we propose a multimodal translation-based approach that defines the energy of a KG triple as the sum of sub-energy functions that leverage both multimodal (visual and linguistic) and structural KG representations. Next, a ranking-based loss is minimized using a simple neural network architecture. Moreover, we introduce a new large-scale dataset for multimodal KG representation learning. We compared the performance of our approach to other baselines on two standard tasks, namely knowledge graph completion and triple classification, using our as well as the WN9-IMG dataset.[1] The results demonstrate that our approach outperforms all baselines on both tasks and datasets.

1 Introduction

Knowledge Graphs (KGs), e.g., Freebase (Bollacker et al., 2008) and DBPedia (Auer et al., 2007), are stores of relational facts, which are crucial for various kinds of tasks, such as question answering and information retrieval. KGs are structured as triples of head and tail entities along with the relation that holds between them. Factual knowledge is virtually infinite and is frequently subject to change. This raises the question of the incompleteness of the KGs. To address this problem, several methods have been proposed for automatic KG completion (KGC, for a survey refer to Wang et al., 2017). In recent years, translation-based approaches have witnessed a great success. Their main idea is to model the entities and their relation as low-dimensional vector representations (embeddings), which in turn can be used to perform different kinds of inferences on the KG. These include identifying new facts or validating existing ones. However, translation-based methods rely on the rich structure of the KG and generally ignore any type of external information about the included entities.

In this paper, we propose a translation-based approach for KG representation learning that leverages two different types of external, multimodal representations: *linguistic* representations created by analyzing the usage patterns of KG entities in text corpora, and *visual* representations obtained from images corresponding to the KG entities. To gain initial insights into the potential benefits of external information for the KGC task, let us consider the embeddings produced by the translation-based TransE method (Bordes et al., 2013) on the WN9-IMG dataset (Xie et al., 2017). This dataset contains a subset of WordNet synsets, which are linked according to a predefined set of linguistic relations, e.g. *hypernym*. We observed that TransE fails to create suitable representations for entities that appear frequently as the head/tail of one-to-many/many-to-one relations. For example, the entity *person* appears frequently in the dataset

Embedding Space	Top Similar Synsets
Linguistic	n02472987_world, n02473307_Homo_erectus, n02474777_Homo_sapiens, 02472293_homo, n00004475_organism, n10289039_man
Visual	n10788852_woman, n09765278_actor, n10495167_pursuer n10362319_nonsmoker, n10502046_quitter, n09636339_Black
Structure (TransE)	_hypernym, n00004475_organism, n03183080_device, n07942152_people, n13104059_tree, n00015388_animal, n12205694_herb, n07707451_vegetable

Table 1: Closest synsets to the person synset (n00007846) according to different embedding spaces.

---

[1] Code and datasets are released for research purposes: https://github.com/UKPLab/starsem18-multimodalKB

*Proceedings of the 7th Joint Conference on Lexical and Computational Semantics (*SEM)*, pages 225–234
New Orleans, June 5-6, 2018. ©2018 Association for Computational Linguistics

as a head/tail of the *hyponym/hypernym* relation; the same holds for entities like *animal* or *tree*. TransE represents such entities as points that are very close to each other in the embedding space (cf. Tab. 1). Furthermore, the entity embeddings tend to be very similar to the embeddings of relations in which they frequently participate. Consequently, such a representation suffers from limited discriminativeness and can be considered a main source of error for different KG inference tasks.

To understand how multimodal representations may help to overcome this issue, we performed the same analysis by considering two types of external information: linguistic and visual. The linguistic representations are created using word embedding techniques (Mikolov et al., 2013), and the visual ones, called visual embeddings, are obtained from the feature layers of deep networks for image classification (e.g., Chatfield et al., 2014) on images that correspond to the entities of the dataset. For the same category of entities discussed above, we observed that both the visual and the linguistic embeddings are much more robust than the structure-based embeddings of TransE. For instance, *person* is closer to other semantically related concepts, such as *Homo_erectus* in the linguistic embedding space, and to concepts with common visual characteristics (e.g., *woman*, *actor*) in the visual embedding space (cf. Tab. 1). Furthermore, the linguistic and the visual embeddings seem to complement each other and hence are expected to enhance KG representations if they can be leveraged during the representation learning process.

The contributions of this paper can be summarized as follows: *(1)* We propose an approach for KG representation learning that incorporates multimodal (visual and linguistic) information in a translation-based framework and extends the definition of triple energy to consider the new multimodal representations; *(2)* we investigate different methods for combining multimodal representations and evaluate their performance; *(3)* we introduce a new large-scale dataset for multimodal KGC based on Freebase; *(4)* we experimentally demonstrate that our approach outperforms baseline approaches including the state-of-the-art method of Xie et al. (2017) on the link prediction and triple classification tasks.

2 Related Work

2.1 Translation Models

TransE (Bordes et al., 2013) is among the earliest translation-based approaches for KG representation learning. TransE represents entities and relations as vectors in the same space, where the relation is considered a translation operation from the representation of the head to that of the tail entity. For a correct triple, TransE assumes that $h + r \approx t$, where h, r, t are the vector representations of the head, relation, and tail, respectively. Additionally, TransE use a dissimilarity measure d to define the energy of a given triple as $d(h+r, t)$. Finally, the representations of KG entities and relations are learned by minimizing a margin-based ranking objective that aims to score positive triples higher than negative triples based on their energies and a predefined margin.

TransE is a simple and effective method, however, the simple translational assumption constrains the performance when dealing with complex relations, such as one-to-many or many-to-one. To address this limitation, some extensions of TransE have been proposed. Wang et al. (2014) introduced TransH, which uses translations on relation-specific hyperplanes and applies advanced methods for sampling negative triples. Lin et al. (2015b) proposed TransR, which uses separate spaces for modeling entities and relations. Entities are projected from their space to the corresponding relation space by relation-specific matrices. Moreover, they propose an extension called CTransR, in which instances of pairs of head and tail for a specific relation are clustered such that the members of the clusters exhibit similar meanings of this relation. Lin et al. (2015a) proposed another extension of TransE, called PTransE, that leverages multi-step relation path information in the process of representation learning.

The above models rely only on the structure of the KG, and learning better KG representations is dependent upon the complexity of the model. In this paper, however, we follow a different approach for improving the quality of the learned KG representation and incorporate external multimodal information in the learning process, while keeping the model as simple as possible.

2.2 Multimodal Methods

Recent advances in natural language processing have witnessed a greater interest in leveraging multimodal information for a wide range of tasks. For instance, Shutova et al. (2016) showed that better metaphor identification can be achieved by fusing linguistic and visual representations. Collell et al. (2017) demonstrated the effectiveness of combining linguistic and visual embeddings in the context of word relatedness and similarity tasks. Regarding KG representation learning, the first and, to the best of our knowledge, only attempt that considers multimodal data is the work of Xie et al. (2017). Their IKRL approach extends TransE based on visual representations extracted from images that correspond to the KG entities. In IKRL, the energy of a triple is defined in terms of the structure of the KG as well as the visual representation of the entities. Our work, while building upon the foundations of Xie et al. (2017), sets itself apart based on the following properties: *(1)* in addition to images, our model integrates another kind of external representation, namely linguistic embeddings for KG entities – thus, adding multimodal information; *(2)* we base our approach on a simple and easily extensible neural network architecture; *(3)* we introduce an additional energy function that considers the multimodal representation of the KG entities; *(4)* we introduce a new large-scale dataset for multimodal KG representation learning.

3   Proposed Approach

We denote the knowledge graph as $\mathcal{G} = (\mathcal{E}, \mathcal{R}, \mathcal{T})$, where $\mathcal{E}$ is the set of entities, $\mathcal{R}$ is the set of relations, and $\mathcal{T} = \{(h, r, t)|h, t \in \mathcal{E}, r \in \mathcal{R}\}$ the set of KG triples. For each head and tail entity $h, r \in \mathcal{E}$, we define three kinds of representations (embeddings): structural $h_s^I, t_s^I \in \mathbb{R}^N$, linguistic $h_w^I, t_w^I \in \mathbb{R}^M$, and visual $h_i^I, t_i^I \in \mathbb{R}^P$, where N, M and P are the corresponding numbers of dimensions. Furthermore, we represent each relation $r \in \mathcal{R}$ as a vector $r_s^I \in \mathbb{R}^N$ in the space of the structural information. The superscript I denotes that these are the input embeddings. Since the different embeddings do not live in the same space, we assume from now on that they can be transformed into a common space using a multilayer network (e.g., h_s^I into h_s, cf. Fig. 1). Following the translational assumption, given a triple (h, r, t), we have

$$h_s + r_s \approx t_s. \tag{1}$$

3.1   Model

In general, previous works such as (Bordes et al., 2013) start from Eq. (1) and build models for minimizing a ranking loss between positive and negative triples that are sampled from the KG. Conventionally, negative triples are sampled by corrupting the head, the tail, or the relation of correct triples. We follow this idea and make it explicit by taking two different "views" on the translational assumption. Apart from the first view through Eq. (1), we can also rewrite the translational assumption as

$$t_s - r_s \approx h_s. \tag{2}$$

We will learn the two views jointly. For each view, we sample specific kinds of negative triples according to which part of the triple has to be predicted. For the head-centric view, we define $\mathcal{T}'_{\text{tail}}$, a set of negative triples that is sampled by corrupting the tail of gold triples. Similarly, for the tail-centric view, we define $\mathcal{T}'_{\text{head}}$, a set of negative triples sampled by corrupting the head of the gold triples:

$$\mathcal{T}'_{\text{tail}} = \{(h, r, t')|h, t' \in \mathcal{E} \wedge (h, r, t') \notin \mathcal{T}\} \tag{3a}$$
$$\mathcal{T}'_{\text{head}} = \{(h', r, t)|h', t \in \mathcal{E} \wedge (h', r, t) \notin \mathcal{T}\}. \tag{3b}$$

Next, we extend the definition of triple energy in order to integrate both the structural and the multimodal representations of the KG entities. For each kind of representation as well as their combination, we define a specific energy function. Subsequently, the final energy of a triple is defined as the sum of the individual energies defined below.

Structural Energy: The structure-based energy of a triple is defined in terms of the structure of the KG as proposed by the TransE approach (Bordes et al., 2013). Accordingly, we define

$$E_S = \|h_s + r_s - t_s\|. \tag{4}$$

Multimodal Energies: The multimodal representation of a KG entity is defined by combining the corresponding linguistic and visual representations. Let $\oplus$ denote the combination operator (more details in Section 3.2). Now, we define the multimodal representations h_m and t_m of the head and the tail entities, respectively, as

$$h_m = h_w \oplus h_i \tag{5a}$$
$$t_m = t_w \oplus t_i. \tag{5b}$$

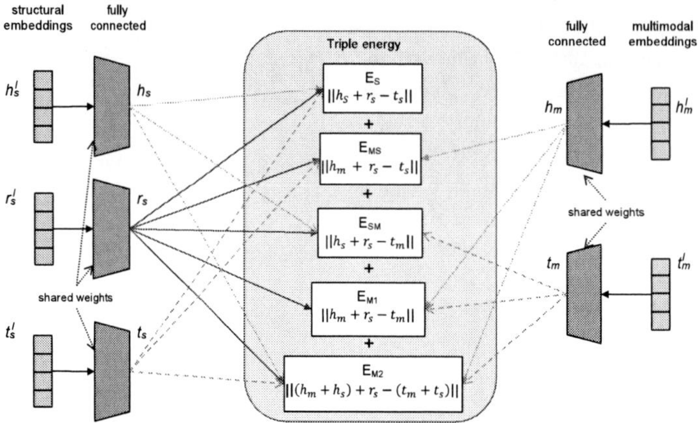

Figure 1: Overview of the neural network architecture for calculating the total triple energy from the different models. The fully connected networks transform the respective input embeddings into a common space.

Next, we transfer the structure-based energy function from Eq. (4) to the multimodal case where it incorporates the multimodal representations under the translational assumption, i.e.

$$E_{M1} = \|h_m + r_s - t_m\|. \tag{6}$$

We then extend the previous energy from Eq. (6) to define another energy function that considers the structural embeddings in addition to the multimodal ones as follows:

$$E_{M2} = \|(h_m + h_s) + r_s - (t_m + t_s)\|. \tag{7}$$

These presented multimodal energies can be understood as additional constraints for the translation model. $M1$ states that the relation corresponds to a translation operation between the multimodal representation of the head and the tail entities once projected into the structural space. $M2$ enforces that same constraint, however, on the sum of the multimodal and the structural embeddings of the head and the tail entities. While Eqs. (4), (6), and (7) cannot be fulfilled at the same time, we found that combining these complementary energies makes the results more robust.

Structural-Multimodal Energies: Next, to ensure that the structural and the multimodal representations are learned in the same space, we follow the proposal of Xie et al. (2017) and define the following energy functions:

$$E_{SM} = \|h_s + r_s - t_m\| \tag{8a}$$
$$E_{MS} = \|h_m + r_s - t_s\|. \tag{8b}$$

Finally, the overall energy of a triple for the head and the tail views are defined as

$$E(h, r, t) = E_S + E_{M1} + E_{M2}$$
$$+E_{SM} + E_{MS}. \tag{9a}$$

Objective Function: For both the head and the tail view, we aim to minimize a margin-based ranking loss between the energies of the positive and the negative triples. The corresponding loss functions are finally defined as

$$\mathcal{L}_{head} = \sum_{(h,r,t)\in\mathcal{T}} \sum_{(h,r,t')\in\mathcal{T}'_{\text{tail}}} \max\big(\gamma + E(h, r, t)$$
$$-E(h, r, t'), 0\big) \tag{10}$$
$$\mathcal{L}_{tail} = \sum_{(h,r,t)\in\mathcal{T}} \sum_{(h',r,t)\in\mathcal{T}'_{\text{head}}} \max\big(\gamma + E(t, -r, h)$$
$$-E(t, -r, h'), 0\big). \tag{11}$$

Here, γ is a margin parameter, which controls the amount of energy difference between the positive and the negative triples. Finally, we aim to minimize the global loss

$$\mathcal{L} = \mathcal{L}_{\text{head}} + \mathcal{L}_{\text{tail}}. \tag{12}$$

To bring the different representations (structural, linguistic, visual) into the same space, we employ a simple feed-forward neural network architecture. The input of the network consists of the structural and the multimodal embeddings of the heads, the tails, and the relations (Fig. 1); the fully-connected layers map these inputs into a common space. Furthermore, we share the weights between

228

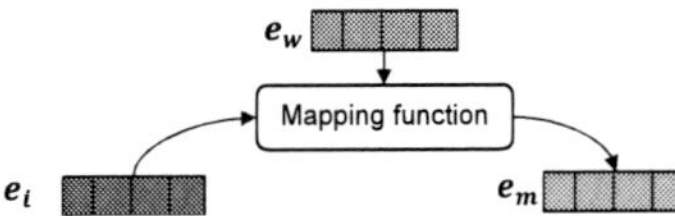

Figure 2: The DeViSE method (Frome et al., 2013).

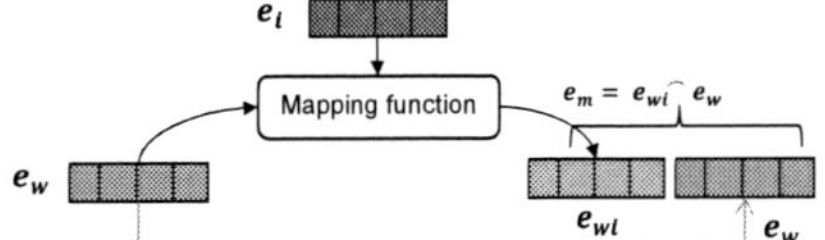

Figure 3: The Imagined method (Collell et al., 2017).

those fully-connected layers that receive the same kind of input. Additionally, the weights are also shared across the head and the tail views.

3.2 Combining Multimodal Representations

To complete the description of our approach, we still need to define the $\oplus$ operator used in Eq. (5) to combine the linguistic and visual embeddings into a single one. To that end, we identified three methods for multimodal representation learning and adapted them to KG entities.

Concatenation Method: The simplest method to create multimodal representations for KG entities is to combine the multimodal embedding vectors by concatenation. Given the linguistic e_w and the visual e_i embeddings of an entity e, we define the multimodal representation $e_m = e_w \frown e_i$, where $\frown$ is the concatenation operator.

DeViSE Method: Next, we consider the deep visual-semantic embedding model (DeViSE) of Frome et al. (2013), which leverages textual data to explicitly map images into a rich semantic embedding space. Given the visual representation of some concept, the goal is to learn a mapping into the linguistic (word) embedding space. The mapped representation can then be used as a multimodal representation for the target entity. Fig. 2 illustrates the application of DeViSE to generating multimodal representations for KG entities.

Imagined Method: Finally, we consider the Imagined method of Collell et al. (2017) for creating multimodal representations of concepts based on their linguistic and visual embeddings. Imagined is similar to DeViSE, however, it applies the reverse procedure. That is, for a given concept Imagined aims to learn a mapping from the linguistic embedding space of that concept into the

visual embedding space. The mapping can be formulated as a linear or nonlinear transformation using a simple neural network, and the objective is to minimize the distance between the mapped linguistic representation and the visual representation of the entities. Subsequently, a multimodal representation is created by applying the learned mapping function on the linguistic representation of the entity and then concatenating the resulting vector with the original linguistic embedding (Fig. 3).

4 Experiments

4.1 Datasets

WN9-IMG: This dataset provided by Xie et al. (2017) is based on WordNet. It contains a collection of triples, where the entities correspond to word senses (synsets) and the relations define the lexical relationships between the entities. Furthermore, for each synset a collection of up to ten images obtained from ImageNet (Deng et al., 2009) is provided.

FB-IMG: To demonstrate the scalability of our approach to larger datasets, we created another dataset based on FB15K (Bordes et al., 2013), which consists of triples extracted from Freebase. For each entity, we crawled 100 images from the web using text search based on the entity labels. To ensure that the crawled images are representative of the corresponding entities, we applied an approach for image filtering based on the Page-Rank algorithm (Page et al., 1999). First, we created a vector representation (embedding) for each image by feeding it into a pre-trained VGG19 neural network for image classification (Simonyan and Zisserman, 2014). The image embeddings consist of the 4096-dimensional activation of the last layer (before the softmax). Next, for each entity we create a similarity graph for the corresponding images based on the cosine similarity between their embedding vectors. Finally, we calculated the PageRank score for each image in the

Dataset	#Rel	#Ent	#Train	#Valid	#Test
WN9-IMG	9	6555	11 741	1337	1319
FB-IMG	1231	11 757	285 850	29 580	34 863

Table 2: Datasets statistics

graph and kept the top 10 results. Tab. 2 gives basic statistics of the two datasets.

4.2 Representations

We now discuss the procedure we followed to obtain different kinds of representations for the entities and relations of the two evaluation datasets.

Structural Representation: This baseline representation is created based on the structure of the KG only, without any external information. In our experiments we created structure representations for the entity and the relations of the two datasets using the TransE algorithm. For both datasets, we trained TransE with 100 dimensions and used the same values for the other hyperparameters as recommended by Bordes et al. (2013).

Linguistic Representation: The linguistic representations of the entities are obtained by applying word embedding techniques. For the FB-IMG dataset, we used a pre-trained word embedding model for Freebase entities as provided by the word2vec framework (Mikolov et al., 2013). The provided embeddings are 1000 dimensional and are trained using the skipgram model over the Google 100B token news dataset. We applied L_2-normalization on the generated embeddings.

The entities of the WN9-IMG dataset correspond to word senses rather than to individual words. In order to create embeddings for the synsets, we used the AutoExtend framework (Rothe and Schütze, 2015), which enables creating sense embeddings for a given sense based on the embeddings of the contained lemmas. For this purpose, we initialized AutoExtend with pre-trained 300-dimensional GloVe embeddings (Pennington et al., 2014). In case where no pre-trained embeddings are found for the sense lemmas, AutoExtend generates zero initialized vectors for the corresponding synsets. In order to provide better representations, we define the embeddings of such synsets by copying the embeddings of the first hyperonym synset that has non-zero AutoExtend embeddings. The linguistic embeddings of WN9-IMG entities (synsets) are 300-dimensional vectors, which were also L_2-normalized.

Visual Representation: For each image of a given KG entity, we created a visual embedding vector using the same procedure as for creating the FB-IMG dataset. This was done using a pre-trained VGG model (Simonyan and Zisserman, 2014). For the WN9-IMG dataset, we used the VGG19 model and extracted the 4096-dimensional vector of the last fully-connected layer before the softmax. For the FB-IMG dataset, which contains much more data than WN9-IMG and in order to speed up the training, we used the more compact VGG-m-128 CNN model (Chatfield et al., 2014), which produces 128-dimensional embedding vector for each image. Next, the visual embeddings are L_2-normalized. We investigated two ways of combining the embedding vectors corresponding to images of a given entity. The first method defines the visual embedding of an entity as the average of the embeddings of all corresponding images. The second method uses the dimension-wise maximum. In our experiments we observed that averaging the embedding vectors outperforms the maximum method. Hence, we only report the results obtained with averaging.

4.3 Experimental Setup

We investigated different sets of hyperparameters for training the model. The best results were obtained using the Adam optimizer (Kingma and Ba, 2014) with a fixed learning rate of 0.001 and batch size of 100. We used the hyperbolic tangent function ($tanh$) for the activation and one fully-connected layer of 100 hidden units. We observed that regularization has a minor effect. In the case of WN9-IMG, we used dropout regularization (Srivastava et al., 2014) with a dropout ratio of 10%; we applied no regularization on the FB-IMG dataset. Regarding the margin of the loss function, we experimented with several values for both datasets $\gamma \in \{4, 6, 8, 10, 12\}$. The best results for both datasets were obtained with $\gamma = 10$.

We investigated different configurations of our approach: *(1) Ling* considers the linguistic embeddings only, *(2) Vis* considers the visual embeddings only, *(3) multimodal* where the visual and the linguistic embeddings are considered according to the presented multimodal combination methods: *DeViSE*, *Imagined*, and the *Concatenation* methods (cf. Sec. 3.2), and *(4) only head* in which we use the head view only and the *concatenation* method for combining the multimodal representations. Here, negative samples are produced by randomly corrupting the head, the tail, or the relation of gold triples.

We compared our approach to other baseline

methods including TransE (Bordes et al., 2013) and IKRL (Xie et al., 2017). For TransE, we set the size of the embeddings to 100 dimensions and followed the recommendations of Bordes et al. (2013) regarding the other hyperparameters. We also implemented the IKRL approach and the best results were achieved by using margins of 8 and 4 for the WN9-IMG and the FB-IMG datasets, respectively. We tested two configurations of IKRL: *(1) IKRL (Vis)* uses the visual representation only (as in the original paper) and initializes the structural representations with our learned TransE embeddings, and *(2) IKRL (Concat)*, which uses the concatenation of the linguistic and the visual embeddings. Please note that we do not apply the attention mechanism for creating image representations as proposed in the IKRL paper (Xie et al., 2017). However, we include that model, referred to as *IKRL (Paper)*, in the comparison.

4.4 Link Prediction

Evaluation Protocol: Given a pair of a head/tail and a relation, the goal of link prediction is to identify the missing tail/head. For each test triple, we replaced the head/tail by all entities in the KG and calculated the corresponding energies in ascending order. Similar to Bordes et al. (2013), we calculated two measures: *(1)* the mean rank (MR) of the correctly predicted entities and *(2)* the proportion of correct entities in the top-10 ranked ones (Hits@10). We also distinguished between two evaluation settings, "Raw" and "Filter". In contrast to the "Raw" setting, in the "Filter" setting correct triples included in the training, validation, and test sets are removed before ranking.

Results: Tab. 3 shows the results on the WN9-IMG dataset. First, we can observe that leveraging multimodal information leads to a significant improvement compared to the structure-only based approach TransE, especially in terms of the mean rank. This conclusion is in accordance with our intuition: although the structural representations become less discriminative after the training for certain kinds of entities (such as the one discussed in Sec. 1), the multimodal representations compensate for this effect, thus the prediction accuracy increases. Regarding the multimodal representations, combining the linguistic and the visual embeddings seems to outperform models that rely on only one kind of those representations. This holds for our approach as well as for IKRL. Re-

Method	MR		Hits@10 (%)	
	Raw	**Filter**	**Raw**	**Filter**
TransE	160	152	78.77	91.21
IKRL (Paper)	28	21	80.90	93.80
IKRL (Vis)	21	15	81.39	92.00
IKRL (Concat)	18	12	82.26	93.25
Our (Ling)	19	13	80.78	90.79
Our (Vis)	20	14	80.74	92.30
Our (DeViSE)	19	13	81.80	93.21
Our (Imagined)	19	14	81.43	91.09
Our (Concat)	**14**	**9**	**83.78**	**94.84**
Our (only head)	19	13	82.37	93.21

Table 3: Link prediction results on WN9-IMG.

garding the multimodal combination method, we surprisingly noticed that the simple concatenation method outperforms other advanced methods like DeViSE (Frome et al., 2013) and Imagined (Collell et al., 2017). This suggests that translation-based approaches for KG representation learning profit more from the raw representations than general purpose pre-combined ones, which are not necessarily tuned for this task.

The evaluation also shows that our approach with the concatenation method outperforms the best IKRL model, IKRL (Concat), which was trained on the same representations as our approach. Additionally, our model outperforms the best performing IKRL model reported in (Xie et al., 2017) with less than half the MR and more than one point in Hits@10. This shows the benefit of our additional energy term coupling structural and multimodal embeddings. To assess the benefit of taking two separate views on the translational assumption, we evaluated the performance of using the head view only. We observe a considerable drop in performance. The MR becomes 5 points higher and the Hits@10 drops by more than one percentage point compared to the same model that is trained using both the head and the tail views.

Compared to WN9-IMG, the FB-IMG dataset has a much larger number of relations, entities, and triples (cf. Tab. 2), thus it better resembles the characteristics of real KG. On the FB-IMG dataset, the superiority of our model compared to the baselines, especially IKRL, becomes even more evident (cf. Tab. 4). Our model performs best and achieves a significant boost in MR and Hits@10 compared to the baselines, while IKRL slightly outperforms TransE in terms of MR only.

Method	MR		Hits@10 (%)	
	Raw	Filter	Raw	Filter
TransE	205	121	37.83	49.39
IKRL (Concat)	179	104	37.48	47.87
Our (Concat)	**134**	**53**	**47.19**	**64.50**

Table 4: Link prediction results on FB-IMG.

Therefore, the results confirm the robustness of our method for large-scale datasets.

Finally, we observe that, in general, the performance boost on the FB-IMG dataset is lower than in the case of the WN9-IMG dataset. This can be explained by the higher scale and complexity of the FB-IMG dataset. Furthermore, the visual representations of the FB-IMG entities are based on images that are automatically crawled from the Web. Accordingly, some of the crawled images may not be representative enough or even noisy, while the images in WN9-IMG have better quality since they are obtained from ImageNet, which is a manually created dataset.

4.5 Triple Classification

Evaluation Protocol: Triple classification is a binary classification task, in which the KG triples are classified as correct or not according to a given dissimilarity measure (Socher et al., 2013). For this purpose a threshold for each relation δ_r is learned. Accordingly, a triple (h, r, t) is considered correct if its energy is less than δ_r, and incorrect otherwise. Since the dataset did not contain negative triples, we followed the procedure proposed by Socher et al. (2013) to sample negative triples for both the validation and the test sets. As a dissimilarity measure, we used the total energy of the triple and determined the relation threshold using the validation set and then calculated the accuracy on the test set.

Results: We measured the triple classification accuracy of our approach using ten test runs. In each run, we sampled new negative triples for both the validation and the test sets. We report the maximum, the minimum, the average, and the standard deviation of the triple classification accuracy.

For WN9-IMG, the results (cf. Tab. 5) show that our approach outperforms the baselines with up to two points in maximum accuracy and around three points in average accuracy. Please note that a direct comparison with IKRL (Paper) is not possi-

Method	Accuracy(%)		
	max	min	avg $\pm$ std
TransE	95.38	89.67	93.35 $\pm$ 1.54
IKRL (Paper)	96.90	–	–
IKRL (Vis)	95.16	88.75	92.57 $\pm$ 1.78
IKRL (Concat)	95.40	91.77	93.56 $\pm$ 1.03
Our (Concat)	**97.16**	**94.93**	**96.10 $\pm$ 0.87**
Our (only head)	95.58	91.78	93.14 $\pm$ 1.09

Table 5: Triple classification results on WN9-IMG.

Method	Accuracy(%)		
	max	min	avg $\pm$ std
TransE	67.13	66.47	66.81 $\pm$ 0.21
IKRL (Concat)	66.68	66.03	66.34 $\pm$ 0.20
Our (Concat)	**69.04**	**68.16**	**68.62 $\pm$ 0.25**

Table 6: Triple classification results on FB-IMG.

ble since we do not have access to the same set of negative samples. Still, the maximum classification accuracy of our approach is higher than that of by IKRL (Paper). Finally, the results confirm that using separate head and tail views leads to better results than using the head view only.

Regarding the FB-IMG dataset, the results in Tab. 6 emphasize the advantage of our approach. Compared to the multimodal approach IKRL, which fails to outperform TransE, our model employs multimodal information more effectively and leads to more than one point improvement in average accuracy compared to TransE.

In conclusion, the conducted evaluation demonstrates the robustness of our approach on both evaluation tasks and on different evaluation datasets.

5 Conclusion

In this paper, we presented an approach for KG representation learning that leverages multimodal data about the KG entities including linguistic as well as visual representations. The proposed approach confirms the advantage of multimodal data for learning KG representations. In future work, we will investigate the effect of multimodal data in the context of advanced translation methods and conduct further research on combining visual and linguistic features for KGs.

Acknowledgments

The first author was supported by the German Federal Ministry of Education and Research (BMBF) under the promotional reference 01UG1416B (CEDIFOR). Other than this, the work has been supported by the DFG-funded research training group "Adaptive Preparation of Information form Heterogeneous Sources" (AIPHES, GRK 1994/1). Finally, we gratefully acknowledge the support of NVIDIA Corporation with the donation of the Tesla K40 GPU used for this research.

References

Sören Auer, Christian Bizer, Georgi Kobilarov, Jens Lehmann, Richard Cyganiak, and Zachary Ives. 2007. DBpedia: A nucleus for a web of open data. In *The Semantic Web*, pages 722–735. Springer.

Kurt Bollacker, Colin Evans, Praveen Paritosh, Tim Sturge, and Jamie Taylor. 2008. Freebase: A collaboratively created graph database for structuring human knowledge. In *Proceedings of the International Conference on Management of Data (ACM SIGMOD)*, pages 1247–1250.

Antoine Bordes, Nicolas Usunier, Alberto Garcia-Durán, Jason Weston, and Oksana Yakhnenko. 2013. Translating embeddings for modeling multi-relational data. In *Proceedings of the 26th International Conference on Advances in Neural Information Processing Systems (NIPS)*, pages 2787–2795.

Ken Chatfield, Karen Simonyan, Andrea Vedaldi, and Andrew Zisserman. 2014. Return of the devil in the details: Delving deep into convolutional nets. In *Proceedings of the British Machine Vision Conference (BMVC)*.

Guillem Collell, Ted Zhang, and Marie-Francine Moens. 2017. Imagined visual representations as multimodal embeddings. In *Proceedings of the 31st Conference on Artificial Intelligence (AAAI)*, pages 4378–4384.

Jia Deng, Wei Dong, Richard Socher, Li-Jia Li, Kai Li, and Li Fei-Fei. 2009. ImageNet: A large-scale hierarchical image database. In *Proceedings of the IEEE Conference on Computer Vision and Pattern Recognition (CVPR)*, pages 248–255.

Andrea Frome, Greg S Corrado, Jon Shlens, Samy Bengio, Jeff Dean, Tomas Mikolov, et al. 2013. De-ViSE: A deep visual-semantic embedding model. In *Proceedings of the 26th International Conference on Advances in Neural Information Processing Systems (NIPS)*, pages 2121–2129.

Diederik Kingma and Jimmy Ba. 2014. Adam: A method for stochastic optimization. *arXiv preprint arXiv:1412.6980*.

Yankai Lin, Zhiyuan Liu, Huan-Bo Luan, Maosong Sun, Siwei Rao, and Song Liu. 2015a. Modeling relation paths for representation learning of knowledge bases. In *Proceedings of the Conference on Empirical Methods in Natural Language Processing (EMNLP)*, pages 705–714.

Yankai Lin, Zhiyuan Liu, Maosong Sun, Yang Liu, and Xuan Zhu. 2015b. Learning entity and relation embeddings for knowledge graph completion. In *Proceedings of the 29th Conference on Artificial Intelligence (AAAI)*.

Tomas Mikolov, Kai Chen, Greg Corrado, and Jeffrey Dean. 2013. Efficient estimation of word representations in vector space. *arXiv preprint arXiv:1301.3781*.

Lawrence Page, Sergey Brin, Rajeev Motwani, and Terry Winograd. 1999. The PageRank citation ranking: Bringing order to the web. Technical report, Stanford InfoLab.

Jeffrey Pennington, Richard Socher, and Christopher D. Manning. 2014. GloVe: Global vectors for word representation. In *Proceedings of the Conference on Empirical Methods in Natural Language Processing (EMNLP)*, pages 1532–1543.

Sascha Rothe and Hinrich Schütze. 2015. AutoExtend: Extending word embeddings to embeddings for synsets and lexemes. In *Proceedings of the 53rd Annual Meeting of the Association for Computational Linguistics (ACL)*, pages 1793–1803.

Ekaterina Shutova, Douwe Kiela, and Jean Maillard. 2016. Black holes and white rabbits: Metaphor identification with visual features. In *Proceedings of the Conference of the North American Chapter of the Association for Computational Linguistics: Human Language Technologies (NAACL-HLT)*, pages 160–170.

Karen Simonyan and Andrew Zisserman. 2014. Very deep convolutional networks for large-scale image recognition. *arXiv preprint arXiv:1409.1556*.

Richard Socher, Danqi Chen, Christopher D Manning, and Andrew Ng. 2013. Reasoning with neural tensor networks for knowledge base completion. In *Proceedings of the 26th International Conference on Advances in Neural Information Processing Systems (NIPS)*, pages 926–934.

Nitish Srivastava, Geoffrey E. Hinton, Alex Krizhevsky, Ilya Sutskever, and Ruslan Salakhutdinov. 2014. Dropout: A simple way to prevent neural networks from overfitting. *Journal of Machine Learning Research (JMLR)*, 15(1):1929–1958.

Quan Wang, Zhendong Mao, Bin Wang, and Li Guo. 2017. Knowledge graph embedding: A survey of approaches and applications. *IEEE Transactions on Knowledge and Data Engineering*, 29(12):2724–2743.

Zhen Wang, Jianwen Zhang, Jianlin Feng, and Zheng Chen. 2014. Knowledge graph embedding by translating on hyperplanes. In *Proceedings of the 28th Conference on Artificial Intelligence (AAAI)*, pages 1112–1119.

Ruobing Xie, Zhiyuan Liu, Huanbo Luan, and Maosong Sun. 2017. Image-embodied knowledge representation learning. In *Proceedings of the 26th International Joint Conference on Artificial Intelligence (IJCAI)*, pages 3140–3146.

Putting Semantics into Semantic Roles

James F. Allen[1,2] **and Choh Man Teng**[1]
[1]Institute for Human and Machine Cognition, 40 S. Alcaniz St., Pensacola FL 32502, USA
[2]Department of Computer Science, University of Rochester, Rochester NY 14627, USA
jallen@ihmc.us, cmteng@ihmc.us

Abstract

While there have been many proposals for theories of semantic roles over the years, these models are mostly justified by intuition and the only evaluation methods have been inter-annotator agreement. We explore three different ideas for providing more rigorous theories of semantic roles. These ideas give rise to more objective criteria for designing role sets, and lend themselves to some experimental evaluation. We illustrate the discussion by examining the semantic roles in TRIPS.

1 Introduction

Semantic roles play a foundational role in most computational approaches to encoding meaning, yet they remain surprisingly ill-defined. For the most part, a role taxonomy is defined by an informal gloss and some examples. In other cases, semantic roles act purely as convenient names for arguments of a predicate, frame or event, but are otherwise uninterpreted. This paper starts from the belief that if we are going to base a representation on semantic roles, they should have consequences independent of the predicate or event they are used in. In particular, we will explore three different aspects that identify criteria one might want in a theory of semantic roles:

1. *Entailment*: We should be able to identify entailments from a role independent of the type that has such roles
2. *Integration with ontology*: Roles should obey the typical entailments in an ontology (e.g., inheritance of properties from parents in the ontology)
3. *Derivability*: The roles that a type has should be derivable from its semantic properties, as revealed by definitions of the type in sources such as dictionaries.

The first property helps ensure that roles are used consistently in a semantic lexicon, the second ensures consistency with an ontology used for rea-

soning, and the third evaluates the semantic interdependence of roles and the types they occur in.

This paper will examine a particular role set, the TRIPS roles sketched in Allen & Teng, (2017)[1]. The first two properties are more formal in nature, but the third allows empirical evaluation, namely, whether the roles of an unknown word sense can be derived from its definition.

2 Preliminaries

Semantic roles have a long history, originating in linguistics as thematic roles (e.g., Fillmore, 1968; Dowty, 1991) and widely adopted in computational linguistics for semantic representations because of their compatibility with frame-based and graph-based (i.e., semantic networks) representations of meaning.

Very roughly, computational approaches can be divided into two classes based on whether one believes there is a single universal set of roles (e.g., LiRICS (Bunt & Rosemary, 2002; Petukhova & Bunt, 2008), VerbNet (Kipper et al., 2008; Bonial et al., 2011)), or whether one believes each type may identify its own unique roles (e.g., FrameNet (Baker et al., 1998)). Straddling a middle ground is PropBank (Palmer et al., 2005), which uses a universal set of role names, but allows each type to define what their roles mean. Our interest is in defining a universal set of roles across all types.

A key distinction that most frameworks make is between the inner (or core or argument) roles and the outer (or relational or adjunct) roles. The core roles identify objects that are typically required to fully specify the content of the type, while relational roles are typically optional but add additional information. For instance, in

The snow melted into a puddle.

The subject of this sentence is clearly a critical argument to the melting event. In fact, we cannot

---

[1] More detail can be found in the TRIPS LF documentation:
trips.ihmc.us/parser/LF%20Documentation.pdf

*Proceedings of the 7th Joint Conference on Lexical and Computational Semantics (*SEM)*, pages 235–244
New Orleans, June 5-6, 2018. ©2018 Association for Computational Linguistics

describe a melting event in a well-formed sentence without mentioning what melted (even if it is vague, as in *something melted*). On the other hand, the result construction realized by *into a puddle* is optional. Typically, roles of time and location are relational roles as they can be applied to almost any event and are usually optional.

But there are differences that go beyond optionality. The core roles semantically are like arguments to a predicate, although they might be optional. The relational roles semantically denote a relationship between an event and some other condition, not an argument. For instance, the phrase *into a puddle* above denotes first a semantic relationship called RESULTING-OBJECT (one of the senses of the word *into*) that takes as one argument the melting event and the other argument the object that the snow becomes, i.e., a puddle. We will elaborate on this later in the paper.

This paper describes three possible ways to establish a more rigorous semantics for a set of semantic roles, and explores each method in terms of the TRIPS semantic roles. In Section 4 we describe the start of an axiomatization of the roles. In Section 5 we describe the integration of the roles with an ontology. And in Section 6 we describe experiments involving derivability, i.e., can the roles that a given verb sense has be derived from its dictionary definition.

3 Overview of TRIPS Semantic Roles

The TRIPS core roles are shown in Table 1. These roles are defined to reflect the causal relationship between the role values and the events they are in. Informally, an AGENT of an event necessarily exerts causal influence to bring about the event. An AFFECTED of an event is necessarily affected or changed in some way by the event but does not cause the event. Objects filling the NEUTRAL and FORMAL roles are acausal, i.e., not necessarily causing or changed by the event. NEUTRAL objects are existent and can be created or destroyed. These include both physical (e.g., a box) and abstract (e.g., an idea) objects. In contrast, FORMAL objects have no temporal existence (e.g., a proposition). Finally, EXPERIENCER is a special class for sentient objects in stative events involving perceptual or cognitive states.

Table 1 summarizes the distinguishing features of each of the roles, and shows correspondences with VerbNet and LiRICS. Note the mappings are nowhere near one-to-one, reflecting differing criteria that are used to define each of the role sets. In some cases, the LiRICS role is not completely clear and is marked with a question mark.

Some differences are differences of granularity (cf: the hierarchical roles in Bonial et al. (2001) and Allen (1995)). For instance, the TRIPS AGENT role only requires a causal relationship to the event, and does not require intentionality of the agent (as in LiRICS which distinguishes between its AGENT and CAUSE roles). TRIPS takes this stance as it seems most verbs with agents would also allow non-intentional causes as well. We believe the intentionality distinction is not signaled in linguistic usage, and should be derived based on commonsense knowledge and reasoning. Thus, we do not make the distinction in the role set.

As another example, VerbNet identifies classes of STIMULUS/EXPERIENCER verbs, as in *The clown amused the children*. Roughly, the STIMULUS role plays a causal role similar to AGENT and the EXPERIENCER plays an AFFECTED role where the object is affected in some cognitive fashion. The TRIPS roleset stays at an abstract level of representation, assigning the clown to AGENT and children to AFFECTED. For similar reasons, TRIPS does not have INSTRUMENT as a core role (although there is a sense of the preposition *with* that captures accomplishing actions with a tool – e.g., *He opened the door with a key*).

Note TRIPS and VerbNet agree on the EXPERIENCER role in some cases, namely with stative verbs. In TRIPS, EXPERIENCER only occurs with stative verbs of perception and cognition.

There is a surprising variety in the VerbNet roles corresponding to the TRIPS roles, partly due to the principle in VerbNet that objects should fill the same role across all the different constructions supported by the verb. For instance, in *The horse jumped over the fence*, the horse is assigned a THEME role because *jump* supports another construction where the horse plays that role, as in *He jumped the horse over the fence*. Using the TRIPS criteria, however, *the horse* is clearly an AGENT in the first, and an AFFECTED in the second.

TRIPS Roles	Properties	Example	VerbNet Roles	Example from VerbNet	LiRICS
AGENT	+causal	**He** pushed the box	AGENT	**Amanda** carried the package	AGENT
			CAUSER	**The bug** causes the chip to give wrong answers …	CAUSE
			INSTRUMENT	**The hammer** broke the window	INSTRUMENT
			STIMULUS	**The clown** amused the children	AGENT?
			THEME	**The horse** jumped over the fence	AGENT
AFFECTED	-causal, +affected	He pushed **the box**	PATIENT	Tony bent **the rod**	PATIENT
			THEME	Carla slid **the books**	
			DESTINATION	Lora buttered **the toast**	
			SOURCE	The doctor cured **Pat** of pneumonia	
			EXPERIENCER	Carrie touched **the cat**	
			PRODUCT	The contractor will build you **a house**	RESULT
			RESULT	David dug **a hole**	
NEUTRAL	-causal, -affected, +existent	I saw **the box**	PIVOT	**Dorothy** needs new shoes	PIVOT
			THEME	We avoided **the ball**	THEME
			STIMULUS	I saw **the play**	THEME
			EXPERIENCER	**I** loved to write.	PIVOT
			LOCATION	We avoided **the area**	THEME?
			TOPIC	Ellen said **a few words**	THEME?
FORMAL	-causal, -affected -existent	I want **to cry**	ATTRIBUTE	He appeared **crazy**	ATTRIBUTE
			STIMULUS	I loved **to write**	THEME
			THEME	I needed **to come**	THEME
			PREDICATE	The bug causes **the chip to give wrong answers …**	THEME
			RESULT	I forced him **to come**	THEME?
EXPERIENCER	-causal, -affected, +cognitive	**He** saw the explosion	EXPERIENCER	**I** saw the play	PIVOT
			AGENT	**The populace** feel that the RIAA has too much power	

Table 1: Key Core Roles and Correlates in Other Rolesets

Note that based on the definitions of the roles, it is common that the same role appears more than once in a sentence. We distinguish these arguments by attaching numbers to them. Thus, in *The box is touching the table* we have two roles NEUTRAL and NEUTRAL1 for *the box* and *the table* respectively. VerbNet uses a similar scheme and labels these arguments THEME and CO-THEME.

Most of the remaining TRIPS roles are relational roles, which as discussed above relate an event to some other property. Linguistically, relational roles are realized by prepositional phrases and other adverbial constructions. Semantically, a relational role identifies causal temporal relationships between the event and the property denoted by the prepositional phrase. As an example, for the sentence *He pushed the box into the corner,* there is an event (*He pushed the box*) that results in a culmination state (*The box is in the corner*). The key characteristic of a RESULT relation is

that the state is caused by the event and starts immediately at the end of the event. Table 2 shows a number of result related roles based on their temporal properties. These three roles differ only in the temporal properties of the caused state.

Note that many cases one might think are SOURCE roles are actually RESULT roles according to their temporal criterion. For instance, in *He lifted the bottle **out of the box**,* the state of being out of the box is true at the end of the event! Using our definitions the SOURCE role seems mostly limited to cases using the preposition *from*.

Note also that the prepositions in these constructions have fully independent word senses, so our representation does not conflate *He put the cup on the box* and *He put the cup in the box*. In contrast, VerbNet assigns *the box* to a DESTINATION role in both and ignoring the preposition.

Other relational roles, which we will not have the space to discuss here, correspond relatively

237

TRIPS Role	Distinctive Properties	Example	VerbNet Role	Example from VerbNet	LiRICS Role
RESULT	E causes R to become true at end of E	He pushed the box **inside the closet**	DESTINATION	Amanda carried the package **to New York**	FINAL LOCATION
			PRODUCT	I kneaded the dough **into a loaf**	RESULT
			RESULT	Tony bent the rod **into a U**	RESULT
SOURCE	E causes R to become not true at start of E	He pushed the box **from the shelf**	INITIAL LOCATION	The book slid **from the table**	INITIAL LOCATION
			SOURCE	The thief stole the paint **from the museum**	SOURCE
TRANSIENT-RESULT	E causes R to be transiently true some time during E	He walked **by the school**	TRAJECTORY	Carla slid the books **across the table**	ATTRIBUTE
			LOCATION	He jumped the horse **over the fence**	THEME

Table 2: Some Result Related Relational Roles and Correlates in Other Rolesets. E denotes the event and R denotes the role under discussion.

well to similar roles in VerbNet, LiRICS and PropBank (e.g., LOCATION, TIME, MANNER, EXTENT, FREQUENCY, …).

4 Axiomatizing Roles

Given the space constraints we cannot present a full axiomatization of the role set. To give a flavor of the axiomatization we look at one core role in particular, namely the AFFECTED role. This introduces most of the formal framework that is used to define all the roles. In addition, we will show the axiomatization of one of the key relational roles, namely the RESULT role.

4.1 The Framework

We start from the formalism developed in Allen & Teng (2013), extended from the interval temporal logic based framework in Allen & Ferguson (1994) and Allen (1984). In this framework, both events and property predicates are reified (cf. Davidson, 1967) with functional relations capturing semantic roles and arguments. Terms, rather than predicates, are temporally qualified. For example, $x@t$ represents "object x over time t".

Objects filling roles of events are temporally situated. For example, *Jack lifted the ball* (over interval t_1) is represented as

$$\exists e.(LIFT(e), time(e)=t_1,$$
$$AGENT(e)=jack_1@t_1,$$
$$AFFECTED(e)=ball_1@t_1)$$

Key to this framework is a theory of scales. For example, $height(o@t)$ maps a temporally situated object to the set of values on the *height* scale that

this object takes over period t. Note that the object o may take different values on a scale sc over a given time interval t. Thus, $sc(o@t)$ is a *set* of values. If sc is not a scale applicable to $o@t$, then $sc(o@t)$ is empty. For example, for all time intervals t, we have $mood(rock_1@t) = \emptyset$.

Adjectives in natural language are typically represented as *Scale Predicates*, which denote (often but not necessarily convex) subsets of values on a corresponding scale. Two examples are *ScalePred(temperature, Cold)* and *ScalePred(mood, Happy)*. Thus, it is true that *John is Happy today* is written as

$$TrueOf(john_1@today, Happy).$$

In this paper, to describe relations between time intervals, we will make use of the *meets* relation, written $t_1{:}t_2$, and *"during or equal"*, written $t_1 \subseteq t_2$, from Allen's temporal relations (Allen, 1983).

For more details, see Allen & Teng (2013).

4.2 The AFFECTED Role

In Allen & Teng (2013), existence is taken as a primitive in the formal framework. We will define this as a scale with dichotomous values: *existent(o@t) = true* if o exists over the time interval t. An object can go in and out of existence at different times. This includes both physical objects such as tables and chairs as well as some abstract objects such as thoughts and orderings.

For some objects, it does not make sense to talk about their existence. These include propositions, properties, scales and scale values. (For example, hungry, five pounds.) For these objects, $\forall t.\ exist$-

ent(o@t) = ∅. Note that the value is ∅, not *false*, meaning the existent scale is not applicable.

Now consider the AFFECTED role of an event. It denotes an object that is casually acted upon in the event by the AGENT of the event and is changed in some way by the event. In "I lifted the box", the box changed location. In "The snow melted", the snow changed state of matter. In "I molded the clay", the clay changed shape.

Each event type (e.g., LIFT, MELT, MOLD) is associated with a specific dimension of change such that every occurrence of a particular event type entails a change in the AFFECTED along that particular dimension. For example, for each MOLD event, the AFFECTED of MOLD changes shape, even though the resulting shape in each instance might differ. This is captured by specifying that all events of the same event type share a scale on which change occurs for the AFFECTED.

We can thus formulate the conditions for AFFECTED as follows. Let *E(e)* denote that *e* is an event occurrence of type *E*. Let *scale(sc)* denote that *sc* is a scale.

$$\forall E \; \exists sc \; \forall e, o, t.$$
$$E(e), scale(sc),$$
$$time(e) = t, \textit{AFFECTED}(e) = o@t$$
$$\Rightarrow \exists t1, t2.$$
$$t1 \subseteq t, \; t1{:}t2,$$
$$sc(o@t1) \neq sc(o@t2)$$

This says the AFFECTED of *e* undergoes at least one change in a scale dimension *sc* characteristic of the event type *E*. There can be more changes, both along the same scale (e.g., the clay changes shape continuously while being molded), or along other dimensions (e.g., the snow changes both shape and volume while being melted).

In the above, t_1 is during or equal t, the time interval of the event, whereas t_2 is met by t_1 but could be during, overlaps, or at the end of t. This allows for changes that are intermittent and may not persist to the end of the event (e.g., flicker, wiggle) and also changes that occur only at the end of the event (e.g., the stick snapped). In the latter case, for AFFECTED objects that only come into existence at the end of the event (e.g., I drew a circle), it is possible that $sc(o@t_1) = ∅$.

Note that the semantics of the roles are defined with respect to completed events. This is captured by the predicate *E(e)*. For example, for *I was drawing a circle but did not finish*, even though the circle never came into existence, the roles are derived not from the progressive formulation but from the corresponding case in which the event has occurred.

4.3 Characteristic Properties of Core Roles

Table 1 lists several properties: *causal, affected, existent*. Each of the core roles can be characterized by a combination of the presence or absence of these properties. The axiomatization of the AFFECTED role indicates how the *affected* property can be defined. The *existent* property is captured by the *existent* scale discussed in the previous section.

The *causal* property is meant to indicate that an object exerts a causal influence. In the transitive case the AGENT causes the event to happen to the AFFECTED (I caused the lifting of the box). The *causal* property is often taken as primitive in other rolesets, but we will outline here how it might be formalized.

We take advantage of the intuition that if X causes an event e, then if we change X in some way we can change the event that occurs. More formally, let sc_E be the scale characteristic of event type E, that is, when an event of type E occurs, its AFFECTED is changed along the scale dimension sc_E. Loosely speaking, when +causal obtains (for an AGENT o_{ag}), there exists some scale sc^* such that a change of o_{ag} on the sc^* scale would entail a change of the AFFECTED o_{aff} on the sc_E scale. In other words, there is some property of the AGENT such that when this property is changed, regardless by what means, some property of the AFFECTED will vary accordingly.

4.4 Wrinkles

A few further considerations complicate the formulation above.

First, existent objects are constantly undergoing changes. For example, an object typically gets older (on the AGE scale) as time passes, even without being involved with any explicit AGENT or EVENT. Such changes (with their associated scales) would trivially satisfy the conditions in the formulation above, such that almost any (existent) object could be a candidate for being an AFFECTED of any EVENT. We call such innocuous changes *Background Changes* and exclude them from consideration.

Second, for some events although the occurrence of the event typically induces a change along the specified scale dimension, this is not always the case. For instance, for the PUSH event, typically the AFFECTED object changes location but in some cases the object might not move. For example, I pushed the door but it was locked. We need to define a notion of canonical or perhaps counterfactual change. This is especially pertinent for events such as PREVENT (I prevented the accident) or MAINTAIN (The pump maintained the air pressure), in which the events in question are meant to induce no change in the object being acted upon.

Third, the NEUTRAL role mostly entails the absence of properties: *not* causal and *not* affected. It would seem then that any existent object could fill this role, even if this object bears no relationship to the event in question. Similarly, in LiRICS for example, the THEME role is defined as

> *"Participant in a state or event that is essential to the event taking place or the state being in effect. In an event, a theme does not have control over the way the event occurs and is not structurally changed by the event."* (Schiffrin & Bunt, 2007).

We need to define the notion of being *relevant* or *essential* to an event to select for the proper objects. The same consideration applies to FORMAL and EXPERIENCER roles as well.

The axiomatization above thus represents our first attempts to formalize the semantic role entailments. We expect further refinements as we explore these issues in depth.

4.5 The RESULT Relational Role

Intuitively a RESULT relates an EVENT and the eventual state. The RESULT only becomes true at the end of the EVENT. For example, in "The cat slid under the table", the cat was not under the table before or during the sliding event, but at the end of the event the cat is under the table.

In contrast, in many approaches the relationship between the event and the resulting spatial predicate is unclear. For example, VerbNet would treat "the table" as the DESTINATION without explicit representation of the spatial relation (under).

RESULTs are often spatial, but they can also be other general states. For example, in "I wiped the desk clean", the result is that the desk is clean.

Resultative constructions apply to intransitive events (e.g., slide) as well as transitive events (e.g., wipe). For intransitive events, the resulting state pertains to the subject of the event (e.g., In *The cat slid under the* table, the result is that *the cat* is under the table), whereas for transitive events, the resulting state pertains to the object of the event (e.g., from *I wiped the desk clean*, the RESULT is that *the desk* is clean).

It is possible to transform intransitive constructions into transitive constructions. For example, in "The dog barked the cat up the tree", the BARK event is normally intransitive, but in the above re-sultative construction, the dog is the AGENT of the BARK event, the cat is the AFFECTED and the RESULT is that the cat is up the tree. (For a treatment of this, see Allen & Teng (2017).)

Thus, the RESULT role can be formalized as follows for a transitive event type E.

$$\exists sc \; \forall e, o, t, P.$$
$$E(e), \; scale(sc), \; ScalePred(sc, P),$$
$$time(e) = t,$$
$$\mathbf{\mathit{AFFECTED}}(e) = o@t,$$
$$\mathbf{\mathit{RESULT}}(e) = P$$
$$\implies \exists t2. \; t : t2,$$
$$TrueOf(o@t2, P),$$
$$\forall t1 \subseteq t. \; {\sim} TrueOf(o@t1, P)$$

For example, for the WIPE event *e* in "I wiped the desk clean", we have *ScalePred(cleanliness, Clean)*, that is, the predicate *Clean* is defined on the *cleanliness* scale. In addition, AFFECTED*(e)* = $desk_1$@*t* and RESULT*(e)* = *Clean*; that is, the desk is clean immediately after the WIPE event but not before.

Similarly, for the intransitive case, the AFFECTED above is replaced by the role filled by the subject, that is, the RESULT is a change in the subject at the end of the EVENT.

Note that an EVENT can have multiple RESULTs. For example, "The cat climbed on the box away from the rising water", in which case the two results combine as a conjunction true immediately after the event.

The scale allowed for each event type constrains the possible interpretations of the text. For example, in "I wiped the table clean", the table can change on the cleanliness scale and thus allows a RESULT construction here. In contrast, in "I wiped the table happy", the mood scale is not applicable to tables, ruling out the RESULT construction. Instead, one would prefer an alternative interpretation using a manner-like construction in which "happy" is used to qualify "I".

5 Integration with an Ontology

The second criterion we set for a theory of semantic roles is integration with an ontology. If semantic roles are to have an impact on deep language understanding and reasoning, they should be integrated with an ontology that supports that reasoning and stores commonsense knowledge. There is a large relevant literature concerning roles in semantic networks (e.g., Hayes, 1980; Thomason & Touretsky, 1991). Essentially such roles are functions from a type (for verbs an event type is one sense of the verb) to another object. If a word

Type	New roles/ *Inherited roles*	Verbs (often in subclasses)
EVENT-OF-ACTION	AGENT	
EVENT-OF-AGENT-INTERACTION	AGENT1 *AGENT*	Meet, collaborate, …
EVENT-OF-CREATION	AFFECTED *AGENT*	Bake, establish, …
EVENT-OF-CAUSATION	AFFECTED, *AGENT*	Push, control, …
MOTION	RESULT *AGENT* *AFFECTED*	Go, disperse, move, …
EVENT-OF-UNDERGOING-ACTION	AFFECTED	Die, inherit, …
EVENT-OF-STATE	NEUTRAL	
POSSESS	NEUTRAL1 *NEUTRAL*	Own, possess, …
HAVE-PROPERTY	FORMAL *NEUTRAL*	Be, seem, …
EVENT-OF-EXPERIENCE	EXPERIENCER *NEUTRAL*	Appreciate, believe, …

Table 3: Some Roles in the Event Ontology (Showing Role Inheritance)

sense S has a semantic role R, then for all instances of S there is an object that fills the R role, i.e.,

$$\forall s.\ S(s) \Rightarrow \exists r.\ R(s,r)$$

This axiom captures what is sometimes called an *essential* role (Palmer, 2006), i.e., a semantic role that must exist even if not specified in the input sentence. Palmer notes that other roles are *obligatory*, that is, they are both essential and linguistically required, and still others are simply *optional* and may or may not be realized at either the linguistic or inferential levels.

A critical foundation of semantic networks is inheritance down type hierarchies, where a subtype "inherits" all properties of its parent types. When viewing this from the perspective of semantic roles, this means any role that is essential for a given type T must also then be essential for all subtypes of T.

Surprisingly, the predominant models of semantic roles do not address such issues in any depth. VerbNet, for instance, creates its classes based on clustering by verb usage patterns, rather than semantic entailments, and has a very limited hierarchical structure defined in terms of extensions in allowed usages. Within these hierarchies, though, it does have inheritance of roles. Propbank, on the other hand, is word based and even semantically very similar verbs have different rolesets (e.g., compare the rolesets for the verbs *constrict, compress* and *squeeze*, which

one would expect would be clustered together in an ontology).

The TRIPS role set is fully integrated with a rich ontology. In this ontology, the concepts are organized both by entailment as well as the semantic roles the verb senses take. Table 3 shows a small part of the upper ontology for events and the roles that are defined for each type and inherited from ancestor types. Note TRIPS allows both essential and optional roles. Both are inherited down the hierarchy, and lower types can make an inherited optional role essential, but not vice versa. Whether a role is obligatory or not is not specified in the ontology, but rather in the lexicon where the words and the argument structures they allow are defined. Furthermore, it employs explanation closure techniques (Schubert, 1994) – if a role is *not* defined as possible in the ontology then the role is not possible.

The integration of roles with an ontology mutually constrains the assignment of roles to verb sense predicates *and* constrains the ontology itself. For instance, if we believe that the verb *disappear* takes the AFFECTED role and not an *AGENT* role, then its word sense cannot be under the EVENT-OF-ACTION or EVENT-OF-STATE hierarchies, but it looks like a good candidate for being under the EVENT-OF-UNDERGOING-ACTION category. Likewise, although you might think the verb *analyze* might take an EXPERIENCER role, if you believe that *analyze* falls under EVENT-OF-ACTION, then it should take the AGENT role instead.

One other aspect that relates to the ontology is selectional preferences. As in many semantic networks, one can also constrain the semantic type of the arguments that can fill a role. For instance, one might say that the event type EAT typically concerns an animate entity (as AGENT) and some comestible substance (as the AFFECTED role). Such knowledge is critical for driving semantic disambiguation during parsing. The TRIPS restrictions are soft constraints, i.e., the parser prefers interpretations that satisfy the constraints, but can construct interpretations that do not. As with roles, the selectional preferences are inherited down the hierarchy, with more specific event types accumulating all the constraints imposed on their ancestors in the hierarchy. We do not have the space to discuss this further here.

Role Chain	Role Identified	Example Word and Definition	Justification
$V \xrightarrow{R} Arg$	R	*wolf*: φ *eat* φ	An unfilled direct role R of the head verb is R
$V \xrightarrow{RESULT} V1 \xrightarrow{GROUND} Arg$	NEUTRAL	*near*: φ *move towards* φ	The ground of the property is not affected by the verb
$V_{change} \xrightarrow{FORMAL} V1 \xrightarrow{AGENT} Arg$	AFFECTED	*jump*: φ *cause [φ to jump]*	The agent of the embedded event is changed by undergoing the cause event

Table 4: A few sample rules for deriving roles from definitions.

6 Derivability in Definitions

The third criterion we explore is derivability. The motivation is as follows: If semantic roles have a semantics independent of their predicates/events, then the semantic properties of roles would not change between a predicate and its definition. For example, consider the word sense corresponding to the predicate for *kill*, defined as *cause to die*. According to our analysis above, *kill* would take two essential roles: AGENT and AFFECTED. The definition, on the other hand, involves a predicate *cause* that takes an AGENT, AFFECTED and a FORMAL role (to die). A highly abbreviated logical form for this definition is shown in Figure 1. While *cause* has three roles, only the FORMAL role is fixed by the definition (i.e., it is the *die* event). The unfilled essential roles in the definition are AGENT and AFFECTED, exactly the roles for *kill*.

Our hypothesis is that given a good definition of a word sense, the essential roles can be derived from that definition automatically. This, of course, has significant impact. If the definitions in WordNet (Fellbaum, 1998) are generally reasonable, we can bootstrap from the items predefined in the TRIPS ontology and lexicon, and derive the semantic roles for any verb in WordNet. Our preliminary evaluation described here indicates that this is a very feasible goal.

To implement this we need a strategy for identifying unfilled semantic roles in a definition. The most common case we have encountered in WordNet definitions is that the unfilled roles are elided in the definition. The TRIPS parser instantiates such gaps in the logical form using its IMPRO construct. Other cases include indicating the unfilled roles by an indefinite pronoun, such as *someone* or *something*.

More complicated cases occur when the roles do not occur at the top level but in an embedded clause, as in one definition of *approach* (*move towards*), shown in Figure 2. The roles for the predicate *Towards* are FIGURE and GROUND, and an IMPRO fills the GROUND role of the predicate. Thus we have a role chain, from the head verb through RESULT and GROUND. We have analyzed such role patterns and created a mapping based on the semantics of the roles. In this case, it would indicate a NEUTRAL role, as the GROUND role is not changed by the event. Table 4 summarizes a few of the most common rules for identifying roles from role chains.

6.1 Experimental Evaluation of Derivability

To test this technique, we built a customized TRIPS system to parse definitions. The main customization was the addition of about a dozen top level syntactic rules that capture the common forms of definitions, which as we have seen contain much ellipsis. Otherwise, the grammar and lexicon are exactly the same as in all the other variants of the TRIPS parser. Our experiment also takes advantage of the fact that the TRIPS ontology has an extensive mapping to WordNet synsets, and uses the WordNet hypernym hierarchy to

Figure 1: Key aspects of the LF for *to cause to die*

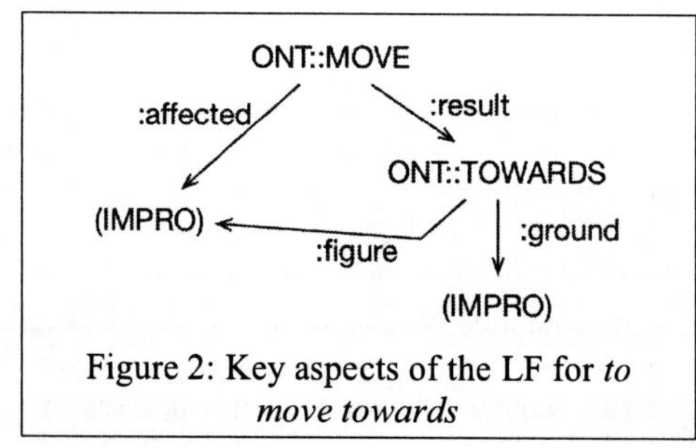

Figure 2: Key aspects of the LF for *to move towards*

identify abstractions. Any WordNet synset can be mapped to its most specific type in the TRIPS ontology (Allen & Teng, 2017).

The experiment was set up as follows. We repeat the following to obtain 40 test cases:

1) Randomly choose a WordNet synset S such that: (a) S has a direct mapping to a TRIPS ontology type T, (b) the TRIPS lexicon has word W with type T that is also in S, and (c) the WordNet definition is not circular.
2) Remove the lexical entry for W from the TRIPS lexicon after recording its essential roles as the gold standard answer.
3) Parse the definition for S and extract the essential roles as described above.
4) Compare the roles from steps 2) and 3) to compute precision and recall.

For a baseline we assigned each verb the AGENT and AFFECTED roles. Table 5 shows the results of the experiment. We obtained 88% precision and 77% recall for our approach, versus 63% and 66% respectively using the baseline assignments. Because a large number of English verbs are simple transitive verbs describing change, the baseline did better than one might expect. Still our approach based on parsing definitions performed far better, lending strong support that our role set passes the derivability test.

Based on a manual analysis of the errors in this experiment, the errors arose from a combination of parse errors, ambiguities, and definitions that are terse and loose. For instance, one sense of *appear* is defined as *to come into sight*. This is ambiguous between entering into some state (the right interpretation here), and the acquisition reading where *sight* is acquired. The parser chose the latter, leading to an assignment of AGENT as the role rather than AFFECTED. We also missed a few roles because of parser errors. For instance, a sense of *pronounce* is defined as *to declare judgement on* (e.g., *they pronounced him unfit*). The parser failed to identify the second gap (i.e., the missing object of the preposition *on*). In addition, this is the one case we found where our strategy for identifying arguments was inadequate. There is an argument to this verb that is the judgement, but this is not signaled by an elided argument or an indefinite pronoun. Thus the gold answer is AGENT, NEUTRAL, FORMAL but our

system was able to identify only the AGENT role.

There are several additional processing steps we could take to improve the performance. For instance, sometimes multiple definitions are presented in WordNet and we could process them all and try to combine them. Currently we only analyze the first one. Also, we could try to verify the roleset by attempting to parse examples that are given in the gloss. Often it seems that the lexicographer depends on the examples to supplement and disambiguate the definitions.

In our error analysis we did not find any example where if we had identified the correct parse of the definition, we would have identified an inappropriate role for the word being defined. This indicates that the semantic roles appear to be consistent across the lexicon and, furthermore, are identifiable by the semantic properties induced by the events in the definitions. In other words, they meet the criterion of derivability!

7 Discussion

We have presented three possible criteria for how one can produce and validate a semantics for a semantic role set. We have illustrated the techniques by looking at the roles in the TRIPS framework. Note we do not claim this indicates the TRIPS roleset is the only roleset that could be useful in linguistic theory and computational semantic models. However, we have shown that the TRIPS roleset is internally consistent and has a set of desirable semantic properties: (1) it is amenable to axiomatization in a temporal logic, (2) it is integrated into an ontology that supports inheritance, and (3) the roles are derivable in the sense that they can be derived for verb senses based on their definitions.

The TRIPS roleset was created by considering the properties of causality, temporality, existence, and sentience. Other researchers choose to create rolesets based on other criteria. We encourage those researchers to attempt to formalize their roles along the dimensions we have defined to create a firm theoretical foundation by which all theories can be compared.

Acknowledgements

This work was supported in part by the DARPA CwC program under ARO contract W911NF-15-1-0542. We also thank the reviewers and Jena Hwang for helpful comments on the paper.

	Our Approach	Baseline
Precision	88.4%	63.4%
Recall	77.2%	65.8%
F1 score	82.4%	64.5%

Table 5: Results in Deriving Rolesets

8 References

Allen, J. F. (1983). Maintaining Knowledge About Temporal intervals. *Communications of the ACM* 26(11):832-843.

Allen, J. F. (1984). Towards a general theory of action and time. *Artificial Intelligence*, 23(2):123-154.

Allen, J.F. (1995). Natural Language Understanding, Benjamin Cummings, Second Edition.

Allen, J. F. and G. Ferguson (1994). Actions and events in interval temporal logic. *Journal of Logic and Computation*, 4(5):531-579.

Allen, J. F. and C. M. Teng (2013). Becoming different: A language-driven formalism for commonsense knowledge. In the 11th International Symposium on Logical Formalizations of Commonsense Reasoning, Cyprus.

Allen, J., and C. M. Teng (2017). Broad coverage, domain-generic deep semantic parsing. *AAAI Workshop on Construction Grammar*, March, Stanford University.

Baker, Collin F., Charles J. Fillmore, and John B. Lowe. (1998). The Berkeley FrameNet Project. In *Proceedings of COLING-ACL'98*, pages 86–90, Montréal, Canada.

Bonial, C., et al. (2011). A Hierarchical Unification of LIRICS and VerbNet Semantic Roles. *5th IEEE Conf. on Semantic Computing (ICSC)*, Palo Alto, CA.

Bunt, H. C. and L. Romary (2002). Requirements on multimodal semantic representations. *Proceedings of ISO TC37/SC4 Preliminary Meeting*, pages 59–68.

Davidson, D. (1967). The Logical Form of Action Sentences. *The Logic of Decision and Action.* N. Rescher. Pittsburgh, University of Pittsburgh Press.

Dowty, D. (1991). Thematic Proto-Roles and Argument Selection, *Language*, Vol 67-3, pp547-619

Fellbaum, C. (1998, ed.) *WordNet: An Electronic Lexical Database.* Cambridge, MA: MIT Press.

Fillmore, Charles (1968) "The case for case", in E. Bach and R. Harms, (eds) *Universals in Linguistic Theory*, Holt, Rinehart, and Winston, New York, 1–90.

Hayes, Pat (1980). The Logic of Frames. In *Reading in Artificial Intelligence,* Margan Kaufman.

Kipper, K., A. Korhonen, N. Ryant, and M. Palmer (2008). A large-scale classification of English verbs. *Language Resources and Evaluation Journal*, vol. 42, pp. 21–40, 2008.

Palmer, M. (2006). *Semantic Processing for Finite Domains,* Cambridge University Press.

Palmer, M., Gildea, D. and Kingsbury, P. (2005). The Proposition Bank: A corpus annotated with semantic roles, *Computational Linguistics Journal*, 31:1.

Petukhova, V. and Bunt, H. (2008). LIRICS Semantic Role Annotation: Design and Evaluation of a Set of Data Categories. *LREC*.

Schiffrin A. and H. C. Bunt (2007). LIRICS Deliverable D4.3. Documented compilation of semantic data categories. http://lirics.loria.fr

Schubert, L.K. (1994). Explanation closure, action closure, and the Sandewall test suite for reasoning about change, *J. of Logic and Computation 4(5)*, Special Issue on Actions and Processes, pp. 679-799

Thomason R. and D. Touretsky (1991). Inheritance Theory and Networks with Roles, in *Principles of Semantic Networks,* Morgan-Kaufmann.

Measuring Frame Instance Relatedness

Valerio Basile
University of Turin
Italy
basile@di.unito.it

Roque Lopez Condori
Université Côte d'Azur,
Inria, CNRS, I3S, France
roque.lopez-condori@inria.fr

Elena Cabrio
Université Côte d'Azur,
Inria, CNRS, I3S, France
elena.cabrio@unice.fr

Abstract

Frame semantics is a well-established framework to represent the meaning of natural language in computational terms. In this work, we aim to propose a quantitative measure of relatedness between pairs of frame instances. We test our method on a dataset of sentence pairs, highlighting the correlation between our metric and human judgments of semantic similarity. Furthermore, we propose an application of our measure for clustering frame instances to extract prototypical knowledge from natural language.

1 Introduction

Frame Semantics has been a staple of artificial intelligence and cognitive linguistics since its first formulation in the '70s (Fillmore, 1976). In particular, frame semantics has been widely adopted as a theoretical backbone for the interpretation of natural language, in order to represent its meaning with formal structures suited for computation. In a nutshell, according to frame semantics, the meaning of a sentence can be represented as a set of situations (*frames*) and the entities involved in them (*frame elements*), each with their own role.

Several approaches have proposed in the past years to automatically interpret natural language in terms of frame semantics (Gildea and Jurafsky, 2002; Thompson et al., 2003; Erk and Padó, 2006, among others). However, the vast majority of these approaches focuses on the extraction of the structure of the frames evoked in the natural language fragment (frames and roles), while leaving the frame elements either underspecified or simply representing them as spans of the original text. In this work, we propose to fully represent the meaning of a natural language sentence with

instantiated frames, where the frame elements are nodes in a knowledge graph.

Moreover, while a great deal of effort has been directed towards the extraction of frames from natural language, not many systems process frames further, to solve downstream tasks in NLP and AI — an example is Sentilo (Recupero et al., 2015), a sentiment analysis system built on top of the frame-based machine reading tool FRED by Presutti et al. (2012).

In this paper we define a quantitative measure to compute the semantic relatedness of a pair of frame instances, and apply it to the task of creating a commonsense knowledge base.

The main contributions of this paper are:

- A novel measure of relatedness between frame instances (Section 3).

- A high-quality data set of natural language sentences aligned to the frame instances evoked by them (Sections 4 and 5).

- A pilot study on the extraction of prototypical knowledge based on frame instance clustering (Section 6).

Before introducing the novel contributions, we describe related work (Section 2), while Section 7 summarizes our conclusions.

2 Related Work

The most relevant to our research is the work of Pennacchiotti and Wirth (2009), which introduces the notion of "frame relatedness" and proposes different types of measures to asses it. These measures are grouped in three categories: i) based on the hypothesis that frames are related if their lexical units are semantically related; ii) corpus-based measures, which suggest that related frames tend to occur in

245

*Proceedings of the 7th Joint Conference on Lexical and Computational Semantics (*SEM)*, pages 245–254
New Orleans, June 5-6, 2018. ©2018 Association for Computational Linguistics

the same or similar contexts (e.g., measured by pointwise mutual information or distributional semantic models); iii) hierarchy-based measures, which leverage the FrameNet hierarchy, assuming that frames are likely related if they are close in the network structure of FrameNet. The results of their experimental tests show high correlation between some of these measures and a dataset of human judgments of semantic similarity.

Subsequent works have taken the measures presented by Pennacchiotti and Wirth (2009) as basis to implement more refined measures. Kim et al. (2013) proposes SynRank, a function to calculate frame relatedness which uses three measures: i) content similarity, based on the overlapping of the terms that evoke the frames, ii) context similarity, defined by neighbor frames within a window in its document, and iii) corpus-based word similarity, which uses the corpus-specific information.

Virk et al. (2016) presented a supervised approach to enrich FrameNet's relational structure with new frame-to-frame relations. To create these new relations, the authors propose to use features based on frame network structure and frame elements (role names similarity by overlap). In addition to these features, the overlap among content words (nouns, verbs, adjectives and adverbs) occurring in verbal definitions of each frame of FrameNet is also used.

More recently, Alam et al. (2017) proposed three measures to compute the semantic relatedness between two frames using the hierarchical structure of the FrameNet graph. These measures are i) path similarity, based on the shortest path between two nodes in the taxonomy, ii) Leacock-Chodorow similarity (Leacock and Chodorow, 1998), which considers the shortest path between two nodes and the depth of the taxonomy and iii) Wu-Palmer similarity (Wu and Palmer, 1994), based on the depths of two nodes in the taxonomy and their least common subsumer. In (Shah et al.) a word sense-based similarity metric is used as a proxy to frame instance relatedness in order to cluster frame instances.

Our method presupposes a formalization of the frame element structure including the entities that fill the semantic roles, akin to the work of (Scheffczyk et al., 2006), which seeks to give the slot fillers semantic type constraints by linking them to a top-level ontology.

To our knowledge, our approach is the first to address the relatedness of instantiated frames that include disambiguated concepts in their frame elements.

3 A Quantitative Measure of Frame Instance Relatedness

In the theory of frame semantics, a *frame* is a prototypical situation uniquely defined by a name, e.g., `Driving_vehicle`, an event involving a vehicle, someone who controls it, the area where the motion takes place, and so on. Frames have *frame elements*, identified by the *role* they play in the frame. Following the example above, `Driver` and `Vehicle` are some of the frame elements expected to be present in a `Driving_vehicle` situation.

Most NLP works on frame semantics are based on FrameNet (Baker et al., 1998), a lexical semantic resource which contains descriptions and annotations of frames. In FrameNet, each frame type defines its own set of frame elements and associated words (known as *lexical units*) which can evoke the frame. FrameNet also lists a set of frame-to-frame relations (e.g. `subframe_of`, `is_causative_of`) according to how they are organized with respect to each other.

We propose a method to compute a numeric score indicating the relatedness of a pair of frame instances. Formally, we define a frame instance fi as a tuple $(f_t, \{(r_1, e_1), ..., (r_n, e_n)\})$, $f_t \in T$, $r \in R, e \in E$, where T is the set of frame types, R is the set of semantic roles, and E is the vocabulary of entities that could fill any given role.

The relatedness between two frame instances fi_1 and fi_2 is computed as a linear combination of the relatedness between the two frame types and the distance between the frame elements contained in the frame instances:

$$firel(fi_1, fi_2) =$$
$$= \alpha ftrel(fi_1, fi_2) + (1-\alpha) ferel(fi_1, fi_2)$$
$$(1)$$

The relatedness $firel(fi_1, fi_2)$ is therefore defined to be a number in the range $[0, 1]$, while the α parameter controls the extent to which the relatedness is weighted towards the frame types or the frame elements. The frame type relatedness $ftrel$ and the frame element relatedness $ferel$ can be computed in several ways, which we detail in the remainder of this section.

3.1 Implementation Details

The method to compute the relatedness of frame instances that we propose is independent from the actual vocabulary of frames, roles and concepts — although for some of the steps precise characteristics of the frame definition are needed, e.g., a set of lexical units. In practice, we use the frame type and element inventory of FrameNet 1.5, containing 1,230 frames, 11,829 lexical units and 173,018 example sentences. As concept inventory, we select BabelNet, a large scale multilingual dictionary and semantic network (Navigli and Ponzetto, 2012). Words in BabelNet belong to one or many BabelNet synsets, each synset defines a sense, thus it represents a potential semantic role filler in a frame element.

3.2 Frame Type Relatedness

Pennacchiotti and Wirth (2009) surveys a number of methods to compute a relatedness score between frames. We implemented the best performing algorithm for frame relatedness among those introduced in the aforementioned paper, namely the *co-occurrence measure* ($ftrel_{occ}$). This algorithm is based on an estimate of the point-wise mutual information (pmi) between the two frames, computed on the basis of their occurrence in an annotated corpus.

Given two frame types ft_1 and ft_2, and a corpus C, the measure is defined as:

$$ftrel_{occ}(fi_1, fi_2) = log_2 \frac{|C_{ft_1,ft_2}|}{|C_ft_1||C_ft_2|} \quad (2)$$

where C_{ft_1} and C_{ft_2} indicate the subsets of contexts in which ft_1 and ft_2 occur respectively, and C_{ft_1,ft_2} the subset of contexts where both frame types occur.

Since a large corpus of frame-annotated natural language is hard to come by and very expensive to produce, the occurrence of a frame type ft_i in a context c is defined as the occurrence of at least one of the lexical units l_{ft_i} associated to that frame type in FrameNet in that particular context:

$$C_{ft_i} = \{c \in C : \exists l_{ft_i} \in c\}$$

$$C_{ft_1,ft_2} = \{c \in C : \exists l_{ft_1} \in c \wedge \exists l_{ft_2} \in c\}$$

While the original method only considers the word part of the lexical units, we computed the occurrence counts on SEMCOR (Landes et al., 1998), a corpus of manually sense-labeled English text (words are annotated with part-of-speech tags and senses from WordNet). By using a disambiguated corpus, we are able to match the lexical units from FrameNet to the sense labels of SEMCOR, overcoming the ambiguity of polysemous words.

We also implement an alternative measure of frame type relatedness, based on distributional semantics ($ftrel_{dist}$ inspired by another of the measures in the same paper by Pennacchiotti and Wirth (2009)). We created vector representations for each frame type by merging the representations of their lexical units in a pre-trained word space model. For each frame type, we compute the average of the vectors in GloVe6B (Pennington et al., 2014), a large word embedding model of English words, corresponding to each lexical unit in the frame. The measure of distributional frame type relatedness between two frame types ft_1 and ft_2 is then given by the cosine similarity between the two respective frame vectors $\vec{ft_1}$ and $\vec{ft_2}$:

$$ftrel_{dist}(fi_1, fi_2) = \frac{\vec{ft_1} \cdot \vec{ft_2}}{||\vec{ft_1}||||\vec{ft_2}||} \quad (3)$$

3.3 Frame Elements Relatedness

The second half of equation 1 corresponds to the relatedness measured between two sets of frame elements, therefore an aggregation step is needed. For each concept corresponding to the frame elements $fe_i \in fi_1$, we compute all the similarity scores with respect to the concepts corresponding to the frame elements $fe_j \in fi_2$, and select the best match. The aggregation by maximum is an approximation of the best match algorithm on bipartite graphs, that is, the measure gives more weight to the most similar pairs of frame elements rather than averaging the similarities of all the possible combinations. The resulting similarities are averaged over all the frame elements. Since this process is asymmetrical, we compute it in both directions and take the average of the results:

$$ferel(fi_1, fi_2) =$$
$$= \frac{1}{2}\Big(\frac{1}{|fi_1|} \sum_{fe_i \in fi_1} \max_{fe_j \in fi_2} csim(fe_i, fe_j) +$$
$$+ \frac{1}{|fi_2|} \sum_{fe_i \in fi_2} \max_{fe_j \in fi_1} csim(fe_i, fe_j)\Big) \quad (4)$$

The function $csim(fe_i, fe_j)$ between concepts is again computed as cosine similarity between vector representations. In this case we leverage the semantic resource NASARI (Camacho-Collados et al., 2016), a concept space model built on top of the BabelNet semantic network. Each vector in NASARI represents a BabelNet synset in a dense 300-dimensional space. The reason to use a different vector space model than the one used for $ftrel_{dist}$ is that NASARI provides representations of disambiguated concepts, which we have from KNEWS, while GloVe6B is a word-based model and the lexical units are not disambiguated.

Note that in equation 4 the semantic roles of the elements are ignored in the computation of the relatedness between frame elements. We therefore extend the definition of frame element relatedness by adding the extra parameter *roles*, acting as a filter: when activated, it sets the relatedness score of a pair of frame elements to zero if they do not share the same role in the frame instance.

4 Evaluation by Text Similarity

To our knowledge, there is no manually annotated dataset of frame instances and their relatedness. In order to circumvent this shortcoming, we propose an indirect methodology for the evaluation of the frame instance relatedness measures we introduced in Section 3. The key idea of our evaluation approach is to measure the relatedness of frame instances extracted from pairs of short texts, for which a gold standard pairwise similarity score is given.

We parse the text with a knowledge extraction system to extract all the frame instances. We then measure the semantic relatedness of the extracted frame instances and compare the outcome with a judgment of pairwise semantic similarity given on the original sentences. The aim of this experiment is to show that our measure of frame instance relatedness correlates with the semantic relatedness of the text that evokes the frame. In other words, we use textual similarity as a proxy for human judgment of relatedness between frame instances.

4.1 Data

The dataset we selected to carry out this experiment is provided by the shared task on Semantic Text Similarity (STS) held at SemEval 2017 (task 1, track 5 English-English) (Cer et al., 2017). The set is composed of 250 pairs of short English sentences, manually annotated with a numerical score from 1 to 5 indicating their degree of semantic relatedness. Examples of sentence pairs from the gold standard set, along with their human judgments of semantic similarity, are shown in Table 1.

Table 1: Examples of the sentence pairs in the SemEval 2017 STS dataset, with numbers indicating their semantic similarity on a scale from 1 to 5.

Sim.	Sentence pair
4.0	There are dogs in the forest.
	The dogs are alone in the forest.
3.4	The boy is raising his hand.
	The man is raising his hand.
1.0	A woman supervisor is instructing
	the male workers.
	A woman is working as a nurse.
0.2	The woman is kneeling next to a cat.
	A girl is standing next to a man.

4.2 Knowledge Extraction

To compute the relatedness score of pairs of frame instances, we need to extract them from the natural language text. For this purpose, we use KNEWS (Knowledge Extraction With Semantics), a fully automated pipeline of NLP tools for machine reading (Basile et al., 2016). The input of KNEWS is an arbitrary English text, and its output is a set of RDF triples encoding the frames extracted from the text by Semafor (Das et al., 2014). KNEWS integrates the Word Sense Disambiguation tool Babelfy (Moro et al., 2014) to extract concept and entities from the input sentences, and maps them to the frame roles provided by Semafor, creating frame instances where the frame types are from FrameNet 1.5 and the frame roles are filled with concepts from BabelNet. An example of the extraction of frame instances from natural language performed by KNEWS is shown in Figure 1. In the example, three frame instances are extracted from the sentence "two men sit on a bench", with frame types `People`, `Cardinal_numbers` and `Being_located`. The frame elements are completed with BabelNet synset identifiers, e.g., the `Theme` of `Being_located` is `bn:00001533n` (man, adult male, male: *An adult person who is male (as opposed to a woman)*[1]) and the `Location` of the same frame instance is `bn:00009850n` (bench: *A long seat for more than one person*[2]).

We ran KNEWS on the 500 sentences from the STS dataset and extracted 1,650 frame instances of 178 different frame types. Each frame instance has on average 1.2 frame elements, for a total of 2,107 roles filled by 457 different types of concepts.

4.3 Frame-based Sentence Similarity

Our aim in this experiment is to assess the relatedness of *sentences* by measuring the relatedness of their corresponding frame instances. Since we have defined (in Section 3) a method to compute the relatedness of *frame instances*, an extra step of aggregation is needed in order to reconcile the measurement for the evaluation. We define the similarity $ssim(s_1, s_2)$ between two sentences $s_1 = \{fi_1^1, ..., fi_n^1\}$ and $s_2 = \{fi_1^2, ..., fi_m^2\}$ as follows:

$$ssim(s_1, s_2) =$$

$$= \frac{1}{2} \Big(\frac{1}{|s_1|} \sum_{fi_i^1 \in s_1} \max_{fi_j^2 \in s_2} firel(fi_i^1, fi_j^2) +$$

$$+ \frac{1}{|s_2|} \sum_{fi_i^2 \in s_2} \max_{fi_j^1 \in s_1} firel(fi_i^1, fi_j^2) \Big) \quad (5)$$

[1] `http://babelnet.org/synset?word=bn:00001533n`

[2] `http://babelnet.org/synset?word=bn:00009850n`

Table 2: Pearson correlation between sentence pair similarity scores predicted by frame instance relatedness and the SemEval STS reference set.

	without role filter		with role filter	
ftrel: alpha	**occ**	**dist**	**occ**	**dist**
1.0	0.526	0.455	0.526	0.455
0.9	0.529	0.465	0.536	0.477
0.8	0.529	0.471	0.544	0.495
0.7	0.525	0.473	0.550	0.510
0.6	0.517	0.471	0.555	0.522
0.5	0.503	0.463	0.558	0.531
0.4	0.484	0.451	0.558	0.538
0.3	0.461	0.436	0.557	0.542
0.2	0.436	0.418	0.554	0.544
0.1	0.410	0.400	0.550	0.545
0.0	0.381	0.381	0.543	0.543

We tested the effect of the α parameter, the frame type relatedness measures $ftrel_{occ}$ and $ftrel_{dist}$, and the filter on semantic roles to investigate their impact on the quality of the relatedness measurement. The result is given in Table 2 in terms of Pearson correlation between the gold standard relatedness scores and the relatedness scores predicted by our method.

Overall, the *occ* measure of frame type relatedness produces better results than *dist*. We find that both halves of equation 1 contribute to the final result, with a sweet stop around $\alpha = 0.4$ that achieves the best performance on this benchmark with $ftrel = occ$ and the filter on the semantic roles. Indeed, enforcing the matching constraint on the semantic roles proves to be a successful strategy. The difference in terms of adherence to the text similarity scores with and without such constraint is significant and consistent across every variation of the other parameters.

4.4 Discussion

It must be stressed that the aim of the experiment presented in this section is not to achieve state of the art performance on the STS task, for which better algorithms based on word similarity and other techniques have been proposed. In fact, many tasks that rely on sentence level semantics can be solved without the need of extracting frame instances. Rather, we show that our method to compute a relatedness score between frame instances works

```
@prefix fbfi: <http://framebase.org/ns/fi->
@prefix fbframe: <http://framebase.org/ns/frame->
@prefix fbfe: <http://framebase.org/ns/fe->
@prefix rdfs: <http://www.w3.org/1999/02/22-rdf-syntax-ns\#>
@prefix bn: <http://babelnet.org/rdf/>

fbfi:People_01b52400 rdfs:type fbframe:People.
fbfi:People_01b52400 fbfe:Person bn:00001533n.
fbfi:Cardinal_numbers_3faa6c9c rdfs:type fbframe:Cardinal_numbers.
fbfi:Cardinal_numbers_3faa6c9c fbfe:Entity bn:00001533n.
fbfi:Being_located_079aed4d rdfs:type fbframe:Being_located.
fbfi:Being_located_079aed4d fbfe:Theme bn:00001533n.
fbfi:Being_located_079aed4d fbfe:Location bn:00009850n.
```

Figure 1: Frame instances extracted by KNEWS from the sentence "two men sit on a bench".

in practice, despite the inevitable shortcomings of the frame extraction process, i.e., wrong and/or missing classifications of frames, roles and concepts. The STS dataset has a strong bias towards people-centric frames. In fact, the most frequent frame type in our collection is People (345 occurrences in 1,650 frame instances), and the most frequent concept is bn:00001533n (*man, adult male, male*, 226 occurrences in 2,107 frame elements).

5 Evaluation on Gold Standard Frame Instances

The evaluation conducted in the first experiment has the advantage of being fully automated. However, measuring frame instance relatedness indirectly through text similarity entails that two distinct effects are measured at once: 1) the relatedness of the frame instances extracted from the text, and 2) the accuracy of the frame instance extraction process. In this section we propose a revised methodology for the evaluation of the frame instance relatedness measure that focuses only on measuring the effect (1), canceling the interference of (2). In short, we manually correct the frame instances extracted with KNEWS from the STS sentence pairs and re-run the evaluation process as described in Section 4. As by-products, we create a gold standard dataset of frame instances aligned with the text that evokes them[3], and we provide an evaluation of the performance of the KNEWS knowledge extraction system.

5.1 Manual correction

We corrected each frame instance individually. For the frame types, they were either confirmed or marked as wrong. In the latter case, the frame instance is discarded from the data set without further process. This was also the procedure applied when an entity was not filling any role for a particular frame instance, due to a parsing mistake. If the frame type was confirmed by the annotator, then the role and sense labels were checked and possibly corrected by replacing them with the correct ones from FrameNet and BabelNet respectively.

We split the STS dataset (250 sentence pairs) in three parts and assigned each of them to an annotator. A subset of 37 frame instances extracted from 10 sentences was annotated by all three annotators in order to compute a measure of inter-coder reliability, resulting in a Fleiss' Kappa of 0.81 on the annotation of frame types, 0.76 for roles, and 0.90 for concepts. Note that the annotation of roles and concepts is only considered when frame types are not discarded by the annotators as wrong.

Once the annotation was finished, we compared the obtained dataset with the one we produced with KNEWS (Section 4.2). The accuracy at the frame instance level (rate of frame instances that were not corrected at all) is 77.1%. More in detail, 79.5% of the frame types were found correct. Among the frame instances with correct frame types, 95.9% of the roles and 82.5% of the concepts were correct. During the manual inspection, we confirmed that Semafor (like most semantic parsers) is

---

[3]We will release the dataset after the review period.

biased towards the most dominant frame for ambiguous forms. The final gold standard set comprises 1,261 frame instances and 1,579 frame elements.

5.2 Text Similarity Experiment with Gold Standard Frame Instances

We repeated the experiment in 4.3, this time computing the pair-wise frame relatedness on the manually corrected frame instances. To provide a fair comparison, we removed the frame instances from the original set corresponding to the frame instances removed during the manual correction. We used the filter on semantic roles described in 4.3 and $ftrel_{occ}$ (the performance patterns we observed were the same as in the original experiment). The results of the experiment are shown in Figure 2. The overall performance is slightly lower than the previous experiment. This can be explained by observing that in this version of the experiment we are using less data, although of higher quality. Due to the structure of the correlation-based evaluation, incorrect frame instances extracted from a pair of sentences contribute to their relatedness score more than missing some frame instances. Also, the dominance bias could play a role, in that we mostly discarded low-frequency frames, for which the relatedness metric we defined could perform less than optimally. An in-depth analysis of this phenomenon (i.e., how does lexical ambiguity interplay with the variance in relatedness scores?) is left for future work.

6 Clustering Frame Instances to Extract Prototypical Knowledge

In the previous sections, we proved that our method for computing a relatedness score between two frame instances correlates well with human judgments of semantic similarity based on the natural language expression of such instances. What we presented is a kind of intrinsic evaluation, which, while helpful in assessing the quality of the solution, does not provide an insight into the motivation to implement a measure of frame instance relatedness, and what open problems could benefit from our approach down the line. To fill this gap, we propose a pilot study on the application of the method introduced in this paper to a down-

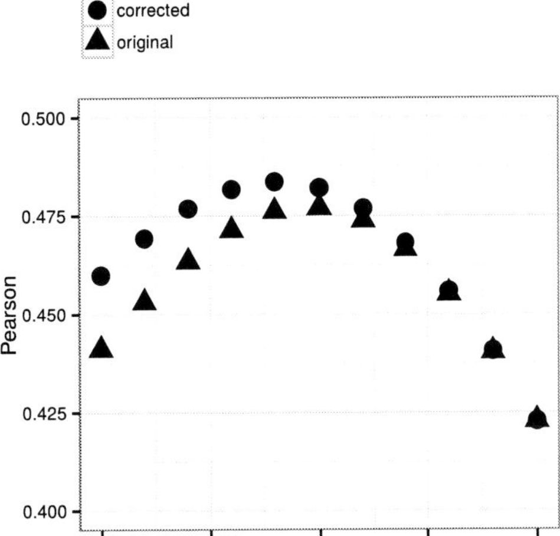

Figure 2: Pearson correlation between sentence pair similarity scores predicted by frame instance relatedness on corrected frame instances and the SemEval STS reference set.

stream task, namely the extraction of common sense knowledge from text, in line with the prototypical knowledge building method in (Shah et al.).

We start by observing that defining a quantitative distance metric between homogeneous instances allows us to apply a clustering algorithm. The result of such clustering is a partition of the original set into subsets that can be either overlapping (*soft clustering*) or non-overlapping (*hard clustering*). Moreover, clusters have a definite shape, with one of the elements being the most central one (called the *clustroid*), and the others being more or less far from the center. We perform a hard clustering of the frame instances collected from the STS dataset and used for the experiment in Section 4.3, and formulate three hypotheses: i) elements close to the center of their respective clusters are the best candidates to represent prototypical frame instances; ii) elements near the border of their respective clusters are less likely to represent prototypical frame instances, and therefore can be filtered out; iii) the size of each cluster influences the prototypicality degree of the elements in its central region, with larger clusters containing more prototypical frame instances near its center.

To cluster the frame instances, we follow

251

Table 3: Random sample of frame instances extracted from the STS dataset.

Cluster size	5
Frame type	Noise_makers (the Noise_maker is an artifact used to produce sound, especially for musical effect)
Role	Noise_maker (this FE identifies the entity or substance that is designed to produce sound)
Concept	Guitar (a stringed instrument usually having six strings; played by strumming or plucking)
Cluster size	40
Frame type	Substance (this frame concerns internally undifferentiated Substances)
Role	Substance (the undifferentiated entity which is presented as having a permanent existence)
Concept	Sand (a loose material consisting of grains of rock or coral)
Cluster size	3
Frame type	Part_inner_outer (This frame concerns Parts of objects that are defined relative to the center or edge of the object
Role	Part
Concept	Center (an area that is approximately central within some larger region)
Role	Whole (an undivided entity having all its Parts)
Concept	Pond (a small lake)

Table 4: Clustroids of randomly selected clusters from the STS dataset.

Cluster size	8
Frame type	Vehicle (the frame concerns the vehicles that human beings use for the purpose of transportation)
Role	Vehicle (is the transportation device that the human beings use to travel)
Concept	Boat (a small vessel for travel on water)
Cluster size	5
Frame type	Biological_area (this frame contains words that denote large ecological areas as well as smaller locations characterized by the type of life present)
Role	Locale (this FE identifies a stable bounded area)
Concept	Forest (the trees and other plants in a large densely wooded area)
Cluster size	35
Frame type	Roadways (This frame involves stable Roadways which connect two stable Endpoints, the Source and the Goal)
Role	Roadway (the Roadway is the roadway that connects locations)
Concept	Road (a way or means to achieve something)

Table 5: Clustroids of the three largest clusters in the dataset.

Cluster size	418
Frame type	People (this frame contains general words for Individuals, i.e. humans)
Role	Person (the Person is the human being)
Concept	Man (an adult person who is male -as opposed to a woman-)
Cluster size	51
Frame type	Clothing (this frame refers to clothing and its characteristics, including anything that people conventionally wear)
Role	Garment (this FE identifes the clothing worn)
Concept	Shirt (a garment worn on the upper half of the body)
Cluster size	50
Frame type	Kinship (this frame contains words that denote kinship relations)
Role	Alter (the person who fills the role named by the Kinship term with respect to the Ego)
Concept	Child (a young person of either sex)

the hierarchical clustering approach, because the number of clusters is not necessary to be known a priori. In particular, we used the version implemented in the SciPy library[4]. We tested different linkage methods for hierarchical clustering (single, complete, average, weighted, centroid, median and ward), observing comparable results in terms of number of clusters and their size distribution. We perform the clustering with average linkage and the best performing parameters of the frame relatedness

---

[4] https://www.scipy.org/

measure (the distance metric for the clustering) according to the experiments in Section 4.

While giving an objective assessment about the prototypicality of a frame instance is somewhat hard, we observe different behavior in line with our hypothesis. The examples reported in Table 3 include quite arbitrary, albeit correct, frame instances. On the other hand, the examples in Table 5 are indeed highly prototypical, e.g., a shirt is a prototypical piece of clothing, while the examples in Table 4 can be placed somewhere in the middle of the prototypicality scale.

7 Conclusion and Future Work

We presented a novel method to compute a quantitative relatedness measure between frame instances, that takes into account the type of the frames, the semantic role of the frame elements, and the entities involved in the frame instances. Based on a test conducted on a gold standard set of sentence pairs, the measure we defined correlates positively with human judgments of semantic similarity. We further apply the relatedness measure to the task of extracting prototypical knowledge from natural language.

One clear bottleneck of our experimental setup is given by the automatic parsing, that does not always reach optimal performances. We believe that a stable measure of relatedness between frame instances will in fact boost the performance of a disambiguation system, acting as a coherence measure for an all-word disambiguation approach. We intend to test such strategy in future work.

The experiment on frame instance clustering for prototypical knowledge extraction presented in Section 6 showed promising results. In future work, we plan to conduct a large-scale experiment following the same principles including an extensive systematic evaluation of the quality of the resulting dataset.

References

Mehwish Alam, Diego Reforgiato Recupero, Misael Mongiovì, Aldo Gangemi, and Petar Ristoski. 2017. Event-based Knowledge Reconciliation using Frame Embeddings and Frame Similarity. *Knowledge-Based Systems*, 135:192–203.

Collin F. Baker, Charles J. Fillmore, and John B. Lowe. 1998. The Berkeley FrameNet Project. In *Proceedings of the 36th Annual Meeting of the Association for Computational Linguistics and 17th International Conference on Computational Linguistics - Volume 1*, ACL '98, pages 86–90, Stroudsburg, PA, USA. Association for Computational Linguistics.

Valerio Basile, Elena Cabrio, and Claudia Schon. 2016. KNEWS: Using Logical and Lexical Semantics to Extract Knowledge from Natural Language. In *Proceedings of the European Conference on Artificial Intelligence (ECAI) 2016*.

José Camacho-Collados, Mohammad Taher Pilehvar, and Roberto Navigli. 2016. Nasari: Integrating explicit knowledge and corpus statistics for a multilingual representation of concepts and entities. *Artificial Intelligence*, 240:36–64.

Daniel Cer, Mona Diab, Eneko Agirre, Inigo Lopez-Gazpio, and Lucia Specia. 2017. Semeval-2017 task 1: Semantic textual similarity multilingual and crosslingual focused evaluation. In *Proceedings of the 11th International Workshop on Semantic Evaluation (SemEval-2017)*, Vancouver, Canada.

Dipanjan Das, Desai Chen, André F. T. Martins, Nathan Schneider, and Noah A. Smith. 2014. Frame-semantic parsing. *Computational Linguistics*, 40:1:9–56.

Katrin Erk and Sebastian Padó. 2006. SHALMANESER - A Toolchain For Shallow Semantic Parsing. In *Proceedings of LREC 2006*.

Charles J. Fillmore. 1976. Frame semantics and the nature of language. *Annals of the New York Academy of Sciences: Conference on the Origin and Development of Language and Speech*, 280(1):20–32.

Daniel Gildea and Daniel Jurafsky. 2002. Automatic labeling of semantic roles. *Comput. Linguist.*, 28(3):245–288.

H. Kim, X. Ren, Y. Sun, C. Wang, and J. Han. 2013. Semantic Frame-Based Document Representation for Comparable Corpora. In *Proceedings of the 13th International Conference on Data Mining*, pages 350–359.

Shari Landes, Claudia Leacock, and Randee I Tengi. 1998. Building semantic concordances. *WordNet: An electronic lexical database*, 199(216):199–216.

C. Leacock and M. Chodorow. 1998. Combining local context and wordnet similarity for word sense identification. In *MIT Press*, pages 265–283, Cambridge, Massachusetts.

Andrea Moro, Alessandro Raganato, and Roberto Navigli. 2014. Entity Linking meets Word Sense Disambiguation: a Unified Approach. *Transactions of the Association for Computational Linguistics (TACL)*, 2:231–244.

Roberto Navigli and Simone Paolo Ponzetto. 2012. BabelNet: The automatic construction, evaluation and application of a wide-coverage multilingual semantic network. *Artificial Intelligence*, 193:217–250.

Marco Pennacchiotti and Michael Wirth. 2009. Measuring Frame Relatedness. In *Proceedings of the 12th Conference of the European Chapter of the Association for Computational Linguistics*, EACL '09, pages 657–665, Stroudsburg, PA, USA. Association for Computational Linguistics.

Jeffrey Pennington, Richard Socher, and Christopher D. Manning. 2014. Glove: Global vectors for word representation. In *Empirical Methods in Natural Language Processing (EMNLP)*, pages 1532–1543.

Valentina Presutti, Francesco Draicchio, and Aldo Gangemi. 2012. Knowledge extraction based on discourse representation theory and linguistic frames. In *Knowledge Engineering and Knowledge Management*, pages 114–129, Berlin, Heidelberg. Springer Berlin Heidelberg.

Diego Reforgiato Recupero, Valentina Presutti, Sergio Consoli, Aldo Gangemi, and Andrea Giovanni Nuzzolese. 2015. Sentilo: Frame-based sentiment analysis. *Cognitive Computation*, 7(2):211–225.

Jan Scheffczyk, Adam Pease, and Michael Ellsworth. 2006. Linking framenet to the suggested upper merged ontology. In *Proceedings of the 2006 Conference on Formal Ontology in Information Systems: Proceedings of the Fourth International Conference (FOIS 2006)*, pages 289–300, Amsterdam, The Netherlands, The Netherlands. IOS Press.

Avijit Shah, Valerio Basile, Elena Cabrio, and Sowmya Kamath S. Frame instance extraction and clustering for default knowledge building. pages 1–10.

Cynthia A Thompson, Roger Levy, and Christopher D Manning. 2003. A generative model for semantic role labeling. In *European Conference on Machine Learning*, pages 397–408. Springer.

Shafqat Mumtaz Virk, Philippe Muller, and Juliette Conrath. 2016. A Supervised Approach for Enriching the Relational Structure of Frame Semantics in FrameNet. In *Proceedings of the 26th International Conference on Computational Linguistics: Technical Papers*, pages 3542–3552, Osaka, Japan. The COLING 2016 Organizing Committee.

Zhibiao Wu and Martha Palmer. 1994. Verbs semantics and lexical selection. In *Proceedings of the 32Nd Annual Meeting on Association for Computational Linguistics*, ACL '94, pages 133–138, Stroudsburg, PA, USA. Association for Computational Linguistics.

Solving Feature Sparseness in Text Classification using Core-Periphery Decomposition

Xia Cui, Sadamori Kojaku, Naoki Masuda, and **Danushka Bollegala**
Department of Computer Science, University of Liverpool
Department of Engineering Mathematics, University of Bristol
{xia.cui, danushka.bollegala}@liverpool.ac.uk
{sadamori.koujaku, naoki.masuda}@bristol.ac.uk

Abstract

Feature sparseness is a problem common to cross-domain and short-text classification tasks. To overcome this feature sparseness problem, we propose a novel method based on graph decomposition to find candidate features for expanding feature vectors. Specifically, we first create a feature-relatedness graph, which is subsequently decomposed into core-periphery (CP) pairs and use the peripheries as the expansion candidates of the cores. We expand both training and test instances using the computed related features and use them to train a text classifier. We observe that prioritising features that are common to both training and test instances as cores during the CP decomposition to further improve the accuracy of text classification. We evaluate the proposed CP-decomposition-based feature expansion method on benchmark datasets for cross-domain sentiment classification and short-text classification. Our experimental results show that the proposed method consistently outperforms all baselines on short-text classification tasks, and perform competitively with pivot-based cross-domain sentiment classification methods.

1 Introduction

Short-texts are abundant on the Web and appear in various different formats such as micro-blogs (Kwak et al., 2010), Question and Answer (QA) forums, review sites, Short Message Service (SMS), email, and chat messages (Cong et al., 2008; Thelwall et al., 2010). Unlike lengthy responses that take time to both compose and to read, short responses have gained popularity particularly in social media contexts. Considering the steady growth of mobile devices that are physically restricted to compact keyboards, which are suboptimal for entering lengthy text inputs, it is safe to predict that the amount of short-texts will continue to grow in the future. Considering the importance and the quantity of the short-texts in various web-related tasks, such as text classification (kun Wang et al., 2012; dos Santos and Gatti, 2014), and event prediction (Sakaki et al., 2010), it is important to be able to accurately represent and classify short-texts.

Compared to performing text mining on longer texts (Guan et al., 2009; Su et al., 2011; Yogatama and Smith, 2014), for which dense and diverse feature representations can be created relatively easily, handling of shorter texts poses several challenges. The number of features that are present in a given short-text will be a small fraction of the set of all features that exist in all of the train instances. Moreover, frequency of a feature in a short-text will be small, which makes it difficult to reliably estimate the salience of a feature using term frequency-based methods. This is known as the *feature sparseness* problem in text classification.

Feature sparseness is not unique to short-text classification but also encountered in cross-domain text classification (Blitzer et al., 2006, 2007; Bollegala et al., 2014), where the training and test data are selected from different domains with small intersection of feature spaces. In the domain adaptation (DA) setting, a classifier trained on one domain (*source*) might be agnostic to the features that are unique to a different domain (*target*), which results in a *feature mismatch* problem similar to the feature-sparseness problem discussed above.

To address the feature sparseness problem encountered in short-text and cross-domain classification tasks, we propose a novel method that computes related features that can be appended to the feature vectors to reduce the sparsity. Specifically, we decompose a feature-relatedness graph into core-periphery (CP) structures, where a core

*Proceedings of the 7th Joint Conference on Lexical and Computational Semantics (*SEM)*, pages 255–264
New Orleans, June 5-6, 2018. ©2018 Association for Computational Linguistics

feature (a vertex) is linked to a set of peripheries (also represented by vertices), indicating the connectivity of the graph. This graph decomposition problem is commonly known as the CP-decomposition (Csermely et al., 2013; Rombach et al., 2017; Kojaku and Masuda, 2018, 2017).

Our proposed CP-decomposition algorithm significantly extends existing CP-decomposition methods in three important ways.

- First, existing CP-decomposition methods consider unweighted graphs, whereas edges in feature-relatedness graphs are weighted (possibly nonnegative) real-valued feature-relatedness scores such as positive pointwise mutual information (PPMI). Our proposed CP-decomposition method can operate on edge-weighted graphs.

- Second, considering the fact that in text classification a particular periphery can be related to more than one core, we relax the hard assignment constraints on peripheries and allow a particular periphery attach to multiple cores.

- Third, prior work on pivot-based cross-domain sentiment classification methods have used features that are frequent in training (source) and test (target) data as expansion candidates to overcome the feature mismatch problem. Inspired by this, we define *coreness* of a feature as the pointwise mutual information between a feature and the source/target domains. The CP-decomposition algorithm we propose will then compute the set of cores considering both structural properties of the graph as well as the coreness values computed from the train/test data.

To perform feature vector expansion, we first construct a feature-relatedness graph, where vertices correspond to features and the weight of the undirected edge connecting two features represent the relatedness between those two features. Different features and relatedness measures can be flexibly used in the proposed graph construction. In our experiments, we use the simple (yet popular and effective) setting of n-gram features as vertices and compute their relatedness using PPMI. We compute the coreness of features as the sum of the two PPMI values between the feature

and the source, and the feature and the target domains.[1] Next, CP-decomposition is performed on this feature-relatedness graph to obtain a set of core-periphery structures. We then rank the set of peripheries of a particular core by their PPMI values, and select the top-ranked peripheries as the expansion features of the core. We expand the core features in training and train a logistic regression-based binary classifier using the expanded feature vectors, and evaluate its performance on the expanded test feature vectors.

We evaluate the effectiveness of the proposed method using benchmark datasets for two different tasks: short-text classification and cross-domain sentiment classification. Experimental results on short-text classification show that the proposed method consistently outperforms previously proposed feature expansion-based methods for short-text classification and even some of the sentence embedding learning-based methods. Moreover, the consideration of coreness during the CP-decomposition improves the text classification accuracy. In cross-domain sentiment classification experiments, the proposed method outperforms previously proposed pivot-based methods such as the structural correspondence learning (SCL) (Blitzer et al., 2006).

2 Related Work

Two complementary approaches for overcoming feature sparseness in text classification can be identified in the literature: (a) expanding the instances by predicting the missing features, and (b) projecting the instances to a dense (potentially lower-dimensional) space and performing the classification task in this projected space. Our work can be categorised to the first group of methods. We next review prior work on both types of approaches.

Man (2014) proposed a feature vector expansion based on frequent term sets (FTS), where they first define the co-occurrence among the features and then the expansion candidates are selected by a pre-defined threshold on frequency. Finally, the features in the original feature vectors are expanded using these frequently co-occurring features. Ma et al. (2016) proposed an improvement based on FTS by introducing the support and confidence to the co-occurrence relationship when

---

[1]In short-text classification experiments, coreness is computed using unlabelled training and test instances.

they create the frequent term sets for expansion.

Our proposed method is related to the pivot selection methods proposed in prior work on unsupervised cross-domain sentiment classification, where common features (called the pivots) are first identified using some heuristic measure, and predictors are learnt that can accurately predict those pivots using the other (non-pivot) features. For example, in spectral feature alignment (SFA) (Pan et al., 2010), a bipartite graph is created between non-pivots (domain-specific) and pivots (domain-independent) then spectral methods are used to learn a projection from domain-specific to domain-independent feature spaces. Blitzer et al. (2006) proposed the frequency (FREQ) of a feature in the source and the target domain as the criterion for selecting pivots for structural correspondence learning (SCL) when performing cross-domain named entity recognition. However, they found (Blitzer et al., 2007) that mutual information (MI) to be a better pivot selection criterion for cross-domain sentiment classification tasks. Bollegala et al. (2015) proposed a feature expansion-based domain adaptation method, where a sentiment sensitive thesaurus (SST) is built using the pointwise mutual information (PMI) between a feature and the source/target domains. The cores identified by CP-decomposition can be seen as playing the role of pivots in cross-domain text classification tasks because cores get expanded by their corresponding peripheries during the feature expansion step. However, one notable characteristic in the proposed method is that we induce cores via CP-decomposition instead of applying heuristic measures such as MI or PMI. As we later see in the experiments, the proposed method outperforms the previous pivot-based feature expansion methods in cross-domain sentiment classification benchmarks.

A complementary approach to overcome feature-sparseness is to learn a (potentially lower dimensional) dense feature representation for the training and test instances that suffer from feature sparseness, and train and evaluate classifiers in this dense feature space instead of the original sparse feature space. Skip-thought vectors (Kiros et al., 2015) encodes a sentence into a lower-dimensional dense vector using bidirectional long short-term memory (bi-LSTM), whereas FastSent (Hill et al., 2016) learns sentence embeddings by predicting the words in the adjacent sentences in a corpus, ignoring the word ordering. Paragraph2Vec (Le and Mikolov, 2014) jointly learns sentence and word embeddings that can mutually predict each other in a short-text such as a paragraph in a document. Sequential Denoising Autoencoder (SDAE) (Hill et al., 2016) transforms an input sentence into an embedding by a look-up table consisting of pre-trained word embeddings and attempts to reconstruct the original sentence embedding from a masked version. Sentence embedding learning methods such as skip-thought vectors, FastSent, SDAE etc. require a large amount of unlabelled texts for training such as 80 million sentence Toronto books corpus, which might not be available for specialised domains. As shown in our experiments, the proposed methods perform competitively with these embedding-based methods, while not requiring any additional training data, other than the small (typically less than 50,000 sentences) benchmark training datasets.

In the CP-decomposition problem, one seeks a partition of vertices into two groups called a core and a periphery. The core vertices are densely interconnected and the peripheral vertices are sparsely interconnected. The core and peripheral vertices may be densely interconnected or sparsely interconnected. Various algorithms have been developed to find a single core-periphery structure (Csermely et al., 2013; Rombach et al., 2017) or multiple core-periphery structures (Kojaku and Masuda, 2018, 2017) in a graph. Many existing algorithms assume that each vertex belongs to only one core-periphery structure. This assumption is problematic for text classification because a peripheral vertex can belong to multiple core-periphery structures. To circumvent this problem, here we present a novel algorithm for the CP-decomposition that allows a peripheral vertex to belong to more than one core-periphery structures. Some existing CP-decomposition algorithms allow peripheral vertices to belong to multiple core-periphery structures (Yan and Luo, 2016; Sardana and Bhatnagar, 2016; Xiang et al., 2018). These algorithms detect non-overlapping communities (i.e., groups of densely interconnected vertices) in a graph. Then, they regard vertices that do not belong to any community as peripheral vertices. Therefore, the detected peripheries might not be strongly related to the associated cores because they are not densely interconnected with the cores in general. Another CP-decomposition algorithm allows communities to overlap and regard the vertices belonging to many communities as a core (Yang and Leskovec, 2014). Then, the detected peripheral vertices may be densely interconnected because they belong to the same community. In contrast to these algorithms, the present algorithm seeks peripheries that are densely interconnected with the associated cores while sparsely interconnected with other peripheral vertices.

To the best of our knowledge, we are the first to apply CP-decomposition to any NLP task, let alone short-text classification. Moreover, our formulation of the CP-decomposition is customised to the needs in the NLP domain such as prioritising linguistically appropriate cores and allows a single periphery to link to multiple cores. We hope that our work will inspire NLP practitioners to use CP-decomposition in related NLP tasks such as information retrieval (Mihalcea and Radev, 2011) (measuring similarity between short-text documents), query suggestion/expansion (Fang, 2008) (suggesting related peripheral terms to a query corresponding to a core).

3 CP-decomposition-based Feature Expansion

Our proposed method consists of three steps: (a) building a feature-relatedness graph (Section 3.1), (b) performing CP-decomposition on the feature-relatedness graph (Sections 3.2 and 3.3) and (c) using the core-peripheries from the decomposition to perform feature expansion (Section 3.4). Next, we describe each of those steps in detail.

3.1 Feature-Relatedness Graph

Given a set of texts, we build a feature-relatedness graph $\mathcal{G}(\mathcal{V}, \mathcal{E}, \mathbf{W})$, where $\mathcal{V}$ is the set of vertices corresponding to the features, $\mathcal{E}$ is the set of undirected edges between two vertices in $\mathcal{G}$ and the weight of the edge $e_{ij} \in \mathcal{E}$ connecting two features i and j is given by the W_{ij} element of the weight matrix $\mathbf{W}$. Let us denote the number of vertices and edges respectively by N and M (i.e. $|\mathcal{V}| = N$ and $|\mathcal{E}| = M$). Different types of features such as n-grams, part-of-speech sequences, named entities, dependency relations etc. can be used as vertices in the feature-relatedness graph. Moreover, different relatedness measures such as co-occurrence frequency, pointwise mutual information, χ^2, log-likelihood ratio etc. can be used

to compute the weights assigned to the edges. For simplicity, in this paper, we represent each text-document using the set of unigrams extracted from that document, and use PPMI to compute a non-negative $\mathbf{W}$. We connect two words if PPMI values between them are greater than zero. This formulation is used for both short-text classification and cross-domain sentiment classification experiments conducted in the paper.

3.2 Core-Periphery Decomposition

Given a feature-relatedness graph $\mathcal{G}$ created using the process described in Section 3.1, we propose a method that decomposes $\mathcal{G}$ into a set of overlapping core-periphery structures. A core-periphery structure assumed in this study consists of one core vertex and an arbitrarily number of peripheral vertices that are adjacent (i.e., directly connected) to the core vertex.[2] Therefore, a core-periphery structure forms a star graph. We further assume that a core belongs only to one core-periphery structure, but a periphery can belong to multiple core-periphery structures.

Let $\mathcal{C} \subseteq \mathcal{V}$ be the set of cores and P_i be the set of peripheries associated with the core $i (\in \mathcal{C})$. We regard that a core-periphery structure is a good pair if the core is adjacent to its peripheries with large edge weights. One goodness measure is the sum of edge weights between the core i and peripheries, which is given by $\sum_{j \in \mathcal{P}_i} W_{ij}$. This quantity should be larger than the value expected from a null model (i.e., randomised graph) for the detected core-periphery structure to be meaningful. We seek $\mathcal{C}$ and $\mathcal{P}_i$ ($\forall i \in \mathcal{C}$) by maximising

$$Q = \sum_{i \in \mathcal{C}} \sum_{j \in \mathcal{P}_i} W_{ij} - \sum_{i \in \mathcal{C}} \sum_{j \in \mathcal{P}_i} \mathbb{E}[W_{ij}], \quad (1)$$

where $\mathbb{E}[W_{ij}]$ is the expected edge weight between vertices i and j in the null model. The first term on the right-hand side of (1) is the total weights of the edges between the cores and peripheries. The second term is the expected value of the first term according to the null model. Therefore, a large positive Q value indicates that cores and peripheries are connected with large edge weights. To compute $\mathbb{E}[W_{ij}]$, we must specify a null model. We consider a simple null model where any pair of vertices is adjacent by an edge with an equal

---

[2]In the remainder of the paper, we refer to core vertices as cores and peripheral vertices as peripheries to simplify the terminology.

expected weight (Erdős and Rényi, 1959). Then, we can rewrite (1) as

$$Q = \sum_{i \in \mathcal{C}} \sum_{j \in \mathcal{P}_i} (W_{ij} - p), \tag{2}$$

where p is the average edge weight of the original graph given by

$$p = \frac{2}{N(N-1)} \sum_{i,j \in \mathcal{V}, i \neq j} W_{ij}. \tag{3}$$

We maximise Q as follows. Given a set of cores $\mathcal{C}$, it is easy to find peripheries that maximise Q. Suppose a core i and a vertex $j \notin \mathcal{P}_i$, which may belong to one or more different core-periphery structures. Adding the vertex j to $\mathcal{P}_i$ increases Q, if $W_{ij} - p$ is positive. Therefore, $\mathcal{P}_i$ associated with core i must be the neighbours of vertex i with an edge weight of $W_{ij} > p$. Therefore, we have

$$\max_{\mathcal{C}} \max_{\mathcal{P}_i, i \in \mathcal{C}} Q = \max_{\mathcal{C}} \sum_{i \in \mathcal{C}} \sum_{j \in \mathcal{V} \setminus \mathcal{C}} \tilde{W}_{ij}, \tag{4}$$

where

$$\tilde{W}_{ij} = \begin{cases} W_{ij} - p & W_{ij} - p > 0, \\ 0 & \text{otherwise.} \end{cases} \tag{5}$$

(4) indicates that the maximisation of Q is equivalent to partitioning of the set of vertices $\mathcal{V}$ into $\mathcal{C}$ and $\mathcal{V} \setminus \mathcal{C}$ such that the sum of edge weights given by (5) between $\mathcal{C}$ and $\mathcal{V} \setminus \mathcal{C}$ is maximised. This is known as the max-cut problem (Goemans and Williamson, 1995). However, solving the max-cut problem is NP-hard (Karp, 1972). Therefore, we use the Kernighan-Lin's algorithm (Kernighan and Lin, 1970) to find a good (but generally a suboptimal) solution.

It should be noted that Q is conserved when we regard $\mathcal{V} \setminus \mathcal{C}$ as the cores and $\mathcal{C}$ as peripheries. This is because Q is the sum of edge weights between $\mathcal{C}$ and $\mathcal{V} \setminus \mathcal{C}$. For example, suppose a graph with a single core-periphery structure as shown in Figure 1(a). By regarding the core as a periphery and vice versa, we have another assignment of the core-periphery structure achieving the same Q value as shown in Figure 1(b). Although Q is the same in the two assignments, we would like to prioritise the core-periphery structure shown in Figure 1(a), because we would like to have a smaller set of cores than peripheries. Therefore, we regard $\mathcal{C}$ as the set of cores if $|\mathcal{C}| < |\mathcal{V} \setminus \mathcal{C}|$; otherwise we regard $\mathcal{C}$ as the set of peripheries.

3.3 Semi-supervised Core-Periphery Decomposition

The objective given by (4) depends only on $\mathcal{G}$ and does not consider any prior linguistic knowledge that we might have about which features are appropriate as cores. For example, for cross-domain sentiment classification, it has been shown that features that express similar sentiment in both source and target domains are suitable as pivots (Blitzer et al., 2007). To incorporate this information, we integrate the *coreness* of words into the objective as follows:

$$\max_{\mathcal{C}} \max_{\mathcal{P}_i, i \in \mathcal{C}} Q = \max_{\mathcal{C}} \sum_{i \in \mathcal{C}} \sum_{j \in \mathcal{V} \setminus \mathcal{C}} \tilde{W}_{ij} + \lambda \sum_{i \in \mathcal{C}} \text{coreness}(i). \tag{6}$$

In (6), $\text{coreness}(i)$ is a nonnegative value that indicates the appropriateness of i as a core. Hyperparameter λ adjusts the importance we would like to give to coreness as opposed to determining cores based on the graph structure. We tune λ using a held out portion of the training data in our experiments. Different measures can be used to pre-computed the coreness values from the train/test data such as FREQ, MI, PMI, PPMI etc, which have been proposed in prior work on DA for selecting pivots (Blitzer et al., 2006, 2007; Bollegala et al., 2015). In this work, we use PPMI to pre-compute the coreness for a word i as follows:

$$\text{coreness}(i) = (\text{PPMI}(i, \mathcal{D}_{\text{train}}) - \text{PPMI}(i, \mathcal{D}_{\text{test}}))^2. \tag{7}$$

Here, $\mathcal{D}_{\text{train}}$ and $\mathcal{D}_{\text{test}}$ are respectively the set of training and test data (or in the case of DA selected from the source and the target domains).

3.4 Feature Expansion

To overcome feature-sparseness in training and test instances, we expand features that are cores by their corresponding peripheral sets. Specifically, for each core $i \in \mathcal{C}$, we sort its peripheries $\mathcal{P}_i$ by their coreness values and select the top-k ranked peripheries as the expansion features for a core i if it appears in a document. The values of these expansion features are set to their PPMI values with the corresponding core after ℓ_1 normalising over the set of expansion features in each instance. The effect of k on performance is experimentally studied later.

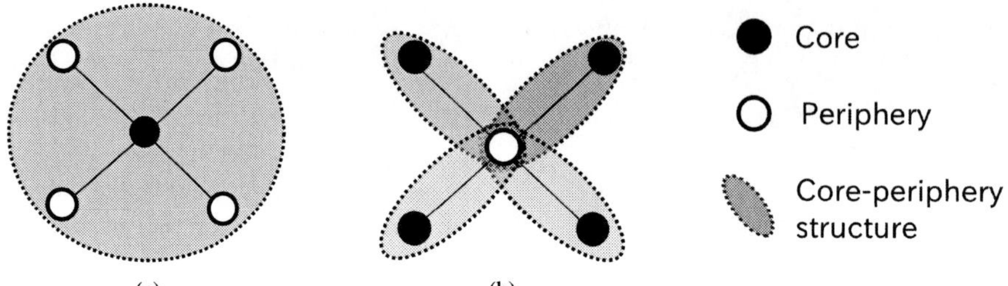

Figure 1: Core-periphery structures with an equal quality, Q. Each filled and empty circles indicate core and peripheral vertices, respectively. Each shared region indicates a core-periphery structure.

Dataset	SCL					CP-decomposition		
	FREQ	MI	PMI	PPMI	No Expansion	Non-overlapping	Overlapping w/o coreness	Overlapping w/ coreness
TR	67.60	66.12	67.44	63.21	78.86	80.34	80.56	**80.86**
CR	77.85	74.83	78.52	75.50	80.87	83.89	83.89	**84.40**
SUBJ	87.65	82.15	85.65	82.75	88.05	89.75	90.15	**90.48**
MR	64.68	58.07	64.26	59.10	73.55	75.23	74.95	**75.66**
AVG	74.45	70.29	73.97	70.14	80.33	82.30	82.39	**82.85**

Table 1: Results for the short-text classification task. For each dataset, the best results are shown in bold.

4 Experiments

We evaluate the proposed method on two tasks: short-text classification (a non-DA task) and cross-domain sentiment classification (a DA task). For short-text classification we use the Stanford sentiment treebank (TR)[3], customer reviews dataset (CR) (Hu and Liu, 2004), subjective dataset (SUBJ) (Pang and Lee, 2004) and movie reviews (MR) (Pang and Lee, 2005). For DA we use Amazon multi-domain sentiment dataset (Blitzer et al., 2007) containing product reviews from four categories: Books (B), DVDs (D), Electronics (E) and Kitchen Appliances (K). Each category is regarded as a domain and has 1000 positive and 1000 negative reviews, and a large number of unlabelled reviews.[4] We train a classifier on 12 domain pairs adapting from source to target (S-T): B-D, B-E, B-K, D-B, D-E, D-K, E-B, E-D, E-K, K-B, K-D, K-E. For the short-text classification datasets, we use the official train/test split.

We represent each instance (document) using a bag-of-features consisting of unigrams. Stop words are removed using a standard stop words list. We train an ℓ_2 regularised binary logistic regression classifier with each dataset, where the regularisation coefficient is tuned via 5-fold cross validation.

Methods	TR	CR	SUBJ	MR
No Expansion	76.31	81.54	88.05	73.35
FTS (Man, 2014)	76.47	62.41	50.15	66.83
SCL (Blitzer et al., 2006)	67.60	78.52	87.65	64.68
SFA (Pan et al., 2010)	60.08	70.13	79.00	59.57
Proposed	**80.86**	**84.40**	**90.48**	**75.66**

Table 3: Proposed vs. feature-based methods for short-text classification.

4.1 Classification Accuracy

We use the classification accuracy on the test data (i.e. ratio between the number of correctly classified test instances and the total number of test instances in the dataset) as the performance evaluation measure. As baselines we evaluate the classification accuracy without expanding features (**No Expansion**), expanding the features by a non-overlapping version of the CP-decomposition method where a single periphery will be assigned to only a single core, overlapping CP-decomposition with and without the consideration of coreness (described respectively in Sections 3.2 and 3.3). We apply SCL with pivots selected from four different criteria (FREQ, MI, PMI and PPMI) for each S-T pair in the DA datasets. Strictly speaking, SCL is a DA method but if we can apply to short-text classification tasks as well if we consider training and test datasets respectively as a source and a target domain and select pivots using some selection criterion. Results on

<hr>

[3]https://nlp.stanford.edu/sentiment/treebank.html

[4]Blitzer et al. (2007) considered 4 and 5 star rated reviews as positive and 1 or 2 as negative in sentiment.

S-T	SCL					CP-decomposition		
	FREQ	MI	PMI	PPMI	No Expansion	Non-overlapping	Overlapping w/o coreness	Overlapping w/ coreness
B-D	72.75	65.50	71.50	69.25	75.00	75.75	**76.75**	76.38
B-E	72.75	71.00	**74.50**	66.00	71.00	71.00	69.75	69.75
B-K	77.25	64.00	**80.50**	77.25	78.25	78.25	77.75	78.00
D-B	71.00	53.00	66.25	65.50	74.00	74.25	74.25	**75.25**
D-E	72.00	67.00	72.75	**74.75**	**74.75**	73.75	73.00	**74.75**
D-K	**79.75**	57.50	79.00	76.75	79.25	78.00	79.25	79.25
E-B	62.75	57.25	66.25	60.25	**69.50**	68.50	68.75	68.75
E-D	64.50	62.75	65.50	62.75	73.25	71.75	73.25	**73.50**
E-K	82.00	77.75	81.25	79.50	**84.25**	84.00	82.50	84.00
K-B	65.75	52.50	68.00	68.75	**70.00**	**70.00**	69.75	69.50
K-D	67.25	53.75	66.75	68.50	72.75	72.00	72.75	**73.63**
K-E	77.25	74.50	74.50	74.75	79.00	79.75	79.00	**80.50**
AVG	72.08	63.04	72.23	70.33	75.08	74.75	74.73	**75.27**

Table 2: Results for DA tasks. For each S-T pair, the best results are shown in bold. The last row shows the average of performance over the 12 S-T pairs.

the short-text and DA tasks are summarised respectively in Tables 1 and 2.

As shown in Table 1, all variants of the CP-decomposition outperform the **No Expansion** baseline and the best performance is reported by the overlapping CP-decomposition considering the coreness values. According to binomial test results, there is no statistical significance in Table 1. SCL performs poorly on this non-DA task, indicating that it is specifically customised for DA tasks.

Table 3 compares the performance of the proposed method (i.e., overlapping version of the CP-decomposition with coreness) against FTS, a previously proposed feature expansion method and DA methods such as SCL and SFA applied to short-text classification. We see that the proposed method consistently outperforms FTS, which uses frequently occurring features as expansion candidates. This result implies that frequency of a feature alone does not enable us to find useful features for expanding sparse feature vectors. The suboptimal performance of SFA and SCL for short-text classification indicates that, despite the fact that the feature-mismatch problem in DA has some resemblance to the feature-sparseness problem in short-text classification, applying DA methods to short-text classification is not effective. On the other hand, as shown in Table 2, proposed method reports equal or the best performance for 10 out of 12 domain pairs indicating that it is effective not only for short-text classification but also for DA. However, the improvements reported in Table 2 are not statistically significant (according to Clopper-Pearson confidence intervals (Clopper

Methods	MR	CR	SUBJ
Skip-thought (Kiros et al., 2015)	**76.5**	80.1	**93.6**
Paragraph2Vec (Le and Mikolov, 2014)	74.8	78.1	90.5
FastSent (Hill et al., 2016)	70.8	78.4	88.7
SDAE (Hill et al., 2016)	74.6	78.0	90.8
CNN (Kim, 2014)	76.1	79.8	89.6
Proposed	75.7	**84.4**	90.5

Table 4: Proposed vs. document-level embedding-based methods for short-text classification.

and Pearson, 1934) computed at $p < 0.01$), implying that CP-decomposition is less effective on DA datasets, which contain longer (on average 5-10 sentence reviews) texts.

We compare the proposed method against the state-of-the-art embedding-based short-text classification methods in Table 4. For skip-thought vectors (Kiros et al., 2015), Paragraph2Vec (Le and Mikolov, 2014), FastSent (Hill et al., 2016) and SDAE (Hill et al., 2016) provided by Hill et al. (2016), we show the published results on MR, CR and SUBJ.[5] CNN represents the convolutional neural network-based document-level embedding learning method proposed by Kim (2014). The proposed method reports the best results on CR, whereas skip-thought does so for MR and SUBJ datasets. An interesting future research direction would be to combine feature-expansion method and document-level embedding methods to further improve the accuracy of short-text classification.

An example feature expansion is shown in Table 5, where 6 cores are expanded by the overlapping version of the CP-decomposition method

---

[5]These methods have not been evaluated on the TR dataset.

Sentence:	The film makes a strong case for the importance of the musicians in creating the motown sound.						
Methods:	Overlapping w/o coreness						Overlapping w/ coreness
Cores:	film	strong	case	musicians	creating	sound	motown
Peripheries:	tribeca	willed	neko	remixers	irritation	puget	discographer
	remakes	fliers	genitive	trombonists	populating	stereophonic	gordy
	grossing	syllabic	accusative	bandleaders	abolishing	nootka	supremes
	slasher	roderick	dative	saxophonists	duopoly	mcmurdo	stax
	blaxploitation	oxidizing	eeml	clarinetists	soundscapes	blaster	dozier

Table 5: An example of cores and top 5 peripheries chosen by overlapping CP-decomposition with/without coreness ($k = 5$). This example sentence in TR is classified incorrectly using the method without coreness (and the **No Expansion** baseline) but correctly after considering coreness.

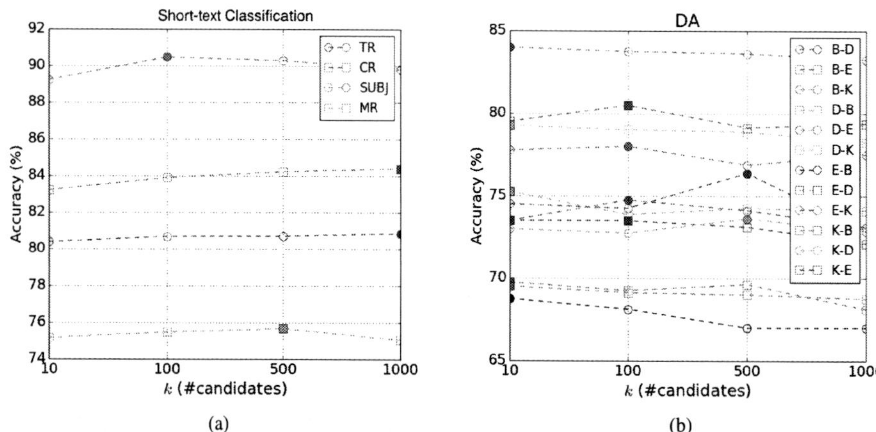

Figure 2: Number of expansion candidates for the proposed method. The marker for the best result for each dataset is filled.

without using coreness and one core with the proposed method. Top 5-ranked peripheries are shown for each core, which are used as the expansion features. We see that many cores are found without constraining the CP-decomposition by coreness, introducing noisy expansions resulting in an incorrect prediction. On the other hand, although by integrating coreness into the CP-decomposition process we have only a single matching core, *motown*, it is adequate for making the correct prediction. *motown* is a music company, which is expanded by a more general periphery *discographer*, which is a type of music performer, helping the final classification. Consideration of coreness improves the classification accuracy in both short-text classification as well as DA.

In both Tables 1 and 2, the non-overlapping version performs poorly compared to the overlapping counterpart. With non-overlapping CP-decomposition, peripheries are not allowed to connect to multiple cores. This results in producing a large number of cores each with a small number of peripheries, which does not help to overcome the feature-sparseness because each core will be expanded by a different periphery.

Figure 2 shows the effect of the number of expansion candidates k on the performance of the proposed overlapping CP-decomposition with coreness. For short-text classification (Figure 2a), the accuracy increases for $k \geq 100$ (TR and CR obtain the best for $k = 1000$). For DA (Figure 2b), $k \leq 100$ yields better performance in most of the domain pairs (10 out of 12). For all 12 domain pairs, the accuracy achieved a peak when $k \leq 500$.

5 Conclusion

We proposed a novel algorithm for decomposing a feature-relatedness graph into core-periphery structures considering coreness of a feature. Our experimental results show that the induced core-periphery structures are useful for reducing the feature-sparseness in short-text classification and cross-domain sentiment classification tasks, as indicated by their improved performance. We hope this research will encourage the society to imply different CP decomposition methods with different tasks in NLP.

References

John Blitzer, Mark Dredze, and Fernando Pereira. 2007. Biographies, bollywood, boom-boxes and blenders: Domain adaptation for sentiment classification. In *Proc. of ACL*. pages 440–447.

John Blitzer, Ryan McDonald, and Fernando Pereira. 2006. Domain adaptation with structural correspondence learning. In *Proc. of EMNLP*. pages 120–128.

Danushka Bollegala, Takanori Maehara, and Ken ichi Kawarabayashi. 2015. Unsupervised cross-domain word representation learning. In *Proc. of ACL*. pages 730–740.

Danushka Bollegala, David Weir, and John Carroll. 2014. Learning to predict distributions of words across domains. In *Proc. of ACL*. pages 613–623.

C. J. Clopper and E. S. Pearson. 1934. The use of confidence or fiducial limits illustrated in the case of the binomial. *Biometrika* 26(4):403–413.

Gao Cong, Long Wang, Chin-Yew Lin, Young-In Song, and Yueheng Sun. 2008. Finding question-answer pairs from online forums. In *Proc. of SIGIR*. pages 467–474.

Peter Csermely, András London, Ling-Yun Wu, and Brian Uzzi. 2013. Structure and dynamics of core/periphery networks. *Journal of Complex Networks* 1(2):93–123.

Cicero dos Santos and Maira Gatti. 2014. Deep convolutional neural networks for sentiment analysis of short texts. In *Proc. of COLING*. pages 69–78.

P Erdős and A Rényi. 1959. On random graphs i. *Publ. Math.* 6:290–297.

Hui Fang. 2008. A re-examination of query expansion using lexical resources. In *Proc. of ACL*. pages 139–147.

Michel X Goemans and David P Williamson. 1995. Improved approximation algorithms for maximum cut and satisfiability problems using semidefinite programming. *Journal of the ACM (JACM)* 42(6):1115–1145.

Hu Guan, Jinguy Zhou, and Minyi Guo. 2009. A class-feature-centroid classifier for text categorization. In *Proc. of WWW*. pages 201–210.

Felix Hill, Kyunghyun Cho, and Anna Korhonen. 2016. Learning distributed representations of sentences from unlabelled data. In *Proceedings of NAACL-HLT*. pages 1367–1377.

Minqing Hu and Bing Liu. 2004. Mining and summarizing customer reviews. In *KDD 2004*. pages 168–177.

Richard. M. Karp. 1972. *Reducibility among Combinatorial Problems*. Springer US, Boston, MA.

Brian W Kernighan and Shen Lin. 1970. An efficient heuristic procedure for partitioning graphs. *The Bell System Technical Journal* 49(2):291–307.

Yoon Kim. 2014. Convolutional neural networks for sentence classification. In *Proceedings of the 2014 Conference on Empirical Methods in Natural Language Processing (EMNLP)*. pages 1746–1751.

Ryan Kiros, Yukun Zhu, Ruslan R Salakhutdinov, Richard Zemel, Raquel Urtasun, Antonio Torralba, and Sanja Fidler. 2015. Skip-thought vectors. In *Advances in neural information processing systems*. pages 3294–3302.

Sadamori Kojaku and Naoki Masuda. 2017. Finding multiple core-periphery pairs in networks. *Physical Review E* 96(5):052313.

Sadamori Kojaku and Naoki Masuda. 2018. Core-periphery structure requires something else in the network. *New Journal of Physics* 40:043012.

Bing kun Wang, Yong feng Huang, Wan xia Yang, and Xing Li. 2012. Short text classification based on strong feature thesaurus. *Journal of Zhejiang University-SCIENCE C (Computers and Electronics)* 13(9):649–659.

Haewoon Kwak, Changhyun Lee, Hosung Park, and Sue Moon. 2010. What is twitter, a social network or a news media? In *Proc. of WWW*. pages 591–600.

Quoc Le and Tomas Mikolov. 2014. Distributed representations of sentences and documents. In *International Conference on Machine Learning*. pages 1188–1196.

Huifang Ma, Lei Di, Xiantao Zeng, Li Yan, and Yuyi Ma. 2016. Short text feature extension based on improved frequent term sets. In Zhongzhi Shi, Sunil Vadera, and Gang Li, editors, *Intelligent Information Processing VIII*. Springer International Publishing, Cham, pages 169–178.

Yuan Man. 2014. Feature extension for short text categorization using frequent term sets. *Procedia Computer Science* 31:663–670. 2nd International Conference on Information Technology and Quantitative Management, ITQM 2014.

Rada Mihalcea and Dragomir Radev. 2011. *Graph-based Natural Language Processing and Information Retrieval*. Cambridge University Press.

Sinno Jialin Pan, Xiaochuan Ni, Jian-Tao Sun, Qiang Yang, and Zheng Chen. 2010. Cross-domain sentiment classification via spectral feature alignment. In *Proc. of WWW*. pages 751–760.

Bo Pang and Lillian Lee. 2004. A sentimental education: Sentiment analysis using subjectivity summarization based on minimum cuts. In *Proceedings of the 42nd annual meeting on Association for Computational Linguistics*. Association for Computational Linguistics, page 271.

Bo Pang and Lillian Lee. 2005. Seeing stars: Exploiting class relationships for sentiment categorization with respect to rating scales. In *Proceedings of the 43rd annual meeting on association for computational linguistics*. Association for Computational Linguistics, pages 115–124.

Puck Rombach, Mason A. Porter, James H. Fowler, and Peter J. Mucha. 2017. Core-periphery structure in networks (revisited). *SIAM Review* 59(3):619–646.

Takeshi Sakaki, Makoto Okazaki, and Yutaka Matsuo. 2010. Earthquake shakes twitter uers: Real-time event detection by social sensors. In *Proc. of WWW*. pages 851–860.

Divya Sardana and Raj Bhatnagar. 2016. Core periphery structures in weighted graphs using greedy growth. In *Proc. 2016 IEEE/WIC/ACM Int. Conf. Web Intelligence Core*. ACM, New York, pages 1–8.

Jiang Su, Jelber Sayyad-Shirabad, and Stan Matwin. 2011. Large scale text classification using semi-supervised multinomial naive bayes. In *Proc. of ICML*.

Mike Thelwall, Kevan Buckley, Georgios Paltoglou, Di Cai, and Arvid Kappas. 2010. Sentiment strength detection in short informal text. *Journal of the Association for Information Science and Technology* 61(12):2544–2558.

Bing-Bing Xiang, Zhong-Kui Bao, Chuang Ma, Xingyi Zhang, Han-Shuang Chen, and Hai-Feng Zhang. 2018. A unified method of detecting core-periphery structure and community structure in networks. *Chaos: An Interdisciplinary Journal of Nonlinear Science* 28(1):013122.

Bowen Yan and Jianxi Luo. 2016. Multicore-periphery structure in networks. Preprint arXiv:1605.03286.

Jaewon Yang and Jure Leskovec. 2014. Overlapping communities explain core–periphery organization of networks. *Proc. IEEE* 102(12):1892–1902.

Dani Yogatama and Noah A. Smith. 2014. Making the most of bag of words: Sentence regularization with alternating direction method of multipliers. In *Proc. of ICML*. pages 656–664.

Robust Handling of Polysemy via Sparse Representations

Abhijit A. Mahabal
Google
amahabal@google.com

Dan Roth
University of Pennsylvania
danroth@seas.upenn.edu

Sid Mittal
Google
sidmittal@google.com

Abstract

Words are polysemous and multi-faceted, with many shades of meanings. We suggest that sparse distributed representations are more suitable than other, commonly used, (dense) representations to express these multiple facets, and present *Category Builder*, a working system that, as we show, makes use of sparse representations to support multi-faceted lexical representations. We argue that the set expansion task is well suited to study these meaning distinctions since a word may belong to multiple sets with a different reason for membership in each. We therefore exhibit the performance of *Category Builder* on this task, while showing that our representation captures at the same time *analogy* problems such as "the Ganga of Egypt" or "the Voldemort of Tolkien". *Category Builder* is shown to be a more expressive lexical representation and to outperform dense representations such as Word2Vec in some analogy classes despite being shown only two of the three input terms.

1 Introduction

Word embeddings have received much attention lately because of their ability to represent similar words as nearby points in a vector space, thus supporting better generalization when comparisons of lexical items are needed, and boosting the robustness achieved by some deep-learning systems. However, a given surface form often has multiple meanings, complicating this simple picture. Arora et al (2016) showed that the vector corresponding to a polysemous term often is not close to any of that of its individual senses, thereby breaking the similar-items-map-to-nearby-points promise. The polysemy wrinkle is not merely an irritation but, in the words of Pustejovsky and Boguraev (1997), "one of the most intractable problems for language processing studies".

Our notion of Polysemy here is quite broad, since words can be similar to one another along a variety of dimensions. The following three pairs each has two similar items: (a) {*ring, necklace*}, (b) {*ring, gang*}, and (c) {*ring, beep*}. Note that ring is similar to all words that appear as second words in these pairs, but for different reasons, *defined by the second token* in the pairs. While this example used different senses of *ring*, it is easy to find examples where a single sense has multiple *facets*: *Clint Eastwood*, who is both an actor and a director, shares different aspects with directors than with actors, and *Google*, both a website and a major corporation, is similar to *Wikipedia* and *General Electric* along different dimensions.

Similarity has typically been studied pairwise: that is, by asking how similar item A is to item B. A simple modification sharply brings to fore the issues of facets and polysemy. This modification is best viewed through the task of *set expansion* (Wang and Cohen, 2007; Davidov et al., 2007; Jindal and Roth, 2011), which highlights the similarity of an item (a candidate in the expansion) to a set of seeds in the list. Given a few seeds (say, {*Ford, Nixon*}), what else belongs in the set? Note how this expansion is quite different from the expansion of {*Ford, Chevy*}, and the difference is one of *Similar How*, since whether a word (say, *BMW* or *FDR*) belongs in the expansion depends not just on how much commonality it shares with *Ford* but on *what* commonality it shares. Consequently, this task allows the same surface form to belong to multiple sets, by virtue of being similar to items in distinct sets *for different reasons*. The facets along which items are similar is implicitly defined by the members in the set.

In this paper, we propose a context sensitive version of similarity based on highlighting shared facets. We do this by developing a *sparse representation* of words that simultaneously captures all

*Proceedings of the 7th Joint Conference on Lexical and Computational Semantics (*SEM)*, pages 265–275
New Orleans, June 5-6, 2018. ©2018 Association for Computational Linguistics

facets of a given surface form. This allows us to define a notion of contextual similarity, in which *Ford* is similar to *Chevy* (e.g., when *Audi* or *BMW* is in the context) but similar to *Obama* when *Bush* or *Nixon* is in the context (i.e., in the seed list). In fact, it can even support multi-granular similarity since while {*Chevy, Chrysler, Ford*} represent the facet of AMERICAN CARS, {*Chevy, Audi, Ford*} define that of CARS. Our contextual similarity is better able to mold itself to this variety since it moves away from the one-size-fits-all nature of cosine similarity.

We exhibit the strength of the representation and the contextual similarity metric we develop by comparing its performance on both set expansion and analogy problems with dense representations.

2   Senses and Facets

The present work does not attempt to resolve the Word Sense Disambiguation (WSD) problem. Rather, our goal is to advance a lexical representation and a corresponding context sensitive similarity metric that, together, get around explicitly solving WSD.

Polysemy is intimately tied to the well-explored field of WSD so it is natural to expect techniques from WSD to be relevant. If WSD could neatly separate senses, the set expansion problem could be approached thus. *Ford* would split into, say, two senses: *Ford-1* for the car, and *Ford-2* for the president, and expanding {*Ford, Nixon*} could be translated to expanding {*Ford-2, Nixon*}. Such a representational approach is taken by many authors when they embed the different senses of words as distinct points in an embedding space (Reisinger and Mooney, 2010; Huang et al., 2012; Neelakantan et al., 2014; Li and Jurafsky, 2015).

Such approaches run into what we term *the Fixed Inventory Problem*. Either senses are obtained from a hand curated resource such as a dictionary, or are induced from the corpus directly by mapping contexts clusters to different senses. In either case, however, by the time the final representation (e.g., the embedding) is obtained, the number of different senses of each term has become fixed: all decisions have been made relating to how finely or coarsely to split senses.

How to split senses is a hard problem: dictionaries such as NOAD list coarse senses and split these further into fine senses, and it is unclear what granularity to use: should each fine sense correspond

to a point in the vector space, or should, instead, each coarse sense map to a point? Many authors (Hofstadter and Sander, 2013, for example) discuss how the various dictionary senses of a term are not independent. Further, if context clusters map to senses, the word *whale*, which is seen both in mammal-like contexts (e.g., "whales have hair") and water-animal contexts ("whales swim"), could get split into separate points. Thus, the different *senses* that terms are split into may instead be distinct *facets*. This is not an idle theoretical worry: such facet-based splitting is evident in Neelakantan et al. (2014, Table 3). Similarly, in the vectors they released, *november* splits into ten senses, likely based on facets. Once split, for subsequent processing, the points are independent.

In contrast to such explicit, prior, splitting, in the Category Builder approach developed here, relevant contexts are chosen given the task at hand, and if multiple facets are relevant (as happens, for example, in {*whale, dolphin, seal*}, whose expansion should rank aquatic mammals highest), all these facets influence the expansion; if only one facet is of relevance (as happens in {*whale, shark, seahorse*}), the irrelevant facets get ignored.

3   Related Work

In this section, we situate our approach within the relevant research landscape. Both *Set Expansion* and *Analogies* have a long history, and both depend on *Similarity*, with an even longer history.

3.1   Set Expansion

Set Expansion is the well studied problem of expanding a given set of terms by finding other semantically related terms. Solutions fall into two large families, differing on whether the expansion is based on a preprocessed, limited corpus (Shen et al., 2017, for example) or whether a much larger corpus (such as the entire web) is accessed on demand by making use of a search engine such as Google (Wang and Cohen, 2007, for example).

Each family has its advantages and disadvantages. "Open web" techniques that piggyback on Google can have coverage deep into the tail. These typically rely on some form of Wrapper Induction, and tend to work better for sets whose instances show up in lists or other repeated structure on the web, and thus perform much better on sets of nouns than on sets of verbs or adjectives. By contrast, "packaged" techniques that work off a preprocessed corpus are faster (no Google lookup needed) and can work well for any part of speech, but are of course limited to the corpus used. These typically use some form of distributional similarity, which can compute similarity between items that have never been seen together in the same document; approaches based on shared memberships in lists would need a sequence of overlapping lists to achieve this. Our work is in the "packaged" family, and we use sparse representations used for distributional similarity.

Gyllensten and Sahlgren (2018) compares two subfamilies within the packaged family: *centrality*-based methods use a prototype of the seeds (say, the centroid) as a proxy for the entire seed set and *classification*-based methods (a strict superset), which produce a classifier by using the seeds. Our approach is classification-based.

It is our goal to be able to expand nuanced categories. For example, we want our solution to expand the set {*pluto, mickey*}—both Disney characters—to other Disney characters. That is, the context *mickey* should determine what is considered 'similar' to pluto, rather than being biased by the more dominant sense of *pluto*, to determine that *neptune* is similar to it. Earlier approaches such as Rong et al. (2016) approach this problem differently: they expand to both planets and Disney characters, and then attempt to cluster the expansion into meaningful clusters.

3.2   Analogies

Solving analogy problems usually refers to proportional analogies, such as *hand*:*glove*::*foot*:*?*. Mikolov et al. (2013) showed how word embeddings such as Word2Vec capture linguistic regularities and thereby solve this. Turney (2012) used a pair of similarity functions (one for *function* and one for *domain*) to address the same problem.

There is a sense, however, that the problem is *overdetermined*: in many such problems, people can solve it even if the first term is not shown. That is, people easily answer "What is the *glove* for the *foot*?". People also answer questions such as "What is the Ganga of Egypt?" without first having to figure out the unprovided term *India* (or is the missing term *Asia*? It doesn't matter.) Hofstadter and Sander (2013) discuss how our ability to do these analogies is central to cognition.

The current work aims to tackle these *non-proportional* analogies and in fact performs better than Word2Vec on some analogy classes used by Mikolov et al. (2013), despite being shown one fewer term.

The approach is rather close to that used by Turney (2012) for a different problem: *word compounds*. Understanding what a *dog house* is can be phrased as "What is the house of a dog?", with *kennel* being the correct answer. This is solved using the pair of similarity functions mentioned above. The evaluations provided in that paper are for *ranking*: which of five provided terms is a match. Here, we apply it to non-proportional analogies and evaluate for retrieval, where we are ranking over all words, a significantly more challenging problem.

To our knowledge, no one has presented a computational model for analogies where only two terms are provided. We note, however, that Linzen (2016) briefly discusses this problem.

3.3   Similarity

Both Set Expansion and Analogies depend on a notion of similarity. Set Expansion can be seen as finding items most similar to a category, and Analogies can be seen as directly dependent on similarities (e.g., in the work of Turney (2012)).

Most current approaches, such as word embeddings, produce a context independent similarity. In such an approach, the similarity between, say, *king* and *twin* is some fixed value (such as their cosine similarity). However, depending on whether we are talking about bed sizes, these two items are either closely related or completely unrelated, and thus context dependent.

Psychologists and Philosophers of Language have long pointed out that similarity is subtle. It is sensitive to context and subject to priming effects. Even the very act of categorization can change the perceived similarity between items (Goldstone et al., 2001). Medin et al. (1993, p. 275) tell a story, from the experimental psychology trenches, that supports representation morphing when they conclude that "the effective representations of constituents are determined in the context of the comparison, not prior to it".

Here we present a malleable notion of similarity that can adapt to the wide range of human categories, some of which are based on narrow, superficial similarities (e.g., BLUE THINGS) while others share family resemblances (à la Wittgenstein). Even in a small domain such as movies, in different contexts, similarity may be driven by who the director is, or the cast, or the awards won. Furthermore, to the extent that the contexts we use are human readable, we also have a mechanism for explaining what makes the terms similar.

There is a lot of work on the context-dependence of human categories and similarities in Philosophy, in Cognitive Anthropology and in Experimental Psychology (Lakoff, 1987; Ellis, 1993; Agar, 1994; Goldstone et al., 2001; Hofstadter and Sander, 2013, for example, survey this space from various theoretical standpoints), but there are not, to our knowledge, unsupervised computational models of these phenomena.

4 Representations and Algorithms

This section describes the representation and corresponding algorithms that perform set expansion in Category Builder (CB).

4.1 Sparse Representations for Expansion

We use the traditional word representation that distributional similarity uses (Turney and Pantel, 2010), and that is commonly used in fields such as context sensitive spelling correction and grammatical correction (Golding and Roth, 1999; Rozovskaya and Roth, 2014); namely,words are associated with some ngrams that capture the contexts in which they occur – all contexts are represented in a sparse vector corresponding to a word. Following Levy and Goldberg (2014a), we call this representation *explicit*.

Generating Representations. We start with web pages and extract words and phrases from these, as well as the contexts they appear in. An aggregation step then calculates the strengths of word to context and context to word associations.

Vocabulary. The vocabulary is made up of words (nouns, verbs, adjectives, and adverbs) and some multi-word phrases. To go beyond words, we use a named entity recognizer to find multi-word phrases such as *New York*. We also use one heuristic rule to add certain phrasal verbs (e.g., *take shower*), when a verb is directly followed by its direct object. We lowercase all phrases, and drop those phrases seen infrequently. The set of all words is called the vocabulary, $\mathcal{V}$.

Contexts. Many kinds of contexts have been used in literature. Levy (2018) provides a comprehensive overview. We use contexts derived from syntactic parse trees using about a dozen heuris-

tic rules. For instance, one rule deals with nouns modified by an adjective, say, *red* followed by *car*. Here, one of the contexts of *car* is MODIFIEDBY#RED, and one of the contexts of *red* is MODIFIES#CAR. Two more examples of contexts: OBJECTOF#EAT and SUBJECTOF#WRITE. The set of all contexts is denoted $\mathcal{C}$.

The Two Vocabulary⇔Context matrices. For vocabulary $\mathcal{V}$ and contexts C, we produce *two* matrices, $M^{\mathcal{V}\to C}$ and $M^{C\to\mathcal{V}}$. Many measures of association between a word and a context have been explored in the literature, usually based on some variant of *pointwise mutual information*.

PPMI (*Positive* PMI) is the typically used measure. If $P(w)$, $P(c)$ and $P(w,c)$ respectively represent the probabilities that a word is seen, a context is seen and the word is seen in that context, then

$$\text{PMI}(w,c) = \log \frac{P(w,c)}{P(w)P(c)} \qquad (1)$$

$$\text{PPMI}(w,c) = max(0, \text{PMI}(w,c)) \qquad (2)$$

PPMI is widely used, but comments are in order regarding the ad-hocness of the "0" in Equation 2. There is seemingly a good reason to choose 0 as a threshold: if a word is seen in a context more than by chance, the PMI is positive, and a 0 threshold seems sensible. However, in the presence of polysemy, especially lopsided polysemy such as *Cancer* (disease and star sign), a "0" threshold is arbitrary: even if every single occurrence of the star sign sense of *cancer* was seen in some context c (thereby crying out for a high PMI), because of the rarity of that sense, the overall PMI between c and (non-disambiguated) *Cancer* may well be negative. Relatedly, Shifted PPMI (Levy and Goldberg, 2014b) uses a non-0 cutoff.

Another well known problem with PPMI is its large value when the word or the context is rare, and even a single occurrence of a word-context pair can bloat the PMI (see Role and Nadif, 2011, for fixes that have been proposed). We introduce a new variant we call *Asymmetric PMI*, which takes frequency into account by adding a second log term, and is asymmetric because in general $P(w|c) \neq P(c|w)$:

$$\text{APMI}(w,c) = \text{PMI}(w,c) + \log \frac{P(w,c)}{P(w)}$$
$$= \log \frac{P(w,c)^2}{P(w)^2 P(c)} \qquad (3)$$

This is asymmetric because $\text{APMI}(c, w)$ has $P(c)$ in the denominator of the extra log term.

What benefit does this modification to PMI provide? Consider a word and two associated contexts, c_1 and c_2, where the second context is significantly rarer. Further, imagine that the PMI of the word with either feature is the same. The word would have been seen in the rarer context only a few times, and this is more likely to have been a statistical fluke. In this case, the APMI with the more frequent term is higher: we reward the fact that the PMI is high despite its prevalence; this is less likely to be an artifact of chance.

Note that the rearranged expression seen in the second line of Equation 3 is reminiscent of $\text{PPMI}^{0.75}$ from Levy et al. (2015).

The second log term in APMI is always negative, and we thus shift all values by a constant k (chosen based on practical considerations of data size: the smaller the k, the larger the size of the sparse matrices; based on experimenting with various values of k, it appears that expansion quality is not very sensitive to k). Clipping this shifted value at 0 produces Asymmetrical PPMI (APPMI):

$$\text{APPMI}(w, c) = \max(0, \text{APMI}(w, c) + k) \quad (4)$$

The two matrices thus produced are shown in Equation 5. If we use PPMI instead of APPMI, these are transposes of each other.

$$
\begin{aligned}
M_{w,c}^{\mathcal{V} \to \mathcal{C}} &= \text{APPMI}(w, c) \\
M_{c,w}^{\mathcal{C} \to \mathcal{V}} &= \text{APPMI}(c, w)
\end{aligned}
\quad (5)
$$

4.2 Focused Similarity and Set Expansion

We now come to the central idea of this paper: the notion of focused similarity. Typically, similarity is based on the dot product or cosine similarity of the context vectors. The pairwise similarity among all terms can be expressed as a matrix multiplication as shown in Equation 6. Note that if we had used PPMI in Equation 5, the matrices would be each other's transposes and each entry in SimMatrix in Equation 6 would be the dot-product-based similarity for a word pair.

$$\text{SimMatrix} = M^{\mathcal{C} \to \mathcal{V}} M^{\mathcal{V} \to \mathcal{C}} \quad (6)$$

We introduce context weighting by inserting a square matrix W between the two (see Equation 7). Similarity is unchanged if W is the identity matrix. If W is a non-identity diagonal matrix, this is equivalent to treating some contexts as more important than others. It is by appropriately choosing weights in W that we achieve the context dependent similarity. If, for instance, all contexts other than those indicative of cars are zeroed out in W, *ford* and *obama* will have no similarity.

$$\text{SimMatrix} = M^{\mathcal{C} \to \mathcal{V}} W M^{\mathcal{V} \to \mathcal{C}} \quad (7)$$

4.3 Set Expansion via Matrix Multiplication

To expand a set of k seeds, we can construct the k-hot column vector S with a 1 corresponding to each seed, and a 0 elsewhere. Given S, we calculate the focus matrix, W_S. Then the expansion E is a column vector that is just:

$$E = M^{\mathcal{C} \to \mathcal{V}} W_S M^{\mathcal{V} \to \mathcal{C}} S \quad (8)$$

The score for a term in E is the sum of its focused similarity to each seed.

4.4 Motivating Our Choice of W

When expanding the set $\{taurus, cancer\}$—the set of star signs, or perhaps the constellations—we are faced with the presence of a polysemous term with a lopsided polysemy. The *disease* sense is much more prevalent than the *star sign* sense for *cancer*, and the associated contexts are also unevenly distributed. If we attempt to use Equation 8 with the identity matrix W, the expansion is dominated by diseases.

The contexts we care about are those that are shared. Note that restricting ourselves to the intersection is not sensible, since if we are given a dozen seeds it is entirely possible that they share family resemblances and have a high pairwise overlap in contexts between any two seeds but where there are almost no contexts shared by all. We thus require a soft intersection, and this we achieve by downweighting contexts based on what fraction of the seeds are associated with that context. The parameter ρ described in the next section achieves this.

This modification helps, but it is not enough. Each disease-related context for *cancer* is now weakened, but their large number causes many diseases to rank high in the expansion. To address this, we can limit ourselves to only the top n contexts (typically, $n = 100$ is used). This way, if the joint contexts are highly ranked, the expansion will be based only on such contexts.

input : $S \subset \mathcal{V}$ (seeds), $\rho \in \mathbb{R}$ (limited support penalty), $n \in \mathbb{N}$ (context footprint)

output: The diagonal matrix W.

```
1  for c ∈ C do
2      // Activation of the context.
3      a(c) ← Σ_{w∈S} M^{V→C}_{w,c}
4      // Fraction of S with context active
5      f(c) ← fraction with M^{V→C}_{*,c} > 0
6      // Score of context
7      s(c) ← f(c)^ρ a(c)
8  end
9  Sort contexts by score s(c)
10 for c ∈ C do
11     if c one of n top-scoring contexts
       then
12         W_{c,c} = f(c)^ρ
13     end
14 end
```

Algorithm 1: Calculating context focus

The {*taurus, cancer*} example is useful to point out the benefits of an asymmetric association measure. Given *cancer*, the notion of *star sign* is not highly activated, and rightly so. If w is *cancer* and c is BORN UNDER X, then $\mathrm{PPMI}(w, c)$ is low (as is $\mathrm{APPMI}(w, c)$). However, $\mathrm{APPMI}(c, w)$ is quite high, allowing us to highly score *cancer* when expanding {*taurus, aries*}.

4.5 Details of Calculating W

To produce W, we provide the seeds and two parameters: $\rho \in \mathbb{R}$ (the *limited support penalty*) and $n \in \mathbb{N}$ (the *context footprint*). Algorithm 1 provides the pseudo-code.

First, we score contexts by their *activation* (line 3). We penalize contexts that are not supported by all the seeds: we produce the score by multiplying activation by f^ρ, where f is the fraction of the seeds supporting that context (lines 5 and 7). Only the n top scoring contexts will have non-zero values in W, and these get the value f^ρ.

This notion of weighting contexts is similar to that used in the SetExpan framework (Shen et al., 2017), although the way they use it is different (they use weighted Jaccard similarity based on context weights). Their algorithm for calculating context weights is a special case of our algorithm, with no notion of *limited support penalty*, that is, they use $\rho = 0$.

4.6 Sparse Representations for Analogies

To solve the analogy problem "What is the Ganga of Egypt?" we are looking for something that is like *Ganga* (this we can obtain via the set expansion of the (singleton) set {*Ganga*}, as described above) and that we see often with *Egypt*, or to use Turney's terminology, in the same domain as *Egypt*.

To find terms that are in the same domain as a given term, we use the same statistical tools, merely with a different set of contexts. The context for a term is other terms in the same sentence. With this alternate definition of context, we produce $D^{C→V}$ exactly analogous to $M^{C→V}$ from Equation 5.

However, if we define $D^{V→C}$ analogous to $M^{V→C}$ and use these matrices for expansion, we run into unintended consequences since expanding {*evolution*} provides not what things *evolution* is seen with, but rather those things that cooccur with what *evolution* co-occurs with. Since, for example, both *evolution* and *number* co-occur with *theory*, the two would appear related. To get around this, we zero out most non-diagonal entries in $D^{V→C}$. The only off diagonal entries that we do not zero out are those corresponding to word pairs that seem to share a lemma (which we heuristically define as "share more than 80% of the prefix". Future work will explore using lemmas). An example of a pair we retain is *india* and *indian*), since when we are looking for items that co-occur with *india* we actually want those that occur with related words forms. An illustration for why this matters: *India* and *Rupee* occur together rarely (with a negative PMI) whereas *Indian* and *Rupee* have a strong positive PMI.

4.7 Finding Analogies

To answer "What is the Ganga of Egypt", we use Equation 8 on the singleton set {*ganga*}, and the same equation (but with $D^{V→C}$ and $D^{C→V}$) on {*egypt*}. We intersect the two lists by combining the score of the shared terms in squash space (i.e., if the two scores are m and d, the combined score is

$$\frac{100m}{99 + m} + \frac{100d}{99 + d} \qquad (9)$$

5 Set Expansion Experiments and Evaluation

5.1 Experimental Setup

We report data on two different corpora.

The Comparison Corpus. We begin with 20 million English web pages randomly sampled from a set of popular web pages (high pagerank according to Google). We run Word2Vec on the text of these pages, producing a 200 dimensional embeddings. We also produce $M^{\mathcal{V} \to \mathcal{C}}$ and $M^{\mathcal{C} \to \mathcal{V}}$ according to Equation 5. We use this corpus to compare Category Builder with Word2Vec-based techniques. Note that these web-pages may be noisier than Wikipedia. Word2Vec was chosen because it was deemed "comparable": mathematically, it is an implicit factorization of the PMI matrix (Levy and Goldberg, 2014b).

Release Corpus. We also ran Category Builder on a much larger corpus. The generated matrices are restricted to the most common words and phrases (around 200,000). The matrices and associated code are publicly available[1].

Using Word2Vec for Set Expansion. Two classes of techniques are considered, representing members of both families described by Gyllensten and Sahlgren (2018). The centroid method finds the centroid of the seeds and expands to its neighbors based on cosine similarity. The other methods first find similarity of a candidate to each seed, and combines these scores using arithmetic, geometric, and harmonic means.

Mean Average Precision (MAP). MAP combines both precision and recall into a single number. The gold data to evaluate against is presented as sets of synsets, e.g., $\{\{California, CA\}, \{Indiana, IN\}, \ldots\}$.

An expansion L consists of an ordered list of terms (which may include the seeds). Define $\mathrm{Prec}_i(L)$ to be the fraction of items in the first i items in L that belong to at least one golden synset. We can also speak of the precision at a synset, $\mathrm{Prec}_S(L) = \mathrm{Prec}_j(L)$, where j is the smallest index where an element in S was seen in L. If no element in the synset S was ever seen, then $\mathrm{Prec}_S = 0$. $\mathrm{MAP}(L) = avg(\mathrm{Prec}_S(L))$ is the average precision over all synsets.

Generalizations of MAP. While MAP is an excellent choice for closed sets (such as U.S. STATES), it is less applicable to open sets (say, POLITICAL

IDEOLOGIES or SCIENTISTS). For such cases, we propose a generalization of MAP that preserves its attractive properties of combining precision and recall while accounting for variant names. The proposed score is $\mathrm{MAP}_n(L)$, which is the average of precision for the first n synsets seen. That it is a strict generalization of MAP can be seen by observing that in the case of US STATES, $\mathrm{MAP}(L) \equiv \mathrm{MAP}_{50}(L)$.

5.2 Evaluation Sets

We produced three evaluation sets, two closed and one open. For closed sets, following Wang and Cohen (2007), we use US States and National Football League teams. To increase the difficulty, for NFL teams, we do not use as seeds dismabiguated names such as *Detroit Lions* or *Green Bay Packers*, instead using the polysemous *lions* and *packers*. The synsets were produced by adding all variant names for the teams. For example, *Atlanta Falcons* are also known as *falcs*, and so this was added to the synset.

For the open set, we use verbs that indicate things breaking or failing in some way. We chose ten popular instances (e.g., *break, chip, shatter*) and these act as seeds. We expanded the set by manual evaluation: any correct item produced by any of the evaluated systems was added to the list. There is an element of subjectivity here, and we therefore provide the lists used (Appendix A.1).

5.3 Evaluation

For each evaluation set, we did 50 set expansions, each starting with three randomly selected seeds.

Effect of ρ and APPMI. Table 1 reveals that APPMI performs better than PPMI — significantly better on two sets, and slightly worse on one. Penalizing contexts that are not shared by most seeds (i.e., using $\rho > 0$) also has a marked positive effect.

Effect of n. Table 2 reveals a curious effect. As we increase n, for US STATES, performance drops somewhat but for BREAK VERBS it improves quite a bit. Our analysis shows that pinning down what a state is can be done with very few contexts, and other shared contexts (such as LIVE IN X) are shared also with semantically related entities such as states in other countries. At the other end, BREAK VERBS is based on a large number of shared contexts and using more contexts is beneficial.

Technique	US States	NFL Teams	*Break Verbs*
W2V HM	.858	.528	.231
W2V GM	.864	.589	.273
W2V AM	.852	.653	.332
W2V Centroid	.851	.646	.337
CB:PPMI; $\rho = 0$	.918	.473	.248
CB:PPMI; $\rho = 3$	**.922**	.612	.393
CB:APPMI; $\rho = 0$	.900	.584	.402
CB:APPMI; $\rho = 3$	.907	**.735**	**.499**
CB:Release Data[†]	.959	.999	.797

Table 1: MAP scores on three categories. The first four rows use various techniques with Word2Vec. The next four demonstrate Category Builder built on the same corpus, to show the effect of ρ and association measure used. For all four Category Builder rows, we used $n = 100$. Both increasing ρ and switching to APPMI can be seen to be individually and jointly beneficial. [†]The last line reports the score on a different corpus, the release data, with APPMI and $\rho = 3, n = 100$.

	5	10	30	50	100	500
US States	**.932**	.925	.907	.909	.907	.903
NFL	.699	.726	.731	.734	**.735**	.733
Break Verbs	.339	.407	.477	.485	.496	**.511**

Table 2: Effect of varying n. APPMI with $\rho = 3$.

5.4 Error Analysis.

Table 3 shows the top errors in expansion. The kinds of drifts seen in the two cases are revealing. Category Builder picks up word fragments (e.g., because of the US State *New Mexico*, it expanded states to include *Mexico*). It sometimes expands to a hypernym (e.g., *province*) or siblings (e.g., instead of Football teams sometimes it got other sport teams). With Word2Vec, we see similar errors (such as expanding to the semantically similar *southern california*).

5.5 Qualitative Demonstration

Table 4 shows a few examples of expanding categories, with $\rho = 3, n = 100$.

Table 5 illustrates the power of Category Builder by considering a a synthetic corpus produced by replacing all instances of *cat* and *denver* into the hypothetical *CatDenver*. This illustrates that even without explicit WSD (that is, separating *CatDenver* to its two "senses", we are able to expand correctly given an appropriate context. To complete the picture, we note that expanding {*kitten, dog*} as well as {*atlanta, phoenix*} contains *CatDenver*, as expected.

Set	Method	Top Errors
US States	W2V	southern california; east tennessee; seattle washington
	CB	carolina; hampshire; dakota; ontario; jersey; province
NFL	W2V	hawks; pelicans; tigers; nfl; quarterbacks; sooners
	CB	yankees; sox; braves; mets; knicks; rangers, lakers

Table 3: Error analysis for US States and NFL. Arithmetic Mean method is used for W2V and $\rho = 3$ and APPMI for Category Builder

Seeds	CB Expansion, $\rho = 3, n = 100$
ford, nixon	nixon, ford, obama, clinton, bush, richard nixon, reagan, roosevelt, barack obama, bill clinton, ronald reagan, w. bush, eisenhower
ford, chevy	ford, chevy, chevrolet, toyota, honda, nissan, bmw, hyundai, volkswagen, audi, chrysler, mazda, volvo, gm, kia, subaru, cadillac
ford, depp	ford, depp, johnny depp, harrison ford, dicaprio, tom cruise, pitt, khan, brad pitt, hanks, tom hanks, leonardo dicaprio
safari, trip[†]	trip, safari, tour, trips, cruise, adventure, excursion, vacation, holiday, road trip, expedition, trek, tours, safaris, journey,
safari, ie[†]	safari, ie, firefox, internet explorer, chrome, explorer, browsers, google chrome, web browser, browser, mozilla firefox

Table 4: Expansion examples using Category Builder so as to illustrate its ability to deal with Polysemy. [†] For these examples, $\rho = 5$

6 Analogies

6.1 Experimental Setup

We evaluated the analogy examples used by Mikolov et al. (2013). Category Builder evaluation were done by expanding using syntactic and sentence-based-cooccurrence contexts as detailed in Section 4.6 and scoring items according to Equation 9. For evaluating using Word2Vec, the standard vector arithmetic was used.

In both cases, the input terms from the problem were removed from candidate answers (as was done in the original paper). Linzen (2016) provides analysis and rationales for why this is done.

6.2 Evaluation

Table 6 provides the evaluations. A few words are in order for the difference between the published scores for Word2Vec analogies elsewhere (e.g., Linzen, 2016). Their reported numbers for common capitals were around 91%, as opposed to around 87% here. Where as Wikipedia is typically used as a corpus, that was not the case here. Our corpus is noisier, and may not have the same level

Seeds	CB Expansion, $\rho = 3, n = 100$
CatDenver, dog	dogs, cats, puppy, pet, rabbit, kitten, animal, animals, pup, pets, puppies, horse
CatDenver, phoenix	chicago, atlanta, seattle, dallas, boston, portland, angeles, los angeles
CatDenver, TigerAndroid	cats, lion, dog, tigers, kitten, animal, dragon, wolf, dogs, bear, leopard, rabbit

Table 5: Expansion examples with synthetic polysemy by replacing all instances of *cat* and *denver* into the hypothetical *CatDenver* (similarly, *TigerAndroid*). A single other term is enough to pick out the right sense.

| | $a{:}b{::}c{:}?$ | Harder $:b{::}c{:}?$ (a withheld) | |
Method	W2V	CB:APPMI	
Corpus	Comp	Comp	Release[†]
common capitals	.872	**.957**	.941
city-in-state	.657	**.972**	.955
currency	.030	**.037**	.122
nationality	.515	**.615**	.655
world capitals	.472	**.789**	.668
family	**.617**	.217	.306

Table 6: Performance on Analogy classes from Mikolov et al. (2013). The first two columns are derived from the same corpus, whereas the last column reports numbers on the data we will release. For category builder, we used $\rho = 3, n = 100$

$term_1$	$term_2$	**What is the $term_1$ of $term_2$?**
voldemort	tolkien	sauron
voldemort	star wars	vader
ganga	egypt	nile
dollar	india	rupee
football	india	cricket
civic	toyota	corolla

Table 7: A sampler of analogies solved by Category Builder.

gories that benefit from very small n (such as BLUE THINGS) or very large n. Similarly, as can be seen in Equation 9, analogy also uses a parameter for combining the results, with no automated way yet to choose it. Future work will prioritize this.

The current work suggests, we believe, that it is beneficial to not collapse the large dimensional sparse vector space that implicitly underlies many embeddings. Having the ability to separately manipulate contexts can help differentiate between items that differ on that context. That said, the smoothing and generalization that dimensionality reduction provides has its uses, so finding a combined solution might be best.

8 Conclusions

Given that natural categories vary in their degree of similarities and their kinds of coherence, we believe that solutions that can adapt to these would perform better than context independent notions of similarity.

As we have shown, Category Builder displays the ability to implicitly deal with polysemy and determine similarity in a context sensitive manner, as exhibited in its ability to expand a set by latching on to what is common among the seeds.

In developing it we proposed a new measure of association between words and contexts and demonstrated its utility in set expansion and a hard version of the analogy problem. In particular, our results show that sparse representations deserve additional careful study.

of country-based factual coverage as Wikipedia, and almost all non-grammar based analogy problems are of that nature.

A second matter to point out is why grammar based rows are missing from Table 6. Grammar based analogy classes cannot be solved with just two terms. For *boy:boys::king:?*, dropping the first term *boy* takes away information crucial to the solution in a way that dropping the first term of *US:dollar::India:?* does not. The same is true for the *family* class of analogies.

6.3 Qualitative Demonstration

Table 7 provides a sampler of analogies solved using Category Builder.

7 Limitations

Much work remains, of course. The analogy work presented here (and also the corresponding work using vector offsets) is no match for the subtlety that people can bring to bear when they see deep connections via analogy. Some progress here could come from the ability to discover and use more semantically meaningful contexts.

There is currently no mechanism to automatically choose n and ρ. Standard settings of $n = 100$ and $\rho = 3$ work well for the many applications we use it for, but clearly there are cate-

Acknowledgments

We are thankful to all the reviewers for their helpful comments and critiques. In particular, Ido Dagan, Yoav Goldberg, Omer Levy, Praveen Paritosh, and Chris Waterson gave us insightful comments on earlier versions of this write up. The research of Dan Roth is partly supported by a Google gift and by DARPA, under agreement number FA8750-13-2-008.

References

Michael Agar. 1994. *Language shock: Understanding the culture of conversation*. William Morrow & Company.

Sanjeev Arora, Yuanzhi Li, Yingyu Liang, Tengyu Ma, and Andrej Risteski. 2016. Linear algebraic structure of word senses, with applications to polysemy. *arXiv preprint arXiv:1601.03764*.

Dmitry Davidov, Ari Rappoport, and Moshe Koppel. 2007. Fully unsupervised discovery of concept-specific relationships by web mining. In *Proceedings of the 45th Annual Meeting of the Association of Computational Linguistics*, pages 232–239, Prague, Czech Republic. Association for Computational Linguistics.

John M. Ellis. 1993. *Language, Thought, and Logic*. Northwestern University Press.

A. R. Golding and D. Roth. 1999. A winnow based approach to context-sensitive spelling correction. *Machine Learning*, 34(1-3):107–130.

Robert L Goldstone, Yvonne Lippa, and Richard M Shiffrin. 2001. Altering object representations through category learning. *Cognition*, 78(1):27–43.

Amaru Cuba Gyllensten and Magnus Sahlgren. 2018. Distributional term set expansion.

Douglas Hofstadter and Emmanuel Sander. 2013. *Surfaces and Essences: Analogy as the Fuel and Fire of Thinking*. Basic Books.

Eric H Huang, Richard Socher, Christopher D Manning, and Andrew Y Ng. 2012. Improving word representations via global context and multiple word prototypes. In *Proceedings of the 50th Annual Meeting of the Association for Computational Linguistics: Long Papers-Volume 1*, pages 873–882. Association for Computational Linguistics.

P. Jindal and D. Roth. 2011. Learning from negative examples in set-expansion. In *ICDM*, pages 1110–1115.

George Lakoff. 1987. *Women, Fire, and Dangerous Things: What Categories Reveal about the Mind*. University of Chicago Press.

Omer Levy. 2018. *The Oxford handbook of computational linguistics*, second edition, chapter Word Representaion. Oxford University Press.

Omer Levy and Yoav Goldberg. 2014a. Linguistic regularities in sparse and explicit word representations. In *Proceedings of the eighteenth conference on computational natural language learning*, pages 171–180.

Omer Levy and Yoav Goldberg. 2014b. Neural word embedding as implicit matrix factorization. In Z. Ghahramani, M. Welling, C. Cortes, N. D. Lawrence, and K. Q. Weinberger, editors, *Advances in Neural Information Processing Systems 27*, pages 2177–2185. Curran Associates, Inc.

Omer Levy, Yoav Goldberg, and Ido Dagan. 2015. Improving distributional similarity with lessons learned from word embeddings. *Transactions of the Association for Computational Linguistics*, 3:211–225.

Jiwei Li and Dan Jurafsky. 2015. Do multi-sense embeddings improve natural language understanding?

Tal Linzen. 2016. Issues in evaluating semantic spaces using word analogies. *arXiv preprint arXiv:1606.07736*.

Douglas L Medin, Robert L Goldstone, and Dedre Gentner. 1993. Respects for similarity. *Psychological review*, 100(2):254.

Tomas Mikolov, Wen-tau Yih, and Geoffrey Zweig. 2013. Linguistic regularities in continuous space word representations. In *Proceedings of the 2013 Conference of the North American Chapter of the Association for Computational Linguistics: Human Language Technologies*, pages 746–751.

Arvind Neelakantan, Jeevan Shankar, Alexandre Passos, and Andrew McCallum. 2014. Efficient non-parametric estimation of multiple embeddings per word in vector space. In *Proceedings of the 2014 Conference on Empirical Methods in Natural Language Processing*.

James Pustejovsky and Bran Boguraev. 1997. *Lexical semantics: The problem of polysemy*. Clarendon Press.

Joseph Reisinger and Raymond J Mooney. 2010. Multi-prototype vector-space models of word meaning. In *Human Language Technologies: The 2010 Annual Conference of the North American Chapter of the Association for Computational Linguistics*, pages 109–117. Association for Computational Linguistics.

Francois Role and Mohamed Nadif. 2011. Handling the impact of low frequency events on co-occurrence based measures of word similarity. In *International Conference on Knowledge Discovery and Information Retrieval*, pages 226–231.

Xin Rong, Zhe Chen, Qiaozhu Mei, and Eytan Adar. 2016. Egoset: Exploiting word ego-networks and user-generated ontology for multifaceted set expansion. In *Proceedings of the Ninth ACM International Conference on Web Search and Data Mining*, pages 645–654. ACM.

A. Rozovskaya and D. Roth. 2014. Building a state-of-the-art grammatical error correction system.

Jiaming Shen, Zeqiu Wu, Dongming Lei, Jingbo Shang, Xiang Ren, and Jiawei Han. 2017. Setexpan: Corpus-based set expansion via context feature selection and rank ensemble. In *Joint European Conference on Machine Learning and Knowledge Discovery in Databases*, pages 288–304. Springer.

Peter D Turney. 2012. Domain and function: A dual-space model of semantic relations and compositions. *Journal of Artificial Intelligence Research*, 44:533–585.

Peter D Turney and Patrick Pantel. 2010. From frequency to meaning: Vector space models of semantics. *Journal of artificial intelligence research*, 37:141–188.

Richard C Wang and William W Cohen. 2007. Language-independent set expansion of named entities using the web. In *Data Mining, 2007. ICDM 2007. Seventh IEEE International Conference on*, pages 342–350. IEEE.

A Supplemental Material

A.1 Lists Used in Evaluating Set Expansion

US States. Any of the 50 states could be used as a seed. The 50 golden synsets were the 50 pairs of state name and abbreviation (e.g., {*California, CA*}).

NFL Teams. Any of the first terms in these 32 synsets could be used as a seed. The golden synsets are: {*Bills, Buffalo Bills*}, {*Dolphins, Miami Dolphins, Phins*}, {*Patriots, New England Patriots, Pats*}, {*Jets, New York Jets*}, {*Ravens, Baltimore Ravens*}, {*Bengals, Cincinnati Bengals*}, {*Browns, Cleveland Browns*}, {*Steelers, Pittsburgh Steelers*}, {*Texans, Houston Texans*}, {*Colts, Indianapolis Colts*}, {*Jaguars, Jacksonville Jaguars, Jags*}, {*Titans, Tennessee Titans*}, {*Broncos, Denver Broncos*}, {*Chiefs, Kansas City Chiefs*}, {*Chargers, Los Angeles Chargers*}, {*Raiders, Oakland Raiders*}, {*Cowboys, Dallas Cowboys*}, {*Giants, New York Giants*}, {*Eagles, Philadelphia Eagles*}, {*Redskins, Washington Redskins*}, {*Bears, Chicago Bears*}, {*Lions, Detroit Lions*}, {*Packers, Green Bay Packers*}, {*Vikings, Minnesota Vikings, Vikes*}, {*Falcons, Atlanta Falcons, Falcs*}, {*Panthers, Carolina Panthers*}, {*Saints, New Orleans Saints*}, {*Buccaneers, Tampa Bay Buccaneers, Bucs*}, {*Cardinals, Arizona Cardinals*}, {*Rams, Los Angeles Rams*}, {*49ers, San Francisco 49ers, Niners*}, and {*Seahawks, Seattle Seahawks*}

Break Verbs. Seeds are chosen from among these ten items: *break, chip, shatter, rot, melt, scratch, crush, smash, rip, fade*. Evaluation is done for MAP_{30} (see Section 5.1). The following items are accepted in the expansion: *break up, break down, tip over, splinter, tear, come off, crack, disintegrate, deform, crumble, burn, dissolve, bend, chop, stain, destroy, smudge, tarnish, explode, derail, deflate, corrode, trample, ruin, suffocate, obliterate, topple, scorch, crumple, pulverize, fall off, cut, dry out, split, deteriorate, hit, blow, damage, wear out, peel, warp, shrink, evaporate, implode, scrape, sink, harden, abrade, unhinge, erode, calcify, vaporize, sag, shred, degrade, collapse, annihilate*. In the synsets, we also added the morphological variants (e.g., {*break, breaking, broke, breaks*}).

A.2 Word2Vec Model Details

The word2vec model on the "comparison corpus" created 200 dimensional word embeddings. We used a skip-gram model with a batch size of 100, a vocabulary of 600k ngrams, and negative sampling with 100 examples. It was trained using a learning rate of 0.2 with Adagrad optimizer for 70 million steps.

Multiplicative Tree-Structured Long Short-Term Memory Networks for Semantic Representations

Nam Khanh Tran[*]
L3S Research Center
ntran@l3s.de

Weiwei Cheng
Amazon
weiweic@amazon.com

Abstract

Tree-structured LSTMs have shown advantages in learning semantic representations by exploiting syntactic information. Most existing methods model tree structures by bottom-up combinations of constituent nodes using the same shared compositional function and often making use of input word information only. The inability to capture the richness of compositionality makes these models lack expressive power. In this paper, we propose *multiplicative tree-structured LSTMs* to tackle this problem. Our model makes use of not only word information but also relation information between words. It is more expressive, as different combination functions can be used for each child node. In addition to syntactic trees, we also investigate the use of Abstract Meaning Representation in tree-structured models, in order to incorporate both syntactic and semantic information from the sentence. Experimental results on common NLP tasks show the proposed models lead to better sentence representation and AMR brings benefits in complex tasks.

1 Introduction

Learning the distributed representation for long spans of text from its constituents has been a crucial step of various NLP tasks such as text classification (Zhao et al., 2015; Kim, 2014), semantic matching (Liu et al., 2016), and machine translation (Cho et al., 2014). Seminal work uses recurrent neural networks (RNN) (Elman, 1990), convolutional neural networks (Kalchbrenner et al., 2014), and tree-structured neural networks (Socher et al., 2011; Tai et al., 2015) for sequence and tree modeling. Long Short-Term Memory (LSTM) (Hochreiter and Schmidhuber, 1997) networks are a type of recurrent neural net-

---

[*] Work done as an intern at Amazon.

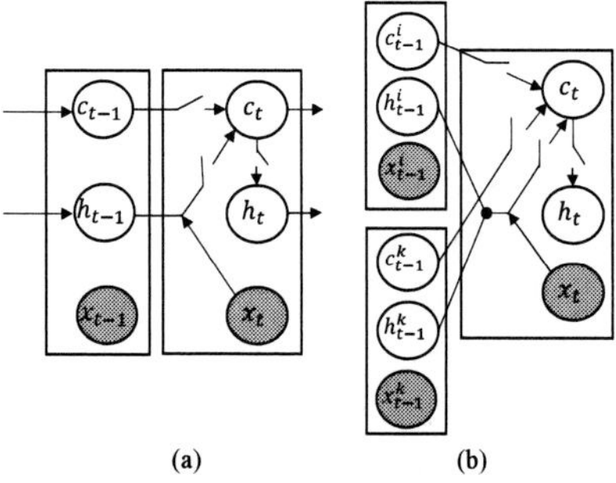

Figure 1: Topology of sequential LSTM and TreeLSTM: (a) nodes in sequential LSTM and (b) nodes in tree-structured LSTM

work that are capable of learning long-term dependencies across sequences and have achieved significant improvements in a variety of sequence tasks. LSTM has been extended to model tree structures (e.g., TreeLSTM) and produced promising results in tasks such as sentiment classification (Tai et al., 2015; Zhu et al., 2015) and relation extraction (Miwa and Bansal, 2016).

Figure 1 shows the topologies of the conventional chain-structured LSTM (Hochreiter and Schmidhuber, 1997) and the TreeLSTM (Tai et al., 2015), illustrating the input (x), cell (c) and hidden node (h) at a time step t. The key difference between Figure 1 (a) and (b) is the branching factor. While a cell in the sequential LSTM only depends on the single previous hidden node, a cell in the tree-structured LSTM depends on the hidden states of child nodes.

Despite their success, the tree-structured models have a limitation in their inability to fully capture the richness of compositionality (Socher et al., 2013a). The same combination function is used for all kinds of semantic compositions, though the

*Proceedings of the 7th Joint Conference on Lexical and Computational Semantics (*SEM)*, pages 276–286
New Orleans, June 5-6, 2018. ©2018 Association for Computational Linguistics

compositions have different characteristics in nature. For example, the composition of the adjective and the noun differs significantly from the composition of the verb and the noun.

To alleviate this problem, some researchers propose to use multiple compositional functions, which are predefined according to some partition criterion (Socher et al., 2012, 2013a; Dong et al., 2014). Socher et al. (2013a) defined different compositional functions in terms of syntactic categories, and a suitable compositional function is selected based on the syntactic categories. Dong et al. (2014) introduced multiple compositional functions and a proper one is selected based on the input information. These models accomplished their objective to a certain extent but they still face critical challenges. The predefined compositional functions cannot cover all the compositional rules and they add much more learnable parameters, bearing the risk of overfitting.

In this paper, we propose *multiplicative TreeLSTM*, an extension to the TreeLSTM model, which injects relation information into every node in the tree. It allows the model to have different semantic composition matrices to combine child nodes. To reduce the model complexity and keep the number of parameters manageable, we define the composition matrices using the product of two dense matrices shared across relations, with an intermediate diagonal matrix that is relation dependent.

Though the syntactic-based models have shown to be promising for compositional semantics, they do not make full use of the linguistic information. For example, semantic nodes are often the argument of more than one predicate (e.g., coreference) and it is generally useful to exclude semantically vacuous words like articles or complementizers, i.e., leave nodes unattached that do not add further meaning to the resulting representations. Recently, Banarescu et al. (2013) introduced Abstract Meaning Representation (AMR), single rooted, directed, acyclic graphs that incorporate semantic roles, correference, negation, and other linguistic phenomena. In this paper, we investigate a combination of the semantic process provided by TreeLSTM model with the lexical semantic representation of the AMR formalism. This differs from most of existing work in this area, where syntactic rather than semantic information is incorporated to the tree-structured models. We seek to answer the question: *To what extent can we do better with AMR as opposed to syntactic representations, such as constituent and dependency trees, in tree-structured models?*

We evaluate the proposed models on three common tasks: sentiment classification, sentence relatedness, and natural language inference. The results show that the multiplicative TreeLSTM models outperform TreeLSTM models on the same tree structures. The results further suggest that using AMR as the backbone for tree-structured models is helpful in the complex task such as for longer sentences in natural language inference but not in sentiment classification, where lexical information alone suffices.

In short, our contribution is twofold:

1. We propose the new multiplicative TreeLSTM model that effectively learns distributed representation of a given sentence from its constituents, utilizing not only the lexical information of words, but also the relation information between the words.
2. We conduct an extensive investigation on the usefulness of lexical semantic representation induced by AMR formalism in tree-structured models.

2 Tree-Structured LSTM

A standard LSTM processes a sentence in a sequential order, e.g., from left to right. It estimates a sequence of hidden vectors given a sequence of input vectors, through the calculation of a sequence of hidden cell vectors using a gate mechanism. Extending the standard LSTM from linear chains to tree structures leads to TreeLSTM. Unlike the standard LSTM, TreeLSTM allows richer network topologies, where each LSTM unit is able to incorporate information from multiple child units.

As in standard LSTM units, each TreeLSTM unit contains input gate i_j, output gate o_j, a memory cell c_j, and hidden state h_j for node j. Unlike the standard LSTM, in TreeLSTM the gating vectors and the memory cell updates are dependent on the states of one or more child units. In addition, the TreeLSTM unit contains one forget gate f_{jk} for each child k instead of having a single forget gate. The transition equations of node j are as follows:

$$\tilde{h}_j = \sum_{k \in C(j)} h_k \,,$$

$$i_j = \sigma \left(W^{(i)} x_j + U^{(i)} \tilde{h}_j + b^{(i)} \right) ,$$

$$o_j = \sigma \left(W^{(o)} x_j + U^{(o)} \tilde{h}_j + b^{(o)} \right) ,$$

$$f_{jk} = \sigma \left(W^{(f)} x_j + U^{(f)} h_k + b^{(f)} \right) , \qquad (1)$$

$$u_j = \tanh \left(W^{(u)} x_j + U^{(u)} \tilde{h}_j + b^{(u)} \right) ,$$

$$c_j = i_j \odot u_j + \sum_{k \in C(j)} f_{jk} \odot c_k \,,$$

$$h_j = o_j \odot \tanh(c_j) \,,$$

where $C(j)$ is the set of children of node j, $k \in C(j)$ in f_{jk}, σ is the sigmoid function, and $\odot$ is element-wise (Hadamard) product. $W^{(*)}$, $U^{(*)}$, $b^{(*)}$ are model parameters with $* \in \{u, o, i, f\}$.[1]

3 Multiplicative Tree-Structured LSTM

Encoding rich linguistic analysis introduces many distinct edge types or relations between nodes, such as syntactic dependencies and semantic roles. This opens up many possibilities for parametrization, but was not considered in most existing syntax-aware LSTM approaches, which only make use of input node information.

In this paper, we fill this gap by proposing multiplicative TreeLSTM, an extension to the TreeLSTM model, injecting relation information into every node in the tree. The multiplicative TreeLSTM model, *mTreeLSTM* for short, introduces more fined-grained parameters based on the edge types. Inspired by the multiplicative RNN (Sutskever et al., 2011), the hidden-to-hidden propagation in mTreeLSTM contains a separately learned transition matrix W_{hh} for each possible edge type and is given by

$$\tilde{h}_j = \sum_{k \subset C(j)} W_{hh}^{r(j,k)} h_k \,, \qquad (2)$$

where $r(j, k)$ signifies the connection type between node k and its parent node j. This parametrization is straightforward, but requires a large number of parameters when there are many edge types. For instance, there are dozens of syntactic edge types, each corresponding to a Stanford dependency label.

To reduce the number of parameters and leverage potential correlation among fine-grained edge types, we learned an embedding of the edge types and factorized the transition matrix $W_{hh}^{r(j,k)}$ by using the product of two dense matrices shared across edge types, with an intermediate diagonal matrix that is edge-type dependent:

$$W_{hh}^{r(j,k)} = W_{hm} \mathrm{diag}(W_{mr} e_{jk}) W_{mh} \,, \qquad (3)$$

where e_{jk} is the edge-type embedding and is jointly trained with other parameters. The mapping from h_k to $\tilde{h}_j$ is then given by

$$m_{jk} = (W_{mr} e_{jk}) \odot (W_{mh} h_k) \,,$$
$$\tilde{h}_j = \sum_{k \in C(j)} W_{hm} m_{jk} \,. \qquad (4)$$

The gating units – input gate i, output gate o, and forget gate f – are computed in the same way as in the TreeLSTM with Eq. (1).[2]

Multiplicative TreeLSTM can be applied to any tree, where connection types between nodes are given. For example, in dependency trees, the semantic relations $r(j, k)$ between nodes are provided by a dependency parser.

4 Tree-Structured LSTMs with Abstract Meaning Representation

Tree-structured LSTMs have been applied successfully to syntactic parse trees (Tai et al., 2015; Miwa and Bansal, 2016). In this work, we look beyond *syntactic* properties of the text and incorporate *semantic* properties to the tree-structured LSTM model. Specifically, we utilize the network topology offered by a tree-structured LSTM and incorporate semantic features induced by AMR formalism. We aim to address the following questions: *In which tasks using AMR structures as the backbone for the tree-structured LSTM is useful? Furthermore, which semantic properties are useful for the given task?*

AMR is a semantic formalism where the meaning of a sentence is encoded as a single rooted, directed and acyclic graph (Banarescu et al., 2013). For example, the sentence "*A young girl is playing on the edge of a fountain and an older woman is not watching her*" is represented as:

---

[1] In Tai et al. (2015), the TreeLSTM defined in Eq. (1) was referred to as *child-sum TreeLSTM*, which is a good choice for trees with high branching factor.

[2] In the rest of the paper, we use the term *TreeLSTM* in a narrow sense to refer to the model corresponding to Eq. (1) and the term *tree-structured LSTM* to include both TreeLSTM and mTreeLSTM, unless specified otherwise.

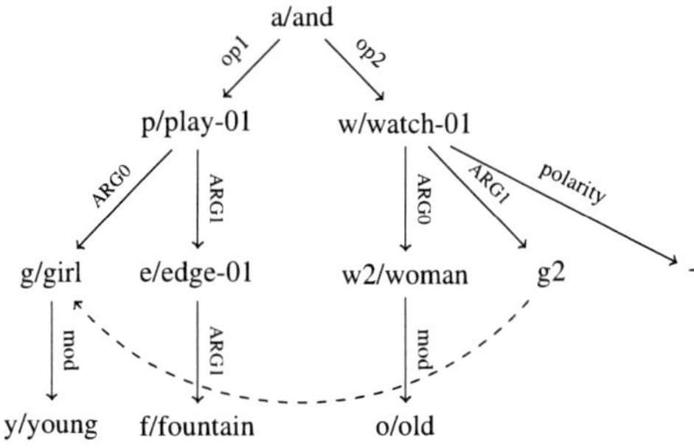

Figure 2: An AMR representing the sentence "A young girl is playing on the edge of a fountain and an older woman is not watching her".

```
(a / and
    :op1 (p / play-01
        :ARG0 (g / girl
            :mod (y / young))
        :ARG1 (e / edge-01
            :ARG1 (f / fountain)))
    :op2 (w / watch-01
        :ARG0 (w2 / woman
            :mod (o / old))
        :ARG1 g
        :polarity -))
```

The same AMR can be represented as in Figure 2, in which the nodes in the graph (also called concepts) map to words in the sentence and the edges represent the relations between words. AMR concepts consist of predicate senses, named entity annotations, and in some cases, simply lemmas of English words. AMR relations consist of core semantic roles drawn from the Propbank (Palmer et al., 2005) as well as fine-grained semantic relations defined specifically for AMR. Since AMR provides a whole-sentence semantic representation, it captures long-range dependencies among constituent words in a sentence. Similar to other semantic schemes, such as UCCA (Abend and Rappoport, 2013), GMB (Basile et al., 2012), UDS (White et al., 2016), AMR abstracts away from morphological and syntactic variability and generalize cross-linguistically.

To use AMR structures in a tree-structured LSTM, we first parse sentences to AMR graphs and transform the graphs to tree structures. The transformation follows the procedure used by Takase et al. (2016), splits the nodes with an indegree larger than one, which mainly present coreferential concepts, to a set of separate nodes, whose indegrees exactly equal one. We use JAMR (Flanigan et al., 2014, 2016), a statistical semantic parser

trained on AMR bank, for AMR parsing.

On one hand, the AMR tree structure can be used directly with the TreeLSTM architecture described in Section 2, in which only node information is utilized to encode sentences into certain fixed-length embedding vectors. On the other hand, since AMR provides rich information about semantic relations between nodes, the mTreeLSTM architecture is more applicable due to its capability of modeling edges in the tree. We evaluate both encoded vectors produced by TreeLSTM and mTreeLSTM on AMR trees in Section 6.

5 Applications

In this section, we describe three specific models that apply the mTreeLSTM architecture and the AMR tree structures described above.

5.1 Sentiment Classification

In this task, we wish to predict the sentiment of sentences, in which two sub-tasks are considered: binary and fine-grained multiclass classification. In the former, sentences are classified into two classes (*positive* and *negative*), while in the latter they are classified into five classes (*very positive, positive, neutral, negative,* and *very negative*).

For a sentence x, we first apply tree-structured LSTMs over the sentence's parse tree to obtain the representation h_r at the root node r. A softmax classifier is then used to predict the class $\hat{y}$ of the sentence, with $\hat{p}_\theta(y \mid x) = \text{softmax}(W^{(s)}h_r)$, where θ is the model parameters and $\hat{y} = \text{argmax}_y \hat{p}_\theta(y \mid x)$. The cost function is the negative log-likelihood of the true sentiment class of the sentence with L2 regularization.

5.2 Semantic Relatedness

Given a sentence pair, the goal is to predict an integer-valued similarity score in $\{1, 2, ..., K\}$, where higher scores indicate greater degrees of similarity between the sentences.

Following Tai et al. (2015), we first produce semantic representation h_L and h_R for each sentence in the pair using the described models over each sentence's parse trees. Then, we predict the similarity score $\hat{y}$ using additional feedforward layers that consider a feature vector x_s consisting of both distance and angle between the pair (h_L, h_R): $\hat{p}_\theta = \text{softmax}(W^{(p)} \sigma(W^{(s)}x_s)), \hat{y} = r^\top \hat{p}_\theta$, where $r^\top = [1, 2, ..., K]$. Similar to Tai et al. (2015), we define a sparse target distribution p

such that the ground-truth rating $y \in [1, K]$ equals $r^\top p$ and use the regularized KL-divergence from $\hat{p}_\theta$ to p as the cost function.

5.3 Natural Language Inference (NLI)

In this task, the model reads two sentences (a premise and a hypothesis), and outputs a judgement of *entailment, contradiction*, or *neutral*, reflecting the relationship between the meanings of the two sentences.

Following Bowman et al. (2016), we frame the inference task as a sentence pair classification. First we produce representations h_P and h_H for the premise and hypothesis and then construct a feature vector x_c for the pair that consists of the concatenation of these two vectors, their difference, and their element-wise product. This feature vector is then passed to a feed-forward layer followed by a softmax layer to yield a distribution over the three classes: $\hat{p}_\theta = \text{softmax}\left(W^{(p)} \sigma\left(W^{(c)} x_c\right)\right)$. The negative log-likelihood of the true class labels for sentence pairs is used as the cost function.

6 Experiments

6.1 Hyperparameters and Training

The model parameters are optimized using Ada-Grad (Duchi et al., 2011) with a learning rate of 0.05 for the first two tasks, and Adam (Kingma and Ba, 2015) with a learning rate of 0.001 for the NLI task. The batch size of 25 was used for all tasks and the model parameters were regularized with a per-minibatch L2 regularization strength of 10^{-4}. The sentiment and inference classifiers were additionally regularized using dropout with a dropout rate of 0.5.

Following Tai et al. (2015) and Zhu et al. (2015), we initialized the word embeddings with 300-dimensional GloVe vectors (Pennington et al., 2014). In addition, we use the aligner provided by JAMR parser to align the sentences with the AMR trees and then generate the embedding by using the GloVe vectors. The relation embeddings were randomly sampled from an uniform distribution in $[-0.05, 0.05]$ with a size of 100. The word and relation embeddings were updated during training with a learning rate of 0.1.

We use one hidden layer and the same dimensionality settings for sequential LSTM and tree-structured LSTMs. LSTM hidden states are of size 150. The output hidden size is 50 for the related-

ness task and the NLI task. Each model is trained for 10 iterations. (We did not observe better results with more iterations.) The same training procedure repeats 5 times with parameters being evaluated at the end of every iteration on the development set. The model having the best results on the development set is used for final tests.

For all sentences in the datasets, we parse them with constituency parser (Klein and Manning, 2003), dependency parser (Chen and Manning, 2014), and AMR parser (Flanigan et al., 2014, 2016) to obtain the tree structures. We compare our mTreeLSTM model with two baselines: LSTM and TreeLSTM. We use the notation (C), (D), and (A) to denote the tree structures that the models are based on, where they stand for constituency trees, dependency trees, and AMR trees, respectively. The code to reproduce the results is available at `https://github.com/namkhanhtran/m-treelstm`.[3]

6.2 Sentiment Classification

For this task, we use the Stanford Sentiment Treebank (Socher et al., 2013b) with the standard train/dev/test splits of 6920/872/1821 for the binary classification sub-task, and 8544/1101/2210 for the fine-grained classification sub-task. We used two different settings for training: *root-level* and *phrase-level*. In the root-level setting, each sentence is a data point, while in the phrase-level setting, each phrase is reconstructed from nodes in the parse tree and treated as a separate data point. In the phrase-level setting we obtain much more data for training, but the root-level setting is closer to real-world applications. For AMR trees, we only report results in the root-level setting, as the annotation cost for the phrase-level setting is prohibitively high. We evaluate our models and baseline models at the sentence level.

Table 1 shows the main results for the sentiment classification task. While LSTM model obtains quite good performance in both settings, TreeLSTM model on constituency tree obtains better results, especially in the phrase level setting, which has more supervision. It confirms the conclusion from Tai et al. (2015) that combining linguistic knowledge with LSTM leads to better performance than sequence models in this task. Table 1 also shows mTreeLSTM consistently outperforms

---

[3]The correctness of our implementation is also suggested by the fact that we have reproduced the results of LSTM and TreeLSTM in Tai et al. (2015), up to small variations.

Model	Phrase-level		Root-level	
	5-class	2-class	5-class	2-class
LSTM	48.0 (1.0)	86.7 (0.7)	45.6 (1.1)	85.6 (0.5)
TreeLSTM(C)	**49.8** (0.8)	**87.9** (0.9)	46.3 (0.7)	**85.8** (0.5)
TreeLSTM(D)	46.9 (0.2)	85.5 (0.4)	46.0 (0.3)	85.0 (0.4)
TreeLSTM(A)	n/a	n/a	44.4 (0.2)	82.9 (0.6)
mTreeLSTM(A)	n/a	n/a	45.2 (0.5)	83.2 (0.5)
mTreeLSTM(D)	47.5 (0.7)	85.7 (0.1)	**46.7** (0.8)	85.7 (0.8)

Table 1: Accuracy on the Stanford Sentiment Treebank dataset with standard deviation in parentheses (numbers in percentage)

Model	Pearson	Spearman	MSE
LSTM	.841 (.004)	.778 (.006)	.304 (.003)
TreeLSTM (C)	.849 (.005)	.790 (.004)	.286 (.010)
TreeLSTM (D)	.863 (.003)	.803 (.002)	.260 (.005)
TreeLSTM (A)	.842 (.002)	.774 (.001)	.299 (.005)
mTreeLSTM (A)	.853 (.001)	.788 (.001)	.279 (.002)
mTreeLSTM (D)	**.872** (.004)	**.814** (.005)	**.244** (.007)

Table 2: Results on the SICK dataset for semantic relatedness task with standard deviation in parentheses

TreeLSTM on the same tree structures in both settings – Whenever a tree structure is applicable to both mTreeLSTM and TreeLSTM, the performance of mTreeLSTM with that tree structure is better. That is, in phrase-level setting, mTreeLSTM (D) outperforms TreeLSTM (D) and similarly in root-level setting, mTreeLSTM (D) and mTreeLSTM (A) perform better than TreeLSTM (D) and TreeLSTM (A), respectively. It demonstrates the effectiveness of the relation multiplication mechanism and the importance of modeling relation information. The TreeLSTM and mTreeLSTM models with AMR trees do not perform well on this task. Synthetic information along goes a long way in determining the sentiment of a sentence. Noisy sentences in this task also impact the accuracy of the AMR parser.

We now dive deep into what the models learn, by listing the composition matrices $W_{hh}^{r(j,k)}$ with the largest Frobenius norms. These matrices have learned larger weights, which are in turn being multiplied with the child hidden states. That child will therefore have more weight in the composed parent vector. In decreasing order of Frobenius norm, the relationship matrices for mTreeLSTM on dependency trees are: conjunction, adjectival modifier, object of a preposition, negation modifier, verbal modifier. The relationship matrices for mTreeLSTM on AMR trees are: negation (`:polarity`), attribute (`:ARG3, :ARG2`), modifier (`:mod`), conjunction (`:opN`). The model learns that verbal and adjective modifiers are more important than nouns, as they tend to affect the sentiment of sentences.

6.3 Sentence Relatedness

For this task, we use the Sentences Involving Compositional Knowledge (SICK) dataset, consisting of 9927 sentence pairs with the standard train/dev/test split of 4500/500/4927. Each pair is annotated with a relatedness score $y \in [1, 5]$, with 1 indicating the two sentences are completely unrelated, and 5 indicating they are very related. Following Tai et al. (2015), we use Pearson, Spearman correlations and mean squared error (MSE) as evaluation metrics.

Our results are summarized in Table 2. The tree-structured LSTMs, both TreeLSTM and mTreeLSTM, reach better performance than the standard LSTM. The model using dependency tree as the backbone achieves best results. The mTreeLSTM with AMR trees obtain slightly better results than the TreeLSTM with constituency trees. The multiplicative TreeLSTM models outperform the TreeLSTM models on the same parse trees, illustrating again the usefulness of incorporating relation information into the model.

Similar to the previous experiment, we list the composition matrices $W_{hh}^{r(j,k)}$ with the largest Frobenius norms. The relationship matrices for dependency trees include: indirect object, marker for introducing a finite clause subordinate to another clause, negation modifier, adjectival modifier, phrasal verb particle, conjunction. The relationship matrices for AMR trees are: patient (`:ARG1`), comparatives and superlatives (`:degree`), agent (`:ARG0`), attribute (`:ARG3`), medium (`:medium`), possession (`:poss`), manner (`:manner`).

6.4 Natural Language Inference

In this task, we first look at the SICK dataset described in the previous section. In this setting each sentence pair is classified into three labels, *entailment, contradiction,* and *neutral.*

In addition to the standard test set, we also report performances of our models on two different

Model	All	LS	Negation
LSTM	77.3 (0.5)	74.6 (1.4)	77.5 (0.4)
TreeLSTM (C)	79.0 (1.4)	78.1 (2.9)	85.3 (1.2)
TreeLSTM (D)	82.9 (0.3)	81.0 (2.6)	84.3 (1.2)
TreeLSTM (A)	82.6 (0.2)	84.0 (1.5)	88.2 (0.4)
mTreeLSTM (A)	83.3 (0.2)	**85.3** (0.4)	**88.5** (0.8)
mTreeLSTM (D)	**84.0** (0.5)	81.6 (1.3)	87.8 (0.8)

Table 3: Accuracy on the SICK dataset for the NLI task with standard deviation in parentheses (numbers in percentage)

Model	Acc (%)
LSTM (Bowman et al., 2015)	77.6
Syntax TreeLSTM (Yogatama et al., 2017)	80.5
CYK TreeLSTM (Maillard et al., 2017) *	81.6
Gumbel TreeLSTM (Choi et al., 2018)	81.8
Gumbel TreeLSTM + leaf LSTM (Choi et al., 2018)	82.6
TreeLSTM (D)	81.0
mTreeLSTM (D)	81.9

Table 4: Results on the SNLI dataset. The first group contains results of some best-performing tree-structured LSTM models on this data. (*: a preprint)

Model	rDim	# Params	Acc (%)
TreeLSTM (A)	n/a	301K	82.6
mTreeLSTM (A)	50	354K	82.7
mTreeLSTM (A)	75	358K	83.1
mTreeLSTM (A)	100	361K	83.6
mTreeLSTM (A)	200	376K	83.0

Table 5: Effects of the relation embedding size on SICK dataset for the NLI task

subsets. The first subset, *Long Sentence (LS)*, consists of sentence pairs in the test set where the premise sentence contains at least 18 words. We hypothesize that long sentences are more difficult to handle by sequential models as well as tree-structured models. The second subset, *Negation*, is a set of sentence pairs where negation words (*not, n't* or *no*) do not appear in the premise but appear in the hypothesis. In the test set, 58.7% of these examples are labeled as *contradiction*.

Table 3 summarizes the results of our models on different test sets. The mTreeLSTM models obtain highest results, followed by TreeLSTM models. The standard LSTM model does not work well on this task. The results reconfirm the benefit of using the structure information of sentences in learning semantic representations. In addition, Table 3 shows that TreeLSTM on dependency trees and AMR trees outperform the models with constituency trees. The dependency trees provide some semantic information, i.e., semantic relations between words at some degrees, while AMR trees present more semantic information. The multiplicative TreeLSTM on AMR trees perform much better than other models on the *LS* and *Negation* subsets. The results on the *LS* subset shows that mTreeLSTM on AMR trees can handle long-range dependencies in a sentence more effectively. For example, only mTreeLSTM (A) is able to predict the following example correctly:
Premise: *The grotto with a pink interior is being climbed by four middle eastern children, three girls and one boy.*
Hypothesis: *A group of kids is playing on a colorful structure.*
Label: *entailment*

Similar to previous experiments, we list the composition matrices with the largest Frobenius norms to get some insights into what the models learn. The relationship matrices for mTreeLSTM on dependency trees are: negation modifier, nominal subject, adjectival modifier, direct object, passive auxiliary, adverb modifier. These matrices for mTreeLSTM on AMR trees are: attribute (`:ARG2`), patient (`:ARG1`), conjunction (`:opN`), location, negation (`:polarity`), domain. In contrast to the sentiment classification task, where adjectives are crucial, the model learns that subjects and objects are important to determine the meaning of sentences.

Furthermore, we evaluate our mTreeLSTM model with SNLI (Stanford Natural Language Inference), a larger NLI dataset (Bowman et al., 2015). It is composed of about 550K/10K/10K sentence pairs in train/dev/test sets. We use dependency tree as the backbone for tree-structured LSTMs. All models in Table 4 use a hidden size of 100 for a fair comparison. The table shows that mTreeLSTM (D) outperforms many other syntax-based TreeLSTM models including TreeLSTM (D), reconfirming our conclusion drawn with SICK.

6.5 Additional Tests and Discussions

Incorporating relation information in the tree-structured LSTM increases model complexity. In this experiment, we analyze the impact of the dimensionality of relation embedding on the model

Model	# Params	Acc (%)
TreeLSTM (D)	301K	82.9
addTreeLSTM (D)	361K	83.4
fullTreeLSTM (D)	1.1M	83.5
mTreeLSTM (D)	361K	84.0

Table 6: Comparison between different methods using relation information on the SICK dataset for the NLI task

size and accuracy. Table 5 shows the model with the relation embedding size of 100 achieves the best accuracy, while the overall impact of the embedding size is mild. The multiplicative TreeLSTM has only 1.2 times the number of weights in TreeLSTM (with the same number of hidden units). We did not count the number of parameters in the embedding models since these parameters are the same for all models.

Table 6 shows a comparison between mTreeLSTM and two other plausible methods for integrating relation information with TreeLSTM. In *addTreeLSTM*, a relation is treated as an additional node input in the TreeLSTM model; In *fullTreeLSTM*, the model corresponds to Eq. (2), where each edge type has a separate transition matrix. Both models achieve better results than TreeLSTM, indicating the usefulness of relation information. While addTreeLSTM and fullTreeLSTM obtain comparable performances, mTreeLSTM outperforms both of them. It is also to note that the number of parameters of mTreeLSTM is much less than those of fullTreeLSTM.

7   Other Related Work

There is a line of research that extends the standard LSTM (Hochreiter and Schmidhuber, 1997) in order to model more complex structures. Tai et al. (2015) and Zhu et al. (2015) extended sequential LSTMs to tree-structured LSTMs by adding branching factors. They showed such extensions outperform competitive LSTM baselines on several tasks such as sentiment classification and semantic relatedness prediction (which is also confirmed in this paper). Li et al. (2015) further investigated the effectiveness of TreeLSTMs on various tasks and discussed when tree structures are necessary. Chen et al. (2017) combined sequential and tree-structured LSTM for NLI and has achieved state-of-the-art results on the benchmark dataset. Their approach uses *n-ary* TreeLSTM based on

syntactic constituency parsers. In contrast, we focus more on child-sum TreeLSTM which is better suited for trees with high branching factor.

Previous works have studied the use of relation information. Dyer et al. (2015) considered each syntactic relation as an additional node and included its embedding to their composition function for dependency parsing. Peng et al. (2017) introduced a different set of parameters for each edge-type in their LSTM-based approach for relation extraction. In contrast to these works, our mTreeLSTM model incorporates relation information via a multiplicative mechanism, which we have shown is more effective and uses less parameters.

AMR has been successfully applied to a number of NLP tasks, besides the ones we considered in this paper. For example, Mitra and Baral (2016) made use of AMR to improve question answering; Liu et al. (2015) utilized AMR to produce promising results toward abstractive summarization. Using AMR as the backbone in TreeLSTM has been investigated in Takase et al. (2016). They incorporated AMR information by a neural encoder to the attention-based summarization method (Rush et al., 2015) and it performed well on headline generation. Our work differs from these studies in the sense that we aim to investigate how semantic information induced by AMR formalism can be incorporated to tree-structured LSTM models, and study which properties introduced by AMR turn out to be useful in various tasks. In this paper, we use the start-of-the-art AMR parser provided by Flanigan et al. (2016) which additionally provides the alignment between words and nodes in the tree.

Though we have considered AMR in this paper, we believe the conclusions we drew here largely apply to other semantic schemes, such as GMB and UCCA, as well. Abend and Rappoport (2017) has recently noted that the differences between these schemes are not critical, and the main distinguishing factors between them are their relation to syntax, their degree of universality, and the expertise they require from annotators.

8   Conclusions

We presented multiplicative TreeLSTM, an extension of existing tree-structured LSTMs to incorporate relation information between nodes in the tree. Multiplicative TreeLSTM allows different compositional functions for child nodes, which makes it more expressive. In addition, we investigated how lexical semantic representation can be used with tree-structured LSTMs. Experiments on three common NLP tasks showed that multiplicative TreeLSTMs outperform conventional TreeLSTMs, illustrating the usefulness of relation information. Moreover, with AMR as backbone, tree-structured models can effectively handle long-range dependencies.

Acknowledgments

We would like to thank Matthias Seeger, Cedric Archambeau, Alex Klementiev, Ralf Herbrich, and anonymous reviewers for their helpful comments.

References

Omri Abend and Ari Rappoport. 2013. Universal conceptual cognitive annotation (UCCA). In *Proceedings of the 51st Annual Meeting of the Association for Computational Linguistics*. ACL, pages 228–238.

Omri Abend and Ari Rappoport. 2017. The state of the art in semantic representation. In *Proceedings of the 55th Annual Meeting of the Association for Computational Linguistics*. ACL, pages 77–89.

Laura Banarescu, Claire Bonial, Shu Cai, Madalina Georgescu, Kira Griffitt, Ulf Hermjakob, Kevin Knight, Philipp Koehn, Martha Palmer, and Nathan Schneider. 2013. Abstract meaning representation for sembanking. In *Proceedings of the 7th Linguistic Annotation Workshop & Interoperability with Discourse*. pages 178–186.

Valerio Basile, Johan Bos, Kilian Evang, and Noortje Venhuizen. 2012. Developing a large semantically annotated corpus. In *Proceedings of the 8th Language Resources and Evaluation Conference*. LREC, pages 3196–3200.

Samuel R. Bowman, Gabor Angeli, Christopher Potts, and Christopher D Manning. 2015. A large annotated corpus for learning natural language inference. In *Proceedings of the 2015 Conference on Empirical Methods in Natural Language Processing (EMNLP)*. EMNLP, pages 632–642.

Samuel R. Bowman, Jon Gauthier, Abhinav Rastogi, Raghav Gupta, Christopher D. Manning, and Christopher Potts. 2016. A fast unified model for parsing and sentence understanding (volume 1). In *Proceedings of the 54th Annual Meeting of the Association for Computational Linguistics*. ACL, pages 1466–1477.

Danqi Chen and Christopher Manning. 2014. A fast and accurate dependency parser using neural networks. In *Proceedings of the 2014 Conference on Empirical Methods in Natural Language Processing*. EMNLP, pages 740–750.

Qian Chen, Xiaodan Zhu, Zhenhua Ling, Si Wei, Hui Jiang, and Diana Inkpen. 2017. Enhanced LSTM for natural language inference. In *Proceedings of the 55th Annual Meeting of the Association for Computational Linguistics*. ACL, pages 1657–1668.

Kyunghyun Cho, Bart van Merrienboer, Caglar Gulcehre, Dzmitry Bahdanau, Fethi Bougares, Holger Schwenk, and Yoshua Bengio. 2014. Learning phrase representations using rnn encoder-decoder for statistical machine translation. In *Proceedings of the 2014 Conference on Empirical Methods in Natural Language Processing*. EMNLP, pages 1724–1734.

Jihun Choi, Kang Min Yoo, and Sang goo Lee. 2018. Learning to compose task-specific tree structures. In *Proceedings of the 32nd AAAI Conference on Artificial Intelligence (AAAI-18)*. AAAI.

Li Dong, Furu Wei, Chuanqi Tan, Duyu Tang, Ming Zhou, and Ke Xu. 2014. Adaptive recursive neural network for target-dependent twitter sentiment classification. In *Proceedings of the 52nd Annual Meeting of the Association for Computational Linguistics (Volume 2)*. ACL, pages 49–54.

John Duchi, Elad Hazan, and Yoram Singer. 2011. Adaptive subgradient methods for online learning and stochastic optimization. *Journal of Machine Learning Research* 12:2121–2159.

Chris Dyer, Miguel Ballesteros, Wang Ling, Austin Matthews, and Noah Smith. 2015. Transition-based dependency parsing with stack long short-term memory. In *Proceedings of the 53rd Annual Meeting of the Association for Computational Linguistics*. ACL, pages 334–343.

Jeffrey L. Elman. 1990. Finding structure in time. *Cognitive Science* 14:179–211.

Jeffrey Flanigan, Chris Dyer, Noah A. Smith, and Jaime Carbonell. 2016. CMU at SemEval-2016 task 8: Graph-based AMR parsing with infinite ramp loss. In *Proceedings of the 10th International Workshop on Semantic Evaluation (SemEval-2016)*. SemEval, pages 1202–1206.

Jeffrey Flanigan, Sam Thomson, Jaime Carbonell, Chris Dyer, and Noah A. Smith. 2014. A discriminative graph-based parser for the abstract meaning representation. In *Proceedings of the 52nd Annual Meeting of the Association for Computational Linguistics (Volume 1)*. ACL, pages 1426–1436.

Sepp Hochreiter and Jürgen Schmidhuber. 1997. Long short-term memory. *Neural Computation* 9(8):1735–1780.

Nal Kalchbrenner, Edward Grefenstette, and Phil Blunsom. 2014. A convolutional neural network for modelling sentences. In *Proceedings of the 52nd Annual Meeting of the Association for Computational Linguistics (Volume 1)*. ACL, pages 655–665.

Yoon Kim. 2014. Convolutional neural networks for sentence classification. In *Proceedings of the 2014 Conference on Empirical Methods in Natural Language Processing*. EMNLP, pages 1746–1751.

Diederik P. Kingma and Jimmy Ba. 2015. Adam: A method for stochastic optimization. In *The 3rd International Conference on Learning Representations*. ICLR.

Dan Klein and Christopher D. Manning. 2003. Accurate unlexicalized parsing. In *Proceedings of the 41st Annual Meeting of the Association for Computational Linguistics*. ACL, pages 423–430.

Jiwei Li, Minh-Thang Luong, Dan Jurafsky, and Eduard Hovy. 2015. When are tree structures necessary for deep learning of representations? In *Proceedings of the 2015 Conference on Empirical Methods in Natural Language Processing*. EMNLP, pages 2304–2314.

Fei Liu, Jeffrey Flanigan, Sam Thomson, Norman M. Sadeh, and Noah A. Smith. 2015. Toward abstractive summarization using semantic representations. In *Proceedings of the Conference of the North American Chapter of the Association for Computational Linguistics*. NAACL.

Pengfei Liu, Xipeng Qiu, Yaqian Zhou, Jifan Chen, and Xuanjing Huang. 2016. Modelling interaction of sentence pair with coupled-LSTMs. In *Proceedings of the 2016 Conference on Empirical Methods in Natural Language Processing*. EMNLP, pages 1703–1712.

Jean Maillard, Stephen Clark, and Dani Yogatama. 2017. Jointly learning sentence embeddings and syntax with unsupervised tree-LSTMs. *CoRR* .

Arindam Mitra and Chitta Baral. 2016. Addressing a question answering challenge by combining statistical methods with inductive rule learning and reasoning. In *Proceedings of the 13th AAAI Conference on Artificial Intelligence*. AAAI, pages 2779–2785.

Makoto Miwa and Mohit Bansal. 2016. End-to-end relation extraction using LSTMs on sequences and tree structures. In *Proceedings of the 54th Annual Meeting of the Association for Computational Linguistics (Volume 1)*. ACL, pages 1105–1116.

Martha Palmer, Daniel Gildea, and Paul Kingsbury. 2005. The proposition bank: An annotated corpus of semantic roles. *Computational Linguistics* 31:71–106.

Nanyun Peng, Hoifung Poon, Chris Quirk, Kristina Toutanova, and Wen-tau Yih. 2017. Cross-sentence n-ary relation extraction with graph LSTMs. *Transactions of the Association for Computational Linguistics* pages 101–115.

Jeffrey Pennington, Richard Socher, and Christopher D. Manning. 2014. GloVe: Global vectors for word representation. In *Proceedings of the 2014 Conference on Empirical Methods in Natural Language Processing*. EMNLP, pages 1532–1543.

Alexander Rush, Sumit Chopra, and Jason Weston. 2015. A neural attention model for abstractive sentence summarization. In *Proceedings of the 2015 Conference on Empirical Methods in Natural Language Processing*. EMNLP, pages 379–389.

Richard Socher, John Bauer, Christopher D. Manning, and Ng Andrew Y. 2013a. Parsing with compositional vector grammars. In *Proceedings of the 51st Annual Meeting of the Association for Computational Linguistics (Volume 1)*. ACL, pages 455–465.

Richard Socher, Brody Huval, Christopher D. Manning, and Andrew Y. Ng. 2012. Semantic compositionality through recursive matrix-vector spaces. In *Proceedings of the 2012 Joint Conference on Empirical Methods in Natural Language Processing and Computational Natural Language Learning*. EMNLP-CoNLL, pages 1201–1211.

Richard Socher, Cliff C. Lin, Andrew Y. Ng, and Christopher D. Manning. 2011. Parsing natural scenes and natural language with recursive neural networks. In *Proceedings of the 28th International Conference on Machine Learning*. ICML, pages 129–136.

Richard Socher, Alex Perelygin, Jean Wu, Jason Chuang, Christopher D. Manning, Andrew Y. Ng, and Christopher Potts. 2013b. Recursive deep models for semantic compositionality over a sentiment treebank. In *Proceedings of the 2013 Conference on Empirical Methods in Natural Language Processing*. ACL, pages 1631–1642.

Ilya Sutskever, James Martens, and Geoffrey Hinton. 2011. Generating text with recurrent neural networks. In *Proceedings of the 28th International Conference on Machine Learning*. ICML, pages 1017–1024.

Kai Sheng Tai, Richard Socher, and Christopher D. Manning. 2015. Improved semantic representations from tree-structured long short-term memory networks. In *Proceedings of the 53rd Annual Meeting of the Association for Computational Linguistics and the 7th International Joint Conference on Natural Language Processing*. ACL, pages 1556–1566.

Sho Takase, Jun Suzuki, Naoaki Okazaki, Tsutomu Hirao, and Masaaki Nagata. 2016. Neural headline generation on abstract meaning representation. In *Proceedings of the 2016 Conference on Empirical Methods in Natural Language Processing*. EMNLP, pages 1054–1059.

Aaron Steven White, Drew Reisinger, Keisuke Sakaguchi, Tim Vieira, Sheng Zhang, Rachel Rudinger, Kyle Rawlins, and Benjamin Van Durme. 2016. Universal decompositional semantics on universal dependencies. In *Proceedings of the 2016 Conference on Empirical Methods in Natural Language Processing*. EMNLP, pages 1713–1723.

Dani Yogatama, Phil Blunsom, Chris Dyer, Edward Grefenstette, and Wang Ling. 2017. Learning to compose words into sentences with reinforcement learning. In *Proceedings of the 5th International Conference on Learning Representations*. ICLR.

Han Zhao, Zhengdong Lu, and Pascal Poupart. 2015. Self-adaptive hierarchical sentence model. In *Proceedings of the 24th International Joint Conference on Artificial Intelligence*. IJCAI, pages 4069–4076.

Xiaodan Zhu, Parinaz Sobhani, and Hongyu Guo. 2015. Long short-term memory over recursive structures. In *Proceedings of the 32nd International Conference on Machine Learning*. ICML, pages 1604–1612.

Author Index

Allen, James, 235

Badaro, Gilbert, 86
Bakarov, Amir, 94
Barbieri, Francesco, 101
Basile, Valerio, 245
Beschke, Sebastian, 54
Bethard, Steven, 167
Bollegala, Danushka, 33, 255
Botschen, Teresa, 225

Cabrio, Elena, 245
Camacho-Collados, Jose, 101
Cheng, Weiwei, 276
Cheung, Jackie Chi Kit, 1, 130
Choi, Jihun, 107
Crouch, Richard, 113
Cui, Xia, 255

Demberg, Vera, 11
Dligach, Dmitriy, 119
Duh, Kevin, 142, 173

El-Hajj, Wassim, 86

Fan, Chuchu, 148
Frassinelli, Diego, 76

Gargett, Andrew, 33
Gimpel, Kevin, 192
Gurevych, Iryna, 65, 225

Hajj, Hazem, 86
Haldar, Aparajita, 180
Hong, Xudong, 11
Hu, Hai, 124

Jundi, Hussein, 86

Köper, Maximilian, 22
Kallmeyer, Laura, 130
Kalouli, Aikaterini-Lida, 113
Kenyon-Dean, Kian, 1
Kim, Taeuk, 107
Kiritchenko, Svetlana, 43, 214
Kojaku, Sadamori, 255

Lee, Sang-goo, 107
Lopez Condori, Roque, 245

Mahabal, Abhijit, 265
Masuda, Naoki, 255
Mei, Hongyuan, 142
Menzel, Wolfgang, 54
Miller, Timothy, 119
Mittal, Sid, 265
Mohammad, Saif, 43, 214
Moss, Larry, 124
Mousselly Sergieh, Hatem, 225

Naradowsky, Jason, 180
Naumann, Daniela, 76
Ning, Qiang, 148

Pierrejean, Benedicte, 154
Poliak, Adam, 180
Precup, Doina, 1

QasemiZadeh, Behrang, 130

Roth, Dan, 148, 203, 265
Roth, Stefan, 225
Rudinger, Rachel, 180

Sagarkar, Manasvi, 192
Samardzhiev, Krasen, 33
Sayeed, Asad, 11
Schulte im Walde, Sabine, 22, 76
Sharp, Rebecca, 167
Shwartz, Vered, 160
Sochenkov, Ilya, 94
Sorokin, Daniil, 65
Springorum, Sylvia, 22
Suvorov, Roman, 94

Tanguy, Ludovic, 154
Teng, Choh Man, 235
Tran, Nam Khanh, 276
Tu, Lifu, 192

Van Durme, Benjamin, 142, 173, 180
Vu, Tu, 160

Wieting, John, 192
Wojatzki, Michael, 214

Yadav, Vikas, 167
Yin, Wenpeng, 203
Yu, Zhongzhi, 148

Zesch, Torsten, 214
Zhang, Sheng, 142, 173